Office Tax Procedures

Process Business Tax Requirements

8 EDITION

Office Tax Procedures

HELEN BOWERS • ROBERT VINTON • ROBYN VIDLER

(t)p

8 EDITION

PEARSON
Education Australia

Pearson Education Australia
Unit 4, Level 3
14 Aquatic Drive
Frenchs Forest NSW 2086

www.pearsoned.com.au

Acquisitions Editors: Andrew Brock, Suzanne Hall
Project Editor: Sandra Goodall
Production Coordinator: Barbara Honor
Copy Editor: Caroline Hunter
Proofreader: Janice Keynton
Indexer: Caroll Casey
Cover and internal design by Liz Nicholson
Cover illustration by Ian McKinnell, Getty Images
Typeset by Midland Typesetters, Australia

Printed in Australia by Ligare Book Printers

1 2 3 4 5 13 12 11 10 09

National Library of Australia
Cataloguing-in-Publication Data

Bowers, Helen, 1938–

Office tax procedures : process business tax requirements / Helen Bowers, Robert Vinton, Robyn Vidler.

8th ed.

9781442501355 (pbk.)

Includes index.

Taxation—Australia.

Value-added tax—Australia.

Business enterprises—Taxation—Australia.

Vinton, Robert, 1955–
Vidler, Robyn.

336.200994

PEARSON
Prentice Hall

An imprint of Pearson Education Australia
(a division of Pearson Australia Group Pty Ltd)

Contents

Preface

'The art of taxation consists in so plucking the goose as to obtain the largest amount of feathers with the least possible amount of hissing.'

Attributed to J B Colbert (1619–83),
Comptroller-General of Finance to Louis XIV of France

Although taxes today are not quite as onerous as those in the days of the French king Louis XIV, there is nevertheless a widespread lack of understanding of how our taxation system works. Many people experience extreme difficulty in determining their taxation liability and in complying with the time frames for lodgement and reporting determined by the Commissioner of Taxation. The Australian Taxation Office (ATO) has made many rulings that indicate how it might treat certain controversial matters, but these are often clouded in uncertainty. In this eighth edition we incorporate many changes to office tax procedures initiated by amendments and adjustments to rates and legislation. During the passage of this decade we have seen some settlement of the major changes that came into effect with *A New Tax System* at the turn of the millennium.

The purpose of this book is to provide a practical guide to taxation, including the requirements of the *Income Tax Assessment Act 1997* and the *Income Tax Assessment Act 1936* (as amended) and other vital Commonwealth legislation that affects all business operations. The book also examines various state taxes (including those of the Australian Capital Territory). This book is not a reference to every section of the tax legislation, nor does it attempt to cover precedents on arcane points of law. What the book does set out to be is a contemporary guide to the real and basic problems of complying with our intricate tax laws. The objective is to provide a very practical explanation of the current relevant issues that businesspeople face in their daily commercial life. In its simplest form, the book sets out to assist not in interpreting the law but rather in complying with the law.

Readership

The book is written for both students and small businesspeople requiring a preliminary and practical understanding of taxation matters. The material should be accessible to readers with little or no knowledge of tax law, although some of the chapters will be more demanding in terms of technical sophistication. In every chapter, references by way of endnotes are made to the relevant sections of the Acts discussed for those wanting to undertake a more rigorous investigation.

Structure and content

The book is written in three parts. The first part deals with federal taxation issues and procedures. All the major tax requirements for business and commerce are explored. This eighth edition includes a new chapter devoted to the completion and lodgement of Business Activity Statements. The second part of the book considers extant state taxes. Requirements differ from state to state, and an attempt has been made to cover each state's general criteria. We have introduced commonalities at the start of the state chapters and these show what is common throughout Australia. In particular, we highlight the process towards harmonisation in state payroll tax laws. The third part of the text is more academically rigorous, since it investigates the importance of electronic communications. We examine business tax reforms, setting out the effects of the consolidation scheme, encompassing modern ethical issues, providing definitions and functions of tax and tax bases, and highlighting problems associated with the various types of taxation. The effectiveness of individual taxation is examined and the consequences of changes to the tax threshold are analysed. Keeping abreast of the explosion in communications technology, this edition pays particular attention to electronic transactions with the ATO through public key technology. The Business Portal, the Tax Agent Portal and the Electronic Commerce Interface are discussed. Readers can also refer to current informative websites and useful telephone contacts.

Copies of relevant forms and explanations of how these should be completed are reproduced in the Appendix with the kind permission of the ATO. Every form has the ATO code in square brackets [ ] and this number can be quoted when requesting forms from the ATO. Alternatively, all ATO forms that are available online may be downloaded from the Internet and the appropriate web addresses are quoted in the text.

At the end of each section of all federal chapters we have introduced Active reflection questions to help deepen your understanding of complex tax law. There are also self-testing questions, and the solutions to both these and the Active reflection questions can be found at the back of the book. In addition, the extensive glossary at the back of the book helps develop a deeper understanding of taxation vocabulary.

The teachers' resources contain up-to-date validation tools that satisfy the audit requirements for student assessments. The resources also include a solutions manual and solutions to the various multiple-choice, quick-and-easy comprehension and more rigorous assessment questions. There are a variety of calculators developed in Excel that can be used to work out many of the complicated taxes, payments and duties.

The book will have achieved its objective if, after studying any chapter, you have an understanding of the basic requirements of the tax laws for that topic and would feel capable of accurately processing any forms for lodgement with the relevant authority.

Acknowledgment is gratefully given to the Australian Taxation Office for its continuing assistance in relation to publications and documents, and to the various State Offices of Revenue, from where much of the state-by-state research material came. Once again we are indebted to our many colleagues who provided constructive comments on the earlier editions that have assisted us in adding to the depth and breadth of knowledge upon which this book is written. Finally, we graciously acknowledge our families, who still, after all these years and editions, continue to encourage the venture.

Helen Bowers
Robert Vinton
Robyn Vidler

How to use this book

Office Tax Procedures: Process Business Tax Requirements, 8th edition, has been carefully planned with the reader in mind. The learning aids within the text are designed to clarify the subject matter and facilitate student learning.

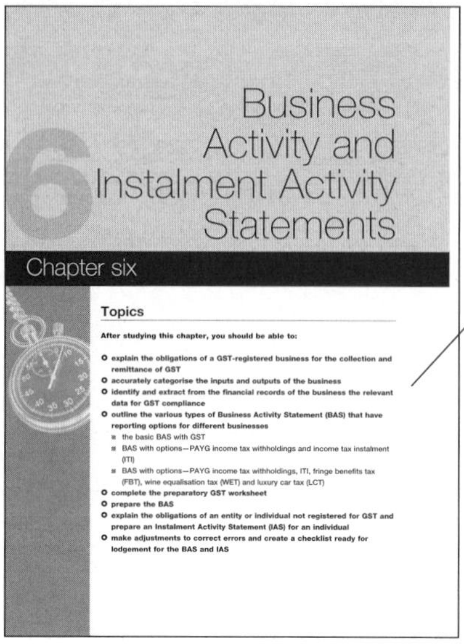
6
Business Activity and Instalment Activity Statements
Chapter six
Topics

Topics establish learning goals and competency standards specific to each chapter.

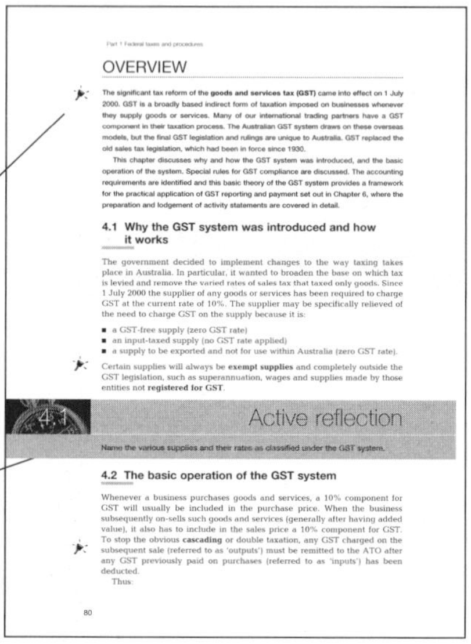
OVERVIEW
4.1 Why the GST system was introduced and how it works
4.1 Active reflection
4.2 The basic operation of the GST system

Overview provides a summary of the content of the forthcoming chapter.

Active reflection consolidates important concepts throughout each chapter.

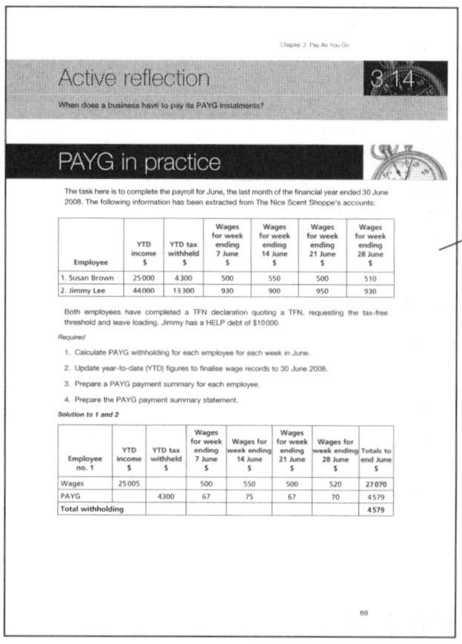
Active reflection 3.14
PAYG in practice

'. . . in practice' provides a practical summary of the key chapter concepts.

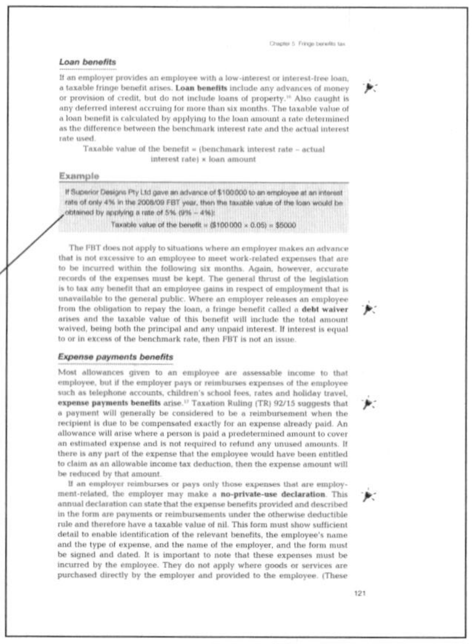
Loan benefits
Example
Expense payments benefits

Examples illustrate key chapter concepts in a practical way.

Key terms are highlighted with key icons in the margins

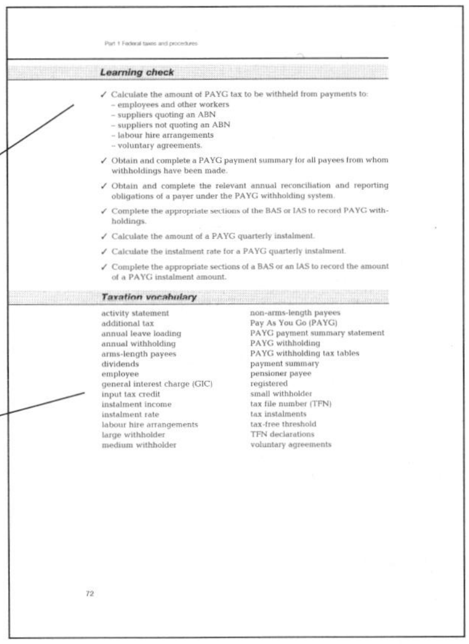

Learning check lists the appropriate skills and knowledge covered within the chapter.

Taxation vocabulary catalogues the key terms highlighted in the chapter, providing a quick review of important terminology.

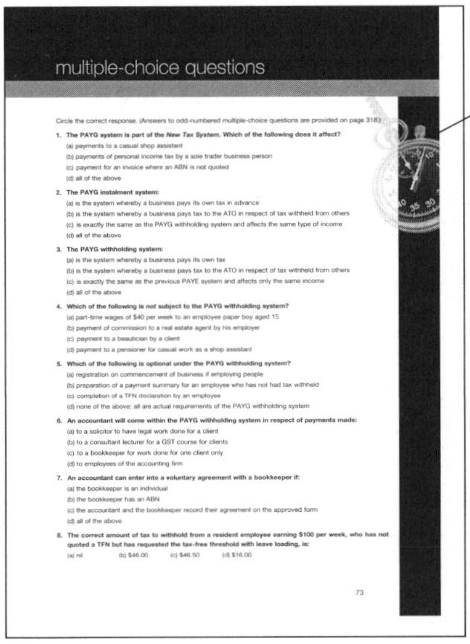

Multiple-choice questions review and evaluate students' understanding of the chapter content. The answers to odd-numbered questions are provided at the back of the book.

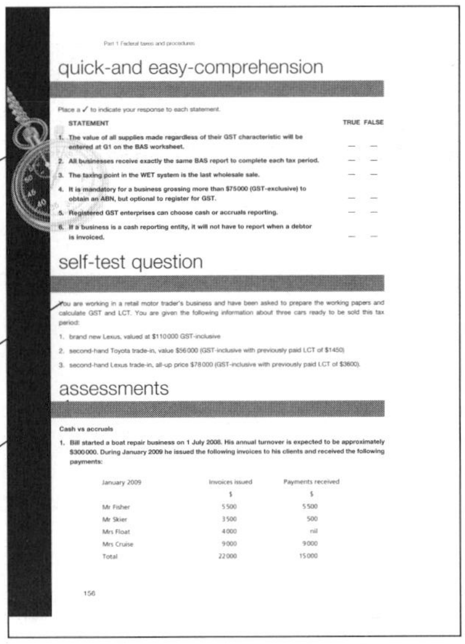

Quick-and-easy comprehension (true and false) questions are provided to further reinforce students' understanding of key chapter concepts.

A **self-test question** (and **solution**) is provided at the end of most chapters to aid student learning.

Assessments are more detailed questions to test a deeper level of student knowledge.

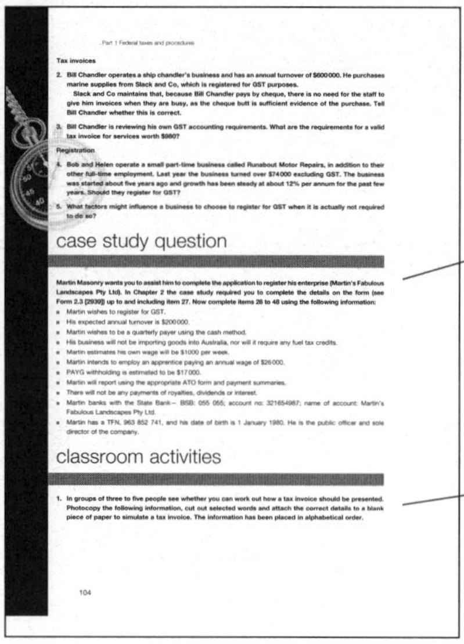
Part 1 Federal taxes and procedures

Tax invoices

2. **Bill Chandler operates a ship chandler's business and has an annual turnover of $600 000. He purchases marine supplies from Slack and Co, which is registered for GST purposes.**
   Slack and Co maintains that, because Bill Chandler pays by cheque, there is no need for the staff to give him invoices when they are busy, as the cheque butt is sufficient evidence of the purchase. Tell Bill Chandler whether this is correct.
3. **Bill Chandler is reviewing his own GST accounting requirements. What are the requirements for a valid tax invoice for services worth $980?**

Registration

4. **Bob and Helen operate a small part-time business called Runabout Motor Repairs, in addition to their other full-time employment. Last year the business turned over $74 000 excluding GST. The business was started about five years ago and growth has been steady at about 12% per annum for the past few years. Should they register for GST?**
5. **What factors might influence a business to choose to register for GST when it is actually not required to do so?**

case study question

Martin Masonry wants you to assist him to complete the application to register his enterprise (Martin's Fabulous Landscapes Pty Ltd). In Chapter 2 the case study required you to complete the details on the form (see Form 2.3 [2939]) up to and including item 27. Now complete items 28 to 48 using the following information:

- Martin wishes to register for GST.
- His expected annual turnover is $200 000.
- Martin wishes to be a quarterly payer using the cash method.
- His business will not be importing goods into Australia, nor will it require any fuel tax credits.
- Martin estimates his own wage will be $1000 per week.
- Martin intends to employ an apprentice paying an annual wage of $26 000.
- PAYG withholding is estimated to be $17 000.
- Martin will report using the appropriate ATO form and payment summaries.
- There will not be any payments of royalties, dividends or interest.
- Martin banks with the State Bank— BSB: 055 055; account no: 321654987; name of account: Martin's Fabulous Landscapes Pty Ltd.
- Martin has a TFN, 963 852 741, and his date of birth is 1 January 1980. He is the public officer and sole director of the company.

classroom activities

1. **In groups of three to five people see whether you can work out how a tax invoice should be presented. Photocopy the following information, cut out selected words and attach the correct details to a blank piece of paper to simulate a tax invoice. The information has been placed in alphabetical order.**

104

Case study questions encourage students to consider the simulated workplace situation of a business. As the student progresses through the text, case study questions are added at the end of each chapter, picking up the themes relevant to that chapter and building on their previous understanding of office tax procedures. This ensures a deeper understanding of the operations of a commercial enterprise.

Classroom activities apply key chapter concepts in a fun, practical way.

Federal taxes and procedures

1

Part one

This part of the book examines the federal taxes collected by the Commonwealth Government through the Pay As You Go procedure, the Medicare levy, the goods and services tax, the fringe benefits tax and the Higher Education Loan Program. An analysis of the Superannuation Guarantee Scheme, the Australian Business Number and the Tax File Number systems, and an overview of the Child Support Agency set out the processes necessary to comply with current legislation covering these important areas. A newly introduced chapter explains the intricacies of preparing Business Activity Statements and Instalment Activity Statements, combining the theory outlined in the first five chapters.

The *Income Tax Assessment Act 1997* together with provisions of the old *Income Tax Assessment Act 1936* and the *Income Tax (Transitional Provisions) Act 1997* cover the main areas of federal taxation addressed in this part of the book. It will be increasingly important for all business managers to take reasonable steps to ensure that they are familiar with changes to tax law and the likely effects these changes will have on their strategic planning. The Commissioner of Taxation in his 2008 address[1] stated that the Australian Taxation Office (ATO) 'effectiveness over the long term requires vision that values the past and challenges the future. We are striving to be both responsive to the present while building and innovating for the future'. It is noteworthy that the ATO is using 'environmental scanning' and is liaising with the Department of Innovation, Industry, Science and Research[2] and other government agencies to research and develop future scenarios and other policies within the broader context of taxation policy effects on business and industry.

Efficient and effective office tax procedures add value to the services offered to individuals and business. The material covered in this part of the book offers support to all those who rely on accurate and easy-to-read resources.

1 Michael D'Ascenzo (2008), 'Sights set on the horizon', *8th International Conference on Tax Administration*, 27 March, Sydney.

2 Dr Terry Cutler (2008), *Innovation: What is it and why it matters*, Department of Innovation, Industry, Science and Research (DIISR).

Introduction

Chapter one

Topics

After studying this chapter, you should be able to:

- **define the liability for taxation**
- **write the equation that produces taxable income**
- **calculate tax payable**
- **list the characteristics of income**
- **describe substantiation requirements**
- **list the rights of a taxpayer when a compliance audit is required.**

OVERVIEW

The successful management of any organisation depends to a large extent on an efficiently and effectively operated office. It acts as the firm's heart, constantly and methodically monitoring the flow of information through the business. It is the point of first contact with the outside environment and can be described as a window through which the firm can be viewed. It is essential, therefore, that the office procedures are planned and controlled so the objectives set by management can be achieved with the maximum efficiency at the minimum cost.

This book is intended as an aid to implementing effective office tax procedures. It deals with the requirements of both federal and state laws. In today's business environment there are many legal requirements for **tax**, and among the most demanding are:

- income tax
- goods and services tax
- fringe benefits tax
- superannuation guarantee requirements
- payroll tax
- transactions duties
- land tax.

Office tax procedures need constant attention if they are to meet the demands of law. **Returns** must be filed by certain dates; payments of PAYG income tax instalments, PAYG withholdings and goods and services tax (GST) must be submitted; and the onerous requirements of **substantiation** must be upheld. All of this demands good planning and constant monitoring. The contemporary accountant will not only be required to answer countless questions from clients regarding the complex commercial laws but will also need to organise office tax procedures to ensure that timely and reliable information is constantly available. Small business entrepreneurs also require assistance in planning their office policies because many have a need to cultivate skills in management to complement the practical ability that has led them to become self-employed.

To keep abreast of all that is happening in tax, visit the **Australian Taxation Office (ATO)** website shown in Figure 1.1 at **www.ato.gov.au** where you will find links to many useful sites.

1.1 Liability for taxation

Taxation has been a part of Australia since the very early days of settlement. Australian tax history tells us that in 1880 the colony of Tasmania was the first to impose a tax on income received from the profits of public companies and that South Australia imposed a general tax on income in 1885. By 1900 all the colonies were collecting **revenue** from some sort of taxation.

The Commonwealth, although collecting income tax nationally since 1915, has been the sole collector of income tax revenue since 1942 and reimburses the states according to the terms of their agreements. The states supplement this by raising their own revenue from payroll taxes, land taxes and transactions duties (stamp duties). With the introduction of *A New Tax System* (ANTS) in July 2000 the states began to share in the revenue collected from the **goods and services tax (GST)** and in return abolished some of their taxes. This is discussed in more detail in Part 2. Until 1989 each state was entitled

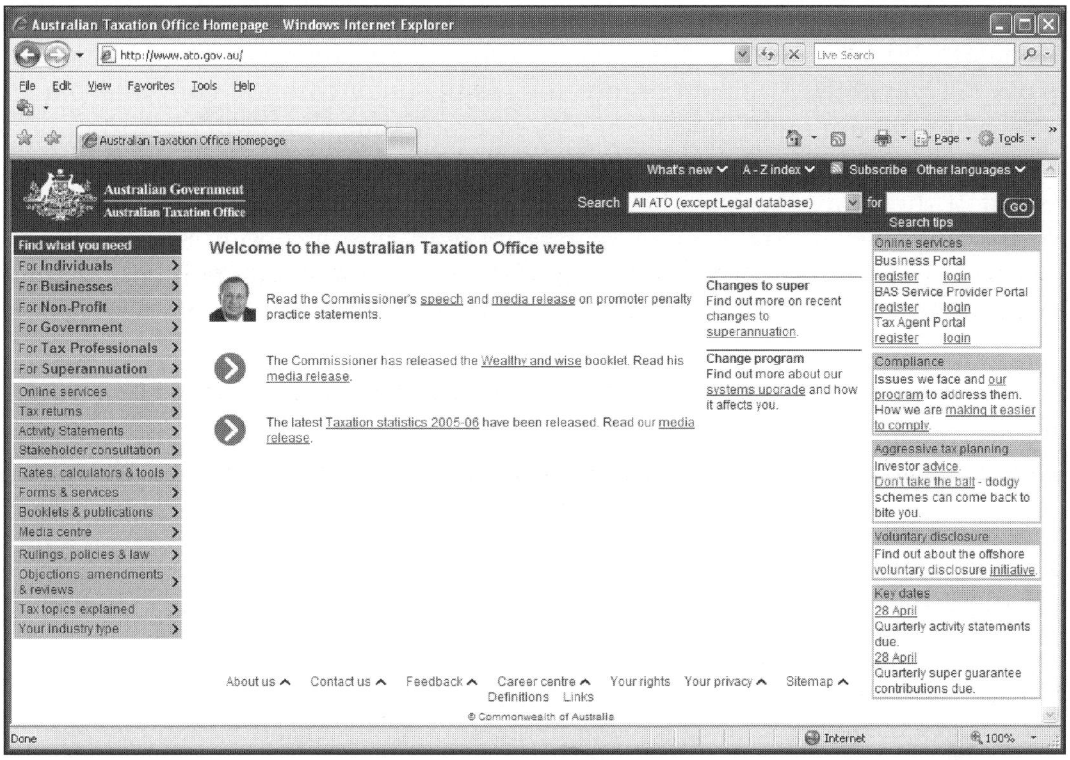

FIGURE 1.1 The ATO's homepage

to impose an additional surcharge on income or to give a rebate, but these options were never taken up and the scheme was dismantled.

The Australian government imposes a tax on revenue by operation of the *Income Tax Assessment Act 1997* (ITAA 1997) and the still-operative provisions of the original *Income Tax Assessment Act 1936* (ITAA 1936) as amended. Throughout the book reference is simply made to 'the Act' for general taxes on revenue, and to 'the GST' when referring to *A New Tax System (Goods and Services Tax) Act 1999*. The provision that is central to the interpretation of the Act is Division 4, which requires tax to be levied each year on income received by any person, whether that person is a **resident** or a **non-resident**.[1] As business tax reform evolves, various new packages of legislation that make up *A New Tax System* and the *New Business Tax System* are replacing some of the old provisions.

Active reflection

In Australia, which level of government has the sole right to impose tax on income?

1.2 Determining taxation liability

The **rates of tax** to be applied to **taxable income** will be those declared by Parliament. To arrive at taxable income, all **assessable income** is added together to obtain the gross assessable income, and then from this amount any **allowable deductions**, either *general* or *specific*, may be subtracted, the result being taxable income. For individual taxpayers, the current tax rates are then applied to ascertain the amount of **prime tax assessed** and also the **Medicare levy**, and these two amounts are added together to produce the **gross tax payable**. After obtaining this result, reconciliation can take place, where any rebate entitlements, offsets or credits may be deducted to obtain the net liability of the taxpayer. (Offsets or rebates are allowed only to the extent of the prime tax payable, and the Medicare levy can never be extinguished by any offsets, rebates or credits with the exception of imputation credits from fully franked dividends and the 30% private health insurance tax credit.) Figure 1.2 depicts the taxing process in simple terms.

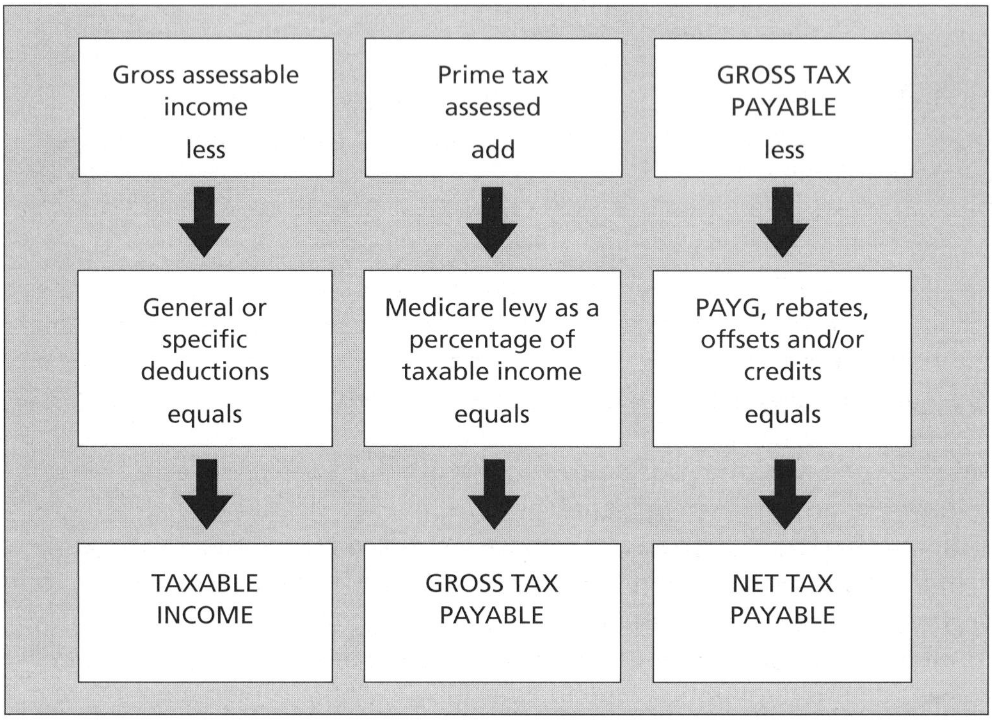

FIGURE 1.2 The taxing process

Offsets and credits. See sections 159H–159Y, Division 17, ITAA 1936.

The levying of income tax takes place every year on income derived from all sources in that year. Company and funds taxpayers will have tax levied on the taxable income as set out in the Act[2] and according to the group to which they belong. All taxpayers are required to **self-assess** their tax liability. Individual taxpayers may become liable for **PAYG income tax instalments**, which are levied on a wage or salary earner's other income, or on a self-employed person's business income. The tax system allows tax to be collected either by instalments or as a lump sum during the year in which the income is derived. Chapter 3 discusses the tax instalment system under PAYG, and Chapter 6 shows how these instalments are recorded on the **Business Activity Statement (BAS)** or **Instalment Activity Statement (IAS)**.

Active reflection

Suppose an individual taxpayer has an annual salary of $65 000, investment income of $3300, allowable deductions of $2700 and PAYG withheld of $15 000. What is the taxpayer's taxable income?

1.3 Characteristics of income

For many years there have been volumes of litigation about the concept of income. Assessable income includes all income from all sources, and generally excludes **receipts** of a capital nature. If receipts are regular, earned by personal exertion or by the utilisation of assets, or if they are received as compensation for some loss, then they are much more likely to be classified as income. They are much less likely to be income if receipts are gifts, windfall gains, compensation for the loss of an asset or a lump sum received. Any proceeds received from a hobby will generally not be considered as income and any associated expenses will not be allowable as general or specific deductions.

To help clarify the complicated sections of the Act, the Commissioner of Taxation will, from time to time, issue *rulings*. These are simply the Commissioner's opinion as to the way a tax law should be interpreted. A **private ruling** initiated by a request from a taxpayer will have application for that taxpayer only, but a **public ruling**, usually initiated by the ATO, will have application for all taxpayers. It is important to understand the distinction between '**capital**' and '**income**'. Capital receipts will be assessed as income only when a **capital gain** is made on the sale or disposal of a capital asset. These capital gains are subject to special taxation rules[3] (see Section 1.6).

There is an important concept in taxation called the **mutuality principle**, which means that any payment to oneself cannot constitute income. Any surplus arising from the transactions of members of a club or an association cannot be classed as income to the club and thus will not be assessable (Federal Court of Australia decision in *Coleambally Irrigation Mutual Co-operative Ltd v Commissioner of Taxation 2004*).

The principle of mutuality provides that where a number of persons contribute to a common fund created and controlled by them for a common purpose, any surplus arising from the use of that fund for the common purpose is not income. This principle, of course, does not extend to include income that is derived from sources outside that group.

If income has been gained from illegal ventures, it cannot escape being assessable. This is quite interesting, because the Commissioner will not allow any deductions against income that has been received from illegal ventures.[4]

If non-cash rewards or incentives are received, the Act sets out special rules to ensure that these benefits, even if non-convertible, are treated as income. Some benefits that are given to employees, such as the use of a company car, will be taxed as a **fringe benefit**[5] with the tax liability accruing to the employer. The separate Act that controls the collection of revenue from fringe benefits will become operative only when there is an **employer–employee relationship**. It can never apply outside this relationship. Employers must calculate their own fringe benefits tax liability and include payments for this tax on their Business Activity Statement (see Chapter 6). Employers must therefore calculate the taxable value of benefits provided to their employees, assess this tax and pay their liability (see Chapter 5).

Some income may be **exempt**.[6] This exempt income is defined under Division 4 of the Act to mean 'income which is exempt from income tax and includes income which is not assessable income'. The exemption of income applies only to the original recipient of that income and does not extend to any people who may receive payment later from that income. If a person receives income from a foreign source, even if foreign tax has been paid on that income, it may be assessable and a foreign tax credit may be allowed.[7]

It has now become a necessity for management systems to promote adequate **internal control**, not only to ensure compliance with all the complex statutory requirements but also to produce the optimal efficiency and effectiveness of the enterprise. Accountants must have a thorough understanding of the basic commercial laws so that they are able to translate these laws into plain language for their clients. Small business entrepreneurs need to be able to cope with the regular requirements of federal and state laws in order to maximise their operational efficiency within the compliance framework of taxation laws.

Active reflection

In Active reflection 1.2 you were asked to determine a taxpayer's taxable income. Would this amount change if the taxpayer had sold his investment in shares at the end of the year for exactly the price he paid for them ($41 250) two years ago?

1.4 Substantiation requirements

Substantiation rules apply to certain expenses incurred, such as the use of a motor vehicle for business, overseas travel and extended domestic travel.[8] Visit the ATO's website at **www.ato.gov.au**, select the 'Tax Professionals' page and then type the word 'substantiation' into the search window. This will give many useful questions and answers on the topic and examples and explanations of the requirements. The rules apply to employees and self-employed persons. The general thrust of the legislation is to ensure that adequate documentation is maintained of all these expenses if they are to be deductible. The Act is quite specific as to the type of details required by the taxpayer and the records that need to be available to the Commissioner on request. Documents do not have to be lodged with returns, but the return form requires a signature from the taxpayer attesting to the fact that all the necessary receipts and records have been kept to substantiate the expenses claimed. For electronic lodgement of tax returns, the taxpayer is required to sign a declaration that attests to the accuracy of the information in the electronic return.

Car expenses require a **log book** if a business percentage is to be claimed. Three options are available to the taxpayer:

- log book records and all documentary evidence of vehicle expenses
- documentary evidence only for a claim of one-third of the vehicle expenses
- no evidence other than odometer readings for a claim of 12% of the car's value, this value being limited by section 42–80 for luxury vehicles.

Car expenses include depreciation on the vehicle but exclude taxi fares or similar expenses.

For business usage of a car when claiming less than 5000 kilometres:

- a rate per kilometre is available to the taxpayer
- opening and closing odometer readings should be recorded.

These kilometre rates are set by the Commissioner each year and are in accordance with the engine capacity of the vehicle. Larger vehicles over one tonne are exempt from these substantiation requirements.

Overseas travel and extended domestic travel require documentary evidence and a travel diary, while meal allowances need documentation unless satisfied by an overtime claim of 'reasonableness'. All documentary evidence should consist of a receipt or an invoice that shows:

- the date of the expense
- the name of the supplier
- the amount and currency of the expense
- the nature of the goods or services supplied
- the date on which the document was made out.

Such evidence should be made out in English or in the language of the country in which the expense was incurred. Taxpayers who use their home office for work must keep a diary for at least a four-week period so that a pattern of use for electricity and gas can be established and depreciation on home office furniture can be calculated. Then either a claim per hour or a percentage of actual cost can be made. Remember to regularly review this estimate.

It is important to remember that not only does a taxpayer have to obtain the relevant documentary evidence, but he or she must also retain car and travel evidence for a standard period of five years after the date on which the return is lodged. If any other expenses are incurred in the course of employment, records must be retained for a period of three years and six months.

Active reflection

What evidence is needed to substantiate home office electricity and gas usage and depreciation on home office furniture?

1.5 Compliance programs

Much of the ATO's work is now carried out in compliance programs. These are sometimes in the form of interviews or **desk audits** conducted at ATO premises, and taxpayers are generally randomly chosen so as to enable statistical information to be gathered and their returns to be checked for adherence to tax laws. These audits are a necessary part of compliance as many ATO requirements are now self-assessed. Taxpayers have certain rights, such as:

- requesting that their tax agent or accountant be present
- requesting a mutually convenient time for the interview
- being allowed reasonable time to gather records
- being afforded an opportunity to explain any circumstances that may prima facie lead to a reduction of penalty tax
- being given a copy of the interview if required
- objecting to any assessment or penalty that may result from the audit.

Taxation requirements mean that you need good office planning to keep all **relevant records** safe. One helpful aid is to use colour-coded paper for different tax years. You can also use a checklist with deadline dates displayed, prepare a lodgement program for each client notifying them of the month you will require their tax information, and perhaps produce a quarterly newsletter from the accounting office to keep clients up to date with significant changes in the law. This, of course, also helps you and your staff to keep abreast of the continuing changes in the legislation. Remember that regular staff training and professional development is a sound investment, even if you have only a very small team.

The Commissioner is committed to the compliance program and is implementing a uniform eligibility test for small businesses, making it easier for them to determine whether they meet the requirements for concessions covering capital gains tax, GST and the Simplified Tax System. The ATO will also aggressively pursue individual taxpayers and small business owners who do not comply with the requirements of the tax legislation. You can check these strategies by logging on to the ATO's website at **www.ato.gov.au**.

Active reflection

It is important to understand taxpayers' rights as well as their obligations. What are three of these rights?

1.6 Capital gains tax

Capital gains tax (CGT) legislation was first introduced into Australia in 1985 and generally applies only to assets acquired after 19 September 1985. This original legislation referred to CGT applying on the disposal of CGT assets.

Since the introduction of the *Income Tax Assessment Act 1997* the CGT provisions, contained in Part 3-1 (general rules) and Part 3-3 (more specialised rules), were rewritten and now three issues must be considered to determine whether CGT applies:

- whether a CGT event[9] has occurred
- whether an exemption or concession applies
- whether a capital gain or a capital loss results.

For assets held prior to 21 September 1999, instead of the 'discount method' taxpayers can choose as an alternative the previous method of adjusting the cost base for inflation using quarterly consumer price indices, but this inflation adjustment was 'frozen' at September 1999. Thus taxpayers are not disadvantaged by this change; they can still choose the method that gives the best result.

In the past, one of the strongest criticisms of CGT was the complexity of the calculation, whereby the capital gain had to be discounted for inflation using the quarterly **consumer price index (CPI)** provided by the Australian Bureau of Statistics. Major amendments, however, were made to CGT to apply from 21 September 1999 and any capital gain on assets held for more than 12 months may now be discounted by:

- 50% for individuals
- 33.3% for certain superannuation funds
- nil for companies.

For a deeper understanding of how CGT works, check out the ATO's website at **www.ato.gov.au**. Select the 'Tax Professionals' page and then choose 'CGT'.

Example of the discount method

For the year ended 30 June 2009 Jan's payment summary shows the following information:

- gross wages of $48 000
- PAYG tax withheld of $9900.

In addition, Jan had bank interest of $1000 and on 1 June 2009 she sold some shares in ABC Ltd for $15 000. These particular shares cost her $9000 when they were purchased on 1 May 2000.

Jan's taxable income for the year ended 30 June 2009 would be:

	$	$
Gross wages		48 000
Interest		1 000
Net capital gain		
Sales value	15 000	
Less cost base	9 000	
Capital gain	6 000	
Less: 50% discount	3 000	
Assessable capital gain		3 000
Taxable income (TI)		**52 000**
Prime tax payable on $52 000	9 600	
Medicare levy payable on $52 000	780	
Gross tax payable		**10 380**
Less: PAYG tax withheld	9 900	
Net tax payable		**480**

Note: If Jan had purchased the shares in ABC Ltd on, say, 1 May 2009 rather than 1 May 2000 (i.e. she had held them for less than 12 months), her taxable income would have been $55 000 and her net tax payable would have been $1425 ($945 greater) because the full amount of $6000 (capital gain) would have been included as income.

It is important to appreciate that the capital gains legislation divides gains and losses into various categories, and any gains or losses can be offset only against their own class of asset.

Capital losses

If the CGT calculation after a CGT event results in a net loss rather than a net gain, this net loss must be used against capital gains in a particular order:

- first in the current year, or
- carried forward (indefinitely) to future years.

Note: Whenever a **capital loss** has to be taken into account and combined with a capital gain, this has to be done before the discount is applied if using the discount method.

Example

- If an individual has a capital gain of $1000 in a particular year, sales value of $5000 less cost base of $4000, and
- a capital loss of $800 in the same year or carried forward (unused) from a previous year,

the net capital gain for tax purposes would be calculated as follows:

	$
Capital gain	1000
Less: Capital loss	800
Capital gain	200
Less: 50% discount	100
Net capital gain for income tax purposes	**100**

As well as the laws regarding income and capital gains, there are various statutory requirements covering GST, payroll taxes, transactions duties, land tax, Tax File Numbers, Australian Business Numbers, higher education support fees and superannuation guarantee levies. The office manager must be aware of all of these. A sound, methodical approach is required when putting a management system in place that will adequately deal with these matters. Perhaps the key to achieving this degree of organisation is, first, an understanding of the business legal requirements and, second, a disciplined strategy for office tax procedures.

1.6 Active reflection

What are the three issues that must be considered to determine whether CGT applies?

Tax in practice

Here is an exemplar of income tax and capital gains tax in practice.

Andrew earns a wage of $65 000 per year, has allowable work-related expenses of $1700 and earns bank interest of $950. Andrew bought some shares for $6500 two years ago and sold them for $10 000, making a capital gain of $3500 for the current year. Last year he made a $1500 loss on the sale of some shares and this was carried forward unused. Andrew had an amount of $15 750 withheld as PAYG tax during the year.

Calculate Andrew's gross assessable income, taxable income, gross tax liability and net tax liability for the year ended 30 June 2009.

	$	$	$
Gross wages		65 000	
Interest		950	
Capital gain			
Sales value	10 000		
Less: Cost base	6 500		
Capital gain this year	3 500		
Less: Carried forward capital losses	1 500		
Net capital gain	2 000		
Discount amount 50% assessable gain		1 000	
Gross assessable income			**66 950**
Less: Allowable deductions			1 700
Taxable income (TI)			**65 250**
Prime tax payable on $65 250		13 575.00	
Add: Medicare levy payable on $65 250		978.75	
Gross tax payable			**14 553.75**
Less PAYG withholding tax		15 750.00	
Net tax refundable (notice the minus result)			**–1 196.25**

Learning check

✓ Calculate the taxable income of an individual, given assessable income and general and specific allowable deductions.

✓ Calculate the Medicare levy, primary tax and net taxation liability for an individual.

✓ Calculate net tax liability after applying available offsets and tax credits.

Taxation vocabulary

allowable deductions
assessable income
Australian Taxation Office (ATO)
Business Activity Statement (BAS)
capital
capital gain
capital gains tax (CGT)
capital loss
consumer price index (CPI)
desk audit
employer–employee relationship
exempt
fringe benefit
goods and services tax (GST)
gross tax payable
income
Instalment Activity statement (IAS)
internal control
log book
Medicare levy
mutuality principle
non-resident
PAYG income tax instalments
prime tax assessed
private ruling
public ruling
rates of tax
receipts
relevant records
resident
returns
revenue
self-assess
substantiation
tax
taxable income

Assumptions

Rates of tax for individuals from 1 July 2009

From $	To $	Rate
Nil	6000	Nil
6001	34 000	Nil plus 15 cents in $ in excess of $6000
34 001	80 000	$4200 plus 30 cents in $ in excess of $34 000
80 001	180 000	$18 000 plus 40 cents in $ in excess of $80 000
180 000	–	$58 000 plus 45 cents in $ in excess of $180 000

From 1 July 2008, the low income tax offset (LITO) increased from $750 to $1200 and begins to phase out at $34 000. Taxpayers eligible for the full LITO will not pay tax until their annual income exceeds $14 000 (up from $11 000).

Medicare levy: Currently 1.5% of taxable income.

Single taxpayers

Nil if taxable income is $17 309 or less. If taxable income is in the range $17 310 to $20 363, then 10% of the excess over $17 309.

Married taxpayers (one spouse only earning) or sole parents

Nil if family has a combined taxable income of $29 207 or less. If the family income is in the range $29 208 to $34 361, then 10% of the excess over $29 207. This range moves up by $2682 from the lower limit for each dependent child or student and $3155 from the upper limit for each dependent child or student. If each spouse derives an income, more complicated rules apply.

A 1% Medicare surcharge applies in addition to the normal Medicare levy if the taxpayer, taxpayer's spouse and all dependants are not covered by private health insurance for private patient hospital care, and if the single taxable income is over the $70 000 threshold or the combined family taxable income is over the $140 000 threshold. Under *A New Tax System (Medicare Levy Surcharge Fringe Benefits) Act 1999*, this levy is imposed on taxable income plus reportable fringe benefits (see Chapter 5). This threshold increases by $1500 for every additional child or dependant. The surcharge will be adjusted pro rata for the number of days in the year that taxpayers and dependants are not fully covered.

Example

For the whole of the year Bob was not covered by private health insurance and he had a taxable income of $98 000 and reportable fringe benefits of $10 000. The Medicare levy and surcharge is calculated as follows:

Basic Medicare levy on taxable income = $98 000 × 1.5% = $1470

Surcharge of 1% on $108 000 = $1080

Therefore total Medicare levy and surcharge = $2550

multiple-choice questions

Circle the correct response. (Answers to odd-numbered multiple-choice questions are provided on page 318.)

1. By what date in the history of Australian taxation were all the colonies collecting income tax?

(a) 1880 (b) 1885 (c) 1900 (d) 1915

2. When did the Commonwealth government formally introduce the national collection of income tax?

(a) 1880 (b) 1885 (c) 1900 (d) 1915

3. Since what year has the Commonwealth been the sole collector of income tax revenue?

(a) 1915 (b) 1936 (c) 1942 (d) 1997

4. The states were entitled to impose an additional surcharge on income, but this was dismantled in:

(a) 1989 (b) 1997 (c) 1999 (d) 2000

5. To clarify certain grey areas of legislation, the Commissioner of Taxation will occasionally issue:

(a) income tax rulings

(b) international agreements (c) income tax regulations

(d) income tax rates

6. A 'resident' is defined in the *Income Tax Assessment Act* as:

(i) a person, other than a company, who resides in Australia

(ii) a person whose domicile is in Australia

(iii) a person who has been in Australia for at least six months

(iv) a company that is incorporated in Australia or carries on business in Australia

(a) (i) only (b) (i) and (ii) only (c) (i), (ii) and (iii) only (d) (i), (ii), (iii) and (iv)

7. A taxpayer has business income of $50 000, other assessable income of $26 000 and allowable general deductions of $10 000. His taxable income is:

(a) $86 000 (b) $76 000 (c) $66 000 (d) $26 000

8. A taxpayer has allowable general deductions of $5000, PAYG withheld of $9630 and a taxable income of $52 510. Her prime tax assessed is:

(a) $910.65 (b) $9630.00 (c) $9753.00 (d) $10 540.65

9. A taxpayer has allowable general deductions of $12 000, PAYG withheld of $8420 and assessable income of $70 100. Her net tax payable is:

(a) $3881.50 (b) $8420.00 (c) $12 301.50 (d) $11 430.00

10. If a single taxpayer with private health cover has assessable income of $112 000 and a taxable income of $102 000, what is the current Medicare levy payable?

(a) $2550.00 (b) $1680.00 (c) $2800.00 (d) $1530.00

11. If a single taxpayer, with no private health cover for any part of the year, has wages of $50 000, other assessable income of $25 000, reportable fringe benefits of $10 000, general deductions allowed of $5000 and PAYG withheld of $7500, the Medicare levy will be:

(a) $1050.00 (b) $1850.00 (c) $2125.00 (d) $1275.00

12. A married taxpayer with two dependent children has an assessable income of $151 000, allowable deductions of $1500 and his wife has no separate net income. The family is not covered by private health insurance. The Medicare levy would be:

(a) $2242.50 (b) $3775.00 (c) $3737.50 (d) $2265.00

quick-and-easy comprehension

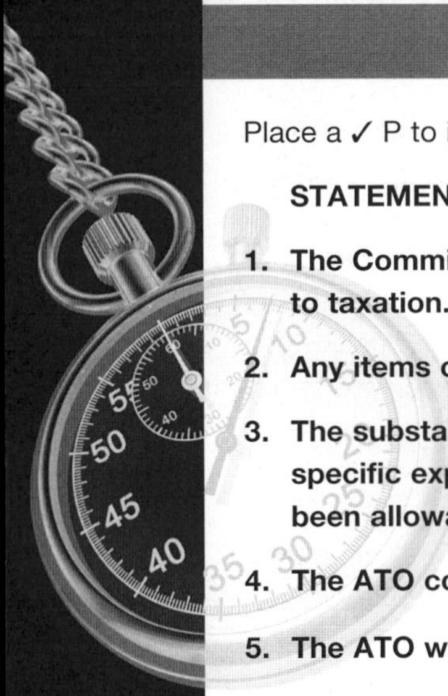

Place a ✓ P to indicate your response to each statement.

STATEMENT	TRUE	FALSE
1. The Commissioner is not concerned with non-income when calculating a liability to taxation.	—	—
2. Any items of income that are not assessable are exempt income.	—	—
3. The substantiation sections of the Act require documentary evidence of general or specific expenses to be retained; otherwise the expense is considered never to have been allowable.	—	—
4. The ATO compliance program randomly selects taxpayers for desk audits.	—	—
5. The ATO will calculate the Medicare levy based on assessable income.	—	—

self-test question

For the year ended 30 June 2009 Renee's payment summary shows wages of $30 000 with tax withheld of $4200. Renee also has bank interest of $2000 and allowable work-related expenses of $100.

On 1 June 2009 Renee sold some shares in XYZ Ltd for $5000. The shares cost her $3000 when purchased on 1 June 2002 and she had a carried forward loss of $250 from the AMP share demerger.

Calculate Renee's tax payable or refundable for the year ended 30 June 2009.

assessments

1. **Draw up a list of the characteristics of income and give a brief description of each characteristic.**
2. **A couple has approached you and asked for assistance in identifying the liability each of them may have with regard to taxation. Write a checklist of the questions you might initially ask.**
3. **Ben is self-employed and his business profit for tax purposes is calculated as $55 500. His wife, Dot, assists him and is paid $5900 per year as a wage. State whether Ben and Dot will be under a liability to lodge a tax return. Would it make a difference if they told you that they had three children, all of whom were dependent?**
4. **Why in most cases are the gains and losses from gambling considered non-income for a taxpayer, thus excluding them from capital gains tax provisions?**
5. **If Ben and Dot said that they were intending to build a holiday cottage using some of the discarded materials from Ben's subcontracting business, how would you advise them to record these transactions in their business books? Are there tax implications of which they should be made aware?**
6. **For the year ended 30 June 2009 Robyn's payment summary shows wages of $60 000 with tax withheld of $14 000. Robyn also has an investment and received interest of $3000. Allowable expenses of $200 related to Robyn's investment income. On 1 May 2009 some shares in Boost Juice Ltd were sold for $12 000. The shares originally cost $9500 when purchased on 1 May 2003 and Robyn had a carried forward loss of $1500 from a previous share capital event. Calculate Robyn's tax payable or refundable for the year ended 30 June 2009.**

case study information

Tom and Jan Masonry are the directors of a construction company, Colossal Constructions Pty Limited. Tom is fully employed as the managing director of operations and Jan takes care of the office and accounting, also on a full-time basis. They have three children: one has just completed a TAFE course and is about to start a landscaping business using a company structure, one is at university and the other is at secondary school. The family lives in a pleasant bungalow on the outskirts of a capital city, not far from their operations yard. Their home address is 10 Pleasant Drive, Forest, STATE 8051. Tom and Jan both work hard in the business. Tom drives a company utility and Jan has a station sedan owned by the company that not only serves to transport the family on outings but is also used occasionally to collect materials for both operations and the office. Jan received an inheritance in July 1998, and immediately invested in a mixed portfolio of shares and a long-term investment at the local bank. Her interest and dividends provide a modest regular addition to her wage income.

Tom and Jan own a holiday cottage by the sea where they spend occasional weekends and their annual holidays. They rent out their cottage for one week at Easter and two weeks at Christmas, a total of three weeks, and the revenue helps to cover local council rates and other charges associated with the cottage. Just recently, in 2008, the couple applied successfully for an investment loan to purchase a residential unit that is rented on a long-term basis through their local real estate agent. This investment will help to fund their future retirement.

Colossal Constructions Pty Limited has grown into a medium-sized enterprise employing 15 people. The company's gross annual income is in excess of $2 million but less than $20 million and its average annual payroll is $720 000. The annual tax withholding is greater than $25 000 but less than $1 million. The company's ABN is 40 915 311 539 and the company is registered for GST.

The address for the service of notices is 35–39 Woodgrove Avenue, Littletown, STATE 8005. The Tax File Number is 12 654 987. Contact details are as follows: telephone 041 693 017; email **tom@colossal.com.au**; and facsimile 041 963 741.

case study questions

1. **Tom earns an annual income of $75 000 as managing director of Colossal Constructions. He has work-related expenses of $2500, all of which are allowable general deductions as he has kept the correct substantiation. His PAYG withholding tax is $22 500 and he is entitled to claim a medical rebate of $1000.**
2. **Tom and Jan received $8000 rent from their new investment unit and incurred $1000 in expenses for the period. They share equally the income and expenses from the investment unit.**
3. **Jan earns $60 000, has $13 000 PAYG withholding tax per year and claims work-related expenses of $320, all of which are allowable deductions.**

Required

For both Tom and Jan, calculate the prime tax payable, the Medicare levy, the gross tax payable and the net tax payable for the year using the current rates. Show your workings.

classroom activities

1. **Group work (approximately 30 minutes)**
   In groups of three to five students, devise five questions relating to tax aspects studied in this chapter. You have approximately seven minutes to do so. Then exchange the questions with another group, and after seven minutes discussion the spokesperson from each group is to give the answers to the questions. The group that wrote the questions can award marks for each correct answer.
2. **Individual web search for news (approximately 40 minutes in a class of 20)**
   Prepare a two-minute talk using any recent material from the ATO's What's new website (accessed via **www.ato.gov.au**). Select the What's new button, making sure that the news has been listed in the last month.
3. **Individual web search for substantiation**
   Make a list of all the substantiation items listed on the ATO's website at **www.ato.gov.au**. Select 'Tax professionals' and search for 'substantiation'. This gives a list of all expenses subject to this rule.
4. **Group web search for Taxpayers' Charter**
   In groups of three to five, look on the ATO's website at **www.ato.gov.au** to find the rights that the ATO promises to uphold. Select 'Booklets and Publications' then 'Taxpayers' Charter'. Discuss the charter and determine whether there are any other rights that you think the ATO should support.

self-test question solution

	$	$	$
Gross wages		30 000.00	
Interest received		2000.00	
Capital gain			
Sales value XYZ shares	5000.00		
Less: Cost base	3000.00		
Capital gain this year	2000.00		
Less: Carried forward capital losses	250.00		
Net capital gain	1750.00		
Discount amount 50% assessable gain		875.00	
Total assessable income			**32 875.00**
Less: Allowable deductions			100.00
Taxable income (TI)			**32 775.00**
Prime tax payable on TI		4016.25	
Add: Medicare levy payable on TI		491.63	
Gross tax payable			**4507.88**
Less: PAYG tax withheld		4200.00	
Net tax payable			**307.88**

Notes

1. A 'resident' is defined in the Act as meaning all of the following:
   - a person, other than a company, who resides in Australia
   - a person whose domicile is in Australia
   - a person who has been in Australia for at least six months
   - a company that is incorporated in Australia or carries on business in Australia.
2. Refer to sections 221AK–221AZU, Part VI Division 1A, of ITAA 1936.
3. See capital gains tax legislation, Divisions 100–152, ITAA 1997.
4. See section 26-5, ITAA 1997.
5. See *Fringe Benefits Tax Assessment Act 1986*.
6. See sections 50, 51 and 52, ITAA 1997.
7. See Division 18, sections 160AE–160AGB, ITAA 1936.
8. See Division 28, ITAA 1997.
9. The CGT events are summarised in sections 104–105 being event A1 to event L, and are not in any particular order. Event A1 on the disposal of a CGT asset is the most commonly used section.

2 The tax file number and Australian Business Number systems

Chapter two

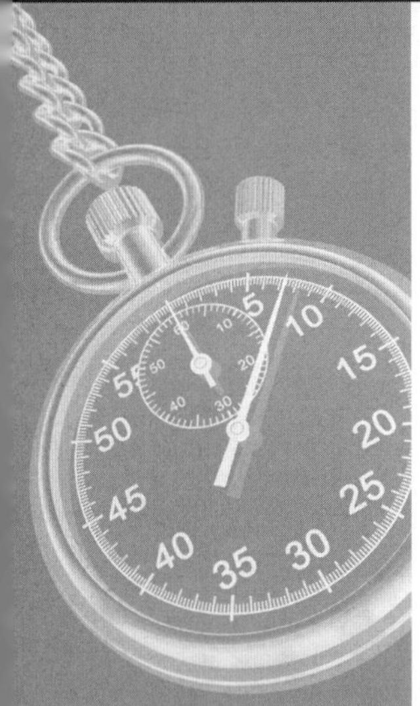

Topics

After studying this chapter, you should be able to:

- **explain what a tax file number (TFN) is and the purpose of the TFN system**
- **explain what an Australian Business Number (ABN) is and the purpose of the ABN system**
- **describe when and how an employee should quote a TFN**
- **explain the obligations of an employer when a TFN is quoted and when a TFN is not quoted**
- **identify the types of investments that require a TFN or ABN to be quoted, and those that are exempt from the requirement**
- **explain the obligations imposed on an investment body in relation to:**
  - the withholding of tax
  - reporting to the tax office and to the investor
- **outline the procedure for applying for a TFN**
- **outline the procedure for applying for an ABN.**

OVERVIEW

The **Australian Taxation Office (ATO)** uses a system of unique identification numbers to distinguish taxpayers. **Tax file numbers (TFNs)** have become the cornerstone on which our national taxation system is built. It is common for these numbers to be used for many other purposes, such as in the area of social security payments. For any system or database to be efficient, it must be possible to access individual records without the threat of there being any mistaken identity, and the ATO is very careful to make sure that its TFN system is secure and efficient.

On 1 July 2000 the ATO began a range of tax reforms in Australia known as *A New Tax System* (ANTS), and one of its major reforms was the introduction of another unique identification number, intended only for taxpayers in business. This number, the **Australian Business Number (ABN)**, is issued only to entities that request registration and can demonstrate that they are carrying on an enterprise. The enterprise can be carried on as an individual, a partnership, a company, a fund or a trust.

Put simply, individuals or entities not carrying on an enterprise (i.e. not in business) are issued only with a TFN, whereas all individuals and entities carrying on an enterprise have both a TFN and an ABN.

This chapter examines how the system works, when **quotation** of a TFN or an ABN is essential and when it is optional, and why there is sometimes withholding tax. Some exemptions to the TFN requirement are identified, along with the notification requirements. The impact of the *Privacy Act* on the quotation of TFNs and ABNs is examined.

2.1 The tax file number system

To be able to clearly identify and distinguish between taxpayers, the ATO issues each taxpayer with a unique number called a *tax file number*. This number, commonly referred to as a *TFN*, is typically a nine-digit number for individuals, partnerships, trusts, companies, superannuation funds and other non-incorporated organisations. It has a built-in mathematical algorithm check to ensure its accuracy.

Each taxpayer is issued with only one TFN, which will not change even if the taxpayer subsequently changes his or her name—as, for example, in marriage. The one practical exception to this rule applies to partnerships. Whenever a new partner is admitted to an existing partnership or an existing partner retires, at law the existing partnership ceases and a new partnership comes into existence. Thus, again at law, as the old partnership has ceased, there is technically the need for a new TFN to be obtained. It seems, however, that the ATO does not strictly enforce this requirement as long as income tax returns are lodged on time and the partnership's net income is correctly distributed to the appropriate partners.

Without such a unique TFN system it would be difficult for the ATO to ensure that:

- the affairs of one taxpayer are not mixed up with those of another
- non-disclosure of income is detected
- checking and matching processes are used efficiently in conjunction with its audit program.

in some cases, the ABN confirmed immediately and a follow-up written notification of the TFN and ABN mailed out to the business later. This is clearly the quickest way to achieve registration. Superannuation funds registering for *A New Tax System* are also required to complete a paper application (which is **downloadable** from **www.abr.gov.au**).

2.1 Active reflection

Advise an individual what he or she must do to obtain a TFN.

2.2 The Australian Business Number system

The Australian government introduced the Australian Business Number system in response to businesses calling for less 'red tape'. The ABN is a single identifying number for a business to use in all of its dealings with government departments and agencies. All entities without branch registration receive an 11-digit ABN, which has a built-in mathematical algorithm check to ensure its accuracy. If an entity has applied for branch registration, it will receive a 14-digit ABN. For companies, the ABN is made up of a nine-digit Australian Company Number (ACN) plus two digits. There are no letters at all in the ABN, only digits.

The business ABN will not cover all dealings with the ATO and government. You still need to quote a TFN when lodging income tax returns and you still need to attend to registration requirements regarding business names.

Since the introduction of *A New Tax System*, it is important for a business to obtain an ABN as soon as possible, for without an ABN any amounts received will be subject to tax being withheld at the rate of 46.5%. Individuals (e.g. employees) need a TFN but not necessarily an ABN, but it would be unusual for a non-individual entity not to need both a TFN and an ABN.

ABNs are necessary for certain business dealings with the ATO, including:

- Pay As You Go system (see Chapter 3)
- lodging a **Instalment Activity Statement** (**IAS**), if required (see Chapter 3, Section 3.7)
- lodging a **Business Activity Statement** (**BAS**) (see Chapter 6)
- **goods and services tax (GST)** (Chapter 4)
- fringe benefits tax (see Chapter 5).

Charities also have to obtain an ABN before they can access certain concessions offered to them under *A New Tax System*.

An entity can apply for more than one ABN if this would assist in accounting for GST and PAYG. For example, where an entity has two interstate branches, each with a separate accounting system, it may be advantageous to have separate ABNs.

The details of all ABN registrations have become part of the **Australian Business Register** that is maintained by the ATO. This register can be accessed from the interactive Business Entry Point (at **www.business.gov.au**).

In the future, it is intended that the Australian Business Register will be used by state, territory and local governments to cover government dealings at all levels. Applicants will be able to:

- register a new business at only one entry point and all registration requirements, at all levels of government, will be attended to
- notify only one government agency of any changes in their business and all levels of government will be notified.

Eventually, it is hoped that the ABN will replace the ACN system at present required under Corporations Law.

To be registered for GST it is necessary to have an ABN and to quote this number on all tax invoices (see Chapter 4, Section 4.2). However, a small business may not be required to register for GST (see Chapter 4, Section 4.3) but may still register for an ABN.

In summary, to ensure compliance for all taxation record-keeping, the ATO requires that all business-to-business transactions be evidenced by an invoice with an ABN quoted, otherwise tax has to be withheld at the rate of 46.5%. (This is discussed fully in Chapter 3, Section 3.4.)

Active reflection

Briefly explain why a business needs an ABN and what the consequences are of not having one.

2.3 Applying for an ABN

Businesses wishing to apply for an ABN have a variety of options, which ultimately will require them to use the appropriate registration application form (see Appendix, Form 2.2 [2938] for individuals and Form 2.3 [2939] for companies, partnerships, trusts and other organisations). This can be done electronically, through:

- the Australian Business Register (**www.abr.gov.au**), if applying only for an ABN
- the Business Entry Point (**www.business.gov.au**), where other government obligations can be accessed as well as applying for an ABN.

Other options for obtaining these application forms are:

- through a tax agent, who will lodge an application using the **Electronic Lodgment Service (ELS)**
- on a paper application form, available from most newsagents or by telephoning the ATO on 13 28 66 between 8 am and 6 pm Monday to Friday.

ABN applications that are lodged electronically are generally processed immediately, whereas paper lodgements may take at least 14 days. If this delay will lead to problems, then, after the application has been lodged, a **safety net letter** can be requested. This letter allows the business to operate in the *New Tax System* for a period of 28 days from the date of issue and to not have tax withheld on monies received for goods and services supplied. Attached to the safety net letter will be a Notice of Withholding Rate Variation. A copy of this notice must be given to each business that pays for goods or services supplied.

Situations that lead to the need for a safety net letter include:

- transactions are being conducted where the withholding tax under PAYG arrangements will create cash-flow hardships for the client
- there are strict time constraints on the incorporation of a new company
- a business transition or contractual transaction has strict time constraints
- reconstructed partnerships have debtor/creditor transactions pending.

To apply for a safety net letter, telephone the Business Tax Reform Infoline on **13 24 78**. The ATO advises when the request is accepted and a safety net letter will be issued by Express Post within one working day.

Who is entitled to an ABN?

To be registered with an ABN, an entity must be one of the following:

- a company registered under Corporations Law in Australia
- a government department or agency
- an **entity** carrying on an **enterprise** in Australia.

An *entity* means an individual (sole trader), a body corporate, a company, a body political, a government body, a partnership, any other unincorporated association or body of persons, a trust or a superannuation fund.

An *enterprise* means any activity:

- in the form of a business
- in the form of an adventure or a concern in the nature of trade
- on a regular or continuous basis, in the form of a lease, licence or grant of an interest in property
- by a trustee of a fund or by an authority or institution to which deductible gifts can be made
- by a charitable institution
- by a religious institution
- by a Commonwealth, state or territory body.

Note, however, that an enterprise *does not* include activities undertaken:

- as an employee, a company director or an office holder or under a labour hire arrangement
- as a private recreational pursuit or hobby
- by an individual or a partnership without a reasonable expectation of profit or gain
- by a member of a local governing body.

It is worth noting that not all entities are entitled to an ABN. To be entitled to an ABN, the entity must meet either criterion 1 or criterion 2 (see below), as set out by the ATO.

For partnerships, where all or most of the partners are individuals there must be a reasonable expectation of a profit being made. If the entity does not meet criterion 1 or 2, it is not entitled to an ABN.

Criterion 1

The entity is entitled to an ABN if it is a:

- company incorporated under the *Corporations Act 2001* in Australia
- charitable institution or trustee of a charitable fund in Australia
- deductible gift recipient in Australia

- religious institution in Australia.

Criterion 2

The entity is entitled to an ABN if it can answer 'yes' to the following statements:

- Its activity is carried out:
  - in the form of a business
  - in the nature of trade
  - in the form of a regular or continuous grant of a lease, licence or interest in property.
- Its activity is carried out in Australia or it makes supplies that are connected with Australia.
- Its activity is not a private recreational pursuit or hobby.

Active reflection 2.3

Outline the procedure that a business taxpayer wishing to obtain an ABN must follow.

2.4 Employee quotation of the TFN

As noted in Section 2.1, the TFN system provides an opportunity for the ATO to check information as disclosed in an income tax return against information it can obtain from other sources, such as:

- its copy of payment summaries (see Chapter 3)
- bank and other financial institutions' details of interest paid
- public companies' details of dividends paid
- reportable fringe benefits (see Chapter 5)
- eligible termination payments
- amounts payable under the Higher Education Loan Program scheme (see Chapter 8).

Thus the Australian taxation system now has a common feature running through it—the opportunity to quote an appropriate TFN. It should be noted, however, that it is not compulsory to quote a TFN; rather, it is an optional system with the following consequences:

- If a TFN is quoted, tax is deducted or withheld at the minimum possible rate as set by the Income Tax Regulations.
- If a TFN is not quoted, tax is deducted or withheld at the maximum possible rate as set by the Income Tax Regulations.

Note: An employee has the opportunity to quote a TFN via the **TFN declaration**. An investor has the opportunity to quote a TFN via an appropriate **TFN notification form**.

If a TFN is not quoted, the employer or investment body must deduct tax at the rate equivalent to the maximum personal tax rates plus Medicare levy (for resident investors). For the year ended 30 June 2009, this is 46.5%, made up of the maximum personal tax rate (45%) and the Medicare levy (1.5%).

In practice, employers refer to the weekly, fortnightly or monthly PAYG withholding tax table (see Chapter 3, Table 3.1) to determine the correct amount of tax to withhold. However, a quick check of the rate appropriate for non-quotation of a TFN will confirm that the percentage is as stated above. Quotation of TFNs has also been extended to provide a more secure system that is less likely to be abused. For example:

- Quotation of TFNs is now a precondition to receiving Centrelink and Veterans' Affairs pensions.
- Quotation of TFNs is now necessary when making payments to the Child Support Agency.

2.4 Active reflection

What are the consequences for an employee who does not quote a TFN to his or her employer?

2.5 Investments subject to the TFN system

The legislation requires the following types of investments to be subject to the TFN system:

- interest-bearing accounts and deposits with financial institutions such as banks and credit unions
- interest-bearing deposits or debentures with government bodies or companies
- monies deposited into the trust account of a solicitor for reinvestment or on-lending
- units in a unit trust, including cash and property trusts
- shares in a public company
- certain investment-related prizes wherein the cash received or credited is classified as income for the purposes of the TFN system.

Investment bodies and banks have forms that you need to use when advising them of a TFN or an ABN. It is necessary to obtain the correct form, complete the details required and submit this to the investment body, *not* the ATO.

2.5 Active reflection

Advise a taxpayer how to inform an investment institution of his or her TFN or ABN.

2.6 Withholding tax

The TFN system has very specific requirements as to the obligations of an investment body in regards to investment-related activities.

Since 1 July 2000 the rules concerning the withholding of tax have been contained within the new PAYG withholding provisions, as well as section 12 of the *Taxation Administration Act 1953* (as amended).

If an investor does not quote a TFN or an ABN where appropriate, the investment body must withhold the appropriate amount from the monies otherwise payable. As outlined in Section 2.1, the current appropriate rate is 46.5%.

For investments held in a business capacity, investors have the option of quoting either their TFN or their ABN. It should be noted, however, that the option of quoting an ABN is available only to an entity that makes an investment in its own name, and where the investment is in the course of its business.

Example

Renee, a sole trader, can quote either her TFN or her ABN in respect of a term deposit of business funds paid in advance by a customer, whereas in relation to a private account to pay private mortgage repayments Renee should quote her TFN only.

The rule requiring tax to be withheld applies irrespective of when the investment was originally made. The withholding tax should be deducted at the time of payment or crediting the income. The monies withheld must be paid to the ATO via the investment body's Business Activity Statement within 21 days of the end of the month in which the payment was made. There are various penalty provisions for failure to comply with the conditions set out above, and they include:

- for failure to remit amounts withheld on time, a fine of $5000 or imprisonment, or both
- for late payment, currently 16%, plus an interest penalty also currently at 16%
- for an investment body that does not deduct the appropriate amount of withholding tax, a penalty of $1000.

It should be noted here that, for resident taxpayers, the fact that TFN withholding tax has been deducted does not mean that the final liability for income tax on the relevant investment income has been assessed. Rather, the net income received has to be '**grossed-up**' to calculate the amount that would have been received had the TFN withholding tax not been deducted. This grossed-up amount then forms part of the recipient's assessable income, which together with all other assessable income, less all allowable deductions, determines the taxable income. It therefore appears at this stage that the relevant investment has been double-taxed. However, this apparently harsh treatment is resolved because, after the calculation of taxable income, the final calculation of the amount payable allows as a credit the amount of withholding tax withheld by the investment body. (Have another look at Figure 1.1 in Chapter 1, showing the taxing process.)

Example

For the year ending 30 June 2009, Jan Masonry's payment summary shows a salary of $39 050, with PAYG withholding tax deductions of $7000. Jan had quoted her TFN to her employer. She also received net bank interest of $535 after the bank had deducted $465 from the interest payable on a fixed-interest term deposit. Jan had not quoted her TFN to the bank. Her allowable deductions were bank fees and charges of $50.

Thus Jan's taxable income for the year ended 30 June 2009 would be:

$$\$39\,050 + \$535 + \$465 - \$50 = \$40\,000$$

Prime tax on taxable income		$4200.00
Add: Medicare levy @ 1.5% of taxable income		$480.00
Gross tax payable		$4680.00
Less: PAYG withholding tax	$7000.00	
TFN withholding tax credit	$465.00	$7465.00
Amount refundable		$2785.00

2.6 Active reflection

How much interest would an individual receive from a 12-month term deposit of $10 000 paying 5% interest if the individual did not quote his or her TFN to the investment body?

2.7 Exemptions to the TFN system

In most cases, a TFN must be quoted if the maximum tax is not to be deducted from any interest or investment income. However, there are also some **exemptions**, which relieve some persons of the need to quote their TFN. These exemptions do not mean exemption from paying income tax. If the taxable income is sufficiently high, tax will be payable.

Children

Investment income only

If a child is under the age of 16 on the 1 January preceding the payment, then for all types of investment income (excluding public company share investments) he or she is exempt from the requirement to quote a TFN, so long as the following conditions are fulfilled:

- the investment body is aware of the age of the investor
- the income from the investment is less than $420 annually.

Pensioners

Investment income only

People receiving all or part of the following Centrelink or Veterans' Affairs pensions or benefits are exempt from the requirement to quote a TFN:

- age pension
- disability support pension
- wife, carer or widow pension
- supporting parent's benefit
- special benefits
- rehabilitation allowance in lieu of the above
- pensions under the *Veterans' Entitlements Act*.

These conditions are applicable only if the investment body is given the recipient's full name and pension or benefit entitlement.

Other

Investment income only

Irrespective of the age of the investor, if the following circumstances exist the recipient is exempt from the requirement to quote a TFN:

- the investment is in an interest-bearing account or deposit, and
- the income from the investment is less than $120 annually.

Public company franked dividends

Regarding dividends from public company shares, the company paying the dividend is not required to withhold any tax in respect of any part of the dividend if that dividend has been declared partially or fully franked and thus has franking credits attached to it. This makes fully franked dividends exempt from the TFN rules and partly franked dividends partly exempt (on a pro-rata basis).

Norfolk Island residents

Bona fide residents of Norfolk Island are exempt from the requirement to quote a TFN in relation to the following types of income:

- investment income from sources within the territory
- investment income from sources outside Australia.

Charities and not-for-profit organisations without a TFN

Companies and unincorporated associations that are exempt from tax, or that do not need to lodge income tax returns and hence do not have a TFN, are also exempt from the requirement to quote a TFN. Again, this is on condition that they supply the following information to the investment body:

- full name
- full address
- the reason for the exempt status.

Unlike tax withheld, non-resident withholding tax is a separate obligation on the payers of interest, dividends etc. It is usually set at different rates: 30% on dividends or 15% if a double tax agreement is in place with the other country, 10% on interest payments and 30% on royalties.

Non-residents

Non-residents (as defined for income tax purposes) are exempt from the requirement to quote a TFN, provided they are liable for non-resident withholding tax on dividends, interest or royalties.

Non-resident withholding tax is the final taxation liability, with the resultant net income then specifically exempt from further taxation.

Note that for other types of income, such as salary or wages, business income or rental income, non-residents will require a TFN to enable the processing of their necessary income tax return.

2.7 Active reflection

Advise a 14-year-old how much interest he or she will receive from a 12-month term deposit of $1000 paying 5% interest if a TFN is not quoted to the investment body.

2.8 Notification requirements

The **TFN reporting system** imposes a number of reporting requirements on investment bodies, and these stipulations reinforce the efficiency of the system. All investment bodies must provide the following reports:

- *A TFN report—to the Commissioner of Taxation.* This report must be made within one month of the end of the previous quarter, covering all investments made within that quarter. An alternative report is allowable here, whereby the investment body reports only those TFNs investors supply to it that do not appear valid, as confirmed by the mathematical algorithm check.
- *Notification of amounts withheld—to the investor.* The investment body must notify the investor of the amount withheld at the same time as it notifies the investor of the details of the net income paid or credited.
- *Remittance of monies withheld—to the Commissioner of Taxation.* As stated previously, any amount withheld from monies paid or payable has to be paid to the ATO within 21 days of the end of the month in which the monies became legally payable.
- *Annual investment income report—to the Commissioner of Taxation.* For each financial year, most investment bodies must provide a written report to the Commissioner on all investments in the investment body. The report is due within four months of the end of the financial year.

  There are exceptions to this requirement, whereby the annual investment income report does not have to report amounts less than the relevant threshold (see Section 2.5), or if there are fewer than 10 investments in the investment body.
- *Annual reconciliation—to the Commissioner of Taxation.* Investment bodies must also provide a reconciliation of (1) amounts deducted during the year for non-quotation of a TFN, along with (2) amounts remitted to the Commissioner. This process accounts for any discrepancies.

2.8 Active reflection

Outline how the ATO can match details provided in an income tax return with actual interest and dividend amounts earned by the taxpayer.

2.9 Privacy safeguards

The ATO is eager to ensure that TFN and ABN information is not used for purposes other than those intended. There are special provisions in the *Taxation Administration Act 1953* authorising maximum penalties of a fine of $10 000 and/or two years' imprisonment for breaches of this requirement. These penalties are for the unauthorised collection, recording, use or disclosure of TFNs.

The *Privacy Act 1988* also imposes security conditions on recipients of TFN information, whereby internal control systems must be established to ensure that such information can be used and accessed by authorised persons only. Recipients of TFNs must ensure that all staff who have access to this information are aware of:

- the need to protect the privacy of TFNs
- how and when TFNs may be collected
- the prohibitions on the use and disclosure of TFNs
- the penalties for breaching the TFN privacy rules.

Access to ABN information does not have the same restrictions. It is public information and can be readily obtained from the Australian Business Register (at **www.abr.gov.au**). The penalty for incorrect use of an ABN—that is, when it is not that entity's valid ABN—comprises a prison sentence of two years.[1]

Active reflection 2.9

What are the consequences of using a person's TFN without authorisation?

TFNs and ABNs in practice

The TFN application for an individual requires proof-of-identity documents. Assume that Mr Pat Malone, born on 30 June 1970, already has a TFN, 100 000 001. He now wants to apply for an ABN, in order to be able to conduct a small part-time cleaning business as a sole trader. He will not employ any staff and believes that his business will bring in approximately $20 000 per annum. Mr Malone is not required to register for GST and he does not wish to do so, so for this exercise only the information needs to be completed to item 22.

Required

Apply for an ABN for Mr Pat Malone using Form 2.2 [2938] in the Appendix.

The solution follows on the next three pages.

multiple-choice questions

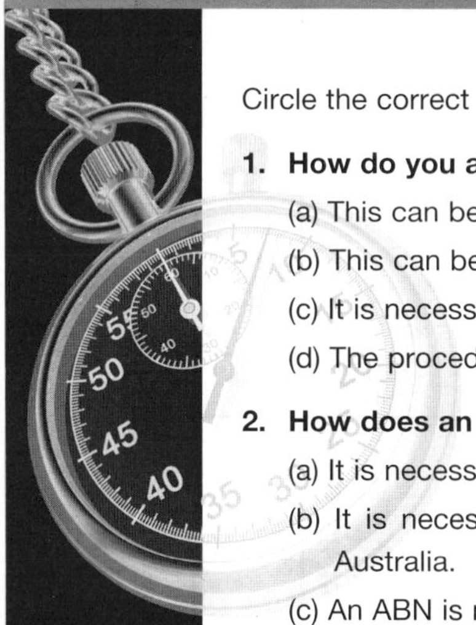

Circle the correct response. (Answers to odd-numbered multiple-choice questions are provided on page 318.)

1. **How do you apply for a TFN?**
   (a) This can be done over the telephone with the ATO.
   (b) This can be done at any post office in Australia.
   (c) It is necessary to complete a standard TFN application/inquiry form.
   (d) The procedure differs depending on whether the application is for an individual or a non-individual.

2. **How does an individual obtain an ABN?**
   (a) It is necessary to complete an application form.
   (b) It is necessary to complete an application form, and show that you are carrying on an enterprise in Australia.
   (c) An ABN is not necessary if you already have a TFN.
   (d) It can be done over the telephone with the ATO.

3. **Which of the following cases would *not* require the provision of proof-of-identity documents for an individual applying for a TFN?**
   (a) a pensioner applying for a TFN
   (b) a 15-year-old applying for a TFN
   (c) a secondary school student applying for a TFN through the school
   (d) proof-of-identity documents are always required when applying for a TFN

4. **Which of the following cases would *not* require the provision of proof-of-identity documents for a non-individual applying for a TFN/an ABN?**
   (a) all non-individual entities
   (b) a partnership applying for a TFN/an ABN
   (c) a company that already has an ACN
   (d) proof-of-identity documents are always required when applying for a TFN/an ABN

5. **Which of the following people do *not* require a TFN?**
   (a) a non-resident earning rental income in Australia
   (b) a school student aged 15 earning part-time employment income
   (c) a pensioner in receipt of the age pension
   (d) a child aged 10 who is in receipt of $200 in bank interest only

6. **Which of the following business entities may require the issuing of another TFN?**
   (a) a company (b) a trust (c) a partnership (d) a superannuation fund

7. **If a TFN or an ABN is required but is not correctly quoted, the amount of withholding tax is set at the rate of:**
   (a) 46.5% (b) 47.0% (c) Nil (d) 48.5%

8. **If a resident taxpayer aged 18 does not quote his/her TFN to a bank when investing $5000 in a term deposit:**
   (a) the bank will not deduct tax because of the age of the taxpayer
   (b) the bank will not deduct tax because term deposits are exempt from the TFN requirements
   (c) the bank will have to deduct 46.5% of all interest paid on the term deposit
   (d) the bank will not deduct tax if the taxpayer declares all the interest in the tax return

9. A person has had $139.50 TFN withholding tax deducted, and received $160.50 net interest for the year. When preparing a tax return he/she will:

(a) have to declare interest of $160.50 only

(b) have to declare $300 interest income and claim $139.50 TFN credit

(c) have to declare $300 interest income and claim $160.50 TFN credit

(d) not declare any interest as TFN tax has already been paid

10. With respect to TFNs:

(a) it is not compulsory for employees to give their TFN to their employer

(b) there are severe penalties for the unauthorised collection, recording or use of a TFN

(c) a non-resident earning rental income from Australia will require a TFN

(d) all of the above are true

11. Which of the following will be able to obtain an ABN?

(a) a schoolteacher whose only source of income is as an employee

(b) a singer who sings only with the church choir

(c) a police officer who also has a private security business earning $5000 in fees

(d) a gambler who bets $1000 per week on the poker machines

12. Which of the following will *not* be able to obtain an ABN?

(a) a partnership consisting of two individuals who themselves do not have ABNs

(b) a partnership consisting of two individuals without a reasonable expectation of profit

(c) a charitable institution

(d) a company registered under Corporations Law in Australia

quick-and-easy comprehension

Place a ✓ to indicate your response to each statement.

	STATEMENT	TRUE	FALSE
1.	**It is possible for two individuals to have the same TFN.**	—	—
2.	**To obtain a TFN all one has to do is fill in a current year income tax return form (without a TFN specified) and the ATO will automatically issue a TFN.**	—	—
3.	**If a sole trader changes from conducting business as an electrician to conducting business as a builder, it is not necessary to apply for another TFN.**	—	—
4.	**If a sole trader changes from conducting business as an electrician to conducting business as a builder, it is not necessary to apply for another ABN.**	—	—
5.	**It is compulsory for all employees and investors to quote their TFN to their employer or investment body.**	—	—
6.	**It is compulsory for all businesses to quote their ABN in all business-to-business transactions.**	—	—
7.	**TFN withholding tax, once paid, is the final taxation liability for the investor.**	—	—
8.	**The withholding tax system for non-residents is the same as the TFN system for resident taxpayers.**	—	—
9.	**Children under 16 are exempt from the need to quote a TFN to investment bodies.**	—	—
10.	**If a company is paying a fully franked dividend, it is required to withhold TFN tax from investors who have not quoted their TFN.**	—	—

self-test question

For the year ending 30 June 2009, Jan Masonry's payment summary shows a salary of $40 000, with PAYG withholding tax of $18 600. Jan did not quote her TFN to her employer. She also received net bank interest of $535 after the bank had deducted $465 from the interest payable on a fixed-interest term deposit. Jan had not quoted her TFN to the bank. Jan's allowable deductions were nil.

Calculate Jan's taxable income for the year ended 30 June 2009 and her net tax payable or amount refundable

assessments

1. **Ben, a student aged 18, does not have a TFN and intends to invest $10 000, being the proceeds from the sale of a car. The annual interest income will be $500. Advise Ben about the taxation implications of:**
   (a) not having a TFN and thus being unable to quote a TFN to the investment body
   (b) applying for a TFN and not quoting it to the investment body
   (c) applying for a TFN and quoting it to the investment body
2. **Using the correct TFN application form (make up details as required):**
   (a) apply for an individual TFN for yourself
   (b) apply for a TFN for a partnership consisting of yourself and a colleague, trading as Superior Surveyors
   (c) apply for a TFN for Builder Bob Pty Ltd
3. **For the year ended 30 June 2009, Audrey Scott's payment summary shows a salary of $40 000, with PAYG withholding deductions of $10 000. Audrey had quoted her TFN to her employer. Audrey also received net bank interest from a fixed-interest term deposit of $1070 after the bank had deducted tax from it of $930. Audrey had not quoted her TFN to this bank. Her allowable deductions totalled $300. Calculate:**
   (a) her taxable income for the year ended 30 June 2009
   (b) the amount of tax payable

case study question

Tom and Jan Masonry's son Martin has just incorporated a company and the following information is available:

- *Martin's Fabulous Landscapes Pty Ltd*, ACN 123 124 125.
- Martin is the sole director, secretary and shareholder of the private company.
- Martin intends to use his home address at 50 Pleasant Drive, Forest, STATE 8051 as the main business address and postal address for the company.
- Neither the company nor Martin has an email address or website address and Martin does not want to register for access to the ATO's online services for business.
- Martin is the authorised contact person for the company and his telephone numbers are: business 08 1234 5678; home 08 1234 6789; fax 08 1234 5677.
- The company is to commence trading as a new business on 1 July 2008.

- Assume that the business operates only in your state and is intended to operate for the long term.
- The company will operate in the construction industry and will derive its business income from property services. The company does not operate an agricultural property.
- The company is a resident of Australia for tax purposes, is not exempt from income tax, is not a not-for-profit organisation and does not want to register for any item included at item 27 on the application form.
- The company intends to use the services of tax agent Bill Smith, tax agent number 11111 222.

Required

Apply for a TFN and an ABN for *Martin's Fabulous Landscapes Pty Ltd* **using Form 2.3 [2939] in the Appendix (ensure you use the printed version of this form for this exercise). For the purposes of this case study question, complete the application only to the end of item 27: Does the entity want to be registered or endorsed for any of the following?**

Note: In Chapter 4 the case study question will ask you to complete the remainder of this application form.

classroom activities

Students are to form into pairs. One student is to take the role of the ATO and have the other student complete the TFN application Form 2.1 [1432] in the Appendix and submit it for discussion.

Then imagine you have created a partnership and using Form 2.3 [2939] in the Appendix apply for a TFN and an ABN.

self-test question solution

$40 000 + $535 + $465 = $41 000

Prime tax on taxable income		$6 900.00
Add: Medicare levy @ 1.5% of taxable income		$615.00
Gross tax payable		$7515.00
Less: PAYG withholding tax	$18 600.00	
TFN withholding tax credit	$465.00	$19 065.00
Amount refundable		$11 550.00

Note: The very large refund is the result of Jan not quoting her TFN to her employer.

Note

1. Section 23, *A New Tax System (Australian Business Number) Act 1999*.

3 Pay As You Go

Chapter three

Topics

After studying this chapter, you should be able to:

- **explain the overall Pay As You Go (PAYG) system and state how it fits into Australia's tax system**
- **outline the PAYG *withholding* system**
- **identify to whom the PAYG *withholding* system will apply**
- **calculate the amount of tax to be withheld under the PAYG *withholding* system**
- **explain the obligations of a payer with respect to**
  - registration under the PAYG *withholding* system
  - TFN declarations
  - reporting and remitting amounts withheld to the ATO
  - preparation of payment summaries for each payee
  - annual reporting to the ATO
- **explain the penalties for non-compliance with the PAYG *withholding* system**
- **outline the PAYG *instalments* system**
- **identify the entities affected by the PAYG *instalments* system**
- **explain the options for calculating the PAYG *instalment***
- **explain how and when PAYG *instalments* are paid to the ATO**
- **explain the procedure for varying the amount of PAYG *instalments*.**

OVERVIEW

The start of many important changes to the administration of the Australian tax system began on 1 July 2000. The **Pay As You Go (PAYG)** system is a significant part of these changes. In the past, one of the biggest criticisms of the various payment-in-advance systems was that there was too much 'red tape'. The new PAYG system streamlined the process, and incorporated the many previous systems into one system. For many businesses it now means one form to complete and a common payment date on either a monthly or quarterly basis depending on the size of the business or the business owner's preference. The new PAYG system replaced 11 previous systems, such as the pay as you earn (PAYE) system, the prescribed payments system (PPS), the reportable payments system (RPS), company instalments and provisional tax.

The PAYG system has two distinct components, known as PAYG *withholding* and PAYG *instalments*. The PAYG withholding component has not required many changes as it is very similar to the well-established *PAYE system* for employers. The PAYG instalment component (the means by which a business pays its own tax) has been modified many times in response to numerous criticisms from the business community. The practical impact of these modifications is that businesses now have some choice in how the PAYG instalment system affects them. Put simply, businesses can do their own calculations and consequently pay PAYG instalments based on their income for the relevant quarter, or they can accept an estimate calculated by the ATO.

Although, under the PAYG system, information is reported to the ATO and income tax is paid to the ATO, taxpayers are still required to lodge an income tax return after the end of the tax year. However, because the PAYG system requires tax to be paid in advance on a regular basis, it follows that any income tax liability that arises on the lodgement of an income tax return may already have been largely met by the advance payments.

The legislation under *A New Tax System Act 1999* requires businesses to lodge activity statements with the ATO and Chapter 6 examines this process in detail. Part of these activity statements cover the PAYG system, wherein a business will be required to report certain information and remit payment to the ATO in respect of tax withheld from salaries, wages and other payments (PAYG withholding) as well as **tax instalments** for the business's own tax (PAYG instalments). Figure 3.1 depicts the PAYG system.

3.1 The PAYG system and how it fits into Australia's New Tax System

The PAYG system is designed to match, for most taxpayers, the payment of tax to the earning of the associated income. On a regular basis, information is provided and tax is paid to the ATO based on simple calculations or estimates. These 'prepayments' are remitted to the ATO via a single reporting requirement, called an **activity statement**. When the income tax year is completed and the final year-end income tax liability has been established (based on taxable income), any amount prepaid under the PAYG system is allowed as a credit against this liability.

The PAYG system is only one part of the various reforms to Australia's *New Tax System*, and the legislation covering it can be found in Schedule 1, Parts 2-5 (PAYG withholding) and 2-10 (PAYG instalments) of the *Taxation Administration Act 1953*.

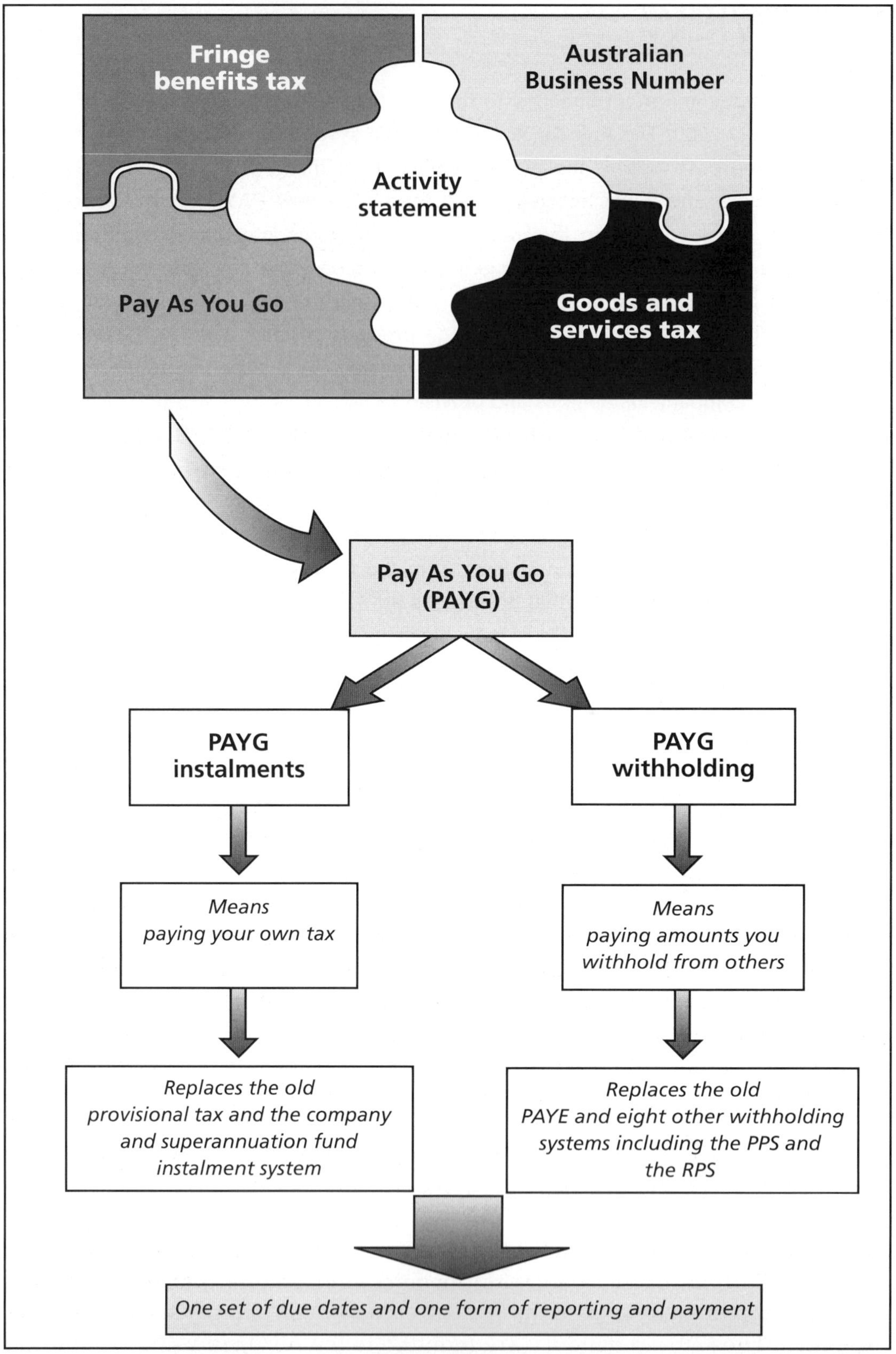

FIGURE 3.1 The PAYG system

Other reforms introduced include:

- the introduction of an Australian Business Number (ABN) system (see Chapter 2)
- the introduction of a goods and services tax (GST) (see Chapter 4)
- the introduction of a Business Activity Statement (BAS) (see Chapter 6)

- reforms to the fringe benefits tax (FBT) system (see Chapter 5).
- The PAYG system has two limbs:
- PAYG withholding
- PAYG instalments.

Active reflection 3.1

What do you understand by the term *PAYG*?

3.2 The PAYG withholding system

To date, the predominant form of taxation in Australia has been income tax, and employee salary and wage income accounts for a large proportion of this revenue. It is therefore logical that the taxation system has an inbuilt feature that causes the amount of tax that will probably be payable to be prepaid wherever possible.

A single form called an activity statement is used to report PAYG instalments and PAYG withholding. A business will use:

- a Business Activity Statement (BAS) if registered for GST
- an Instalment Activity Statement (IAS) if not registered for GST.

Employers already have to do various calculations in order to determine the amount of wages payable to each employee. Thus this is obviously a perfect opportunity for employers to also estimate the amount of income tax (and Medicare levy) payable for each employee and to remit these amounts to the ATO on a regular basis.

For many years a well-established scheme known as the PAYE system applied, whereby employers were compelled by law to deduct income tax from the wages of employees and to remit this amount to the ATO on a regular basis. After 30 June each year, the employer had to prepare a 'group certificate' for each employee. The employee used the certificate to complete his or her own income tax return for the year. This system was widely understood by business but was limited to collecting tax in respect of employees. During the 1980s and 1990s various other payment in advance and reporting systems were introduced, such as the PPS and the RPS, all of which had a different set of rules and had application only to certain industries.

Since 1 July 2000 the previous withholding systems have been combined into the one system known as the **PAYG withholding** system, with one set of rules and common dates for remittance of monies to the ATO. The PAYG withholding system draws heavily on the old system's framework, but it does have its own paperwork, jargon and procedures.

The process of withholding is one that requires a business or payer to deduct amounts from payments to others and remit these monies to the ATO on a regular basis. The payer must then prepare a PAYG **payment summary** for each payee at the end of the tax year, and this summary must show, inter alia:

- the total of gross payments made
- the total of income tax withheld.

Payees use this information to help prepare their annual income tax return, and are able to claim back the amount of income tax withheld when their income tax return is processed. The introduction of the new tax system saw the opportunity to extend this system of withholding, not only to the traditional employer/employee payments but also to:

- payments under **labour hire arrangements**
- payments under **voluntary agreements**
- payments where an ABN has not been properly quoted.

Active reflection

Explain to whom the PAYG withholding system applies.

3.3 Who is affected by the PAYG withholding system?

Most business operators are probably affected to some extent by the PAYG withholding system. More specifically, any business, not-for-profit organisation or government agency that makes payments to workers has to comply with some aspect of the PAYG withholding system.

The most obvious group affected by the PAYG withholding system is employers. Employers paying salaries and wages to employees are essentially required to carry out various tasks, as follows:

- collect **TFN declarations** from employees quoting their **tax file number (TFN)** and other relevant details to help establish the correct amount of tax to withhold (see Appendix, Form 3.1 [3092])
- complete the employer details of the TFN declaration and send it to the ATO within 14 days of receipt, or, if no TFN declaration is received, notify the ATO of this within 14 days
- withhold tax from each salary or wage payment as per withholding tax tables provided by the ATO
- remit those amounts withheld to the ATO on a regular basis, usually in conjunction with a monthly or quarterly activity statement (see Chapter 6)
- at year-end provide each employee with a PAYG payment summary in ATO format showing the gross amount earned, the total tax withheld and other required information
- after year-end provide the ATO with a **PAYG payment summary statement**, which provides a synopsis of PAYG payment summaries issued during the financial year to payees.

Businesses should ensure that they understand the full extent of the PAYG withholding system, as penalties for late lodgement of the above requirements accrue at the rate of $110 for each four-week period (to a maximum of $550). In some circumstances the penalties are larger.

Types of withholding

Table 3.1 shows the payments or events that are subject to the PAYG withholding system and ultimately require the collection or recovery of income tax and other liabilities.

TABLE 3.1 SUMMARY OF WITHHOLDING PAYMENTS

Item	Withholding payment	Section
1	A payment of salary etc to an employee	12-35
2	A payment of remuneration to the director of a company	12-40
3	A payment of salary etc to an office-holder (e.g. a member of the Defence Force)	12-45
3A	A payment to a religious practitioner	12-47
4	A return-to-work payment to an individual	12-50
5	A payment that is covered by a voluntary agreement	12-55
6	A payment under a labour hire arrangement or a payment specified by regulations	12-60
9	An unused leave payment	12-90
10	A social security or similar payment (e.g. old age pension)	12-110
11	A Commonwealth education or training payment	12-115
12	A compensation, sickness or accident payment	12-120
13	A payment arising from an investment where the recipient does not quote its TFN or, in some cases, its ABN	12-140
14	Investor becoming presently entitled to income of a unit trust	12-145
15	A payment for a supply where the recipient of the payment does not quote its ABN	12-190
16	A dividend payment to an overseas person	12-210
18	An interest payment to an overseas person	12-245
20	An interest payment derived by a lender in carrying on business through overseas permanent establishment	12-255
21	A royalty payment to an overseas person	12-280
22A	A departing Australia superannuation payment	12-305
22B	A payment (of a kind set out in the regulations) to a foreign resident	12-315
22C	A payment (of a kind set out in the regulations) received for a foreign resident	12-317
23	A mining payment	12-320
24	A natural resource payment	12-325
25	A payment by a managed investment trust	12-385
26	A payment by an intermediary	12-390

Source: Schedule 1, section 10-5 of the *Taxation Administration Act 1953*.

Payments to employees as salary and wages

Under the PAYG withholding system, the term **employee** has the normal meaning of the word, in that an employee is a person who receives payment in the form of a salary or wages in return for work or services rendered.

Typically the employer–employee relationship is a master–servant relationship. A detailed determination of whether a worker is an employee or not is outside the scope of this book; however, if in doubt, an ATO brochure, *PAYG withholding guide no. 2: How to determine if workers are employees or independent contractors (NAT 2780)*, has guidelines that may help determine whether or not the payment is to an employee and hence subject to the PAYG withholding system. Check the ATO's website (**www.ato.gov.au**) for some further definitions. A payment to an independent contractor (i.e. not an employee) will not usually be subject to withholding when the contractor provides an invoice quoting an ABN.

Payments under labour hire arrangements

It is fairly common for a business to contract with a labour hire firm to provide labour or services to that business. The labour hire firm does not actually perform the work; rather, it contracts with a worker to provide the required labour or service to the business. The problem in the past has been that the worker was actually not an employee of the labour hire firm or an employee of the business. Under the PAYG withholding system, the labour hire firm must withhold tax from payments it makes to its workers for performing labour or services for its clients. This means that a firm must withhold tax from payments made to workers even if the labour hire aspect is not the sole, or even the main, business of the firm.

Example

Colossal Constructions Pty Ltd contracts with Builders Labour Hire Pty Ltd to provide labour at one of its building sites for a three-week period at a rate of $1000 per week.

Builders Labour Hire Pty Ltd

Builders Labour Hire Pty Ltd engages Bill Carson to do a three-week assignment at Colossal Constructions Pty Ltd and pays him $800 per week.

Bill Carson

Bill Carson performs services for the three-week period at a building site of Colossal Constructions Pty Ltd.

Colossal Constructions Pty Ltd

The ATO labour hire requirements are that Builders Labour Hire Pty Ltd has to deduct PAYG withholding tax from its $800 weekly payments to Bill Carson.

However, this rule does not apply if labour hire is only incidental to the business.

Example

Labour hire arrangements incidental to a business

Assume that an accountant arranges for a solicitor to perform work for one of the accountant's clients. This would be incidental to the accountant's normal business activities, and consequently the PAYG withholding system would not apply to the payment from the accountant to the solicitor, as long as the solicitor quoted an ABN on the invoice. If the accountant regularly arranged for a bookkeeper to assist various clients, then the PAYG withholding system would apply to the payments from the accountant to the bookkeeper.

Payments under voluntary agreements

To benefit from the administrative and cash flow advantages that the system provides, a business and an individual contract payee with an ABN can enter into a voluntary agreement to have the PAYG withholding system apply. Because the payee and payer both have an ABN, technically the PAYG system would not apply. However, this voluntary agreement overrides the GST/ABN system. The agreement must be in writing and in the approved form, and must quote the individual contractor's ABN. Copies of the agreement must be retained by both parties for five years beyond the last payment subject to the agreement. Either party may terminate the agreement in writing at any time. (See Appendix, Form 3.2 [2772].)

It is important to note that only an individual (i.e. a sole trader) can enter into a voluntary agreement with a business (see Figure 3.2). It is also necessary that the individual has an ABN.

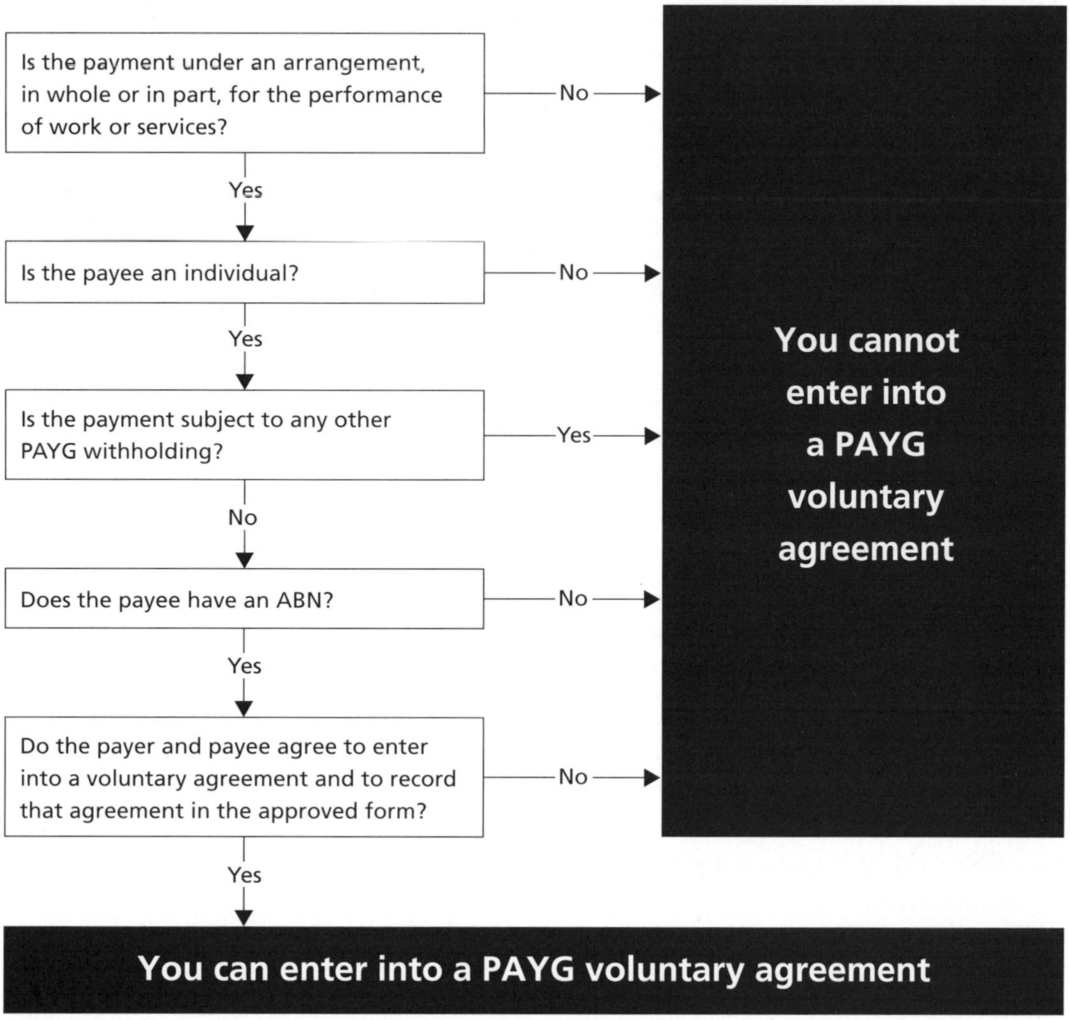

FIGURE 3.2 Voluntary agreement flow chart

Source: PAYG withholding voluntary agreement fact sheet, ATO (www.ato.gov.au/taxprofessionals) © Commonwealth of Australia, reproduced by permission.

Since the introduction of this voluntary agreement system in July 2000, very few businesses have taken up the opportunity to benefit from the administrative and cash-flow advantages that the system provides. The advantage to payees is that tax is paid by having the payer withhold an agreed amount. This enables the payee to avoid having to make payments under the PAYG instalments system in respect of that income (see Section 3.13). The advantage to the payer is that the voluntary payments under PAYG usually fall outside the GST system. Thus the payer does not have the cash-flow disadvantage of having to fund the GST amount, only to claim it back in the next Business Activity Statement. The rate of withholding will be either the payee's instalment rate as notified by the ATO (see Section 3.13) or a flat rate of 20%.

Note that, under a voluntary agreement, if the payer is not entitled to a full GST **input tax credit** for the goods or services being supplied, then GST does apply.

3.3

Active reflection

Outline the various tasks an employer is required to carry out in respect of the PAYG withholding system.

3.4 Calculating the amount of tax to be withheld

Withholding tax from salary and wages

Having determined that it is necessary to withhold income tax from a salary or wage payment, the next step is to determine the amount of tax to withhold. To assist employers in this regard, the ATO makes available various standard tables setting out the amount of tax that should be withheld. As discussed previously, the circumstances of one employee will be different from those of another, and consequently employees advise their employer of various details via a TFN declaration. These details include the choice to quote a TFN, the desire to claim (or not to claim) the **tax-free threshold**, and whether other items such as family tax benefits and tax offsets should be taken into consideration.

The various **PAYG withholding tax tables** are printed in such a way that the one appropriate table can accommodate the variations that may occur, namely:

- TFN quoted, tax-free threshold claimed and leave loading applicable to this employee
- TFN quoted, tax-free threshold claimed and leave loading not applicable to this employee
- TFN quoted, but tax-free threshold not claimed (this would be appropriate if it was an employee's 'second job').

The instructions to these tables also advise that if a payer is making a payment to a payee who has not (1) quoted a TFN, (2) claimed an exemption from quoting a TFN or (3) advised that a TFN has been applied for, then the payer must withhold an amount equal to 46.5% of the payment, ignoring any cents. (Note that if a payee advises the ATO that he/she has applied for a TFN, then the ATO allows a period of 28 days for the payer to withhold tax as if a TFN had been provided. At the end of this 28-day period, the payer must begin to withhold tax at the 46.5% rate unless the ATO advises otherwise. This would continue until the payee advises the employer of his/her TFN.)

These tables are not always reproduced on 1 July in each tax year but are subject to change at any time if Parliament changes the tax rates. The current tables in the book are for payments made on or after 1 July 2008. It is important for employers to ensure that the most current table is always used. The commencement date for each table is shown at the top of the first page. (See Appendix, Form 3.3 [1005] (weekly rates), Form 3.4 [1006] (fortnightly rates) and Form 3.5 [1007] (monthly rates).)

At the ATO's website (**www.ato.gov.au**) there are online calculators to determine the correct amount of tax to withhold.

Example

To determine the correct amount of tax that Superior Services Pty Limited should withhold, the wages and other records of three employees are provided.

Name	TFN quoted	With tax-free threshold with leave loading	Wage ($)	Period
Mary Jones	Yes	Yes	265.00	Week
Bill Jack	Yes	No	400.00	Fortnight
Tom Jones	No	Yes	923.00	Month

Use the extract from the PAYG withholding tax tables provided in Table 3.2 to calculate for each employee:

- the correct amount of withholding tax
- the resultant net amount payable to the employee.

Rates as at 1 July 2008

Name	Gross wage ($)	Tax withheld ($)	Net wage ($)	Period
Mary Jones	265.00	12.00	253.00	Week
Bill Jack	400.00	66.00	334.00	Fortnight
Tom Jones	923.00	429.00	494.00	Month

Note: 'Leave loading' refers to **annual leave loading**, adjusting for small amounts of extra tax each week.

TABLE 3.2 THREE SCHEDULES OF PAYG TAX

(a) WEEKLY TAX TABLE

Weekly earnings	With tax-free threshold with leave loading	With tax-free threshold no leave loading	No tax-free threshold
1	**2**	**3**	**4**
261	11.00	11.00	48.00
262	12.00	11.00	48.00
263	12.00	11.00	48.00
264	12.00	11.00	49.00
265	12.00	12.00	49.00
266	12.00	12.00	49.00
267	12.00	12.00	49.00
268	12.00	12.00	49.00
269	13.00	12.00	50.00
270	13.00	12.00	50.00

the amount otherwise withheld and is calculated on all earnings, including taxable allowances, bonuses and commissions. However, it is not calculated on lump sum termination payments. The ATO provides tables for each of the above pay periods—weekly, fortnightly and monthly—and the tables provide for whether or not the tax-free threshold is claimed by the employee.

Thus, for an employee paid weekly the HELP weekly tax table would be used, calculating the withholding amount by adding:

- the appropriate amount to be withheld from the standard weekly PAYG withholding tax table, and
- an additional HELP component using the formula $y = ax$ and calculated as per Table 3.3, where y = weekly HELP component, x = weekly earnings rounded down to whole dollars plus 99 cents and a = percentage. The final amount is rounded to the nearest dollar.

TABLE 3.3 WEEKLY TAX TABLE FOR HELP DEBTS

(a) TAX-FREE THRESHOLD CLAIMED

Weekly earnings, *x*	**Percentage, *a***
$0–$798.99	0
$799–$890.99	4.0
$891–$981.99	4.5
$982–$1032.99	5.0
$1033–$1110.99	5.5
$1111–$1202.99	6.0
$1203–$1265.99	6.5
$1266–$1393.99	7.0
$1394–$1484.99	7.5
$1485 and over	8.0

(b) NO TAX-FREE THRESHOLD CLAIMED

Weekly earnings, *x*	**Percentage, *a***
$0–$481.99	0
$482–$572.99	4.0
$573–$663.99	4.5
$664–$715.99	5.0
$716–$792.99	5.5
$793–$885.99	6.0
$886–$948.99	6.5
$949–$1075.99	7.0
$1076–$1167.99	7.5
$1168 and over	8.0

Example

John has advised his employer that he wishes to claim the tax-free threshold with leave loading and has a HELP liability. His weekly earnings are $848.80. Applying the rules as above in the first step results in an amount of $149 PAYG withholding. The second step requires us to drop off the 80 cents and add 99 cents to arrive at $848.99. Reading Table 3.3, we multiply $848.99 by 4% to obtain $33.96, and rounding to the nearest whole dollar results in an amount of $34 being the additional HELP component. The total tax withheld for the week is therefore $149 + $34 = $183.

Refer to Appendix Form 8.1 [2173] (PAYG withholding HELP weekly tax table) to confirm the amount of $34. Note that the calculation and the tax tables sometimes differ slightly, but a discrepancy of a dollar or two is immaterial.

Amount of withholding tax where no ABN is quoted on an invoice

Another withholding situation exists for businesses, not-for-profit organisations and government organisations. If such an organisation is about to make a payment for goods or services to another business, not-for-profit organisation or government organisation that has not quoted an ABN on its invoice, that organisation must withhold tax at the top marginal tax rate plus the Medicare levy (currently 46.5%).

Active reflection

Advise an employer of two basic factors that determine how much weekly PAYG to withhold from an employee's wage.

3.5 Registering for PAYG withholding

If an employer makes payments from which tax must be withheld, the employer must register with the ATO by the day on which it is first required to withhold payment under the PAYG withholding system.

If the business is not **registered** for PAYG withholding, the ATO preprinted activity statements may have deleted the PAYG withholding section or may have overprinted the section with the words 'You are not required to complete this option'.

If the business already has an ABN, it is possible to register for PAYG withholding by telephoning the Business Tax Reform Infoline on **13 24 78** or by completing an 'Add a new business account' form (see Appendix, Form 3.7 [2954]).

If the business does not yet have an ABN but will need to obtain one, this can be applied for at the same time as registering for PAYG withholding by registering electronically through the Business Entry Point at **www.business.gov.au**. Alternatively, it is possible to complete an application form (see Appendix, Form 2.2 [2938] for an individual, or Form 2.3 [2939] for companies and other organisations).

Care must be taken when making payments for goods and services. If a payee has not quoted an ABN on an invoice, the business must withhold 46.5% of the amount to be paid, and therefore will also then be required to register for PAYG withholding immediately. Once registration for PAYG withholding has been processed by the ATO, the next Instalment Activity Statement will be printed to allow the business to report and pay PAYG withholding liability.

Active reflection

Do all businesses have to register for PAYG withholding?

3.6 TFN declarations

In order that the amount of tax to be withheld is calculated at the lowest possible rate, a payee should give a fully completed TFN declaration to the payer. (See Appendix, Form 3.1 [3092].)

It should be noted, however, that it is not compulsory for a TFN declaration to be provided, as a payee can choose not to do so. If a properly completed TFN declaration is provided with a TFN quoted, the payer will withhold tax at the lowest amount as specified in the ATO tables. If a properly completed TFN declaration is not provided, the payer must withhold tax at 46.5% of the amount to be paid.

The TFN declaration is the official way for employees to advise their employer of:

- their TFN, which then relieves the employer of the responsibility for withholding tax at the maximum rate
- their authorisation for their employer to give their TFN to the trustee of their superannuation fund
- their residential status (residents pay less tax than non-residents)
- their desire to claim the tax-free threshold from this employer
- their desire to take into their withholding tax calculation the effect of various tax offsets and any family tax assistance they may be entitled to (and hence have the benefit of the tax offset during the tax year, rather than receiving the tax offset as a lump sum benefit in the year-end tax assessment)
- their liability under HELP.

Resident taxpayers do not pay tax on their first $6000 of taxable income, and they can choose the employer (one only at any particular point in time) to whom this $6000 tax-free threshold will apply.

If a payer receives a properly completed TFN declaration, the payer must use the information contained on the form to help calculate the amount of tax to withhold. The payer must complete the employer section of the form and send it to the ATO within 14 days of receipt.

Remember, if a properly completed TFN declaration is not received, the payer must withhold tax at the top marginal tax rate plus Medicare levy (currently 46.5%).

TFN declarations are required for the following payments:

- payments for work and services, including payments to employees, company directors and office-holders, payments under return-to-work schemes and labour hire arrangements, and payments specified by regulation
- benefit and compensation payments
- retirement payments and annuities, and eligible termination payments.

Active reflection

Outline the information that an employee provides to his or her employer via a TFN declaration.

3.7 Reporting and remitting amounts withheld to the ATO

Businesses are required to report and pay PAYG amounts withheld to the ATO via an activity statement (see Chapter 6). This form has been designed so that businesses can account for all amounts withheld using the one reporting system. These amounts may be withheld from salary and wage payments or from amounts withheld under a voluntary agreement, or because a payment was made to a business when an ABN was not quoted. Whatever the reason for withholding, the amounts are sent to the ATO at the same time, via an activity statement that has been appropriately completed with the business details. Table 3.4 sets out the dates on which reporting and payment of the PAYG withholding must take place.

TABLE 3.4 PAYMENTS UNDER THE PAYG WITHHOLDING SYSTEM

	Due date		
Period	**Up to $25 000 annual withholding pay quarterly**	**$25 000 to $1 million annual withholding pay monthly**	**More than $1 million annual withholding**
July August September	28 October	21 August 21 September 28 October	Amounts withheld from Saturday to Tuesday are payable on the following Monday. Amounts withheld from Wednesday to Friday are payable on the following Thursday.
October November December	28 February	21 November 21 December 28 February	
January February March	28 April	21 February 21 March 28 April	
April May June	28 July	21 May 21 June 28 July	

The ATO customises and issues activity statements in the month before the end of each quarter, as follows:

- All businesses registered for GST are issued with a *Business Activity Statement* on either a monthly or a quarterly basis.
- All businesses *not* registered for GST are issued with an *Instalment Activity Statement* on either a monthly or a quarterly basis.

- All businesses registered for GST that report GST on a quarterly basis but have to report PAYG withheld on a monthly basis are issued with a monthly *Instalment Activity Statement* for the first two months of each quarter and a *Business Activity Statement* for the final month of each quarter.
- When the due date for payment falls on a public holiday, the ATO allows payment to be made on the next working day.

The following is a summary of ATO requirements:

- If a business has an **annual withholding** of $25 000 or less (**small withholder**), and consequently is required to report and make quarterly payments, it can do so using the quarterly Business Activity Statement issued by the ATO.
- If a business has an annual withholding in the range of $25 001 to $1 million (**medium withholder**), it is required to report and make monthly payments for PAYG withheld. If the entity is also a quarterly GST payer, then for the month at the end of each quarter the quarterly Business Activity Statement will be used for both its GST and its PAYG obligations. For the two other months of each quarter it will receive a monthly Instalment Activity Statement for each month, which needs to be completed only in relation to PAYG withholding. If the entity is a monthly GST payer, the Business Activity Statement will collect all the GST and PAYG information and payments each month.
- If a business has an annual withholding greater than $1 million (**large withholder**), it is required by the ATO to electronically transmit PAYG withholdings as shown in Table 3.5.

TABLE 3.5 DUE DATES: WITHHOLDING OVER $1 MILLION P.A.

Sat	Sun	Mon	Tue	Wed	Thu	Fri	Sat	Sun	Mon	Tue	Wed	Thu
withholdings									pay here			
				withholdings								pay here

Active reflection

Advise an employer of the requirements for remitting amounts of PAYG withholding to the ATO.

3.8 Preparing payment summaries, showing payments made and tax withheld

The PAYG withholding system requires employers who make payments to employees to report these on a payment summary, which must be issued to the employee or payee after the end of the tax year. (See Appendix, Form 3.8 [46] and Form 3.9 [3223].)

PAYG payment summaries are issued by the ATO without serial numbers, and the year-ending box is left blank so that any unused payment summaries can be retained and used the following year. Many employers now issue their payment summaries directly from their electronic payroll systems that have been certified by the ATO.

The PAYG withholding system requires payers of certain types of payments to withhold amounts from any payments paid. These guidelines do not apply where amounts have been withheld from payments made:

- under labour hire or other specified payment arrangements
- under voluntary agreements to withhold
- for supplies where an ABN is not quoted
- that are eligible termination payments (ETP).

Separate payment summaries and guidelines are available for each of these types of payments.

The following guidelines apply to payers who make payments to payees (irrespective of whether tax was actually withheld) who are employees, company directors or office-holders, receive a pension or annuity, receive compensation, sickness or accident payments, or receive return-to-work payments.

Guidelines, payment summary: individual non-business

The ATO-supplied payment summary consists of three copies (see Appendix, Form 3.8 [46]). The original is forwarded to the ATO, the second copy is given to the payee and the third copy is to be retained by the payer. Both the payer and the payee must retain their copy of the payment summary for five years.

How to prepare a payment summary: individual non-business

When preparing a payment summary by typewriter or printer, the payer can type over and through the boxes. However, each field of information must fall within the boundaries of the appropriate row(s) of boxes. When preparing a payment summary by hand, payers must write each letter or number in a separate box and are requested to use BLOCK LETTERS and a black pen. Not all information fields need to be completed. For example, where an amount has not been paid or withheld, that field should be left blank.

All amounts should be shown in whole dollars. If an amount includes cents, the cents must be truncated (i.e. disregarded). For example, the amount of $100.60 should be shown as $100.

The information cannot be changed on the payment summary after it has been given to the payee or after the summary information has been forwarded to the ATO.

If an error is detected after giving the payment summary to the payee or the ATO, the payee should be advised by letter of the correct information and a copy of this correspondence kept. A copy of the letter should also be forwarded to the ATO at the following address: Australian Taxation Office, Locked Bag 1515, Upper Mt Gravatt, QLD 4122.

If an error is detected before giving the payment summary to the payee or the ATO, the old payment summary should be destroyed and a new payment summary completed.

If the payee loses the payment summary, a new one must not be issued; he or she should simply be given a certified copy (of the employer copy) or a signed statement showing all the details from the lost payment summary.

Guidelines for completing fields on payment summary

Payment summary for year ending 30 June

This is a compulsory field, and the year must be shown as a four-digit figure. For example, the year ending 30 June 2009 must be shown as 2009 and not 09.

Reportable fringe benefits amount

This field should be completed if the total taxable value of certain fringe benefits provided to the payee in the FBT year (1 April to 31 March of the same year as the payment summary) exceeds $3000 (as from 1 April 2007; see Section 5.1, Chapter 5). The amount must be grossed-up using type 2 (non GST) factor of 1.8692 (because an employee would not be entitled to claim back GST credits if they had paid the amount themselves) and the value must be shown in whole dollars only. For example, a reportable fringe benefits amount of $4178.45 would be truncated to $4178.

Payer's ABN or withholder payer number

This is a compulsory field, as all payers must have either an ABN or a withholder payer number.

Payee's tax file number

This is a compulsory field and must show the TFN quoted by the payee. In specific circumstances, the following codes should be used to substitute for a TFN:

- 111 111 111 if a new payee has not made a TFN declaration, but 28 days have not passed
- 333 333 333 if the payee is under 18 years of age and earns $112 or less per week
- 444 444 444 if the payee is a Commonwealth government **pensioner payee**
- 000 000 000 if the payee chooses not to quote a TFN and has not claimed an exemption from quoting one.

Total tax withheld (whole dollars)

The total tax withheld must be shown in whole dollars. If the total amount includes cents, the cents must be truncated (i.e. disregarded). For example, $12 672.70 would be shown as $12 672.

Total tax withheld—whole dollars only in words

The amount of total tax withheld should be written in words in the field provided. For example:

Thousands	Hundreds	Tens	Units
TWELVE	SIX	SEVEN	TWO

Gross payments

This must include all amounts of salary, wages, bonuses and commissions paid to the payee as an employee, a company director or an office-holder. Gross payments also may include pensions and annuities, compensation, and sickness or accident pay. These amounts must be shown in whole dollars only; again, if an amount paid includes cents, the cents must be disregarded. The following amounts should also be included in gross payments:

- allowances to compensate for specific working conditions and payments for special qualifications or extended hours
- allowances paid to cover expenses that are not tax-deductible for the payee, for example normal home-to-work transport expenses
- holiday pay or bonuses
- amounts paid for unused long service leave, unused holiday pay and other leave-related payments that accrued after 17 August 1993, unless the amount was paid because the payee ceased employment under an approved early retirement scheme, invalidity or bona fide redundancy (see notes on lump sum payments below).

The following should not be included in gross payments: amounts that are shown separately as Community Development Employment Project (CDEP) salary or wages, allowances, lump sum payments, return-to-work payments or amounts shown at the 'Other income' field.

CDEP salary or wages

This is the amount of salary or wages paid to the payee for a CDEP wages grant. This amount must be shown in whole dollars.

Other income

Shown in this field are any amounts paid to the payee that are exempt income and/or foreign-source salary and wage income.

Allowances

This field shows payments made to cover the payee's work-related expenses, for example tool and motor vehicle allowances, including car expense payments on a cents-per-kilometre basis. The type of allowance should be indicated using abbreviations that are clear and understandable because the ATO does not have a standard list of abbreviations. There is provision for up to four allowances, which should be shown separately. If more than four allowances were paid, the term 'VARIOUS' should be printed in the details block and the sum of all allowances paid should be shown in the 'Total allowances' box. This amount should not be included as part of gross payments.

Lump sum payments

These amounts must be shown in whole dollars. Amounts shown in the lump sum payments field must not be included in the gross payments field. Each lump sum payment must be recorded against the appropriate payment type, and there are four types of lump sum payments, detailed as follows.

A Amounts paid for:

- unused long service leave that accrued after 15 August 1978 but before 18 August 1993
- unused holiday pay and other leave-related payments that accrued before 18 August 1993
- unused long service leave, unused holiday pay and other leave-related payments that accrued after 15 August 1978 if the amount was paid because the payee ceased employment under an approved early retirement scheme, because of invalidity or because of a bona fide redundancy.

B Amounts paid for unused long service leave that accrued before 16 August 1978.

D The tax-free component of a bona fide redundancy payment or an approved early retirement scheme payment. For more information, see the *ETP Guide on Redundancy of an Employee*, available through the ATO's website.

E Amounts paid for back payment of salary and wages that were accrued more than 12 months ago. Any return-to-work payments should also be shown in this field.

Union fees etc

Amounts paid to unions or professional associations on behalf of the payee must be shown here. If payments have been paid to more than one union or professional association, the term 'VARIOUS' should be printed in the box where 'name of organisation' is indicated.

For more detailed information on payment summaries and the PAYG system, telephone the Small Business Hotline on **13 28 66** or visit the ATO's website at **www.ato.gov.au** to download information. Refer to the form *How to complete the PAYG payment summary—individual non-business (NAT 3388).*

Lump payment 'C' no longer exists. It has been replaced by an ETP statement.

3.8 Active reflection

How do employees know how much income they have earned and how much tax has been withheld to enable them to fill in their tax return after the end of the financial year?

3.9 Annual reporting to the ATO

After finalising the payment summary for each payee, the last step in the process is to complete the annual reporting requirements as per section 16-153 of the *Taxation Administration Act 1953*.

The PAYG withholding system may require a payer to prepare two reports, each with a different due date:

1. For large withholders and reports prepared without a tax agent, the PAYG payment summary statement is due by 14 August each year (see Appendix, Form 3.10 [3447]). It is to be used in respect of payments for salary and wages for:
   - work or services
   - eligible termination payments, retirement payments and annuities
   - compensation and benefits payments.
2. A report due by 31 October in respect of payments for:
   - a supply where an ABN is not properly quoted
   - dividends, interest and royalties.

The reports have to be in the required format and enable the ATO to reconcile amounts remitted during the year for tax withheld with amounts shown on the payment summaries, and to check the accuracy of income tax returns subsequently lodged by payees.

The ATO gives a concession to registered tax agents aimed at easing their workload. Agents are allowed extra time to prepare PAYG payment summary statements in respect of payments for salary and wages. Where there are employees not related to the owners of the business (**arms-length payees**), these statements are to be lodged by 30 September. If the employees are **non-arms-length payees** (only payees related to the owners of the business), the lodgement date is the due date of the business's income tax return, which may not be until May or June of the following year.

Active reflection 3.9

After having given PAYG payment summaries to all employees, how does an employer advise the ATO of such details?

3.10 Penalties for non-compliance

Section 16 of the *Taxation Administration Act 1953* imposes various penalties for non-compliance. The penalty amount is calculated in accordance with a statutory formula (for example, false or misleading statement penalties) or in multiples of a 'penalty unit'. The penalty unit is currently $110. The Act now has uniform penalties:

- relating to statements, unarguable positions and schemes
- for failing to lodge documents on time
- for failing to withhold amounts as required (under the PAYG withholding system) and
- for failing to meet other tax obligations.

Some examples are as follows:

- Failure to withhold: the penalty amount is equal to the amount that the business should have withheld from the payment.
- Failure to register: five penalty units.
- Failure to notify of an amount withheld such as failure to retain or produce declarations as required: 20 penalty units.
- Failure to remit tax withheld by the due date: the **general interest charge (GIC)**[2] will apply daily, with the penalty set by dividing the total of the base interest rate plus 7% by the number of days in that calendar year. The base interest rate is the monthly average yield of 90-day bank accepted bills. At the time of writing the penalty rate was 14.75% per annum from the due date to the date of payment (this rate varies as it is indexed every quarter). Interest charges apply whether or not a penalty applies.

Active reflection 3.10

What is the penalty for failing to notify the ATO of an amount withheld?

3.11 An outline of the PAYG instalments system

The introduction of Australia's *New Tax System* provided an opportunity to streamline the way in which businesses, or taxpayers with income that does not have tax withheld at source, pays their tax in advance. It should be remembered that all aspects of the PAYG system are designed to ensure that income tax is largely prepaid in advance of the actual liability established on the lodgement of an income tax return for the tax year. The reason for this is because income tax is based on taxable income, and this can be established only when an income tax return is completed. Thus, monthly or quarterly PAYG instalments paid by a taxpayer are subsequently taken into account in the yearly income tax assessment.

As previously discussed under the PAYG withholding system (Sections 3.2–3.10), since 1 July 2000 employees have had to prepay income tax by having it withheld from their wages or salary by their employer. This amount is then remitted to the ATO by the employer, on a monthly or quarterly basis. Employees still have to lodge an income tax return at the end of the tax year, but are allowed credit for the amount of tax withheld.

Under the PAYG instalment system, a taxpayer with business and/or investment income also has to prepay income tax by remitting a quarterly estimate or instalment to the ATO. The taxpayer still has to lodge an income tax return at the end of the tax year, but is allowed credit for the amount of tax paid. Thus, the dual payment and reporting for business of its own tax as well as tax withheld from others is one of the features of the PAYG system.

Active reflection

Briefly outline the operation of the PAYG instalment system.

3.12 Identifying entities affected by PAYG instalments

Taxpayers with business or investment income are required to pay PAYG instalments if they have **instalment income** for the quarter and have been notified by the ATO of their **instalment rate**. Ultimately, the ATO advises affected taxpayers either by issuing them with a quarterly Instalment Activity Statement (IAS) if they are not registered for GST or by including a PAYG instalment section on their Business Activity Statement (BAS) for each of the quarters ended March, June, September and December. Put simply, if the ATO does not issue an activity statement outlining PAYG instalment obligations, no PAYG instalments are required.

Entities that may be affected by PAYG instalments are:

- individuals in business conducted as a sole trader
- individuals in business conducted as a partnership[3]
- individuals with investment income
- companies
- beneficiaries
- trustees

- superannuation funds
- a body corporate.

The PAYG instalment system does *not* apply to charities, as long as they are endorsed as income-tax-exempt charities and have obtained an ABN. This endorsement requirement enables the ATO to validate those charities that are entitled to the tax-free concession. Forms for endorsement can be obtained from the ATO.

Active reflection 3.12

Name three entities that are affected by PAYG instalments.

3.13 Options for calculating PAYG instalments

The PAYG instalment system has undergone numerous changes since it began but has now settled down. Quarterly payers using either an IAS or BAS now have two options. If an option is not chosen, the ATO uses option 1. The option used for the first quarter of each tax year must be used for the remainder of that year.

Option 1

The taxpayer pays a PAYG instalment amount that is calculated by the ATO using the taxpayer's latest income tax return. This option is available to all individuals and to companies and superannuation funds with business and investment income of $1 million or less.

It is vitally important that these forms are completed accurately and all instructions are followed carefully. If this is not done, payments to the ATO may not be processed correctly.

Option 2

The taxpayer calculates his or her own PAYG instalment amount using the quarterly instalment income multiplied by the rate provided by the ATO. This option is available to all taxpayers unless they have chosen option 1.

The instalment rate for option 2 will be advised by the ATO as a percentage to two decimal places and preprinted on the entity's quarterly activity statement. The ATO will work out the instalment rate for a business from the income tax information it has for the most recent year of income, and this is calculated by dividing the business tax payable by the business instalment income of that year. Even if the rate is advised as 0%, and thus no instalment payment is required, the actual instalment income must be reported.

This approach therefore bases PAYG instalments on actual income earned, which obviously aligns the amount of tax payable more closely to income than did previous systems.

Instalment income includes:

- gross sales or fees received during the period

Learning check

- ✓ Calculate the amount of PAYG tax to be withheld from payments to:
  - employees and other workers
  - suppliers quoting an ABN
  - suppliers not quoting an ABN
  - labour hire arrangements
  - voluntary agreements.
- ✓ Obtain and complete a PAYG payment summary for all payees from whom withholdings have been made.
- ✓ Obtain and complete the relevant annual reconciliation and reporting obligations of a payer under the PAYG withholding system.
- ✓ Complete the appropriate sections of the BAS or IAS to record PAYG withholdings.
- ✓ Calculate the amount of a PAYG quarterly instalment.
- ✓ Calculate the instalment rate for a PAYG quarterly instalment.
- ✓ Complete the appropriate sections of a BAS or an IAS to record the amount of a PAYG instalment amount.

Taxation vocabulary

activity statement
additional tax
annual leave loading
annual withholding
arms-length payees
dividends
employee
general interest charge (GIC)
input tax credit
instalment income
instalment rate
labour hire arrangements
large withholder
medium withholder
non-arms-length payees
Pay As You Go (PAYG)
PAYG payment summary statement
PAYG withholding
PAYG withholding tax tables
payment summary
pensioner payee
registered
small withholder
tax file number (TFN)
tax instalments
tax-free threshold
TFN declarations
voluntary agreements

multiple-choice questions

Circle the correct response. (Answers to odd-numbered multiple-choice questions are provided on page 318.)

1. **The PAYG system is part of the *New Tax System*. Which of the following does it affect?**
   (a) payments to a casual shop assistant
   (b) payments of personal income tax by a sole trader business person
   (c) payment for an invoice where an ABN is not quoted
   (d) all of the above

2. **The PAYG instalment system:**
   (a) is the system whereby a business pays its own tax in advance
   (b) is the system whereby a business pays tax to the ATO in respect of tax withheld from others
   (c) is exactly the same as the PAYG withholding system and affects the same type of income
   (d) all of the above

3. **The PAYG withholding system:**
   (a) is the system whereby a business pays its own tax
   (b) is the system whereby a business pays tax to the ATO in respect of tax withheld from others
   (c) is exactly the same as the previous PAYE system and affects only the same income
   (d) all of the above

4. **Which of the following is *not* subject to the PAYG withholding system?**
   (a) part-time wages of $40 per week to an employee paper boy aged 15
   (b) payment of commission to a real estate agent by his employer
   (c) payment to a beautician by a client
   (d) payment to a pensioner for casual work as a shop assistant

5. **Which of the following is optional under the PAYG withholding system?**
   (a) registration on commencement of business if employing people
   (b) preparation of a payment summary for an employee who has not had tax withheld
   (c) completion of a TFN declaration by an employee
   (d) none of the above; all are actual requirements of the PAYG withholding system

6. **An accountant will come within the PAYG withholding system in respect of payments made:**
   (a) to a solicitor to have legal work done for a client
   (b) to a consultant lecturer for a GST course for clients
   (c) to a bookkeeper for work done for one client only
   (d) to employees of the accounting firm

7. **An accountant can enter into a voluntary agreement with a bookkeeper if:**
   (a) the bookkeeper is an individual
   (b) the bookkeeper has an ABN
   (c) the accountant and the bookkeeper record their agreement on the approved form
   (d) all of the above

8. **The correct amount of tax to withhold from a resident employee earning $100 per week, who has not quoted a TFN but has requested the tax-free threshold with leave loading, is:**
   (a) nil (b) $46.00 (c) $46.50 (d) $16.00

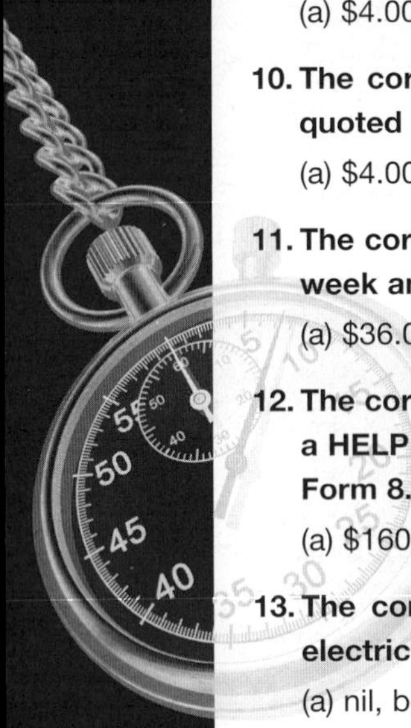

9. The correct amount of tax to withhold from a resident employee earning $400 per fortnight, who has quoted a TFN but has not requested the tax-free threshold, is:

(a) $4.00 (b) $26.00 (c) $66.00 (d) $186.00

10. The correct amount of tax to withhold from a resident employee earning $832 per month, who has quoted a TFN and has requested the tax-free threshold with leave loading, is:

(a) $4.00 (b) $52.00 (c) $139.00 (d) nil

11. The correct amount of additional tax to withhold for HELP from a resident employee earning $800 per week and claiming the tax-free threshold is:

(a) $36.00 (b) nil (c) $32.00 (d) $32.04

12. The correct total amount of tax to withhold from a resident employee earning $883 per week, who has a HELP liability, has quoted a TFN and has requested the tax-free threshold with leave loading, is (use Form 8.1 [2173] from the Appendix of this book):

(a) $160.00 (b) $35.00 (c) $195.00 (d) $395.00

13. The correct amount of tax a builder should withhold from a payment of $400 to a subcontracted electrician, who has quoted a TFN and an ABN and has requested the tax-free threshold, is:

(a) nil, because the PAYG withholding system applies only to employees

(b) nil, because the opportunity to request the tax-free threshold applies only to employees

(c) $186.00

(d) $194.00

14. The correct amount of tax a builder should withhold from a payment of $400 to a subcontracted electrician, who has not quoted an ABN, is:

(a) nil, because the PAYG withholding system applies only to employees

(b) nil

(c) $186.00

(d) $194.00

15. The correct amount of tax instalment to deduct from an employee paid $1100 monthly, who has quoted an ABN only and wishes to claim the tax-free threshold, is:

(a) $95.00 (b) $533.00 (c) $511.00 (d) $511.50

16. The correct amount of tax instalment to deduct from an employee paid $400 weekly, who has quoted a TFN and wishes to claim the tax-free threshold with loading and a $500 dependant tax offset, is:

(a) $39.00 (b) $49.00 (c) $29.00 (d) $10.00

quick-and-easy comprehension

Place a ✓ to indicate your response to each statement.

STATEMENT	TRUE	FALSE
1. PAYG is the name given to the system whereby all taxpayers pay their tax liability without the need to lodge an income tax return.	—	—
2. The PAYG withholding tables are a combined amount to cover not only income tax liability but Medicare levy liability as well.	—	—
3. It is possible for an employer to deduct less than the prescribed amount to withhold, if the employer has the appropriate authority from the ATO.	—	—
4. It is not possible for an employer to deduct more than the prescribed amount to withhold, even if the employer has authority to do so from the employee.	—	—

5. A business and an individual contract worker with an ABN can make a voluntary agreement to have tax withheld even though there is not an employer–employee relationship. — —

6. A business with an annual PAYG withholding liability of $100 000 will have to report and pay quarterly. — —

7. A business with an annual PAYG withholding liability of $2 000 000 will have to report and pay monthly. — —

8. All businesses subject to the PAYG instalment system have to make quarterly payments of income tax. — —

self-test question

Complete the payroll for June, the last month of the financial year ended 30 June 2009. The following information is given:

Employee	YTD income $	YTD tax withheld $	Wages for week ending 7 June $	Wages for week ending 14 June $	Wages for week ending 21 June $	Wages for week ending 28 June $
Michelle	25 000	3700	450	450	500	510
Renee	37 000	7500	730	860	850	730

Both employees have completed a TFN declaration quoting a TFN, requesting the tax-free threshold and leave loading. Renee has a HELP debt of $16 000.

1. Calculate PAYG withholding for each employee for each week in June.
2. Update year-to-date figures to finalise wage records to 30 June 2009.

assessments

1. Bill Layer, a subcontractor to Superior Services Pty Ltd, has decided to employ two labourers to cope with his increased workload. One labourer will be on a full-time basis and the other on a casual basis. Bill has never employed people before.

Explain to Bill in simple terms how the PAYG withholding system works and advise him of any specific requirements to which he should attend.

2. Bill Layer follows your advice, and comes to you for help in working out the wages for his first week as an employer. The ATO has sent Bill a Business Activity Statement and a weekly tax instalment table. The two employees have given Bill TFN declarations showing that they are residents, quoting their TFNs and stating that they both wish to claim the tax-free threshold. Neither employee wishes to claim any tax offsets.

A check of Bill's wages book shows that the full-time employee earned $100 per day for five days, and the casual employee earned $80 per day for two days.

(a) Advise Bill of the appropriate amount of tax to deduct for each employee for this first week.

(b) Advise Bill of the net amount to pay each employee.

(c) Assuming that Bill pays the full-time employee $500 per week for the next three months and does not re-employ the casual employee, what would be the total tax withheld for the quarter?

(d) If Bill is registered as a small withholder and has to lodge quarterly Business Activity Statements, what further advice would you give him?

3. Superior Services Pty Ltd is registered as a PAYG withholder and remits PAYG withholding on a monthly basis. All employees are paid weekly (with leave loading applicable to annual leave).

(a) Complete the wages book for the last week in July.

Name	TFN	Tax-free threshold	Tax offset $	Gross wages $	Tax $	Net wages $
S. Avery	yes	yes	nil	350		
P. Fill	yes	yes	nil	800		
G. Kent	yes	no	nil	200		
H. Pole	no	yes	nil	325		
C. Set	no	no	nil	180		
D. Wood	yes	yes	1040	400		

(b) If the total tax withheld for the first three weeks of July (excluding the above amounts) was $3000, explain the procedure to remit the required amount to the ATO.

4. Using the following pro-forma, which contains the details of one employee of Helpers Pty Ltd, create a worksheet for the company's other two employees (see below).

Name: Mary Smith			
Gross salary, wages, bonus etc.	$1000 per week	52 weeks	$52 000
Allowances			
Entertaining		$1040	
Total allowances			$1 040
Tax withheld			$15 600

Employees

- **Mary Smith, who earns:**
  - **a salary of $1000 per week (before tax of $300 is withheld) for 52 weeks**
  - **plus an allowance of $20 per week for entertaining clients for 52 weeks.**
- **Bill Smith, who earns:**
  - **a gross salary for the year of $30 000**
  - **overtime payments of $3000**
  - **holiday pay and leave loading of $2500.**
- **Bill has had tax of $10 200 withheld during the year.**
- **Harry Smith, who earns:**
  - **a gross salary for the year of $40 000**
  - **bonuses for the year of $2000**
  - **a remote area allowance of $1500**
  - **a travel allowance of $500.**
- **Harry has had tax $12 600 withheld during the year.**

5. Using the information from your completed worksheet for problem 4, prepare a payment summary for each employee.

case study question

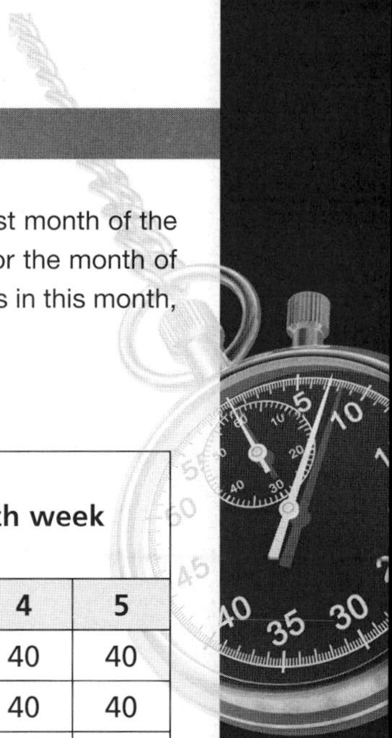

Colossal Constructions Pty Ltd requires you to complete the payroll to 31 July 2009, being the first month of the new financial year. You have been provided with the employees' information and hours worked for the month of July. In the last week of July, Ron Lim was paid for eight hours sick leave. There are five pay weeks in this month, and the information is contained in the table below.

Payroll information, July 2009

Employee	Tax no.	Tax scale column	Hourly rate $	Hours worked each week				
				1	2	3	4	5
Adams, Kylie	000000005	3	20.60	40	40	40	40	40
Anderson, Mary	000000007	3	15.00	40	32	40	40	40
Hill, Peter	000000009	3	15.00	40	40	40	40	40
Jones, Mark	000000006	3	17.80	40	40	40	40	40
Lim, Ron	000000010	3	15.00	40	40	40	24	40
Little, John	000000008	3	20.00	40	40	40	40	40
Masonry, Jan	000000002	3	$1150 per week					
McAllister, Mark	Not quoted	5	15.00	40	40	40	40	40
Parker, Janet	000000003	3	21.60	40	40	40	40	40
Masonry, Tom	000000001	3	$1450 per week					
Singh, Lyn	000000004	3	21.60	40	40	40	40	40
Student, Ned	000000012	4	13.00	10	10	12	6	8

You will need to use the weekly PAYG withholding tax tables in Appendix, Form 3.3 [1005].

Required

1. **Calculate PAYG withholding for each employee for each week of July.**
2. **Set out an appropriate report for Colossal Constructions Pty Ltd that shows clearly the total wages for the month and the total PAYG withholding tax due. This will enable the relevant data to be transferred to the activity statements.**

Note: In the Chapter 6 case study you will use this data again to calculate superannuation guarantee requirements.

classroom activities

1. **Using Form 3.8 [46] 'PAYG payment summary' from the Appendix, make up and complete all necessary details and then use this form to complete an income tax return for the taxpayer concerned.**
2. **PAYG puzzle. The following sets of letters represent words important in PAYG. Find the solution to these letter puzzles and then write a brief explanation of the word. The answer has been given for the first one.**

SMY	SuMmarY	This word refers to the payment **summary** given to each employee at the end of the tax year.
WHG		
VUT		
SLR		
AEN		
THE		
VAO		
RSR		
RRN		
PAY		
ILN		

self-test question solution

Employee Michelle	YTD income $	YTD tax withheld $	Wages for week ending 7 June $	Wages for week ending 14 June $	Wages for week ending 21 June $	Wages for week ending 28 June $	Totals to end June $
Wages	25 000		450	450	500	510	**26 910**
PAYG		3700	59	59	71	74	3 963
Total withholding							3 963

Employee Renee +HELP	YTD income $	YTD tax withheld $	Wages for week ending 7 June $	Wages for week ending 14 June $	Wages for week ending 21 June $	Wages for week ending 28 June $	Totals to end June $
Wages	37 000		730	860	850	730	**40 170**
PAYG		7500	143	184	181	143	8 151
HELP			29	39	38	29	135
Total withholding							**8 286**

Notes

1. The ATO has prepared technical guides to instalment rates, notional tax and variations. You can obtain these guides by telephoning the Business Tax Reform Infoline on **13 24 78** or by visiting **www.taxreform.ato.gov.au**.
2. See ITAA 1997, section 25-5(1). The Explanatory Memorandum to Act 11 of 1999 (which inserted the GIC provisions) explains that the total debt made up of the outstanding tax and the GIC is calculated as an amount *A*, which if invested at an effective rate of *i*% per period for *N* periods, will accumulate to $A + (1 + i)^n$.
3. A partnership is not required to pay income tax, so consequently it is not required to pay PAYG instalments; rather, each partner is required to include a proportion of the partnership's instalment income in his/her individual instalment income.

4

Goods and services tax

Chapter four

Topics

After studying this chapter, you should be able to:

- **explain how the goods and services tax (GST) system works and why it was introduced**
- **outline the method of collection of GST and the goods and services to which the tax applies**
- **describe the basic operation of the system, and identify:**
  - the rate of tax
  - the taxing point
  - timing of payments
  - taxable supplies
  - input tax credits
- **describe the registration process**
- **illustrate the accounting requirements for GST**
- **identify GST-free supplies**
- **identify input-taxed supplies**
- **explain the treatment of goods and services subject to special rules.**

Example

The sales price of $110 for an item of goods or a service should be shown clearly to the customer as GST-inclusive: that is, $110. The ACCC guidelines state that it is prohibited to display the price as $100 + 10% GST.

If the customer needs to calculate the GST component within the purchase price, this can be done by taking one-eleventh of the price, as explained in the following calculation:

Purchase price × 1/11

That is, in the above example $110 × 1/11 = $10 GST.

State duties legislation imposes a stamp duty liability on insurers in relation to insurance policies they sell. The law dictates that state stamp duties on insurance premiums are charged on the GST-inclusive price of the premium. This is also the case for imported goods; GST is charged on the total cost of the import and this includes import duty.

The taxing point

The taxing point is very simple, and is applied every time a supply of goods or services is made, unless under the legislation the goods or services are specifically excluded from having GST imposed. The price for goods and services must be shown inclusive of the GST component.

As previously discussed, the supplier of the goods or services has the responsibility for remitting GST to the tax office on a 'net' basis. Therefore, it is necessary for a business purchasing goods to be able to quantify the amount of GST applicable to all inputs so that it can claim amounts as input tax credits.

When a business supplies goods or services to another business, it is required to provide a cash receipt docket or credit invoice known as a **tax invoice**. As well as the usual information contained in invoices, this document includes a statement that the price is GST-inclusive; alternatively, it shows the amount of GST applicable.

Under current guidelines, the actual amount of GST applicable does not have to be shown separately, but there are specific rules for invoices over $1000, and these are now discussed in more detail.

Tax invoices

If necessary, and to assist a business in calculating the 'net' GST to be remitted, the legislation has a provision to allow the recipient of the supplied goods or services to request that the supplier issue a tax invoice within 28 days of the supply. Tax invoices are the critical evidence needed in order to claim input tax credits. Tax invoices for supplies with a value greater than $75 (GST-exclusive) but less than $1000 must show the following details:

- the supplier's **Australian Business Number (ABN)** (see Chapter 2, Section 2.2)
- the GST-inclusive price of the taxable supply
- the words 'tax invoice' stated prominently (see Figure 4.2)
- the date of issue of the tax invoice
- the name of the supplier
- a brief description of each thing supplied
- when GST is exactly one-eleventh of the total price, a statement that GST has been included within the total price charged.

Tax invoices for supplies with a value of $1000 or more must also show these additional items:

- the name of the recipient

- the address or ABN of the recipient
- the quantity of the goods or the extent of the services supplied.

It should be noted that businesses do not have to 'request' a tax invoice; rather, they will be provided with an invoice or a receipt that complies with the GST requirements.

For purchases of supplies with a value less than $75 (GST-exclusive), businesses can claim input tax credits without a formal tax invoice.

The Nice Scent Shoppe **TAX INVOICE**

ABN 45 727 605 968
Shop 11 North Arcade
Glen Iris Shopping Centre
214 Rocklands Road
Woodgrove NSW 2078

DATE 31/07/2008
INVOICE # 5036

BILL TO Dr George Button
Medical Centre
PO Box 44
Terrigal NSW 2260

CUST ABN	**P.O. #**	**TERMS**	**DUE DATE**
57 316 260 790	**1656**	**Net 15 days**	**17/08/2008**

QTY	**DESCRIPTION**	**PRICE PER UNIT (ex GST)**	**GST**	**AMOUNT (ex GST)**
8	Medium floral arrangement	75.00	60.00	600.00
8	Small floral arrangement	55.00	44.00	440.00
			SUBTOTAL	**$1040.00**
			GST TOTAL	**104.00**
Thank you for your business			**Total including GST**	**$1144.00**

FIGURE 4.2 Tax invoice (cash receipt) with a value over $1000

The timing of payments

The actual timing of the due date for remittance of GST to the ATO will depend on the annual GST turnover of the business and the choice of option, if available:

- Businesses with an annual GST turnover of $20 million or more have to remit GST on a monthly basis.
- Businesses with an annual GST turnover of less than $20 million are allowed to remit on a quarterly basis for each of the three-monthly periods ended 30 September, 31 December, 31 March and 30 June; however,

there are some options available (see below). It should be noted that these businesses may choose to be monthly remitters if they wish.

For those businesses above the $20 million **gross annual turnover** criterion, a common due date of the 21st of the month following the end of the month applies to:

- GST
- Pay As You Go withholding taxes (PAYGWT)
- Pay As You Go income tax instalments (PAYGITI) of the entity
- fringe benefits tax (FBT) instalments
- **wine equalisation tax (WET)** and
- **luxury car tax (LCT)**.

Entities with an annual GST turnover of less than $20 million have some options available. Table 4.1 sets out the dates for entities that are able to choose quarterly lodgement, and also choose option 1, to report and calculate GST details quarterly. With option 2, GST is calculated quarterly but reported annually (refer to Appendix, Form 6.2 [4195]. The annual GST return is due when the income tax return is due. If the business is not required to lodge an income tax return, the annual GST return is due on 28 February of the next year.

TABLE 4.1 LODGEMENT DATES FOR QUARTERLY GST PAYERS

	Due date
Quarter 1 (July–September)	28 October
Quarter 2 (October–December)	28 February
Quarter 3 (January–March)	28 April
Quarter 4 (April–June)	28 July

Under option 3 an instalment calculated by the ATO is payable each quarter with a reconciliation at the end of the year. This also requires an annual GST return to be lodged with the income tax return. If a BAS has been damaged or mislaid, businesses can contact the ATO on **13 24 78** and request a replacement form. Businesses can also use the Business Portal to lodge their activity statements electronically. Chapter 14 sets out some of the benefits of using the **electronic lodgement service**.

Active reflection

Give an example of how GST works using the following information:

(a) a business purchased $22 000 of materials for use in manufacture
(b) the business sold goods to a customer for $33 000
(c) the business found that there was no ABN on one invoice totalling $440 that it received from a supplier
(d) the business turns over more than $2 million each year but less than $20 million.

4.3 The registration requirements

The ABN

With the advent of GST came the opportunity to introduce another control into the Australian taxation system, the ABN. All businesses have a tax file number (TFN) (see Chapter 2, Section 2.1), which has been the cornerstone of the income tax system. The ABN is another identification number, and it is compulsory for most businesses to:

- lodge a formal application to obtain an ABN
- lodge a formal application to register for GST
- use their ABN in all GST transactions.

The simple rule is that all businesses dealing with other businesses need to have an ABN. In addition to this, businesses with an annual turnover (exclusive of GST) of $75 000 or more are required to register for GST. If the ATO agrees that a business exists, the business will be registered for GST irrespective of whether it is conducted as an individual, a partnership, a trust, a company or other.

The ABN has become the cornerstone of the GST system, and further reforms the existing taxation system. If a business cannot obtain an ABN:

- it will not be able to register or participate in the GST system
- tax of 46.5% will be deducted at source from all business income.

Note: It is possible to register for an ABN without registering for GST, but it is not possible to register for GST without an ABN. Refer to Chapter 2, Section 2.3, outlining details on applying for an ABN. ABNs can be checked at the website **www.abr.business.gov.au**.

If a business has a GST-exclusive annual turnover under $75 000, registration is optional.

GST annual turnover

The critical requirement for the need to register for GST is **GST annual turnover**. If this is in excess of $75 000, the business must register. This is an expansive definition, because it is calculated with reference to:

- the current month's taxable supplies plus the previous eleven months' taxable supplies, or
- the current month's taxable supplies plus the next eleven months' projected taxable supplies.

A business must apply for registration within 21 days of either of the above current or projected $75 000 annual turnover tests being met.

A business that is not registered:

- will not have to charge GST to its customers, but
- will not be able to claim input tax credits for GST paid on purchases.

Exceptions

There are some exceptions to the GST registration rules:

- Not-for-profit bodies are required to register only if their annual turnover is $150 000 or more.
- Registration is required irrespective of annual turnover for:
  - taxi operators

- resident agents acting for non-residents
- representatives of **incapacitated entities** (e.g. representatives of bankrupt or liquidated entities).

Active reflection

Explain when an entity is required to register for GST.

4.4 Identifying taxable supplies, GST-free supplies and input-taxed supplies

To understand GST, it is necessary to understand the terminology used within the legislation. The sale of goods or services is referred to as the 'supply of goods or the supply of services'. GST has to be charged by a registered business on all taxable supplies.

A **taxable supply** occurs whenever:

- a business is registered or required to be registered for GST
- a supply is made for consideration
- a supply is made in the ordinary course of business
- the supply is connected with Australia.

It is interesting to note that a taxable supply also occurs when an employee pays an employer for part of a fringe benefit (see Chapter 5). The employer is then obliged to include one-eleventh of that payment in its next BAS. Examples of taxable supplies are given in Table 4.2.

TABLE 4.2 EXAMPLES OF TAXABLE SUPPLIES

Advertising	Fuel sales
All processed foods	Goods retail and wholesale
Asset sales for business	Internet services
Books and magazines	Leasing
Commercial waste services	Postage, printing and stationery supplies
Commercial renting or leasing (see note in Table 4.4)	Professional development
	Supplying subcontractors
Debt collection	Services, all business services (see list of services in Table 4.5)
Electricity and gas supplies	
Forfeited security deposits	Telephone services

The term **GST-free supply**, as the words suggest, covers the situation where the supply is totally free of GST—in other words, it is zero-rated (Division 38). A supply is GST-free when:

- the supplier does not have to charge GST on the supply, and
- the supplier is able to claim input tax credits, if applicable, on inputs to the business.

Examples of GST-free supplies are given in Table 4.3.

TABLE 4.3 EXAMPLES OF GST-FREE SUPPLIES

Legislation section	Examples
Subdivision 38-A	All fresh food ready to eat
Subdivision 38-B	Health as defined by the *Health Act*
Subdivision 38-C	Education delivered by eligible institutions
Subdivision 38-D	Child care
Subdivision 38-E	Exports and other supplies for consumption outside Australia
Subdivision 38-F	Religious services
Subdivision 38-G	Non-commercial activities of charitable institutions
Subdivision 38-H	Raffles and bingo conducted by charitable institutions
Subdivision 38-I	Water and sewerage
Subdivision 38-J	Supplies of going concerns
Subdivision 38-K	Transport and related matters (for overseas passengers and imports and exports)
Subdivision 38-L	Precious metals
Subdivision 38-M	Supplies through inwards duty-free shops
Subdivision 38-N	Grants of freehold and similar interests by governments
Subdivision 38-O	Farm land
Subdivision 38-P	Cars for use by persons with disabilities in getting to and from work or running a business

Source: *The GST Act (1999)*.

The term **input-taxed supply**, as the words suggest, implies that GST is applicable in some form. The *inputs* or acquisitions to the business may have GST embedded, but if the *outputs* or supplies are for a particular purpose they will not have any GST embedded in them, and no GST can be reclaimed on the inputs. Examples of input-taxed supplies are given in Table 4.4.

The principle of a supply being input-taxed is explained as follows:

- the supplier does not have to charge GST on the supply, but
- the supplier is *not able* to claim input tax credits, if applicable, on inputs to the business.

TABLE 4.4 EXAMPLES OF INPUT-TAXED SUPPLIES

Input-taxed supply	Definition
Money	Lending, borrowing, making an advance or granting credit
Accounts	Creating, keeping or closing savings, cheque or deposit accounts
Debt security	Creation or other dealing in a security for a debt
Shares	Allotment, issue, transfer, assignment or receipt of securities
Futures	Dealings of a futures contract through a futures exchange
Superannuation	Creation, transfer or dealing in an interest in a superannuation fund

Input-taxed supply	Definition
Life insurance	Provision, transfer or assignment of a life insurance policy
Hire purchase (HP)	Provision of credit provided as a separate charge under an HP agreement
Residential rent (see note below)	Renting or leasing out of **residential premises**
Residential premises (see note below)	The sale of used real property if it is residential premises and is to be used predominantly for residential accommodation
Note: The sale of new residential premises (previously neither sold nor subject to a long-term lease) is excluded from being input-taxed; hence, such sales are a taxable supply with input tax credits also available to the supplier if registered for GST (unless the margin scheme is used in calculating GST liability; see Section 4.7). For a rented boat to be classified under this category it must be permanently attached to the shore and unable to be moved in the water. It is not good enough just to remove the motor!	

For example, if a bank buys a quantity of paper on which to record transactions, it cannot claim the input tax credit embedded in the cost of that paper. Input-taxed supplies and their related legislative sections are outlined in Table 4.6.

Table 4.5 outlines supplies that are *not* financial supplies, and hence are subject to GST.

TABLE 4.5 FINANCIAL SUPPLIES SUBJECT TO GST

Other GST supplies	Definition
Advice	Advice including advice in respect of financial supplies such as money, accounts, debt securities and shares
Insurance	All insurance other than life insurance
Legal services	Legal services of a solicitor in the course of a professional practice
Accounting	Accounting services by an accountant in the course of a professional practice
Tax agents	Management of tax affairs by a registered tax agent
Safe custody	Safe custody for cash, documents or other things
Payroll	A supply of a payroll service

TABLE 4.6 EXAMPLES OF INPUT TAX SUPPLIES

Legislation section	Input-taxed supply
Subdivision 40A	Financial supplies
Subdivision 40B	Residential rent
Subdivision 40C	Residential premises
Subdivision 40D	Precious metals
Subdivision 40E	School tuckshops and canteens

Active reflection

Give three examples of each of the following:
(a) taxable supplies
(b) GST-free supplies
(c) input-taxed supplies.

4.5 Accounting requirements for GST

The first question to consider is whether GST accounting has to be done:

- on a cash basis, or
- on an accruals basis.

The answer to this has been addressed under the legislation by a simple rule. If a business has an annual turnover of *less* than $2 million, the cash basis can be used. If its annual turnover is *greater* than $2 million, the accruals basis applies and must be adopted.

Example

To understand the concept of 'cash versus accruals' accounting, consider the following:

- In period 1, Bee Enterprises makes a credit sale of $110 and issues an invoice to Rex Dresses.
- In period 2, Rex Dresses pays the $110.

Does Bee Enterprises recognise the sale:

- in period 1, when it made the sale, or
- in period 2, when it was paid for the sale?

Under the GST system the answer is:

- using the *cash* basis (annual turnover of less than $2 million), in period 2
- using the *accruals* basis (annual turnover of more than $2 million), in period 1.

Thus, in the above example:

1. If both businesses have an annual turnover of *less* than $2 million:
   - Bee Enterprises will have to remit GST to the ATO 28 days after the end of period 2.
   - Rex Dresses will be able to claim input tax credits within its own GST remittance to the ATO 28 days after the end of period 2.
2. If both businesses have an annual turnover of *more* than $2 million:
   - Bee Enterprises will have to remit GST to the ATO 28 days after the end of period 1.
   - Rex Dresses will be able to claim input tax credits within its own GST remittance to the ATO 28 days after the end of period 1.

In this example, the cash-flow implications of having to pay 10% GST to the ATO *before* the cash is actually received from the customer could be disastrous for the business.

GST has changed the way we do business in many circumstances, and the impact of this tax system has been quite significant. One thing seems clear: the preparation of more regular data in order to comply with GST has almost certainly improved many accounting information systems. There are now genuine management benefits accruing from this periodic preparation of financial statements and cash-flow forecasts.

4.5 Active reflection

Using the following information, explain how the accounting requirements for GST impact on the way a business operates:

(a) The business turns over less than $2 million each year, but more than $75 000.

(b) During the quarter the business received cash of $100 000 for taxable supplies and was owed $35 000 from invoiced customers.

(c) In that same quarter the business purchased $10 000 trading goods for cash and owed $5000 to suppliers for invoiced trading goods.

(d) The business has written off $500 as a bad debt.

4.6 GST accounting methodology

This section demonstrates the accounting treatment of GST within a business using a simple example. It explains how to implement the legislative GST principles for the accruals method. The cash method of reporting on the BAS is carried out solely through the operation of a cash book, and thus requires very little explanation. Chapter 6 has examples of manual cash book accounting.

The basic mechanics of debits and credits are a necessary foundation for the GST accounting methods to be fully understood. Underlying all the GST rules is the fact that accounts must be able to isolate the GST input tax credits available to be netted off against output tax payable. Only the GST-exclusive amounts of the ledger accounts must be left for a final analysis of the entity's financial position.

Adjustments are placed in the BAS only when they relate to activities of a previous period. These are more fully explained in Chapter 6, Section 6.5.

All accounts in the entity's ledger should reflect only the GST-exclusive amount, as the GST will be cleared with completion of every BAS. It is also necessary for revenue and expense accounts to be transferred to the profit and loss account every BAS period.

You need to classify all accounts as follows:

Sales or supplies you make	Purchases or acquisitions made
Taxable	Non-capital including GST
GST-free	Non-capital GST-free
Input-taxed	Non-capital for making input-taxed supplies
GST-free exports	Capital including GST
	Capital GST-free
	Capital for making input-taxed supplies

Wages and superannuation are excluded from GST, as are cash drawings. Drawings of goods should be treated separately as they require an adjustment of GST. There is no distinction between capital and revenue for GST purposes, so all accounts may be subject to the classifications as above.

The balance sheet accounts that support the GST clearing account

Asset

Input tax credits

Asset

Input tax credit adjustment

Liability

GST output tax payable

Liability

GST output tax payable adjustment

These four basic GST accounts will be used to illustrate how the amounts are manually recorded. It has to be remembered that the types of accounts required will largely depend on the activities of the entity. In a computerised accounting system, these four accounts would probably all be entered as sub-accounts of the **GST clearing account**, generally considered a liability account. All the balances can be transferred into this clearing account to determine the exact amount required to be forwarded to the ATO, or the amount that can be expected as a refund.

Measuring

GST clearing account

The purchase of assets has to be dealt with carefully, because the BAS requires total capital purchases, GST included, to be reported separately from other purchases, at G10. To ensure that amounts are recorded accurately in the books of the business, open a capital asset purchases control account, into which can be placed all assets purchased in the period, GST-inclusive. Once the BAS is completed for the period, each asset can be transferred to the relative asset account, and the GST input tax credit can be transferred to the GST clearing account.

Asset

Capital asset purchases control

Asset sales are included in the BAS calculation worksheet along with all other supplies, sales revenue and other income. The portion of GST embedded in these supplies can be posted to the output tax payable account when the initial entry is made. Original entries can be made to an asset disposal account. This account should be balanced off to determine the gain or loss only after the BAS has been completed for the **tax period**.

Accounting information

Primary information collected from source documents of OTP Pty Ltd is as follows:

Account	Ref	Dr $	Cr $
Taxable sales			110 000
Export sales			50 000
Residential rent received			10 000
Commercial rent received			33 000
Bottled water sales			2 000
Interest received			650
Accounting fees		1 100	
Bank fees		770	
Depreciation		15 000	
Other operating expenses		77 000	
Rent expenses (residential)		1 000	
Rent expenses (commercial)		4 400	
Superannuation		5 400	
Wages and salaries		60 000	

Other information during the quarter

- Purchase made of a new photocopy machine for the office, paying $2200. The old one, which was bought for $1200 and had a book value of $600, was sold for $550 cash.
- $110 of taxable supplies was returned to the entity. These supplies had been sold in the previous BAS period.
- A discount of $22 was given for creditable purchases purchased in the last BAS period.
- A bad debt of $88 of taxable supplies, owing for 13 months, was written off (available only to accruals (non-cash) payers).

To fully understand what amount actually ends up in the ledger accounts of the business we will use the information given for OTP Pty Ltd above. The extra columns shown on the right-hand side of Table 4.7 give the amount of GST extracted, and state whether it is GST payable or creditable. The GST-exclusive amount of the transaction in any supply or creditable acquisition is shown in the left-hand columns. This allows us to see how the recording process is carried out.

TABLE 4.7 ACCOUNTING FOR GST-EXCLUSIVE INFORMATION FOR OTP PTY LTD

Account	Dr $	Cr $	Input tax credit Dr	Input tax credit Cr	Output tax payable Dr	Output tax payable Cr
Taxable sales		100 000				10 000
Export sales		50 000			GST-free	
Residential rent received		10 000			Input-taxed	
Commercial rent received		30 000				3 000
Bottled water sales		2 000			GST-free	
Sale of asset		500				50
Interest received		650			Input-taxed	
Accounting fees	1 000		100			
Bank fees	770		No GST in the price			
Depreciation	15 000		Excluded			
Other operating expenses	70 000		7 000			
Rent expenses (residential)	1 000		Input-taxed			
Rent expenses (commercial)	4 000		400			
Superannuation	5 400		Excluded			
Wages and salaries	60 000		Excluded			
Totals	**157 170**	**193 150**	**7 500**			**13 050**
*Photocopy machine acquired	2 200		*The $200 input tax credit will be transferred directly to the clearing account after entering the BAS information			
Total capital purchases	**2 200**					
Adjustments (that occurred in a prior BAS period)			**Input tax credit adjustment** Dr	Cr	**Output tax payable adjustment** Dr	Cr
Discount received adjustment		20		2		
Bad debts adjustment	80				8	
Sales returns adjustment	100				10	
Total adjustments	**180**	**20**		**2**	**18**	

Note: Chapter 6 gives a detailed explanation of the obligations for BAS reporting and payment.

General comments

As you can see from the example above, the supplies *to* one business *from* another business retain the same characteristics. It is a good idea to think of these in terms of the flow-through effect, presented in Figure 4.3.

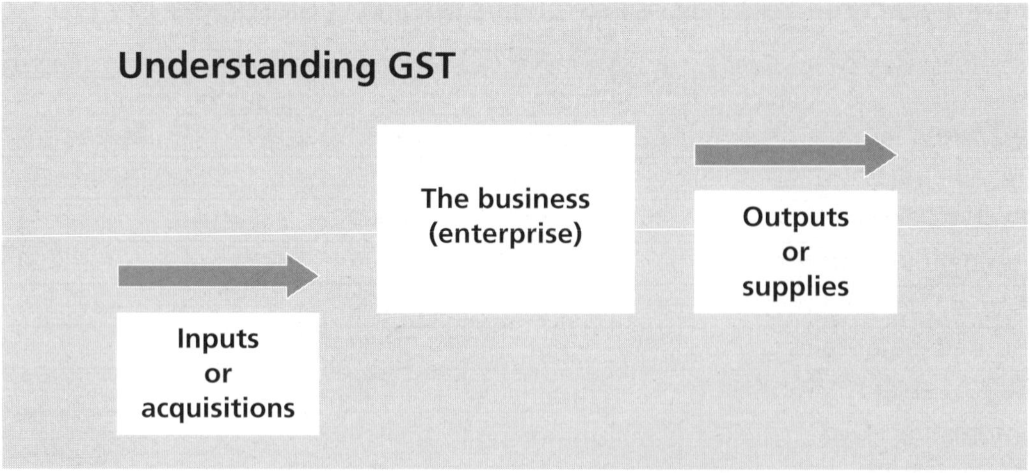

FIGURE 4.3 The operation of a business

Example

Abby Pty Ltd is a timber merchant.

Bailey Pty Ltd is a furniture maker.

Club Pty Ltd is a furniture wholesaler/exporter.

Transaction	Input GST $	Output GST $	GST payable $ (net)
Abby Pty Ltd			
Sells timber to Bailey Pty Ltd for $110		10	
GST payable to the ATO			10
Bailey Pty Ltd			
Buys timber from Abby Pty Ltd for $110	10		
Sells furniture to Club Pty Ltd for $550		50	
GST payable to the ATO			40
Club Pty Ltd			
Buys furniture from Bailey Pty Ltd for $550	50		
Exports furniture for $700		nil	
GST refund			(50)
TOTAL	**60**	**60**	**nil**

4.6 Active reflection

If, for the BAS quarter, a GST-registered business had inputs costing $217 000, of which $2500 did not have GST embedded in the tax invoices, what would be the input tax credit available?

4.7 Treatment of goods and services subject to special rules

The underlying principle of GST is that the supplier is the party responsible for charging and remitting GST to the ATO. This principle is not practical for goods imported from overseas suppliers. Thus, for imported goods, it is the receiver or importer who is responsible for calculating and remitting the GST.

The value of a taxable importation is the sum of:

- the customs value of the goods
- any customs duty payable
- the amount paid or payable to transport the goods to the port or airport of final destination in Australia
- the insurance cost for that transport, and
- any wine equalisation tax payable.

GST on taxable importations is 10% of the market value derived from the above list. GST is payable on all importations that are taxable importations, regardless of who produces them. However, any tax credits are available only to those receivers or importers who are registered, or required to be registered, for GST purposes. However, a cash-flow problem may arise for the importer, as follows:

- GST has to be paid before the goods can be released from customs.
- The first opportunity to claim the corresponding input tax credit will not be until at least 21 days after the end of the monthly or quarterly tax period.

As a result, subject to certain eligibility criteria, and if the importer is registered for GST, the importer may be able to defer making the GST payment by participating in the government's Deferred GST Scheme. This scheme enables the importer to defer the payment of GST on taxable importations until the first BAS is lodged after the goods have been imported into the country for home consumption. (Refer to the Australian Customs Notice No. 99/66.)

To obtain more information about deferring GST on imports, telephone the ATO's Deferred GST Scheme Helpline on **1300 130 915**. More information is also available at **www.ato.gov.au**, where you can select 'Businesses' then 'GST essentials' and 'Importation and international issues'.

Special rules concerning the grouping of companies

Companies within a 90% **common ownership group** can apply for approval as a GST group. The practical implication of this is that the GST group is treated for GST purposes as a single entity.

The **representative member** becomes liable for all GST matters affecting the group:

- lodging the GST return
- paying GST for the group
- claiming input tax credits for the group.

The representative member is liable for the GST on any taxable supplies made by the group and claims GST credits for any **creditable acquisitions** or **creditable importations** made by members of the group.

An entity that wishes to join a GST group, or a proposed GST group, must satisfy all the membership requirements of the GST Act[1] and must be registered for GST. All companies wishing to form a GST group must also have the same tax period, must account for GST on the same basis and must not belong to any other GST group. However, each member of the group will quote its own ABN on tax invoices or adjustment notes for any taxable supplies or taxable importations it makes.

Note: The applicable GST annual turnover thresholds are calculated for the group as a whole. All taxable supplies between group members are excluded from GST.

Special rules concerning rental property

The GST treatment of rent from a residential property is different from that for a commercial property:

- Residential rental is an input-taxed supply.
- Commercial rental is a normal GST taxable supply.

As shown previously in the accounting treatment of GST transactions, it is important that these accounts be kept separate in the ledger so that accurate reporting can take place.

Special rules concerning second-hand goods

Entities that deal in **second-hand goods** would commonly buy these goods from non-registered sellers. Thus they would not be entitled to input tax credits. As a concession, the legislation provides for **notional input tax credits** that can be built into the calculation of 'net' GST payable. The amount of a notional input tax credit is one-eleventh of the consideration that the business provides or is liable to provide for the acquisition of the goods.

If the owner of the second-hand goods is registered, then the sale to a second-hand dealer will be a taxable supply and the normal GST rules will apply.

Example

If a retailer accepts from a customer (who is not registered for GST) a second-hand boat as part payment for a new craft, a notional input tax credit is available when the boat is subsequently sold by that retailer. If, for example, $3300 was given for the boat trade-in, and after cleaning it up it was sold the following week for, say, $3608, this is the outcome:

Date	Details	Amount $	Input tax $	Output tax payable $
4 July	Second-hand boat as trade-in	3300		
11 July	Sold second-hand boat	3608		328
11 July	Notional input tax credit now available		300	
	Net GST payable to the ATO	28		

In most cases, the trade-in will be from a private customer who is not registered for GST. The notional input tax credit is available only when the boat is sold. If the boat was not sold until 1 October, the notional credit would be available as at 1 October. If the retailer sold the boat for less than the trade-in, say $3080, the retailer's notional input tax credit would become $280, which is the same as output tax payable; thus, no GST would actually be paid at all. If the trade-in was from another business that is registered for GST, no notional credit would be needed. The retailer would ask the other business for a tax invoice for the $3300 and would be entitled to an input tax credit at the time of payment (if registered for GST as a cash payer) or at the time of invoicing (if registered for GST as an accruals payer).

Special rules concerning the sale of real property subject to GST

Under the normal rules, the supply of real property (sale of vacant land, new residential premises or commercial premises) is subject to GST of one-eleventh of the supply. The **margin scheme** operates to allow one-eleventh GST to be paid on the *difference* between the selling price and the purchase price, under certain circumstances.[2]

Even if the taxpayer acquired the real property before the commencement of GST in July 2000, the vendor can still use the margin scheme, but there are some important criteria that need to be met:

The vendor must be registered (or required to be registered) for GST.

The post-GST purchase must have been from a taxpayer who calculated his/her GST liability using the margin scheme.

No input tax credit must be claimed on the purchase.

If the real property was acquired prior to 30 June 2000, the margin scheme uses the value of the land as at 1 July 2000 or the date the vendor applied for registration for GST. Thus, it is important that the land has been valued as at 1 July 2000 or no later than the end of the tax period in which the settlement occurs. If a valuation is not obtained, the ATO defaults to the purchase price, and this could substantially increase the GST payable. The law also states that the taxpayer is required to obtain a certified professional valuation. For sales of real property made under contracts entered into on or after 29 June 2005, suppliers and purchasers of real property must agree in writing to use the margin scheme by the time the property is supplied (usually at settlement). If the margin scheme is used, no input tax credit is available to the purchaser.[3]

Active reflection 4.7

What is the value of the following taxable importation of a yacht, and how much GST will be applicable?

- **Customs value: $500 000**
- **Customs duty: $2000**
- **Insurance premium:$10 000**

4.8 Penalties

The introduction of GST signified a change in the taxing process in Australia. It shifted the emphasis from direct taxation (i.e. income tax) to an indirect value-added tax. The suppliers of goods or services charge GST on the supply but have to remit to the ATO only the net amount after deducting any input tax credits. This prevents the tax cascading. If taxpayers fail to correctly report the amount they are required to remit or do not meet other tax obligations, then they may be liable to penalties and/or interest charges. The uniform penalty provisions[4] consist of the following penalties:

- those relating to statements, unarguable positions and schemes
- failing to lodge documents on time
- failing to withhold amounts as required (under the PAYG withholding system or the GST system)
- failing to meet other tax obligations.

The ATO deals severely with false or misleading statements if the statements are made intentionally or recklessly. It is very important that taxpayers take reasonable care that all their statements and documents lodged with the ATO are prepared in good faith. The amount of any penalty will depend on the ATO's assessment of the taxpayer's behaviour and the factors set out in the legislation that increase or reduce the penalty. The base penalty amount that applies is a percentage of the shortfall amount. The shortfall amount is the difference between the correct tax liability or credit entitlement and the liability or entitlement worked out using the information provided to the ATO. The percentage used is determined by the behaviour that gave rise to the shortfall amount. Behaviour is classified under the following headings:

- Failure to take reasonable care: the base penalty amount is 25% of the shortfall.
- Recklessness: the base penalty amount is 50% of the shortfall.
- Intentional disregard: the base penalty is 75% of the shortfall.

In all cases, obviously the penalty is on top of paying the shortfall.

4.8 Active reflection

What penalty applies for making false and misleading statements that result in a GST shortfall of $1000? Set out the scenario for each of the cases explained in the section above.

GST in practice

To enable the practitioner to answer the GST questions that will arise from time to time, it is necessary to fully understand the implications of this complex legislation. This 'GST in practice' is a challenging question that may assist in extending your understanding of these laws.

Assume that Company A and Company B both buy and sell goods in Australia and overseas. Company A has an annual turnover of $20.7 million, while Company B, which is 90% owned by

Company A, has an annual turnover of $10.5 million. Quite often the companies have interactive trading events, and these are always carried out adhering to the principle of arms-length transactions. Set out a GST scenario for both companies, calculate the PAYG instalment income and tax that would be paid in the year, and complete the cost of inputs for each company using the following partial information:

Company A: subject to an ATO instalment rate of 2.76%			
Annual turnover GST-inclusive		20 700 000	
(20% of turnover has no GST)			
Total supplies			20 700 000
Importations base value		3 105 000	
Customs duty (on base value)	12%		
Import insurance costs (on base)	3%		
GST on imports			
Payroll		950 000	
PAYG withholdings tax		171 000	
Superannuation		85 500	
All other inputs with GST		13 500 000	
Total acquisitions			?
Company B (90% controlled by A)			
Annual turnover GST-inclusive		10 500 000	
(14% of turnover has no GST)			
Total supplies			10 500 000
Importations base value		2 100 000	
Customs duty (on base value)	12%		
Import insurance costs (on base)	3%		
GST on imports			
Payroll		670 000	
PAYG withholdings tax		120 600	
Superannuation		60 300	
All other inputs with GST		5 000 000	
Total acquisitions			?

Scenario solution

Company A would have to register for GST. It would be an accruals payer and would be required to lodge and pay with monthly reports for GST, PAYG withholdings tax and PAYG instalment tax. The company would also be required to pay the GST on importations, and this amount is 10% of the total value of the importations, customs duty and insurance costs. If Company A traded with Company B, their transactions would be subject to GST and each one would collect and pay GST output tax payable and receive input tax credits for inputs that were taxable.

Company B would have to register for GST. It would also be an accruals payer, but in this case it could choose to lodge and pay with quarterly reports for GST and PAYG instalment tax. However, PAYG withholdings tax would have to be reported and paid monthly. Company B would also be required to pay the GST on the total value of importations at the rate of 10%. Similarly all of Company B's inter-company trades with Company A would be subject to GST, and each would collect and pay GST output tax payable and receive input tax credits for inputs that were taxable.

Company A	ATO-advised PAYG tax instalment rate: 2.76%					Instalments income	Tax instalments paid p.a.
Annual turnover GST-inclusive			20 700 000		16 560 000	15 054 545	
(20% of turnover has no GST)	20%				4 140 000	4 140 000	
Total supplies				20 700 000	20 700 000	19 194 545	529 769
Importations base value	15%	3 105 000					
Customs duty	12%	372 600					
Import insurance costs	3%	93 150					
Total value of imports for GST			3 570 750				
GST on imports	10%		357 075				
Payroll			950 000				
PAYG withholdings tax			171 000				
Superannuation			85 500				
All other inputs with GST			13 500 000				
Total acquisitions				18 634 325			
Company B (90% controlled by A)	ATO-advised PAYG tax instalment rate: 1.97%						
Annual turnover GST-inclusive			10 500 000		9 030 000	8 209 091	
(14% of turnover has no GST)	14%				1 470 000	1 470 000	
Total supplies				10 500 000	10 500 000	9 679 091	190 678
Importations base value	20%	2 100 000					
Customs duty	12%	252 000					
Import insurance costs	3%	63 000					
Total value of imports for GST			2 415 000				
GST on imports	10%		241 500				
Payroll			670 000				
PAYG withholdings tax			120 600				
Superannuation			60 300				
All other inputs with GST			5 000 000				
Total acquisitions				8 507 400			

There is a possible benefit from grouping for GST, because Company B is 90% owned by Company A. If both entities satisfy the membership requirements of a GST group and both are registered and meet the other membership requirements as per section 48-10 of the GST Act, they could form a GST group. However, they would have to ensure that:

- they have the same tax period—so Company B would have to choose monthly reporting and payment of GST
- the accounts for GST are kept on the same basis, and
- neither belongs to any other GST group.

Each member of the group would quote its own ABN on tax invoices or adjustment notes for any taxable supplies or taxable importations it makes. Either Company A or Company B could be the representative member.

Learning check

✓ Complete the GST section of the ABN application form.

✓ Calculate the GST-inclusive and GST-exclusive price of an item. Correctly display the price in accordance with ACCC guidelines.

✓ Classify business transactions into taxable or creditable, GST-free, input-taxed, capital or non-capital acquisitions.

✓ Calculate the correct amount of increasing or decreasing balancing adjustment.

✓ Calculate the correct amount of GST to be reported using the:
- cash method
- accruals method.

✓ Design a tax invoice for transactions:
- under $1000
- over $1000.

Taxation vocabulary

Australian Business Number (ABN)
cascading
common ownership group
creditable acquisitions
creditable importations
electronic lodgement service
exempt supplies
goods and services tax (GST)
gross annual turnover
GST annual turnover
GST clearing account
GST-free supply
incapacitated entities
input tax credits
input-taxed supply
luxury car tax (LCT)
margin scheme
notional input tax credits
output tax payable
registered for GST
representative member
residential premises
second-hand goods
taxable supply
tax invoice
tax period
wine equalisation tax (WET)

multiple-choice questions

Circle the correct response. (Answers to odd-numbered multiple-choice questions are provided on page 318.)

1. GST replaced sales tax, which was levied on:

(a) services only
(b) goods and imports
(c) imports only
(d) goods and services and imports

2. The GST is levied on:

(a) services only
(b) goods and imports
(c) imports only
(d) goods and services and imports

3. If a supply is GST-free, the rate of tax is:

(a) 0% (b) 10% (c) 9.09% (d) no rate is applied

4. If a supply is input-taxed, the rate of tax is:

(a) 0% (b) 10% (c) 9.09% (d) no rate is applied

5. GST avoids double taxation by allowing businesses to:

(a) claim input tax credits
(b) pay only the output tax
(c) pay only the input tax
(d) claim output tax credits

6. Businesses that export all goods and services will only:

(a) claim output tax credits
(b) pay the output tax
(c) pay the input tax
(d) claim input tax credits

7. GST is often referred to as:

(a) a turnover tax (b) a cascading tax (c) a value-added tax (d) a sales tax

8. The introduction of GST means that the tax base is:

(a) narrowed (b) broadened (c) direct (d) cascading

9. A tax invoice is required only if:

(a) the sale is under $75
(b) an input tax credit is to be claimed
(c) the sale is over $1000
(d) a customer requests one

10. A tax invoice is not required if:

(a) the sale is under $75
(b) an input tax credit is to be claimed
(c) the sale is over $1000
(d) a customer requests one

11. If a business that has purchased taxable supplies cannot obtain an ABN from the seller, tax will be deducted at source by the purchasing business at the rate of:

(a) 10.0% (b) 20.0% (c) 30.0% (d) 46.5%

12. If tax is deducted at source by Company X because a tax invoice has not been provided by Company Y, then the amount actually paid to Company Y is:

(a) noted in the BAS as GST-free
(b) noted in the BAS as input-taxed
(c) noted in the BAS under the PAYG withholdings section
(d) not reported in the BAS at all.

quick-and-easy comprehension

Place a ✓ to indicate your response to each statement.

STATEMENT	TRUE	FALSE
1. **If a business advertises the price of its product or service, that price has to be GST-exclusive.**	—	—
2. **Input tax credits are available only to GST-registered businesses.**	—	—
3. **The taxing point in the GST system is the last wholesale sale.**	—	—
4. **GST is not a tax on business; it is the end user that pays.**	—	—
5. **The sale of new residential premises is input-taxed.**	—	—
6. **A notional input tax credit can be built into the GST calculations under certain conditions.**	—	—

self-test question

Jack has operated his plumbing business since 1993. He has an ABN and is registered for GST. He purchased a work van in 1997 but has decided to trade in his old van for a brand-new one.

Using the information below, set out for Jack any GST implications in the chart of accounts. Jack lodges an activity statement monthly as a cash payer.

- The original cost of his work van was $29 000.
- The new work van will cost a total of $46 970.
- The trade-in offered for the old van is $5830.
- Jack will borrow $35 000 from a financier.
- Any balance remaining will be met by Jack with his own cash.

assessments

Cash vs accruals

1. **The company Marina Shores Pty Ltd provided the following information for the year ending 30 June 2009. All its purchases were creditable purchases and no taxable supplies were GST-free or input-taxed.**

   Show how Marina Shores should account for GST, assuming the business uses:

   (a) the cash basis

   (b) the accruals basis

Quarter ending	Sales (including GST)	Purchases (including GST)	Received (from debtors)	Paid (to creditors)
	$	$	$	$
September 2008	11 000	5 500	nil	nil
December 2008	11 550	6 050	nil	5 500
March 2009	13 200	7 150	11 000	6 050
June 2009	14 300	7 700	12 100	6 600

Tax invoices

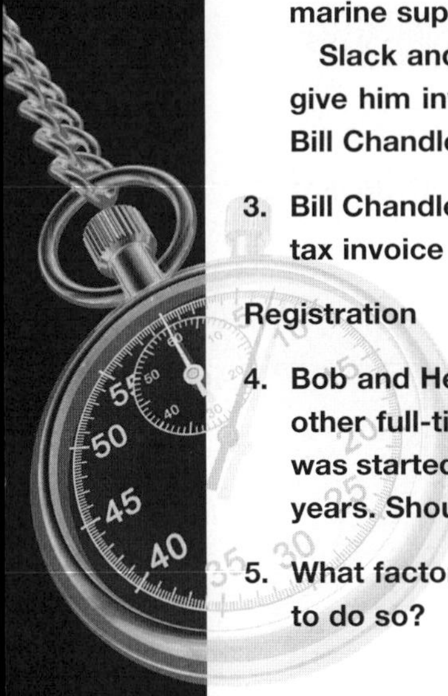

2. **Bill Chandler operates a ship chandler's business and has an annual turnover of $600 000. He purchases marine supplies from Slack and Co, which is registered for GST purposes.**

   Slack and Co maintains that, because Bill Chandler pays by cheque, there is no need for the staff to give him invoices when they are busy, as the cheque butt is sufficient evidence of the purchase. Tell Bill Chandler whether this is correct.

3. **Bill Chandler is reviewing his own GST accounting requirements. What are the requirements for a valid tax invoice for services worth $980?**

Registration

4. **Bob and Helen operate a small part-time business called Runabout Motor Repairs, in addition to their other full-time employment. Last year the business turned over $74 000 excluding GST. The business was started about five years ago and growth has been steady at about 12% per annum for the past few years. Should they register for GST?**

5. **What factors might influence a business to choose to register for GST when it is actually not required to do so?**

case study question

Martin Masonry wants you to assist him to complete the application to register his enterprise (Martin's Fabulous Landscapes Pty Ltd). In Chapter 2 the case study required you to complete the details on the form (see Form 2.3 [2939]) up to and including item 27. Now complete items 28 to 48 using the following information:

- Martin wishes to register for GST.
- His expected annual turnover is $200 000.
- Martin wishes to be a quarterly payer using the cash method.
- His business will not be importing goods into Australia, nor will it require any fuel tax credits.
- Martin estimates his own wage will be $1000 per week.
- Martin intends to employ an apprentice paying an annual wage of $26 000.
- PAYG withholding is estimated to be $17 000.
- Martin will report using the appropriate ATO form and payment summaries.
- There will not be any payments of royalties, dividends or interest.
- Martin banks with the State Bank— BSB: 055 055; account no: 321654987; name of account: Martin's Fabulous Landscapes Pty Ltd.
- Martin has a TFN, 963 852 741, and his date of birth is 1 January 1980. He is the public officer and sole director of the company.

classroom activities

1. **In groups of three to five people see whether you can work out how a tax invoice should be presented. Photocopy the following information, cut out selected words and attach the correct details to a blank piece of paper to simulate a tax invoice. The information has been placed in alphabetical order.**

Date:	**Quantity of goods sold**
Date:	Quantity of goods sold
Description of goods	Sold to:
Description of goods	**Sold to:**
GST	Sub-total
GST	**Sub-total**
GST	Swaggies ABN: 12 234 456 678
GST	**Swaggies ABN: 12 234 456 678**
Including	Tax
Including	**Tax**
Invoice no. 651	**Total**
Invoice no. 651	Total
Native Art Supplies ABN: 98 874 456 632	Unit price
Native Art Supplies ABN: 98 874 456 632	**Unit price**

The entity supplying the goods for sale:	*The entity purchasing the goods from Swaggies Head Office:*
Swaggies Head Office 361 Manly Road Manly NSW 2095	Native Art Supplies 112 Mt Wilga Parade East Wahroonga NSW 2076
Swaggies Head Office 361 Manly Road Manly NSW 2095	**Native Art Supplies 112 Mt Wilga Parade East Wahroonga NSW 2076**

The transaction details

15 Akubra hats @ $87.99 each
10 bark paintings @ $57 each

2. Now try the giant crossword.

Across

1 Short for a powerful nation. 2
7 Expressing position or time of day. 2
10 This form is filed monthly or quarterly. 8, 8, 9
15 The ATO requests you use this to fill out the forms. 3
16 If you are a PAYG payer, you probably pay them. 5
18 Used as a preposition in sentences. 2
19 We walk on them. 4
21 The summit or upper part. 3
23 If only we had more of it! 4
24 Either! 2
25 Sometimes we do this to accounts. 6
26 Use a broom to sweep them.6
27 Where we send our taxes. 3
28 GST is the abbreviation for it. 5, 3, 8, 3
34 Japanese currency. 3
35 A way to bring events to the public at home. 8
36 GST classification for residential rent. 5, 5
37 If your car breaks down, you may need one. 3
41 You have a choice. 8
45 Used for catching. 3
46 Something that will happen. 5
49 Abbreviation for number. 2
50 Initials of consumer watchdog. 4
51 The proportion of GST embedded in a taxable supply. 3, 8
52 What the ATO calls tax avoidance schemes. 5
53 Used when expressing a ratio. 2
54 Short for compact disk. 2
55 Clever, talented or robust. 4
57 Abbreviation for advice that will come. 3
59 Long narrow strap as a means of control. 4
61 Used in GST to indicate outputs of the business. 8
62 If you are not an 'accruals' payer, you will be this type. 4
63 These are GST-free and placed at G2 on the BAS calculation sheet. 7
64 It is attracted to the light. 4
65 When the BAS is completed, you may need this cuppa! 3
66 Worn by a judge. 1, 3
67 The ATO may have to call them in to investigate fraud. 6
68 Short for Office Tax Procedures. 3
71 Often used to mark a page. 3
72 This is said when there is no limit. 3
73 The expenditure tax system recently introduced. 3
74 If turnover is over $2 million, you must be this payer. 8
75 Maybe the Commissioner uses one on his golf day! 3
76 In the UK it is not called GST! 3
77 Private principal ones do not normally attract GST, land tax or CGT. 10

Down

2 Good information may be put to many ________ 4
3 GST-free supplies have this rating. 4
4 Fresh food is classified as this. 3,4
5 If it is no good, you throw it in this. 3
6 It's on your face and on a needle. 3
7 The past tense for 'eat'. 3
8 The number, one more than nine. 3
9 If you are, then you must charge GST. 10
11 The name given to business acquisitions. 6
12 You make one if you want an ABN. 11
13 All these tax changes keep you on them! 4
14 In overdraft, then in credit! Your cash account may do this. 6
17 The green light says it. 2
18 The annual amount to determine if required to register for GST. 8
20 Necessary to claim input tax credits. 3, 7
22 A preposition meaning 'from', 'out of'. 2
23 Have morning tea on it. 4
29 The word used to indicate goods and services supplied. 7
30 This tax ceased on 1 July 2000. 5, 3
31 She is this to her siblings. 6
32 The limit or conclusion. 3
33 If you are in business, you probably need one. 3
38 The second limb of PAYG laws. 10
39 If it isn't taxed. 3,7
40 If your acquisitions are this, you may get an input tax credit. 10
42 When sale documents are prepared but not finalised. 7
43 Abbreviation for number. 2
44 Engaged in commerce. 10
47 Abbreviation for the top position in a firm. 3
48 If you worry about the GST too much, you may get one! 5
52 A bridge needs a lot of them. 8
56 Rebounding sound. 4
58 With *A New Tax System* (ANTS) we have been as busy as one. 3
59 A cunning person may commit one. 4
60 Abbreviation for the first state. 3
61 When the Commissioner has done this, most of us listen. 6
65 You declare that the information supplied to the ATO is this. 4
69 Most of us have to pay it. 3
70 Short for personal computer. 2
72 If we have eyes, then we can. 3
75 Stands for 'tax determination'. 2

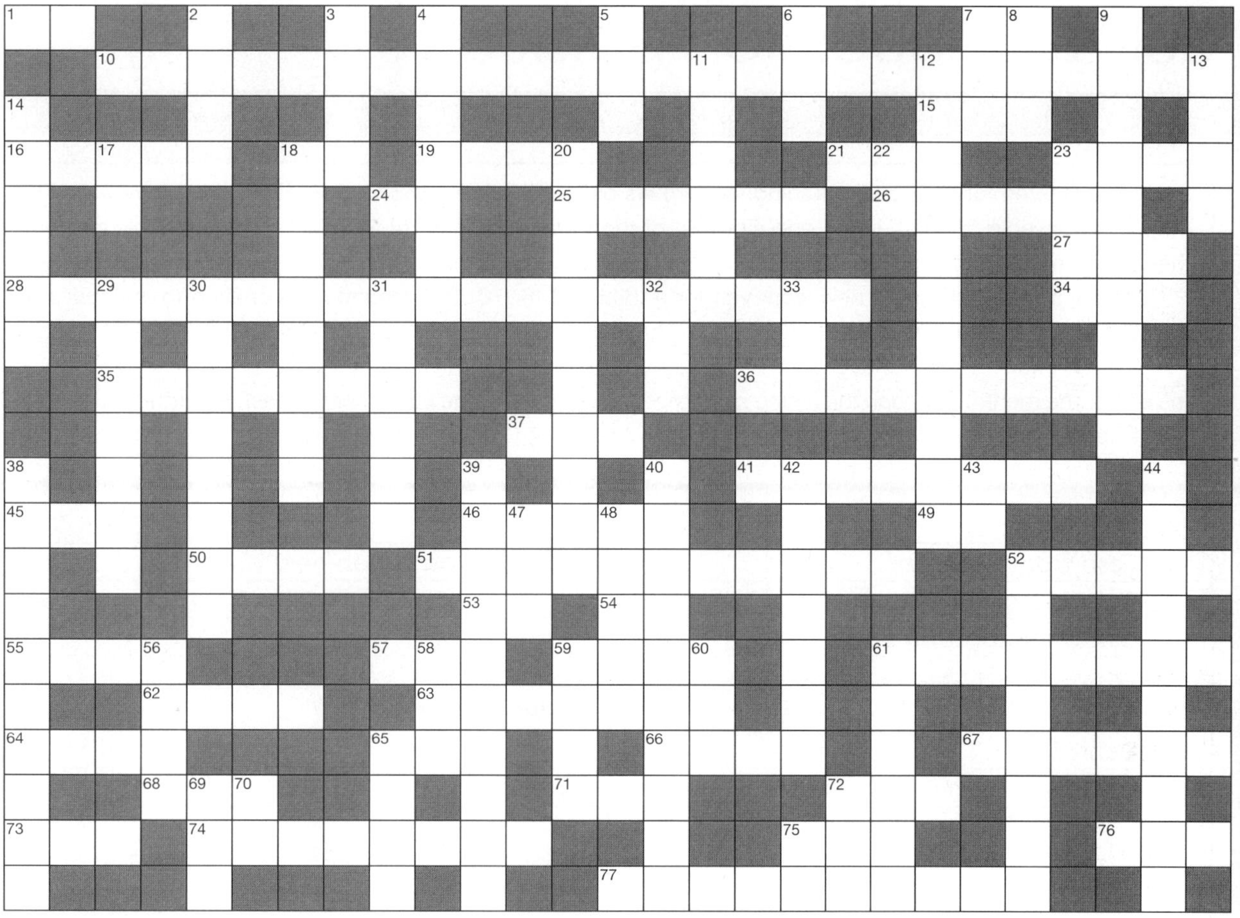

self-test question solution

Jack is registered for GST and is trading (selling) his old work van for $5830, therefore he will owe the ATO output tax payable of $530, being one-eleventh of the trade-in amount of $5830. Thus the real return from the sale of the old van is $5300.

Jack is also purchasing a new work van for a total of $46 970. This means he is entitled to an input tax credit of $4270, being one-eleventh of $46 970. Thus the real cost of the new van for Jack is $42 700.

The net effect of this transaction is a refund from the ATO of $3740, to be received within 14 days from the end of the month. Although the timing might not line up exactly, the movement of cash and other accounts might be as follows:

Bank account

	Debit $		Credit $
Cash from financier	35 000	Net cash outlay on new van	41 140
Refund from ATO	3 740		
Own cash contributed	2 400		

New work van account (asset)

Debit $			Credit $
Original cost (net of GST)	42 700		

GST control account

	Debit $		Credit $
Input tax credit	4 270	Output tax payable	530
		Refund to Bank from ATO	3 740
	4 270		4 270

Old work van account (asset)

	Debit $		Credit $
Original cost in 1997	29 000	Trade-in received (net of GST)	5 300
Profit on disposal	430	Accumulated depreciation	24 130
	29 430		29 430

Financier account (liability)

	Debit $		Credit $
		Cash loan for two years	35 000

Notes

1. Grouping membership requirements are set out in section 48-10 of the GST Act.
2. An interesting margin scheme case to examine is *Brady King Pty Ltd v Commissioner of Taxation (2008)* FCA 81.
3. This is contained in section 75-10 (3b) of the GST Act.
4. The legislative provisions for the imposition of failure to lodge (FTL) penalties are contained in Division 286 of the *Taxation Administration Act 1953*.

Fringe benefits tax

Chapter five

Topics

After studying this chapter, you should be able to:

- **define what is meant by a 'fringe benefit'**
- **outline the reporting requirements of fringe benefits**
- **indicate the rate of fringe benefits tax and identify who the liability rests with**
- **describe how GST is integrated with fringe benefits tax**
- **explain the method of assessment of fringe benefits tax**
- **outline the method of payment of fringe benefits tax**
- **list the different types of benefits that give rise to fringe benefits tax.**

OVERVIEW

The taxing of employee fringe benefits (**fringe benefits tax**, or FBT) came into force in the mid-1980s with the implementation of the *Fringe Benefits Tax Assessment Act 1986* (FBT Act) and its regulations. It is really not a tax on income because, by its operation, it taxes the **non-cash benefits** that are paid by an employer to an employee, with the liability falling on the employer to pay the tax. The critical underlying feature is that there must be an **employer–employee relationship**. It is essentially a tax on employers, and double taxing is avoided by ensuring that the benefit is not taxed as income in the hands of the employees.

In this chapter we discuss the process regarding the reporting requirements for fringe benefits under the *A New Tax System (Fringe Benefits Reporting) Act 1999* (see **www.ato.gov.au**, and then select 'Tax Professionals—homepage' followed by 'Fringe Benefits Tax'). A fringe benefit is explained and the interaction of the FBT with the GST is examined. Other areas studied are the FBT rate of tax, the types of benefit given to employees and how taxable values are calculated. In Chapter 6 you will see the special area of the Business Activity Statement where FBT is reported and how the FBT instalment paid to the ATO can be varied, if necessary.

'FBT in practice' looks at the aggregate and grossed-up values from the examples given in the chapter and calculates the employer's FBT liability for the year.

Employer–employee relationship means any benefit that, if bestowed on a person and if paid in cash, would have been classified as salary or wages as far as PAYG is concerned. The meaning also extends to past and future employees.

5.1 Reporting requirements

The reporting requirements for fringe benefits, brought in by the operation of the *A New Tax System (Fringe Benefits Reporting) Act 1999*, affect both the reporting of benefits given to employees and the calculation of the Medicare levy surcharge. Employers are required to calculate the taxable value of fringe benefits provided in respect of each employee's employment and to record the grossed-up taxable value on the employee's payment summary where the taxable value amount exceeds $2000 (raised from $1000 on 1 April 2007). This value will be included in the income tests used to determine liability for various surcharges, levies and other income-related obligations.

Example

Assume that Jan works for Superior Designs Pty Ltd and received an expense payment fringe benefit of $1950 in the 2008/09 tax year. The taxable value is below $2000 so this will not be a reportable amount. But if Jan also received the use of a car during the tax year, and the taxable value of the car benefit amounted to $2050, then the total taxable value of all Jan's benefits would amount to $4000 and the reportable value would be $4000 × 1.8692 = $7477. Note that the lower type 2 gross-up factor is always be used for this calculation. (See Section 5.2 for an explanation of gross-up factors.)

In addition, a Medicare levy surcharge may be imposed under the *A New Tax System (Medicare Levy Surcharge Fringe Benefits) Act 1999*. This surcharge is based on taxable income as well as the reportable fringe benefits totals for a year of income of a person who is a resident of Australia at any time during the year of income and does not have adequate private patient hospital cover. The amount that employers calculate and report to the ATO on payment summaries as the grossed-up value is now the amount that is included in the taxable wages for payroll tax purposes (see Chapter 10).

Example

Let us assume that Jan, in the above example, has a taxable income of $95 000. She is not covered by private health insurance so the Medicare levy of 1.5% will be charged on taxable income of $95 000 and the surcharge of 1% of $102 477 added. Thus the total Medicare levy payable is:

$95 000 × 1.5%	$1425.00
$102 477 × 1%	$1024.77
Total Medicare levy payable	$2449.77

Active reflection

Suppose during the year an employee received benefits with a taxable value of $4500. What amount would appear on the employee's payment summary at the 30 June?

5.2 The operation of the FBT system

Fringe benefits tax is a separate tax payable by employers on any benefits they provide to employees, over and above salary and wages amounts. FBT is also independent of the liability of the employer to income tax, which means that, even if an employer has losses for income tax purposes and consequently no income tax is payable, there could still be a liability to pay FBT. The tax file number (TFN) for income tax returns and FBT returns is identical for all employers, whether a sole trader, a partnership or a corporation.

Benefits and fringe benefits

The definition of a **benefit** includes any right (including real or personal property), privilege, service or facility that is—or is to be at some time in the future—provided under an arrangement for or in relation to:

- the performance of work whether with or without the provision of property
- the provision of, or the use of, facilities for entertainment, recreation or instruction
- the conferring of rights, benefits or privileges for which remuneration is payable in the form of a royalty or similar demand.

The definition also includes contracts of insurance and money loans. So it is very broad and catches just about any benefit that an employer could bestow on an employee. The *Tax Laws Amendment (2006 Amendments No. 1) Act 2006* states that any foreign-sourced income of temporary residents in Australia is exempt from income tax in Australia. The definition of a fringe benefit in section 136(1) of the FBT Act now excludes benefits to 'exempt visitors', so it is assumed that fringe benefits to temporary residents will also be exempt from FBT.

If a benefit is applied to an associate or family member of the employee or some other person, it will be taxable. A benefit given by an associate of the employer can also be caught by the provisions of the FBT Act, if the benefit is given by the associate with the agreement of the employer or some other third party who has entered into an arrangement with the employer to provide that benefit. An interesting point is that the employer providing the benefit does not necessarily have to be an Australian resident for FBT to apply.

A fringe benefit will not arise unless there is an agreement of some kind between the employer and the third party. Note that it is the actual employer who is liable for the tax rather than the third party giving the benefit. Thus we might say that the benefit must be provided 'in respect of employment' or fall under the 'arranger' provisions if it is to be taxable.[1] For example, a benefit given to a partner in a partnership cannot be classified as a fringe benefit because there is no employer–employee relationship, and a birthday gift given by a husband to his wife whom he employs in his small business is the result of a family relationship and therefore cannot have the characteristic of a fringe benefit.

As a general rule, if an employee contributes to or reimburses the employer for any part of the benefit given, the **taxable value** of that benefit will decrease by that amount. (See the example in Section 5.5.) Certain benefits may fall under what has become known as the **otherwise deductible rule**, which states that the taxable value of a benefit may be reduced where expenditure, which an employee might have incurred in obtaining that benefit, would have been deductible by that employee for income tax purposes. This approach by the ATO is backed by a large body of case law already established, which clearly states that if an expense is allowable as a deduction under income tax law it cannot be considered a fringe benefit.

Fringe benefits tax applies to benefits that are provided to employees resident in Australia, except those whose wages are exempt from income tax. If a non-resident receives salary or wages that are Australian-sourced, then any benefit received will be subject to FBT. For example, an overseas airline will be liable for FBT on benefits given to any of its employees who carry out their employment in Australia, unless they fall under the in-house benefits mentioned below.

If FBT is payable on a benefit, then the benefit is not income in the hands of the employee. In most instances if FBT has not been paid on a benefit then it will be assessable income to the employee.[2] There appears to be the option of an agreement between the employer and employee as to how a benefit will be taxed.

A benefit provided in respect of employment

The most common benefits that are subject to FBT are motor vehicles, free or low-interest loans, payment of employees' private expenses such as HELP debts or school fees, free or subsidised housing, living-away-from-home allowances, airline transport, car parking and tax-exempt bodies' entertainment fringe benefits. Some of these are examined in more detail in Section 5.5. Amounts of FBT paid by the employer are available as income tax deductions.[3]

Example

If an employer has entered into an agreement with an employee to pay the HELP debt for the employee's daughter who is attending university, this benefit is provided in respect of employment and, consequently, is a fringe benefit.

Exempt benefits

Fringe benefits tax is not payable in respect of **exempt benefits**. A minor benefit[4] with a taxable value below $300 (raised from $100 on 1 April 2007) is exempt if it is irregular. Some other exempt benefits include in-specie contributions paid by the employer to superannuation funds (from 1 July 2007), free or discounted commuter travel, the provision of emergency health care, work-related items provided to employees (mobile phone, briefcase, one laptop computer per year, electronic diary), newspapers and periodicals for work, and recreational and child-minding facilities. Taxi travel that originates or ends at the place of work is also exempt. Some employers, such as religious institutions, public benevolent bodies, international organisations and foreign governments, are also exempt from FBT.

If a firm provides goods and meals consumed on its premises by an employee in one working day, then these are exempt from FBT.[5] The first $1000 of the aggregate taxable value of certain in-house benefits given to an employee in a year is also exempt from FBT.[6] Services, goods and other property provided to employees that are of a kind the employer sells in the ordinary course of its business are examples of this type of benefit. Another example is airline transport benefits provided to airline and travel industry employees.

Interaction of FBT with GST

On 1 July 2000 significant changes to the FBT calculations and reporting came into effect as a result of the *A New Tax System (Fringe Benefits) Act 2000*. These changes to the FBT Act regarding the taxable value coincided with the introduction of the GST. FBT is calculated on the **grossed-up value** of the benefit, and this must include GST where input tax credits are available to the employer.

In order to avoid allowing employers the benefit of GST input credits for goods and services purchased by them for the private use of their employees, a GST-inclusive gross-up has been introduced, called *higher type 1 factor*. This effectively recovers the input tax credit that was obtained by the employer in providing a fringe benefit.

Employers are able to apply the original FBT *lower type 2 factor* in situations where GST input tax credits are not available. The GST-inclusive gross-up applies in all other situations. A payment or contribution by an employee to an employer towards the cost of a fringe benefit is treated as a taxable supply for GST purposes. In these situations the GST payable on the taxable supply is one-eleventh of the payment or contribution made by the employee to the employer, and is attributed to the tax period in which the payment is received. These rules also apply to payments or contributions towards the cost of exempt benefits.

If an employer gives a benefit to an employee and the employee does not have to pay tax on that benefit, then the benefit is really a net benefit in the employee's hands. The real value of the benefit is considered to be the **net benefit** plus the **untaxed portion** of that benefit. So, when calculating the FBT payable, the aggregate amount of all benefits paid in that **FBT year** (see Section 5.3) must be grossed-up by the higher gross-up formula (type 1) if the employer is entitled to input tax credits on the benefits paid, or the lower gross-up formula (type 2) if no input tax credits can be claimed. The gross-up formulae are applied to the aggregate taxable values as follows:[7] All amounts are rounded to the nearest dollar.

Type 1—with GST

$$\frac{\text{FBT} + \text{GST}}{(1 - \text{FBT}) \times (1 + \text{GST}) \times \text{FBT}} = 2.0647$$

Type 2—without GST

$$\frac{1}{1 - \text{rate of FBT tax for the year of tax}} = 1.8692$$

To help in the understanding of this taxing procedure, two scenarios are given in the example below. The first represents a cash benefit given to the employee, and thus is taxable in the hands of the employee, and the second represents a fringe benefit paid in respect of employment. We show that it makes no difference how the amount is taxed, as the ATO still ends up with the same amount of tax revenue.

Example

Suppose an employer paid $535 in subscriptions fees for an employee, thus giving a fringe benefit to that employee for the FBT year ended 31 March 2009. Grossing up for FBT and GST by a factor of 2.0647 brings the amount to $1104.59. The FBT rate of 46.5%, equal to the top marginal income tax rate plus the Medicare levy, is applied so that the employer's tax payable on the benefit would be as follows:

FBT payable = $1104.59 × 46.5% = $514

The employer will be given a tax deduction for the amount of FBT paid, being $514, as well as receiving a deduction of $486 (the net benefit after the $49 GST input tax credit—that is, one-eleventh of $535).

1. Income of $1000 is paid out in cash to the employee.

Cost to the employer:	$1000 before tax
Value to employee:	$1000 before tax

Tax payable by the employee: ($1000 × 0.465) = $465

$535 is available after tax if the employee has a marginal tax rate of 46.5%. Thus the employee would be able to pay the subscription fees of $535.

2. The employer decides to give the employee a fringe benefit by paying the subscription fees of $535.

Value to employee:	$535
Cost to employer:	
Net cost of the benefit given to the employee ($535 less input tax credit of $48)	$486
FBT payable $535 × 2.0647 × 0.465	**$514**
Total cost to employer:	$1000

The employer will pay $514 FBT but receives $49 as a GST input tax credit. Thus the tax collected by the government is $465 either way.

5.2 Active reflection

Give three examples of taxable fringe benefits, two of exempt benefits and two of in-house benefits.

5.3 The FBT year and rates of tax

The **fringe benefits standard year (FBT year)** is the 12-month period from 1 April to the following 31 March and returns are required to be lodged on an annual basis by 21 May in the next FBT year. Payment is by self-assessment, calculated to the nearest dollar,[8] and paid in **quarterly instalments**. The information is required on the BAS, and, unless the FBT amount on which the instalment is calculated is less than $3000 (see section 111 of the FBT Act), quarterly payments of tax should be made, using the employer's most recent base year or estimated on the current year benefits. For more information and forms, go to **www.ato.gov.au** and search under 'FBT'. You can also obtain information by telephoning the ATO on **1300 720 092**.

The dates when instalments of FBT are due for non-deferred BAS payers are 21 July, 21 October, 21 January and 21 April, with the annual return to be lodged by 21 May in the following year.

In Chapter 6 you will see that the dates on which the quarterly instalments of FBT are due coincide with all other business tax payments, being 28 July, 28 October, 28 February and 28 April. (See Appendix, Form 5.1 [1067].) The rate of FBT is set by the government and equates with the top marginal individual tax rate plus the Medicare levy.[9] For the FBT year ended 31 March 2007 and later years the rate is set at 46.5%.

Another rate within the legislation that is necessary for various calculations, such as the taxable value of both car and loan fringe benefits, is the **benchmark interest rate** (sometimes referred to as the *statutory interest rate*), set at 9% for 2008/09.[10] It is known as the large bank housing lenders' variable interest rate on loans for housing for owner occupation, last published by the Reserve Bank of Australia before the commencement of the year of tax. Check the Reserve Bank's website on **www.rba.gov.au/Statistics/Bulletin/index.html** at 31 March each year and open Table F5, 'Indicator lending rates', to keep up to date with this annual rate. The new rate will be the interest rate published in late March for the month of February. For further information, telephone the ATO on **13 33 28**.

Active reflection 5.3

Outline the FBT standard year, the current rate of FBT and the current benchmark interest rate.

5.4 Family businesses

The 'family business' makes up quite a large percentage of Australian small businesses, and benefits provided to a family member often fall outside the FBT laws. For example, a wedding gift given to an adult child who has worked for the business in the past cannot be said to be liable for FBT, but remember it is also non-deductible as an expense. The benefit was not provided in respect of employment, because it would have been given even if the firm had not employed the adult child. On the other hand, a motor vehicle given to a family member who works as a marketing agent for the business would attract FBT on the amount used for private purposes. Since 4 December 1997, the payments made to shareholders or associates in private companies have been exempt from FBT. However, strict deemed dividend rules now apply to these payments.

Special considerations apply and each case is considered on its merits, so the Commissioner will examine the details closely to determine the liability for FBT. In general, if the business is gaining allowable tax deductions for the expenditures on the benefit being given, this benefit is probably liable for FBT. If the family member pays all the private expenditure and the asset providing the benefit is not treated as a business asset, it would seem to be outside the FBT requirements.

5.4 Active reflection

Give an example of a benefit in a family business that would (a) fall outside the FBT laws and (b) be caught by the legislation.

5.5 Examples of taxable fringe benefits

It is beyond the scope of this book to deal with all the benefits that may arise in an employer–employee relationship. However, for the purposes of understanding how taxable values are calculated and how the FBT works, this section looks at three types of benefit and gives some examples of assessing FBT liability with:

- car fringe benefits[11]
- loan benefits
- expense payments benefits.

The cost of a car will include any *non*-business accessories such as CD player, GPS, special wheel trims and sun roof, but does not include any business accessories such as a mobile phone for a salesperson or windscreen protectors for a stock agent.

The cost of the car for FBT purposes is *not* limited by the legislation for claiming input tax credits, depreciation or calculating luxury car tax. So a $200 000 car benefit would attract FBT based on the full value of the car.

Car fringe benefits

To determine what a 'car' is for FBT purposes, note the definition given in the FBT Act, which states that it is a motor car, station wagon, panel van, utility truck or similar vehicle, or any other road vehicle. The Commissioner has given a ruling that motor cycles and similar vehicles do not qualify for FBT. The legislation provided that, for FBT years commencing on or after 1 April 1995, panel vans and utilities designed to carry loads of 1 tonne or more would no longer meet the definition of a car.

If an employee (or associate) has the private use of the car, or even if the car is available for private use, a benefit will arise. The same general principles of deductibility apply in determining whether a benefit arises. If a car is kept at or near the employee's place of residence, it will be deemed to be available for private use and thus a benefit will arise. An exemption applies to taxis and to unregistered vehicles used in the business. Two methods are available for valuing **car fringe benefits**: the statutory formula method[12] and the operating cost method.[13] While the employer is free to elect to use either method, the operating cost method requires that a **log book** be kept accurately by the employee for at least 12 consecutive weeks in the first FBT year of tax and thereafter every five years. Each year the **business percentage** must be reviewed for its accuracy.

Statutory formula method

The problem the Commissioner faced when deciding how to tax a motor vehicle was the determination of the actual value of the benefit to the employee. In this **statutory formula** method, the value of the car benefit is based on a percentage of the base value of the car.

The **base value** of the car is its original purchase price, GST-inclusive, paid by the employer, and includes any fitted extras that are not required for business purposes. Any **non-business accessories**, added subsequent to the car being purchased, would increase the base value of the car for FBT purposes. Dealer delivery charges are included in the base value, but registration and stamp duty are not. If the car is leased, the base value is the market value at the commencement of the lease. In both the cases above, the base value of the car will be depreciated by one-third after the car has been held for four years. The reduction applies at the beginning of the first FBT year following the fourth anniversary of its acquisition.

The statutory formula method uses a **statutory fraction** that depends on the total annual kilometres travelled during the FBT year and reflects any days that the car was not available for private use:

$$\text{Taxable value of the benefit} = \frac{ABC}{D} - E$$

where:

A is the base value of the car, which is (i) the cost of the car to the employer not including registration or (ii) the base value of a leased car, or (iii) where at the beginning of the FBT year the car has been owned or leased by the employer for more than four years, the cost is two-thirds of either (i) or (ii).

B is the relevant statutory fraction where the **annualised** number of whole kilometres travelled during the year of tax was (i) more than 40 000—0.07, (ii) not less than 25 000 and not more than 40 000—0.11, (iii) not less than 15 000 and not more than 24 999—0.20, and (iv) any other case—0.26.[14]

C is the number of days during the year on which a car fringe benefit was provided in relation to the car.

D is the number of days in the FBT year.

E is the amount (if any) of the recipient's payments.

Example

Assume that Superior Designs Pty Ltd has given a car to a sales employee and during the FBT year the car was available for the employee's private use. The following information is given:

FBT year ending 31 March 2009

- Car available for use for the whole year
- Date of purchase: 1 October 2004
- Length of time held at start of FBT year 1 April 2008: 3 years 6 months
- Cost price of car (in this case the base value) including GST: $35 000

- Number of days that the car was available for private use (assuming the car was off the road for 25 days): 340
- Number of days in the FBT year: 365
- Total kilometres clocked during the FBT year: 28 000
- Employee payments as per the required declaration: $150

$$\text{Taxable value of the benefit} = \frac{\$35\,000 \times 0.11 \times 340}{365} - \$150$$

This equals $3436.

By using the information given, you can work out the taxable value of the car benefit, remembering that sometimes it will be necessary to annualise the kilometres if the car was purchased or sold during the year.[15]

Operating cost method

This method attempts to be more specific in valuing the benefit and uses specific costs. If an employer elects to use this method rather than the statutory formula method, the employee must keep a log book for a continuous period of at least 12 weeks during the log book year so that the actual business percentage use of the vehicle can be obtained. The log book need only be kept once every five years. The business percentage should, however, be reviewed every year. The **odometer** readings of the total kilometres travelled during the period must also be recorded. Once established, this same business percentage may be used in subsequent years provided the employee keeps the opening and closing odometer readings in the year of tax, and so long as the business percentage remains a reasonable estimate in the year of tax. The formula for **operating cost** method is:

$$\text{Taxable value of the benefit} = (C \times [100\% - BP]) - R$$

where:

C   is the operating costs, GST-inclusive.
BP is the business percentage use ascertained from the log book.
R   is the recipient's payments (if any).

Unfortunately, it is not quite as simple as that, because component C covers such things as:

- actual costs such as repairs, registration (**pro rata**), fuel, maintenance, normal car insurance (pro rata) and, if leased, leasing charges
- deemed costs of depreciation (18.75% pro rata for vehicles purchased after 1 July 2002 and 25% for those purchased after 9 May 2006) and imputed interest. (These are relevant only if the car is owned rather than leased.)

It is necessary to identify the current benchmark interest rate for the deemed costs in this method, and it is mandatory that the employer retain the log books and relevant records for a period of five years from the date of the FBT assessment. Employees must be instructed carefully in the records required, which have now become consistent with the income tax substantiation rules. Figure 5.2 shows how the log book might look. Mandatory records for the log book are as follows:

- the employer's estimate of business kilometres and business percentage use, and the nomination of replacement cars
- the details of the log book period—that is, the dates of the 12-week period
- the date on which each journey began and ended
- the number of kilometres travelled in the course of each journey
- the purpose of each journey.

Date ended	Opening odometer	Closing odometer	No. of km	Purpose of journey	Driver name (optional)	Date of entry (optional)		Comments (entries to be made as soon as possible)

FIGURE 5.2 Motor vehicle log book—every business journey

Note: The vehicle's odometer reading must be taken every 31 March so that the total annual kilometres can be assessed. If there is a change in the business usage, the employer may estimate the business percentage, making sure that the patterns of use and seasonal variations are taken into account.

types of benefits are subject to valuation under property or residual fringe benefit rules.)

The application of the otherwise deductible rule will produce different results depending on whether (i) the payment was simply made without any reference to the business-related element of the expense payment fringe benefit, or (ii) the reimbursement by the employer was intended to be in respect of the business-related element. The following example will explain the two applications.

Example

This is a challenging example that may be covered more fully in further FBT studies.

Application 1

- An employee of Superior Designs Pty Ltd incurred telephone expenditure of $500, of which 80% was employment-related (and tax-deductible) and 20% was private.
- Superior Designs Pty Ltd always pays $350 towards the telephone accounts of its employees regardless of the amount of business use.
- The taxable value of the expense payments fringe benefit without the otherwise deductible rule would be $350.

Apply the otherwise deductible rule.

Steps	Calculation	Result
1. Employee's gross expenditure:		$500
2. Notional amount that the employee can claim as a tax deduction:	$500 × 80%	$400
3. Actual amount of employee's tax claim is 80% of the difference between actual expenditure and the reimbursement paid:	($500 – $350) × 80%	$120
4. Subtract the actual amount (step 3) from the notional amount (step 2) to arrive at the amount by which the taxable value may be	$400 – $120	$280

Thus the taxable value of the payment of $350 may be reduced by $280 = $70.

Application 2

- An employee of Superior Designs Pty Ltd incurred telephone expenditure of $500, of which 80% was employment-related (and tax-deductible) and 20% was private.
- Superior Designs Pty Ltd pays $350 towards the telephone account of its employees after considering the extent of each employee's telephone business use and being careful to avoid reimbursing private calls.
- The taxable value of the expense payments fringe benefit without the otherwise deductible rule would be $350.

Apply the otherwise deductible rule.

Steps	Calculation	Result
1. Employee's gross expenditure:		$500
2. Notional amount that the employee can claim as a tax deduction:	$500 × 80%	$400

- Assuming that input tax credits are available on the other benefits:
  - Grossed-up value of the car fringe benefit = $1898 × 2.0647 = $3919
  - Grossed-up value of the expense payments benefit = $70 × 2.0647 = $145
  - Total grossed-up value = $9345.79 + $3919 + $145 = $13 409.

FBT payable = $13 409 × 0.465 = $6235

The employer must then send quarterly instalments of $1559 ($6235 ÷ 4) to the ATO each 28 July, 28 October, 28 February and 28 April. The balance (if any) should accompany the next annual FBT return due by 21 May in the next year of tax. If the total FBT on which the instalments are based is less than $3000, quarterly instalments are not required. From 1 July 2008 a statement of account is available. See Form 5.2 [ICP] in Appendix.

Learning check

✓ Complete the registration process for an employer who will provide fringe benefits.

✓ Calculate the grossed-up value of taxable benefits, and the FBT tax payable.

✓ Calculate the taxable value of motor vehicle fringe benefits, using both the statutory formula method and the operating cost method.

✓ Calculate the grossed-up value and the FBT payable in respect of the motor vehicle fringe benefit.

✓ Calculate the tax deduction available to an employer resulting from the provision of a taxable benefit and the payment of the FBT liability.

✓ Complete an FBT taxation return.

Taxation vocabulary

annualised
base value
benchmark interest rate
benefit
business percentage
car fringe benefits
closing adjusted value (CAV)
debt waiver
employer–employee relationship
exempt benefits
expense payments benefits
fringe benefits standard year (FBT year)
fringe benefit
grossed-up value
loan benefits
log book
net benefit
non-business accessories
non-cash benefits
no-private-use declaration
odometer
opening adjusted value (OAV)
operating cost
otherwise deductible rule
pro rata
quarterly instalments
statutory formula
statutory fraction
taxable value
untaxed portion

multiple-choice questions

Circle the correct response. (Answers to odd-numbered multiple-choice questions are provided on page 318.)

1. **For a liability to FBT to arise, there must be an employer–employee relationship. Which of the following is *not* such a relationship?**
   (a) the working son of a partner in a partnership
   (b) the working spouse of a partner in a partnership
   (c) the working partner in a partnership
   (d) the working typist in a partnership

2. **Which of the following represents an employer–employee relationship?**
   (a) The chief executive officer of a company
   (b) The accountant called in to audit a company's accounts
   (c) The subcontractor delivering materials for a job on site
   (d) The subcontractor providing goods and services, 60% of which are goods

3. **If there has been an arrangement between a third party and an employer to provide a benefit to an employee of the employer, the liability for that benefit falls on:**
   (a) the employee
   (b) the employer
   (c) the employee and the employer evenly
   (d) neither the employee nor the employer

4. **If there has been an arrangement for a benefit to be given to an employee of a third party, the liability for the payment of FBT falls on:**
   (a) the employee
   (b) the employer
   (c) the employee and the employer evenly
   (d) the third party

5. **Which of the following fringe benefits would be grossed-up using the type 2 factor of 1.8692?**
   (a) benefits of housing
   (b) motor vehicle reportable payment benefits on the payment summary
   (c) amounts paid for employee private telephone expenses
   (d) benefits derived from the private use of a motor vehicle

6. **Which of the following fringe benefits would be grossed-up using the type 1 factor of 2.0647?**
   (a) benefits of a loan
   (b) motor vehicle reportable payment benefits on the payment summary
   (c) amounts paid for employee HELP fees
   (d) benefits derived from a weekend away at a Gold Coast resort.

7. **If Superior Designs Pty Ltd had an aggregate taxable value of $16 300 in the 2008/09 FBT year, half of which gave input tax credits to the firm, the grossed-up value would be:**
   (a) $33 654 (b) $33 173 (c) $32 061 (d) $30 467

8. **If Superior Designs Pty Ltd had a grossed-up taxable value of $27 625 for the 2008/09 FBT year, and all payments had input tax credits attached, the aggregate taxable value would be:**
   (a) $14 779 (b) $13 380 (c) $13 813 (d) $12 846

9. **If a $40 000 car was purchased for a vet employed in a country practice and the car had accessories**

fitted (portable telephone $880, special racing wheels $1400, farmer's tow bar $685, CD player $1370 and GPS navigation system $2750), the base value of the car for statutory formula purposes would be $40 000 plus:

(a) $3630 (b) $2770 (c) $3650 (d) $3455

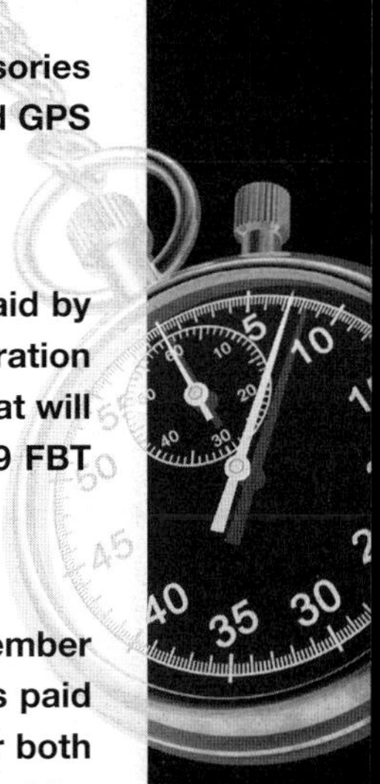

10. If a $42 000 car was purchased for a dentist employed in a city practice and the car had accessories fitted (portable telephone $880, racing wheels $1400, farmer's tow bar $685, CD player $1370 and GPS navigation system $2750), the base value of the car for statutory formula purposes would be:

(a) $46 805 (b) $45 455 (c) $44 280 (d) $48 205

11. Registration of $605 and insurance of $1700, being advance annual premiums, were amounts paid by the employer on 1 October 2007 for a car given to an employee for private use. Then $650 registration and $1800 insurance were paid on 1 October 2008. What is the total amount for both expenses that will be included in any calculation of costs under the car operating expense method for the 2008/09 FBT year?

(a) $2398 (b) $2305 (c) $2378 (d) $2450

12. If registration of $520 was paid on 1 November 2007 and insurance of $1500 was paid on 1 December 2007, for a car given to an employee for use throughout 2008/09, and then $595 registration was paid on 1 November 2008 and $1750 insurance was paid on 1 December 2008, what is the amount for both expenses that will be included in any calculation of costs under the car operating expense method for the 2008/09 FBT year?

(a) $2230 (b) $2020 (c) $2345 (d) $2135

quick-and-easy comprehension

Place a ✓ to indicate your response to each statement.

STATEMENT	TRUE	FALSE
1. If an associate of an employer enters into an arrangement with that employer to provide a benefit to an employee of the employer, the liability for FBT will fall on the associate.	—	—
2. An irregular benefit of less than $100 is exempt from FBT.	—	—
3. If an employee works for a bank and is given a loan at the lowest commercial interest rate, the FBT rules do not apply.	—	—
4. If an employee who has control of a company car uses it only to go to and from work and keeps it in the neighbour's garage, then FBT does not apply.	—	—
5. Assuming that all fringe benefits have GST input tax credits attached, and the grossed-up value of fringe benefits is $26 028, the aggregate taxable value must be $13 925.	—	—

self-test question

Assume that Marina Pty Ltd has given a car to an employee and during the FBT year the car was available for private use for 244 days. The following details are available:

FBT year ending 31 March 2009

- Date of purchase: 1 July 2008, owned for a total of 274 days in the FBT year.
- Non-business accessories fitted: $1800
- Business accessories fitted: $2200

- Cost price of car: $35 000
- Number of days the car was off the road: 30
- Number of days in the FBT year: 365
- Total kilometres clocked since purchased during the FBT year: 9500
- Percentage business use from log book: 70%
- Employee payments as per the required declaration: $150

Use the above information to answer this challenging question.

(a) By applying the statutory formula to the information, work out:
   (i) the taxable value of the car fringe benefit
   (ii) the grossed-up value of the benefit
   (iii) the amount of fringe benefits tax payable on the car fringe benefit

(b) Who has the liability to pay the fringe benefits tax?

assessments

1. If a car travelled 23 000 kilometres during the last seven months of the FBT year 2008/09, calculate the annualised kilometres.

2. If a car travelled 23 000 kilometres during the last seven months of the FBT year 2008/09, what would be the statutory percentage for use in the statutory formula?

3. Assume that AG Enterprises Pty Ltd has given a car to a sales employee and during the FBT year the car was available for private use. The following information is given:
FBT year ending 31 March 2009

- **Date of purchase: 1 July 2004**
- **Non-business accessories fitted: $2300**
- **Cost price of car: $39 000**
- **Number of days the car was available for private use: 365**
- **Number of days in the FBT year: 365**
- **Total kilometres clocked during the FBT year: 23 500**
- **Employee payments as per the required declaration: nil**

By applying the statutory formula to the information, work out the taxable value of the car fringe benefit.

4. Assume that Stephen's Surf Shop Pty Ltd has given a car to a sales employee and during the FBT year the car was available for private use. The following information is given:
FBT year ending 31 March 2009

- **Date of purchase: 1 July 2002**
- **Non-business accessories fitted: $1920**
- **Cost price of car: $51 000**
- **Number of days that the car was available for private use: 365**
- **Number of days in the FBT year: 365**
- **Total kilometres clocked during the FBT year: 19 000**
- **Employee payments as per the required declaration: $220**

Apply the statutory formula to the information and work out the taxable value of the car fringe benefit. What is the GST implication when the employee pays the employer $220 towards the cost of the car's maintenance?

5. An employer paid $300 towards the telephone expenses of $550 incurred by an employee, and this amount was intended to cover the 60% business use estimated by the employee. Calculate the taxable value of the benefit using the otherwise deductible rule. Would your answer change if the employer paid $300 towards the telephone expense, regardless of the business-use element? Show your workings.

case study questions

1. **Assume that the details provided in this question relate to the motor vehicle used by Jan Masonry. Colossal Constructions Pty Ltd has given Jan a car and during the year the car was available for private use. The following information is given:**
   FBT year ending 31 March 2009

   - Car available for use during the holding period, (i.e. the 243 days)
   - Date of purchase: 1 August 2008
   - Non-business accessories fitted: $1800
   - Cost price of car: $45 000
   - Number of days the car was available for private use: 243
   - Number of days in the FBT year: 365
   - Total kilometres clocked during the FBT year: 13 000
   - Employee payments as per the required declaration: $440

   Apply the statutory formula to the information and work out the taxable value of the car fringe benefit.

2. **Assume that the information in this question relates to a sales rep employed by Colossal Constructions, who has private use of the car. Which method would you suggest Colossal Constructions adopt for the valuation of car fringe benefits in 2008/09?**
   FBT year ending 31 March 2009

   - Car available for use for the whole year
   - Date of purchase: 1 October 2003
   - Length of time held at commencement of FBT year 1 April 2008: 4 years 6 months
   - Cost price of car (in this case the base value): $37 000
   - Number of days that the car was available for private use: 335
   - Number of days in the FBT year: 365
   - Total kilometres clocked during the FBT year: 33 000
   - Employee payments as per the required declaration: $230
   - Business percentage as per log book: 70%
   - Benchmark interest rate: 9%
   - Fuel $3230, repairs $650, pro-rata registration $520 and insurance $795: $5195

3. **Colossal Constructions Pty Ltd supplies some details for the 2008/09 FBT year of tax that relates to benefits supplied to three employees:**

   - car fringe benefits taxable value: $8051
   - loan fringe benefits taxable value: $1800
   - telephone expense payment taxable value: $1060
   - value of a small basket of flowers given to a sick employee: $95.

   (a) Calculate the aggregate taxable value and the grossed-up value of all benefits for the FBT year of tax.
   (b) Calculate the amount of FBT that Colossal Constructions will owe for the 2008/09 FBT year.
   (c) What reportable amount would be shown on the employees' payment summaries as at 30 June 2009?
   (d) Complete Form 5.1 [1067] in the Appendix, using the above details.

classroom activities

Examine the square below with nine compartments, each containing a letter. These nine letters make a word related to fringe benefits. How many words of four letters or more can you make from the letters shown? In making a word, each letter must be used once only. Each word must contain the letter in the shaded box. There must be no plurals or verb forms ending with 's', no words with initial capitals and no words with a hyphen or an apostrophe.

Y	U	S
R	T	O
T	A	T

Hint: 13 words is good and more than 35 words is excellent!

self-test question solution

Business percentage use	70%				
Start of FBT year	1 April 2008		STATUTORY FORMULA METHOD		
FBT year rate	46.5%		Taxable value of benefit	=	$\frac{A\,B\,C}{D} - E$
No. of days held for use	244	C	Taxable value	=	**$6246**
No. of days in FBT year	365	D	Start of next FBT year : 1 April 2009		
Date purchased	1 July 2008				
Original cost	$35 000				
Total kilometres travelled	9500				
Statutory fraction	0.26	B			
Kilometres annualised	12 655				
Employee contributions	$150	E	Age of car		
Benchmark interest rate	9%		at start of FBT year	0	years
Base value of car	**$36 800**	A			
Cost plus accessories	$36 800				
Accessories for car	$1800		No. of days owned to end of FBT year = 274		
Opening adjusted value	$35 000		No. of days car off road in FBT year = 30		
Depreciation rate	25%				

Km	Rate
0	0.26
15 000	0.20
25 000	0.11
40 000	0.07

Special note: Employer must pay output tax payable on employee contribution **$14**

(a) (i) The taxable value of the car = **$6246**.

(ii) The grossed-up value using type 1 factor of 2.0647 = **$12 896**.

(iii) The amount of fringe benefits tax payable is 46.5% × $12 896 = **$5997**.

(b) This is payable by the employer, **Marina Pty Ltd**.

Notes

1. See section 136(1) of the FBT Act for the definitions. The arranger provisions became operative on 1 April 1998. A fringe benefit will arise only if it is provided under an arrangement that involves an agreement of some kind between the employer and the third party, or the employer is involved in a particular way with the provision of the benefit.
2. An examination of section 26(e) of the *Income Tax Assessment Act 1936* sets out the benefits in relation to employment that will be subject to income tax in the hands of the employee, and specifically states any benefit that is not a fringe benefit.
3. The years prior to 1994/95 specifically excluded FBT from being an allowable deduction by the operation of section 51(4) of the *Income Tax Assessment Act 1936*.
4. Public ruling TR 2007/12.
5. Refer to section 41 of the FBT Act.
6. Refer to section 62 of the FBT Act.
7. See Part IIA, Division 1, section 5B of the FBT Act.
8. In the FBT Act, section 101(4) states that all amounts are to be to the nearest dollar. Section 103 gives the dates for the quarterly payments. Section 104 states that notice of the instalment must be on the form approved by the Commissioner—that is, the Business Activity Statement.
9. The rate is set out in section 6 of the *Fringe Benefits Act 1986*, as amended.
10. Section 136(1) of the FBT Act states that the benchmark interest rate is defined as 'the large bank housing lenders variable interest rate on loans for housing for owner occupation, last published by the Reserve Bank of Australia before the commencement of the year of tax'.
11. See Part III, Division 2, sections 7–13 of the FBT Act.
12. See section 9 of the FBT Act.
13. See section 10 of the FBT Act.
14. See Division 2, section 9(2)(c) of the FBT Act.
15. To annualise the kilometres travelled by the car during the FBT year of tax, refer to Division 2, section 9(2)(d) of the FBT Act:

$$\frac{\text{km travelled during holding period} \times \text{days in year}}{\text{days in holding period}}$$

16. Division 4, sections 16–19 of the FBT Act.
17. Division 5, sections 20–24 of the FBT Act.

6 Business Activity and Instalment Activity Statements

Chapter six

Topics

After studying this chapter, you should be able to:

- **explain the obligations of a GST-registered business for the collection and remittance of GST**
- **accurately categorise the inputs and outputs of the business**
- **identify and extract from the financial records of the business the relevant data for GST compliance**
- **outline the various types of Business Activity Statement (BAS) that have reporting options for different businesses**
  - the basic BAS with GST
  - BAS with options—PAYG income tax withholdings and income tax instalment (ITI)
  - BAS with options—PAYG income tax withholdings, ITI, fringe benefits tax (FBT), wine equalisation tax (WET) and luxury car tax (LCT)
- **complete the preparatory GST worksheet**
- **prepare the BAS**
- **explain the obligations of an entity or individual not registered for GST and prepare an Instalment Activity Statement (IAS) for an individual**
- **make adjustments to correct errors and create a checklist ready for lodgement for the BAS and IAS**

OVERVIEW

In Chapter 4 the GST system was explained and an outline of the method and timing of GST collection showed that businesses are subject to registration and lodgement requirements depending on their **gross annual turnover** (GST-inclusive). All businesses that have an annual turnover of $75 000 or more ($150 000 for not-for-profit entities) must be **registered for GST**. This means that there are very few enterprises that are not registered for GST.

In this chapter we examine how data is extracted from the firm's financial records for GST compliance and entered into the **Business Activity Statement (BAS)**. The various types of BAS are investigated in order to understand how the ATO personalises the various forms for each business, depending on the details the business has provided to the ATO. This makes it much easier for an enterprise to prepare and lodge its activity statements.

This chapter draws together the theory from Chapters 2–5 to provide a practical application of reporting and remitting **Pay As You Go income tax withholdings (PAYG-ITW)**, **Pay As You Go income tax instalments (PAYG-ITI)**, GST, **fringe benefits tax (FBT)**, **wine equalisation tax (WET)** and **luxury car tax (LCT)**, thus adding a deeper learning element to the preparation and lodgement of these activity statements. The examples provided in the chapter should invoke experiential learning and ongoing discussion on the practical application of complex GST theory, allowing participants to learn from their shared experiences.

6.1 The obligations of registered entities for collecting and remitting GST

Statutory laws have been enacted to ensure that the collection and remittance of taxes is carried out in the most equitable manner. The obligations of GST-registered entities in assisting with the transfer of funds to government are quite onerous; however, such an excuse for non-compliance can never be a defence. Before any 'net' calculations of GST owing can be made, it is essential for any business to establish whether:

- the **cash method** or the **accrual accounting method** applies
- the quarterly or monthly **tax period** applies.

While the actual delivery of goods or services (making of a supply) triggers the application of GST, the actual timing of the liability is dictated by the above criteria. There are significant cash-flow benefits to be gained from adopting the cash method and the quarterly tax period. Take another look at the example in Chapter 4, Section 4.5.

The GST term *annual turnover* is not necessarily the same as accounting annual turnover. It is simply the total charged for all supplies a business makes for consideration, exclusive of GST and any **input-taxed supplies**.

The appropriate thresholds in respect of annual turnover are as follows:

- If the business has an annual turnover of more than $75 000, it needs to register for GST.
- If the business has an annual turnover of less than $2 million, it can use the cash method. If its annual turnover is more than $2 million, the accrual accounting method must be used.
- If the business has an annual turnover of less than $20 million, it will have

a quarterly tax period. If its annual turnover is more than $20 million, it will have a monthly tax period.

Note: Even if a business has a turnover greater than $2 million, it can apply to the ATO for permission to use the cash method.

The actual amount of GST payable is GST **output tax payable** less **input tax credits** (remember the two-sided coin in Chapter 4, Section 4.2?). However, the net amount payable for the tax period may be increased or decreased by any adjustments for that interval. In practice, there is often a need to adjust tax invoices or amounts owing in order to take into account changed circumstances, such as a dispute with a customer or the return of goods. The GST return accommodates this by allowing for upward or downward adjustments, as shown in Section 6.5.

Such an adjustment necessarily leads to a compliance issue. Any adjustment that alters the sales value (and hence the GST applicable) must have a formalised **adjustment note** so that the two parties concerned can adjust their GST returns. Refer to Section 6.6 for a more detailed explanation of adjustments. The already existing credit note procedure commonly used by most businesses is usually sufficient to comply with ATO requirements.

Active reflection

Briefly set out the main thresholds that determine the obligations facing an entity wishing to register for GST.

6.2 Revising the status of supplies under GST

Taxable, input-taxed, GST-free and exempt supplies were examined in detail in Chapter 4 and once these four categories are understood, identifying and extracting the accounting information for the preparation of the BAS will be made much easier. At the heart of GST compliance is a thorough knowledge of how the inputs and outputs of the business are categorised. In Chapter 4 we explained that a GST-registered business uses the following rules for these four categories of supplies:

The tax invoice received by the business provides the critical evidence that supports any input tax credits claimed on the BAS. The tax invoice must comply with the legislation and state clearly the amount of GST embedded in the supply of goods and services. Refer to Chapter 4, Section 4.2.

1. Supplies that are **taxable** have one-eleventh GST embedded.
2. Supplies that are **input-taxed** are exempt supplies as no GST is embedded in the outputs and any GST in the inputs used to produce the supplies cannot be claimed as a credit.
3. Supplies that are **GST-free** have a zero rate of tax, and all supplies of services and goods in this category do not have GST embedded. However, input tax credits are available on inputs to produce these supplies.
4. Supplies that are **exempt** or **excluded** are not included on the BAS.

The industry in which the business operates is irrelevant, as these categories apply to all businesses and are vital for completing the BAS correctly. If you are still unsure about these categories, before continuing with this chapter revisit Chapter 4, Section 4.4, and re-examine the various examples given of the different categories of inputs and outputs.

Active reflection 6.2

The main sales and services of a marina business comprise storage fees, sales of petrol and boat stores. The business also has a boat broking segment, building special craft for sale to an overseas buyer. In the corner of the property is a cottage from which residential rent is collected every month. Categorise the marina's inputs and outputs by giving two examples of a transaction, one revenue and one capital, for as many of the four supplies categories that you can.

6.3 Identifying and extracting relevant data for BAS compliance

We begin this section by examining the information from OTP Pty Ltd, given in the example in Chapter 4, Section 4.6. The firm's output items are classified in Table 6.1 and its inputs are classified in Table 6.2.

TABLE 6.1 OUTPUTS OF OTP PTY LTD

ACCOUNT	Primary data totals		ALL INCOME AND REVENUE			
	Inputs Dr	Outputs Cr	Taxable	Exports	GST-free	Input-taxed
Sales and supplies		110 000	110 000			
Export supplies		50 000		50 000		
Other GST-free supplies		2 000			2 000	
Residential rent		10 000				10 000
Commercial rent		33 000	33 000			
Interest received		650				650
Sale of asset		550	550			
Total outputs		206 200	143 550	50 000	2 000	10 650
Codes on Worksheet		G1		G2	G3	G4

We will assume that the business operates in the tourism services industry. The business supplies retail services both in Australia and overseas. The business also owns a residential flat from which rent is received, as well as having a commercial tenant in its shop next door. For the convenience of its customers the business sells bottled water. The business pays wages to employees, and may possibly have a liability for FBT.

Tables 6.1 and 6.2 are simulated spreadsheets and you will notice that the amounts are GST-inclusive. Most BAS calculations are made easier if the GST-inclusive amounts are entered into the report. You will also notice that these amounts have been classified into the four categories explained in Section 6.2. Once you have this information at hand, then it is a fairly straightforward matter of completing the BAS worksheet and transferring the final amounts into the BAS report for the ATO.

Add G6 + G7	**G8**
Divide G8 by 11	**G9**
The amount at G9 is the GST payable and is the amount at 1A on the BAS	
GST amounts the ATO owes you from purchases	
Capital purchases (GST-inclusive)	**G10**
Other purchases (GST-inclusive)	**G11**
Add G10 + G11	**G12**
Purchases for making input-taxed sales and income and other supplies	**G13**
Purchases without GST in the price	**G14**
Total estimated private use of purchases + non-income tax-deductible purchases	**G15**
Add G13 + G14 + G15	**G16**
G12 – G16	**G17**
Adjustments (must be total GST-inclusive)	**G18**
Add G17 + G18	**G19**
Divide G19 by 11	**G20**
The amount at G20 is a GST credit, shown at 1B on the BAS	

Note: See Appendix, Form 6.1 [4203] for a plain BAS calculation worksheet.

Entering information into the BAS worksheet

The information is entered into the BAS calculation worksheet as follows:

- Add the total amounts of supplies, and output tax payable, and place in G1.
- Enter the total export sales into G2.
- Enter the total other GST-free supplies into G3.
- Enter the total input-taxed supplies into G4.
- Capital purchases, GST-inclusive, must go into G10.
- Enter the total of all other purchases plus the total of input tax credits into G11.
- Enter purchases for making input-taxed supplies into G13.
- Enter purchases with no GST in the price into G14, things such as inputs from a business not registered for GST or bank fees.
- Enter the estimated private use of purchases and/or non-tax-deductible purchases, such as entertainment expenses, into G15.
- The adjustments are treated as follows:
- **Input tax credit adjustments**, plus the amount of the ledger account (in other words, the full GST-inclusive amount of the adjustment), go into G18 if the effect is to increase the credits available; otherwise, place in G7 if the effect is to reduce previous credits claimed.
- **Output tax payable adjustments**, GST-inclusive, are treated similarly to the input tax credit adjustments. If the effect is to increase output tax paid, then place the amount in G7, and if the adjustment is meant to decrease output tax previously paid, place the adjustment in G18.

Special entries will sometimes be made through the general journal. These might be drawings of goods for private use or adjustments for bad debts that have been unpaid for at least 13 months. For an accruals payer, a bad debt adjustment is entered into the accounts through the general journal. Cash payers do not have bad debt adjustments.

Now let us look at the completed worksheet.

The completed BAS worksheet

Assume that OTP Pty Ltd is an accruals payer. The net GST payable is $5334 ($13 052 – $7718).

GST calculation worksheet for BAS
(If you want to use the calculation sheet method to work out GST amounts)

Tax period: 01/04/2009 to 30/06/2009
Name: OTP Pty Ltd

Do not lodge the calculation sheet with your BAS
We recommend you file it with a copy of the BAS to which it relates

Show amounts at these labels on your BAS

GST amounts you owe the Tax Office from sales

G1	Total sales (including any GST)		G1 $	206200 .00	G1 on the BAS
G2	Export sales	G2 $ 50000 .00			G2 on the BAS
G3	Other GST-free sales	G3 $ 2000 .00			G3 on the BAS
G4	Input taxed sales	G4 $ 10,650 .00			
G5	G2 + G3 + G4		G5 $	62650 .00	
G6	Total sales subject to GST (G1 minus G5)		G6 $	143550 .00	
G7	Adjustments (if applicable)		G7 $	22 .00	
G8	Total sales subject to GST after adjustments (G6 + G7)		G8 $	143572 .00	
G9	GST on sales (G8 divided by eleven)		G9 $	13052 .00	1A in the Summary section of the BAS

GST amounts the Tax Office owes you from purchases

G10	Capital purchases (including any GST)	G10 $ 2200 .00			G10 on the BAS
G11	Non-capital purchases (including any GST)	G11 $ 84270 .00			G11 on the BAS
G12	G10 + G11		G12 $	86470 .00	
G13	Purchases for making input taxed sales	G13 $ 1000 .00			
G14	Purchases without GST in the price	G14 $ 770 .00			
G15	Estimated purchases for private use or not income tax deductible	G15 $ .00			
G16	G13 + G14 + G15		G16 $	1770 .00	
G17	Total purchases subject to GST (G12 minus G16)		G17 $	84700 .00	
G18	Adjustments (if applicable)		G18 $	198 .00	
G19	Total purchases subject to GST after adjustments (G17 + G18)		G19 $	84898 .00	
G20	GST on purchases (G19 divided by eleven)		G20 $	7718 .00	1B in the Summary section of the BAS

Now go to the GST section on the front of the BAS and follow the instructions on the form. You will need to transfer amounts from this calculation sheet to the BAS.

NAT 5107-06.2006

FIGURE 6.1 The completed BAS worksheet

Source: ATO interactive BAS worksheet NAT5107 © Commonwealth of Australia, reproduced by permission.

PAYG-ITW and PAYG-ITI

In Chapter 3, Section 3.7 the overview of the reporting and remitting requirements for GST-registered entities explained that there are three classes of withholdings tax remitters:

1. small withholders (less than $25 000 withholding tax per year)—quarterly BAS
2. medium withholders (between $25 000 and $1 million per year)—monthly IAS and either monthly or quarterly BAS
3. large withholders (over $1 million per year)—lodge electronically as per the weekly schedule.

Many businesses fall into the bracket of being quarterly BAS payers and monthly PAYG withholdings payers and increasingly they are lodging using **electronic funds transfer**. Theses entities are registered as cash payers (under $2 million annual turnover) and medium withholders (PAYG withholding tax per year over $25 000 and under $1 million). This means that every quarter for the June, September and March quarters the BAS will collect all the information including the PAYG tax and be due and payable 28 days after the end of the quarter. The monthly IAS reports are to be reported and paid 21 days after the end of every other month. However, the BAS for the December quarter is not due until 28 February and this report will contain the PAYG withholding tax for the month of December. Strangely enough, the PAYG withholding tax for the month of January falls due and payable by 21 February, some seven days before the December quarterly BAS. This is a special note that should be on the checklist of all BAS preparers from these entities.

At the time of quarterly BAS reporting and lodgement, a business may be required to pay PAYG instalments of income tax. This topic is covered in some detail in Chapter 3, Sections 3.11–3.14, and in Table 6.5 we briefly revise which entities are affected. You will recall that the options available are dependent on the entity's amount of business or investment income. For option 1 the ATO calculates the amount due and payable and for option 2 the ATO advises a percentage rate to be applied to the quarterly gross income (GST-exclusive).

TABLE 6.5 ENTITIES AFFECTED BY PAYG TAX INSTALMENTS

Type of entity	GST-registered	Type of report	Amount of business or investment income	Option available	Eligible for annual instalments
Sole trader	Yes	BAS	Under $1 m	Both 1 and 2	No
Sole trader	No	IAS	N/A	Both 1 and 2	Yes, if last year's tax under $8000
Company	Yes	BAS	Under $1 m	Both 1 and 2	No
Company/sole trader	Yes	BAS	Over $1 m	2 only	No
Individual	No	IAS	Under $1 m	Both 1 and 2	Yes, if last year's tax under $8000

Individual in a business partnership	No	IAS	Under $1 m	Both 1 and 2	Yes, if last year's tax under $8000
Individual in a business partnership	Yes	BAS	Under $1 m	Both 1 and 2	No
Beneficiary	No	IAS	Under $1 m	Both 1 and 2	Yes
Trustee	Yes	BAS	Under $1 m	Both 1 and 2	No
Superannuation fund	Yes	BAS	Under $1 m	Both 1 and 2	No
Body corporate	Yes	BAS	Under $1 m	Both 1 and 2	No

For eligible persons such as sportspeople, farmers and professional artists there is another option, option 3, which enables payments each year rather than quarterly or monthly. For such people the unique design of the form will allow option 3 to be selected.

If an entity is entitled to use either option 1 or option 2, the BAS or IAS will allow option 2 to be varied if necessary. It is important that, if this is done, a reason code is given that identifies the taxpayer's changed circumstances. (Refer to Table 3.6 in Chapter 3.) Figure 6.2 shows an example of option 2, with an alteration to the percentage rate calculated by the ATO. The reason for the variation is given as a 'significant change in trading conditions'.

PAYG income tax instalment

☑ **Option 2: Calculate PAYG instalment using income tax times the rate**

PAYG instalment income **T1** $192,650

T2 9.81 %

OR

New varied rate **T3** 5.26 %

T1 × T2 (or × T3) **T11** $10,133

Write the T11 amount at 5A in the Summary section

Reason code for variation **T4** 23

FIGURE 6.2 Extract from OTP's BAS report

FBT

If an entity is liable for FBT of more than $3000 per year, the ATO will calculate the amount of quarterly instalment and this will be preprinted at F1 on the quarterly BAS. For amounts less than this threshold, an annual payment is due when lodging the annual FBT return (see Appendix, Form 5.1 [1067]). In cases where there are changes to employees or to the circumstances of benefits provided to employees, there is an opportunity for the FBT instalment to be varied on the BAS, as shown in Figure 6.3. If this is done, once again it is important to give a reason code. The following codes should be used:

Codes for varying FBT

22 Current business structure not continuing

30 Change in fringe benefits for employees

31 Change in employees with fringe benefits
32 Fringe benefits rebate now claimed

Fringe benefits tax liability < $3000—instalment not required					
Fringe benefits ATO instalment pre-printed on BAS	**F1**	$5 000	Varied fringe benefits tax instalment amount	**F3**	$3 000
Estimated total fringe benefits tax payable for year	**F2**	$12 000	Reason for variation	**F4**	**31**
Transfer your elected fringe benefits tax instalment to 6A on the BAS					

FIGURE 6.3 Extract from BAS report

WET

Wine equalisation tax is levied on all **assessable dealings** of the sale of wine. WET affects wine manufacturers and wholesalers; however, retailers do not have a WET liability unless they make their own **wholesale sales** of wine. WET is a value-based tax on wine consumed in Australia. The most common assessable dealings are:

1. wholesale sale of wine
2. retail sale of grape wine
3. retail sale of wine that is not grape wine (apple cider etc.)
4. application to own use connected with retail sale of grape wine
5. application to own use connected with retail sale of wine that is not grape wine.

The WET is calculated as follows. For (1), the amount is 29% of the GST-exclusive price of the supply of wine. For (2) and (4) two methods may be used: either 29% of half the retail price including GST or 29% of the weighted average wholesale price (the **weighted average** is calculated with WET and GST included in the calculation). For (3) and (5) the amount is 29% of half the retail price including GST.

The only time the weighted-average price method can be used is if, during the tax period in which the liability to pay WET arises, at least 10% by value of all sales of grape wine are in fact wholesale sales. If this condition is satisfied, the weighted average price method can be adopted for particular assessable dealings as in (2) and (4) above. However, these retail transactions must be of the same vintage as the grape wine to which the dealing relates, and must be produced from the same grape varieties, or the same blend of grape varieties, as the grape wine to which the dealing relates.

Example

Sandalford Wines have cellar door retail sales and use wine for promotional purposes. They sell more than 10% of their grape wines to wholesalers, so they are able to calculate WET on their assessable dealings for (2) and (4) above using either of the methods outlined. They choose the weighted average price method for their Margaret River Range. Sandalford must apply this method to all cellar door sales and application to own-use of this Margaret River Range. The weighted average cost cannot be applied to any wholesale sales of the Margaret River Range.

The calculations for WET are not carried out on the BAS worksheet. These amounts must be inserted directly into the BAS at 1C and 1D from working papers. WET owing is calculated and inserted at 1C. If the business is entitled to a Commonwealth producer rebate, the amount of this rebate is entered at 1D. Under this producer rebate, producers of wine may be entitled to a rebate of 29% of the wholesale value of eligible **rebateable dealings**. These dealings may include wholesale sales, cellar door and mail order retail sales, wine used for tastings and promotions, and other applications to own-use. Other adjustments can be made on the BAS at either 1C or 1D if the necessity arises. If the business has nothing to report, the boxes should be left blank.

Input tax credits can be claimed for the cost of purchasing new motor vehicles to the extent that they are used in the business. The limit for claiming these credits is the same as the luxury car threshold, which was $57 180 for 2008–09 and is subject to change each year. Farmers and tourism operators receive LCT rebates.

LCT

A luxury car tax of 33% applies to the sale of all motor vehicles with a GST-inclusive price above the ATO **luxury car threshold**; for the 2008/09 year this threshold was set at $57 180. It is adjusted each year, so BAS preparers must be careful to keep up-to-date.[1] Like WET, the calculations for LCT are not carried out on the BAS worksheet. The LCT amounts must be inserted directly into the BAS at 1E and 1F from working papers.

To explain how this tricky tax is calculated, we will give you an example.

Example

Assume a motor trader has a new luxury car for sale priced at $99 000, including GST. This is subject to LCT because the value is above the luxury car threshold.

Luxury car tax	
Luxury car threshold 2008/2009	$57 180.00
Motor vehicle sale price before LCT, including GST	$99 000.00
LCT rate	33%
Amount exceeding threshold	$41 820.00
Excess amount GST-exclusive	$38 018.18
LCT applied to excluded amount	$12 546.00
Enter the whole dollars only of LCT at 1E on the BAS	**12 546**
Therefore, the new sale price is $99 000 plus $12 546	$111 546

Unfortunately, it does not end there. If a motor trader sells a car that has previously been sold with LCT attached, then this must be extracted from the all-up price along with the GST to determine the correct amount of LCT payable. The following example shows how GST and LCT are calculated for a vehicle that previously had LCT paid.

Example

Assume a motor trader has a used luxury car for sale with an all-up price of $89 600, and the amount includes GST and previously paid LCT of $4165.

Used motor vehicle sale price, including GST and previously paid LCT	$89 600.00
GST of 10% plus LCT rate of 33%	43%
Amount exceeding the luxury car threshold	$32 420.00
Amount after removing the GST and LCT from excess	$22 671.33
Apply LCT of 33% to excluded amount	$7 481.54
Previously paid LCT	$4 165.00
Deduct previously paid LCT from new LCT amount	$3 316.54
Enter whole dollars of LCT owing at 1E on BAS	**3316**

Now calculate the GST payable on this sale

Used motor vehicle all-up sale price, including GST and LCT	$89 600.00
Remove from the price the LCT just calculated	$86 283.46
Calculate one-eleventh of this amount	$7 843.95
Amount of GST payable on this used car sale, whole dollars	**7843**

The car still sells for the same all-up price but the trader has correctly estimated the GST and LCT that will be paid to the ATO on this sale.	All-up price $89 600.00 GST in the price $7 843 LCT in the price $3 316

Amounts of adjustments can be made at 1E on the BAS for such things as using the car for private purposes, increasing the price of the car or recovering a bad debt. If there are any refundable amounts of LCT due, these should be entered at 1F, and could be due to a decrease in the price of the car, a cancelled sale or perhaps the writing off of a debt that has been bad for more than 12 months. If the business has nothing to report, the boxes should be left blank.

6.4 Active reflection

In active reflection 6.3 you were given some basic data to complete the BAS worksheet. Now we are adding some information that will require you to complete the summary boxes for the BAS report. Use Form 6.2 [4195] in the Appendix. You must determine the GST-exclusive gross sales and apply the ATO rate given to find the quarterly tax instalment amount. Finally, find out the BAS report net amount owing or refundable for the quarter.

Additional information for the BAS report	
Wages paid in the quarter	44 000
PAYG withholding tax	9 243
PAYG instalment income rate advised from the ATO	3.5%
FBT instalment amount	2101

6.5 Entities not registered for GST

Some small entities are not required to register for GST and have to complete an Instalment Activity Statement, either quarterly or annually. No GST is embedded in any supplies they make and the GST that is implanted in their inputs is simply absorbed as part of the cost of their goods and expenses. However, they may have obligations to remit PAYG withholding tax, to pay an income tax instalment or to pay an instalment of FBT. They will need to have an ABN, otherwise they will temporarily lose 46.5% of any supplies of goods and services they make.

The IAS is similar to the BAS, but no GST is reported. The IAS generally deals only with PAYG withholdings and PAYG instalments of tax. It may record FBT but almost certainly would not require WET or LCT reporting.

Active reflection 6.5

A taxpayer who is not registered for GST has to pay quarterly instalments of tax based on business income. The ATO has advised that a rate of 9.6% applies to gross business income and option 2 has been selected. The taxpayer's accounts for the first quarter show gross sales of $15000, but for the second quarter they are only $10000. Calculate income tax instalment for both quarters.

6.6 Adjustments and correction of errors in the BAS

Adjustments

The following are examples of adjustments:

- A customer returns goods for a refund or credit.
- A customer is incorrectly charged GST on goods or services that should not have included GST.
- A debt for a taxable supply becomes bad and is written off.
- A customer uses an early payment discount.

These adjustments are not treated as errors and must be handled according to the GST legislation. If the cash method can be adopted, it will eliminate the need for most adjustments. Adjustments are only ever placed in the BAS when they relate to activities of a previous period. Any adjustments for the current period should be put straight into the GST control account. However, if adjustments do take place in a later period, the adjustment accounts must be used and the amounts transferred to the appropriate boxes on the BAS. Adjustments for input tax credits can also take place, based on the change in use of purchases over time.

Correction of errors

Some errors, omissions or mistakes can be corrected in a future BAS, to either increase or decrease GST payable and input tax credits. There are time limits in which corrections are allowed to be made on the next BAS and also value limits. Table 6.6 sets out these limits, which correspond to the size of the business. Where a mistake or an omission relates to an earlier BAS that falls outside the time or correction limits, it must be corrected by completing a Revised Activity Statement.

TABLE 6.6 TIME LIMITS FOR CORRECTIONS TO THE BAS

Entity's annual turnover	Time limit for corrections	Correction limit
Less than $20 m	Up to 18 months (18 monthly BASs, 6 quarterly BASs or 1 annual GST return)	Less than $5000
$20 m to less than $100 m	Up to 3 months (3 monthly BASs)	Less than $10 000
$100 m to less than $500 m	Up to 3 months (3 monthly BASs)	Less than $25 000
$500 m to less than $1 b	Up to 3 months (3 monthly BASs)	Less than $50 000
$1 b and over	Up to 3 months (3 monthly BASs)	Less than $300 000

If the business is small and chooses the option of paying GST by instalments for a full year, it accounts for GST on an annual basis and reports GST in an annual GST return. Where a mistake is made in that return, subject to the correction limits set out in Table 6.6, this can be corrected in the next annual GST return. (Note that correcting mistakes in this way may inflate the next year's Commissioner-notified GST instalment amount.) The correction limits correspond to the size of the business.

Note that the correction limits are the net effect of the total of all errors occurring in the earlier BASs. They are the maximum amount of corrections that can be made on a later BAS. For more information, telephone **13 28 66** or obtain a fax by telephoning **13 28 60**. The form *Goods and services tax—how to complete your activity statement (NAT 7392)* contains all the instructions and is a useful resource.

Active reflection

Briefly outline what a small GST-registered entity must do to comply with GST laws if an error of $4000 was made in its BAS six months ago.

6.7 Penalties for failing to lodge or late lodgement

There is now a uniform administrative penalty for failure to lodge all types of taxation returns, statements, notices or other documents by the required date. This is referred to as a failure to lodge on time (FTL) penalty,[2] but it is not the same as the general interest charge applied to late payments of tax. The FTL penalty was applied to various documents during the transitional period from 1 July 2000 to 1 July 2002, but the Commissioner took a concessional approach towards taxpayers during that time. However, since 1 July 2002, any document due but not lodged on time automatically incurs a penalty.

The FTL penalty is calculated as follows:

- Small entities are liable to a penalty of $110 for each period of 28 days (or part thereof) that lodgement is overdue.
- Medium entities are liable to a penalty of $220 for each period of 28 days (or part thereof) that lodgement is overdue.
- Large entities are liable to a penalty of $550 for each period of 28 days (or part thereof) that lodgement is overdue.

The maximum penalty per BAS that can be imposed is for a total of five periods. Thus for small entities the maximum penalty for BAS/Q3 is $550, as shown below. After 28 September no more penalties will accrue to that particular BAS.

Q3 BAS January to March due by	28/4	
Penalty if not submitted by	28/5	$110
Penalty if not submitted by	28/6	$110
Penalty if not submitted by	28/7	$110
Penalty if not submitted by	28/8	$110
Penalty if not submitted by	28/9	$110

Active reflection 6.7

For small entities, a penalty of $110 applies for each period of 28 days (or part thereof) that lodgement is overdue. What is the amount of the penalty as at 28 June for a small business that failed to lodge a BAS for the third quarter? Would it be different if the date were 6 July?

BAS in practice

To enable the practitioner to answer the BAS questions that will arise from time to time, it is necessary to fully understand the implications of this complex legislation. The following examples of BAS in practice may assist in this regard.

The Nice Scent Shoppe is owned and operated as a sole trader by Jenny who is registered for GST. The business lodges quarterly BAS returns, pays by electronic funds transfer and has elected to use option 1, to report and calculate GST quarterly (see Chapter 4, Section 4.2). The books of account show the following information for the quarter July to September:

The Nice Scent Shoppe (GST-inclusive)	**July to September**
Income	$
Taxable supplies	78601.75
Expense	
Purchase of trading goods	19858.52
Creditable acquisitions	13441.39
Depreciation expense	4377.00
GST-free	193.22
No GST in the price	746.09
Payroll expenses	20269.62
Total expense	58885.84
Other information	
1. Capital expenditure (new)	1925.00
2. Owner gives her motor vehicle to the business at market value	15004.00
3. Sale of asset previously purchased in 1999 for $10100 now written down to $2090	2200.00
4. An employee repays Jenny for private use petrol	55.00
5. Quarterly PAYG withholdings	3012.00

Now let us see how the data is sorted and what is included in the BAS and what is left out. The first comment to make is that both depreciation of $4377 and payroll of $20269.62 must be excluded from the BAS worksheet shown as Figure 6.4. Note: The payroll and any PAYG tax withheld are entered in the relevant boxes on the final BAS summary report (see Figure 6.5).

The Nice Scent Shoppe BAS calculation worksheet		
GST amounts owed to the ATO from sales In this box include $78601 taxable supplies, the $2200 proceeds from the sale of the asset and also the $55 repaid by the employee for petrol. Rounded figures are used.	G1	$80857
Exports: nothing is recorded here so leave G2 blank.	G2	
Other GST-free supplies: leave G3 blank.	G3	
Input-taxed sales and income and other supplies: leave G4 blank.	G4	
Add G2 + G3 + G4 (This has a nil total, so leave G5 blank.)	G5	
G1 – G5	G6	$80857
Adjustments (must be total, GST-inclusive): in this box place only those adjustments that will increase the GST liability.	G7	
Add G6 + G7	G8	$80857
Divide G8 by 11 and round to the nearest whole dollar.	G9	$7351
Note: The amount at G9 is the GST payable and is shown at 1A on the BAS		
GST amounts the ATO owes you from purchases		
Capital purchases (GST-inclusive): here you must record the total paid for the new (or second-hand) capital items.	G10	$1925
Other purchases (GST-inclusive): in this box you place all other purchases, including any amounts that may also fit into G13, G14 and G15.	G11	$34239

Add G10 + G11	G12 $36164
Purchases for making input-taxed sales and income and other supplies: there were no purchases that fell into this category.	G13
Purchases without GST in the price: place the amounts of $746.09 and $193.22 in this box and round up or down.	G14 $939
Total estimated private use of purchases + non-income tax-deductible purchases: the owner has not taken any goods or other items out of the business, so leave this box blank.	G15

Figure 6.4 Insertions to BAS worksheet

Option 1 Quarterly GST			Amounts you owe the ATO		
Total sales and income and other supplies including capital (GST-inclusive)	**G1**	80857	GST on sales or GST instalment	**1A**	7351
Does this amount at G1 include GST? Mark with X	**Yes**	X	Wine equalisation tax	**1C**	
			Luxury car tax	**1E**	
Exports	**G2**	0	PAYG tax withheld	**4**	3012
Other GST-free supplies	**G3**	0	PAYG income tax instalment	**5A**	
Capital acquisitions (GST-inclusive)	**G10**	1925	FBT instalment	**6A**	
All other acquisitions (GST-inclusive)	**G11**	34239	~~Deferred company/fund instalment~~	**7**	
			1A + 4 + 5A + 6A + 7	**8A**	10363

These boxes represent the various ones on the BAS form, so follow the numbering.

Amounts the ATO owes you		
GST on purchases	**1B**	3202
Wine equalisation tax refundable	**1D**	
Luxury car tax refundable	**1F**	
Credit from PAYG income tax variation	**5B**	
Credit from FBT variation	**6B**	
1B + 5B + 6B	**8B**	3202

Payment or refund?

Is 8A more than 8B? (indicate with an X)

Yes, then write the result of 8A minus 8B at 9. This is the amount payable to the ATO.	X
No, then write the result of 8B minus 8A at 9. This amount is refundable to you (or offset against any other tax debt you have).	

Payment due

9 7161

Figure 6.5 Completing the boxes on the BAS summary

Learning check

- ✓ Identify individual compliance and other requirements for Activity Statements
- ✓ Recognise and apply GST implications and code transactions
- ✓ Report on payroll activities, in particular pay as you go income tax withheld (PAYG-ITW)
- ✓ Report on other amounts payable, pay as you go income tax instalments (PAYG-ITI), fringe benefits tax (FBT), wine equalisation tax (WET) and luxury car tax (LCT)
- ✓ Complete and reconcile the Business Activity Statement and Instalment Activity statement
- ✓ Prepare Activity Statements for lodgement

Taxation vocabulary

accounts method
accrual accounting method
adjustment note
assessable dealings
Business Activity Statement (BAS)
calculation worksheet method
cash method
electronic funds transfer
excluded
exempt
fringe benefits tax (FBT)
gross annual turnover
GST-free
input tax credit adjustments
input tax credits
input-taxed
input-taxed supplies
Instalment Activity Statement (IAS)
luxury car tax (LCT)
luxury car threshold
output tax payable
output tax payable adjustments
Pay As You Go income tax instalment (PAYG-ITI)
Pay As You Go tax withholdings (PAYG-ITW)
rebateable dealings
registered for GST
taxable
tax period
weighted average
wholesale sale
wine equalisation tax (WET)

multiple-choice questions

Circle the correct response. (Answers to odd-numbered multiple-choice questions are provided on page 318.)

1. The threshold for trading enterprises to register for GST is:

(a) $75 000 (b) $2 million (c) $20 million (d) $100 000

2. The threshold for the tax period is:

(a) $75 000 (b) $2 million (c) $20 million (d) $100 0001

3. Joe's Wholesale Wine business keeps working papers on all the taxes payable every quarter. His accounts show that in the tax period he had assessable dealings valued at $220 000 (GST-inclusive). The amount of GST entered into 1A is:

(a) $20 000 (b) $50 000 (c) $58 000 (d) $63 800

4. With reference to Joe's Wholesale Wine business in question 3, what amount of WET will be entered into 1C?

(a) $20 000 (b) $50 000 (c) $58 000 (d) $63 800

5. The only time the weighted-average price method can be used for calculating the WET is if, during the tax period in which the liability to pay WET arises, at least ____ by value of all sales of grape wine are in fact wholesale sales.

(a) 10% (b) 33% (c) 29% (d) 50%

6. For businesses wishing to use the cash basis to account for GST, the threshold is:

(a) $75 000 (b) $2 million (c) $20 million (d) $100 000

7. It will be compulsory for most businesses to:

(a) lodge a formal application to obtain an ABN

(b) lodge a formal application to register for GST

(c) use their ABN in all GST transactions

(d) all of the above

8. If a GST-registered business purchased a new photocopy machine for $3300 to be used exclusively in the office, the input tax credit would be:

(a) nil (b) 1/11th of $3300 (c) 1/11th of $3000 (d) 10% of $3300

9. If a non-GST-registered business purchased a new photocopy machine for $3300 to be used exclusively in the office, the input tax credit would be:

(a) nil (b) 1/11th of $3300 (c) 1/11th of $3000 (d) 10% of $3300

10. Think about the way we described GST as a double-sided coin in Chapter 4. Focusing just on the 'output tax' side of the GST coin, if a GST-registered business sold an old photocopy machine for $3300, the output tax payable would be:

(a) nil (b) 1/11th of $3300 (c) 1/11th of $3000 (d) 10% of $3300

quick-and easy-comprehension

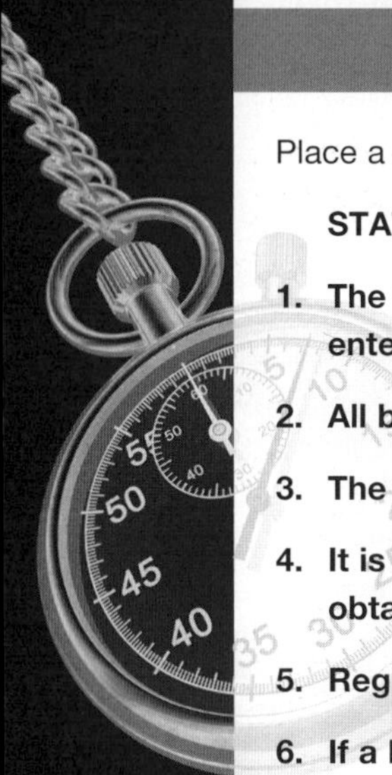

Place a ✓ to indicate your response to each statement.

STATEMENT	TRUE	FALSE
1. The value of all supplies made regardless of their GST characteristic will be entered at G1 on the BAS worksheet.	—	—
2. All businesses receive exactly the same BAS report to complete each tax period.	—	—
3. The taxing point in the WET system is the last wholesale sale.	—	—
4. It is mandatory for a business grossing more than $75 000 (GST-exclusive) to obtain an ABN, but optional to register for GST.	—	—
5. Registered GST enterprises can choose cash or accruals reporting.	—	—
6. If a business is a cash reporting entity, it will not have to report when a debtor is invoiced.	—	—

self-test question

You are working in a retail motor trader's business and have been asked to prepare the working papers and calculate GST and LCT. You are given the following information about three cars ready to be sold this tax period:

1. brand new Lexus, valued at $110 000 GST-inclusive
2. second-hand Toyota trade-in, value $56 000 (GST-inclusive with previously paid LCT of $1450)
3. second-hand Lexus trade-in, all-up price $78 000 (GST-inclusive with previously paid LCT of $3600).

assessments

Cash vs accruals

1. **Bill started a boat repair business on 1 July 2008. His annual turnover is expected to be approximately $300 000. During January 2009 he issued the following invoices to his clients and received the following payments:**

January 2009	Invoices issued	Payments received
	$	$
Mr Fisher	5 500	5 500
Mr Skier	3 500	500
Mrs Float	4 000	nil
Mrs Cruise	9 000	9 000
Total	22 000	15 000

During January, cash sales of repair kits amounted to $3000 and cash sales of soft drinks amounted to $110. Ignoring input tax credits and tax period implications, what is Bill's GST liability for the month of January?

Wine equalisation tax

2. At Coriole Winery in South Australia the spectacular views are framed by an ancient range of hills running down to the sea. The winery has significant cellar door sales; however, it sells most of its wine wholesale. One harvest of Shiraz brought the following revenue to the winery in a tax period:

Details of sales	$
Cellar door retail wine sales	45 500
Wholesale wine sales	350 000
Gift shop sales	22 000
Application to own use from shiraz harvest @ retail price	11 440

All amounts given for sales include GST but not WET. The weighted-average cost of the retail sales and the application to own use is 45% of the GST plus WET inclusive price.

Calculate the amount of GST output tax payable and WET payable that will be recorded on the BAS for the period.

BAS worksheet

3. From the following information complete the BAS worksheet using Form 6.1 [4203] and determine the net GST payable or refundable.

ACCOUNT	**Primary data**	
	Inputs $	Outputs $
Sales and supplies		250 000
Export supplies		10 000
Other GST-free supplies		700
Residential rent		4 000
Commercial rent		5 500
Interest received		600
Sale of asset		12 000
Totals outputs		282 800
Accounting fees	880	
Bank fees	120	
Cleaning	700	
Electricity	1 200	
General expenses	125 000	
Hire purchase expenses	900	
Interest paid on loans	250	
Rent expenses (commercial)	4 100	
Rent expenses (residential)	2 200	
Superannuation	6 750	
Wages and salaries	77 000	
New office security cameras	15 000	
New oven for residence	920	
Totals inputs	235 020	

4. **Using the results from completing the BAS worksheet in the previous question and the following additional information, complete the BAS summary report using Form 6.2 [4195]. Complete the PAYG tax withheld and calculate the PAYG instalment using option 2. The entity will not vary the ATO rate.**

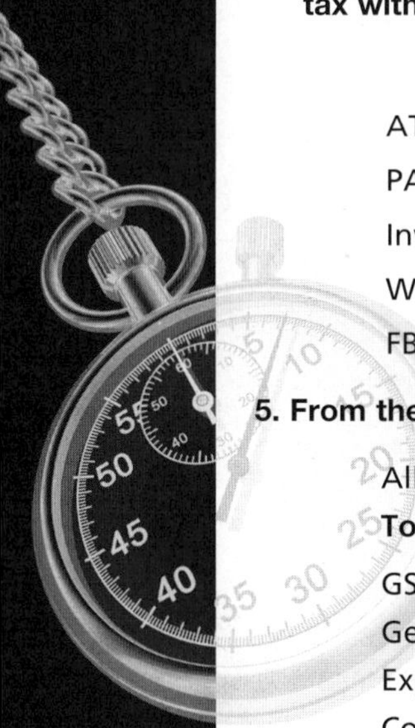

ATO PAYG instalment rate	6.20%
PAYG tax withheld (included in $77 000)	$14 630
Invoice from supplier (No ABN)	$450
WET tax has been calculated at:	$31 250
FBT instalment	$3265

5. **From the following information, complete the BAS summary report using Form 6.2 [4195].**

All Revenue	
Total receipts including GST	293 450.00
GST output tax payable	17 718.18
General fees	137 181.82
Exports	80 000.00
Commercial rent	38 909.09
Residential rent	15 150.00
Interest received	200.00
GST-free sales	3 200.00
Asset sales	1 090.91
Equals total receipts	293 450.00

All Expenditure	
Total payments including GST	188 890.00
GST input tax credits	9 727.27
Accounting fees	2 000.00
Bank fees	910.00
Commercial rent expenses	4 545.45
Residential rent expenses	2 500.00
Operating expenses	86 727.27
Superannuation	6 480.00
Wages and salaries (gross)	72 000.00
Purchase assets	4 000.00
Equals total expenditure	188 890.00

case study questions

1. **The following raw data (GST-inclusive) has been recorded by Colossal Constructions Pty Ltd. This entity has chosen the option to report and pay GST every quarter. There are no credit transactions. The ATO has advised a PAYG instalment rate of 2.67%. Tom Masonry has asked you to sort out the information using the BAS worksheet and prepare the BAS report for the period 1 January 2009 to 31 March 2009.**

Account details	**Amount ($)**
Sales of goods	635 200
Sales of services	11 000
Residential rent received	4 400

Commercial rent received	14 300
Interest received	110
Export sales	122 000
Advertising paid	1 770
Bank fees	55
Commercial rent expenses	231
Depreciation	10 500
Electricity	4 440
Insurance premiums, business	3 130
Interest paid	622
Motor vehicle costs	5 880
Purchase timber (inventory purchases)	209 900
Rates, council and water	660
Residential rent expenses	121
Superannuation paid	14 650
Subscriptions	44
Telephone	1 330
Wages and salaries	172 150

Other information

- Purchased a new photocopy machine for $1100 cash.
- Sold the old photocopy machine for $220 cash.
- For use in the delivery of timber, Tom Masonry sold the company a motor vehicle with a market value of $17 950.
- PAYG withholdings for the month $12 650.
- Fringe benefits for the quarter $3200.

Complete the BAS calculation worksheet using the interactive form from the ATO's website. Determine the GST payable or refundable and complete the BAS summary report Form 6.2 [4195] in the Appendix.

2. **What might happen if the BAS for Colossal Constructions Pty Ltd is not lodged on time?**

classroom activity

Noughts and crosses[3]

Students are assigned to one of two teams, either 'noughts' or 'crosses', with team members sitting together. A noughts and crosses grid is shown below. Within each cell of the grid is a topic from the chapter:

Input-taxed supplies	ABN or no ABN	Tax invoices
Taxable supplies	Net GST	Input tax credits
Output tax payable	GST-free	BAS

Students are to spend a few minutes devising questions and their solutions for each cell. Hence, with two teams of, say, nine students, each student can be responsible for devising one or more questions for a different cell.

The lecturer will ask an initial question and the first team to answer correctly will be the team to begin the game. For example, having answered the initial question correctly, team 'noughts' may decide that it will select the central 'Net GST' cell. The team 'crosses' must then ask a question on Net GST. If the answer from team 'noughts' is judged by the lecturer to be appropriate, a nought will be placed over the central cell. The team 'crosses' then chooses a cell and must answer a question on the topic of that cell, asked by the 'noughts' team. If the team gets the question right, a cross is placed in that cell. The teams take it in turn to ask questions, until one team achieves a line (either straight or diagonal) of noughts or crosses.

There are no restrictions on the nature of questions asked, and students should enjoy the diversity of questions that emerge. For example, one team could ask the other team diagrammatic questions that require one of the students to volunteer to demonstrate something on the whiteboard. The lecturer will have a few reserve questions in case some questions are judged inappropriate. These questions may or may not be relatively straightforward to answer.

self-test question solution

Motor vehicle sale price, GST-inclusive	$110 000.00	**Car 1**
LCT rate	33%	
Amount exceeding threshold	$52 820.00	
Amount GST-exclusive	$48 018.18	
Apply LCT to excluded amount	$15 846.00	
Enter whole dollars only of LCT at 1E on BAS	**15 846**	
Therefore the new sale price is	$125 846.00	
GST payable on this vehicle	**10 000**	
Calculations for used cars with previously paid LCT		**Car 3**
Used motor vehicle all-up sale price, including GST and previously paid LCT	$78 000.00	
GST of 10% plus LCT rate of 33%	45%	
Amount exceeding the threshold	$20 820.00	
Amount after removing GST and LCT from excess	$14 559.44	
Apply LCT of 33% to excluded amount	$4 804.62	
Previously paid LCT	$3 600.00	
Deduct previously paid LCT from new LCT amount	$1 204.62	
Enter whole dollars of LCT owing at 1E on BAS	**1 204**	
Now calculate the GST payable on this sale		
Used motor vehicle all-up sale price, including GST and LCT	$78 000.00	
Remove LCT from the price just calculated	$76 795.38	
Calculate one-eleventh of this new amount	$6 981.40	
Amount of GST payable on this used car sale	**6 981**	

Note: Car 2 is $56 000 and is this under the luxury car tax threshold, so no LCT is payable.

Notes

1. The luxury car tax threshold is the car depreciation limit that applies under Subdivision 42-B of the *Income Tax Assessment Act 1997*. This amount may change from year to year.
2. The legislative provisions for the imposition of FTL penalties are contained in Division 286 of the *Taxation Administration Act 1953*.
3. This activity has been adapted from the game devised by Caroline Elliott, Department of Economics, Lancaster University Management School, United Kingdom.

Superannuation guarantee levy

7

Chapter seven

Topics

After studying this chapter, you should be able to:

- **explain the government's purpose in imposing the superannuation guarantee levy**
- **determine the minimum level of superannuation support to be provided by an employer**
- **identify payments subject to the superannuation guarantee levy**
- **identify any exemptions that might apply to the superannuation guarantee levy**
- **explain the application of the government's initiative of choice of superannuation fund and the consequence of non-compliance by employers**
- **explain the consequences for an employer who fails to pay:**
  - the minimum level of superannuation support
  - to a complying fund
  - by the prescribed time
- **explain the calculation and components that make up the superannuation guarantee charge**
- **explain the application of the superannuation co-contribution.**

OVERVIEW

The tax laws now make it mandatory for all employers to provide a level of superannuation support for most **employees**, with very limited exceptions. This legislation covers compulsory and voluntary contributions, the former designed to ensure that all employers contribute a minimum amount for the future support of their employees. It is referred to as the **superannuation guarantee levy**. The commencement date of the superannuation guarantee levy was 1 July 1992 and there have been various changes in its application since that date. Since 1 July 2003, compulsory superannuation contributions have to be paid into a complying superannuation **fund** or retirement savings account on a quarterly basis, by the twenty-eighth day after the end of the quarter. In 2005 employees were given the freedom to choose their superannuation fund and, after the passage of the *Superannuation Legislation Amendment (Simplification) Act 2007*, significant changes to voluntary contributions came into force from 1 July 2007. These changes affect individuals (including self-employed persons), as well as businesses.

Statistics from the Australian Prudential Regulation Authority (APRA) (accessed at **www.apra.gov.au**) show that, at the end of June 2008, total superannuation assets increased by 0.6% for the year to $1.17 trillion. Contributions to superannuation funds in the 2008 quarter totalled $25.1 billion, with $17.5 billion being contributions from employers and $7.5 billion being from member contributions. The balance of approximately $100 million included spouse contributions and government co-contributions.

This chapter explains how the superannuation guarantee levy works, and how it affects all employers. Payments that are required under these laws are identified and any exemptions are explained. Finally, the chapter looks at the consequences of not complying with the legislation and thus having to pay the *superannuation guarantee charge*.

7.1 The superannuation guarantee levy

The superannuation guarantee levy was announced in the 1991 budget and was part of the then Labor government's Retirement Incomes Policy. The authority for the conduct of this scheme is to be found in the *Superannuation Guarantee (Administration) Act 1992* (SGAA) and the *Superannuation Guarantee Charge Act 1992*, which applied from 1 July 1992.

The Commissioner of Taxation is responsible for administering this legislation. The government's intention here is to ensure that all employers provide a minimum level of superannuation for employees. In terms of government policy, the provision of adequate superannuation is considered essential for Australians to be able to maintain their living standards into retirement, while not being a massive burden on the social security system.

The pool of funds created by such superannuation payments is also seen as desirable for Australia, because these forced savings may assist in decreasing our level of foreign debt. Over time, the massive injection of funds into superannuation has assisted the government's collection of revenue. Currently tax of 15% is levied on the taxable income of all superannuation funds, and contributions to a superannuation fund are considered to form part of a fund's taxable income. If an employer pays the appropriate amount for each employee into a complying fund by the statutory date, a tax deduction is available to the employer for this superannuation guarantee levy. However, if any of the above three requirements of amount, fund or date are not correctly met, the employer will be subject to a **superannuation guarantee charge** for any shortfall. This charge is not an allowable tax deduction, and, in all cases, will be greater than the amount that would otherwise have been payable. Since 1 July 2005, it has also been a requirement that employers offer a choice of funds; otherwise they will pay an increased superannuation guarantee charge.

It should be noted that the new taxation and preservation arrangements applying to Australia's superannuation system since 1 July 2007 have had far-reaching implications for superannuation in Australia, with the main concessions relating to the taxation treatment of superannuation lump sum amounts and pensions in the hands of retirees aged 60 years or over.

The greater part of this chapter is concerned with the necessary calculations to ensure that the minimum superannuation contribution has been met.

The maximum tax-deductible or concessional contribution that an employer or self-employed person can make is limited to $50 000 per financial year[1] These contributions include employees' salary sacrifice amounts. Contributions over this amount will be taxed at 31.5%, which is on top of the 15% contributions tax paid by the fund. Together these equal the tax rate of 46.5%, being the highest marginal rate plus Medicare levy. Between 1 July 2007 and 30 June 2012 transitional arrangements are in place for tax-deductible or concessional contributions up to a maximum of $100 000 per financial year for people aged 50 years or over. In these cases, no extra tax at the 31.5% rate will be charged until contributions exceed the $100 000 per financial year threshold.

There is a limit of $150 000 per financial year on non-deductible contributions for those persons under the age of 65 years. These contributions are after-tax amounts paid into a fund by an individual. As a concession individuals are able to contribute up to $450 000 over any three-year period. Any contributions over this limit will attract a penalty tax rate of 46.5% on any excess. However, those people over the age of 65 years must meet a work test in order to contribute non-deductible contributions up to $150 000 per year. The three-year option is not available to them. The impact of this from a retirement planning perspective is to ensure that contributions to a superannuation fund are spread over a person's working life rather than compacting the contributions into the last few years before retirement.

Active reflection 7.1

What was the main reason for implementing the superannuation guarantee levy legislation in Australia?

7.2 The liability of employers

The ATO has made it clear that it makes good sense for businesses to provide superannuation support for their employees, particularly when these payments are tax-deductible. This is far better than paying the superannuation guarantee charge, which will be a greater amount and will not be tax-deductible.

A work test requires a person to have worked at least 40 hours within 30 consecutive days in a financial year. People who are aged between 65 and 74 must meet the work test to be allowed to make personal superannuation contributions.

To ensure that employers have help in meeting their superannuation guarantee obligations, and hence do not have to pay the charge, the ATO has prepared numerous fact sheets and its website offers many explanations and examples on superannuation obligations for employers.

Who is an employee for superannuation guarantee purposes?

Generally, employees are individuals who receive payment in the form of a salary or wages in return for their **labour** or services. An employer should make superannuation contributions on behalf of all its employees (subject to the exemptions listed below). People engaged under a contract that is wholly or principally for their labour may also be considered to be employees even if their ABN is quoted. For more information, refer to the *Superannuation Guarantee Ruling 2005/1: Who is an employee?*

Exemptions

Persons aged 70 to 74 inclusive who are working at least 10 hours per week can make personal superannuation contributions for themselves, but employers are not required to make contributions for them.

Superannuation support does not have to be provided for some limited categories of employees, and these are:

- employees paid less than $450 (before tax) in a calendar month
- employees aged over 70 years
- employees under 18 years of age working not more than 30 hours per week
- resident employees paid by non-resident employers for work done outside Australia
- non-resident employees paid for work done outside Australia
- some foreign executives who hold certain visas or entry permits under the Migration (1993) Regulations and Migration Regulations 1994 (for further information, contact the Superannuation Infoline on **13 10 20**)
- employees paid to do work of a domestic or private nature, for not more than 30 hours per week (e.g. part-time nanny or housekeeper)
- employees who receive payments under the Community Development Employment Program (CDEP)
- a member of the Army, Navy or Air Force Reserve, which is not required to provide superannuation support
- employees temporarily working in Australia for an overseas employer who are covered by a Bilateral Superannuation Agreement (a Certificate of Coverage must be presented in order to obtain this exemption).

Generally, the extended definition of 'employee' for superannuation guarantee purposes is very similar to the definition contained in the PAYG provisions of the *Income Tax Assessment Act 1997*. There are, however, some significant differences:

- People who receive payments for contracts (see Chapter 3), but who enter into a contract wholly or principally for their labour, are employees for superannuation guarantee purposes, even though they may not be treated as employees for PAYG purposes. This includes a sole trader (even if he or she has an ABN) who is engaged wholly for his or her labour.
- If a person is an employee at common law, then that person is an employee for superannuation guarantee purposes. However, the common law meaning is extended via subsections 12(2)–(11) of the SGAA to include

as employees certain contractors, directors, artists and sportspersons, and excludes certain domestic or private workers.
- The common law test for the existence of an employment relationship is mainly the **control test**. That is, a person performing labour will be considered to be in an employment relationship when that person does not have control over decisions as to how, when, where and who is to perform the labour.
- A subsidiary test that can be used when the control test is inconclusive is the **integration test**—that is, whether a person providing labour or services does so as an individual carrying on his or her own business (contract for service) or individually as an integral part of another's business organisation (contract of service).
- The Superannuation Guarantee legislation establishes that a person who has entered into a contract principally for his or her labour is an employee of the other party to the contract, even if he or she classifies himself or herself as a **contractor**. However, there are various exceptions to this rule, namely:
  - If the principal has a contract, not with the individual who will do the work but with a company, trustee or partnership, then the person providing the labour will not be an employee of the principal. Note also here that the worker could be an employee of the company, trustee or partnership.
  - A contract is a contract for a person's labour only if that particular person must do the work. If the contract leaves the person free either to do the work personally or to have any part of it done by another person(s), then again the person providing the labour will not be an employee under the terms of the contract.

Records

Employers are free to choose the format of their records, but they must keep, for five years, records in English that adequately explain the amount of superannuation provided for each employee.

The records can be examined by the ATO and there are penalties for failing to keep accurate records. If an employer is liable to pay the superannuation guarantee charge, that employer will also have to keep details of the calculations required in the superannuation guarantee charge statement (see Section 7.9).

Note that if an employer is required to pay award superannuation, further record-keeping provisions may apply, and it is prudent to check the relevant award or regulations.

Active reflection 7.2

List three categories of employees for whom employers may not have to pay the superannuation guarantee levy.

7.3 The minimum level of employer contributions

There is no flat dollar statutory minimum level of employer contributions. Since 1 July 2008, to simplify matters, all employers are required to calculate the superannuation guarantee levy only on an employee's **ordinary time earnings (OTE)**. Thus, the only way a contribution amount can be determined for any contribution period is by the application of the following formula:

Employee's ordinary time earnings (OTE) × charge percentage

Ordinary time earnings

Ordinary time earnings is the total of an employee's earnings for ordinary hours of work, and includes over-award payments, any paid leave, commissions and shift allowances. Table 7.1 identifies whether various payments form OTE and/or salary or wages.[2]

It is important to note that an employer needs to use salary or wages rather than OTE in calculating each individual superannuation guarantee shortfall (see Section 7.9).

TABLE 7.1 CHECKLIST FOR SALARY OR WAGES/OTE

Payment type	Salary or wages?	OTE?
Allowances paid (other than a reimbursement of expenses)	Yes	Yes
Reimbursement of expenses (e.g. travel costs)	No	No
Expense allowance that is paid with the expectation that it will be fully expended in producing income, e.g. car allowance paid to real estate agents	No	No
Bonuses that do not relate to specific performance criteria (e.g. Christmas bonuses)	Yes	No
Other bonuses	Yes	Yes
Commissions	Yes	Yes
Over-award payments	Yes	Yes
Shift loading	Yes	Yes
Overtime	Yes	No
Casual loading	Yes	Yes
Benefits subject to fringe benefits tax	No	No
Workers compensation payments, including top-up payments, where no work is performed	No	No
Workers compensation payments, including top-up payments, paid by the employer where work is performed	Yes	Yes
Top-up payments when serving on jury duty or with reserve forces etc.	Yes	No
Payments when on maternity or paternity leave	Yes	No
Pay for annual holiday leave taken	Yes	Yes
Government (wage) subsidies (e.g. job start allowance)	Yes	Yes
Annual leave loading	Yes	No
Pay for sick leave taken	Yes	Yes

Payment type	Salary or wages?	OTE?
Pay for long service leave taken	Yes	Yes
Accrued annual leave, long service leave and sick leave paid as a lump sum on termination	Yes	No
Payments in lieu of notice	Yes	No
Redundancy payments	Yes	No
Other payments made by an employer on termination of employment	Yes	No
Director's fees	Yes	Yes
Payments for performance in, or provision of services relating to, entertainment, sport, promotions, films, discs, tapes, TV or radio	Yes	Yes
Payments to a contractor who is an employee under the SGAA (labour portion only)	Yes	Yes
Dividends	No	No
Partnership and trust distributions	No	No
Payments for entering into a restraint of trade agreement	No	No
Payments for domestic or private work under 30 hours per week	No	No

Charge percentage

In its earlier years of application the superannuation guarantee requirements were phased in through various changes to the **charge percentage**. Since the year ended 30 June 2003, the contribution rate has remained at 9%.

Example

For the year ended 30 June 2009, Mary Lou's OTE is $30 000. The level of contribution necessary by her employer would therefore be:

$$\$30\,000 \times 9\% = \$2700$$

Maximum superannuation contribution base

The amount of employer superannuation support is calculated on a quarterly **contribution period** commencing on 1 July, 1 October, 1 January and 1 April each year. To limit the amount of superannuation guarantee levy or superannuation guarantee charge that any employer must pay for each employee, the legislation sets a maximum contribution per quarter that is indexed annually. Table 7.2 sets out these maximum contributions over the last four years; however, check each year for the updated amount. Employers do not have to provide support for any part of earnings above this quarterly maximum limit.

TABLE 7.2 MAXIMUM CONTRIBUTIONS PER QUARTER

Income year	Per quarter maximum contribution base
2008/2009	$38 180
2007/2008	$36 470
2006/2007	$35 240
2005/2006	$33 720

Source: Data from www.ato.gov.au/superprofessionals.

7.3 Active reflection

List three types of earnings on which an employer would ***not*** have to pay the superannuation guarantee levy.

7.4 Paying contributions into a complying fund

To satisfy the requirements of the superannuation guarantee legislation, employees' contributions must be paid into a complying superannuation fund or retirement savings account. A complying fund is a superannuation fund that complies with the federal government's rules. To qualify as a complying fund, APRA must issue a notice to the trustee of the fund. This notice states whether it is a complying fund and is designed to protect employees from funds that are not run according to standards set by the *Superannuation Industry (Supervision) Act 1993* and ensure that benefits are fully **vested** and **preserved** on behalf of employees. 'Vested' means that the superannuation benefit belongs to the employees when they leave the fund, for example if they move jobs or stop working. 'Preserved' means that the benefit is payable only on retirement at 55 years of age or over.

Many employers also have an award obligation to pay into a specified fund. Employers who fail to pay into such a fund may not be meeting award obligations. It is wise to check any relevant industrial award for details.

Since 1 July 1997, banks, building societies, credit unions and life insurance companies have been able to provide superannuation in the form of a retirement savings account. To satisfy the requirements of the superannuation guarantee legislation, employers are able to open a retirement savings account to accept contributions for an employee. All retirement savings accounts are required to comply with the government's compliance rules.

How to check whether a superannuation fund complies

The fund's trustees or managers should be able to confirm whether the fund complies. The fund should indicate that it intends to accept superannuation guarantee contributions and continue to meet government standards. Contributors need to confirm this before they make any superannuation guarantee contributions to the fund and keep a record of this advice. To obtain further information on the compliance of a particular superannuation fund, you can check the Register of Complying Super Funds (ROCS) at **www.ato.gov.au/super** or telephone the Superannuation Infoline on 13 10 20.

Active reflection

What is meant by the term *complying superannuation fund*?

7.5 Choice of superannuation fund

Commencing on 1 July 2005 was the much awaited initiative that provided many employees with the right to choose their superannuation fund or retirement savings account. Prior to this, the employer was usually able to comply with the superannuation guarantee requirements by making the appropriate contributions to any complying fund.

Under Financial Services Reform legislation, it is illegal for employers (unless they are licensed financial advisers) to advise employees about which fund to choose.

To comply with the 'choice of superannuation fund' requirements, employers should follow four steps:

1. Identify eligible employees.
2. Identify an appropriate employer fund.
3. Provide a standard choice form to eligible employees.
4. Act on each employee's choice.

Identify eligible employees

All employers must offer a **choice of fund** to an employee unless the employee is covered under:

- a certified agreement, or
- an Australian workplace agreement, or
- a state award or industrial agreement.

Identify an appropriate employer fund

All employers must nominate a 'default' employer fund that will accept contributions if the employee does not wish to make his or her own choice of fund. The employer fund does not need to be the same fund for all employees; however, it must be a complying fund and also meet the insurance requirements by offering minimum life insurance coverage that depends on the age of the employee.

Provide a standard choice form to eligible employees

The standard choice form (NAT 13080) has to be provided to:

- all eligible existing employees
- all eligible new employees within 28 days of commencement of employment.

The standard choice form needs to include details of the default employer fund to which the employer will make superannuation guarantee contributions if the employee does not choose a fund.

Act on each employee's choice

Once an employee provides the employer with all the required information concerning his or her choice of complying fund, the employer has two months to comply with this choice. For the remaining time of employment, this choice remains in force.

The consequences of non-compliance by employers

Employers who do not comply with the 'choice of superannuation fund' obligations may become liable for an additional liability known as *choice liability*. The choice liability is an additional 25% of amounts incorrectly contributed; however, it is capped at $500 per notice period per employee. This liability may arise through the failure of an employer to:

- pay a contribution to the correct fund
- provide an employee with a standard choice form in the required timeframe.

7.5 Active reflection

How does an employer comply with the 'choice of super fund' requirements?

7.6 Self-assessment of liability and the contribution period

The superannuation guarantee applies to all employers, including:

- all government departments, their statutory authorities and municipal bodies
- non-resident employers who have employees working in Australia
- Commonwealth and tax-exempt Commonwealth authorities
- tax-exempt organisations, such as charities
- family companies and trusts and partnerships paying salaries or wages.

The superannuation guarantee is part of the ATO's **self-assessment** system. The calculation and subsequent payment of any superannuation guarantee liability are left up to the employer; hence any person or business making payments to any individuals for their labour or services must ensure that they are complying with this legislation. No employer is exempt from the superannuation guarantee.

7.6 Active reflection

Briefly describe how an employer self assesses their superannuation guarantee liability.

7.7 When and how to pay into a complying fund

Each complying superannuation fund has specific requirements as to how payments should be made. Broadly, however, the employer is required to complete an application form, and each employee needs to complete an employee application form. Payment methods thereafter are usually very flexible, with payments being as simple as operating a bank account. Contributions are generally made by cheque, together with an accompanying contribution statement or form showing how much of the amount paid relates to particular employees.

Superannuation is tax-deductible only when paid, not when incurred. Thus, to be able to claim an income tax deduction in the same year to which the June quarter payment relates, it must be paid by 30 June of that tax year.

Since 1 July 2003, superannuation contributions have to be made at least every quarter, with the legislation now requiring sufficient superannuation contributions to have been made by the dates as shown in Table 7.3.

TABLE 7.3 SUPERANNUATION CONTRIBUTION DUE DATES

Quarter	Due date
1 July to 30 September	28 October
1 October to 31 December	28 January
1 January to 31 March	28 April
1 April to 30 June	28 July

Active reflection 7.7

When would an employer have to make superannuation guarantee levy payments for wages paid for January, February and March 2009?

7.8 The superannuation guarantee charge

If the minimum contribution for each employee for any particular contribution period is not made, or the choice of superannuation fund obligations are not met, the non-deductible superannuation guarantee charge will apply and it will be necessary to lodge a **superannuation guarantee statement** (see Section 7.9). If the minimum contribution is not paid to a complying fund, there are many disadvantages, including the following:

- The charge is non-deductible.
- The amount of charge an employer has to pay will usually be much greater than the minimum amount otherwise payable (see Section 7.3), because the charge includes interest and an administration fee.
- There are penalties for late payment and failure to provide a superannuation guarantee statement.

Active reflection 7.8

Is the superannuation guarantee charge tax-deductible?

7.9 Calculating and submitting the superannuation guarantee charge

The superannuation guarantee statement (NAT 9600) must be lodged by the fourteenth day of the second month following the end of the relevant quarter, as shown in Section 7.10. The superannuation guarantee charge must be paid at the same time. The charge will usually amount to more than might otherwise have been payable, because it consists of three parts:

1. the total of the employer's individual **superannuation guarantee shortfalls** for the year plus any choice liability applicable
2. a nominal interest component (10%)
3. an administration component.

Shortfall component and choice liability component

Whenever the amount of superannuation support in any contribution period is less than the minimum prescribed amount, the calculation of a shortfall component is necessary. The calculation for establishing the individual shortfall for each employee is:

Employee salary/wages × employee individual shortfall percentage

The shortfall percentage is the difference between the charge percentage, currently at 9%, and the actual percentage (of the OTE) already contributed by the employer.

The calculation of any shortfall for an individual employee is the first and essential step in calculating the superannuation guarantee charge. To assist in the correct calculation of any shortfall, an instruction guide accompanies the superannuation guarantee statement.

Example

For the 2008/09 financial year employer Allen & Co's charge percentage is 9%. Rob is an employee who has been provided with superannuation support equivalent to 4% of his OTE.

Assume that Rob's OTE for the quarter ended 31 March 2009 is $10 000.

Amount of contributions paid: $400 (400 ÷ 10 000 = 4%)

Rob's individual shortfall percentage is: 9% – 4% = 5%

Rob's individual shortfall for the quarter is: 5% × $10 000 = $500

Allen & Co would also have to pay interest (10% of the shortfall; section below) and an administration fee of $20 (see below).

Since the introduction of the legislation for 'choice of superannuation fund', the calculation of the superannuation guarantee charge shortfall has become more complex where it includes a choice liability. To assist employers, the ATO provides an excellent set of six examples that cover the range of possibilities that could exist. These can be read in the publication *How to complete the superannuation guarantee charge statement—quarterly (NAT 9600)*, available on the ATO's website.

Nominal interest component

The **nominal interest component** is considered necessary to compensate for the loss of earnings on contributions not made by an employer during the year. The rate at which the nominal interest is calculated is equal to the rate as set in the *Taxation (Interest on Overpayments) Act 1983*. The rate is currently set at 10%.

Since 1 July 2003, interest has been calculated on the employer's shortfall amount from the first day of the relevant quarter to the date when the superannuation guarantee charge is payable or the superannuation guarantee statement is lodged, whichever is later.

Example

Assume that employer A's total individual shortfalls for the quarter ended 30 September 2008 are $10 000. Employer A lodges a superannuation guarantee statement on 28 November 2008. The interest component calculation is as follows:

$$\$10\,000 \times 10\% \times (150 \div 365) = \$410.95$$

Note: There are 150 days from 1 July 2008 to 28 November 2008 (not counting 28 November). The 10% interest component is an annual rate and consequently the calculation must be carried out on a per daily basis.

Administration component

The **administration component** is levied to offset some of the costs to the ATO of administering the superannuation guarantee charge—that is, the cost of collecting the charge, and the costs associated with redistributing such funds to the benefit of the relevant employees. Before 1 July 2003, there was a fixed administration fee of $50 and an additional $30 charge for each employee for whom there was a shortfall. Since 1 July 2003 the fixed administrative fee has been removed and the $30 charge for each employee has been reduced to $20 per quarter per employee.

Example

An employer has individual superannuation guarantee shortfalls in respect of 10 employees in a particular quarter. The administration component of the charge is $20 × 10 = $200.

Active reflection 7.9

When is the superannuation guarantee charge due to be paid?

The change to the law in 2008 generally allows an employer to offset superannuation contributions paid late to a superannuation fund on behalf of an employee against the superannuation guarantee charge assessment. The offset relates only to late contributions for that employee for the relevant period. See form NAT 14899.

7.10 Superannuation guarantee late payment tax offset

Superannuation guarantee laws were drafted in such a way that the ATO was prohibited from exercising some discretion for late contributions (even if they were late by only a few days). This strict treatment often meant that an employer who missed paying the correct amount of superannuation for an employee and who tried to correct the mistake and pay the shortfall into the superannuation fund account was considered by the ATO as not having complied with the law. This had the effect of 'double paying' superannuation, because the amount of shortfall also had to be paid to the ATO. The government has now made changes to the superannuation guarantee laws to provide some relief in such circumstances by way of a **late payment tax offset**.

These changes ensure that late contributions still count towards reducing the required superannuation guarantee charge payments of an employer. If an employer makes a late contribution to a superannuation fund for an employee, before the due date for lodgement of the employer's superannuation guarantee charge statement (NAT 9599 quarterly; refer Section 7.11), the employer can elect to have this contribution used to reduce the amount of superannuation guarantee charge liability that relates to that employee. This means that employers may be liable only for the interest and administration components.

Note that:

- any late contribution cannot be applied to offset the administration component of the superannuation guarantee charge
- no part of the late payment tax offset is an allowable tax deduction for income tax purposes.

Active reflection

Which part of the late portion of the superannuation guarantee levy may be used to offset the superannuation guarantee charge liability?

7.11 Lodging the superannuation guarantee statement

This statement is the formal basis for self-assessing the liability for the superannuation guarantee charge. If an employer calculates that there is a liability for the superannuation guarantee charge for any contribution period, the following should be done for each quarter:

- Calculate the charge payable.
- Lodge a superannuation guarantee statement—quarterly (see Appendix, Form 7.1 [9599]).
- Pay the superannuation guarantee charge by the due date, as follows:

Quarter	Due date
1 July to 30 September	28 November
1 October to 31 December	28 February
1 January to 31 March	28 May
1 April to 30 June	28 August

Active reflection 7.11

If an employer is late paying his June quarter superannuation contribution levy, when would he need to pay the superannuation guarantee charge?

7.12 Superannuation guarantee penalties

If an employer does not lodge a superannuation guarantee statement by the due date, or fails to pay the superannuation guarantee charge required, various additional penalties can be imposed. These include penalties for late payment (a **general interest charge**, or **GIC**), for late lodgement of the superannuation guarantee statement, for failing to provide statements or other information when required, for failing to keep records or for entering into avoidance arrangements.

General interest charge

This is an additional charge imposed when the superannuation guarantee charge is not paid by the due date. It is intended to encourage employers to pay on time. It also compensates employees for the late contribution of funds to their nominated superannuation fund. It is calculated from the date of lodgement of the superannuation guarantee statement until the charge is paid in full.

The general interest charge is an allowable tax deduction in the year in which it is incurred or paid.

The general interest charge will apply daily, with a penalty set by dividing the total of the base interest rate plus 7% by the number of days in that calendar year. The base interest rate is the monthly average yield of 90-day bank-accepted bills. At the time of writing, the penalty rate was approximately 14.75% per annum from the date due to the date of payment. This percentage is updated quarterly and can be checked on the ATO's website.

Other penalties applicable

All of the following penalties will be considered by the ATO according to the facts of each case examined. The penalties may then be varied accordingly. An employer may be able to qualify for a 20% reduction in penalties if, after being informed by the ATO of a compliance review, there is an immediate disclosure of non-compliance. Cooperation during a compliance review will further reduce the penalty imposed. An employer may also possibly qualify for an 80% reduction by voluntarily lodging a superannuation guarantee statement and paying the superannuation guarantee charge before the ATO recognises the failure to lodge. Penalties paid by an employer are not tax-deductible.

Not following reporting requirements

Failing to report contributions to employees attracts up to 30 penalty units per employee. Currently, a penalty unit equals $110. If a false or misleading report is made, a penalty of up to 12 months' imprisonment can be applied.

Having a 'tax shortfall amount'

If an employer pays an amount of superannuation guarantee that is less than it should have been, there is a 'tax shortfall amount'. If the tax shortfall amount is a result of making a false and misleading statement, the base penalty amount that can be imposed is 75% of the tax shortfall.

Failing to keep records

Failing to keep records adequately attracts a penalty that is capped at $3300.

Not providing a statement when required

Failing to provide a statement when required attracts a late lodgement penalty capped at 200% of the amount of the charge payable.

Entering into avoidance arrangements

If an employer has entered into an arrangement to reduce or avoid liability for the superannuation guarantee charge, a penalty of 50% of the charge avoided will be applied.

7.12 Active reflection

What is the penalty for an employer who fails to keep adequate superannuation guarantee levy records?

7.13 What happens if the employer pays the charge?

Since 1 July 2003, if the ATO is satisfied that all account details are accurate regarding entitlement for superannuation recovered under the charge, this is paid directly into the employee's superannuation nominated account. Where this does not occur, the ATO will send a letter to the employee with a contribution reference number that can be quoted so that the nominated fund can claim the entitlements.

7.13 Active reflection

If an employer paid the superannuation guarantee charge—a shortfall of $10 000, an administration charge of $200 and a nominal interest charge of $370—what amount would be paid by the ATO into the employee's superannuation accounts?

7.14 Superannuation co-contribution

From 1 July 2003 the government introduced a 'helping hand' to assist and motivate low-income earners to provide for their own superannuation from after-tax income, known as the superannuation **co-contribution**. This is in addition to superannuation contributions made by employers under the superannuation guarantee scheme. It is not necessary to apply for the superannuation co-contribution. If a taxpayer is eligible to receive the co-contribution (see below), and has made personal super contributions during the financial year, the ATO is able to calculate any co-contribution amount the taxpayer is to receive once his or her income tax return and superannuation fund information have been processed. The ATO then sends a letter to the taxpayer giving details of the superannuation co-contribution to be received. Since 1 July 2007 the ATO has indexed income thresholds to the average weekly ordinary time earnings (AWOTE) and the co-contribution has also been extended to include self-employed persons.

Eligibility for the super co-contribution[3]

To be eligible for the superannuation co-contribution, taxpayers need to meet the following requirements:

- They must have made a personal contribution to their superannuation.
- They must earn less than $60 342 (assessable income plus any reportable fringe benefits) per year.
- 10% or more of their total income must come from eligible employment, running a business or a combination of both.
- They must be under 71 years of age.
- They must not be a holder of an eligible temporary resident visa at any time during the year.

Two further points are of note:

1. Entitlement to co-contribution does not include contributions that are being claimed as tax deductions.
2. The superannuation fund must hold the contributor's TFN on file.

Calculation of the amount of co-contribution

If a taxpayer earned $30 342 or less in the 2008/09 tax year, the government would contribute one and a half times the personal superannuation contributions up to a maximum of $1500 per financial year. The lowest amount of co-contribution payable by the government is $20 per financial year. That means that a taxpayer on an income of, say, $22 000 who contributes only $10, will receive $20 as the co-contribution amount and not $15.

Example

If a taxpayer earns $22 000 per year and makes personal super contributions of $321 during that year, he or she will be entitled to a super co-contribution of $482 ($321 × 1.5), making a total contribution of $803 for that year.

If the taxpayer's income for co-contribution purposes is more than $30 342 but less than $60 342 per year, the super co-contribution will be adjusted based on the formula represented in Table 7.4. There is an inverse relationship between the amount of an individual's contribution and the minimum relevant income level where shading-in begins. The minimum threshold at which the government's co-contribution starts to diminish can be found by multiplying the individual contribution by $30 and deducting this from the top threshold. This minimum relevant income amount goes up by $30 for every $1 less than $1000 that the taxpayer contributes.

Example

If a taxpayer earns $46 342 per year and makes personal super contributions of $500 during that year, he or she will be entitled to a government super co-contribution of $700, making a total contribution for the year of $1200. The shading-in loss from the maximum government co-contribution ($750 in this case) does not begin until the taxpayer's income reaches $45 342.

If this same taxpayer contributed only $200, the shading-in would not begin until the relevant income reaches $54 342 (this is $200 × $30 less than the top threshold of $60 342, well above the taxpayer's relevant income of $46 342). Thus, the taxpayer would receive the maximum co-contribution of $300 from the government. If you check Table 7.4 you can see these amounts.[4]

TABLE 7.4 SUPERANNUATION CO-CONTRIBUTIONS

	If your personal super contribution is:			
	$1000	$800	$500	$200
And your income is:	Your super co-contribution will be:			
$30 342 or less	$1 500	$1 200	$750	$300
$30 342	$1 500	$1 200	$750	$300
$31 342	$1 450	$1 200	$750	$300
$32 342	$1 400	$1 200	$750	$300
$33 342	$1 399	$1 200	$750	$300
$34 342	$1 300	$1 200	$750	$300
$35 342	$1 250	$1 200	$750	$300
$36 342	$1 200	$1 200	$750	$300
$37 342	$1 150	$1 150	$750	$300
$38 342	$1 100	$1 100	$750	$300
$39 342	$1 050	$1 050	$750	$300
$40 342	$1 000	$1 000	$750	$300
$41 342	$950	$950	$750	$300
$42 342	$900	$900	$750	$300
$43 342	$850	$850	$750	$300
$44 342	$800	$800	$750	$300
$45 342	$750	$750	$750	$300
$46 342	$700	$700	$700	$300
$47 342	$650	$650	$650	$300
$48 342	$600	$600	$600	$300
$49 342	$550	$550	$550	$300
$50 342	$500	$500	$500	$300
$51 342	$450	$450	$450	$300
$52 342	$400	$400	$400	$300
$53 342	$350	$350	$350	$300
$54 342	$300	$300	$300	$300
$55 342	$250	$250	$250	$250
$56 342	$200	$200	$200	$200
$57 342	$150	$150	$150	$150
$58 342	$100	$100	$100	$100
$59 342	$50	$50	$50	$50
$60 342	$0	$0	$0	$0

Source: Data from **www.ato.gov.au/superprofessionals**, 'Superannuation co-contributions'.

Active reflection 7.14

A taxpayer has an assessable income of $48 342 and reportable fringe benefits of $4000 and has personally contributed $1000 in superannuation. What amount of government co-contribution will this taxpayer receive, and what is the total amount that the taxpayer's super fund will receive for that year?

7.15 Lost members register

The ATO requires regulated superannuation funds (other than self-managed superannuation funds) to provide it with details of members that they cannot contact. These details are stored on what has become known as the **lost members register**. The lost members register is a central register of superannuation fund members and retirement savings account holders who were unable to be contacted at their last known address.

A employee may be a lost member of a superannuation fund if:

- the fund has been unable to contact the employee and has received returned unclaimed mail
- the employer made contributions for the employee to a fund and in the past two years the fund has not received any further contributions
- the employee's account was transferred from another fund and no new address has been found for this employee in the past two years.

To see whether any funds may be available in the lost members register, a person can complete the 'Searching for lost super' form' (see Appendix, Form 7.2 [2476]), which is available from the superannuation section of the ATO's website (**www.ato.gov.au/superprofessionals**) under 'Super Seeker', or contact the current superannuation fund administrators and ask them to do a search via **SuperMatch**.

SuperMatch

To help superannuation funds and individuals to control the large amounts of unmatched superannuation that now exist in the Australian superannuation system, the ATO has introduced SuperMatch, which is an electronic commerce interface (ECI) designed to provide superannuation funds with electronic access to data held on the lost members register, unredeemed superannuation guarantee vouchers and the superannuation holding account reserve.[5] SuperMatch has many benefits:

- Superannuation monies can be consolidated into the one account, with the resulting benefits of compound interest.
- It helps members to trace their superannuation entitlements.
- Interest can be earned on money previously held in superannuation vouchers and account reserves by transferring it into a superannuation fund account.

Security measures have been implemented that require superannuation funds to obtain ATO authorisation and a digital certificate and to sign a formal agreement before access to SuperMatch will be granted. All users must also obtain written authorisation from the member prior to requesting a search. To gain ATO authorisation to SuperMatch, send an email to **SuperMatch@ato.gov.au**. In all cases the enquirer is required to disclose details of the organisation's name, address, TFN, ABN, type of organisation (e.g. superannuation fund, financial adviser, tax agent), contact person, contact telephone number, email address and the reason for requiring access. For more information on digital certificates, contact the ESD Technical Support Centre by telephoning **1300 139 373** or email the ATO at **esd.help@ato.gov.au**.

7.15 Active reflection

If you leave your employer and cannot remember the fund into which your superannuation contributions were paid, briefly state how you might go about finding your lost superannuation.

Superannuation in practice

Employers have to calculate and pay superannuation guarantee contributions on a quarterly basis. The following example of the superannuation guarantee levy in practice shows what is required of an employer.

Michelle Fitness conducts her business as a sole trader and has two employees. She pays superannuation guarantee payments in respect of her employees to ABC Superannuation Fund. Michelle uses OTE as the earnings base for superannuation guarantee purposes.

For the quarter ended 31 March 2009, Michelle's wage records reveal the following in respect of her two employees:

Details of payments for the quarter	Lisa Smith	Renee Jones
Ordinary wages actually paid	$6100	$5250
PAYG tax withheld from ordinary wages	$1400	$1000
Overtime payment for additional work in January 2009		$500
PAYG tax withheld from overtime pay		$200
Fringe benefits provided	$1500	nil
Reimbursement of train fares to attend a training course	$25	
Bonus for being the most productive employee	$250	

Calculation of OTE for the quarter

Details of OTE payments for the quarter	Lisa Smith	Renee Jones
Ordinary wages actually paid	$6100	$5250
PAYG tax withheld from ordinary wages	$1400	$1000
Overtime payment for additional work in January 2009		
PAYG tax withheld from overtime pay		
Fringe benefits provided		
Reimbursement of train fares to attend a training course		
Bonus for being the most productive employee	$250	
Total OTE for superannuation purposes	$7750	$6250

Lisa Smith	$7750 × 9%	=	$720.00
Renee Jones	$6250 × 9%	=	$562.50
TOTAL			$1260.00

This amount must be paid by 28 April 2009.

Learning check

✓ Establish the current rate of the superannuation guarantee.

✓ Calculate the earnings base of an employee for the purposes of the superannuation guarantee.

✓ Calculate the correct level of quarterly contributions for the earnings base salary.

✓ Outline the quarterly reporting obligations that are required of an employer.

✓ Ensure that the level of contributions does not exceed the age-based statutory limits.

✓ Complete a superannuation guarantee statement for an employer.

✓ Calculate the amount of the superannuation guarantee charge.

✓ Access the ATO's website and locate the lost members register.

✓ Compile a list of at least five public complying superannuation funds.

✓ Calculate the super co-contribution for an employee.

Taxation vocabulary

administration component
charge percentage
choice of fund
co-contribution
contractor
contribution period
control test
employees
fund
general interest charge (GIC)
integration test
labour
late payment tax offset
lost members register
nominal interest component
ordinary time earnings (OTE)
preserved
self-assessment
superannuation guarantee charge
superannuation guarantee levy
superannuation guarantee shortfall
superannuation guarantee statement
SuperMatch
vested

multiple-choice questions

Circle the correct response. (Answers to odd-numbered multiple-choice questions are provided on page 318.)

1. **The superannuation guarantee levy aims to:**
   (a) lower the foreign debt
   (b) increase government revenue
   (c) provide funds for investment
   (d) provide support benefits for employees

2. **The superannuation guarantee levy:**
   (a) is exactly the same amount as would be payable under the superannuation guarantee charge
   (b) is paid on an annual basis
   (c) is paid on a quarterly basis and has to be paid by the end of each quarter
   (d) is paid on a quarterly basis and has to be paid by the 28th of the month following the quarter

3. **For superannuation guarantee purposes, an employee does not include:**
   (a) a common law employee
   (b) an individual contracted wholly or principally for his or her labour
   (c) a contract for an individual's labour plus materials of a minor amount
   (d) a partner in a partnership when the contract is between the partnership and a third party

4. **Which of the following is *not* an employee for superannuation guarantee purposes?**
   (a) an employee of a government department
   (b) an individual builder who has been contracted wholly or principally for his or her labour
   (c) a babysitter engaged to look after children part-time
   (d) a company director

5. **The control test for superannuation guarantee levy purposes assists in the determination of:**
   (a) who is an employee for superannuation guarantee levy purposes
   (b) whether the fund is properly controlled
   (c) the actual percentage payable per employee
   (d) nothing; it has no relevance to the superannuation guarantee levy

6. **Which of the following employees is exempt from the superannuation guarantee levy?**
   (a) a clerk earning $500 per week
   (b) a receptionist earning $500 per month
   (c) an assistant aged 17 working 15 hours per week
   (d) an aide aged 61 earning $500 per fortnight

7. **For the quarter ended 30 June 2009, the correct amount of superannuation levy that an employer should contribute in respect of an employee who has OTE of $10 000 for the quarter is:**
   (a) $900 (b) $1800 (c) $900 less the employee's own contributions
   (d) $1800 less the employee's own contributions

8. **For the quarter ended 30 June 2009, the correct amount of superannuation levy that a payer should contribute in respect of a quarterly payment of $10 000 to a subcontractor trading as a genuine company is:**
   (a) $1800 (b) $900 (c) nil
   (d) not applicable, as the superannuation guarantee levy applies only if the parties have entered into a voluntary agreement

9. The 'choice of superannuation fund' obligations:

(a) allow employers to choose which employees will receive superannuation contributions

(b) allow employees to choose how much superannuation they want an employer to pay

(c) provide most employees with the right to choose the superannuation fund or retirement savings account that will receive their superannuation guarantee levy contributions

(d) provide employers with the right to choose the superannuation fund or retirement savings account that will receive their employees' superannuation guarantee levy contributions

10. The superannuation co-contribution is payable to:

(a) an employee with a taxable income under the top threshold who personally contributes to superannuation

(b) an employee with assessable income under the top threshold who personally contributes to superannuation

(c) an employee who only has employer superannuation support

(d) self-employed persons only

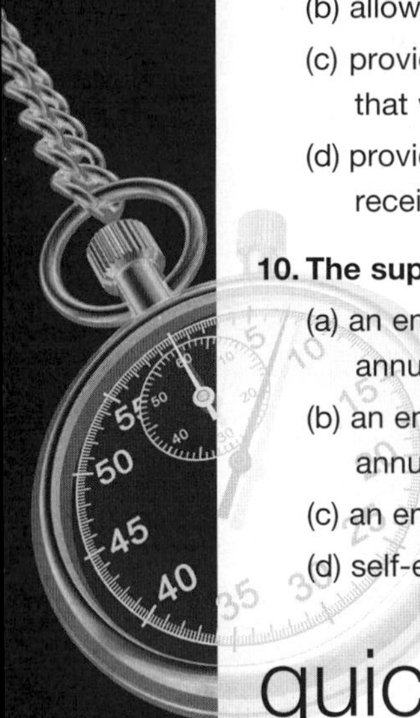

quick-and-easy comprehension

Place a ✓ to indicate your response to each statement.

STATEMENT	TRUE	FALSE
1. Payment of superannuation in Australia is compulsory for all Australians.	—	—
2. Employers can choose which employees they want to make superannuation contributions for.	—	—
3. The superannuation guarantee charge does not apply if the two parties agree that there is no employment relationship between them.	—	—
4. The superannuation guarantee levy requirements do not apply to weekly drawings paid to partners in a partnership.	—	—
5. There are no exempt employers for superannuation guarantee levy purposes.	—	—
6. If an employer has to pay the superannuation guarantee charge, the ATO will arrange for the appropriate amount to be credited to affected employees.	—	—
7. To satisfy the superannuation guarantee levy requirements, contributions to any superannuation fund would be acceptable.	—	—
8. The government has introduced the superannuation co-contribution to assist all employees.	—	—

self-test question

For the quarter ended 30 June 2009, Colossal Constructions Pty Ltd's wage records reveal the following in respect of the firm's two employees:

Details of payments for the quarter	Matthew Janes	Stephen Laurie
Ordinary net wages actually paid	$25 100	$23 300
PAYG tax withheld from ordinary gross wages	$5 500	$4 700

Overtime net payment for additional work in May		$500
PAYG tax withheld from gross overtime pay		$150
Fringe benefits provided	$2900	nil
Reimbursement of train fares to attend a training course	$25	
Bonus for being the most productive employee	$250	

Set out the following superannuation liability of the firm for the quarter ended 30 June 2009:

(a) total OTE for each employee

(b) amount of superannuation for each employee

(c) total amount of superannuation payable

(d) the date by which this payment is due

assessments

1. Set out the limited categories of employees for whom superannuation contributions do not have to be made.

2. (a) Calculate the minimum amount of superannuation contributions that Builder Bob Ltd should pay for the quarter ended 30 June 2009 given the following information:

Name	Age	Hours per week	Quarterly OTE
R. Tam	25	40	$29 000
T. Lam	49	55	$40 000
F. Mal	18	40	$17 000
G. Mat	76	25	$12 000
H. Tat	15	10	$7 000

(b) When would these amounts have to be paid?

(c) When would these amounts have to be reported to the employees?

3. (a) Using the information given in question 2, and assuming that only the following amounts have been paid in the quarter, calculate the superannuation guarantee charge that Builder Bob Ltd will be required to pay.

Name	Date paid	Payment
R. Tam	30.6.2009	$3000
T. Lam	28.7.2009	$3000
F. Mal	28.8.2009	$850
G. Mat	30.6.2009	nil
H. Tat	30.6.2009	$1500

(b) When would the superannuation guarantee statement need to be lodged in respect of the above and payment of the charge made?

case study questions

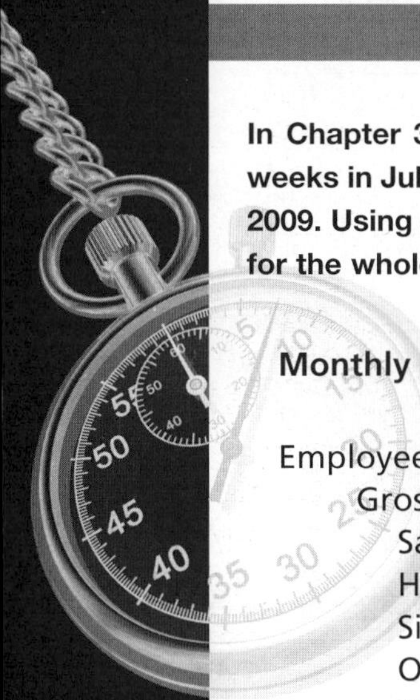

In Chapter 3 you were required to complete the payroll for Colossal Constructions Pty Ltd for the five weeks in July 2009. You are now given the totals taken from the payroll register for August and September 2009. Using all the information for July, August and September, calculate the superannuation contribution for the whole company for the quarter ending 30 September 2009.

Monthly summary

	1 August to 28 August
Employee wages, taxes and adjustments	
Gross pay	
Salaries	16 000.00
Hourly pay	30 005.00
Sick pay	112.50
Overtime pay	164.80
Holiday loading	302.40
Total gross pay	46 584.70
Taxes withheld	
PAYG tax	–13 843.00
Total taxes withheld	–13 843.00
Net pay	32 741.70
Employer super contributions	
Superannuation at 9% for August	?

Monthly summary

	4 September to 25 September
Employee wages, taxes and adjustments	
Gross pay	
Salaries	11 620.00
Hourly pay	32 869.40
Sick pay	945.60
Overtime pay	135.00
Holiday loading	0.00
Total gross pay	45 570.00
Taxes withheld	
PAYG tax	–11 364.00
Total taxes withheld	–11 364.00
Net pay	34 206.00
Employer super contributions	
Superannuation at 9% for September	?
Total employer superannuation for July, August and September	?

classroom activity

In groups of three to five people, use an Internet search engine to find information on five superannuation funds into which you might like your employer to place your super contributions. Write a paragraph on each of these funds.

self-test question solution

Calculation of OTE for the quarter

Details of OTE payments for the quarter	Matthew Janes	Stephen Laurie
Net ordinary wages actually paid	$25 100	$23 300
PAYG tax withheld from gross ordinary wages	$5500	$4700
Overtime net payment for additional work in May 2008		$500
PAYG tax withheld from gross overtime pay		$150
Fringe benefits provided	$2900	nil
Reimbursement of train fares to attend a training course	$25	
Bonus for being the most productive employee	$250	
Total OTE for superannuation purposes	$30 850	$28 000

Note: No superannuation is required to be paid on those amounts in the shaded cells.

(a) Total OTE for Matthew = $30 850; for Stephen = $28 000.

(b) Superannuation for Matthew = $30 850 × 9% = $2776.50; for Stephen = $28 000 × 9% = $2520.00.

(c) Total amount of superannuation payable = $2776.50 + $2520.00 = $5296.50.

(d) This amount must be paid by 28 July 2009.

Notes

1. A 'superannuation contribution' is a payment to a superannuation fund that, if made by an employer, is generally concessionally taxed.
2. See Superannuation Guarantee Ruling 94/5 from the ATO.
3. The relevant income for co-contribution purposes is defined in section 8 of the *Superannuation (Government Co-Contribution for Low Income Earners) Act 2003* as being a person's assessable income plus any reportable benefits for that year of income.
4. For those interested in formulae this is how the government co-contribution (GC) is calculated. First, determine the relevant income threshold (RIT). RIT is dependent upon the amount contributed, so for every dollar the contribution (C) decreases, RIT goes up by a factor of 30 (f).

   $$RIT = UT - (C \times f)$$

   where: UT = upper indexed threshold

   f = factor by which lower indexed threshold increases as contributions decrease

   If the relevant income (RI) is within the range of UT for the year and RIT as determined above, then:

   $$GC = (C \times gf) - ((RI - RIT) \times r) \text{ (or \$20, whichever is the greater)}$$

   where: gf = government co-contribution uplift factor

   r = rate of loss from the MGC for every dollar of RI over the RIT

   MGC = maximum government co-contribution amount = (C * gf)

   If RI is less than both RIT and the lower indexed threshold (LT), then apply:

   $$GC = C \times gf \text{ (or \$20, whichever is the greater)}$$
5. The superannuation holding account reserve was designed to protect small superannuation amounts until they could be transferred into a complying fund or retirement savings account. This special account was closed on 30 June 2006 because there are now many superannuation funds and retirement savings accounts able to accept and protect small amounts.

8 Higher education support

Chapter eight

Topics

After studying this chapter, you should be able to:

- **identify the types of higher education students who are eligible for higher education support**
- **explain how the higher education fees are assessed**
- **identify how reportable fringe benefits affect higher education loan payments**
- **illustrate the three methods of payment of Higher Education Loan Program (HELP) debts and examine any advantages or disadvantages that may be associated with these methods**
- **identify when taxpayers become liable to make repayments through the tax system and review the effect of the annual indexation of HELP debts.**

OVERVIEW

In May 2003 the government introduced a new framework for higher education: *Our Universities: Backing Australia's Future*. The integrated package of reforms was established to reinforce four key education principles: sustainability, quality, equity and diversity. On 19 December 2003 the *Higher Education Support Act 2003* received royal assent. The new course and student funding arrangements started on 1 January 2005 and as of 1 June 2006 all accumulated HECS debts became accumulated HELP debts. The **Higher Education Loan Program (HELP)**[1] now covers assistance to eligible students with support for HELP debts in the following areas: **HECS-HELP**, for units of study with a higher education provider; **FEE-HELP**, for the payment of tuition fees with an accredited provider; and **OS-HELP**, for the payment of full-time oversees tuition that is part of a course of study accredited in Australia.

In September 2007 the *Higher Education Support Amendment (Extending FEE-HELP for VET Diploma, Advanced Diploma, Graduate Diploma and Graduate Certificate Courses) Act 2007* came into force. Schedule 1A provides for loans, called **VET FEE-HELP** assistance, to be made available to students enrolled in certain accredited **vocational education and training (VET)** courses.

The Commonwealth now pays to the approved higher education providers money to be used in delivering courses to new and continuing students. Students are offered a *Commonwealth-supported place* or a *fee-paying place*. Most domestic students are offered a supported place. The government provides a **Student Learning Entitlement (SLE)** scheme so that students can access education through a supported place for up to seven years' equivalent full-time undergraduate study. The aim of the support is for students entitled to SLE to gradually use up their entitlement. Extra government support will be available for those students who are studying longer than seven years in certain degrees or who take an honours year. Each student contributes towards the cost of his or her education, and this contribution is determined by the university. Many postgraduate students receive **postgraduate exemption scholarships** that allow them to carry out research free of any HELP fees.

The government pays universities varying amounts for each undergraduate degree being undertaken at the university. However, universities can set their own contribution amounts to be paid by students within set bands.[2] Students are liable to pay the university for a place in a course either up-front or by seeking assistance through HELP. The four packages of assistance (HECS-HELP, FEE-HELP, OS-HELP and VET FEE-HELP) allow students to defer payment until such time as they are earning a wage or salary. Students may also pay an amount voluntarily at any time against the debt.

8.1 Definitions and assessment procedures

The Higher Education Funding Act 1988 that came into effect on 1 January 1989 gradually phased out the previous bands of student contributions. Under the legislation, most students undertaking higher education had a liability to pay a contribution under HELP. When the new laws came into effect in January 2005, the old scheme was integrated with the new. The higher education contribution scheme does *not* apply to students enrolled in:

- certificate courses at TAFE institutions
- courses at higher institutions that are funded by TAFE

- fee-paying postgraduate courses
- non-award courses
- courses at the Marcus Oldham College of Farm Management
- courses to gain industrial experience as part of a course
- postgraduate or honours courses given HELP exemption by either their institution or an education authority
- courses at Avondale College that are not funded by the Commonwealth
- courses at the University of Notre Dame for which students are enrolled on a fee-paying basis
- students from overseas who are full-fee paying.

Under the support legislation, the higher education providers decide how much they require students to contribute towards their undergraduate courses. The key to calculating student contributions is an **equivalent full-time student unit (EFTSU)**. Providers may set the support fee for a course of study anywhere from zero to the maximum. If a student is undertaking only a **half-year program**, the EFTSU is halved. If a student is doing less than the **standard annual program**, the support charge is proportionally less; if the student is doing more, the support charge is greater. The academic institution calculates the student's workload for each half-year and the fees are set within the band under which the student is enrolled. A full-time program consists of a set number of units, and each unit is given a weighting, which represents a fraction of the total workload associated with the standard annual program or EFTSU.

Equivalent full-time student unit refers to the average full-time student program of study for one year.

For example, if eight equally **weighted units** make up a full-time program for one year, then each unit will carry a weight of 0.125. The combined weights of the units being undertaken in a half-year represent the workload or proportion of the standard annual program on which the support contribution is calculated. If some units are full-year units, the weight is assumed to be distributed equally over each half-year, making half the support charge for that unit payable in the first semester.

If students are in a Commonwealth-supported place, they make only a contribution towards the cost of their education (known as the *student contribution*), while the Australian government contributes the majority of the cost. If students are not Commonwealth-supported, they will pay tuition fees, which are not subsidised by the government. Fee-paying undergraduate places are additional to Commonwealth-supported places.

Example

Julie is enrolled in a three-year bachelor degree program in humanities, and at her particular institution students are expected to complete this course in three years. Her university has set the contribution fee at $5000. This means that a standard full-time program for each year would be one-third of the subjects required to complete the degree. For Julie's course, this means eight subjects every year, or four every half-year.

If Julie undertakes four subjects in both the first and second semesters, this would be a standard annual program. When enrolling in February 2009 Julie elected to complete four subjects in each semester, but before 31 March (the **census date**) she decided to withdraw from one subject. This meant that in semester 1 Julie was undertaking only three subjects and the fee would be proportionally less:

$$\$5000/8 \times 3 = \$1875 \text{ (not } \$2500\text{)}$$

In semester 2 Julie wanted to catch up, so she undertook an overload and enrolled in five subjects. Thus the fees would be calculated as:

$$\$5000/8 \times 5 = \$3125$$

The standard annual program of study in each semester has been altered proportionally to match Julie's workload.

If a student chooses subjects across other disciplines, the amount of the fees is calculated according to each amount set by the university for the discipline under which the unit falls. Suppose that in the first semester Julie chose four units of study, three subjects from humanities and one from law (set by the university at $8000, with eight subjects to be undertaken each year). The fee calculation would be as follows:

$$3 \times \$625 + 1 \times \$1000 = \$2875$$

All calculations for HELP must be rounded to the nearest dollar.

The census dates each academic year are 31 March for semester 1 and 31 August for semester 2. The academic institutions must notify the student of the liability owed for HECS-HELP. These dates are withdrawal dates and should not be confused with the academic withdrawal dates of the institution.

Institutions send a written notice after each census date to the students enrolled advising of the **HELP assessment**, and giving 14 days to have the calculation checked if necessary. The ATO cannot alter a deferred debt without written advice from the institution concerned.[3] If a student withdraws from a course, it must be with a written application to the institution before the census date in the semester. If a student enrols at more than one institution and does not withdraw the unwanted placement by the census date, a double liability will accrue. If a student fails a subject(s), this makes no difference to the liability for the contribution fee.

Active reflection 8.1

Explain to a student who has just commenced a course of study at a university in your capital city why it is important to advise the university of changes to her program.

8.2 Methods of payment of HELP debts

At the time of enrolment, students must indicate to the institution how they wish to pay their **HELP debt**. Students can choose one of the following three methods of payment by completing a **payment options form**.

Method 1: Up-front payment

Australian citizens and holders of a permanent humanitarian visa may choose an **up-front payment** of their contribution HECS-HELP charges to the institution at the time of enrolment and thus be entitled to a discount of 20%, paying only 80% of the estimated liability assessed.

New Zealand citizens and holders of other permanent visas do not have access to HELP loans. These students must pay their student contributions or tuition fees up-front without a discount.

Chapter 3, Part 3-3 of the *Higher Education Support Act 2003* allows for taxpayers to apply for fee help assistance.

After the census date, the institution will advise students of the correct assessment based on the study program. With this method, once paid the option cannot be changed until the next semester. One very important aspect is that these HELP payments are not tax-deductible.[4] HELP is an allowable deduction only to an employer taxpayer who has made the payment subject to fringe benefits tax.[5]

Method 2: Deferred payment

With the **deferred payment** method, the HELP liability can be deferred until such time as the student's taxable income reaches a minimum level. (Refer to Chapter 3, Section 3.4.) When electing this method the student is required to provide a TFN to the university. If the student does not have a TFN, an application for one must be made to the ATO. This deferred payment option to eligible supported students may be in respect of HECS-HELP, FEE-HELP, OS-HELP or VET FEE-HELP.

The Commonwealth government pays the contribution to the education provider, and this really represents a 'loan' that must then be repaid through the tax system. If a student chooses the deferred payment option but later decides to pay up-front, this must be done before the census date in the semester, otherwise the option will remain unchanged until the next semester. Options can be changed at the beginning of a semester by completing a new payment options form, which is supplied by the educational institution.

If a taxpayer has a HELP debt and begins full-time employment, this debt must be declared on the taxpayer's TFN declaration form (NAT 3092). If the taxpayer is already in employment and acquires a HELP debt, a withholding declaration (NAT 3093) must be completed to advise the employer of the changed circumstances of employment. Once the weekly gross wage exceeds the threshold, the employer will deduct an amount for debt and remit this to the ATO on the PAYG Instalment Activity Statement. (See Chapter 3.)

Method 3: Voluntary part-payments that attract a bonus

Students may make a voluntary part-payment of their debt. If this amount is $500 or more paid up-front, the debt for the course is reduced by 110% of the payment made. For example, a $500 payment up-front would be recorded with a bonus of $50 and would become $550 off the debt.

8.2 Active reflection

Explain the various payment options available to students who have a HELP liability.

8.3 Liability and indexing of HELP debts

If the deferred payment option has been selected, the actual yearly amount of repayment for the HELP debt is based on a repayment income calculated to include:

- the taxable income for that year of income
- any negative gearing loss related to rental income for that year of income
- the person's total **reportable fringe benefits** for the year of income.

The ATO will add back rental losses and any reportable fringe benefits to taxable income to establish the amount of *HELP repayment income (HRI)*. For example, if a taxpayer's assessable income is $55 000, rental losses of $10 000 produce a taxable income of $45 000 and reportable fringe benefits are $2500, then the ATO will calculate the debt based on an HRI of $57 500.

If a student has chosen to defer payment of the debt liability, then repayment of the loan will begin when his or her taxable income reaches the minimum level (see Form 8.1 [2173]). The debt repayment is calculated from a table that takes a percentage of the HRI each year towards the debt (see Table 8.1). These rates are indexed each year using the **consumer price index (CPI)**, and you can check them by visiting the website **www.backingaustraliasfuture.gov.au/student_info.htm**.

TABLE 8.1 HELP REPAYMENT SCHEDULE, 2008/09

For 2008/09 HELP repayment incomes in the range:	Percentage rate to be applied to total HELP repayment income
Below $41 595	Nil
$41 595–$46 333	4.0%
$46 334–$51 070	4.5%
$51 071–$53 754	5.0%
$53 755–$57 782	5.5%
$57 783–$62 579	6.0%
$62 580–$65 873	6.5%
$65 874–$72 492	7.0%
$72 493–$77 247	7.5%
$77 248 and above	8.0%

The repayment for any year depends on the repayment taxpayer's income. As this income rises, so too does the repayment of the debt. The ATO will send the taxpayer a **HELP information statement** dated 1 June, which shows the value of the debt owed. For taxation returns, the debt incurred in semester 1 of a new enrolment year must be added to the debt shown on the statement received, to calculate the total debt. From this is deducted any voluntary payments that have been made after 1 June.

The fact that a HELP debt exists must then be indicated on the taxpayer's return of income. Once the Commissioner issues a notice of assessment with a HELP debt repayment on that notice, that debt becomes due and payable.[6]

For example, in 2009, if a taxpayer had a taxable income of $50 000, with no rental losses and no reportable fringe benefits, and a debt of $3316, the taxpayer would be required to pay only $2250 ($50 000 × 4.5%) of that debt.[7] The remaining balance of $1066 would be carried forward to the next tax year, but any part of the debt older than 11 months would be subject to indexing. The **index number** for a quarter is the All Groups CPI number, being the weighted average of the eight capital cities, published by the Australian Statistician in respect of that quarter. The index used on 1 June each year is obtained as follows: add the four quarters to 31 March in the current financial year and divide by the total of the four quarters to 31 March of the preceding year. In the 2008 year the June HELP debts index number was 2.8%, as shown in Table 8.2.

TABLE 8.2 CONSUMER PRICE INDEX FOR HELP DEBTS OVER 11 MONTHS OLD

Year	Q1 June	Q2 Sept	Q3 Dec	Q4 Mar	Aggregate	Index number rounded to one decimal place
2005/06	148.4	149.8	150.6	151.9	600.7	
2006/07	154.3	155.7	155.5	155.6	621.1	3.4%
2007/08	157.5	158.6	160.1	162.2	638.4	2.8%

The HELP information statement is issued to inform current and former students of their outstanding debt and the indexation that has been applied to that debt. (Check the Australian Bureau of Statistics website, **www.abs.gov.au**, for these indices.) From 1 June 2009, all debts incurred between January and June 2008 will be indexed and become part of the accumulated HELP debt. Debts incurred between July 2008 and June 2009 will also become part of the accumulated HELP debt, but will not be indexed until 1 June 2010.

If a taxpayer dies, any amount included as an education debt on a notice of assessment issued by the Commissioner must be paid from the deceased taxpayer's estate. The remainder of any debt is automatically cancelled. For example, if a taxpayer died with a current HELP debt of $4063, and the last notice of assessment issued showed a HELP repayment of $2000, the taxpayer's estate would be required to pay only $2000 of the total HELP debt. The remaining balance of $2063 would be cancelled.

If you believe that the HELP details shown on a notice of assessment are incorrect, you may seek an explanation from the ATO either by phone or by interview. If a formal objection is to be lodged, it must be made within four years after the service of notice of assessment.[8]

8.3 Active reflection

For the year ended 30 June 2009, a student has a HELP liability of $11 000, a taxable income of $50 000 and reportable fringe benefits of $5000. What is the amount of HELP repayment that will be issued on the student's tax assessment for that year?

HELP in practice

In this exercise we will assume that costs for a commerce degree are set at $7500 and the indexation years are 2006, 2007 and 2008.

Bill was accepted by City University to undertake a commerce degree, and the fee set by the university was $7500. The course had 10 units per year for three years, making a total of 30 units to complete the degree. Bill enrolled in five commerce units in the first semester and was given his tax invoice for the contribution. Before 31 March that year he withdrew from one unit. He then added that unit to his student load in the second semester so that he could complete 10 units in the first year. In second semester he elected to study one unit from law as part of his program of six units. The university had set the fee for law courses at $8000, and the law course also had 30 units in the program. Bill decided to defer his contribution for the first year and as a supported eligible student took out a HECS-HELP loan. He received assistance from his grandmother in the second and third years and elected to pay up-front for the remainder of his study. Now that Bill has finished his degree he has obtained a very good job and his first-year income is $50 000.

Required

1. Calculate the amounts Bill would have incurred as his HELP debt in his first year of study.
2. What is the amount that Bill must repay now in his first year of working? Assume that the HRI is as in this text and the CPI indexing amounts are as follows:

   2.4% in Bill's second year of study
   3.4% in Bill's third year of study
   2.8% in Bill's first year of working.

Solution

Year	Unit fee	No. of units	Total fee	Index factor	Indexed amount
Year 1					
Sem 1	$750	4	$3000		
Sem 2	$800	1	$800		
	$750	5	$3750		
Total			$7550		
Year 2					
1 June:	index only the debt that is 11 months old, $3000			2.4%	$72.00
Year 3					
1 June:	the total debt is indexed			3.4%	$259.15
Year 4					
1 June:	the total debt is indexed			2.8%	$220.67
Total owing at end			$8101.82		$551.82

1. In the first year of study Bill would have incurred a HECS-HELP debt of $7550.
2. Bill will pay 4.5% of his higher education repayment income as repayment of the HELP debt. $50 000 × 4.5 % = $2250. The remaining debt is $5851.82 and this will continue to be indexed each year until the debt is repaid.

Learning check

✓ Calculate the HECS-HELP liability for a student:
- for a full-time enrolment
- for a part-time enrolment
- for a mixed qualification enrolment.

✓ Calculate the discount for an up-front HECS-HELP payment:
- for full payment
- for partial payment.

✓ Calculate the amount of taxable income for a student for the purposes of repaying the HELP debt.

✓ Calculate the annual repayment amount based on taxable income, the required up-front payment to discharge a HELP debt and a lump sum payment.

✓ Calculate the correct weekly PAYG instalment deduction for an employee with a HELP debt.

Taxation vocabulary

census date
consumer price index (CPI)
deferred payment
equivalent full-time student unit (EFTSU)
FEE-HELP
half-year program
HECS-HELP
HELP assessment
HELP debt
HELP information statement
Higher Education Loan Program (HELP)
index number
OS-HELP
payment options form
pay up-front
postgraduate exemption scholarships
reportable fringe benefits
standard annual program
Student Learning Entitlement (SLE)
VET FEE-HELP
vocational education and training (VET)
weighted units

multiple-choice questions

Circle the correct response. (Answers to odd-numbered multiple-choice questions are provided on page 318.)

1. **Academic institutions estimate HECS-HELP of Commonwealth-supported places by calculating the EFTSU. This is based on the:**
   (a) undergraduate annual program
   (b) postgraduate annual program
   (c) student full-time annual program
   (d) student part-time annual program
2. **The census dates set for HECS-HELP Commonwealth-supported places each year are:**
   (a) 31 January and 30 June
   (b) 31 March and 31 August
   (c) 30 June and 31 August
   (d) 31 August and 31 January
3. **If a student enrols at more than one institution, the student's HECS-HELP debt will be:**
   (a) exempt at the second place
   (b) halved at both places
   (c) levied at both places
   (d) levied at the first place for both places
4. **Students must repay their HELP debt by:**
   (a) method 1 (b) method 2 (c) method 3 (d) by choosing method 1, method 2 or method 3
5. **The HELP repayment income (HRI) as assessed by the ATO will include:**
   (a) reportable fringe benefits
   (b) rental losses from negative gearing
   (c) wages under the PAYG system
   (d) all of the above
6. **If a student has a HELP debt of $8000 and in the year ended 30 June 2009 earned $45 000, the repayment amount set by the ATO would be:**
   (a) $8000 (b) $2250 (c) $360 (d) $1800
7. **If a Commonwealth-supported student decided to pay up-front for a HECS-HELP semester debt of $3418 calculated at enrolment, the amount to pay would be:**
   (a) $2573 (b) $2734 (c) $3076 (d) $3418
8. **If a student voluntarily offered to pay $500 off her HELP debt, the debt would be reduced by:**
   (a) $550 (b) $500 (c) $600 (d) nil
9. **If a student earned $55 000 in the year of income and had a HELP debt of $2500, the amount that must be repaid for the 2009 year is:**
   (a) $553 (b) $2500 (c) $3575 (d) $3025
10. **If a student deferred his HELP debt, it would result in consumer price indexing:**
    (a) at once
    (b) after six months
    (c) after 11 months
    (d) after the course is finished

quick-and-easy comprehension

Place a ✓ to indicate your response to each statement.

STATEMENT	TRUE	FALSE
1. For a taxpayer who chooses method 2 for repayment of HELP, as taxable income rises so too does the HELP repayment component.	—	—
2. New Zealand citizens can defer their HELP debt.	—	—
3. HELP debt is calculated by the ATO on taxable income plus any reportable fringe benefits.	—	—
4. The only part of HELP debt that must be repaid is that part shown on the notice of assessment issued by the Commissioner in any year.	—	—
5. If a taxpayer dies owing a HELP debt, the family will have to repay that debt.	—	—

self-test question

You have a graduate employee working for you for the year ended 30 June 2009 and he is earning $850 each week. He has indicated on his declaration that he has a HELP debt of $12 000. How much should you deduct each week from his pay under PAYG withholding laws?

assessments

1. Bill has just enrolled as a domestic student in a veterinary science undergraduate degree course and will take six subjects this semester. The EFTSU at his institution is a standard annual program based on 50 units over five years, and the charge set by the provider for the year 2009 is $9500. Answer the three questions below.

(a) If Bill chooses repayment method 1, what is the fee amount payable for the first semester?

(b) If Bill chooses repayment method 2, what is the HELP liability assessed for the first semester?

(c) If Bill voluntarily pays $450 to the ATO in the second semester, how much will be credited to his HELP debt account?

2. Julian studied for three years before gaining his degree in accounting. He always deferred his HELP charges. He then went overseas for two years on a long working holiday. His father sent him the HELP information statements that the ATO kept issuing every 1 June and the latest one showed that he had an accumulated debt of $9756. He had earned much more than this in Europe, and now that he has returned to Australia he has asked for your help in deciding what to do. He will be starting his new job in Sydney next week. What do you advise?

case study question

Tom and Jan Masonry have a son, Joe, who has just enrolled at university in a building degree undergraduate course. The course will take three years to complete and this first semester Joe will take six subjects. If the EFTSU at his institution is a standard annual program based on 30 units over three years, what weighting will each of Joe's units carry this semester for HELP purposes?

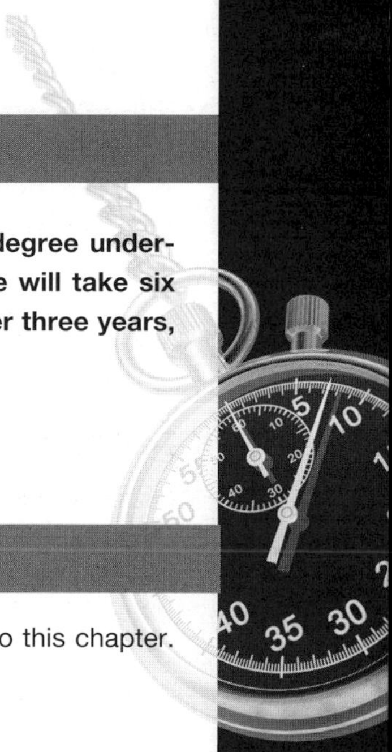

classroom activity

Inside the grid vertically, horizontally, diagonally, forwards and backwards are 18 words related to this chapter. See how many words you can find.

C	E	F	T	S	U	Z	D	M	G	S	I
E	O	X	Z	U	P	D	E	B	T	L	K
N	G	M	C	P	L	C	N	U	Q	S	W
S	Q	E	M	P	M	Q	D	B	L	P	X
I	R	T	A	O	H	E	L	P	S	D	V
S	U	H	O	R	N	Y	B	P	E	L	S
D	P	O	J	T	B	W	T	F	R	O	R
A	V	D	U	E	C	A	E	Y	B	X	E
T	M	N	K	D	U	R	G	A	F	A	H
E	I	U	P	F	R	O	N	T	L	X	G
T	Z	E	L	E	Q	D	E	O	K	T	I
S	W	I	D	B	S	X	Z	N	L	P	H

self-test question solution

The extra PAYG amount that should be withheld each week from your graduate employee's pay is $850 × 4% = $34

Notes

1. Details about HELP debts are contained in Part 4-1, Division 137 of the *Higher Education Support Act 2003*.
2. The 2008 student contribution bands and ranges for students commencing undergraduate degrees on or after 1 January 2008 are as follows:

Student contribution band	2008 student contribution range (per EFTSL) (for students commencing on or after 1 January 2008)
Band 3 (law, dentistry, medicine, veterinary science, accounting, administration, economics, commerce)	\$0–\$8499
Band 2 (mathematics, statistics, computing, built environment, health, engineering, science, surveying, agriculture)	\$0–\$7260
Band 1 (humanities, behavioural sciences, social studies, foreign languages, visual and performing arts)	\$0–\$5095
National priorities (education, nursing)	\$0–\$4077

For Commonwealth-supported students who commenced a course of study before 1 January 2008, the maximum student contribution that may be charged for accounting, administration, economics and commerce units is $7260.

3. Some universities set their own withdrawal or census dates that may be different (earlier) than the HECS-HELP census dates of 31 March and 31 August each year.
4. See section 26-20 of the *Income Tax Assessment Act 1997*.
5. See the *Fringe Benefits Tax Assessment Act 1986* and *A New Tax System (Fringe Benefits Reporting) Act 1999*. Since 1 April 1994 the law allows the HELP paid on behalf of an employee to be deductible, but it will also give rise to a taxable value of a benefit provided. No liability for GST is attached to HELP, thus no input tax credits are available to the employer.
6. The HELP liability is classed as a tax for the purposes of the 'interest on overpayments' provisions of the *Income Tax Assessment Act 1936*.
7. This amount of $2500 is an example of the HELP debt that would appear on the notice of assessment issued to the taxpayer. The balance of the HELP debt is not at present due and payable.
8. See Part IVC of the *Taxation Administration Act 1953*.

Child Support Agency

9

Chapter nine

Topics

After studying this chapter, you should be able to:

- **indicate the nature and role of the Child Support Agency (CSA)**
- **identify which persons are eligible for the Child Support Scheme, and set out the method for applying for child support**
- **indicate the options available for either party if there is dissatisfaction with the support assessment made by the CSA**
- **explain the obligations of employers under this scheme and how the employer is notified of these obligations.**

OVERVIEW

From 1 July 2008 the child support scheme changed dramatically. All parents who pay or receive child support are affected, even those who have drawn up private agreements. The Child Support Scheme, operating through the authority of the *Child Support (Registration and Collection) Act 1988*, the *Child Support (Assessment) Act 1989* and the *Child Support Legislation Amendment (Reform of the Child Support Scheme—New Formula and Other Measures) Act 2006*, collectively known as the Child Support Act, has as its aims and objectives to ensure that the support of children is shared fairly by the parents of those children, that the parents are equally responsible, that at least one parent will support the child and that a custodian receives assistance with support. The Scheme is administered by the **Child Support Agency (CSA)**, a section of the Department of Family and Community Services, which works closely with the ATO.

In 2004 the Australian government funded a ministerial taskforce to look into the Child Support Scheme. The taskforce released a report called *In the Best Interests of Children—Reforming the Child Support Scheme*. The main recommendations of the report were:

- a need for greater emphasis on shared parental responsibility and the importance of both parents remaining actively involved in parenting after separation
- a new method of calculating child support payments.

These recommendations have been implemented in three stages and were finally completed in 2008 as a direct result of the new legislation.

Under the new scheme, parents who have significant care of their children are advised to lodge a **parenting plan** with the CSA. This plan is used by both Centrelink and the CSA to calculate any benefits or payments. Alternatives to this are verbal or written agreements or a court order. The CSA acts as a mediator in many cases where it may be stressful for the parties to communicate. At all times, the welfare of the child or children is paramount.

This chapter examines the liability for child support and how this may affect the obligations of the employer. The method of application for assistance is set out. An example of how child support is calculated in a simple case is given in 'CSA in practice' at the end of the chapter, and finally the chapter looks at how the support will be paid and the methods available for parents where they disagree with the amount of child support calculated by the CSA.

A 'custodian' means any person who has daily care of the child; he or she need not be a parent of the child.

9.1 Child support liability

Parents who have separated, or any other persons who should be paid child support, need to understand how the CSA determines the liability for **child maintenance**. Any **custodian** can ask the CSA for a child **support assessment** and collection of supporting payments. Either the custodian or the **paying parent** can lodge a **child support agreement** if an arrangement has been privately agreed, but it is not a requirement of law. However, to ensure that the terms of the agreement are documented, it is quite a good idea to lodge this accord even if there is no requirement for the CSA to order collections or payments.

It is important to note that every person who is liable to pay child support under the *Child Support (Assessment) Act 1989* during a year of income is required to lodge a tax return for that year.

Application for an assessment is made using a special request form,[1] and the option is available for the support payments to be collected through the CSA via the Department of Social Security.

The forms used by all child support parties can be downloaded from the CSA's website (**www.csa.gov.au/forms/**) and either posted or sent electronically to the CSA. A new worksheet and calculator are available online for parents who separated after 1 July 2008 or who asked for a new child support calculation after this date.

It is desirable to apply for assessment, particularly if it is possible that payments will not be made regularly by the paying parent. Once an election is made to have the CSA collect **support payments**, this will remain in force for the whole time the recipient is receiving a payment from Centrelink.

Active reflection 9.1

Set out the major reasons why the child support legislation was introduced.

9.2 Separation of parents

The scheme was originally divided into two categories, based on the date of birth of the youngest child in the family or the date of separation of the parents.

- *Parents who separated on or after 1 October 1989, or have a child born after that date.* In this case there are two ways in which the scheme can apply:
  (a) A private agreement can be made between the parents, and if they wish this can be lodged with the CSA.
  (b) In the absence of such an agreement, the CSA can assess how much child support should be paid and a formula is used that has been developed in consultation with community groups (see Section 9.3). It is generally the person who has daily care of the children who will ask for assistance from the CSA.
- *Parents who separated before 1 October 1989 and do not have a child born on or after that date.* This section no longer applies to any child born prior to this date as he or she would be greater than 18 years of age and this Act would not apply[2] unless another order has been requested to allow the child to finish school or because of mental or physical impairment.

Western Australia is the only Australian state that has not referred to the Commonwealth its power to make laws about children whose parents are not married. This means that the Western Australian Parliament retains its powers to make laws about Western Australian children whose parents have never been married (WA ex-nuptial children), including child support laws. However, in October 2007 the WA Parliament passed laws to ensure a uniform code for child support throughout Australia.

For any child born while the parents were not married, documentary proof of parentage must be provided to ensure that the paying parent is in fact the parent who should support the child. This proof can be the child's birth certificate, a statutory declaration and adoption certificate or a court document.

For more information, telephone the CSA on **13 12 72** for general inquiries, **13 11 07** for automated quick information, or, for a free fax, dial **1800 062 610**. Explore the website at **www.csa.gov.au/guide/index.htm**, where a guide will explain many of the more complicated sections of the current changes and is available in PDF format at **www.csa.gov.au/schemereforms/reference-guide.aspx**. There are many worked examples in the guide that help in understanding these new laws.

- carers who receive child support but who are not the parent of the child
- parents who are not Australian residents or have other special circumstances.

Income variations

If either parent estimates that their income will drop by 15% or more, they may request a new assessment. The *Child Support (Assessment) Act 1989* provides a number of modifications to the basic formula. There are 10 different reasons why the CSA may vary a child support amount and these can be found on CSA's website if more information is required.

Active reflection

Calculate the child support percentage for a parent whose support income percentage is 65% and cost percentage is 45%.

9.4 Child support payments

The protected earnings rate is defined as the amount prescribed by regulation (section 4(1)). The weekly rate is prescribed as 75% of the maximum fortnightly basic rate of the Newstart Allowance, payable on 1 January each year, to a person who is over 21 and partnered, and has no dependent children (regulation 3).

The *Child Support (Registration and Collection) Act 1988* requires the employer to:

- deduct the child support amount specified (referred to as a **garnishee** order by the ATO)
- advise the employee in writing how much child support was deducted
- send the deduction to the CSA by the seventh of the month following the month in which the deductions were made
- advise the CSA of:
  - any variations in amounts deducted and reasons for the variations
  - any business changes such as change of name, address or ownership.

An employer will not be allowed to make child support deductions from wages below a minimum amount. This is referred to as the **protected earnings amount**. (See the Protected Earnings Amount Table on the CSA's website for the current amount.) The employer has an obligation to respect the employee's privacy. It is illegal to discriminate against an employee or a prospective employee because of his or her child support responsibilities. Any employer receiving a Notice Pursuant to Section 72A must make the payments that are prescribed in that notice.

Active reflection

How is child support collected from an employee and paid?

9.5 Agreements

It is important that parents with children from a previous relationship take action, if possible, to obtain child support for children in their care. Under the new scheme there are two types of agreements: binding agreements and limited agreements.

Binding agreements are those that:

- are in writing and signed by both parents
- are made after the parents have sought independent legal advice
- contain a certificate from the independent lawyer for each parent
- can be for any amount, even if it is less than the formula amount, if both parties agree
- can be ceased only by the forming of another binding agreement or by a court order.

For those parents receiving Family Tax Benefit Part A, this is based on the CSA's formula amount and is reviewed every three years.

Limited agreements are different to binding agreements in the following ways:

- there is no requirement for parents to obtain legal advice
- there must be a CSA formula assessment already existing
- the child support amount must be equal to or greater than the amount assessed by the CSA formula.

Finally, a new CSA **notional assessment** will be made every three years or when requested by a parent, and if the change is greater than 15% then either parent may end the agreement and request a new one.

Active reflection 9.5

What are the major differences between the two types of agreements that parents can make for child support?

9.6 Reassessment, change and maintenance action

Some examples of the grounds put forward for reassessment are:

- the complex nature of the parents' finances
- the special needs of a child
- the high costs of access
- other necessary commitments of either parent
- child support being provided as other benefits, such as payment of school fees.

If the custodian has a court order or court-registered agreement for the payment of either child or spouse maintenance, application for reassessment can be made using the appropriate form. Check the website at **www.csa.gov.au/**, where all the forms required can be obtained, and also keep up to date with any amounts that are regularly adjusted by the CSA.

9.6 Active reflection

Name five reasons why a parent may ask for a reassessment by the CSA.

CSA in practice

The simple example of the new child support amount is best calculated using a worksheet. For this case we have reproduced Table 3A from Schedule 1 of the Act.

Information

- John and Edith separated in 2007. They have three children aged 10, 6 and 3. (Refer to Table 3A below.)
- Edith is the primary carer and they have a child support assessment.
- John's taxable income for 2006/07 was $22 000. He also received $28 000 in foreign income.
- Edith's taxable income was $25 000 and she also had $2000 in net rental losses and $3000 in reportable fringe benefits.
- John cares for the three children between 14% and 34% of the time.
- Neither John nor Edith support any other children.

TABLE 3A COST OF CHILDREN, 2008: CHILDREN AGED 12 YEARS AND UNDER (APPORTIONED BETWEEN PARENTS)

Parents' combined child support income	1 child	2 children	3 or more children
$0–$27 378	17c for each $1	24c for each $1	27c for each $1
$27 379–$54 756	$4654 + 15c for each $1 over $27 378	$6571 + 23c for each $1 over $27 378	$7392 + 26c for each $1 over $27 378
$54 757–$82 134	$8761 + 12c for each $1 over $54 756	$12 868 + 20c for each $1 over $54 756	$14 510 + 25c for each $1 over $54 756
$82 135–$109 512	$12 046 + 10c for each $1 over $82 134	$18 344 + 18c for each $1 over $82 134	$21 355 + 24c for each $1 over $82 134
$109 513–$136 890	$14 784 + 7c for each $1 over $109 512	$23 272 +10c for each $1 over $109 512	$27 926 + 18c for each $1 over $109 512
Over $136 890	$16 700	$26 010	$32 854

Step 1 *Work out the child support income for each parent.*		
Parent's adjusted taxable income amount John = \$22 000 + \$28 000 = \$50 000 Edith = \$25 000 + \$2000 + \$3000 = \$30 000	**John** \$50 000	**Edith** \$30 000
Deduct self-support amount (\$18 252 for 2008)	\$18 252	\$18 252
Deduct a relevant dependant child amount (Neither John nor Edith have any other children)	Nil	Nil
Deduct a multi-case allowance amount	Nil	Nil
= Each parent's child support income amount	\$31 748	\$11 748
Step 2 *Determine the parent's combined child support income.*		
Add each parents child support income	\$31 748 + \$11 748	
= Combined child support income	\$43 496	
Step 3 *Calculate each parent's support income percentage.*		
Each parent's child support income	\$31 748	\$11 748
Each parent's child support income divided by the combined child support income	\$31 748 / \$43 496	\$11 748 / 43 496
= Each parent's support income percentage	73%	27%
Step 4 *Determine each parent's share of the care of the child (or children).*		
Each parent's share of the care of the child (or children)	14–34%	66–86%
Step 5 *Calculate each parent's cost percentage.*		
Use the percentage care from Step 4: refer to Table 9.1 in Section 9.3 above.	24%	76%
Step 6 *Determine each parent's child support percentage.*		
Each parents income percentage (from Step 3)	73%	27%
Less each parent's cost percentage (from Step 5)	24%	76%
= Each parent's child support percentage	49%	–49%
Step 7 *Work out the cost of the child (or children).* (Note: as John's child support percentage is positive, he needs to pay child support to Edith.)		
Total cost of three children less than 12 years of age as per the costs of children Table 3A = \$7392 + 0.26(\$43 496 – \$27 378)	\$11 583	
= Cost of each child (\$11 583 ÷ 3)	\$3861	
Step 8 *Work out the child support payable.*		
Each parent's child support percentage	49%	0%
Multiply the total cost of the children in Step 7 by the child support percentage (from Step 6) = \$11 583 × 49% (John only)	\$5676	
Amount of child support payable. **John is liable to pay Edith child support of \$1892 for each of the three children.** **This makes a total of \$5676 each year.**		

Learning check

- ✓ Calculate a simple basic formula for child support.
- ✓ Identify those separated parents who may be eligible for child support.
- ✓ Identify the obligations of employers with regards to a Notice Pursuant to Section 72A.
- ✓ Complete the forms necessary to advise the CSA of missed child support deductions, remittance of child support and changes of details of employees.

Taxation vocabulary

adjusted income
child maintenance
Child Support Agency (CSA)
child support agreement
child support formula
child support income
child support percentage
combined support income
cost percentage
costs of children tables
custodian
Family Tax Benefit
fixed annual rate
garnishee
income support payment
indexation factor
Maintenance Income Test
minimum annual rate
notional assessment
parenting plan
paying parent
percentage of care
protected earnings amount
self-support amount
support assessment
support income percentage
support payments

multiple-choice questions

Circle the correct response. (Answers to odd-numbered multiple-choice questions are provided on page 318.)

1. **The CSA operates to ensure that:**
   (i) separated parents are equally responsible for the support of their children
   (ii) at least one separated parent is responsible for the support of the children
   (iii) separated parents pay their fair share of support for their children
   (iv) the custodian receives assistance in supporting the children in daily care
   (a) (i) only (b) (i) and (ii) only (c) (i), (ii) and (iii) only (d) all of the above
2. **The CSA operates as part of:**
   (a) the ATO
   (b) the Department of Family and Community Services
   (c) Centrelink
   (d) the various state governments
3. **Child support assessments can be altered:**
   (a) only by the Child Support Review Office
   (b) by one dissatisfied parent lodging a declaration
   (c) only by lodging an agreement by both parties
   (d) by either agreement or the Child Support Review Office
4. **Payment for child support must be made:**
   (a) weekly (b) monthly (c) quarterly (d) yearly
5. **Parent A cares for their child 57% of the time and has a support income of $22 000. Parent B cares for their child 43% of the time and has a support income of $52 000. The child support percentage for Parent B is:**
   (a) 41% (b) 29% (c) –31% (e) 30%

quick-and-easy comprehension

Place a ✓ to indicate your response to each statement.

	STATEMENT	TRUE	FALSE
1.	**The custodian is the only person permitted to lodge a child support agreement.**	—	—
2.	**The CSA will act as a mediator in cases where it is stressful for the parents to communicate.**	—	—
3.	**After an assessment has been made, the paying parent is given the option of contributing to the support of the child.**	—	—
4.	**Parents who separated before 1 October 1989 and do not have a child born on or after that date may still be able to access child support assistance.**	—	—
5.	**The CSA collects spouse maintenance for a separated person.**	—	—

assessments

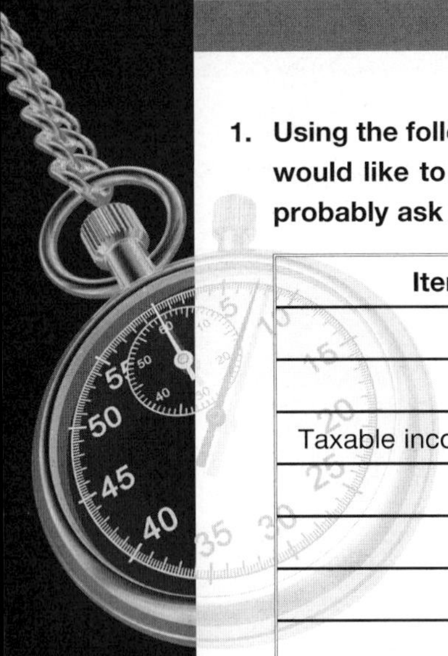

1. **Using the following checklist that has been designed for your office, fill in the remaining items that you would like to discuss with a client who wants to know about child support. For example, you would probably ask about the client's taxable income, third on the list.**

Item to discuss	Yes ✓	No ✓	Comments
Taxable income (client)	✓		$53 000

Other comments:

2. **Set out briefly the definitions of the following:**
   (a) combined support income
   (b) limited agreements
   (c) binding agreements
3. **How is the Family Tax Benefit affected by the new Child Support Scheme?**

case study questions

1. **Tom Masonry has asked you to explain 'protected earnings'. Use an example to show Tom what happens when an employer is required to garnishee wages for child support.**
2. **One of Colossal Constructions' employees, named Jim, separated from his wife in February 2006. An order from a support assessment has been sent to Tom Masonry requiring him to make a monthly deduction of $350 for child support from Jim's wages. Tom has asked you to advise him of his liabilities with regard to that order. What difference would it make if Jim were actually a subcontractor to the company, not an employee?**

classroom activity

Suppose that in a certain four-week period Tom Masonry could not deduct the $350 each week as required by the Notice Pursuant to Section 72A. Download the form concerning variations to child support deductions from www.csa.gov.au/forms/1648.pdf and complete the variation details.

Notes

1. See section 27(1) of the *Child Support (Assessment) Act 1989*.
2. See section 12 of the *Child Support (Assessment) Act 1989*.

State taxes and procedures

2

Part two

This part of the book examines the most common taxes levied by the various state governments and the Australian Capital Territory, collectively referred to as the 'states'. While the Commonwealth government at present collects all the income tax revenue and gives a proportion of this to each state, the states must also collect revenue to augment their expenditure. It is beyond the scope of this book to examine all the various taxes levied by the states.

Chapter 10 examines payroll tax, Chapter 11 transactions duties and Chapter 12 land tax. There is no 'In practice' segment in these chapters as each state has different rates, thresholds and requirements. However, the generic questions at the end of each chapter will allow the tax principles of each state to be applied. In each of the chapters an overview of the particular type of tax will be given and the commonalities listed. The subsections then set out specific details relating to Victoria, South Australia, Queensland, Western Australia, Tasmania, the Australian Capital Territory and New South Wales.

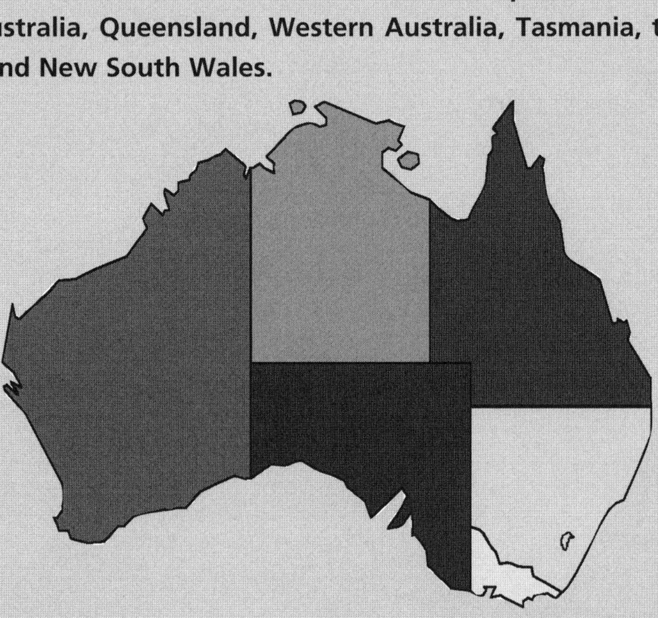

10

Payroll tax

Chapter ten

Topics

After studying this chapter, you should be able to:

- **examine the states' move towards harmonisation of payroll tax laws**
- **define and explain the nature of payroll tax, setting out what is taxed and when**
- **identify who is required to register for payroll tax purposes and explain the procedure for registration**
- **define 'wages' for the purpose of the various state Acts and identify what remuneration falls within this definition**
- **list any payments that are not subject to payroll tax**
- **explain the term 'general exemption' and set out how this affects payroll tax assessed, the deduction where employers are grouped and the calculation across state boundaries.**

OVERVIEW

Until 1971 the Commonwealth was the sole collector of **payroll tax**. In that year, each state took up the legislation through its own *Pay-roll Tax Act 1971*, together with its amendments and regulations. By 2008 the move towards harmonising all state payroll tax laws had begun with new and amended legislation operative in all of the states. However, most of the tax rates remain different.

'Employer' means any person who pays or is liable to pay any wages and includes the Crown in right in the state of Western Australia and a person who is an employment agent.

Payroll tax is payable by **employers** and is levied on the wages paid or payable, with monthly remittance of tax being required in most cases. The collection of this tax revenue helps the states to meet the costs of public services such as health, education, law and order, and public safety. Public institutions such as charities, religious and educational bodies and local government non-business activities are generally exempt from paying payroll tax.[1]

All the states require that every employer maintain proper books of account and that these records be held for a period of five years from the payroll dates. These books must be made available to officers of the Revenue Department if an inspection is required.

There has been a good deal of debate about the definition of 'payroll', and most of the states have been involved in a process of reviewing this definition and expanding it for taxing purposes. There is some degree of variance in tax rates, with both deduction and marginal rate systems being used. Most states, however, have fairly standard reporting policies. The most common practice is the use of online monthly return forms with an estimate of the general exemption already on the form or an embedded calculation as the details are completed. In the twelfth month, reconciliation to actual wages will determine the correct amount, if any, of the concession or threshold.

This chapter examines the registration procedures for liable employers, followed by the grouping provisions and calculation of payroll tax. It then looks at the current definitions of wages in each of the states that vary from the harmonised rules, and finally considers those wages that are at present exempt and the implications of third-party payments. As with all the chapters on state taxes, each state is dealt with fully in turn. Many of the questions at the end of the chapter are generic, although some are state-specific.

The chapter begins with an overview of the common characteristics of payroll tax legislation including grouping provisions between the states and the move towards harmonisation. It then considers Victoria, South Australia, Queensland, Western Australia, Tasmania, the Australian Capital Territory and New South Wales. Each section follows the same order, allowing an interstate comparison of the topics covered. See Table 10.1 for a quick rate reference guide.

TABLE 10.1 PAYROLL TAX: A QUICK STATE-BY-STATE RATE REFERENCE GUIDE

State	Payroll tax rate	Annual general exemption	Monthly general exemption
Victoria	4.95%	$550 000	$45 833
South Australia	5.00%	$552 000	$46 000
Queensland	4.75%	$1 000 000	$83 333
Western Australia	5.50%	$750 000	$62 500
Tasmania	6.10%	$1 010 000	$84 167
Australian Capital Territory	6.85%	$1 500 000	$125 000
New South Wales	5.75%	$623 000	$51 917

Commonalities

Registration

All employers are required to register for payroll tax purposes when weekly payrolls pass a certain threshold. The term **general exemption (GE)** is used in this chapter to apply to the payroll threshold as it is given in each state. Various terms have been used in the state pamphlets to describe this, such as 'prescribed amount', 'small business deduction' and 'business concession amount'. Now with the move towards harmonisation, most states have adopted the same terminology, so the meaning is common among all states.

Grouping provisions

All the states have introduced **grouping provisions**, which class as members of the one group any persons, corporations or companies that are deemed to be related to one another. The general thrust of all payroll tax legislation is to deem 50% or more common control as a group as per the *Corporations Act 2001* (Cwlth). Grouping affects the threshold available and members of the group are still required to register separately if any **taxable wages** are paid in that particular state. Generally, the state payroll tax will be paid only on the taxable wages paid in that particular state, but as a group member the threshold may not be available as it can be given only once for any particular group. The ACT has now joined the other states in allowing a designated group employer to claim the whole of the tax-free threshold on behalf of all members of the primary group. Previously the ACT used a special procedure for determining the group tax liability that shared the threshold among members. All employers in the group remain jointly and severally liable for payroll tax.

A designated group employer in relation to a group means the member of that group who for the time being is the designated member of that group.

Definition of wages

The definition of **wages** appears to be reasonably standard across Australia and could be said to include any wages, salary, commissions, bonuses and allowances paid or payable, whether at piecework rates or otherwise and whether paid or payable in cash or in kind to any employee. This definition now includes wages paid to apprentices unless expressly exempt by a particular state. Employment agents are deemed to be the employer, and as such they are liable for payroll tax on wages paid to another person who is engaged to perform services for a client. A *salary sacrifice* is the conversion of a cash component of a salary package into some other kind of remuneration. It is liable for payroll tax as it is classified as a payment in 'cash or kind for the services of an employee'. Payments made by a third party, or received by someone other than the employee, are taxable if they are paid in relation to an employee's services. All of the states have adopted the definition of a fringe benefit[2] and all now use the lower **grossed-up value** (type 2 factor; see Chapter 5, Section 5.2) of the **taxable value** of that benefit for payroll tax purposes. Also included in the definition of wages are **superannuation contributions** that are paid by the employer to an eligible fund, and any travelling and meal allowances paid to an employee, to the extent that they exceed a certain set rate per kilometre or amount per day for overnight accommodation.

Harmonisation

The first state to enact new payroll tax laws was Western Australia's *Pay-roll Tax Assessment Act 2002*. In 2007 the governments of Victoria, Queensland, Tasmania and New South Wales began the process of harmonisation of payroll tax legislation. The ACT has also brought into harmonisation many aspects of its payroll tax legislation. The new Victorian and New South Wales Acts became operative from 1 July 2007 and have already produced the initial harmonised Revenue Rulings for quite a number of areas of the legislation. In a bid to help reduce red tape for taxpayers, key aspects of the New South Wales and Victorian legislation were adopted by South Australia, Queensland and Tasmania effective from 1 July 2008 and by the ACT from 17 September 2008.

With reference to harmonising the grouping provisions, it appears that the entity entitled to claim the threshold in each state will be termed the 'designated group employer'. This employer must pay or have paid wages in excess of the threshold in that state to be eligible for nomination.

Payments of expenses for employees will be excluded only up to the prescribed limits set by the ATO each year and adopted by the states as part of harmonising their legislation. The following definitions are part of the new harmonised laws and standardise these expense allowances:

The motor vehicle exempt rate is the rate prescribed under the federal tax legislation in the *Income Tax Assessment Act 1997* (Cwlth) section 28-25. The exempt rate for daily travel allowance expenses is determined using the lowest capital city rate for the lowest salary band for the year. This is determined by the Commissioner of Taxation of the Commonwealth for the *Income Tax Assessment Act 1997* (Cwlth) section 900-50.

- *Motor vehicle allowances:* the exempt component is calculated using the formula: $E = K \times R$

  Where:

  E is the exempt component

  K is the number of business kilometres travelled during the financial year

  R is the exempt rate.

  The exempt rate is the rate prescribed under the federal income tax legislation for calculating a deduction for car expenses for a large car using the cents per kilometre method in the financial year immediately preceding the financial year in which the allowance is paid or payable.
- *Accommodation allowance:* the exempt rate for overnight accommodation allowances may be set by each state; however, in the absence of any such rate being expressly determined it is the total reasonable amount for daily travel allowance expense using the lowest capital city rate for the lowest salary band for the financial year as determined by the Commissioner of Taxation. These determinations are made by the Commissioner in June of each year and they set out the amounts that the Commissioner considers are reasonable for the following income year in relation to claims made for travel allowance expenses.

10.1 Victoria

Registration and collection procedures

Both Victoria and New South Wales now operate payroll tax under similar legislation, although the rates of tax remain different. An employer is required to register for payroll tax under the *Payroll Tax Act 2007* (Vic) and the *Taxation Administration Act 1997* (Vic) when the gross Australian wages exceed the monthly threshold of $45 833. Registration must be made within seven days of the end of the month in which the wages as defined first exceed the threshold. The method of calculation of tax is by the single marginal rate of 4.95% after the GE of $550 000 per year has been exceeded.

Example

A firm pays $85 000 wages for the month. The payroll tax for that month, prima facie, would be $1938.75, that is, $39 167 ($85 000 – $45 833) × 4.95%.

See the Victorian government's website (**www.sro.vic.gov.au**) for more information.

Group members—methods of calculation

Groups operate in Victoria with a **designated group employer (DGE)** system. Group provisions apply in Victoria, and the group must nominate a DGE. The following example shows how the system works.

Example

Suppose that a firm pays wages of $85 000 every month in Victoria but also belongs to a group. The group's total Australian wages amount to $4 000 000 per annum. If the firm is nominated as the DGE, the payroll tax payable on the Victorian wages, calculated after arriving at the GE, would be:

$$\text{GE available} = \text{GE} - \left[\frac{\text{Total interstate wages}}{\text{Total Australian wages}} \times \text{GE}\right]$$

$$\text{GE available} = \$550\,000 - \left[\frac{\$2\,980\,000}{\$4\,000\,000} \times \$550\,000\right]$$

$$= \$550\,000 - \$409\,750 = \$140\,250$$

Payroll tax is then calculated for the month using the notional yearly GE of $140 250, giving $11 688 per month. Thus wages of $85 000 less the GE allowed of $11 688 gives taxable wages of $73 313 × 4.95%, which is $3629 in payroll tax for that month. The concession is actually based on estimated wages, and will in fact be documented on the preprinted monthly return forms. An adjustment takes place at the end of the financial year.

The State Revenue Office is encouraging customers to lodge their reconciliation electronically. If a firm cannot do so, it can telephone **(03) 9628 0060** to discuss alternative arrangements.

If the firm used in the example is *not* the DGE, the full 4.95% on the wages in Victoria will be payable. That is, $85 000 × 4.95% is $4208 in payroll tax for the month.

Definition of wages

As well as the general definition of wages, Victoria also includes **accrued annual leave** paid on termination. Before January 1996 this was exempt; however, after this date it became taxable, and therefore is apportioned accordingly.

Directors' fees are taxable and the provisions operate to tax payments where contracts are essentially for labour and where the contractor works predominantly for a principal. This seems to follow the general principles established by the ATO regarding the concept of labour. It is also important to remember that it is the **gross wage** that is taxable; thus it includes employees' own contributions to a superannuation scheme, as well as any other deductions from the pay of employees. If GST is included in a wage paid, then the GST amount is excluded from payroll tax.

The employer's or group employer's total Australian wages paid or payable are subject to payroll tax when they exceed the prescribed threshold.

Exempt wages and third-party payments

In Victoria, wages paid that are prescribed **workers compensation** payments (not make-up pay) are exempt. **Termination payments** to either former employees or their estates that are paid as compensation for loss of employment as a result of forced redundancy or severance are also exempt. Gratuitous payments and payments to employees for leave to give service in the Defence Forces or to fight bushfires are also free from payroll tax.[3]

Exemptions from payroll tax include charities, religious and educational bodies, and local government non-business activities. The *Education and Training Reform Act 2006* exempts the wages of 'new entrant' apprentices and trainees approved by the Commission. The Act extends exemption to wages paid or payable for maternity and adoption leave and applies to female employees taking paid maternity leave in respect of a pregnancy. It does not apply to male employees taking paid paternity leave. The adoption leave exemption is applicable to both male and female employees taking paid adoption leave. The exemption applies irrespective of whether the leave is taken before or after the birth or adoption. Wages are also exempt wages if they are paid or payable to an Aboriginal person who is employed under an employment project.

10.2 South Australia

Registration and collection procedures

An employer, whether or not as a group member, is liable, under the *Pay-roll Tax Act 1971* (SA), the *Pay-roll Tax Regulations 2001*, the *Pay-roll Tax (Harmonisation Project) Amendment Act 2008* and the *Taxation Administration Act 1996* (SA), to apply for registration and to lodge returns and payments of tax within seven days of the close of the month in which the taxable wages are paid or payable. These taxable wages are so liable if the monthly amount exceeds the threshold of \$46 000, although for ease of administration RevenueSA recommends registration when the employer's wages bill consistently exceeds \$10 615 per week. The method of calculation is by a single marginal rate of 5.0% on the amount per year that exceeds the GE of \$552 000. The government has announced that this rate will drop to 4.95% on 1 July 2009.

Example

A firm pays \$85 000 wages for the month. The payroll tax for that month, prima facie, would be \$1950; that is, \$39 000 (\$85 000 – \$46 000) × 5.0%.

Payroll tax payments can now be made via the Internet. Once established, the taxpayer can log onto the site at **www.bizgate.sa.gov.au** using the allocated number, and then enter wage and deduction details. For more information, telephone **(08) 8226 3793** or search the website at **www.treasury.sa.gov.au/revenuesa** for details.

Group members—methods of calculation

Groups in South Australia operate with a **designated group employer (DGE)** system. Grouping provisions operate with the nomination of a DGE, who must then determine the availability of the GE as a proportion of total Australian wages. All other group members will pay a flat rate of 5.0% tax on all South Australian wages.

Example

Suppose that a firm pays wages of \$85 000 every month in South Australia but also belongs to a group. The total Australian wages of the group is \$4 000 000 per annum. The GE that the firm can claim is calculated as follows:

$$GE = \$522\,000 - \left[\frac{\$2\,980\,000}{\$4\,000\,000} \times \$522\,000 \right]$$

The notional annual GE is \$140 760. The monthly GE would be \$11 730. Thus, the payroll tax payable for the month is 5.0% × (\$85 000 less \$11 730), which is \$3664.

If the employer was *not* the DGE, then the payroll tax payable would be \$85 000 × 5.0% = \$4250.

Definition of wages

South Australia also includes in the definition of wages for payroll tax purposes, **termination payments** to either former employees or their estates. Other items now included in wages paid or payable are amounts paid under certain contracts for service. This seems to follow the general principles established by the ATO regarding the concept of labour. It is also important to remember that it is the **gross wage** that is taxable; thus it includes employees' own contributions to a superannuation scheme, as well as any other deductions from the pay of employees.

Service contract payments are liable unless they are for 90 days or less in the financial year, or they are provided by a contractor offering services to the general public. Any GST amount in the wages paid is disregarded for payroll tax purposes. Employment agents are also liable, as are all non-cash benefits. If in doubt about any item, employers should seek specific clarification from RevenueSA on **(08) 8204 9880**.

Exempt wages and third-party payments

All the states exempt wages paid as **workers compensation** payments. In South Australia, ex-gratia payments and payments to employees for leave to give service in the Defence Forces are also free from payroll tax. The exemptions apply to all public benevolent bodies and local government non-business activities. Fire-fighters' wages are also exempt under the *Fire and Emergency Services Act 2005*.

Additional exempt third-party payments are wages paid or payable to an employee engaged under a contract of training that is registered under the *Training and Skills Development Act 2008*. Contracts where the contractor

Exempt wages and third-party payments

All the states exempt wages paid as **workers compensation** payments. Payments in lieu of notice, redundancy or severance paid in Queensland to either former employees or their estates are treated as exempt for payroll tax purposes. Wages of apprentices employed under the *Vocational Education, Training and Employment Act 2000* are exempt while they are working as apprentices or trainees. Ex-gratia payments and payments to employees for leave to give service in the Defence Forces are also free from payroll tax. For more information, check **www.osr.qld.gov.au/** or telephone the revenue office on **1300 301 546** or request a Rev-Q-Fax on **1300 300 089**.

Although the exemptions also apply to charities, religious and educational bodies and local government non-business activities, certain conditions apply.

Queensland applies a penalty of 75% of the amount assessed to late payment of payroll tax and this may be increased by 20% if required by the Commissioner. Check out the website **www.osr.qld.gov.au/taxes/payroll/index.shtml** for Queensland payroll tax changes.

10.4 Western Australia

Registration and collection procedures

In Western Australia payroll tax is collected under the *Pay-roll Tax Assessment Act 2002* (WA) and its regulations and amendments, and any employer who, during a month, pays or is liable to pay wages anywhere in Australia at a level in excess of $14 423 per week may be liable for payroll tax. If an employer is a member of a group, and during a month pays or is liable to pay any wages, then within seven days after the close of that month the employer must apply for payroll tax registration. The single marginal rate is presently set at 5.5%.

Employers who are registered or who have applied for registration will self-assess their payroll tax and furnish returns each month based on an estimate of the previous year's actual wages paid. For more information, check the website at **www.dtf.wa.gov.au/cms/dtf_index.asp** or telephone the payroll tax enquiry line on **(08) 9262 1300**; for a fax call **(08) 9262 1348**.

The annual wages threshold is applied to determine whether an employer is liable for payroll tax, and this GE amount has been set at $750 000 per year or $62 500 per month.

Example

A firm pays $85 000 wages for the month. It is subject to a tax rate of 5.5% that is applied to the amount of payroll above the threshold. The amount per month that will be subject to tax is as follows:

$22 500 ($85 000 – $62 500) × 5.5% = $1238

Group members—methods of calculation

In Western Australia, an employer who is a member of a group is required to pay tax only on the payroll paid or payable in Western Australia. It is mandatory for an employer who has, or is a member of a group that has, an expected payroll tax liability equal to or greater than $100 000 per annum to lodge and pay their payroll tax return via WA Revenue Online (ROL). From 1 July 2009 the Western Australian Commissioner will have the discretion to de-group certain commonly controlled family entities if they are run independently. An example would be where one brother operates a plumbing business while the other brother runs a hair salon. These are considered stand-alone businesses that should not be caught under the common grouping provisions.

Example

Suppose that AB Pty Ltd pays wages of $85 000 every month in Western Australia but also belongs to a group. The group's total Australian wages amount to $4 000 000. If AB Pty Ltd was nominated as the **designated group employer (DGE)**, the GE would be:

$$\text{GE available} = \left[\frac{\text{Total WA wages}}{\text{Total Australian wages}} \times \text{GE}\right]$$

$$\text{GE available} = \left[\frac{\$1\,020\,000}{\$4\,000\,000} \times \$750\,000\right]$$

GE available for the year to the DGE = $191 250

Payroll tax is then calculated for the month as follows:

WA wages	$1 020 000
Less GE	$191 250
Taxable p.a.	$828 750

Thus, $69 063 monthly taxable wages at 5.5% is $3798 in payroll tax. This amount would be paid each month and reconciliation will take place after 12 months when actual wages are known.

If the firm was not the DGE, then 5.5% of total wages paid in Western Australia would be payable—that is, $4675 ($85 000 × 5.5%) each month.

Definition of wages

Also included in the definition of wages in Western Australia are payments for **long service leave**, **accrued annual leave** and **accrued sick leave** paid to an employee on termination, eligible termination payments and golden handshakes. Some wages paid or payable under certain service contracts might also be included in payroll tax amounts. If an employer–employee relationship exists between the employer and the contract worker, payments to that worker are classified as wages. The definition of taxable wages also includes **superannuation contributions** paid by the employer. It is important to remember that it is the **gross wage** that is taxable; thus it includes employees' own contributions to a superannuation scheme, as well as any other deductions from the pay of employees.

As explained in the section above on harmonisation, travelling and overnight accommodation allowances over and above prescribed rates are liable, unless they are directly reimbursed to the employee.

Exempt wages and third-party payments

All the states exempt wages paid as **workers compensation** payments. In Western Australia, payments to employees for leave to give service in the Defence Forces are free from payroll tax. Payroll tax is not payable on any component of wages that is directly attributed to the GST.

Exemption from payroll tax is given for wages paid to all apprentices under the *Industrial Training Act 1975*. The exemptions apply also to charities, religious and educational bodies, and local government non-business activities.

There are also **anti-avoidance provisions** that allow the Commissioner of Payroll Tax to serve a notice of intention to deem a person an employer for payroll tax purposes.

10.5 Tasmania

Registration and collection procedures

The legislation for these calculations is contained in Schedule 1 of the *Payroll Tax Act 2008 (Tas)*.

The *Payroll Tax Act 2008* came into effect on 1 July 2008 and ensures that any employer who pays wages exceeding $19 423 per week must register for payroll tax purposes. The GE of $1 010 000 is now available to all employers, and the excess over this amount is currently taxed at the rate of 6.1%.

Example

Assume the following:

- An employer pays Tasmanian taxable wages of $1 020 000.
- The employer is *not* a member of a group, does not pay interstate wages and has been a registered employer for the full year. (If registered for only part of the year, the GE is reduced proportionately.)
- The current threshold (GE) is $1 010 000 and the tax rate is 6.1%.

Payroll tax payable annually will be:

(1 020 000 – 1 010 000) × 6.1%
= $10 000 × 6.1%
= $610

Now assume the following:

- This employer has other interstate Australian wages totalling $1 320 000 per annum.
- The employer is *not* a group member and has Tasmanian taxable wages of $1 020 000.
- The employer was a registered employer for the full year.

The GE will have to be reduced as follows:

$$\text{GE available} = \text{GE} - \left[\frac{\text{Total interstate wages}}{\text{Total Australian wages}} \times \text{GE}\right]$$

$$\text{GE available} = \$1\,010\,000 - \left[\frac{\$1\,320\,000}{\$2\,340\,000} \times \$1\,010\,000\right]$$

Thus the GE available = $579 744
Payroll tax payable annually will be:
($1 010 000 – $579 744) × 6.1%
$440 256 × 6.1% = $26 856

Group members—methods of calculation

The tax liabilities for Tasmanian firms are now similar to other states, and if an employer is a member of a group, the general exemption may be claimed by the **designated group employer (DGE)** using the calculations and formulae outlined in the following example.

Example

Assuming the firm in the first example is a member of a group, it is the DGE and is registered for the whole of the financial year. Other members of the group have Tasmanian wages of $1 480 000. Therefore the GE is calculated as follows:

$$\text{GE available} = GE - \left[\frac{\text{Total interstate wages}}{\text{Total Australian wages}} \times GE\right]$$

$$\text{GE available} = \$1\,010\,000 - \left[\frac{\$1\,320\,000}{\$3\,820\,000} \times \$1\,010\,000\right]$$

GE available = $660 995

Thus payroll tax payable annually for this DGE is:

($1 020 000 – $660 995) × 6.1%

$359 005 × 6.1% = $21 899

The monthly amount payable would be approximately $1825.

All other group members must pay payroll tax on their total wages as they are not eligible for any GE.

Definition of wages

Other items now included in Tasmanian wages paid or payable are amounts paid under certain contracts for service. This seems to follow the general principles established by the ATO regarding the concept of labour. Contracts are liable unless they are for 90 days or less in any financial year, or are provided by a contractor offering services to the general public at a cost that exceeds $500 000 per year. It is also important to remember that it is the **gross wage** that is taxable; thus it includes employees' own contributions to a superannuation scheme, as well as any other deductions from the pay of employees. Any GST embedded in wages will not be taken into account for payroll tax.

Any termination payments, either voluntary or forced, that are in respect of employment will be included in payrolls for taxing. **Superannuation contributions** paid by the employer are part of taxable wages for payroll tax purposes. For more information, check the website at **www.tres.tas.gov.au/** or telephone **(03) 6233 6154**.

Exempt wages and third-party payments

All the states exempt wages paid as **workers compensation** payments. In Tasmania, payments to either former employees or their estates in the form of golden handshakes or special severance pay will be exempt from payroll tax, as this is considered by Tasmania to be outside the meaning of the term 'in respect of employment'.[4] Payments to employees for leave to give service in the Defence Forces are also free from payroll tax.

A rebate is available for wages paid to apprentices under the Tasmanian Trainee Apprentice Incentive Scheme (TTAIS) if it is within the meaning of the *Vocational and Educational Training Act 1994*. However, these rebates are being phased out and will disappear totally by 2010.

The exemptions extend to partnership drawings and apply to charities, religious and educational bodies and local government non-business activities. The *Taxation Administration Act 1997* (Tas) has operated since 1 July 1998 and administers all payroll tax.

Anti-avoidance provision

The legislation contains an **anti-avoidance provision** in respect of contracts (section 3B) to help curb certain schemes that use artificial arrangements to qualify for exclusion under sections 3A(4)(b) and (c) (the 90 days and 180 days provisions). The Commissioner has the power to exclude certain 'relevant contracts' under the provision of the Act. If the Commissioner is not satisfied that the businesses of the parties to the contracts are:

- carried on independently of each other, and
- carried on without an intention of avoiding or evading payment of payroll tax,

the Commissioner may determine that the contracts are 'relevant contracts' for payroll tax purposes (Payroll Tax Guide to Employers, 2008, p. 13).

10.6 Australian Capital Territory

Registration and collection procedures

The *Payroll Tax Act 1987* as amended by the *Payroll Tax Amendment Act 2008* deems that employers making payments exceeding \$28 846 per week must register for payroll tax purposes. Interacting with this legislation is the *Taxation Administration Act 1999*. The ACT allows an employer to claim a GE of \$1 500 000. This threshold is available to all employers, and the tax is calculated using the current rate of 6.85%.

Example

Assume that an ACT employer pays monthly taxable wages of \$140 000, has been a registered employer for the full year and is not a member of a group. The amount of payroll tax for the month, prima facie, would be calculated as follows: (\$140 000 – \$125 000) × 6.85% = \$15 000 × 6.85% = \$1028.

Group members—methods of calculation

In the ACT, there is now a scheme whereby a **designated group employer (DGE)** can claim the whole of the tax-free threshold on behalf of all members of the primary group.

The DGE must be liable to pay payroll tax for the whole of the financial year; otherwise the amount of GE available will be reduced proportionately. The GE is also affected by all wages paid in Australia and will be reduced as follows:

The ACT Payroll Tax legislation for these calculations is contained in the *Taxation Administration Act 1999*, section 139.

$$\textit{GE available} = GE - \left[\frac{\textit{Total interstate wages}}{\textit{Total Australian wages}} \times GE \right]$$

Example

Assume that the firm in the first example is the nominated DGE and has annual wages of $1 680 000. The other group member in ACT pay wages of $820 000. The group's Australia-wide wages are $3 820 000. The group's ACT taxable wages total $2 500 000 therefore the interstate wages total $1 320 000. Assume the DGE firm was liable for payroll tax for the whole year of 365 days. Using the above equation the calculation of the GE available to the DGE is as follows:

$$\textit{GE available} = \$1\,500\,000 - \left[\frac{\$1\,320\,000}{\$3\,820\,000} \times \$1\,500\,000 \right]$$

GE available = $981 675

Note: The other ACT firm must pay 6.85% of $820 000.

The DGE pays payroll tax as follows:

($1 680 000 – $981 675) × 6.85%

$698 325 × 6.85% = $47 835 per year.

Definition of wages

Wages, for the purpose of determining ACT payroll tax liability, include all employer-funded **superannuation contributions** made on and since 1 July 1996. Other items now included in wages paid or payable are amounts paid under certain contracts for service. Since 1 July 2000 the payments made under a service contract have the payroll tax liability calculated on the payment less any GST component. This seems to follow the general principles established by the ATO regarding the concept of labour and the treatment of GST. Contracts are liable unless they are for 90 days or less in any financial year, or are provided by a contractor offering services to the general public at a cost that exceeds $500 000 per year. It is also important to remember that it is the **gross wage** that is taxable; thus it includes employees' own contributions to a superannuation scheme, as well as any other deductions from the pay of employees.

Any termination payments, either voluntary or forced, that are in respect of employment will be included in payrolls for taxing.

Exempt wages and third-party payments

All the states exempt wages paid as **workers compensation** payments. In the ACT, payments in lieu of notice, ex-gratia payments and payments to employees who are 'new starters' (that is, employed in industry for the first time) and who are undertaking eligible training as set out in the *Training and Tertiary Education Act 2003* are exempt wages. Payments for leave to give service in the Defence Forces are also free from payroll tax.

Penalties

Division 2 of Part 5 of the *Taxation Administration Act 1999* sets out the circumstances in which a tax default may incur the imposition of penalty tax. The rate of penalty tax will be dependent on the circumstances surrounding the tax default. Interest will be charged on any overdue payment of tax. Interest rates are reviewed every six months. For more information, telephone **(02) 6207 0085** or **(02) 6207 0088**, or request a facsimile from **(02) 6207 0090**.

Also go to **www.revenue.act.gov.au**, where there is updated information on payroll tax in the ACT.

10.7 New South Wales

Registration and collection procedures

In 2007 the governments of New South Wales and Victoria began the process of harmonisation of payroll tax legislation. The initial harmonised Revenue Rulings for quite a number of areas of the legislation have been issued and these two states are gradually bringing all their payroll tax laws into synchronisation.

Any employer who pays or is liable to pay wages, either in cash or kind, as defined in the *Payroll Tax Act 2007* and the *Taxation Administration Act 1996* (NSW), where the value of those wages exceeds the threshold level of $623 000 per annum, is liable to register for payroll tax.[5] If the monthly wages exceed $51 917, the employer must register within seven days of the end of that month. The method of calculation is a single marginal rate of 5.75%, down on 1 January 2009 from 6.0%. The rate will be further reduced to 5.65% from 1 January 2010. The first $623 000 is given as a GE. Check the website at **www.osr.nsw.gov.au** for rate changes.

It is important to note that, irrespective of where the wages are paid, if they are for services wholly performed in New South Wales then payroll tax is payable in New South Wales.

Example

A firm pays $85 000 wages for the month of January 2009. The payroll tax for that month, prima facie, would be $1902; that is, ($85 000 – $51 917) × 5.75%. = $33 083 × 5.75%.

Group members—methods of calculation

In New South Wales since 1 July 2003 the grouping definition also includes 'the carrying on of a trust'.

Grouping affects the GE available. Members of a group are still required to register separately if any **taxable wages** are paid in that particular state. Generally, the state payroll tax will be paid only on the taxable wages paid in that particular state, but as a group member the GE may not be available because it can be given only once for any particular group. The groups operate with a **designated group employer (DGE)** system.

In New South Wales one member may claim the threshold and the other members must then pay tax at the flat rate of 5.75% on total taxable wages. If the group also pays wages in other states, the GE must be reduced by the ratio of the group's **interstate wages** to Australian wages, as follows:

$$\textit{GE available} = \textit{GE} - \left[\frac{\textit{Total interstate wages}}{\textit{Total Australian wages}} \times \textit{GE} \right]$$

Example

	$
The DGE firm's total wages per annum	1 020 000
Total Australian group wages	4 000 000
Interstate wages	2 980 000
GE available	158 865
Taxable wages for the firm if nominated DGE	861 135
Payroll tax due on taxable wages for year	**49 515**

If the firm was not the nominated DGE in the group, then tax would be payable on the total firm's wages for the year, resulting in a payroll tax liability of $58 650.

Definition of wages

Since 1 July 2003 the definition of wages in New South Wales has been extended to include any distribution to a person as a beneficiary under a trust in lieu of wages for work done by that person for the trust. Work that constitutes the provision of services to the trustee of the trust, or for the purposes of a business conducted by the trustee of the trust, will be considered to be work done for the trust. Payroll also includes golden handshakes and the distributions or payments made to members of trusts for services rendered.

For more information on New South Wales FBT payroll, check the website at **www.osr.nsw.gov.au/**. To ease compliance, businesses can use one-twelfth of the previous year's FBT values, then make an adjustment at the end of the payroll tax year. Other items now included in wages paid or payable are amounts paid under certain service contracts. This seems to follow the general principles established by the ATO regarding the concept of labour. It is also important to remember that it is the **gross wage** that is taxable; thus it includes employees' own contributions to a superannuation scheme, as well as any other deductions from the pay of employees. Any GST component embedded in these payments is ignored for payroll tax calculations.

For the purposes of calculating payroll tax, all wages paid in every state by an employer or group must be taken into account to enable the correct rate of tax to be applied. The New South Wales portion of taxable wages will then be liable to tax. Service contracts are liable unless they are a type of service that is required by an employer for less than 180 days in a financial year. These payments are exempt even though an individual contractor may have worked for more than 90 days in the same financial year.[6]

Policy payments of accident insurance, made for key person employees, are *not* exempt from payroll tax. It is considered that payments of this nature fall within the definition of salary and wages under the legislation.

Accrued sick leave, **accrued annual leave** and **long service leave** paid as lump sums on termination of employment are included in the definition of wages for payroll tax purposes.

Exempt wages and third-party payments

New South Wales exempts **workers compensation** payments and reimbursement of the exact amount of an employee's receipted business expense. Previously, wages paid or payable to an employee who is registered under the *Apprenticeship and Traineeship Act 2001* were fully exempt. New arrangements for the payment of payroll tax for apprentices and trainees in

New South Wales took effect from 1 July 2008 and thus the exemption no longer applies. All employers are now required to include wages and salaries paid to apprentices and new entrant trainees in their payroll tax calculation. A rebate scheme replaces the exemption and is offset against monthly payroll tax payments.

Payments to employees for leave to give service in the Defence Forces are exempt. Exemptions also apply to charities, religious and educational bodies and local government non-business activities. The wages paid to volunteer members of a rural fire brigade under the *Rural Fires Act 1997* are exempt from payroll tax.

On 1 July 2006 a new scheme called the Payroll Tax Incentive Scheme commenced. This scheme is planned to act as an incentive to employers in areas where unemployment is highest. Eligible areas may be found on the website **www.business.nsw.gov.au/ptis**. The scheme is planned to run until 30 June 2009, although employers who are already in the scheme at this date may remain in it until 2011. The following table outlines the benefits to employers:

Year	1	2	3	4	5
Percentage rebate	100%	100%	100%	66.6%	33.3%
Maximum rebate	$144 000	$144 000	$144 000	$95 904	$47 952

Employers will still need to pay the payroll tax liability, but will then be able to claim a rebate from the Department of State and Regional Development.

Avoidance

The new amendments ensure that, where a company has not paid its payroll tax as required in a notice of assessment, the Chief Commissioner of State Revenue can serve notice on the directors and certain former directors, stating that they will be jointly and severally liable to the tax if the default has not been rectified within a specified period. These amendments are in reply to the so-called phoenix companies—businesses wound up by the directors to avoid paying debts. In most cases the same directors or other persons associated with the business would start another company to carry on the same business, thus avoiding the tax. This practice has been a particular concern in the construction industry.

Learning check

- ✓ Obtain relevant payroll taxation rates from the State Revenue Office.
- ✓ Complete a payroll taxation registration.
- ✓ Calculate the monthly remuneration amount for an employer and the corresponding payroll taxation liability.
- ✓ Calculate the annual remuneration amount for an employer and the subsequent payroll tax payable or refundable.
- ✓ Complete a reconciliation.

Taxation vocabulary

accrued annual leave
accrued sick leave
anti-avoidance provisions
designated group employer (DGE)
employers
general exemption (GE)
gross wage
grossed-up value
grouping provisions
interstate wages
long service leave
payroll tax
superannuation contributions
taxable value
taxable wages
termination payments
wages
workers compensation

multiple-choice questions

Circle the correct response. (Answers to odd-numbered multiple-choice questions are provided on page 318.)

1. **A single employer in your state must register when the taxable payroll reaches a set amount in any:**
   (a) week (b) month (c) quarter (d) year
2. **Any group employer must register:**
   (a) when wages paid or payable are less than the GE
   (b) when wages paid or payable are greater than the GE
   (c) when wages paid or payable are equal to the GE
   (d) regardless of the GE
3. **A member of a group who is the designated group employer pays 75% of the group's total annual wages of $950 000. The annual threshold is set at $600 000, so the monthly exemption available will be:**
   (a) $450 000 (b) $37 500 (c) $50 000 (d) nil
4. **A member of a group who is not the designated group employer pays 75% of the group's total wages of $950 000. The annual threshold is set at $600 000, so the monthly exemption available will be:**
   (a) $450 000 (b) $37 500 (c) $50 000 (d) nil
5. **If an employee received fringe benefits of $29 000 being the taxable value of a motor vehicle benefit and $10 000 being the taxable value of a loan benefit, what amount would be considered part of the definition of wages for the firm's payroll tax?**
   (a) $39 000 (b) $72 897 (c) $74 852 (d) $80 522

quick-and-easy comprehension

Place a ✓ to indicate your response to each statement.

STATEMENT	TRUE	FALSE
1. Workers compensation payments are exempt from payroll tax.	—	—
2. Accrued sick leave, annual leave and long service leave are exempt payments.	—	—
3. Payrolls must include Australia-wide wages for general exemption calculations.	—	—
4. Local government non-business employers are required to register only if their payroll exceeds the threshold.	—	—
5. Wages paid in public benevolent institutions are exempt Australia-wide.	—	—

assessments

1. **A non-DGE firm, which is 39% controlled by an interstate corporation, pays wages of $35 000 every week in your state. Apply the payroll tax laws for your state and calculate any annual liability the firm may have.**

2. A non-DGE firm, which is 89% controlled by an interstate corporation, pays wages of $35 000 every week in your state. Apply the payroll tax laws for your state and calculate any annual liability the firm may have.

3. A DGE firm, which is 89% controlled by an interstate corporation, pays wages of $35 000 every week in your state, and the group's other Australian wages (all paid outside your state) are estimated at $2 850 000. Apply the payroll tax laws for your state and calculate any annual liability the firm may have.

4. The following list represents monthly payments made by an employer entitled to the threshold. However, the firm is not a DGE nor a group member. Determine the amounts that would be included for payroll tax purposes and the monthly payroll tax payable in your state.

Details of monthly payments	**$**
Net wages paid to employees	125 000
PAYG tax withheld	31 215
Superannuation paid for employees	14 065
Contractor payments for labour supplied	34 000
Contract payments for materials supplied	51 250
Taxable value of fringe benefits	6 000
Total payments	**261 565**

5. How does your state value fringe benefits for payroll tax purposes? Using $15 000 as the taxable value of the benefit for one year, show the amount to be included in the payroll in one month.

6. If a firm paid wages of $1 550 000 a year in your state, a total of $3 250 000 Australia-wide and was not a member of a group, set out the payroll tax liability showing what amount might be due and payable in that year.

classroom activities

A significant word in the payroll tax legislation containing 12 letters is spelled out in the puzzle below, row by row, starting at the top left-hand corner. Each letter in the word is represented by a number between 1 and 9 as shown in the following alphabet key. You will need to first solve the number puzzle to find the keys to unlocking the word. The numbers around the puzzle grid represent the totals of the rows or columns. Once you have worked out the numbers for the three rows, match these numbers to the alphabet key to find the word. Note that some numbers may represent more than one letter. For example, the number 5 could be E, N or W.

Alphabet key

A	B	C	D	E	F	G	H	I	J	K	L	M
1	**2**	**3**	**4**	**5**	**6**	**7**	**8**	**9**	**1**	**2**	**3**	**4**
N	O	P	Q	R	S	T	U	V	W	X	Y	Z
5	**6**	**7**	**8**	**9**	**1**	**2**	**3**	**4**	**5**	**6**	**7**	**8**

Puzzle

	5	7		30
1				13
2		6	5	22
12	16	22	15	

Notes

1. For further information on the various state taxes a very good publication that may be of some assistance is D. Collins & N. Warren (2007), *The States and the GST: Demystifying Australian Federal/State Financial Arrangements*, Australian Tax Research Foundation, Sydney, Information Series 4.
2. For the purposes of payroll tax, a fringe benefit means a fringe benefit under the *Fringe Benefits Tax Assessment Act 1986* (Cwlth). Since 1 July 2003 the value of fringe benefits is the value returnable to the ATO on the fringe benefits return. This means that the amount returnable for payroll tax is the same as the returnable grossed-up amount for the ATO, and this helps simplify compliance for employers.
3. In Victoria rulings are issued to clarify those areas where the definitions seem unclear. Golden handshakes and termination payments made because of voluntary retirement are all classified as part of an employer's payroll.
4. The Commissioner of State Taxes in Tasmania now issues rulings so that various aspects of the payroll laws that are contentious will be clarified.
5. New South Wales registrations can be carried out online, or the office issues a General Client Registration Form that covers registration for all state taxes.
6. See Payroll Tax Ruling PTA020 issued for the Chief Commissioner of State Revenue in New South Wales.

Dutiable transactions (stamp duties)

11

Chapter eleven

Topics

After studying this chapter, you should be able to:

- **define and explain the nature of duty and dutiable transactions**
- **identify the types of transactions that attract duty**
- **list any concessions that are available**
- **explain the method of assessment of duty on dutiable transactions**
- **briefly set out the penalties for avoidance of duty.**

OVERVIEW

An ad valorem tax rate is expressed as a percentage of the value of the commodity in question. A specific rate is expressed as a fixed money sum per unit of weight or volume (e.g. $10 per litre). A flat rate is a set amount regardless of weight, volume or percentage.

Duty is a tax imposed in respect of certain documents and transactions. It may be imposed at a fixed tax rate or specific rate, at a flat rate or at an ad valorem rate.

The documents evidencing some transactions must be sent to the Stamp Duties Office for official stamping with an impressed stamp, while other transaction documents may have adhesive stamps affixed to them that are then cancelled by a signature and date across them. In most cases, every part of a dutiable document is liable for duty, and these should be lodged with the Stamp Duties Office within a specified time of signing, generally within two months of an event, otherwise a penalty might attach to them.

Most states operate their Duties Office as part of the State Revenue Office. Opinions may be sought on duty, and written advice or assessments will be issued. Many states have introduced bar coding and lodgement numbers to speed up the assessment and advice and enable fast-tracking of documents through the Duties Office. The states that have enacted new Duties Acts have significantly departed from the old legislation regarding the instruments and transactions liable to duty and various procedures in the payment of that duty. Only South Australia has yet to replace the old legislation.

In this chapter the sections are divided according to the type of transaction, and then an overview of this dutiable event is given, with the current applicable rates. The final section examines the assessment procedures and the penalties that might arise. As with the previous chapter, each state is addressed in turn: Victoria, South Australia, Queensland, Western Australia, Tasmania, the Australian Capital Territory and New South Wales.

The First Home Owner Grant scheme

A 2008 initiative of the Commonwealth government has raised the **First Home Owner Grant (FHOG)** scheme, which gives eligible first home buyers a grant to assist with the purchase of their home. The grant is $14 000 for an existing dwelling or $21 000 for a newly constructed home. Each state administers this legislation in conjunction with concessions on duty payable on these purchases. As part of the Intergovernmental Agreement on the Reform of Commonwealth–State Financial Relations signed in June 1999, the states and territories agreed to provide financial assistance to Australians who are buying their first home through the establishment of the First Home Owner Grant.

The FHOG scheme was established to offset the effect of the GST on home ownership. It is an ongoing scheme with no end date yet specified. The FHOG is not means-tested nor is it restricted by the purchase price of the property. As well as the State Revenue Offices, a number of financial institutions help administer the FHOG, as long as these institutions are approved by the government of that state. The grant is a one-off payment payable by the various governments to eligible first home owners.

Eligibility criteria

To be eligible to receive the FHOG, the following eligibility criteria must be satisfied:

- Each applicant and his or her partner must have a contract to purchase an existing home or to build a new home that is signed on or after 1 July 2000.

- Each applicant and his or her partner must not have already received a grant under a *First Home Owner Grant Act 2000*, in any state or territory of Australia.
- Each applicant and his or her partner must not have owned residential property, either jointly, separately or with some other person prior to 1 July 2000, in any state or territory of Australia.
- Each applicant and his or her partner must not have owned and occupied a residential property, either jointly, separately or with some other person on or after 1 July 2000, in any state or territory of Australia.
- Each applicant must be a natural person (not a company).

Most of the states also require the applicant to be 18 years of age or over.

11.1 Victoria

Duty is payable under the operation of the *Duties Act 2000* (Vic) and this Act applies to a wide variety of documents that evidence commercial and private transactions.

Transfer of dutiable property

Transfer of property includes leaseholds from the Crown. Duties payable on transactions of property are set out in Table 11.1.

TABLE 11.1 RATES ON DUTIABLE TRANSACTIONS: VICTORIA

Range ($)	Base amount ($)	Percentage per $1 above lower limit of range
0–25 000	–	1.4% of the dutiable value
25 000–130 000	350	Plus 2.4% of that part of the dutiable value that exceeds $25 000
130 000–960 000	2870	Plus 6.0% of that part of the dutiable value that exceeds ~~$960 000~~ 130000
Over 960 000	–	5.5% of the dutiable value.

For more information, telephone **(03) 9628 6777**.

First Home Bonus

On 1 May 2004 the Victorian government introduced a **First Home Bonus** of $5000, which was reduced to $3000 in 2005. However, in 2007 the government reinstated the $5000 bonus for new homes while keeping $3000 for the purchase of existing homes. In the 2008 budget the government extended this $3000 bonus for both purchased or newly constructed homes in regional Victoria. This extra bonus is in addition to either the $3000 or $5000 entitlement. For example, if an eligible couple purchased an existing home in regional Victoria after 6 May 2008 then they would receive $6000. If they constructed a new home in regional Victoria they would receive $8000. The bonus is available to all **first home purchasers** who are at least 18 years old and who may not qualify for the First Home Owner Grant paid under Commonwealth law. Some families may qualify for both.

Since 1 January 2006 eligible applicants had the choice as to whether they receive the First Home Bonus or the **Principal Place of Residence**

(PPR) concession as shown in Table 11.2. However, since the budget in 2008 applicants can now receive both the First Home Bonus and the PPR concession if the home is both a first home and their PPR. The exemption is available only if certain eligibility criteria are met, as follows:

- The applicant must reside in the home as the principal place of residence.
- The applicant must not have previously owned a home in any part of Australia.

The government charges duty as shown in Table 11.1 on the conveyance of all property in Victoria. If the purchase price of the principal place of residence is between $130 000 and $550 000, then Table 11.2 shows how PPR duty is calculated:

TABLE 11.2 PRINCIPAL PLACE OF RESIDENCE DUTY

Dutiable value of the PPR	Rate of duty
$130 000 to $440 000	$2870 plus 5% of that part of the dutiable value that exceeds $130 000
$440 000 to $550 000	$18 370 plus 6% of that part of the dutiable value that exceeds $440 000

The Victorian government has stated that the First Home Bonus is in place until 30 June 2009. First homebuyers with families have the option of a full duty exemption in lieu of the First Home Bonus when they purchase property worth not more than $150 000, with a partial exemption available for property worth not more than $200 000. The example sets out the duty concession.

Example

Concessions for first homes purchased after 1 July 2008

1. Purchasing an existing home on the land [s.62(3)]

Ted and Greta, who have one child aged 15 months, buy their first home in St Kilda on 1 July 2008 for $165 000. The concession is calculated as follows:
15 480 – (387 × DV/5000)
= 15 480 – (387 × 165 000/5000)
= 15 480 – 12 771
Concession = $2709

2. Buying the land and starting construction before transfer [s.62(4)]:

Ted and Greta buy vacant land for $75 000 and then enter into a contract to have a $90 000 dwelling built before the final transfer. The dutiable value (DV) is $165 000. The PPR rate payable would be $4620. The concession is calculated as follows:
$4620 × (387 [200 000 – DV])/(250 [DV – 72 600])
= $4620 × 0.58636
Concession = $2709

3. Buying the land and starting construction within three years of settlement: [s.63(3)]

Ted and Greta buy land for $75 000 and within three years build a house costing $90 000. They pay duty of $1550 on the land transfer. They calculate their first home concession as follows:
$1550 × (387 [200 000 – DV])/(250 [DV – 72 600])
= $1550 × 0.58636
Concession = $908.86
Duty is then $1550 – $908.86 = $641.14. As the couple have already paid duty of $1550, they will receive a refund of $908.86.

Exemptions available

In certain circumstances, charitable organisations whose earnings are retained and not distributed will be exempt from duty.[1] Concession card holders may be eligible for a full exemption of duty if the home is under $330 000 or partial exemption or a refund of stamp duty if the value of their home is under $440 000.

Motor vehicle registrations

Duty is based on the value of the motor vehicle (refer to Table 11.3).

TABLE 11.3 DUTY ON MOTOR VEHICLE REGISTRATIONS: VICTORIA

Passenger cars, new and used motor vehicle range ($)	Amount of duty per $200 or part thereof of excess ($)
Passenger cars	
0–57 009	5
$57 010 and over	10
All other new vehicles (all values)	5
All used vehicles	8

The provisions impose duty on applications for registration, and applications for transfer of registration, of motor vehicles and heavy trailers. For more information about these provisions, contact the Technical Advice branch on **(03) 9628 6606**.

Insurance premiums

State taxes and duties are generally calculated on GST-inclusive prices.

Insurance premium duty is based on the sum assured, and the general rate is 10% of the previous month's premiums, payable by the insurance company. No duty is payable on workers compensation or commercial marine insurance.

Duty payable on life insurance is taxed once only at 5% of the first year's premium. Duty is payable on the value of compulsory third party premiums at a rate of 10%.

Agreements

There is no duty payable on agreements under hand, but a $10 duty is payable on agreements under seal. Deeds of settlement have a duty of $200, and a deed not otherwise chargeable has a duty of $10. Rental businesses charge 1.5% of rental income in excess of $80 000 per annum.

Share transfers

Duty on the transfer of quoted marketable securities ceased on 1 July 2001 in accordance with the Intergovernmental Agreement on the Reform of Commonwealth–State Financial Relations. The duty on **off-market transactions** ceased on 1 July 2002.

Hiring arrangements

Hire of goods duty was abolished on 1 January 2007.

Mortgages and loan securities

Duty on most **mortgages** and **loan securities** ceased on 1 July 2004.

Congestion levy

The congestion levy applies to all 'off-street' parking spaces used for parking cars or larger vehicles within a specified area in the Melbourne central business district. It is an annual charge indexed each year by the CPI. For 2008 the amount was $820. Some exemptions apply, including residential spaces, car spaces for drivers with disabilities and spaces relating to exempt bodies.

Avoidance

Where the Commissioner is of the opinion that a mistake of fact has occurred in an assessment of duty, or there has been incorrect, incomplete or misleading information provided, a reassessment can be made.

Penalties are in place to prevent taxpayers from circumventing the duty laws to place themselves in a more beneficial position than that of their fellow taxpayers.

11.2 South Australia

In South Australia stamp duty is collected through the operation of the *Stamp Duties Act 1923* (SA), its amendments and regulations. This Act requires a person to lodge a statement with the Commissioner when a transaction has occurred that:

- results in a change of ownership of a legal or equitable interest in land
- changes ownership of a business or changes the goodwill of a business
- changes an interest in a partnership.[2]

Since 1 July 2005, all mortgages or mortgage refinancing taken out for the purpose of securing a loan for **home acquisition or improvement** have been exempt from stamp duty. This does not apply where a loan is taken out for other purposes as well as the above. Other instruments exempted from stamp duty since 1 July 2006 include the following:

- deeds
- caveats
- trustee appointments
- applications to register or transfer the registration of a motor vehicle pursuant to a will
- other minor conveyances.

Contracts and conveyances

Stamp duties payable on **contracts** and **conveyances** are set out in Table 11.4.

TABLE 11.4 DUTY ON CONTRACTS AND CONVEYANCES: SOUTH AUSTRALIA

Range ($)	Base amount ($)	Percentage per $1 above lower limit of range
0–12 000	nil	1.00
12 001–30 000	120	2.00

30 001–50 000	480	3.00
50 001–100 000	1 080	3.50
100 001–200 000	2 830	4.00
200 001–250 000	6 830	4.25
250 001–300 000	8 955	4.75
300 001–500 000	11 330	5.00
Over 500 000	21 330	5.50

Rebate for new home units in Adelaide

The duty rebate scheme has been extended and is now available to purchasers on the transfer of new residential home units in the city of Adelaide. These units must be new dwellings on individual allotments of 350 square metres or less. The target area is bordered by the North, East, South and West Terraces.

The maximum rebate will be $1500 and is a flat rate. A purchaser who is a first home buyer may be eligible for this rebate as well. Basically this means that a first home buyer of a new home unit in the target area, with a value of $99 000 or less, would be free of any duty. For more information, telephone the South Australian Revenue Office on **(08) 8226 3750** or send a fax to **(08) 8226 3734**.

First home purchases

There is now a First Home Bonus Grant of $4000 available to all first home buyers in South Australia. This replaces the previous concessional scale. All eligible buyers will receive the full $4000 up to $400 000 and it phases out at $450 000. There are certain criteria for eligibility, including the following:

- Applicants must be natural persons (i.e. not a corporation etc.).
- Applicants must be the sole purchasers.
- No party to the application may have owned a dwelling in Australia before this purchase.
- Applicants must occupy the dwelling within 12 months of the purchase.

Example

Terry and Vicky apply for a concession on the purchase of their first home in Glenelg, valued at $350 000. Using the rates shown in Table 11.3, duty of $13 830 would normally apply.

$11 330 + (5% × [$350 000 – $300 000])

$11 330 + (5% × $50 000 = $13 830)

The full bonus of $4000 is available, so Terry and Vicky will pay:

$13 830 – $4000 = $9830

Terry and Vicky would also most likely qualify for the Commonwealth FHOG of $14 000, in which case they would still have $4170 of their grant to put towards paying for their home.

Exemptions available

The transfer of an interest in the **matrimonial home** is exempt from duty, and a rebate of up to $3000 is available for new medium-density dwellings in some specified locations. If there is a transfer by way of a gift to charitable organisations, the ordinary duty is waived and only a nominal duty is charged.

Motor vehicle registrations

Duty on motor vehicles[3] is based on the value of the vehicle. In South Australia, there is a sliding scale, as shown in Table 11.5.

TABLE 11.5 DUTY ON MOTOR VEHICLE REGISTRATIONS: SOUTH AUSTRALIA

Private passenger vehicle range ($)	**Base amount of duty ($)**	**Amount of duty per $100 or part thereof of excess ($)**
0–1000	Minimum 5	1
1001–2000	10	2
2001–3000	30	3
3001 and over	60	4
Commercial vehicles and farmers' tractors 2.5 tonnes or more The above rates apply up to 2000, but over this amount:	30	3

Insurance premiums

State taxes and duties are generally calculated on GST-inclusive prices.

Life insurance premiums duty in South Australia is in the form of a licence, being calculated as $1.50 per $100 of net premiums of the previous year. General duty is payable in the form of a monthly licence and is calculated at $11 per $100 or part thereof of the net premiums of the previous year. Amounts must be rounded up to the nearest dollar before calculating the duty. It is interesting to note that workers compensation insurance duty is not excluded.

Agreements

There is no charge for agreements under hand, but there is a charge of $10 for agreements under seal.

Share transfers

Duty on the transfer of quoted marketable securities ceased on 1 July 2001. Duty is still payable on unlisted transactions. **Off-market transactions** attract a duty of 60 cents per $100 of value or part thereafter. This rate will be reduced by half to 30 cents per $100 from 1 July 2009 and is due to be abolished from 1 July 2010.

Hiring arrangements

With the hire of goods, duty is calculated on the hiring charges exclusive of GST.

Duty of 0.6% is payable on rental contracts where the total amount is in excess of $6000 per month as at 1 July 2008. This duty will be abolished on 1 July 2009. A rate of 0.25% applies to all commercial hire and financing of equipment. This rate will be abolished on 1 July 2009. There is no duty on hire purchase agreements.

The leasing of land and commercial properties is exempt from duty, if the average annual rent does not exceed $50 000. These provisions became operative on 1 January 2002.

Mortgages and loan securities

Since 1 July 2005 all **mortgages** over residential property have been exempt from mortgage stamp duty. For other non-residential loans duty is charged according to the sum secured and since 1 July 2007 has been payable at the following rates:

- up to the first $400: nil
- from $400 to $6000: $10
- over $6000: $10 plus 15 cents in every $100 or part thereafter.

From 1 July 2009 the duty payable for mortgage transactions will be abolished.

Avoidance

Where the Commissioner is of the opinion that a mistake of fact has occurred in an assessment of duty, incorrect, incomplete or misleading information has been provided or a duty needs to be recovered, a reassessment can be made. The penalty provisions have been amended to ensure that if taxpayers seek to circumvent the provisions of the *Stamp Duties Act 1923* (SA), they will not be in a more favourable position than those taxpayers who meet their obligations.

For more information, visit the South Australian Treasury's website at **www.revenuesa.sa.gov.au/**.

11.3 Queensland

On 1 March 2002 the *Duties Act 2001* and the *Taxation Administration Act 2001* (TAA) superseded the *Stamp Act 1894*, which was Queensland's oldest tax legislation. Prior to this date, the *Revenue Laws Amendment Act (No. 2) 1995* had some impact on stamp duties in Queensland. The 2001 Acts had significant changes and these are outlined below.

Transactions duties on the transfer of property

Duty is payable on the transfer of real property and is set out in Table 11.6.

TABLE 11.6 RATES ON DUTIABLE TRANSACTIONS: QUEENSLAND

Range ($)	Base amount ($)	Percentage per $1 above lower limit of range
0–5000	nil	
5001–75 000		1.5
75 001–540 000	1050	3.5
540 001–980 000	17 325	4.5
More than 980 000	37 125	5.25

Home and first home purchases

Since 1 May 2004 all purchasers of private principal residences(PPR) have been given concessions of duty. In the 2008 budget the government raised this threshold to $350 000. These rates are shown in Table 11.7. The PPR concession is capped at $3500. From 1 September 2008 the first home purchase threshold was raised to $500 000, below which first home buyers pay no duty at all. This first home concession duty decreases by $875 for every $5000 increase in the first home purchase, phasing out at $550 000.

Since 1 January 2007 there has been a First Home Duty Concession for the purchase of vacant land that is valued at less than $250 000.

TABLE 11.7 CONCESSION DUTY ON PPR PURCHASES: QUEENSLAND

Range ($)	Base amount of concessional duty for all PPR home buyers ($)	Percentage per $1 above lower limit of range
Up to 350 000	nil	1.00
350 001–540 000	3500	3.50
540 001–700 000	10 150	4.50
700 001–980 000	17 350	4.50
Over 980 000	29 950	5.25

Example

Tim and Julie apply for a concession on the purchase of their home in Kedron valued at $600 000. Using the rates in Table 11.6, duty of $20 025 would normally apply for this conveyance, as follows:

$17 325 + ($4.5 × [$600 000 – $540 000 / 100]) = $20 025

However, because of the PPR home concession rates, Tim and Julie's duty payable will be much less. Refer to the Table 11.7:

$10 150 + ($4.5 × [$600 000 – $540 000 / 100]) = $12 850

Exemptions and concessions

In the 2008 budget the government announced that they were extending the transfer duty home concession to retirement village residents who adopt lease and sub-lease occupancy arrangements. Exemptions of duty are available for educational, charitable, public benevolent and religious institutions. There is also exemption from duty on special transactions arising from the breakdown of a marriage.

Motor vehicle registrations

Motor vehicle duty is based on the rates shown in Table 11.8:

TABLE 11.8 DUTY ON MOTOR VEHICLE REGISTRATIONS: QUEENSLAND

Type of vehicle	Duty payable on value
Hybrid vehicles with any number of cylinders	$2 for each $100 or part of $100
Vehicles with 1 to 4 cylinders or 2 rotors and a steam vehicle	$3 for each $100 or part of $100
Vehicles with 5 or 6 cylinders or 3 rotors	$3.50 for each $100 or part of $100
Vehicles with 7 or more cylinders	$4 for each $100 or part of $100

Insurance premiums

Duty on life insurance premiums has been abolished and these sections omitted from the Act.

State taxes and duties are generally calculated on GST-inclusive prices.

The general insurance premiums attract duty of 7.5% for class 1 and 5.0% for class 2 (for premiums paid on or after 1 August 2004), while workers compensation, comprehensive motor vehicle insurance and professional indemnity all carry duty of 5%. For motor vehicle third-party insurance there is a flat charge of 10 cents per dollar.

Agreements

There are no duty charges for agreements under hand or seal.

Share transfers

Duty on unlisted marketable securities was abolished on 1 January 2007. Shares not listed on the Australian Stock Exchange attracted a duty of 60 cents per $100 or part thereof.

Hiring arrangements

Lease duty was abolished on 1 January 2006 and hire duty was abolished on 1 January 2007.

Mortgages and loan securities

Duty on **mortgages** and **loan securities** was abolished in full from 1 July 2008.

Avoidance

Where the Commissioner is of the opinion that a mistake of fact has occurred in an assessment of duty, incorrect, incomplete or misleading information has been provided or a duty needs to be recovered, a reassessment can be made.

11.4 Western Australia

Since 1 July 2008 stamp duties have been collected under the operation of the *Duties Act 2008* (WA) and its amendments and regulations. Changes in Western Australia's stamp duty laws have been implemented to remove many of the administrative provisions from the old Act, transferring them to the *Taxation Administration Act 2003* (WA).

Contracts and conveyances

Stamp duties payable on **contracts** and **conveyances** are set out in Table 11.9.

TABLE 11.9 NORMAL DUTY ON CONTRACTS AND CONVEYANCES: WESTERN AUSTRALIA

Range ($)	Base amount ($)	Percentage per $1 above lower limit of range
0–80 000	Nil	1.90
80 001–100 000	1 520	2.85
100 001–250 000	2 090	3.80
250 001–500 000	7 790	4.75
Over 500 000	19665	5.15

These rates are subject to change, so it is wise to check the website at **www.dft.wa.gov.au/** for the latest postings.

Residential and first home purchases

There is a new rate scale for the purchase of private principal residences (PPR). This is shown in Table 11.10 as follows:

TABLE 11.10 RESIDENTIAL DUTY ON CONTRACTS AND CONVEYANCES: WESTERN AUSTRALIA

Range ($)	Base amount ($)	Percentage per $1 above lower limit of range
0–120 000	Nil	1.90
120 001–150 000	2 280	2.85
150 001–360 000	3 135	3.80
360 001–725 000	11 115	4.75
Over 725 000	28452	5.15

The existing first home buyer concessions (exempting purchases of vacant land up to $300 000 and established homes up to $500 000) remain in place. Special rates are offered to a purchaser of a *first* home. This rate of stamp duty applies where the value of the home does not exceed $600 000 or the value of vacant land does not exceed $400 000. A duty of $22.51 per $100 or part thereof above $500 000 and up to $600 000 is payable. The workings of this first home scheme are shown in the example below. Since 1 July 2004 the special concession for homes above the twenty-sixth parallel no longer applies.

Example

John and Mary have applied for a concession on the purchase of their first home, in Carnarvon, valued at $550 000. Using the rates in Table 11.9, duty of $22 240 would normally apply for the conveyance. However, because this is their first home, John and Mary will be entitled to a concessional duty of: ([$550 000 – 500 000]/100) × $22.51 = $11 255. If John and Mary had purchased their first block of vacant land and it was below $400 000, the duty would have been nil for the first $300 000 and $13.01 per $100 above $300 000. If the purchase was not a *first home* but rather for a new home, the duty would be $20 140 as per Table 11.10.

Exemptions and concessions available

Some exemptions are available on transactions concerning charitable bodies, and these are set out in the schedules to the Act.[4] A concessional rate applies to principal residences and business undertakings valued at $200 000 or less. This general concession is 1.5% on the first $100 000 and 4.39% on any excess amount up to $200 000.

Transfer of interest in the matrimonial home from one spouse to joint ownership is also exempt, so long as the Stamp Duties Office values the property.

Motor vehicle registrations

From 1 July 2008, where the market value of a motor vehicle does not exceed $25 000, a rate of 2.75% of the market value will be charged on transfer. Between $25 000 and $50 000 the calculation is as follows:

$$\text{Factor} = 2.75\% + \frac{\text{market value} - \$25\,000}{\$6666.66}$$

Then multiply the factor by the market value.

In cases where the market value of the vehicle is more than $50 000, it is 6.5% of the market value.

Example

Suppose that a light vehicle has a market value of $40 000. The duty to transfer ownership is as follows:

$$\text{Factor} = 2.75\% + \frac{\$40\,000 - \$25\,000}{\$6666.66} = 5.0\%$$

Then 5% × $40 000 = $2000 duty payable.

For the transfer of a licence for a heavy vehicle, the amount of duty is the lesser of:

(a) 3% of the dutiable value and

(b) $12 000.

Insurance premiums

Life insurance premiums and workers compensation premiums are exempt from duty. Note also that **annuities** are exempt. General insurance premiums and duty on third-party motor vehicle premiums attract 10% duty.

State taxes and duties are generally calculated on GST-inclusive prices.

Agreements

There is no duty on agreements under hand, but there is a $5 charge on all agreements under seal.

Share transfers

The *Financial Relations Agreement (Consequential Provisions) Act 1999* (WA) was assented to on 13 December 1999. This Act provides that stamp duty will not apply to the transfer of any marketable security that is quoted on a recognised stock exchange on or after 1 July 2001. Transfers of unlisted securities have not attracted duty since 1 January 2004.

Hiring arrangements

Hire duty has been abolished since 1 January 2007 on both new and existing contracts.

Mortgages and loan securities

On 1 July 2008 **mortgage duty** was abolished.

Avoidance

Where the Commissioner is of the opinion that a mistake of fact has occurred in an assessment of duty, incorrect, incomplete or misleading information has been provided or a duty needs to be recovered, a reassessment can be made.

11.5 Tasmania

In Tasmania the *Duties Act 2001* and the *Debits Duties Act 2001* replaced the *Stamp Duties Act 1931*. Duty is levied under these Acts and applies to instruments executed or transactions effected on or after 1 July 2001.

Transfer of dutiable property

Duty is payable on transfer of **dutiable property** as set out in Table 11.11.

TABLE 11.11 RATES OF DUTY ON PROPERTY TRANSFERS: TASMANIA

Range ($)	Base amount ($)	Percentage per $1 above lower limit of range
0–1300	minimum 20	–
1301–10 000	20	1.5
10 001–30 000	150	2.0
30 001–75 000	550	2.5
75 001–150 000	1675	3.0
150 001–225 000	3925	3.5
Over 225 000	6550	4.0

Duty on business conveyances was abolished on 1 July 2008.

Home purchase concession

For contracts for first homes entered into after 20 May 2004 and having a total value of no more than $350 000, the Tasmanian government offers a first home concession of $4000. This concession is available to all new first home purchasers who also qualify for the Commonwealth First Home Owner Grant. For home values up to $350 000, an amount of either the duty calculated or $4000 will be available, whichever is the lesser amount. A concession of a maximum of $2400 is also available for the purchase of vacant land up to the value of $175 000.

Example

Dave and Sally can apply for a concession on the purchase of their first home in Boat Harbour, valued at \$220 000, because the value is less than \$350 000. Using the rates set out in Table 11.11, duty of \$6375 will apply for the conveyance:

\$3925 + 3.5% (\$70 000) = \$6375

Dave and Sally can apply for the \$4000 home concession, which means they will pay \$2375 for duty on the contract.

Note: If Dave and Sally's home was valued at \$100 000 with duty of only \$2425 applicable, their concession would be \$2425 and not \$4000.

Exemptions available

Mortgages transferred to trustees of a registered friendly society, the Tasmanian Museum and Art Gallery or a municipal corporation are all given exemptions, with certain conditions attached.

Motor vehicle registrations

There is a sliding scale for stamp duty on new car sales (see Table 11.12). The amounts are all based on the value of the vehicle.

TABLE 11.12 DUTY ON MOTOR VEHICLE REGISTRATIONS: TASMANIA

	Base amount of duty (\$)	Amount of duty per \$100 or part thereof of excess (\$)
Passenger vehicle range (\$)		
Under 600	20	
600–34 999		3
35 000–40 000	1050	11
Over 40 000		4
All other vehicles		
Commercial vehicles		3
Heavy vehicles		1

Credit card transactions

Duty is payable by the credit card provider and is \$0.15 for each taxable credit card debit.

Insurance premiums

Stamp duty for life insurance premiums is based on the sum assured and is as follows:

- up to \$2000: 10 cents per \$200
- over \$2000: \$1 plus 20 cents per \$200.

State taxes and duties are generally calculated on GST-inclusive prices.

General premiums and term policies are all at the rate of 5%, while there is a \$6 flat charge on all third-party motor vehicle insurance premiums. Mortgage insurance policies attract a 2% charge on the premium.

Agreements

In this state agreements under hand or seal attract a duty of $20 for all amounts.

Share transfers

Duty on the transfer of quoted marketable securities ceased on 1 July 2001 in accordance with the Intergovernmental Agreement. Duty is still payable on unlisted securities for land-rich corporations. Unlisted transactions attract a duty of 60 cents per $100 of value or part thereafter.

Hiring arrangements

Duty on the hire of goods has been abolished.

Mortgages and loan securities

Mortgage duty rates were abolished on 1 July 2008.

Avoidance

Where the Commissioner is of the opinion that a mistake of fact has occurred in an assessment of duty, incorrect, incomplete or misleading information has been provided or a duty needs to be recovered, a reassessment can be made. The Tasmanian government introduced a new general anti-avoidance provision (GAAP) that applies to schemes entered into with the sole or dominant purpose of obtaining a tax benefit. Penalties are incurred under the *Taxation Administration Act 1997*.

For more information, check the website at **www.treasury.tas.gov.au** and keep up to date with legislation changes. You can telephone **(03) 6233 3407** or fax the Tasmanian Treasury on **(03) 6223 2755.**

11.6 Australian Capital Territory

In the Australian Capital Territory the *Duties Act 1999* and the *Taxation Administration Act 1999* now operate. Duty is levied under these Acts and will apply to instruments executed or transactions effected on or after 1 July 2000. All instruments or transactions before this date fall under the old legislation.

Transfer of dutiable property

Duty is calculated on the greater of the purchase price or the market value of the property and is set out in Table 11.13.

TABLE 11.13 RATES OF DUTY ON PROPERTY TRANSFERS: ACT

Range ($)	Base amount ($)	Percentage per $1 above lower limit of range
0–100 000	minimum 20	or 2.00 per $100
100 001–200 000	2 000	3.50
200 001–300 000	5 500	4.00
300 001–500 000	9 500	5.50
500 001–1 000 000	20 500	5.75
Over 1 000 001	49 250	6.75

Home purchase concession

In the ACT the first home concession is given for eligible home buyers of either houses or vacant land to build a house. The ACT uses two tables to calculate this concession. Table 11.14 shows the concessional values for houses and Table 11.15 shows the values for vacant blocks of land. The upper and lower thresholds (used to calculate the rate to apply per $100) are updated in the ACT every six months and can be found in the *Taxation Administration Act 1999*, s. 139 Determination of amounts payable under tax laws. In the 2008 budget the government announced that the upper threshold for homes would rise from $390 000 to $412 000 and for vacant land from $215 400 to $227 600. The lower thresholds rose to $333 000 for homes and $185 300 for vacant land. Other threshold changes may take place for January 2009 so check the web for new rates. The eligible applicants must also satisfy a combined income test of $120 000, which increases by $3330 for each additional dependent child, to a maximum of $136 650 per annum.

TABLE 11.14 DUTY CONCESSIONS ON TRANSFER OF ELIGIBLE PROPERTY: ACT

Dutiable value	Concessional duty payable
Up to $333 000	$20
$333 001 to $412 000	$19.80 for each $100 or part thereof by which the dutiable value exceeds $333 000
Over $412 000	no concession

TABLE 11.15 DUTY CONCESSIONS ON AN ELIGIBLE VACANT BLOCK: ACT

Dutiable value	Concessional duty payable
Up to $185 300	$20
$185 301 to $227 600	$15.60 for each $100 or part thereof by which dutiable value exceeds $185 300
Over $227 600	no concession

Property that is jointly owned attracts a pro rata concession.

Example

James and Liz can apply for a concession on the purchase of their first home in Woden, valued at $355 000. They are eligible applicants with a combined family income of $100 000 and two dependent children. Using the rates set out in Table 11.14, the following duty will apply:

$$\$19.80 \times \left(\frac{\$355\,000 - \$310\,000}{100}\right) = \$4356$$

The Affordable Housing Action Plan includes other initiatives to assist people to own homes.

Exemptions and concessions available

A duty concession is now available for people on aged or disability pensions and Veteran's Gold Card holders. This initiative recognises that older persons often incur significant costs when 'downsizing' their accommodation. The government also recognised extra costs that many disabled people may face. This new 2008 budget measure available for a period of three years from 1 July 2008 provides a one-off exemption of duty on the purchase of property up to median price, to eligible concession card holders. Duty paid on the establishment of trusts over non-dutiable property and the establishment of or amendment to superannuation instruments was abolished from 1 July 2008.

Motor vehicle registrations

Duty is levied at the rate of $3 for each $100 or part thereof of the purchase price or market value of the motor vehicle, whichever is greater.

For a passenger vehicle with a value over $45 000, the duty payable is $1350 plus $5 for each $100 or part thereof in excess of $45 000 of the purchase price or market value of the vehicle, whichever is greater.

Debits tax

Debits duty was abolished on 1 July 2005.

Insurance premiums

State taxes and duties are generally calculated on GST-inclusive prices.

Duty on general insurance contracts is calculated at the rate of 10% of the net premiums received. Duty on life insurance is payable on:

- the sum insured at $1 on the first $2000, and $0.20 for every $200, or part thereof, in excess of $2000;
- temporary or term insurance policies at 5% of the first year's premium;
- life insurance riders at 5% of the first year's premium; and
- insurance in the event of the disablement of the insured by accident or sickness at 10% of the premium paid.

General premiums and term policies are all at the rate of 8%, while there is a $6 flat charge on all third-party motor vehicle insurance premiums. More details and can be obtained from the ACT government's website (at **www.revenue.act.gov.au**).

Agreements

In this state agreements under hand or seal attract a duty rate of $20, for all amounts.

Share transfers

Unlisted transactions attract a duty of 60 cents per $100 of value or part thereafter or $20, whichever is the greater. This duty will cease on 1 July 2010.

Hiring arrangements

Hire duty ceased on 1 July 2007 and lease duty will cease on 1 July 2009.

Mortgages and loan securities

There is no duty on **mortgages** and **loan securities**.

Avoidance

Where the Commissioner is of the opinion that a mistake of fact has occurred in an assessment of duty, incorrect, incomplete or misleading information has been provided or a duty needs to be recovered, a reassessment can be made.

For more information, check the website at **www.revenue.act.gov.au** and keep up to date on legislation changes. You can also telephone **(02) 6207 0081** or fax the ACT Treasury on **(02) 6207 0090**.

11.7 New South Wales

Duty is collected in New South Wales under the *Duties Act 1997* (NSW) and the *Taxation Administration Act 1997* (NSW) on all transfers and transactions that are **dutiable transactions** for the purposes of the Act. It is immaterial whether a dutiable transaction is effected by a written instrument or by any other means, including electronic means (section 9, Chapter 2, Part 1[10] of the Duties Act). All references are to the *Duties Act 1997*.

Transfer of dutiable property

Transfer duty is payable on the transfer of all **dutiable property** and marginal rates are applied every $100 or part of the excess thereof above the lower limit of the range. Duty is calculated on the dutiable value of the property, which is the higher of the consideration (if any) for the property and the market value of the property. Transfer duty is payable on dealings with dutiable property, such as:

- land in New South Wales
- land use entitlement
- transferable floor space
- a business asset—goodwill of a New South Wales business and intellectual property and certain statutory licences or permissions, if transferred with the goodwill of a New South Wales business (due to be abolished on 1 July 2012)
- a statutory licence or permission under New South Wales law (due to be abolished on 1 July 2012)
- a poker machine entitlement within the meaning of the *Gaming Machines Act 2001* (NSW) (due to be abolished on 1 July 2012)
- goods, if the subject of a dutiable transaction together with dutiable property (other than stock in trade, goods under manufacture, raw materials for manufacture, goods held or used in connection with land used in primary production, livestock and registered motor vehicles)
- a partnership interest, being an interest in a partnership that has partnership dutiable property
- options to purchase land
- interests in any of the above dutiable property
- domain names, considered to be 'intellectual property' and dutiable property under the Duties Act.

Transfers of intellectual property in isolation will not be subject to duty, but if sold with a business then duty on intellectual property, registered designs or copyright, statutory licences or permissions will be payable.

Table 11.16 sets out the duties applicable for property transfer. Principal residences valued at $3 million or more will attract a duty of $150 490 plus 7% on the excess over $3 million.

TABLE 11.16 TRANSFER DUTY ON DUTIABLE PROPERTY: NEW SOUTH WALES

Range ($)	Base amount ($)	Percentage per $1 above lower limit of range
0– 14 000	minimum 10	1.25
14 001–30 000	175	1.50
30 001–80 000	415	1.75
80 001–300 000	1 290	3.50
300 001–1 000 000	8 990	4.50
Over 1 000 000	40 490	5.50

Note: Principal residences attract a one-off duty on the excess over $3 million. Where the dutiable value of residential land exceeds $3 million, the duty payable is $150 490 plus $7 for every $100, or part by which the dutiable value exceeds $3 million.

First home benefits

There are currently two schemes operating in New South Wales to assist first home buyers. The first of these is known as the **First Home Plus** scheme. This can be explained as assistance to eligible people to acquire their first home by allowing them concessions on the documentation involved in the dutiable transaction. Normally, the duty payable would be as per dutiable property in Table 11.16, but a concession is obtainable for first purchasers who meet the conditions of being 18 years of age and who have not previously owned land or property anywhere in Australia. There are no income or assets tests applicable and the thresholds are as follows:

- homes in all areas: $500 000 phasing out at $600 000
- land in all areas: $300 000 phasing out at $450 000.

Any first home purchaser who satisfies all the necessary criteria will be able to claim the concessions as shown in Table 11.17.

TABLE 11.17 FIRST HOME PLUS CONCESSIONAL RATES

Range ($)	Base amount ($)	Percentage per $1 above the lower limit of range
0–500 000	nil	
500 001–509 999	nil	22.49
510 000–519 999	2 249	22.49
520 000–529 999	4 498	22.49
530 000–539 999	6 747	22.49
540 000–549 999	8 996	22.49
550 000–559 999	11 245	22.49
560 000–569 999	13 494	22.49
570 000–579 999	15 743	22.49
580 000–589 999	17 992	22.49
590 000–599 999	20 241	22.49
600 000 and over	22 490	normal rates apply as per Table 11.16

The duty for a property with a dwelling is payable at the rate of 22.49% of the dutiable value of the eligible property less \$112 450. The duty for vacant land is payable at the rate of 10.49% of the eligible dutiable value of the vacant land less \$31 470. The threshold is \$300 000, under which no duty is payable. Table 11.18 shows the rates applicable for this first purchase.

TABLE 11.18 RATES FOR FIRST PURCHASE OF VACANT LAND

Range (\$)	Base amount (\$)	Percentage per \$1 above the lower limit of range
0–300 000	nil	
300 001–309 999	nil	plus 10.49
310 000–319 999	1 049	10.49
320 000–329 999	2 098	10.49
330 000–339 999	3 147	10.49
340 000–349 999	4 196	10.49
350 000–359 999	5 245	10.49
360 000–369 999	6 294	10.49
370 000–379 999	7 343	10.49
380 000–389 999	8 392	10.49
390 000–399 999	9 441	10.49
400 000–409 999	10 490	10.49
410 000–419 999	11 539	10.49
420 000–429 999	12 588	10.49
430 000–439 999	13 637	10.49
440 000–449 999	14 868	10.49
450 000 and over	15 735	normal rates apply as per Table 11.16

Example

(a) Tony and Jill pay \$525 000 for their first home so will pay duty as follows:

(\$525 000 × 22.49%) – \$112 450 = \$5622.50

Or, reading the Table 11.17:

\$4498 + ([\$525 000 – \$520 000] × 22.49%) = \$5622.50

(b) Tony and Jill pay \$375 000 for their first vacant block of land:

\$7343 + ([\$375 000 – \$370 000] × 10.49%) = \$7867.50

You will notice that Tony and Jill would pay more duty if they purchased land rather than buying an established home, because the threshold for land is lower.

The second grant available is called the **First Home Plus One** scheme and is for people who enter into a contract to purchase property where one of the buyers has previously owned property. This scheme came into effect on 1 May 2007 and is available only to an eligible first home buyer who acquires at least 50% of the property being purchased. The eligibility criteria are the same as for the First Home Plus scheme. It is important to note that if the home buyer's partner has previously received a First Home Plus grant, then this concession is not available.

Exemptions available

The major exemption is the waiving of duty that would be payable on the transfer of a residential home from single to joint ownership between spouses. Another exemption is available on the conveyance of property as a result of a Family Court order. Certain charities that are not conducted on a commercial basis are also exempt. No duty is chargeable under the legislation on a transfer of dutiable property made pursuant to, or in accordance with, the rules of (a) an association of employees or employers registered as an organisation under the Commonwealth *Workplace Relations Act 1996*, or (b) an industrial union of employers or employees registered under the *Industrial Relations Act 1996*.

Transfer rate of duty

The note in Table 11.16 shows that the marginal rate of purchaser transfer duty increases from 5.5% to 7% on that part of the purchase price of a residential property in excess of $3 million. This duty replaces the premium property land tax that was levied each year on multimillion-dollar residential property values.

Motor vehicle registrations

Duty is payable on all new motor vehicles, based on the GST-inclusive value of the vehicle, and is $3 per $100 or part thereof. Most dealers have an exemption on new vehicle stock and demonstration vehicles, but not on delivery vehicles. The test is that vehicles must be offered for sale. The marginal value of luxury motor vehicles over $45 000 attracts duty of 5%. This means that a luxury vehicle priced at $50 000 will attract duty of $1350 plus $5 for every $100 over $45 000—that is, a total duty of $1600. This duty is payable by the purchaser of the motor vehicle.

Insurance premiums

State taxes and duties are generally calculated on GST-inclusive prices.

General insurance premiums attract duty of 9% for all Type A premiums, while Type B premiums such as motor vehicle insurance, aviation, disability, income and occupational indemnity are 5%. Type C premiums of livestock and crop insurance are set at 2.5%.

Life insurance is based on the sum assured, and is as follows:

- on the first $2000 or part thereof: $1
- $2000 and over: $1 plus 20 cents per $200.

The duty on term insurance or riders is 5% of the first-year premium. **Annuities** are exempt from duty.

Instruments

Most instruments relating to superannuation are liable to duty of $20. Transfer of property from one superannuation fund to another charges duty at an **ad valorem rate** or $200, whichever is the lesser. An instrument that varies a public unit trust scheme charges duty of $10. Other concessional rates of duty are calculated at varying rates according to the nature of the agreement.

Share transfers

Duty on the transfer of quoted marketable securities ceased on 1 July 2001 and for securities not listed on the Australian Stock Exchange, duty will be abolished on 1 January 2009.

Hiring arrangements

Hire duty was abolished effective from 1 July 2007 and duty on leases was abolished for lease instruments first executed on or after 1 January 2008.

Mortgage duty

Effective from 1 September 2007 **mortgage duty** is not payable on owner-occupied housing where the borrowers are natural persons. On 1 July 2008 mortgage duty was abolished on investment housing where the borrowers are natural persons. From 1 July 2009 all mortgage duty will be abolished.

Parking space levy

Parking space levy became operative on 1 July 2007 and is used to support public transport infrastructure and also to discourage the use of car parking spaces in the Sydney central business district. It is levied on owners of car spaces every 1 July and is payable on 1 September each year. Category 1 car space rates are $930 per space and Category 2 are $460 per space.

Category 1: The levy applies to liable spaces in the City of Sydney, North Sydney and Milsons Point business districts at the rate of $930 per liable space per annum from July 2007. Category 2: The levy applies to liable spaces in the Bondi Junction, Chatswood, Parramatta and St Leonards business districts at the rate of $460 per liable space per annum for the year from July 2007. These rates are indexed to the Consumer Price Index (CPI) each year.

Avoidance

The Duties Act is aimed at preventing schemes that result in the loss of duty revenue to New South Wales. One such scheme involved transferring shares in a company incorporated in New South Wales and listed on a New South Wales register to a Victorian register. In Victoria a declaration of trust was made out that attracted a fixed rate of duty of $200. This declaration stated that the owner on the register held the shares on behalf of another person. The shares were then transferred to that other person in Western Australia for a transaction duty of only $5.

Penalties

If the duty is not paid within the specified time of three months after the liability arises, default tax will be levied through the operation of the *Taxation Administration Act 1996.*

Where the Commissioner is of the opinion that a mistake of fact has occurred in an assessment of duty or there has been incorrect, incomplete or misleading information provided, a reassessment can be made. The board of review may extend the time for payment or write off the duty in cases of severe hardship.

Learning check

- ✓ Obtain relevant duties (stamp duty) scales from the State Revenue Office.
- ✓ Calculate the stamp duty payable on a range of contracts, including:
  - transfer of real property
  - transfer of motor vehicles.

Taxation vocabulary

ad valorem rate
annuity
contracts
conveyances
dutiable property
dutiable transactions
First Home Bonus
First Home Owner Grant (FHOG)
First Home Plus
First Home Plus One
first home purchasers
fixed tax rate
home acquisition or improvement
loan securities
matrimonial home
mortgage duty
mortgages
off-market transactions
paid up-front
Principal Place of Residence (PPR)
specific rate

multiple-choice questions

Circle the correct response. (Answers to odd-numbered multiple-choice questions are provided on page 318.)

1. **To be eligible to receive the First Home Owners Grant, which of the following criteria must be satisfied?**
   (a) None of the applicants must have already received a grant for a first home
   (b) None of the applicants must have owned a home and occupied it previously, anywhere in Australia
   (c) Each applicant must be a natural person
   (d) All of the above apply

2. **Of the following statements, which apply to the First Home Owners Grant?**
   (a) In some states it is means tested
   (b) It is due to finish on 1 July 2010
   (c) It is a Commonwealth government initiative administered by the states
   (d) It is a one-off payment of $5000

3. **If duty of 2.5% ad valorem was payable on a contract for the sale of 100 tonnes of goods worth $25 per tonne, the duty rate would be expressed as:**
   (a) $0.625 (b) $6.25 (c) $62.50 (d) $625.00

4. **If specific duty of 2.5% was payable on a contract for the sale of 100 tonnes of goods worth $25 per tonne, the duty rate would be expressed as:**
   (a) $0.625 (b) $6.25 (c) $62.50 (d) $625.00

5. **The first home owner concession base is nil at $500 000 and ceases with $20 000 normal duty payable at $600 000. If a home's purchase price is $520 000, what is the amount of concessional duty payable on the purchase price?**
   (a) $4000 (b) $20 000 (c) $16 000 (d) nil

quick-and-easy comprehension

Place a ✓ to indicate your response to each statement.

STATEMENT	TRUE	FALSE
1. Duty is not payable if there is only a verbal agreement.	—	—
2. If a document or statement is not produced for stamping, both parties may be liable for penalties.	—	—
3. First home buyers receive special treatment, under certain circumstances, for duty payable.	—	—
4. The only way duty can be paid is by having a document or statement assessed.	—	—
5. In all states duty on property transfers, contracts and conveyances that are not first homes will always be payable regardless of the value.	—	—

assessments

1. **A couple with one small child aged three years and a family taxable income of $50 000 purchased their first home for $400 000. Calculate the duty payable for them in your state.**
2. **Explain the home owner concessions available in your state and list any thresholds over which the concessions will not be available.**
3. **A new four-cylinder passenger vehicle valued at $47 000 is subject to duty. Calculate the duty in your state.**
4. **List the bodies and organisations that will generally be given an exemption from stamp duty by the Commissioner.**
5. **What rates apply to insurance premiums in your state?**

case study questions

1. **Colossal Constructions Pty Ltd has just acquired a new hybrid motor vehicle to be used for deliveries. The total purchase price was $52 000 and Tom has asked you to check the stamp duty calculation before he pays the final invoice. What amount should be charged for duty on that tax invoice in your state?**
2. **The company has purchased for $305 000 a vacant block of land next to the factory yard. What is the amount of duty in your state for this transfer of real property?**

classroom activities

Complete the duty crossword.

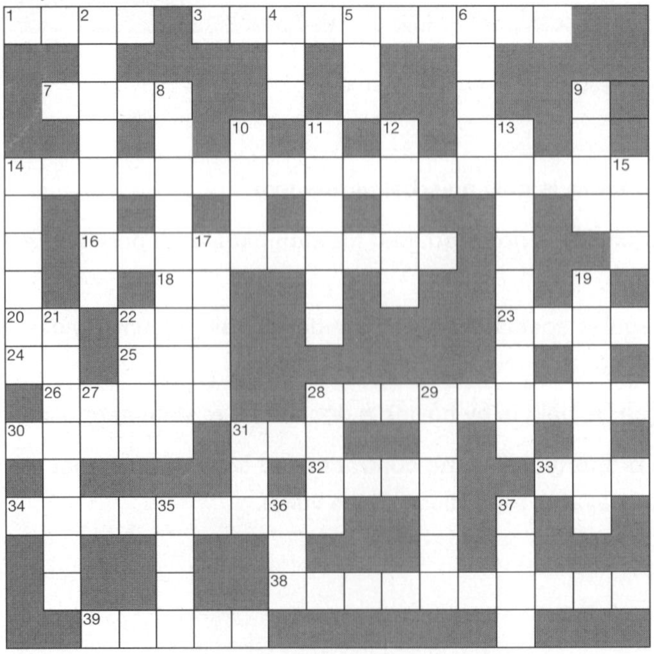

Across

1 A tax imposed in respect of certain documents and transactions. 4
3 These institutions are mostly exempt from duty. 10
7 When you apportion something you pro ----. 4
14 Duty is calculated on their GST-inclusive price. 9, 8
16 If you have these, no duty is payable. 10
18 You use this when it applies to yourself. 2
20 Abbreviation for dutiable securities. 2
22 Australia is surrounded by it. 3
23 This helps you find the crossword answer. 4
24 When employing, we are required to take this into account. 2
25 Abbreviation for a well-known explosive powder. 3
26 In Adelaide there is a rebate for the purchase of new ones. 5
28 Victoria abolished the duty payable on these on 1 July 2004. 9
30 These form that famous cross. 5
31 These operations of the Reserve Bank do not have duty. 3
32 There are plenty of these, with one on the emblem. 4
33 This bird is on the Australian emblem. 3
34 The capital of Victoria. 9
38 Beautiful one day, perfect the next! 10
39 The duty payable is calculated on this. 5

Down

2 Duty is payable when this happens with property. 8
4 These galleries are exempt from duty. 3
5 Intergovernmental Agreement on Reform (2001). 3
6 This pearl of a town in WA is north of Carnarvon. 5
8 There is generally no duty on these 'under hand'. 10
9 If the purchase of this is the first, the duty is mostly less. 4
10 What you do when you take a picture. 4
11 States abolished this financial tax on 1 July 2005. 6
12 The Commonwealth gives $14 000 to eligible home buyers. 5
13 These institutions had their duty abolished in July 2001. 9
14 Information gained through working in a firm. 6
15 Perhaps Qld and WA have a lot of this during the year. 3
17 There is no duty on this food ready to eat. 5
19 In all states, duty incurred by these institutions will be exempt. 7
21 It is a cross in the sky over Australia and on our flag. 8
22 States do this when they meet with the Commonwealth. 4
27 The letters on a form when something does not apply. 2
28 The states collect revenue but all say they need ______. 4
29 You have to cross this water to get to the state. 6
31 Abbreviation for a tax office in one state. 3
35 Even these agreements are subject to duty. 4
36 Abbreviation for the Cairns area of Australia. 3
37 If this happens to real property, duty will apply. 4

Notes

1. Reference should be made to the Third Schedule to the *Duties Act 2000*.
2. See section 71(e) of the *Stamp Duties Act 1923*.
3. Refer to the *Stamp Duties (Miscellaneous) Act 1995* that came into effect on 23 November 1995.
4. See the Schedule to the *Duties Act 2008.*

12 Land tax

Chapter twelve

Topics

After studying this chapter, you should be able to:

- **define and explain the nature of land tax**
- **identify the taxable value of land for land tax purposes**
- **identify who is liable to pay land tax**
- **identify any concessions or exemptions that may apply**
- **explain the calculation and assessment of land tax.**

OVERVIEW

The Commonwealth government introduced the *Land Tax Assessment Act* in 1910, and it operated throughout Australia for the financial years ending 30 June 1911 to 30 June 1952. Since that time, each state has either enacted its own land management statutes or used the existing 1910 legislation to collect **land tax** on any **rateable land**. Land tax is levied in all of the states and the Australian Capital Territory, but not in the Northern Territory, and is considered a **first charge** on the land. There are some quite significant variations in land tax between the states and the Australian Capital Territory (collectively referred to as the states), which are highlighted in this chapter. It would be an enormous task to examine every aspect of each state's land tax system rigorously, but it is hoped that by studying this chapter students will have a much greater appreciation of the nature of land tax and the method of assessment.

In the following sections each state's procedures are highlighted in turn. For each state the nature and operation of land tax are examined, with specific attention focused on the timing of the taxing point, the tax-free thresholds and rates of tax, exemptions that may apply and how the taxable value of land is determined. Finally, returns and assessments are briefly considered.

Some things are common to all states and the next section gives the interstate commonalities.

Commonalities

General interpretation

The word **ownership** is generally defined to mean a person who jointly or severally, whether at law or equity, is entitled to:

- the land for any estate of **freehold** in possession, or
- receive any rents or profits arising from that land.

Liability for land tax thus falls on the owner of the property. Consequently, having entered into or 'exchanged' a contract for sale does not normally change ownership for land tax purposes. All the land in the state owned by a person will be aggregated for land tax purposes. Section 81.5 of the *GST Act 1999* (Cwlth) dictates that there is no GST on land tax.

Liabilities

All of the states allow some amount as a general exemption before applying the various rates of tax. Primary production land is exempt in New South Wales, Victoria, South Australia, Western Australia and Tasmania, but in Queensland special conditions apply. The Crown is not considered the owner of land for land tax purposes, so any person who is leasing Crown land will be liable for the tax.

Valuations

The taxable value for land tax purposes is the value of the land only, without any buildings or improvements. Some states refer to these **valuations** as the *unimproved capital value*; other states refer to this as the *site value*. Any draining, excavation or reclaiming would be considered part of the land value.

12.1 Victoria

Interpretation

Land tax is levied in Victoria under the operation of the *Taxation Administration Act 1997* (Vic) and the *Land Tax Act 2005* (Vic). Any owner, either solely or jointly, owning land with a taxable value of $225 000 or more must pay land tax.

Liabilities and exemptions

Liability for land tax in Victoria falls on the owners of all land owned in Victoria, except exempt land, as at midnight on 31 December of the year preceding the year of assessment and is assessed on a calendar year basis. That is, land owned on 31 December 2009 will give rise to land tax payable for the 2010 assessment, with assessments being issued between February and June each year. It is important to understand that is if land is sold on, say, 1 January 2010, the seller would still be liable for the 2010 land tax calculated on landholdings as at 31 December 2009.

There are several exemptions from land tax that may apply. The most common exemptions are the principal place of residence and land used for primary production. But if primary production land is in the metropolitan area, it is exempt only if it is used by the owner who works most of the time in the primary production being carried out on the land. This may, in some cases, be extended to relatives of the owner. Exemptions are also provided for charitable, religious and educational bodies and commercial retirement villages. Note that commercial nursing homes, residential rental properties and boarding houses providing low-cost permanent accommodation are all liable for tax. Land used for charitable purposes, mines, land held by ex-servicepersons' associations, municipalities, public statutory authorities, friendly societies, and organisations that provide or promote outdoor sporting, recreation or cultural activities may be exempt. Refer to the State Revenue Office of Victoria—Land Tax General Information website at **www.sro.vic.gov.au** for more information on land tax exemptions. The current rates are as shown in Table 12.1; however, also check **www.sro.vic.gov.au** for any changes to rates.

TABLE 12.1 LAND TAX RATES: VICTORIA

Taxable value ($)	Add ($)	Tax payable ($)
0–250 000	–	nil
250 000–599 999	275	Plus 0.20% of the excess over 250 000
600 000–999 999	975	Plus 0.50% of the excess over 600 000
1 000 000–1 799 999	2 975	Plus 0.80% of the excess over 1 000 000
1 800 000–2 999 999	9 375	Plus 1.30% of the excess over 1 800 000
3 000 000 and over	24 975	Plus 2.25% of the excess over 3 000 000

Example

Rateable land owned at midnight on 31 December 2008 is valued for land tax purposes at $700 000:

2009 land tax payable = $975 + ([$700 000 – $600 000] × 0.5%) = $1475

Valuations

The taxable value of land is used as the basis on which land tax is calculated. In Victoria, the taxable value of land is the municipal site value provided by the relevant municipality. Valuations may be made by a rating authority within the meaning of the *Valuation of Land Act 1960* (Vic), or by the Valuer-General or a valuer nominated by the Valuer-General.

Returns and assessments

All the states issue assessments for land tax purposes. In Victoria for the first return, persons who own land that is rateable must lodge an initial return for land tax. Where land is owned jointly by a number of owners and is above the general threshold, an assessment notice will be issued. This is called the **primary assessment**. If the landowner is also a sole owner of other land, then that individual assessment, which carries part of the jointly owned land tax, is deemed to be a **secondary assessment**. A **rebate of tax** from the jointly owned property will prevent double taxation, and will be the lesser of:

- the taxpayer's share of the tax payable on the jointly held land, or
- the taxpayer's share (as the secondary taxpayer) of the tax on the joint ownership as a proportion of all land interests.

Under the *Taxation Administration Act 1997*, interest and a penalty tax will apply to late payments. These penalty rates are equivalent to those charged under federal tax laws. The rates will change periodically at 1 January or 1 July each year, so check by telephoning the State Revenue Office of Victoria on **(03) 9628 6480**.

Taxpayers are generally given 28 days to pay after the issue of an assessment. If the land tax bill is more than $200 and is received before 31 March, the taxpayer can elect to pay in three equal instalments over a 12-week period.

Since the 2006 tax year arrangements have been in place for land tax on trusts. A surcharge has been introduced that applies to Victorian landholdings of trusts between $25 000 and $3 million as shown in Table 12.2, and after this amount normal rates apply as per Table 12.1.

TABLE 12.2 TRUSTS LAND TAX RATES: VICTORIA

Taxable value ($)	Add ($)	Tax payable ($)
0–24 999		nil
25 000–249 999	82	Plus 0.375% of the excess over $25 000
250 000–599 999	926	Plus 0.575% of the excess over $250 000
600 000–999 999	2938	Plus 0.875% of the excess over $600 000
1 000 000–1 799 999	6438	Plus 1.175% of the excess over $1 000 000
1 800 000–2 999 999	15 838	Plus 0.7614% of the excess over $1 800 000
3 000 000 and over	24 975	Plus 2.25% of the excess over $3 000 000

Trusts that hold land purchased before 31 December 2005 and that nominate a beneficiary are not required to pay the surcharge.

12.2 South Australia

Interpretation

Land tax is levied in South Australia under the *Land Tax Act 1936* (SA) and the *Taxation Administration Act 1996* (SA). Land tax for the ensuing financial year is levied on land that is owned as at midnight on 30 June each year. Land ownership, site value and land use are used to calculate land tax. Thus, if you were the owner of a parcel of land on 30 June 2009 but sold that land the next day, you would still be liable for the land tax for the financial year ending 30 June 2010. A threshold exemption of $110 000 applies before the tax rates are levied. The revenue collected from this land tax is used to assist in the provision of education, police and other social services in the state.

Liability and exemptions

Liability for land tax in South Australia falls on the owners of all land owned in South Australia, except exempt land, as at midnight on 30 June of the year preceding the year of assessment and is assessed on a financial year basis. That is, land owned on 30 June 2009 will give rise to land tax payable for the 2010 assessment.

All owners of land are liable for a tax to be levied, but there is an exemption for principal private residences and land used for primary production. Land owned by more than one person is taxed separately from other land that may be held by any one of the **joint owners**.

Exemptions are provided for charitable, religious and educational bodies, and commercial retirement villages. Note that commercial nursing homes, residential rental properties and boarding houses providing low-cost permanent accommodation are all liable for tax. The current rates are shown in Table 12.3; check **www.revenuesa.sa.gov.au** for any changes that may occur.

TABLE 12.3 LAND TAX RATES: SOUTH AUSTRALIA

Taxable value ($)	Add ($)	Tax payable ($)
0–110 000	–	nil
110 001–350 000	–	0.30% of the excess over 110 000
350 001–550 000	720	Plus 0.70% of the excess over 350 000
550 001–750 000	2 120	Plus 1.65% of the excess over 550 000
750 001–1 000 000	5 420	Plus 2.40% of the excess over 750 000
1 000 001 and over	11 420	Plus 3.70% of the excess over 1 000 000

Example

Rateable land owned at midnight on 30 June 2008 and valued for land tax purposes at $700 000 is taxed, after deducting the threshold, as follows:

Land tax payable = $2120 + ($700 000 – $550 000) × 1.65% = $4595

Valuations

In South Australia, the State Valuation Office determines the site value under the *Valuation of Land Act 1971* (SA), which is based on industry-recognised valuation processes that take into account sales and related market evidence.

Owners who are dissatisfied with the valuation of land may object to the Valuer-General, but the objection must contain full and detailed grounds on which the objection is based, and must be lodged within 60 days of the date of the service of notice of the land tax assessment.

Returns and assessments

All the states issue assessments for land tax purposes. In South Australia, persons who own land that is rateable are simply issued with an assessment for land tax. There are no return forms required to be completed and no variation forms. Land tax is calculated on the total of all taxable land values, where the total site values exceed the threshold. If more than one property is owned, the total tax is apportioned to each property depending on its site value:

$$\frac{\text{Site value of property}}{\text{Total taxable site value}} \times \text{total land tax payable} = \text{land tax for particular site}$$

Information for the assessment of land tax is mostly gained from the records that are maintained at the Department of Environment and Natural Resources. While annual returns giving information are not required, changes in ownership must be notified to Revenue Office SA along with any change of address. Accounts for land tax assessed are sent out between October and March in the financial year in which the tax is assessed. The assessment carries an assessment number that corresponds with the Valuer-General's valuation folio.

Taxpayers are given 30 days to pay land tax after assessment, and if the tax is not paid when it falls due it will be increased with a penalty tax. Land tax may also be paid in instalments. These penalty rates are equivalent to those charged under federal tax laws. The rates will change periodically at 1 January or 1 July each year, so check the ATO's website at **www.ato.gov.au** for more information.

12.3 Queensland

Interpretation

The operation of land tax in Queensland takes place under the *Land Tax Act 1915* (Qld) as amended by the new laws contained in the *Land Tax Amendment Act 2003* (Qld), and interacts with the *Taxation Administration Act 2001* (Qld). Every individual who is a resident of Australia is given a statutory exemption up to $600 000. If the holder of land is not an individual, but rather a company, trust or absentee landlord, the threshold is up to $350 000. Values under these thresholds are not taxed, but aggregate values above the threshold are taxable, and the threshold cannot be applied as a deduction. There are, however, special concessions for companies and trustees.

Liability and exemptions

Liability for land tax in Queensland falls on the owners of all land owned in Queensland, except exempt land, as at midnight on 30 June of the year preceding the year of assessment and is assessed on a financial year basis. That is, land owned on 30 June 2009 will give rise to land tax payable for the 2010 assessment. It is important to understand that if land is sold on, say, 1 July 2009, the seller would still be liable for 2010 land tax calculated on landholdings as at 30 June 2009.

Land tax is levied on the aggregate unimproved value of all land owned in Queensland by joint or several persons. While the general threshold exemption applies, there are conditions attached to the exemption of private principal residences, primary production land, charitable and educational bodies, and commercial retirement villages. Commercial nursing homes, residential rental properties and boarding houses providing low-cost permanent accommodation are all liable for tax.

For more information, telephone the Queensland Revenue Office on **1300 300 3734**. Queensland's current land tax rate structure is shown in Tables 12.4 and 12.5; however, **www.osr.qld.gov.au** should be checked regularly for changes to rates.

TABLE 12.4 LAND TAX RATES FOR INDIVIDUALS: QUEENSLAND

Taxable value ($)	Add ($)	Tax payable ($)
Less than 600 000	nil	nil
600 000–999 999	500	Plus 1.00% of the excess over 600 000
1 000 000–2 999 999	4 500	Plus 1.65% of the excess over 1 000 000
3 000 000 or more	1.25% of full taxable value	

TABLE 12.5 LAND TAX RATES FOR COMPANIES, TRUSTS AND ABSENTEE LANDLORDS: QUEENSLAND

Taxable value ($)	Add ($)	Tax payable ($)
Less than 350 000	nil	nil
350 000–2 249 999	1 450	Plus 1.70% of the excess over $350 000
2 500 000 or more	1.50% of full taxable value	

Example

Rateable land owned by a resident individual as at midnight on 30 June 2008 and valued for land tax purposes at $700 000 is taxed, after deducting the threshold exemption of $600 000, as follows:

$$\text{Land tax} = \$500 + ([\$700\,000 - \$600\,000] \times 1.00\%) = \$1500$$

The land tax amount of $1500 can be paid by cheque or BPAY®; a telephone call to the taxpayer's financial institution will assist in setting up these payment options.

Valuations

The unimproved value of land for calculating land tax is determined under the *Valuation of Land Act 1944* (Qld). These values are updated in March each year. The aggregated unimproved value of all Queensland freehold land owned by a land tax payer is used for the purposes of levying land tax. In 1997/98 Queensland introduced a three-year averaging of land values. The average unimproved taxable value is the *lesser* of:

- the current unimproved land value, or
- the average of the unimproved land values for the last three years.

Since 1 July 2007 the Queensland government has placed a 150% cap on the unimproved value of land for land tax purposes. The conditions that apply until the end of the 2009/2010 financial year are as follows:

- the land is not subdivided land that qualifies for the 40% discounting on unimproved value under section 3CA of the *Land Tax Act 1915*
- the land is not newly created parcels of freehold land that do not have an unimproved value for the previous 30 June, and
- the lesser of the unimproved value or averaged unimproved value is more than 150% of the relevant unimproved value of the land for the previous 30 June.

Example

Suppose the unimproved values are given as follows:

Average of three years	2008	2007	2006
$511 667	$900 000	$335 000	$300 000
Capping at 150%		$502 500	

A big increase in the unimproved land value occurred in 2008. The **average unimproved value (AUV)** of $511 667 is greater than 150% of the 2007 value, so the capping of 150% is applied to the previous 2007 unimproved value to give $502 500 for the 2008/2009 year of tax.

Returns and assessments

All the states issue assessments for land tax purposes. For the first return, persons who own land that is rateable must lodge an initial return for land tax. In Queensland, if there are five or more **joint owners** of taxable land, a single assessment is made and no deduction is allowed. These joint owners will not be assessed separately. If there are fewer than five joint owners, separate assessments are issued to the joint owners, including any other interests in jointly owned land with fewer than five owners.

The minimum assessment for Queensland is $1200, and to be assessed with this amount a resident natural person would have taxable land valued at $600 000 or above. Any person owning land that is rateable is liable to supply details to the Commissioner of Land Tax and to lodge a return with details of the land so owned. Once this initial return has been lodged, the information will be used for assessments each year unless the details are changed. Any changes in the information given must be notified to the Commissioner immediately. Taxpayers are generally given 30 days to pay land tax after an assessment is issued, and a penalty of 12% per year from the due date applies to late payments.

12.4 Western Australia

Interpretation

The *Land Tax Act 2002* (WA) and the *Land Tax Assessment Act 2002* (WA) came into effect on 1 July 2002. The revenue collected from land taxes is used in Western Australia to help support education, health, public safety, and law and order.

Liability and exemptions

Liability for land tax in Western Australia falls on the owners of all land owned in Western Australia, except exempt land, as at midnight on 30 June of the year preceding the year of assessment and is assessed on a financial year basis. That is, land owned on 30 June 2009 will give rise to land tax payable for the 2010 assessment. It is important to understand that is if land is sold on, say, 1 July 2009, the seller would still be liable for 2010 land tax calculated on landholdings as at 30 June 2009.

All owners of land in Western Australia are liable for land tax, and this is based on ownership and usage of land. The Metropolitan Region Improvement Tax (MRIT) is a special-purpose **property tax** raised on all land located in the metropolitan region that is subject to land tax. The metropolitan region includes the following local governments: Armidale, Bassendean, Bayswater, Belmont, Cambridge, Canning, Claremont, Cockburn, Cottesloe, East Fremantle, Fremantle, Gosnellis, Joondalup, Kalamunda, Kwinana, Melville, Mosman Park, Mundaring, Nedlands, Peppermint Grove, Perth, Rockingham, Serpentine-Jarrahdale, South Perth, Stirling, Subiaco, Swan, Victoria Park, Vincent and Wanneroo. The rate for this special tax is 15 cents in every $1 of taxable land value in excess of $300 000. It is collected on behalf of the Western Australian Planning Commission, and the revenue collected helps in financing the cost of providing land for roads, open spaces, parks and other public facilities.

Land may be exempt or entitled to a concession if it is used as a residence or being constructed as a residence, used by an owner's disabled relative, used by a rural business, used by not-for-profit societies, clubs and associations or by religious and educational bodies, used by a mining tenement, used by a retirement village or an aged-care facility, or used as a caravan park, park home site or camping ground.

The rating structure at present is shown in Table 12.6. These rates are reviewed annually, so it is wise to check **www.dtf.wa.gov.au** for any changes to these rates.

TABLE 12.6 LAND TAX RATES: WESTERN AUSTRALIA

Taxable value ($)	Add ($)	Tax payable ($)
0–300 000	–	nil
300 000–1 000 000	–	0.10% of the excess over 300 000
1 000 000–2 200 000	700	Plus 0.50% of the excess over 1 000 000
2 200 000–5 500 000	6 700	Plus 1.30% of the excess over 2 200 000
5 500 000–11 000 000	49 600	Plus 1.55% of the excess over 5 500 000
11 000 000 and over	134 850	Plus 2.30% of the excess over 11 000 000

Example

Rateable land in the metropolitan area owned at midnight on 30 June 2008 and valued for land tax purposes at $700 000 is taxed as follows:
Land tax payable = ([$700 000 – $300 000] × 0.10%) = $400

Because the land was in the metropolitan area additional MRIT would be:

($700 000 – $300 000 × 0.15%) = $600

Total land tax and MRIT would be $400 + $600 = $1000

Valuations

The Valuer-General values all land for land tax purposes annually under the *Valuation of Land Act 1978* (WA), the relevant value being the unimproved value. This can be described as the amount that the land might be expected to bring under normal sale conditions, if no improvements or structures were on that land.

Returns and assessments

All the states issue assessments for land tax purposes. For the first return, persons who own land that is rateable must lodge an initial return for land tax. Landowners cannot receive a rebate if they sell their land, as it is not considered to be a pro rata payment. Any person, company or trust who owns land in Western Australia may be liable for land tax. If you owned one lot alone, and owned a second lot jointly with Bill and a third lot jointly with Bob, each of these lots would be assessed separately.

There are three options for payment:

1. payment of the whole amount, with a 3% discount allowed, within 49 days of notice of the assessment
2. payment in two instalments, at 49 days and at 98 days after the notice of assessment
3. payment in three instalments, at 49 days, at 98 days and at 147 days after the notice of assessment.

If an assessment is not paid or the accompanying assessment variation is not completed and lodged by the due date, a penalty will apply automatically.

12.5 Tasmania

Interpretation

The operation of land tax in Tasmania is administered by the State Revenue Office (under the *Land Tax Act 2000* (Tas) and the provisions of the *Taxation Administration Act 1997* (Tas). It is interesting to note that in Tasmania, unlike in some other states, if only a portion of the principal residence is used privately, the land tax will be applied pro rata to tax only the business use.

Liability and exemptions

Liability for land tax in Tasmania falls on the owners of all land owned in Tasmania and is based on the ownership of land as at 1 July of each financial year. The State Revenue Office does not apportion land tax where land is sold during the financial year. However, if the property is sold after 1 July, Section 40(1) of the *Land Tax Act 2000* enables the seller to recover a proper proportion of land tax from the new owner, equivalent to the ratio of the number of days that the land was owned to the number of days in the financial year. Any recovery of paid land tax pursuant to Section 40 of the Act is not initiated by the State Revenue Office, rather by the owner or his or her representative. This normally occurs at settlement and is usually part of the sale agreement conditions.

The following land is exempt from Tasmanian land tax: principal residence land, which is the property where the owner lives; primary production land that is used substantially for primary production; property owned and used for religious purposes; property owned and used by charitable institutions; property owned and used by a private hospital or rest home; aboriginal land used principally for aboriginal cultural activities; land subject to a conservation covenant; and parks and gardens held or owned by local government that are available for use by the general public.

There are four types of land valuations: RES is residential land; RUR is rural land; IND is industrial; and COM is commercial. General rates apply to any land that is not a principal residence or rural land, and tax is levied on all commercial, industrial and vacant land, as well as land used for residential rental properties and commercial retirement villages. The current rates shown in Table 12.7 are liable to be adjusted annually, so check **www.treasury.tas.gov.au** for any changes that may have taken place.

TABLE 12.7 GENERAL RATES ON LAND: TASMANIA

Taxable value ($)	Add ($)	Tax payable ($)
Less than 25 000		nil
25 000–350 000	50.00	Plus 0.55% of the excess over 25 000
350 000–750 000	1837.50	Plus 2.00% of the excess over 350 000
750 000 or more	9837.50	Plus 2.50% of the excess over 750 000

Example

If a property is owned at midnight on 1 July 2008 and the land is valued at $700 000, land tax would be payable as follows:

Land tax = $1837.50 + ([$700 000 – $350 000] × 2.0%) = $8837.50

Valuations and adjustment factors

Land tax is calculated on the **assessed land value** of all taxable properties held by the owner. The assessed land value is the land value of the property multiplied by an **adjustment factor**. The land value and adjustment factors are determined periodically by the Valuer-General under the *Land Valuation Act 1971* (Tas). This attempts to bring all properties in the state into a common valuation band for land tax purposes. These factors are determined for each land category of the municipality. There is no right of appeal against the adjustment factors, but a general right of appeal is available on the Valuer-General's land values. Land is revalued on a cyclical basis approximately every five years and the adjustment factors will reflect movements in the market as at 30 June each year. For more information, visit **www.treasury.tas.gov.au/** or telephone the Tasmanian Treasury on **(03) 6233 2731**.

Returns and assessments

All the states issue assessments for land tax purposes. For the first return, persons who own land that is rateable must lodge an initial return for land tax.

All those persons who own land that is not exempt are liable to furnish details of that land for the levying of land tax. Returns must be lodged with initial details of all land owned in Tasmania, and assessments will be issued each year to the owner unless variations are advised.

Under the *Taxation Administration Act 1997*, interest and penalty tax will apply to late payments. These penalty rates are equivalent to those charged under federal tax laws. These rates will change periodically at 1 January or 1 July each year. Failure to make suitable arrangements for the payment of land tax may result in the sale of the property. If a land tax account is not paid by the due date, a penalty tax of up to 75%, plus any interest, may be charged.

12.6 Australian Capital Territory

Interpretation

The *Land Tax Act 2004* (ACT) has been in operation since 1 July 2004 to levy land tax on land that is owned in the ACT. In the ACT, unlike other states, it is assessed on a quarterly rather than an annual basis and is based on the status of the property on the liability dates of 1 July, 1 October, 1 January and 1 April. General rates revenue in the ACT is used to fund essential community services, and currently contributes approximately 50% of the overall costs of providing these services, the balance being derived from general revenue sources and Commonwealth funding. All owners of non-residential properties are liable for land tax, irrespective of whether the property is rented.

If the property has been rented but is temporarily vacant on a liability date, it may continue to be liable. This would be the case if the property remained vacant for the whole quarter. If the owner notifies the Commissioner for ACT Revenue in writing before the end of the vacant quarter that the property has not been and will not be rented in that quarter, the tax liability may not arise.

Liability and exemptions

The principal residence and primary production land are exempt from land tax. General rates apply to any land that is not a principal residence or rural land, and tax is levied on all commercial, industrial and vacant land, as well as land used for residential rental properties and commercial retirement villages. The rates are liable to be adjusted annually, so check **www.revenue.act.gov.au** for the most current rates. Land tax is assessed for the whole quarter on the **average unimproved value (AUV)** and there is no daily pro-rating of liability within a quarter. The tax is calculated every quarter using the following formula:

(number of days in the quarter/number of days in the year) × AUV × tax rate

The rates shown in Table 12.8 are for both residential and commercial properties. The land tax rates are based on a sliding scale and depend on the AUV of the property.

TABLE 12.8 RATES ON LAND: ACT

AUV ($)	Residential rate	Commercial rate
Less than 75 000	0.60%	0.89%
75 001–150 000	0.89%	0.89%
150 001–275 000	1.15%	1.25%
275 001 and over	1.40%	1.59%

Example

If a residential property is owned at midnight on 1 January 2009 and valued at an AUV of $700 000 for land tax purposes, the March quarterly payment would be payable as follows:

$$\text{March 2009 land tax payable} = (\$700\,000 \times 1.40\%) \times \frac{90}{365} = \$2416.44$$

If the property were a commercial one, the amount of tax would be $2744.38.

Exemptions are available for charitable, religious and educational bodies, commercial nursing homes and boarding houses providing low-cost permanent accommodation.

Valuations

Land tax is calculated on the AUV, which is defined in Section 9 of the *Land Tax Act 2004* as the average unimproved value of the parcel of land valued under the *Rates Act 2004* (ACT). These values are assessed independently by qualified contract valuers engaged by the ACT Revenue Office. The values follow market prices, so the average unimproved value of each block is assessed by examining the price for which similar properties have recently sold, and, if possible, the selling price of unimproved land in the particular area will be used as a comparison. Adjustments are then made for any individual differences, such as size, location, aspect and view, as this may increase or decrease the value of a block of land.

If an owner is dissatisfied with a newly determined unimproved land value of the property, he or she may lodge an objection to the rates assessment only, and not to the land tax assessment. If the objection to the rates assessment is successful and the unimproved land value is changed, the land tax assessment will automatically be recalculated based on the new AUV.

Returns and assessments

If a taxpayer is liable for land tax in the ACT, it is a requirement to advise the Commissioner for ACT Revenue via a 'Notification of Rental Status of Property for Land Tax Purposes' form within 30 days if a residential property purchased, or in which there is an interest, is rented or becomes rented. The taxpayer is also required to advise the Commissioner of any changes in circumstances that may render any such property liable for land tax within 30 days of the change occurring. Assessments will be issued each quarter to the owner unless variations are advised.

Failure to provide the required information and giving false or misleading information are serious offences and may lead to additional interest and penalties. If a land tax account is not paid by the due date, compounding interest charges, which may be subject to change during the year, are calculated and imposed on unpaid amounts on the 16th day of each month.

12.7 New South Wales

Interpretation

Land tax is levied in New South Wales under the *Land Tax Act 1956* (NSW), the *Land Tax Management Act 1956* (NSW) and the *Taxation Administration Act 1996* (NSW). Any owner, either solely or jointly, possessing taxable land with an unimproved value greater than the threshold must pay land tax.

Liability and exemptions

Liability for land tax in New South Wales falls on the owners of all land owned in the state, except exempt land, as at midnight on 31 December of the year preceding the year of assessment and is assessed on a calendar year basis. That is, land owned on 31 December 2009 will give rise to land tax payable for the 2010 assessment, with assessments being issued between February and June each year. It is important to understand that is if land is sold on, say, 1 January 2010 the seller would still be liable for 2010 land tax calculated on landholdings as at 31 December 2009. **Joint owners** are also liable.

The primary principal residence of any person is exempt from land tax if it is owner-occupied. Special concessions apply for those persons who live on the site of their business.[1] Other exemptions apply to primary production land; charitable, religious and educational bodies; commercial retirement villages; educational institutions; not-for-profit societies; clubs and associations; commercial nursing homes; and boarding houses providing low-cost permanent accommodation.

Table 12.9 sets out the current land tax rates; however, it is a good idea to check **www.osr.nsw.gov.au** regularly for any changes that may occur.

It is important to remember that any business use of private residential premises will render the exemption void. Land tax will be assessed in full, on the property value.

TABLE 12.9 LAND TAX RATES: NEW SOUTH WALES

Taxable value ($)	Add ($)	Tax payable ($)
0–359 000	0	nil
359 001 and over	100	Plus 1.6% of the excess over 359 000

Land tax in New South Wales is calculated using an average of the last three years' values. Calculating the threshold for 2008 is shown in Table 12.10.

TABLE 12.10 APPLYING THE THREE-YEAR AVERAGING FOR THE THRESHOLD

Year of value	Indexing values ($)
For the 2006 land tax year	352 000
For the 2007 land tax year	356 000
For the 2008 land tax year	369 000
Threshold average for 2008	**359 000**

Example

Rateable land owned at midnight on 31 December 2008 and valued for land tax purposes at $700 000 will attract land tax as follows:

Land tax = $100 + ([$700 000 – 359 000] × 0.016) = $5556

Where the amount of land tax calculated is less than $100, no land tax will be payable. All calculations should be rounded *down* to the nearest 10 cents.

An option for payment of land tax is a discount of 1.5% available if full payment for the year is made within 30 days of the assessment notice being served. The discount does not apply to payments in arrears, interest or penalty tax.

Valuations

The taxable value of each parcel of land will generally be the average of the land value applying for the current tax year and the two land values that applied for the prior two land tax years. Where a parcel of land has been created only recently (for example, by a subdivision), then the average value will be based only on the land value as it existed at subdivision. The threshold will be indexed each year and it will also be averaged using the new indexed amount and the thresholds from the previous two years. Where the average threshold is less than the previous year's threshold, then the previous year's threshold will be used.

The Valuer-General has the sole responsibility for determining the value for land tax under the *Valuation of Land Act 1916* (NSW), and the Chief Commissioner calculates land tax based on these values, which are recorded in the Register of Land Values. There is the right of appeal to the NSW Land and Environment Court against any land values. An entry in the register is taken to be the value of the land for the purposes of land tax in New South Wales.

Returns and assessments

All the states issue assessments for land tax purposes. Persons who own land that is subject to land tax in New South Wales must lodge an initial return for land tax, unless they have already done so in a previous year. Once an initial return has been lodged, an assessment will be issued to the landowner every year on the information given in that initial return. Further returns are not necessary, unless circumstances change. For this purpose, a **variations only return** is always attached to every land tax assessment, and if there is any change in the ownership of land this form must be lodged, generally online.

Once the assessment notice has been issued, the landowner is given the option of either paying by instalments on the due dates or paying the full assessment by the due date. Where a taxpayer is individually assessed on land that has also been included in another assessment, a credit of tax payable is allowed as a deduction to prevent double taxation. Under the Taxation Administration Act 1996, interest and penalty tax will apply to late payments. These penalty rates are equivalent to those charged under federal tax laws. The rates will change periodically at 1 January or 1 July each year. Check **www.osr.nsw.gov.au** for more details. The market rate component of the interest rate for late payments of land tax is determined by reference to the 90-day bank-accepted bill rate.

Learning check

- ✓ Calculate the assessable land tax base for a taxpayer.
- ✓ Obtain relevant land tax rates from the State Revenue Office.
- ✓ Calculate the land tax payable for a taxpayer.

Taxation vocabulary

adjustment factor
assessed land value
average unimproved value (AUV)
first charge
freehold
joint owners
land tax
ownership
penalty
primary assessment
property tax
rateable land
rebate of tax
secondary assessment
valuations
variations only return

multiple-choice questions

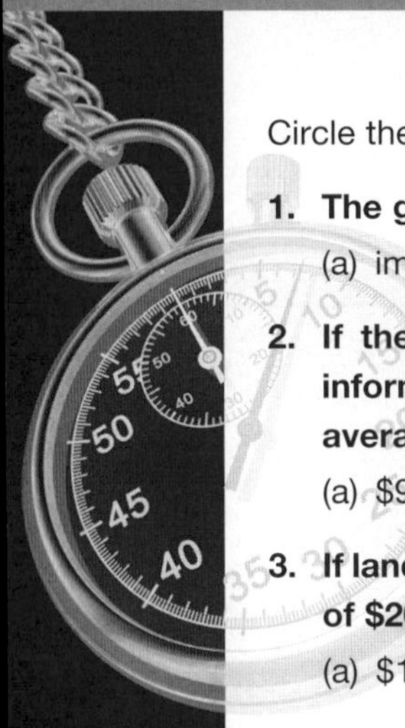

Circle the correct response. (Answers to odd-numbered multiple-choice questions are provided on page 318.)

1. **The general value of land for land tax purposes in all Australian states is defined as:**
   (a) improved (b) adjusted (c) unimproved (d) equalised
2. **If the threshold is averaged over three years, calculate the current threshold using the following information: 2008 year $950 000, 2007 year $335 000, 2006 year $300 000, 2005 year $285 000. The current average threshold would therefore be:**
   (a) $950 000 (b) $528 333 (c) $467 500 (d) $306 667
3. **If land tax of 1.9% was levied on a property valued for that purpose at $450 000, and a general exemption of $200 000 was available, the tax assessed would be:**
   (a) $10 000 (b) $3800 (c) $4750 (d) $8550
4. **If land tax of 1.9% was levied on a property valued for that purpose at $450 000 (and a general exemption of $200 000 was available), but there was also a property levy of 0.15%, the tax assessed would be:**
   (a) $1300 (b) $4100 (c) $4175 (d) $5425
5. **The word 'ownership' is generally defined for land tax purposes to mean:**
   (a) a person who is jointly entitled to the land for any estate of freehold in possession
   (b) a person who is severally entitled to receive any rents or profits from that land
   (c) a person who jointly or severally is entitled to the land for any estate of freehold in possession or to receive any rents or profits from that land
   (d) a person who jointly or severally has placed a claim on the land

quick and easy comprehension

Place a ✓ to indicate your response to each statement.

STATEMENT	TRUE	FALSE
1. The value of land for land tax purposes is the 'unimproved value'.	—	—
2. All owners of land will be liable for land tax.	—	—
3. In Queensland, conditions apply to all exemptions.	—	—
4. The valuation of land subject to land tax in each state is valued by the particular State Revenue Office.	—	—
5. All the revenue collected from land tax is used for land development.	—	—

assessments

1. **If you were asked to tell a client about the basic land tax facts in your state, what items would you place on your checklist?**

Item to discuss	Yes ✓	No ✓	Comments

2. If a landowner had two properties, one the principal residence land valued at $850 000 and the other a weekend cottage with a land value of $700 000, what would be the tax assessed (if any) in your state?

3. Andrew runs a marina, and before he built the wharves he was permitted to dredge and reclaim an area of 100 square metres, which meant that his property increased in size. Would he be issued with a new land valuation for his marina? Set out the reasons for your answer.

case study question

Tom Masonry's company Colossal Constructions Pty Ltd is situated on a large block of land in an industrial estate that is valued for land tax purposes at $550 000. Tom and his wife, Jan, built their jointly owned home on land valued at $680 000. Tom and Jan also own a holiday unit at the beach with a land value of $210 000 ($105 000 each). Set out the land tax liability for Tom as it would apply in your state. What liability will the company have, if any?

classroom activity

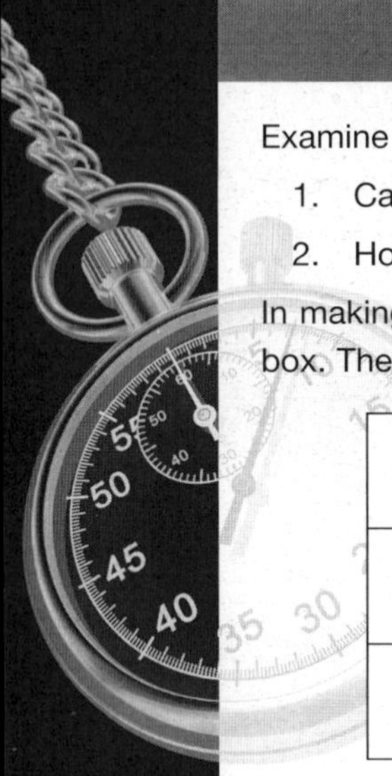

Examine the square below with nine compartments, each containing a letter.

1. Can you find the nine letter word that relates to land tax?
2. How many words of three letters or more can you make from that word?

In making a word, each letter must be used once only. Each word must contain the centre letter in the shaded box. There must be no words with a hyphen or an apostrophe.

T	V	I
U	A	N
A	O	L

A total of 13 words is good, 20 is great and 26 is excellent.

Note

1. Refer to section 9C of the *Land Tax Management Act 1956* for reductions in tax.

New directions for tax reforms

3

Part three

This part of the book goes a little deeper into the meaning of taxation. Chapter 13 contains definitions and the latest statistics from the ATO. It examines the effectiveness of taxation and its function, and looks at the different types of taxation that could be used. Chapter 14 examines how the changing structure of taxation in Australia has benefited many in this first decade of the third millennium and how our embracement of the electronic era has made compliance quicker and easier. However, the Commissioner of Taxation sent a warning to all taxpayers in 2008 when he stated:

> Australians who seek to conceal their tax obligations leave other Australians to bear a greater tax burden. There is no philosopher's stone that, through alchemy, transforms Australian or foreign source income derived by an Australian resident into non-taxable income in Australia by the mere transmission through, or concealment in, a tax haven. Abusive arrangements of this kind, if left unchecked, undermine community confidence in our tax system as well as the system's integrity.[1]

The benefits of accessing the ATO Business Portal are also outlined in Chapter 14, where we discuss the constantly evolving technology that enables businesses to transmit documents and tax payments directly to the ATO. Finally, some interesting websites to visit are listed, some of the latest findings in taxation research are examined, in particular the usefulness of the tax-free threshold, and references for further reading are provided.

1 Media release by Michael D'Ascenzo, Commissioner of Taxation, March 2008. Available online at **www.ato.gov.au**.

13

Tax criteria

Chapter thirteen

Topics

After studying this chapter, you should be able to:

- **define a tax and state the difference between tax and tax expenditure**
- **define the tax base and identify the three broad types of base available for taxing**
- **examine the issues of consolidation and entity taxation**
- **state the function of taxation**
- **distinguish between vertical and horizontal equity.**

launched an aggressive program to investigate offshore tax havens and now Australia has begun a comprehensive program to negotiate tax information exchange agreements with a number of countries.[5] Significant changes to the taxing of superannuation have been introduced[6] and current discussions are assessing possible new directions for business taxes. The Commissioner also believes that the ongoing challenge for the ATO is to better connect with and engage taxpayers and their agents to promote good compliance behaviour and, in doing so, ensure that the tax system is operating fairly. The latest tax reforms are aimed at offering significant tax relief and a reduction in compliance costs, and will help alleviate some of the added workload of implementing the GST.

13.3 Business tax reforms

In general, the federal government's aim is to design a taxation system that will contribute to economic growth. The objectives of the reform measures are:

- to create a durable and flexible business taxation architecture
- to incorporate an integrated design process of policy, legislative design and administration
- to generate external involvement via the Board of Taxation
- to establish a more neutral and **equitable** taxation system
- to reduce the cost of compliance on taxpayers
- to develop a far simpler system for small businesses
- to create equal footing between small and large investors
- to encourage more investment through a more competitive capital gains regime.

13.4 Entity taxation

The federal government has made one of its goals the reform of our taxation system. Among various proposals, one area that has attracted the government's focus is the appropriate entity to be taxed. As the government has found, it is extremely difficult to design a perfect tax system. The traditional criteria for judging a tax system were outlined in the Asprey Report some 25 years ago. A tax system should be:

- **efficient**
- equitable or fair
- simple: clearly understood by the taxpayer and easy to administer
- flexible: for example, the receipts of tax should be able to counter the ups and downs in the economy.

For the government to be able to administer the taxation system, revenue must be collected without too much difficulty. The taxing system draws resources from the private sector, and these should be about equal to the resources made available for public use. The government must also be aware of the problems of taxes that are **shifted backwards**. The fringe benefits tax is in this category. Thus the government has the task of attempting to administer and collect revenue in the simplest way so as to minimise waste. Wasting resources occurs in the costs of complying with and administering taxation. Sometimes very equitable taxes, such as capital gains tax and fringe benefits tax, are also fairly complex and costly.

The concept of entity taxation can best be explained by the following example.

Example

If an individual owns an asset in his or her own name, any resulting income is clearly attributable to that individual. However, if the individual interposes another entity (e.g. a company) between himself or herself and the asset, the question then becomes: who derives the income? There can be three alternatives to this dilemma:

- The interposed entity is taxed on the income, and distributions to the individual are also subject to tax without regard to the tax previously paid by the entity.
- The entity accounts for the income, but is not subject to tax. This income is attributed to the individual, who is then liable for the tax at individual rates. This is similar to a partnership distribution.
- The interposed entity is taxed on the income and distributions to the individual are also subject to tax, but in this case relief from double taxation is offered by way of imputation credits or tax offsets.

This whole area is so complex, particularly in the area of trusts, that the government temporarily shelved these ideas. Instead it introduced a limited regime, which is referred to as consolidation measures.

13.5 Consolidation

The former Howard government decided to introduce **consolidation**—that is, taxing wholly owned groups as single entities—as part of its Business Tax Reform. Prior to consolidation, each company in a wholly owned group was treated as a separate entity for income tax purposes. This meant that each entity had to separately account for all intra-group transactions and debt and equity interests. For business, this meant extra compliance costs. From the community's perspective, this seemed to provide opportunities for **tax avoidance** through artificial arrangements.

The consolidation measures have been developed by designing legislation and administrative processes in parallel with policy development. The government is fine-tuning the consolidation arrangements in consultation with the business community. Thus, this area is continually evolving and subject to change.

Any business group can consolidate, regardless of size. This is so even if a business consists of two or more eligible entities. The head entity of a consolidated group must be a company; it cannot be a trust or a partnership. Most small businesses use straightforward structures and will not be affected by the consolidation regime, because consolidation is relevant only where a company wholly owns one or more other entities. Consolidation is not relevant to the business activities of individuals.

In summary, the key points are as follows:

- The consolidation regime commenced on 1 July 2002.
- A consolidated group is treated as a single entity for income tax purposes.

- The head company pays PAYG instalments and self-assesses a single annual income tax liability on behalf of the whole group.
- Consolidation does not affect other tax obligations such as GST, FBT and PAYG withholding.
- A consolidated group can be formed by a single Australian-resident head company and all its eligible wholly owned Australian-resident subsidiaries.
- The subsidiaries may be companies, partnerships or trusts.
- Participation is optional.
- In most cases, the existing grouping provisions for wholly owned groups will be replaced by the consolidation rules.
- Corporate groups must consolidate if they want access to any form of single entity treatment.
- The head company notifies the ATO of its decision to consolidate (when it lodges the group's first consolidated income tax return).
- The head company must notify the ATO when subsidiary members leave or join the group, or if the consolidated group ceases to exist.
- A decision to consolidate, once notified, is irrevocable.

The merging of separate entities or businesses into one reporting entity is addressed by the Australian Accounting Standards Board (AASB 3, paragraph 4). The result of nearly all business combinations is that one entity, the acquirer, obtains control of one or more businesses from an acquiree. For present purposes, business combinations include parent–subsidiary relationships in which the acquirer is the parent and the acquiree is the subsidiary of the acquirer. For an excellent coverage of all consolidation issues, see the publications on the Consolidation homepage of the ATO's website. The *Consolidation Reference Manual* contained therein has been designed for easy updating as new information becomes available.

13.6 The functions of taxation

Taxes are used to raise revenue for all the objectives that the government has set out. Taxation is also used as a fiscal tool to alter policy, such as giving subsidies to industry, filmmaking, research and development, farming and so on. In addition, tax can be used for the purposes of redistribution, because without the public sector intervention, distribution of income would be unacceptable. This, however, is not a powerful tool for taxation. Taxing can be used to effect resource allocation, such as in pollution taxes and crude oil tax, for efficient use.

As tax reforms are under way, what are the criteria or standards against which we can judge the system? How well does the tax system perform its function of creating equity? The *Income Tax Assessment Act 1997* (Cwlth) has been built up progressively to replace some provisions of the *Income Tax Assessment Act 1936* (Cwlth). However, the current focus is on other tax reforms and consolidation.

13.7 Vertical and horizontal equity

Equity is the 'fairness' of the tax system. Tax researchers have traditionally categorised it as vertical equity and horizontal equity.

Vertical equity

Vertical equity means that persons in different situations should be treated differently by the tax system. Vertical equity advocates progressive taxation and embodies the principle that those who earn more should pay more in tax. However, it is often very difficult for governments to agree on the level of progressivity.

Horizontal equity

Horizontal equity means that persons in the same situation should be treated the same by the tax system. This treats the ability of people to pay as equal if they earn the same amount. But suppose that a single person who does not have to provide for dependants has a wage of $40 000 per year. Can we say that this person has the same ability to pay as a person earning $40 000 per year but who has to provide for a spouse and children?

Benefit equity

We also can speak about **benefit equity**, and this is defined as meaning that those who receive benefits should pay accordingly. An example is a **poll tax**, where in local government areas those people who live and enjoy the benefits of the particular area—such as parks, libraries and footpaths—should contribute to the maintenance and provision of these public goods. Instead of taxing a house with the payment of rates, the people living in the house are taxed with a poll tax, as they are the ones who benefit from the area and its services. Despite the enormous problems that this tax caused in Britain, it is generally considered to be a fairly equitable tax.

Taxation vocabulary

benefit equity
consolidation
efficient
equitable
expenditure base
horizontal equity
income base
poll tax
progressive tax
proportional tax
regressive tax
shifted backwards
tax avoidance
tax base
tax burden
tax evasion
tax incidence
unit
vertical equity

Further reading

ATO (2007), 'Compliance program 2007/2008', Australian Taxation Office, Canberra. Available online at **www.ato.gov.au/content/56734.htm**

Bevan, C. (2000), 'A traveller's guide through stage 1 of the reforms', in *Taxation in Australia*, 34 (10), April.

Carey, A. et al. (2008), *Australian GST Handbook 2008–2009*, Thomson, Sydney.

CCH Income Tax Guide (2008), CCH Australia Limited, Sydney.

Collins, D. & Warren, N. (2007), 'The states and the GST: demystifying Australian federal/state financial agreements', Information Series no. 4, Australian Tax Research Foundation, Sydney.

Collins, D. J. (1989), 'Taxation of fringe benefits', in J. Head (ed.), *Australian Tax Reform in Retrospect and Prospect*, Australian Tax Research Foundation, Sydney.

Deutsch, R. L. et al. (2008), *Australian Tax Handbook*, Australian Tax Practice, Sydney.

Freebairn, J., Porter, M. & Walsh, C. (eds) (1989), *Saving and Productivity: Incentives for the 1990s*, Allen & Unwin, Sydney.

Groenewegen, P. (1984), *Public Finance in Australia: Theory and Practice*, Prentice Hall, Sydney.

Head, J. & Krever, R. (1997), 'Introduction and summary', in J. Head & R. Krever (eds), *Taxation Towards 2000*, Conference Series no. 19, Australian Tax Research Foundation, Sydney, pp. xiii–xlii.

Miller, B. (2004), 'Another draft GST ruling on exports of "things"', in *Taxation in Australia*, 38 (9), April.

Pender, H. (1997), *The Joy of Tax: Australian Tax Design, Directions for Long Term Reform*, Research Study no. 26, Australian Tax Research Foundation, Sydney.

Ralph Committee Report on Business Taxation Reform (July 1999). Available online at **www.rbt.treasury.gov.au**

Rawls, J. (1971), *A Theory of Justice*, Harvard University Press, Cambridge, MA.

Vann, R. (2001), 'Australia's policy on entity taxation', *A Journal of Taxation Policy, Law and Reform*, 16 (1).

Warren, N. (2004), *Tax Facts, Fiction and Reform*, Research Study no. 41, Australian Tax Research Foundation, Sydney.

Notes

1. See J. P. Smith (1990), *Taxing Popularity: The Story of Taxation in Australia*, Canberra Federalism Research Centre, Australian National University, Canberra.
2. Refer to 'Submission to the 2009 federal budget process' (2008), Business Coalition for Tax Reform.
3. The full report on these statistics can be seen at **www.ato.gov.au**
4. Refer to the paper by R. Webb, 'Public finance and vertical fiscal imbalance', Economics, Commerce and Industrial Relations Group, 15 October 2002. Available online at **www.aph.gov.au/LIBRARY/Pubs/rn/2002-03/03rn13.htm**, accessed 23 March 2008.
5. Michael D'Ascenzo (2008), 'Tax havens and tax administration'. Available online at **www.ato.gov.au/content/downloads/LBI_46908_Tax_Havens_w.pdf**, accessed 23 March 2008.
6. L. Nielson, (2007), 'Superannuation and taxation 2007–2008', Research Paper no. 2, August. Available online at **www.aph.gov.au/library/pubs/rp/2007-08/08rp02.pdf**, accessed 23 March 2008.

The electronic era

14

Chapter fourteen

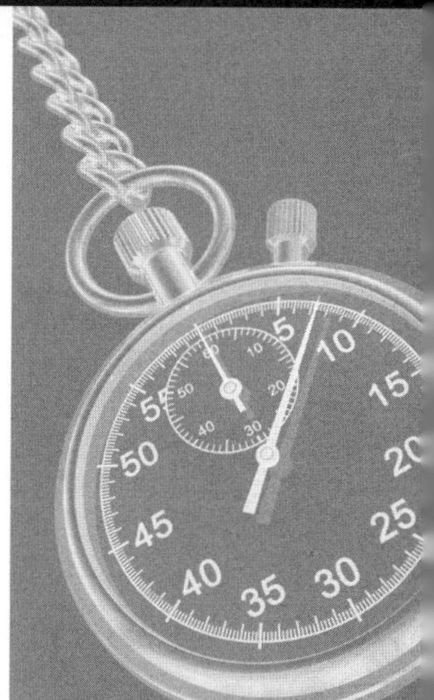

Learning outcomes

After studying this chapter, you should be able to:

- **understand the electronic era and its effect on the business environment**
- **outline the access available to ATO portals for tax agents, businesses and individuals**
- **examine the documents and forms available on the ATO's website**
- **identify other websites that can be searched**
- **outline the tax and business reforms that are currently taking place in Australia**
- **examine the arguments for and against the tax-free threshold.**

OVERVIEW

As this first decade of the third millennium draws to a close, we are experiencing an ever-expanding electronic environment, where most of our business, education and leisure activities involve using the Internet. Taxation is a part of this, and this chapter looks at some of the exciting advances that access to the Internet can offer taxpayers. The chapter also examines some of the websites that can provide businesses with information and assistance, and discusses the more interesting aspects of accessing the Tax Portal and Business Portal and using the Electronic Commerce Interface. Finally, the chapter touches on reforms to taxation and current theories in taxation, such as the effects of raising the income tax threshold and avoiding bracket creep.[1]

14.1 Electronic communications

The ATO, like any other business entity, is keen to be as efficient as possible so that tangible benefits might accrue to taxpayers and the system in general. The Commissioner of Taxation has stated that managing the ATO's relationships with taxpayers and monitoring the continuous improvements to the way the ATO deals with taxpayers is of the utmost importance. To further this philosophy, developments in electronic service delivery are being constantly upgraded to provide cutting-edge services to accountants and taxpayers.

It is well known that the ATO already receives the majority of annual income tax returns electronically, principally through the **Electronic Lodgment Service (ELS)** with tax agents. Initiatives such as **electronic funds transfer (EFT)**, telephone banking, interactive messaging and the ability to electronically register and lodge both returns and forms have increasingly become part of an integrated package.

Public key technology

Public key technology (PKT) is a modern cryptographic technique based on accepted international standards. The technology uses **common-use signing interface (CSI)** with a digital authentication certificate, an electronic signature and a highly secure level of data protection, through the use of authentication and encryption keys. Data is transmitted through a Virtual Private Network (VPN). It enables Internet Protocol (IP) traffic to travel securely over a public Transport Control Protocol (TCP)/IP network by encrypting all traffic from one network to another. A VPN uses 'tunnelling' to encrypt all information at the IP level.

PKT provides the electronic equivalent of all the features of postal or physical document transmission. Taxpayers wishing to take part in this electronic transmission service will be issued with their unique digital certificate once certain requirements have been met.

In a PKT system there are one or more unique key pairs. Each of these pairs has a private key and a public key. The private key must be used only by the key holder. The public key is used by other parties with whom the key holder communicates over the Internet. Key holders may make their public key freely available, but they should not disclose their private key. The keys are used to encrypt a transaction before it is sent over the Internet and to decrypt it on receipt. Once encrypted, the transaction can be decrypted only by the corresponding key. A unique electronic signature must also be used: this identification authenticates the sender and ensures that the contents of a document cannot be repudiated. The ATO will provide the taxpayer with an electronic signature only after rigorous identity checks have been carried out, and the ATO will not accept transactions unless the taxpayer's electronic signature is verified.

FIGURE 14.1 The CSI sign-in certificate

When using the *Application to Register for the New Tax System*, there is a question that relates to electronic transmissions. It asks whether the applicant would like to use the ATO's Internet-based e-commerce system. If the answer is 'yes', then the ATO will issue the applicant with a digital certificate, and private and public keys. The digital certificate and keys will be issued via the post, and a **personal identification code (PIC)** to decrypt the keys and a certificate on the applicant's personal computer will come by separate mail accompanied by detailed instructions to guide the user through the process. Once this is done correctly, the signing and encryption of transactions is largely automatic, managed by a straightforward password control. Figure 14.1 shows an example of a digital certificate sign-in screen. By entering the PIC, entry to the Tax Portal is gained.

14.2 Using the Internet for business

Electronic transactions between taxpayers and the ATO are transmitted via the Internet. The ATO guarantees a high level of security and confidentiality of taxpayer information by using the latest technology, which ensures:

- *authentication:* that the recipient can be fully confident that senders are who they say they are

- *confidentiality:* that the content of the communication cannot be read by anyone other than the recipient
- *integrity:* that the content of the communication cannot be tampered with in transit
- *non-repudiation:* that the sender cannot later deny the communication and its content.

There are many other sites that are useful for business:

- Australian Bureau of Statistics: **www.abs.gov.au**
- Australian Competition and Consumer Commission: **www.accc.gov.au**
- Australian Customs Service: **www.customs.gov.au**
- Australian Taxation Studies Program, University of New South Wales: **www.atax.unsw.edu.au**
- Australasian Legal Information Institute publishes free legal information: **www.austlii.edu.au**
- Case judgements and decisions from the High Court and Federal Court of Australia: **http/scaleplus.law.gov.au**
- Federal Treasury home page: **www.treasury.gov.au**

The Tax Agent Portal

The ATO has been operating the **Tax Agent Portal** for some time. It is a web-based support system that enables tax agents to interact directly with client files at the ATO. This service is password-protected using a digital certificate, and agents can use the messaging, email and key updates to help keep abreast of new developments. From November 2008 tax agents must have a digital certificate to access this service, because the old ID and password entry has been discontinued.

When agents log into the Tax Agent Portal using CSI as shown above, they are able to enter, update or delete their clients' financial institution account details for their activity statement roles. Another service available to agents is the Online Access Manager (OAM), which enables the creation of separate user accounts so that staff members can access the Tax Agent Portal with their own unique certificates. The benefit of this in a tax practice is that it creates internal control procedures to monitor who is accessing the portal and when. When a staff member leaves the practice, or no longer requires access to the portal, it is much easier to manage the change.

Increasingly the Tax Agent Portal has become a key element of the tax agent's professional library. The website includes a wide range of ATO forms, which are available to be downloaded for completion. These are called 'smart forms', and provide technological assistance with completion. Other advances include calculation programs for such things as HELP, PAYG withholding tax, FBT, capital gains tax, superannuation co-contributions and child support.

The ATO introduced the pre-filling of tax forms in 2008 to assist tax agents and their clients by removing the need for them to find and supply a range of information. The pre-filled information that is available through the Tax Agent Portal includes:

- ATO-held data on HELP and prior year deductions
- payment summaries in cases where the employer provided details to the ATO electronically (in 2008, any employer who provided timely electronic information had details loaded for pre-filling)

- private health insurance details from Medicare
- dividend and interest information from financial institutions.

The Business Portal

The **Business Portal** is available to help enterprises view up-to-date running balances on their accounts and check their lodgements and payments to the ATO. Businesses can access their activity statements, income tax accounts, fringe benefits tax accounts, excise accounts and some superannuation accounts. The portal also allows businesses to:

- view their statement of account and payment options
- update business details
- transfer funds between their accounts
- communicate with the ATO through a secure mailbox.

A business's digital certificate can be used for all online services with the ATO and it is attached to the business's ABN. The business's digital certificate can also be used to transact information relevant to that ABN in the private portion of the Australian Business Register at **www.abr.gov.au** and with the electronic commerce interface (ECI).

The electronic commerce interface

The **electronic commerce interface (ECI)** enables businesses to go online to deal electronically with the ATO 24 hours a day, seven days a week, and is both fast and secure. The ECI is designed to allow businesses to lodge TFN declarations, PAYG tax withholding annual reports, lodging or collecting investment body reports and lodging or collecting superannuation reports. It also enables businesses to check the accuracy of their reports before they are transmitted. This facility saves many hours of work in detecting errors in documents such as annual payroll reconciliation reports. The software necessary to run ECI is available either on CD-ROM or via a download from the ATO's website at **www.ato.gov.au**. For more information about the software, visit **http://eci.ato.gov.au** or telephone the electronic products infoline on **1300 139 051**. Or visit the ATO's website and read the extensive guidelines on the ATO's ECI software and accounting software packages.

New developments

The new Standard Business Reporting website, shown in Figure 14.2, is being developed by the ATO to assist businesses with all their reporting obligations and it is hoped the website will be fully operational by 2010. Keep an eye on this new initiative that will help centralise all types of business reporting.

Individual taxpayers

The ATO's website currently provides guided access to a wide range of publications, rulings, legislation and other information to assist professionals, businesspeople and individuals in tax matters. There is also a facility for taxpayers to lodge their tax return directly through the eTax website at **www.etax.com.au/**, and taxpayers can request information from Centrelink about child-care offsets and family tax payments.

At a lower level of technology, but of immediate assistance, is the 'Fax from Tax' service, whereby taxpayers are able to have a wide range of information

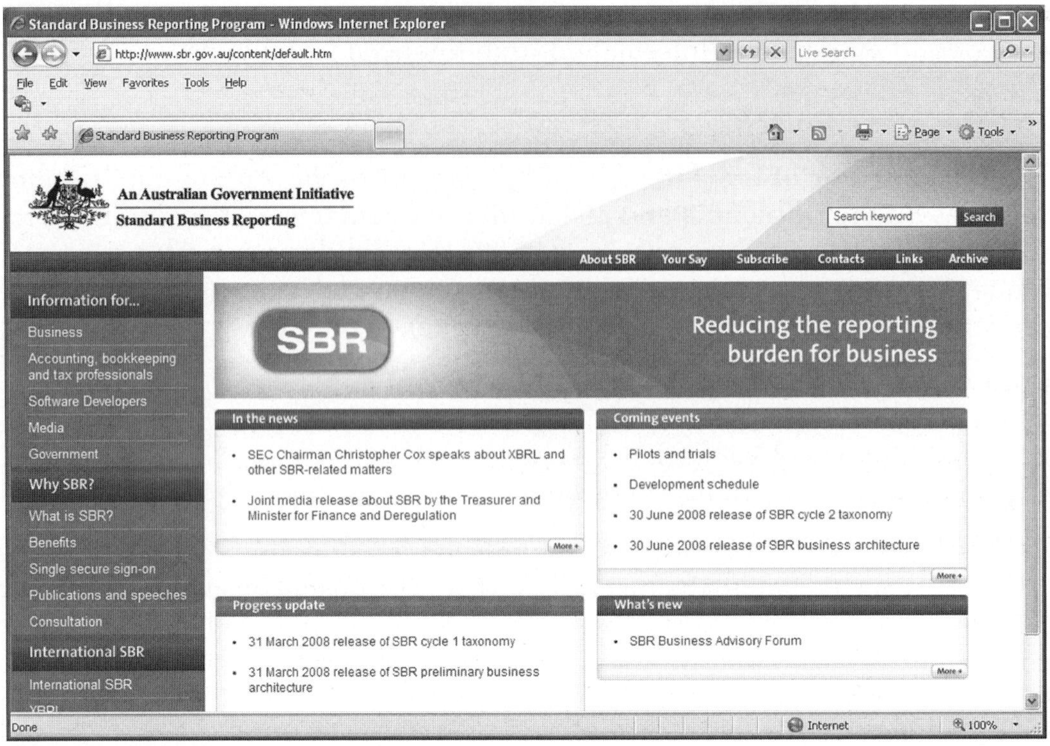

FIGURE 14.2 The ATO's new Standard Business Reporting website

sheets faxed to them by telephoning **13 28 60**. The widespread availability of this technology opens up many opportunities. For example, an agent may request that a particular form be faxed directly to a client. Electronic business is consistent with professional best practice, and person-based communications are set to become a thing of the past.

14.3 Electronic forms

Some commonly used ATO forms can be downloaded from the ATO's website at **www.ato.gov.au**. The intelligent **electronic forms** have been designed to allow on-screen interaction. The user can download the appropriate form (which includes an inbuilt expiry date) and then operate the 'intelligence' of the form. Special programming capabilities incorporated in the software validate details such as TFNs and ABNs and accurately calculate the family tax allowance. The electronic form can be filled in on-screen. Users can access their databases for information and then save the completed form on their hard drive and/or print the (partially) completed form from their printer.

Benefits to ATO clients include:

- improved timely access to current forms
- reduced storage and disposal costs for holding ATO forms
- validation and error correction available online at the time of keying
- on-screen completion assistance available as 'help files' or 'informative messages'.

14.4 The case for taxation reforms

If meaningful and durable reforms are to be made to our taxation system, perhaps governments need to put aside the single-minded pursuit of short-term redistributive policies and change the approach to designing an optimal tax system, one which ensures that national interests are paramount—not vested or sectional interests. The trade-offs between equity and efficiency must be fully assessed and all the measures and procedures that will assist in implementing a practical and workable tax system need to be explored. The results of the change in the tax mix from a narrow income-based system to a more broad-based consumption tax have brought long-term managerial benefits to many Australian businesses.

Many of the OECD countries have for a long time imposed a tax on wealth, whereas Australian states abolished this tax some two decades ago. Death duty was imposed because of the difficulties of assessing changes in the wealth of the living. There is no theoretical concept of income that can be used as a measure of an individual's wealth increase, and in fact the Commissioner of Taxation does not have an exhaustive definition of income. But if, under the income tax system, an all-embracing tax is consistently levied on investment income of all types, there should not be any need for a supplementary tax on wealth or wealth transfers.[2]

One significant problem that must be addressed is the effect that taxation has on the incentive to work. One of the reasons why people work is to be paid so that they can enjoy some leisure time, which is unpaid. But this leisure time does have a value for them, and if the marginal tax rate goes up then people are tempted to substitute more leisure time for work, because the value of leisure time goes up. The real disposable income goes down, and this can cause people to work harder to try to maintain income levels, so the average tax rate rises. These two effects work in opposite directions. Governments are constantly debating this issue but are loath to do anything about bracket creep, where taxpayers are automatically nudged up into a higher marginal income tax bracket when wage increases are granted due to **inflation**.

New models have been offered to help reduce the minimisation schemes, one suggesting that the present tax-free threshold should be abolished and marginal rates introduced from 15% to a high of 36%. The opposite has in fact occurred, as the threshold was last raised in July 2003. The top two thresholds of the income tax system have been increased substantially and the corresponding marginal tax rates were recently cut to 40% and 45%. The change in the government at the end of 2007 may signal some changes to the future tax rates system.

14.5 The tax-free threshold

The **tax threshold** (or tax-free threshold) has two main effects:

1. it contributes to the overall progressivity of the rate scale
2. it gives some protection to low-income earners.

The threshold has to be judged as being progressive because the provision of a zero rate followed by positive rates results in a greater proportion of tax being paid as income rises.[3] This means that the average tax rate, while constantly rising, is always below the marginal tax rate when there is a threshold. Apart from the equity considerations, the fact that there is a threshold removes a large number of people from the liability to taxation, thus removing some of the administration problems associated with processing income tax returns. Research on these issues is gathering pace. Buddelmeyer and Kalb added to this debate when they posed the following questions:

> Examining the tax reform more closely, two questions rise to the fore. Firstly, are all components of the policy changes contributing to the same extent to the positive labour supply response? Secondly, are there better ways to lighten the tax burden while at the same time maximising labour force participation?[4]

With the low-income offset, people can participate in the workforce at present and earn approximately $210 per week without being taxed. But this threshold is an expensive gift of the government because of the revenue lost. If the threshold were not available, there would be billions of dollars extra in tax revenue.[5] However, there would also be some serious equity problems that would have to be solved.

When studying tax proposals, researchers are trying to keep the tax revenue neutral.[6] That means looking at each different option that would change or shift the tax liability, assuming that each would bring in the same amount of revenue to the government. Obviously, when tax rates change, so too does people's behaviour, and thus subjective judgements must be made about what might happen in these cases. However, the following discussion assumes that revenue changes will be neutral.

What would happen if the threshold were to be eliminated? The research by Elizabeth Savage shows that the abolition of the threshold is likely to create a much more efficient system but at a considerable cost to equity and thus an average social welfare loss.[7] It is argued that eliminating the threshold would mean that the marginal tax rate would be able to be lowered by about 5% but that many more people would have to file tax returns. In addition to increased administration costs, the problems of compensating those on lower incomes would also increase. There seems no escaping the fact that this action would merely shift the tax burden to the middle-income earners. Even lowering the threshold would still result in a loss of social welfare.

The threshold was last raised in July 2003. Research shows that this has probably caused a decrease in efficiency but an increase in equity in society. But, again, the problem in Australia is that the increased threshold may lead to more **income-splitting** to take advantage of the higher tax-free portion of income, thus undermining horizontal equity. This could drive a wedge into the social gains.

Some proposals have suggested a **clawback** of the threshold, which would mean that persons on higher income would not receive this tax-free concession. This would be the same as transferring some of the middle-class income to the lower class. There do seem to be arguments in favour of the clawback, as it might address both equity and efficiency concerns.[8] Interestingly, the government superannuation co-contribution, discussed in Chapter 7, is available on assessable income, not taxable income. However, as many researchers indicate, policy design in these areas is very difficult because it is hard to achieve both equitable and efficient outcomes. Some researchers have suggested **joint taxing**, where household incomes are combined for tax purposes.

The introduction of *A New Tax System* was aimed at eliminating the dominance of vested and sectional interests that tend to create two types of taxpayers:

1. those who are unable to change their circumstances, such as employees
2. those who can choose tax-effective structures and arrangements that are purely tax-driven.[9]

There is now a much wider debate on these issues between tax professionals and the government and also on the issues of compliance costs for business. Some interesting statistics were produced recently by ATO researchers:

- The average wage earner paid 17.5% tax on additional earnings in 1954 but paid 45% in 2005.
- A taxpayer had to earn 19 times the average earnings to pay the highest tax rate in 1954, compared with only 1.3 times the average in 2005.

An important implication of all these factors is that any accounting office must be managed in such a way as to provide its clients with a cost-effective and efficient service, one that will be reliable and offer value for money. The office must know what forms a business or an individual requires, and when and how often they must be submitted. Tax professionals must bear in mind that by their actions they will directly affect the **compliance costs** of both their own office and their clients.[10] As professionals, they have the direct responsibility for educating their clients and providing a level of technical competence that supports these issues.

The authors hope that this book will assist in making office tax procedures and processing business tax requirements less complicated and a little more logical. Advocates in the current debate about our taxation system suggest it may benefit from a complete overhaul, so perhaps it is wise to keep in mind Einstein's famous quote: 'Things should be as simple as possible, but not simpler.'

Taxation vocabulary

bracket creep
Business Portal
clawback
common-use signing interface (CSI)
compliance costs
electronic commerce interface (ECI)
electronic forms
electronic funds transfer (EFT)
Electronic Lodgement Service (ELS)
income-splitting
inflation
joint taxing
personal identification code (PIC)
public key technology (PKT)
Tax Agent Portal
tax threshold

Notes

1. Sometimes referred to as that nasty fiscal affliction where even modest wage earners are pushed into a higher tax bracket because of inflation.
2. Refer to J. Head (1997), 'Wealth taxation, capital income taxation and proposals for consumption tax reform', Chapter 22 in J. Head & R. Krever (eds), *Taxation Towards 2000*, Australian Tax Research Foundation Conference Series no. 19, Australian Tax Research Foundation, Sydney, pp. 603–14.
3. Peter Whiteford gives an excellent critique of the threshold and alternatives in his paper in the Australian Tax Research Foundation Conference Series no. 8, pp. 229–30.
4. Hielke Buddelmeyer and Guyonne Kalb, (2007), 'Tax changes the work equation', *The Australian Financial Review*, 18 October, p. 79. Available online at **http://melbourneinstitute.com/news/news/**, accessed 6 April 2008.
5. This proposal was suggested by G. Bascard, J. Cox & M. Porter (1985), 'The Draft White Paper. (Should there be an 'Option D'?)', paper for the National Taxation Summit, Centre of Policy Studies, Monash University. In this paper it was proposed that the threshold be abolished.
6. Of particular assistance is the paper written by Elizabeth Savage when she was at the Department of Economics at Sydney University. See Elizabeth Savage (1993), 'Tax reform and the tax-free threshold', *Journal of Taxation Policy, Law and Reform*, pp. 115–37.
7. Savage, ibid., p. 117.
8. 'The need for tax reform', with detailed discussions and recommendations, appeared in the *Australian Taxpayer's Association Journal* on 16 March 1998; P. Whiteford, 'Equity, tax reform and redistribution', Research Paper no. 28, Department of Treasury.
9. N. Rametse & J. Pope (2002), 'Start-up tax compliance costs of the GST: empirical evidence from Western Australian small businesses', *Australian Tax Forum*, 17 (4), pp. 407–22.
10. CPA Australia (2003), *Small Business Survey Program: Compliance Burden*, CPA Australia, Melbourne.

Chapter 1

1.1 Since 1942 the Commonwealth government has been the sole collector of tax on income and, while the states also originally had rights, these were relinquished in 1989.

1.2

		$
Assessable income	Salary	65 000
	Investments	3 300
Total assessable income		68 300
Less allowable deductions		2 700
Taxable income		**65 600**

1.3 No, this would not change the taxable income because the sale of the investment is of a capital nature. Also, because the price received matched the cost, no capital gain was made.

1.4 Taxpayers who use their home office for work must keep a diary for at least a four-week period so that a pattern of use can be established. Then they can claim either per hour or a percentage of the actual costs. All records must be in English and a review of usage should be made regularly.

1.5 Any three of the following:

- requesting that the agent or accountant be present
- requesting a mutually convenient time for the interview
- being allowed reasonable time to gather records
- being afforded an opportunity to explain any circumstances that may prima facie lead to a reduction of penalty tax
- being given a copy of the interview, if required
- objecting to any assessment or penalty that may result from the audit.

1.6 The three issues are:

- whether a CGT event has occurred
- whether an exemption or concession applies
- whether a capital gain or a capital loss results.

Chapter 2

2.1 Because proof-of-identity documents are required, the individual would need to obtain form Nat 1432 and provide the proof-of-identity documents as stated on that form.

2.2 All businesses need to quote an ABN on their tax invoice. If an ABN is not quoted in a business-to-business transaction, then the payer has to withhold tax at the rate of 46.5% and forward this amount to the ATO.

2.3 There are various ways to obtain an ABN, including completing form Nat 2939 and lodging it with ATO and electronically lodging with the Australian Business Register at **www.abr.gov.au**.

2.4 Employers have to withhold 45.6% of any wages and pay such amounts to the ATO.

2.5 It is necessary to obtain the correct notification form from the investment institution, complete this form and submit it to the investment body.

2.6 $10 000 @ 5% = $500
$500 × 46.5%= $232.50
$500 – $232.50 = $267.50 net amount received by taxpayer

2.7 $1000 @ 5% = $50

2.8 Investment bodies have to send a report to the ATO advising about certain investments within their institution.

2.9 The penalty is a $10 000 fine or two years' imprisonment, or both, for breaches of TFN requirements under the *Taxation Administration Act 1953*.

Chapter 3

3.1 There are two limbs to this system:
- PAYG instalments
- PAYG withholding.

3.2 Predominantly the system applies to payments by an employer to an employee. However, it can also apply to a payment from one business to another business where an ABN is not quoted.

3.3
- Collect the TFN declaration, complete it and send it to the ATO.
- Withhold tax from employees' wages as per tables.
- Remit the amounts withheld to the ATO.
- At the end of the year, give each employee a PAYG payment summary.
- After the year-end send the ATO a PAYG Payment Summary Statement providing a synopsis of all PAYG payment summaries issued during the year.

3.4 First, the amount of the wage; and second, whether the employee has provided a TFN declaration and (a) has quoted his or her TFN and (b) wishes to claim the tax-free threshold.

3.5 No, only businesses that employ people have to register for PAYG withholding. Thus a sole trader that does not employee workers would not need to register.

3.6 (a) TFN, (b) the desire to claim the tax-free threshold or not and (c) various other matters such as claiming tax offsets and having a HELP liability.

3.7 A registered PAYG withholder remits to the ATO via a Business Activity Statement if registered for GST or an Instalment Activity Statement if not registered for GST. These amounts must be remitted to the ATO.

3.8 All employers have to provide a PAYG payment summary that shows details of income earned and tax withheld from all employees.

3.9 Via a PAYG Payment Summary Statement due to be sent to the ATO by 14 August each year.

3.10 The penalty is 20 penalty units—that is, $2200.

3.11 A taxpayer with business or investment income prepays tax by remitting an estimate of quarterly tax with a credit allowed at year end.

3.12 Any three of the following:
- individuals in a business conducted as a partnership
- individuals with investment income
- companies
- beneficiaries
- trustees
- superannuation funds
- a body corporate.

3.13 Option 1, use the simple amount calculated by the ATO; or option 2, use the percentage rate advised by the ATO and multiply this by the business's calculation of its GST-exclusive quarterly instalment income.

3.14 Most businesses report and pay PAYG instalments quarterly, but it is possible to pay annually under certain circumstances.

Chapter 4

4.1
- Taxable supplies—taxed at 10% of value
- GST-free supplies and exported supplies—zero rated
- Input-taxed supplies—no rate is applied
- Exempt supplies—outside the GST system

4.2

(a) It can claim a $2000 input tax credit.
(b) GST payable is $3000
(c) It must withhold 46.5% of the invoice total—$204—and remit this to the ATO. The supplier receives only $236. However, the supplier will have a tax credit of $204 when lodging its next tax return.
(d) The business will be an accruals payer and can choose to lodge quarterly.

The total payable to the ATO for the quarter is $1000 net GST plus $204 ABN withheld. Total of $1204.

4.3 An entity must register for GST as soon as it has grossed $75 000 over the past 11 months plus the current month, or will be likely to gross over $75 000 for the next 11 months plus the current month.

4.4

(a) Taxable supplies: fees from accounting services, receipts from sale of goods, receipts from sale of assets.
(b) GST-free supplies: any fresh food ready for consumption, exports of goods or services, medicines.
(c) Input-taxed supplies: interest received, residential rent received, sale of used residential property.

4.5

(a) It will be a cash payer and may even be able to pay quarterly and lodge annually.
(b) The GST payable, $9091, is calculated only on the $100 000 cash received. No GST is payable on customers' amounts outstanding until the cash is received.
(c) Input tax credits of $909 can be claimed on the $10 000 cash paid for goods. The $5000 still owing will give input tax credits only when the liability is paid.
(d) If the business is a cash payer, there is no effect on the BAS.

4.6 The business would be able to claim $19 500 in input tax credits. That is, $217 000 less $2500 = $214 500, and take one-eleventh of this to get $19 500.

4.7 Total value for GST is $512 000. GST of $51 200 must be added to make the total importation value of the yacht = $563 200. GST must be paid before the yacht can be collected from Customs.

4.8 Scenario 1. Penalty is $1000 plus $250. Failure to take reasonable care—base penalty amount is 25% of the shortfall.
Scenario 2. Penalty is $100 plus $500. Recklessness—base penalty amount is 50% of the shortfall.
Scenario 3. Penalty is $100 plus $750. Intentional disregard—base penalty is 75% of the shortfall.

Chapter 5

5.1 The amount of $4500 would be grossed up by the lower type 2 gross-up factor of 1.8692, reporting an amount of $8411 on the payment summary.

5.2 *Taxable fringe benefits:* provision of a car available for private use; payment of HELP fees at university; an advance of money for an extended period at reduced interest rates.
Exempt benefits: small irregular benefits under $300; provision of emergency health care.
In-house benefits: provision of goods and services to employees of the kind the business produces in the ordinary course of operations, under $1000 per year, such as meals in a hotel and flights in an airline.

5.3 The FBT standard year is from 1 April to 31 March. The current rate of tax is 46.5%. The current benchmark interest rate is 9% for 2008/09.

5.4

(a) Any benefit that is not provided in respect of employment, such as a birthday gift of an overseas airline ticket to a son who works in the business. This is a non-deductible expense.
(b) If a benefit is provided in respect of employment, and the expense is an allowable deduction, such as a daughter being give the use of a business vehicle available for private use, then this is subject to FBT.

5.5 The annualised km would be: 15 000 × 365/151 = 36 258 km. (Be careful here because using months gives a round 36 000, which is incorrect.) The statutory fraction to be used is: 0.11.

5.6 All of the following must be satisfied:

- the employer is not a government body or is not income-tax exempt at any time during the current year
- the Commissioner has not issued a notice requiring the employer to resume keeping records
- the employer was in business for the whole of the base year
- FBT records were kept in the base year
- the FBT return for the base year was lodged by the due date
- the aggregate fringe benefits amount in the base year does not exceed the exemption threshold
- the employer has elected that the record-keeping exemption arrangements apply in all years from the most recent base year to the current year

- the aggregate fringe benefits amount for benefits provided in the current year is not more than 20% greater than it was in the most recent base year, unless the difference is $100 or less.

Chapter 6

6.1 The entity has to take account of the following thresholds in respect of annual turnover:

- If the business has an annual turnover of more than $75 000, it needs to register for GST.
- If the business has an annual turnover of less than $2 million, it can use the cash method. If its annual turnover is more than $2 million, the accrual accounting method must be used.
- If the business has an annual turnover of less than $20 million, it will have a quarterly tax period. If its annual turnover is more than $20 million, it will have a monthly tax period.

6.2

Transaction	Revenue	Capital	Category
Fees received for berths on the marina	✓		Taxable supplies—one-eleventh embedded in the supply
Sales of petrol and diesel	✓		Taxable supplies—one-eleventh embedded in the supply
Sale of an old work boat		✓	Taxable supplies—one-eleventh embedded in the supply
Sales of milk and bread stores	✓		GST-free
Sales of special craft to overseas buyer	✓		GST-free
Residential rent received	✓		Input-taxed—no GST is embedded in the revenue
New hot water heater for the residence		✓	Input-taxed—any GST embedded in the cost must be absorbed by the business
Repair to the residential kitchen	✓		Input-taxed—any GST embedded in the cost must be absorbed by the business
Repair to the marina kitchen	✓		Taxable supplies—one-eleventh embedded in the supply can be claimed back as a credit
Wages paid to the staff at the marina	✓		Excluded from the GST calculations and reporting

6.3 BAS WORKSHEET

Supplies you have made			Acquisitions you have made		
Total sales and income and other supplies including capital (GST-inclusive)	**G1**	149 210	Capital acquisitions (GST-inclusive)	**G10**	1200
Exports	**G2**	10 000	All other acquisitions (GST-inclusive)	**G11**	72 688
Other GST-free supplies	**G3**	1 000	**ADD G10 + G11**	**G12**	73 888
Input-taxed sales and income and other supplies	**G4**	8 010	Acquisitions for making input taxed sales and income and other supplies	**G13**	2 200
ADD G2 + G3 + G4	**G5**	19 010	Acquisitions with no GST in the price	**G14**	88
G1 minus G5	**G6**	130 200	Total estimated private use of acquisitions + non-income tax deductible acquisitions	**G15**	
Adjustments (must be total transaction value, i.e. GST-inclusive)	**G7**		**ADD G13 + G14 + G15**	**G16**	2 288
ADD G6 + G7	**G8**	130 200	**G12 minus G16**	**G17**	71 600
Divide **G8** by 11	**G9**	11 836	Adjustments (must be total transaction value, i.e. GST-inclusive)	**G18**	
			ADD G17 + G18	**G19**	71 600
			Divide **G19** by 11	**G20**	6 509
Rounded down					
Net GST payable		**5 327**			

6.4 BAS SUMMARY REPORT

Option 1 Quarterly GST		
Total sales and income and other supplies including capital (GST-inclusive)	**G1**	149 210
Does this amount at G1 include GST? Mark with X	**Yes** **X**	
Exports	**G2**	10 000
Other GST-free supplies	**G3**	1 000
Capital acquisitions (GST-inclusive)	**G10**	1200
All other acquisitions (GST-inclusive)	**G11**	72 688

GST-exclusive gross sales	135 374
ATO rate given From 1 July 2008	3.50%

These boxes represent the basic layout of the BAS form

Note: The PAYG instalment income is calculated as follows:

Total receipts – GST – net asset sale

$149 210 – $11 836 – $2000 = $135 374

Amounts you owe the ATO		
GST on sales or GST instalment	**1A**	11 836
Wine equalisation tax	**1C**	
Luxury car tax	**1E**	
PAYG tax withheld	**4**	9 243
PAYG income tax instalment	**5A**	4 738
FBT instalment	**6A**	2 101
~~Deferred company / fund instalment~~	**7**	
1A + 4 + 5A + 6A + 7	**8A**	27 918

Amounts the ATO owes you		
GST on purchases	**1B**	6 509
Wine equalisation tax refundable	**1D**	
Luxury car tax refundable	**1F**	
Credit from PAYG income tax variation	**5B**	
Credit from FBT variation	**6B**	
1B + 5B + 6B	**8B**	6 509

Payment or refund?

Is 8A more than 8B? (indicate with an X)

Yes, then write the result of 8A minus 8B at 9. This is the amount payable to the ATO.	**X**
No, then write the result of 8B minus 8A at 9. This amount is refundable to you (or offset against any other tax debt you have).	

		Payment due
	9	21 409

6.5 Quarter 1: apply 9.6% to $15 000 = $1440. Quarter 2: apply 9.6% to $10 000 = $960.

6.6 The business in this case is within the time limit of 18 months and under the dollar limit of $5000 for the correction of errors. In this case, the correction can be made in the next BAS lodged. Outside the time and value limits a Revised Activity Statement must be lodged.

6.7 The penalty is $110 for each 28 days or part thereof that the lodgement is overdue, making a total penalty of $220 to 28 June. Yes, it would make a difference if the date was 6 July. The penalty would go up by another $110 to a total of $330.

Chapter 7

7.1 The Australian government enacted the superannuation guarantee levy in an effort to get employers to assist employees in providing for their retirement.

7.2 Any three of the following:
- employees paid less than $450 (before tax) in a calendar month
- employees aged 70 years and over
- employees under 18 years of age working not more than 30 hours per week
- resident employees paid by non-resident employers for work done outside Australia
- non-resident employees paid for work done outside Australia.

7.3 Any three of the following:
- expense allowance paid with the expectation that it will be fully expended in producing income
- accrued annual leave, long service leave and sick leave paid as a lump sum on termination
- annual leave loading
- bonuses not relating to specific performance criteria
- reimbursements of expenses
- overtime
- benefits subject to FBT
- workers compensation payments when no work is performed
- payments on maternity/paternity leave.

7.4 This means that:
- the super fund complies with the federal government's rules
- APRA has issued a notice to the trustee of the fund stating that the fund complies
- benefits are vested and preserved for the benefit of the employees
- it is not run contrary to the standards set by the *Superannuation Industry (Supervision) Act 1993*.

7.5 An employer needs to follow four steps:
(a) identify eligible employees
(b) identify an appropriate employer fund
(c) provide a standard choice form to eligible employees
(d) act on each employee's choice.

7.6 The superannuation guarantee is part of the ATO's self-assessment system. The employer is responsible for the calculation and subsequent payment of any superannuation guarantee liability.

7.7 The payments must be made by 28 April 2009.

7.8 No, it is not tax-deductible.

7.9 An employer needs to pay the superannuation guarantee charge and lodge a superannuation guarantee statement by the fourteenth day of the second month following the end of the relevant quarter. The superannuation guarantee charge must be paid at the same time as the superannuation guarantee statement is lodged.

7.10 Under the new law, which applied from 1 January 2006, if an employer makes a late contribution to a superannuation fund for an employee, before the due date for lodgement of the employer's *superannuation guarantee charge statement*, the employer can elect to have this contribution used to reduce the amount of superannuation guarantee charge liability that relates to that employee. This means that employers may be liable only for the administration component and interest.

7.11 He would need to pay as soon as possible after the due date of 28 July to avoid further interest charges.

7.12 Failing to keep records that adequately explain the amount of superannuation provided for each employee will attract a penalty of up to $3300.

7.13 The amount paid to the superannuation funds would be the shortfall of $10 000.

7.14

Superannuation co-contribution calculator	
Government contribution uplift factor	1.5
Shading-in rate decreasing maximum co-contribution	0.05
Maximum co-contribution available	$1 500
Lower indexed income amount	$30 342
Upper indexed income amount	$60 342
Enter total assessable income	$48 342
Add: reportable fringe benefits	$4 000
Total relevant income for co-contribution	$52 342
Enter actual personal contribution	$1 000
Government co-contribution given	$400
Total superannuation contribution to fund	$1 400

7.15 You can search using the ATO's online service called 'Super Seeker', making sure you provide your TFN, full name and date of birth. You can email the ATO at **SuperMatch@ato.gov.au** and perhaps complete the 'Lost super' form.

Chapter 8

8.1 Universities charge undergraduate students a contribution for the course they are undertaking. The key to calculating student contributions is an equivalent full-time student unit (EFTSU). If the student enrols in a particular program and then changes it, she may be charged incorrectly. Furthermore, if she withdraws from a course, she must make a written application to the institution before the census date in the semester. If she enrols at more than one institution and does not withdraw the unwanted placement by the census date, a double liability will accrue.

8.2 *Method 1: Pay up-front.* Australian citizens and holders of a permanent humanitarian visa may choose to pay their HECS-HELP contribution to the institution at the time of enrolment and thus be entitled to a discount of 20%, paying only 80% of the estimated liability assessed.
Method 2: Deferred payment. With this method, the HELP liability can be deferred to such time as the student's taxable income reaches a minimum level. The student is required to provide his or her TFN to the university when electing this method.
Method 3: Voluntary payments that attract a bonus. Students may make a part-payment of their debt. If this voluntary amount is $500 or more, the debt for the course is reduced by 110% of the payment made.

8.3

Taxable income	$50 000
Reportable fringe benefit	$5 000
Repayment income	$55 000
Percentage rate to be applied	5.5%
HELP repayment (5.5% × $55 000)	**$3 025**

Chapter 9

9.1 The major reasons are to ensure that:
- both parents contribute to the support of their children
- support is shared
- the custodial parent receives assistance with support.

9.2 The two main ways are:
- private agreement
- Child Support Agency assessment.

9.3

Parent's support income percentage for child	65%
minus	
Parent's cost percentage for child	45%
Child support percentage	20%

9.4 If an order has been sent to an employer (referred to as a *garnishee* order by the ATO), the *Child Support (Registration and Collection) Act 1988* requires the employer to:
- deduct the child support amount specified
- advise the employee in writing how much child support was deducted
- send the deduction to the CSA by the seventh of the month following the month in which the deductions were made
- advise the CSA of:
  - any variations in amounts deducted and reasons for the variations
  - any business changes such as change of name, address or ownership.

9.5 *Binding agreements* are those that:
- are in writing and signed by both parents
- are made after the parents have sought independent legal advice
- contain a certificate from the independent lawyer for each parent
- can be for any amount, even if it is less than the formula amount, if both parties agree

- can be ceased only by the forming of another binding agreement or by a court order.

For those parents receiving Family Tax Benefit Part A, this is based on the CSA's formula amount and is reviewed every three years.

Limited agreements are different to binding agreements in the following ways:

- there is no requirement for parents to obtain legal advice
- there must be a CSA formula assessment already existing
- the child support amount must be equal to or greater than the amount assessed by the CSA formula.

9.6 The five reasons are:

- the complex nature of the parents' finances
- the special needs of a child
- the high costs of access
- other necessary commitments of either parent
- child support being provided as other benefits, such as payment of school fees.

multiple-choice answers to odd-numbered questions

Chapter 1
1. c
3. c
5. a
7. c
9. a
11. b

Chapter 2
1. d
3. c
5. d
7. a
9. b
11. c

Chapter 3
1. d
3. b
5. d
7. d
9. a
11. c
13. b
15. c

Chapter 4
1. b
3. a
5. a
7. c
9. d
11. d

Chapter 5
1. c
3. b
5. b
7. c
9. b
11. c

Chapter 6
1. a
3. a
5. a
7. c
9. a

Chapter 7
1. d
3. d
5. a
7. a
9. c

Chapter 8
1. c
3. c
5. d
7. b
9. b

Chapter 9
1. d
3. d
5. b

Chapter 10
1. a
3. c
5. b

Chapter 11
1. d
3. c
5. a

Chapter 12
1. c
3. c
5. c

See below for further explanations to some questions.

Chapter 1

MCQ 7

Assessable income	Deductions
50 000	10 000
26 000	
0	
76 000	10 000

Therefore the taxable income is $76 000 – $10 000 = **$66 000**

MCQ 9

Assessable Income	Deductions
70 100	12 000
0	
70 100	12 000

The taxable income is $70 100 – $12 000 = **$58 100**

Workings

Raw data TI		Base	Rate margin
58100	25000.00	2850	0.3
Prime tax	11430.00		
Medicare levy	871.50		**MCQ**
Gross tax payable	12301.50		Q9
Less:			
Enter PAYG	8420.00		
TFN credit			
Medical rebate			
Offsets			
	8420.00		
Net tax payable	**3881.50**	←	

Chapter 2

MCQ5

A school student age 10 in receipt of $200 bank interest only. *A non-resident earning rental income from Australia will not need to quote a TFN to enable the gross flow of rental income to continue. They will need a TFN, however, to be able to lodge the yearly income tax return.*

Chapter 3

MCQ11

4% of $800.99 = $32 (ignoring cents)

Chapter 7

MCQ9

Since 1 July 2005 most employees have the right to choose the superannuation fund or retirement savings account that will receive their SGL contributions.

appendix

The following ATO forms[1] have been included in this Appendix in order to assist the experienced student to readily locate and compare the various forms. Their inclusion here also ensures that the most up-to-date forms are able to be incorporated into publishing deadlines.

The forms in the Appendix have been referenced to show:

- the chapter number;
- the sequential reference to the form within the chapter; and
- the 'NAT' number for the form, as issued by the ATO.

1 © Commonwealth of Australia, reproduced by permission.

Form 2.1 [1432] TFN application—individual

Australian Government
Australian Taxation Office

Tax file number application or enquiry for an individual

ABOUT TAX FILE NUMBERS

The tax file number (TFN) is a unique number issued by the Tax Office to individuals and organisations to help the Tax Office administer the tax and other Australian Government systems.

Only one TFN is issued to you for your lifetime. Once a TFN has been issued to you, there is no need to apply for a new one if your circumstances change, for example, if you move interstate, change jobs, change your name in any way, have investments, or claim government benefits. However, you should advise us of any change to your name or address.

WHO SHOULD COMPLETE THIS APPLICATION

Complete this application if you:

- have never had a TFN
- are not sure if you have a TFN, or
- have a TFN but cannot find it on any of your tax papers (you may need to provide full proof of your identity).

WHO SHOULD NOT COMPLETE THIS APPLICATION

Do not use this application if you are a:

- permanent migrant or a temporary visitor to Australia and have a visa to work or remain in Australia indefinitely. You can apply for a TFN online at **www.ato.gov.au** As a permanent migrant or temporary visitor, you do not need to physically provide proof of identity documents if you apply online, or
- non-resident and need a TFN for purposes other than employment. Please use the *Tax file number application for an individual living outside Australia* (NAT 2628). You do not need a TFN for interest, dividends or royalty payments as these are subject to non-resident withholding tax.

BEFORE COMPLETING THIS APPLICATION

Make sure that you have the necessary proof of identity documents. We cannot issue you with a TFN unless you provide these documents. The list of acceptable documents is on page ii of these instructions.

WHEN COMPLETING THIS APPLICATION

- Make sure you answer all the questions, otherwise we may need to contact you for missing information. This may delay you receiving your TFN.
- Print clearly, using a black pen only.
- Use BLOCK LETTERS and print one character in each box.
- Place X in all applicable boxes.
- Do not use whiteout or covering stickers.
- Sign next to any corrections with your **full signature** (not initials).

This will ensure that your details are recorded correctly when the application is processed.

AFTER COMPLETING THIS APPLICATION

- **Sign the declaration at the end of the application.** Make sure you have read the privacy statement on page ii.
- Provide acceptable original documents that prove your identity. We cannot issue you with a TFN unless you provide these documents. See page ii for a list of acceptable documents.
- Lodge your completed application.

If you are:

- 12 years or under, your parent or guardian **must** sign on your behalf
- 13 to 15, you or your parent **or** guardian **must** sign, or
- 16 years or older, **you must** sign.

Where a **parent or guardian** signs the application, they must provide:

- their own full proof of identity documents (see page ii)
- the applicant's proof of identity documents, and
- a document showing the relationship (for example, full birth certificate, guardianship papers or Medicare card).

LODGING YOUR APPLICATION

In person

You can take the completed application and original proof of identity documents to your nearest Tax Office shopfront. Phone **13 28 61** between 8.00am and 6.00pm, Monday to Friday, to make an appointment.

If you need a TFN to claim benefits from Centrelink or the Department of Veterans' Affairs, you can authorise the Tax Office to advise these agencies of your TFN or you can lodge your application directly with them. You will need to provide them with the proof of identity documents needed for your income support payment or benefit.

Mail

Send your completed application, and original proof of identity documents to:

Australian Taxation Office
PO Box 9942
MOONEE PONDS VIC 3039

WHEN WILL YOU RECEIVE YOUR TFN?

Within **28 days** of receiving your completed application, we will:

- return your original documents by registered mail to the postal address shown on this application, and
- mail your TFN to your postal address.

Please do not ask about your application or lodge another application during that time.

MORE INFORMATION

If you need help completing this application or you have difficulty providing enough proof of identity documents, you can:

- visit **www.ato.gov.au**
- phone **13 28 61** between 8.00am and 6.00pm, Monday to Friday.

To enquire about a TFN

If you have lost your TFN or are not sure you have one:

- look for your TFN on any correspondence from the Tax Office or contact your tax agent.
- if you still cannot find your TFN, you can phone **13 28 61** between 8.00am and 6.00pm, Monday to Friday.

If you do not speak English and need help from the Tax Office, please phone the Translating and Interpreting Service on **13 14 50**.

If you have a hearing or speech impairment and have access to appropriate TTY or modem equipment, please phone **13 36 77**. If you have a speech impairment and do not have access to TTY or modem equipment, please phone the Speech to Speech Relay Service on **1300 555 727**.

NAT 1432-12.2005

Form 2.1 [1432] *continued*

PROOF OF IDENTITY REQUIREMENTS

When you lodge your application or are signing on behalf of an applicant, you must provide current documents that prove your identity. We will accept only **unaltered original documents** (not photocopies).

> ❗ If you do not provide full proof of identity documents we cannot issue you with a TFN.

If the documents you provide are in a previous name you must provide a document that shows how your name was changed (for example, marriage certificate, deed poll, change of name certificate).

Where a parent or guardian signs the application, they must provide their own full proof of identity, the applicants proof of identity documents and a document showing the relationship (for example, full birth certificate, guardianship papers or Medicare card).

If an original document is in a language other than English, you must provide a written translation certified as a true and correct copy by an authorised translation service such as the Department of Immigration and Multicultural and Indigenous Affairs (DIMIA), an appropriate embassy or professional translation service.

If you are aged 16 or over, you must provide:

A + **B** + **B** One category **A** and two different category **B** documents.

If you are under 16, you must provide:

A + **B** One category **A** and one category **B** document

Category A documents

- ABC Australian **full** birth certificate. If you have changed your name you must also provide a link document such as a marriage certificate, deed poll or change of name certificate
- ACC Australian citizenship certificate/Extract from Register of Citizen by Descent
- AFP Overseas passport with evidence of Australian immigration status

Category B documents

Only one type of driver licence or student identification card can be used.

- BAP Australian passport
- BDL Australian driver licence with your photo and signature and current address that matches the details provided on this application, **or**
- BDP Australian learner permit with your photo and signature and current address that matches the details provided on this application
- BMC Medicare card
- BFI Account statement from an Australian bank, credit union or building society less than one year old with your name and current home address that match the details provided on this application. Note: credit card statements are not acceptable
- BFL Australian firearm licence
- BTS Tertiary student identification card with your photo and signature issued from an Australian government accredited education authority, **or**
- BSS Secondary student identification card with your photo and signature issued from an Australian government accredited education authority

For under 16-year-olds only

Category B documents can include **one** of the following which must be less than one year old and issued by an Australian government accredited education authority

- BEC Secondary examination certificate
- BEA Record of achievement
- BER Examination report

Privacy

We are authorised by the *Income Tax Assessment Act 1936* to ask for the information on this application. We need this information to help us administer laws relating to taxation and superannuation.

Where authorised by law to do so, we may give this information to other government agencies which administer laws relevant to your particular situation. Depending on your situation these agencies could include Centrelink, the Australian Federal Police, the Child Support Agency, the Department of Veterans' Affairs, the Department of Immigration and Multicultural and Indigenous Affairs, the Department of Family and Community Services, and the Department of Education, Science and Training.

We may check proof of identity information supplied with the issuing agencies.

ii

Form 2.1 [1432] ***continued***

Australian Government
Australian Taxation Office

Tax file number application or enquiry for an individual

1432 1205

TAX OFFICE USE ONLY

WHEN COMPLETING THIS APPLICATION
- Use a **black pen** and **print clearly** in BLOCK LETTERS.
- Answer all questions and place X in the applicable boxes.
- Do not use whiteout or covering stickers.
- Sign next to any corrections with your **full signature** (not initials).

1 Have you ever: (Place X in ONE box only)
- had a tax file number (TFN)
- applied for a TFN before, or
- lodged a tax return in Australia?

No → Go to question 2

Not sure / Yes → Provide details where possible.

What year did you last deal with the Tax Office? Year

Details (for example tax return)

Please provide your details as they were when you last dealt with the Tax Office. (If the same as current details write 'same').

Family name at that time

First given name

Other given names

Postal address for tax matters at that time

Suburb/town

State/territory

Postcode

Name of your tax agent at that time (if applicable)

2 Why do you need a TFN? (Place X in ONE box only)

To give to your employer

To lodge an income tax return

To give to your bank or financial institution

To claim family tax benefit

To apply for a loan under the Higher Education Loan Programme (HELP)

For Child Support Agency payments

To apply for an Australian business number (ABN) or register for another business account, eg goods and services tax (GST)

To give to Centrelink → Do you authorise us to send your TFN to Centrelink? Yes → Lodge your application through Centrelink; No

To give to the Department of Veterans' Affairs (DVA) → Do you authorise us to send your TFN to DVA? Yes → Lodge your application through DVA; No

Other reason (please describe)

3 What is your full name?

Title: Mr Mrs Miss Ms Other

Family name

First given name

Other given names

4 What is your sex? Male Female

5 What is your date of birth? Day / Month / Year

OFFICE USE ONLY

NAT 1432-12.2005

IN CONFIDENCE – when completed

Page 1

Form 2.1 [1432] *continued*

6 Have you ever had another name?

No ☐ Go to question 7. Yes ☐ Provide details below.

Type of name? (Place X in ONE box only)

☐ your previous married name ☐ the name on your birth certificate ☐ a shortened version of your name

☐ your name before marriage ☐ an anglicised name ☐ an assumed name (known as) ☐ your skin name, or

☐ other

Other name

Title: Mr ☐ Mrs ☐ Miss ☐ Ms ☐ Other

Family name

First given name

Other given names

If you have more names, attach a separate sheet of paper giving full names and types. Do not include nicknames.

7 Do you have a spouse (married or de facto)?

No ☐ Go to question 8. Yes ☐ Provide details below.

Spouse's family name

Spouse's first given name

Spouse's other given names

Spouse's date of birth Day / Month / Year

Check that you have given your name before marriage or previous married name at question 6, if applicable.

8 What is your postal address in Australia? (Your TFN will be sent to this address)

For example, write your home address, your post office box or your tax agent's postal address.

Suburb/town

State/territory

Postcode

9 What is your home address? (This must be a permanent street address, for example, 123 Smith St.)

This cannot be a post office box, RMB, RSD or other delivery point address. If you are a temporary visitor, your home address may be your home country address (see question 11). Write 'As above' if same as postal address at question 8.

Suburb/town/locality

State/territory

Postal code

Country if outside Australia

10 Were you born in Australia?

Yes ☐ No ☐ Which country were you born in?

What date did you arrive in Australia? Day / Month / Year

If you are a permanent migrant or temporary visitor to Australia, you may be eligible to apply for a TFN online at **www.ato.gov.au** (see instructions for more information).

Page 2 **IN CONFIDENCE – when completed**

Form 2.1 [1432] *continued*

11 Are you an Australian resident for tax purposes?

An Australian resident for tax purposes is generally someone who has always lived in Australia or someone who has come to Australia and lives here permanently.
If you are on a working holiday or backpacking, you are unlikely to be an Australian resident.
If you are an overseas student enrolled to study in Australia for more than six months, you may be an Australian resident for tax purposes. You **must** provide proof of your student status.

Yes ☐ No ☐

12 Do you have a tax agent?

No ☐ Go to question 13. **Yes** ☐ Provide details below.

Tax agent's business name

Tax agent's phone number

Tax agent's registration number

Name of person you deal with

13 Where can we contact you or leave a message if we need more information?

Daytime phone number

Mobile number

Email address

14 If we need more information to process your application, do you want us to contact a relative or friend who can help us? (This may be because of language difficulties, your age, illness or infirmity).

The contact person must be aged 16 or over.

No ☐ Go to the declaration.

Yes ☐ Provide details below.

If you are 15 or under and completing this application, you **must** provide details of a contact person.
If you are a parent or guardian and completing this application, please give your own contact details.

Name of person we should contact

Their daytime phone number

Please make sure you sign the declaration below.

Declaration

Please read the privacy statement on page ii of the instructions before signing the application.

If you are:

- 12 years or under, your parent or guardian **must** sign
- 13 to 15, you or your parent or guardian **must** sign, or
- 16 or over, you **must** sign.

There are penalties for deliberately giving false and misleading information or for deliberately making a false or misleading statement. There are also penalties for the unauthorised use of a TFN.

I declare that the information given on this application is true and correct.

Signature

Date Day / Month / Year

If you are legally entitled to sign on behalf of the person applying for a TFN, please provide your full name:

A person signing on behalf of the applicant must provide:

- their own full proof of identity documents
- the applicant's proof of identity documents (see page ii of the instructions), and
- a document showing the relationship (for example, full birth certificate, guardianship papers or Medicare card).

Completing a TFN application on behalf of the applicant does not give you authority to ask about other tax matters for the applicant.

See the front page of the instructions for details of where to lodge your completed application.

IN CONFIDENCE – when completed

Page 3

Form 2.2 [2938] ABN application—individual

SHEET 1 OF 3 Initial sheet here

Australian Government
Australian Business Register
Australian Taxation Office

Application for ABN registration for individuals (sole traders)

Complete this application if you are a sole trader who needs an Australian business number (ABN)

- Use the Instructions to help you complete this application.
- Use a black pen and BLOCK LETTERS.
- Place X in ALL applicable boxes.
- Read 'Instructions to help you complete this application'.

See Instructions **page 2**

Before completing this application check that you are entitled to an ABN

You **ARE NOT ENTITLED** to an ABN if any of the following statements are true.

- [ ] Your activity is carried out as an employee or in connection with earning payment as a company director, office holder or under a labour hire arrangement.

  An employee is a person who receives a salary or wage in return for work or services rendered.

  You are not considered an employee for ABN registration purposes if you have your own business and you receive a salary or wage from an activity related to your business.

- [ ] Your activity is a private recreational pursuit or hobby.

- [ ] Your activity is conducted as a member of a local government body, for example, as an elected member of a city, town or shire council.

29380507

You **ARE ENTITLED** to an ABN if all of the following statements are true.

- [ ] Your activity is carried out in the:
  - form of a business
  - nature of trade, or
  - form of a regular or continuous grant of a lease, licence or interest in property.

- [ ] Your activity is carried out in Australia or you make supplies that are connected with Australia.

- [ ] You have a reasonable expectation that a profit will be made from your activity.

If you want to discuss your entitlement to an ABN phone **13 28 66** between 8.00am and 6.00pm, Monday to Friday.

Form 2.2 [2938] ***continued***

Section A: **Sole trader information**

1 What is your name?

Title: Mr ☐ Mrs ☐ Miss ☐ Ms ☐ Other ☐

Family name

First given name

Other given name/s

Date of birth (Day / Month / Year)

Sex: Male ☐ Female ☐

2 What is your trading name?

See Instructions **page 4**

Your trading name is the name you trade under, or that you are known as by your suppliers or customers. It may be the name that is used in advertising and on business cards. You may have registered this name with other government departments.

As above ☐ If your trading name is the same as your name, cross this box.

3 Do you have more than one trading name?

See Instructions **page 4**

No ☐ Yes ☐ ▶ Provide details of the additional trading names on a separate sheet of paper. Please ensure that any separate pages include the name of the sole trader applying for this ABN.

4 Do you have a tax file number?

See 'Proof of Identity' on **page 4** of the instructions

No ☐ ▶ Have you applied for a tax file number? ▶ No ☐ ▶ You must provide documents to prove your identity. These must be supplied with this application.

Yes ☐

Yes ☐ ▶ Please provide the tax file number.

(You are not required by law to quote a tax file number, but not quoting it may increase the risk of administrative error or delay this registration.)

IN CONFIDENCE – when completed

Form 2.2 [2938] ***continued***

SHEET 3 OF 3 Initial sheet here

Section E: **Reason for application**

13 Why are you applying for an ABN? (select ONE reason only)

See Instructions **page 5**

New business in Australia
You have set up, or are about to set up, a new business and have never had an ABN using the same business structure in Australia.

Is this your first time in business in Australia? No Yes

Bought existing business
You have bought or taken over an existing business.

Is this your first time in business in Australia? No Yes

What is the previous owner's ABN?

Contractor or subcontractor
You are contracting or subcontracting your services.

Is this your first time working as a self-employed contractor or subcontractor in Australia? No Yes

To receive payment for services
You need an ABN to receive payment for services.

Is this your first time working as a self-employed provider of services in Australia? No Yes

Recommenced business
You have recommenced in business as a sole trader.

What ABN was used previously?

Change in business structure
The legal structure of your business has changed, for example, from a partnership to a sole trader.

What ABN was used previously?

Other circumstances – only select this reason if none of the above apply.

Please provide details below

29380707

IN CONFIDENCE – when completed

Form 2.2 [2938] *continued*

Section F: **Business activity details**

14 From what date do you require an ABN? See Instructions page 6

- This date should be when you start setting up the business, not when you start trading.
- If the date is in the future, you will not receive your ABN until that date.

The date cannot be more than six months into the future.

Day / Month / Year

15 If you intend for your business activity to be for less than three months, on what date do you expect to cease business?

If you register for GST, you will need to complete monthly activity statements.

Day / Month / Year

16 Do you have more than one business location in Australia? No ☐ Go to question 18 Yes ☐

17 In which states or territories do you have business locations? (Place X in ALL applicable boxes)

All ☐ New South Wales ☐ Victoria ☐ Queensland ☐ Western Australia ☐

South Australia ☐ Tasmania ☐ Northern Territory ☐ Australian Capital Territory ☐

18 What is the main industry that you operate in? (Place X in ONE box only) See Instructions page 6

Agriculture ☐ Forestry ☐ Fishing (including aquaculture) ☐ Mining ☐ Manufacturing ☐

Electricity, gas, water and waste ☐ Construction ☐ Wholesale trade ☐ Retail trade ☐ Accommodation and food services ☐

Transport, postal and warehousing ☐ Information media and telecommunications ☐ Financial and insurance services ☐ Rental, hiring and real estate services ☐ Professional, scientific and technical services ☐ Administrative and support services ☐ Public administration and safety ☐

Education and training ☐ Health care and social assistance ☐ Arts and recreation services ☐ Other services ☐

19 Describe the main activity from which you derive the majority of your business income. See Instructions page 7

Also describe the main goods produced or the main services provided.

20 Do you operate an agricultural property? No ☐ Yes ☐

An agricultural property is land where the breeding, keeping, cultivation or growing of animals, crops, fruit or vegetables (except forest trees or marine life) is undertaken.

Section G: **Taxation details**

See Instructions page 9

21 Are you a resident of Australia for tax purposes? No ☐ Yes ☐

22 Do you want to be registered for any of the following? See Instructions page 9

(Place X in ALL applicable boxes)

Luxury car tax ☐ Fringe benefits tax ☐ Wine equalisation tax ☐

Form 2.2 [2938] *continued*

Section H: **Goods and services tax (GST)**

You cannot register for GST if you are not carrying on an enterprise.

Some sole traders are required by law to register, while others may choose to voluntarily register for GST.

It is recommended that you read *GST for small business* (NAT 3014) if you are unfamiliar with GST.
See 'Useful products and services' on page 16 of the instructions for information on how to obtain this guide.

23 Are you required by law to register for GST?

You are required to register if you:

- are carrying on an enterprise and its GST turnover is $75,000 or more (see question 26)
- supply taxi or limousine travel for fares
- are a representative of an incapacitated entity (where the incapacitated entity is registered or required to be registered), or
- are a resident agent acting for a non-resident (where the non-resident is registered or required to be registered).

No ☐ **Yes** ☐ ▶ Go to question 25

24 If you are not required to register for GST, are you volunteering to register? See Instructions **page 10**

If you are not required by law to register for GST you can choose to register voluntarily if you are carrying on an enterprise, or intend to carry on an enterprise, in the near future.

No ☐ ▶ Go to section J: **Pay as you go (PAYG) withholding** **Yes** ☐

25 What is your date of registration for GST?

When you are required by law to register for GST, your date of registration is the date when: Day ☐☐ / Month ☐☐ / Year ☐☐☐☐

- your GST turnover met or exceeded the threshold turnover of $75,000
- you commenced supplying taxi or limousine travel for fares
- you commenced representing an incapacitated entity, or
- you commenced in your capacity as a resident agent for a non-resident.

Where you are volunteering to register for GST, you may choose your date of registration.

❗ The date of registration for GST cannot be before the ABN registration date provided at question 14.

26 What is your GST turnover? See Instructions **page 10**

Your GST turnover is the greater of your current and projected GST turnovers, which are calculated as:

- current GST turnover is the value of all supplies made or likely to be made in the current month plus the previous 11 months
- projected GST turnover is the value of all supplies made or likely to be made in the current month plus the next 11 months.

(Place X in ONE box only)

$0 to $74,999 ☐ $75,000 to $149,999 ☐ $150,000 to $1,999,999 ☐ $2 million to $19,999,999 ☐

$20 million and over ☐ ▶ You must select 'monthly' at question 27, register for online services at question 9, and provide an email address at question 8.

27 How often will you lodge your activity statements? See Instructions **page 10**

If your GST turnover is:

- $20 million or more you must lodge your activity statement monthly
- less than $20 million you can choose to lodge your activity statement either quarterly or monthly.

If you are registering voluntarily, you may choose to lodge your activity statement either monthly, quarterly or annually.

Monthly ☐ Quarterly ☐ Annually ☐

28 Do you intend to account for GST on a cash basis or a non-cash (accrual) basis? See Instructions **page 11**

There are two ways for accounting for GST. They are: Cash ☐ Non-cash (accrual) ☐

- cash basis – accounting for GST on a cash basis means you account for the GST for your sales when you receive payment for them
- non-cash (accrual) basis – accounting for GST on a non-cash basis (accruals) means that you will account for GST on your sales when you have issued an invoice or received any part of the payment, whichever occurs first.

Not all sole traders are allowed to account for GST on a cash basis.

You must read page 11 of the instructions before nominating the cash basis.

29 Do you import goods or services into Australia?

No ☐ **Yes** ☐ ▶ Read page 11 of the instructions if you want information about deferring GST on imports.

IN CONFIDENCE – when completed

Page 7

Form 2.2 [2938] *continued*

Section I: **Fuel tax credit**

See Instructions **page 11**

A fuel tax credit can be claimed for diesel and petrol used in eligible business activities.

Diesel and petrol when used in:

- road transport (in vehicles with a gross vehicle mass greater than 4.5 tonne)
- generation of electricity.

Diesel only when used in:

- rail or marine transport
- certain primary production activities (for example, agriculture, fishing and forestry)
- mining.

In addition, other fuels (including diesel, petrol, kerosene, heating oil and toluene) are eligible when used:

- in burner applications such as heating
- for any other non-fuel use such as a solvent or as an ingredient in the manufacture of other products (for example, paints or plastic).

You cannot claim a fuel tax credit for fuel used for road transport in a vehicle with a gross vehicle mass of 4.5 tonne or less.

30 Do you need to register for a fuel tax credit?

To register for a fuel tax credit, you must also be registered for GST.

No ☐ Go to Section J: **Pay as you go**

Yes ☐

31 From what date do you expect to be eligible for a fuel tax credit?

This date cannot be before the GST registration date, provided at question 25, or 1 July 2006, when the fuel tax credit commenced.

Day / Month / Year

☐☐ / ☐☐ / ☐☐☐☐

32 Which fuels do you expect to use in your eligible business activities?

(Place X in ALL applicable boxes)

Diesel ☐ Petrol ☐ Other ☐

33 Will you be using diesel or petrol in a road transport vehicle with a gross vehicle mass greater than 4.5 tonne?

No ☐

Yes ☐

IN CONFIDENCE – when completed

Form 2.2 [2938] *continued*

Section J: **Pay as you go (PAYG) withholding**

See Instructions page 12

You will need to register for PAYG withholding if you are required to withhold amounts from payments you make to payees such as:

- employees (salary and wage) — Please note, you are not an employee of your business.
- contractors or subcontractors under a voluntary agreement, or
- labour hire workers.

You will also need to register if you are required to withhold an amount from payments to:

- suppliers who have not provided an ABN, or
- certain non-residents.

34 Are you required by law to register for PAYG withholding?

See Instructions page 13

No ☐ Go to question 39

Yes ☐ On what date will withholding commence? Day __ / Month __ / Year ____

This date cannot be before the ABN registration date provided at question 14.

35 How many employees do you estimate you will pay?

☐☐☐,☐☐☐

This information is used to provide you with the correct number of payment summaries at the end of the financial year.

Do not include people under a voluntary agreement or labour hire arrangement.

36 What amount do you expect to withhold from payments to your payees each year?

$ ☐☐☐,☐☐☐,☐☐☐ .✕✕

This amount is called the estimated annual withholding amount. It is used to determine how often you will pay amounts withheld to the Tax Office.

Where the withholding amount is expected to be:

- less than or equal to $25,000 you will be required to pay quarterly
- between $25,001 and $1,000,000 you will be required to pay monthly, or
- greater than $1,000,000 you will be required to pay more frequently. (If you fall in this group we will send you more information.)

37 How will you provide your PAYG withholding payment summary annual report to the Tax Office?

At the end of each year sole traders are required to lodge an annual report if they have made withholding payments. There are different annual reports for different payments made. Sole traders who have employees and other workers will need to lodge a PAYG withholding payment summary annual report.

This annual report may be lodged by paper, using forms supplied by the Tax Office, or electronically.

Please indicate the method you plan to use to lodge your PAYG withholding payment summary annual report.

Paper form supplied by the Tax Office ☐ Go to question 39 — Electronically ☐

38 How will you provide payment summaries to your payees?

See Instructions page 13

Print your own payment summaries ☐ — Use payment summaries supplied by the Tax Office ☐

39 Will you pay royalties, dividends or interest to non-residents, or report investment income paid to Australian residents?

No ☐ Yes ☐

See Instructions page 13

Form 2.2 [2938] *continued*

Section K: **Financial account details**

40 What are your financial institution account details for Tax Office refunds?

Refunds will only be paid directly into a recognised financial institution account located in Australia. The account details provided must be held by:

- you (solely or jointly)
- your registered tax agent, or
- a legal practitioner acting as your trustee or executor.

If you do not provide these details we cannot refund money owed.

BSB code (6 digits only) Account number

Full account name

Is the account held by: you ☐ you jointly with others ☐ your tax agent ☐ a legal practitioner as your trustee or executor ☐

If the account you wish to nominate for refunds is not one of the four complying account options presented above, you can request the Commissioner of Taxation to exercise his discretion to pay electronic funds into the account of a third party. For more information phone **13 28 66** between 8.00am and 6.00pm, Monday to Friday.

Form 2.2 [2938] *continued*

Section L: **Declaration** – must be completed by the sole trader or a person authorised to act on behalf of the sole trader

Before you sign this form

Please check that you have provided accurate and complete information.

See Instructions **page 13**

Penalties

Please be aware that penalties may be imposed for giving false or misleading information.

Privacy

The collection of information on this form by the Australian Business Registrar and the Commissioner of Taxation is authorised by taxation law for the administration of those laws. Some information may be made publicly available and some may be passed to other government agencies. Further details are given on page 14 of the instructions.

Name of signatory

Position held (for example, owner, proprietor, tax agent)

I declare that:

- *(where this application has not been completed by the sole trader) I am authorised by the sole trader to complete this application on their behalf*
- *the sole trader is entitled to registration, and*
- *the information given on this form is accurate and complete.*

Signature

Day / Month / Year

How to lodge your application

Keep a copy of this application for your own records and return the completed original to the following address:

Australian Taxation Office
PO Box 3000
ALBURY NSW 2640

IN CONFIDENCE – when completed

Form 2.3 [2929] ABN application—non-individual

SHEET 1 OF 3 Initial sheet here

Australian Government
Australian Business Register
Australian Taxation Office

Application for ABN registration for companies, partnerships, trusts and other organisations

Complete this application if you need an Australian business number for an entity such as a company, partnership, trust or other organisation

- Refer to the Instructions to help you complete this application.
- Initial the form where directed.
- Check that the entity is entitled to an Australian business number (ABN). See Instructions **page 4**
- Use a black pen and BLOCK LETTERS. See Instructions **page 5**
- Place X in all applicable boxes.

Section A: **Entity information**

1 Type of entity (place X in one box only) See Instructions **page 6**

When the term 'entity' is used, it refers to the company, partnership, trust or other organisation applying for this ABN.

Australian public company ☐	Family partnership ☐	Other unincorporated entity ☐
Australian private company ☐	Other partnership ☐	Cooperative ☐
Other incorporated entity ☐	Limited partnership ☐	Strata title ☐
Discretionary trust – trading ☐	Fixed unit trust ☐	Public unit trust – listed ☐
Discretionary trust – investment (includes charitable trusts) ☐	Hybrid trust ☐	Public trading trust ☐
Discretionary trust – services management ☐	Corporate unit trust ☐	Cash management trust ☐
Fixed trust ☐	Public unit trust – unlisted ☐	Deceased estate ☐

29390408

2 What is the entity's name? See Instructions **page 7**

The entity's name is the name that appears on all official documents or legal papers.

It may be different from the name that the entity trades under. For example:

- partnership – Ann L Citizen, Greg P Jones and Brian J Smith
- company – AXY Pty Ltd
- trust – Smith Family Trust (do not provide the name of the trustee of the trust).

NAT 2939-04.2008

IN-CONFIDENCE – when completed

Page 1

Form 2.3 [2929] *continued*

3 What is the entity's trading name?

See Instructions **page 7**

The entity's trading name is the name that it trades under or is known as by its suppliers or customers. It may be the name that is used in advertising and on business cards. The entity may have registered this name with other government departments.

As above ☐ If the entity's trading name is the same as the entity name at question 2, cross this box.

4 Does the entity have more than one trading name?

See Instructions **page 7**

No ☐

Yes ☐ ▶ Provide details of the additional trading names on a separate sheet of paper and include with this application. Include the name of the entity (as provided at question 2) on each sheet.

5 Does the entity have an Australian Company Number or an Australian Registered Body Number?

See Instructions **page 7**

No ☐

Yes ☐ ▶ What is its Australian Company Number (ACN) or Australian Registered Body Number (ARBN)?

6 Is the entity a subsidiary company?

See Instructions **page 8**

A subsidiary company is one that is controlled by another company.

No ☐

Yes ☐ ▶ What is the ACN or ARBN of its ultimate holding company?

7 Does the entity have a tax file number?

See Instructions **page 8**

No ☐ ▶ Does the entity want to apply for a tax file number? ▶ No ☐ Yes ☐

Yes ☐ ▶ Provide the tax file number (You are not required by law to quote a tax file number, but not quoting it may increase the risk of administrative error or delay this registration.)

The Commissioner of Taxation may issue a tax file number whenever it is necessary to do so under Australian tax laws.

Section B: **Address details**

8 Where is the entity's main business location or address?

See Instructions **page 8**

This must be a street address, for example, 123 Smith St.

It cannot be a post office box number, roadside mail bag, roadside delivery or other delivery point address but it can be a home address if the entity operates a home-based business.

Suburb/town/locality

State/territory

Postal code

Country if outside Australia

IN-CONFIDENCE – when completed

Form 2.3 [2929] *continued*

SHEET 2 OF 3 Initial sheet here

9 What is the entity's postal address for service of notices and correspondence?

This is the address where government departments and agencies will send notices and correspondence.

As above ☐ If the entity's postal address is the same as the business address, cross this box.

Suburb/town/locality State/territory Postal code

Country if outside Australia

10 What is the entity's email address for correspondence? See Instructions **page 8**

Use BLOCK LETTERS and print one character per box. Provide only one email address.

Section C: **Online (internet) services**

See Instructions **page 8**

Going online is a fast, convenient and secure way to do business with us. We offer a range of online services to make it easier for businesses to comply.

You can go online to lodge and revise activity statements, perform some superannuation transactions, request payment summary report information, update your ABN details on the Australian Business Register and access the Business Portal.

Some entities **must register** for the Tax Office's online services.

29390508

11 Does the entity wish to register for access to the Tax Office's online services for business?

No ☐

Yes ☐ You must provide an email address at question 10. We will send you a CD-ROM and more information about your online services registration.

Section D: **Contact details**

12 Who is the authorised contact person for the entity? See Instructions **page 9**

Provide details of a person who may be contacted for further information. They must be authorised to make changes or update information on behalf of the entity, for example, a tax agent.

Title: Mr ☐ Mrs ☐ Miss ☐ Ms ☐ Other

Family name

Preferred name

Position held

Business hours phone number (a contact number must be provided)

Mobile phone number

After hours phone number

Fax number

Email address of contact person (use BLOCK LETTERS)

Preferred language, if other than English. We may not be able to speak to the contact person in their preferred language.

IN-CONFIDENCE – when completed

Page 3

Form 2.3 [2929] *continued*

13 If the entity's tax agent is the authorised contact, provide their registration number.

This number may be found on an income tax return prepared by the tax agent.
If this number cannot be found, leave this blank.

14 Does the entity want to nominate more than one contact person?

No

Yes ▸ Provide details of additional contact people on a separate sheet of paper.
Include the name of the entity that is applying for this ABN (as provided at question 2) on each sheet.

Section E: **Reason for application**

15 Why is the entity applying for an ABN? (select one reason only)

See Instructions **page 9**

New business in Australia The entity has set up, or is about to set up, a new business and has never had an ABN using the same business structure in Australia.	Is this the entity's first time in business in Australia?	No	Yes
Bought existing business The entity has bought or taken over an existing business.	Is this the entity's first time in business in Australia? What is the previous owner's ABN?	No	Yes
Contractor or subcontractor The entity is contracting or subcontracting its services.	Is this the first time the entity has been engaged as a contractor or subcontractor in Australia?	No	Yes
To receive payment for services The entity needs an ABN to receive payment for services.	Is this the first time the entity has received payment for services in Australia?	No	Yes
Recommenced business The entity has recommenced business using the same legal structure and it wants to use its previous ABN.	What ABN was used previously?		
Change in business structure The legal structure of the entity has changed, for example, from a sole trader to a company.	What ABN was used previously?		
Other circumstances – only select this reason if none of the above apply.	Provide details below.		

Section F: **Business activity details**

16 From what date does the entity require its ABN?

See Instructions **page 9**

- This date should be when the entity starts setting up the business, not when it starts trading.
- If the date is in the future, you will not receive the entity's ABN until that date.

! The date cannot be more than six months into the future.

Day / Month / Year

17 If the entity intends that its business activity be for less than three months, on what date does the entity expect to cease business?

! If you register for GST, the entity will need to complete monthly activity statements.

Day / Month / Year

18 Does the entity have more than one business location in Australia? No ▸ Go to question 20. Yes

IN-CONFIDENCE – when completed

Form 2.3 [2929] *continued*

SHEET 3 OF 3 Initial sheet here

19 In which states or territories does the entity have business locations? (place X in all applicable boxes)

All ☐ New South Wales ☐ Victoria ☐ Queensland ☐ Western Australia ☐

South Australia ☐ Tasmania ☐ Northern Territory ☐ Australian Capital Territory ☐

20 Is the entity owned or controlled by Commonwealth, state, territory or local government? No ☐ Yes ☐

See Instructions **page 9**

21 What is the main industry that the entity operates in? (place X in one box only)

See Instructions **page 10**

Agriculture ☐
Forestry ☐
Fishing (including aquaculture) ☐
Mining ☐
Manufacturing ☐
Electricity, gas, water and waste ☐
Construction ☐
Wholesale trade ☐
Retail trade ☐
Accommodation and food services ☐
Transport, postal and warehousing ☐
Information media and telecommunications ☐
Financial and insurance services ☐
Rental, hiring and real estate services ☐
Professional, scientific and technical services ☐
Administrative and support services ☐
Public administration and safety ☐
Education and training ☐
Health care and social assistance ☐
Arts and recreation services ☐
Other services ☐

22 Describe the main activity from which the entity derives the majority of its business income.

See Instructions **page 11**

Also describe the main goods produced or the main services provided.

23 Does the entity operate an agricultural property?

An agricultural property is land where the breeding, keeping, cultivation or growing of animals, crops, fruit or vegetables (except forest trees or marine life) is undertaken.

No ☐ Yes ☐

29390608

Section G: **Taxation details**

See Instructions **page 12**

24 Is the entity a resident of Australia for tax purposes? No ☐ Yes ☐

25 Is the entity exempt for income tax purposes? No ☐ Yes ☐

26 Is the entity a non-profit organisation? No ☐ Yes ☐

27 Does the entity want to be registered or endorsed for any of the following?

(Place X in all applicable boxes)

Deductible gift recipient ☐ Tax concession charity or income tax exempt fund ☐ Luxury car tax ☐

Fringe benefits tax ☐ Wine equalisation tax ☐

IN-CONFIDENCE – when completed

Page 5

Form 2.3 [2929] *continued*

Section H: **Goods and services tax (GST)**

Entities cannot register for GST if they are not carrying on an enterprise.

Some entities are required by law to register, while others may choose to voluntarily register for GST.

It is recommended that you read *GST for small business* (NAT 3014) if you are unfamiliar with GST.
For information on how to obtain this guide, see 'Useful products and services' on page 21 of the instructions.

28 Is the entity required by law to register for GST?

An entity is required to register if it:

- is carrying on an enterprise and its GST turnover (see instructions for question 31) is $75,000 or more ($150,000 or more if the entity is a non-profit organisation)
- supplies taxi or limousine travel for fares
- is a representative of an incapacitated entity (where the incapacitated entity is registered or required to be registered), or
- is a resident agent acting for a non-resident (where the non-resident is registered or required to be registered).

No ☐

Yes ☐ ▶ Go to question 30.

29 If the entity is not required to register for GST, is the entity volunteering to register?

See Instructions **page 14**

An entity which is not required by law to register for GST can choose to register voluntarily for GST if it is carrying on an enterprise or intends to carry on an enterprise in the near future.

No ☐ ▶ Go to section J: **Pay as you go (PAYG) withholding.**

Yes ☐

30 What is the entity's date of registration for GST?

See Instructions **page 14**

If an entity is required by law to register for GST, its date of registration is the date that:

- its GST turnover met or exceeded the registration turnover threshold of $75,000 (or $150,000 for non-profit organisations). The turnover threshold is GST-exclusive.
- it commenced supplying taxi or limousine travel for fares
- it commenced representation of an incapacitated entity, or
- it commenced in its capacity as a resident agent for a non-resident.

An entity that is voluntarily registering for GST, can choose its date of registration.

! The date of registration for GST cannot be before the ABN registration date provided at question 16.

Day / Month / Year

☐☐ / ☐☐ / ☐☐☐☐

31 What is the entity's GST turnover?

See Instructions **page 14**

The entity's GST turnover is the greater of its current and projected GST turnovers.

- Current GST turnover – the value of all supplies made or likely to be made in the current month plus the previous 11 months.
- Projected GST turnover – the value of all supplies made or likely to be made in the current month plus the next 11 months.

(Place X in one box only)

$0 to $74,999 ☐ $75,000 to $149,999 ☐ $150,000 to $1,999,999 ☐ $2 million to $19,999,999 ☐

$20 million and over ☐ ▶ If your GST turnover is greater than $20 million, you must select 'Monthly' at question 32, register for online services at question 11, and provide an email address at question 10

32 How often will the entity lodge its activity statements?

See Instructions **page 15**

If the entity's GST turnover is:

- $20 million or more, it must lodge monthly
- less than $20 million it can choose to lodge monthly or quarterly.

An entity that is registering voluntarily, can choose to lodge either monthly, quarterly or annually.

Monthly ☐ Quarterly ☐ Annually ☐

Form 2.3 [2929] *continued*

33 Does the entity intend to account for GST on a cash or a non-cash (accruals) basis?

See Instructions **page 15**

- Cash basis – the entity accounts for the GST on its sales when it receives payment for them
- Non-cash (accruals) basis – the entity will account for the GST on its sales when it has issued an invoice or received any part of the payment, whichever occurs first.

Not all entities are allowed to account for GST on a cash basis.

You must read page 15 of the instructions before nominating the cash basis. Cash ☐ Non-cash (accrual) ☐

34 Does the entity import goods or services into Australia?

No ☐ Yes ☐ ▸ You may be eligible to defer GST on imports, see instructions on page 15.

Section I: **Fuel tax credits**

See Instructions **page 16**

From 1 July 2008, most fuel used in your business is eligible for fuel tax credits, including fuel used in equipment, tools, machinery and heavy vehicles.

The only exceptions are:

- fuel used in vehicles of 4.5 tonne gross vehicle mass (GVM) or less travelling on a public road (for example, passenger cars, small delivery vans or utes), and
- alternative fuels.

35 Does the entity need to register for fuel tax credits?

To register for fuel tax credits, the entity must also be registered for GST.

No ☐ ▸ Go to Section J: **Pay as you go (PAYG) withholding.**

Yes ☐

36 From what date is the entity eligible for fuel tax credits?

This date cannot be before the date you have provided at question 30 (date of GST registration) or 1 July 2006 (when fuel tax credits commenced).

Day Month Year

☐☐ / ☐☐ / ☐☐☐☐

37 Which fuel does the entity use in its business activities?

(Place X in all applicable boxes)

Diesel ☐ Petrol ☐ Other ☐

38 Does the entity use fuel in a vehicle with a GVM greater than 4.5 tonnes travelling on a public road?

No ☐

Yes ☐

Form 2.3 [2929] *continued*

Section J: **Pay as you go (PAYG) withholding**

See Instructions **page 16**

Register for PAYG withholding if the entity is required to withhold amounts from payments it makes to payees such as:

- employees (salary and wages)
- contractors or subcontractors under a voluntary agreement, or
- labour hire workers.

The entity will also need to register if it is required to withhold an amount from payments:

- to suppliers who have not provided an ABN
- of investment income to Australian residents, or
- of royalties, dividends, interest or fund payments to non-residents.

39 Is the entity required by law to register for PAYG withholding?

See Instructions **page 17**

No ☐ Go to question 44.

Yes ☐ When will withholding commence?

This date cannot be before the date provided at question 16 (for ABN registration).

Day / Month / Year

40 How many employees does the entity estimate it will pay?

This information is used to provide you with the correct number of payment summaries at the end of the financial year.

Do not include people under a voluntary agreement or labour hire arrangement.

41 What amount does the entity expect to withhold from payments to its payees each year?

$ ☐☐☐,☐☐☐,☐☐☐.✕

This is the estimated annual withholding amount and is used to determine how often the entity will pay withholding amounts to us.

Where the withholding amount is expected to be:

- less than or equal to $25,000, the entity will be required to pay quarterly
- between $25,001 and $1,000,000, the entity will be required to pay monthly, or
- greater than $1,000,000, the entity will be required to pay more frequently.

(If the entity falls in this group we will send you more information.)

42 How will the entity provide its PAYG withholding payment summary annual report to the Tax Office?

Entities that have made withholding payments, have to lodge an annual report with us at the end of each year. There are different annual reports for different payments made. Entities that have employees and other workers will need to lodge a PAYG withholding payment summary annual report.

This annual report can be lodged electronically, or by paper using forms we supply.

Indicate the method you plan to use to lodge the entity's PAYG withholding payment summary annual report.

Paper form supplied by the Tax Office ☐ Go to question 44. Electronically ☐

43 How will the entity provide payment summaries to its payees?

See Instructions **page 17**

Print its own payment summaries ☐ Use payment summaries supplied by the Tax Office ☐

44 Will the entity pay royalties, dividends, interest or fund payments to non-residents, or are you an investment body that will pay investment income to Australian residents?

See Instructions **page 17**

No ☐

Yes ☐

IN-CONFIDENCE – when completed

Form 2.3 [2929] *continued*

Section K: **Financial account details**

45 What are the entity's financial institution account details for Tax Office refunds?

Refunds will only be paid directly into a recognised financial institution account located in Australia.
The account details provided must be held by:

- the entity (solely or jointly)
- the entity's registered tax agent, or
- a legal practitioner acting as trustee or executor for the entity.

! If you do not provide these details, we cannot refund money owed.

BSB number (must be 6 digits) Account number

Full account name – for example, JQ Citizen. Do not show the account type, such as cheque, savings, mortgage offset.

Is the account held by: the entity ☐ the entity jointly with others ☐ a tax agent for the entity ☐ a legal practitioner as trustee or executor for the entity ☐

If the account you wish to nominate for refunds is not one of the four complying account options presented above, you can request the Commissioner of Taxation to exercise his discretion to pay electronic funds into the account of a third party. For more information phone **13 28 66** between 8.00am and 6.00pm, Monday to Friday.

Section L: **Associates of the entity**

These questions collect information about all individuals and organisations associated with the entity.

Examples of types of associates are:

- companies – the public officer and all directors (individuals only)
- partnerships – all partners (may be individuals, companies, trusts or a combination)
- trusts – all trustees (may be individuals or companies)
- other organisations – all office bearers, for example, president, treasurer or secretary (individuals only), or public officer (if applicable).

Tax file number (TFN) disclosure

We are authorised by the *A New Tax System (Australian Business Number) Act 1999* to ask you to provide tax file numbers on this form. You are not required by law to quote a TFN, but not quoting it increases the risk of administrative error and may delay this registration. If we cannot identify an associate from the information you provide, you may be contacted for more information.

If an individual who is a public officer, director, office bearer, partner or trustee chooses not to disclose their TFN, they must provide on a separate sheet of paper their residential address with the application. Similarly, if an entity other than an individual chooses not to disclose its TFN, it must provide on a separate sheet of paper its business address, the date it commenced, registered or became incorporated and, if applicable, its ACN or ARBN with the application.

46 If the entity is a company, who is its public officer?

Companies must provide details of their public officer.

Every company is required to appoint a public officer, for tax purposes only, within three months of commencing a business. A public officer must be a natural person of at least 18 years of age, who is appointed by a company and answerable for all actions on behalf of the company for tax-related purposes. Examples include record keeping and submitting company tax returns.

Title: Mr ☐ Mrs ☐ Miss ☐ Ms ☐ Other

Family name

First given name

Other given names

Public officer's TFN (refer to the above disclosure)

Date of birth: Day / Month / Year

Sex: Male ☐ Female ☐

Is the public officer also a director of the company? No ☐ Yes ☐ ▶ Do not provide the public officer's name again at question 47.

IN-CONFIDENCE – when completed

Page 9

Form 2.3 [2929] *continued*

47 Who are the individuals associated with the entity?

Individuals associated with the entity must be provided here:

- companies must provide all directors
- partnerships must provide all partners
- trusts must provide all trustees, and
- other organisations must provide all office bearers.

Title: Mr Mrs Miss Ms Other

Family name

First given name Other given names

Individual's TFN (refer to the disclosure on page 9)

Date of birth: Day / Month / Year Sex: Male Female

Position held: Director Trustee Partner Office bearer of a club/association

Title: Mr Mrs Miss Ms Other

Family name

First given name Other given names

Individual's TFN (refer to the disclosure on page 9)

Date of birth: Day / Month / Year Sex: Male Female

Position held: Director Trustee Partner Office bearer of a club/association

Title: Mr Mrs Miss Ms Other

Family name

First given name Other given names

Individual's TFN (refer to the disclosure on page 9)

Date of birth: Day / Month / Year Sex: Male Female

Position held: Director Trustee Partner Office bearer of a club/association

Title: Mr Mrs Miss Ms Other

Family name

First given name Other given names

Individual's TFN (refer to the disclosure on page 9)

Date of birth: Day / Month / Year Sex: Male Female

Position held: Director Trustee Partner Office bearer of a club/association

If you need to provide information for more individuals associated with the entity, provide the relevant details on a separate sheet of paper. Ensure that any additional pages include the name of the entity that is applying for this ABN.

Page 10 **IN-CONFIDENCE – when completed**

Form 2.3 [2929] *continued*

48 What are the organisations associated with the entity? (partnerships and trusts only)

- All non-individual partners of a partnership must be provided here.
- All company trustees of a trust must be provided here.

Full name of the associated organisation

TFN (refer to the disclosure on page 9)

ACN/ARBN

Position held: Trustee Partner

Full name of the associated organisation

TFN (refer to the disclosure on page 9)

ACN/ARBN

Position held: Trustee Partner

Full name of the associated organisation

TFN (refer to the disclosure on page 9)

ACN/ARBN

Position held: Trustee Partner

Full name of the associated organisation

TFN (refer to the disclosure on page 9)

ACN/ARBN

Position held: Trustee Partner

If you need to provide information for more organisations associated with the entity, provide the relevant details on a separate sheet of paper. Ensure that any additional pages include the name of the entity that is applying for this ABN.

IN-CONFIDENCE – when completed

Page 11

Form 2.3 [2929] *continued*

Section M: **Declaration** – must be completed by an individual authorised by the entity

Before you sign this form
Check that you have provided accurate and complete information. See Instructions **page 18**

Penalties
Penalties may be imposed for giving false or misleading information.

Privacy
We are authorised by taxation laws, including the *A New Tax System (Australian Business Number) Act 1999* to collect the information requested on this form. We need this information to help us administer those laws. Some of the information collected will appear on the Australian Business Register. Selected information may be made publicly available and some may be passed to other government agencies, including Commonwealth, state, territory and local government agencies authorised by law to receive it. Further details are given on page 19 of the instructions.

Name of signatory

Position held (for example, director, tax agent, trustee or partner)

Business hours phone number

I declare that:
- *I am authorised by the entity to complete this application on its behalf*
- *the entity is entitled to registration, and*
- *the information given on this form is accurate and complete.*

Signature

Day / Month / Year

How to lodge your application

Send your completed application, including any attachments to:
Australian Taxation Office
PO Box 3000
ALBURY NSW 2640

Make a copy of your application for your own records before you mail it.

Form 3.1 [3092] Withholding tax

ORIGINAL – Tax Office copy

Australian Government
Australian Taxation Office

www.ato.gov.au

Tax file number declaration

This declaration is NOT an application for a tax file number.

- Use a black or blue pen and print clearly in BLOCK LETTERS.
- Print X in the appropriate boxes.
- Read all the Instructions before you complete this declaration.

30920708

Section A: To be completed by the PAYEE

1 What is your tax file number (TFN)?

See *Privacy of information* on page 5 of the Instructions.

OR I have made a separate application/enquiry to the Tax Office for a new or existing TFN.

OR I am claiming an exemption because I am under 18 years of age and do not earn enough to pay tax.

OR I am claiming an exemption because I am in receipt of a pension, benefit or allowance.

2 What is your name? Title: Mr Mrs Miss Ms

Surname or family name

First given name

Other given names

3 If you have changed your name since you last dealt with the Tax Office, show your previous family name

4 What is your date of birth? Day / Month / Year

5 What is your home address in Australia?

Suburb or town

State Postcode

6 On what basis are you paid? (Select only one.)

Full-time employment | Part-time employment | Labour hire | Superannuation income stream | Casual employment

7 Are you an Australian resident for tax purposes? Yes No — You must answer **No** at question 8.

8 Do you want to claim the tax-free threshold from this payer?

Only claim the tax-free threshold from one payer.

If you have more than one source of income and currently claim the tax-free threshold from another payer, do **not** claim it now.

Yes No — Answer **No** at questions 9 and 10 unless you are a non-resident claiming a senior Australians, zone or overseas forces tax offset.

9 Do you want to claim the senior Australians tax offset by reducing the amount withheld from payments made to you?

Yes — Complete a *Withholding declaration* (NAT 3093), but only if you are claiming the tax-free threshold from this payer. If you have more than one payer, see page 3 of the Instructions. No

10 Do you want to claim a zone, overseas forces, dependent spouse or special tax offset by reducing the amount withheld from payments made to you?

Yes — Complete a *Withholding declaration* (NAT 3093). No

11 (a) Do you have an accumulated Higher Education Loan Programme (HELP) debt?

Yes — Your payer will withhold additional amounts to cover any compulsory repayments. No

(b) Do you have an accumulated Financial Supplement debt?

Yes — Your payer will withhold additional amounts to cover any compulsory repayments. No

DECLARATION by payee: *I declare that the information I have given is true and correct.*

Signature

Date Day / Month / Year

There are penalties for deliberately making a false or misleading statement.

Once Section A is completed and signed, give it to your payer.

Section B: To be completed by the PAYER (if you are not lodging via electronic media)

1 What is your Australian business number (ABN) or your withholding payer number? Branch number (if applicable)

2 If you don't have an ABN or withholding payer number, have you applied for one?

Yes No — See 'More information' on page 6 of the Instructions.

3 What is your registered business name or trading name (or your individual name if not in business)?

DECLARATION by payer: *I declare that the information I have given is true and correct.*

Signature of payer

Date Day / Month / Year

There are penalties for deliberately making a false or misleading statement.

4 What is your business address?

Suburb or town

State Postcode

5 Who is your contact person?

Business phone number

6 If you no longer make payments to this payee, print X in this box

Return the completed original Tax Office copy to:

For WA, SA, NT, VIC or TAS
Australian Taxation Office
PO Box 795
ALBURY NSW 2640

For NSW, QLD or ACT
Australian Taxation Office
PO Box 9004
PENRITH NSW 2740

Payers can lodge this information to us electronically or by paper within 14 days of receipt. Ensure you keep a copy in a secure place.

TAXPAYER-IN-CONFIDENCE (when completed)

NAT 3092-07.2006

Form 3.2 [2772] Voluntary agreement for PAYG

Australian Taxation Office ATO

A Voluntary Agreement for PAYG Withholding

ORIGINAL
PAYER'S COPY

Part A - Payee Details

1. Payee's Australian Business Number (ABN)
2. Full name of payee (must be an individual)

Title: Mr Mrs Miss Ms

Surname or family name

First given name

Other given names

Payee's date of birth / /

3. Trading name (if applicable)
4. Phone number
5. Postal address

Suburb/Town

State/Territory Postcode

6. Are you registered for GST (please cross box) Yes No

Part B - Payer Details

1. Payer's Australian Business Number (ABN)
2. Full legal name of the business or organisation
3. Trading name (if applicable)
4. Phone number
5. Postal address

Suburb/Town

State/Territory Postcode

6. Would you be entitled to a full GST input tax credit for supplies from the payee in the absence of this agreement? (please cross one of the boxes)

Yes No

Part C - Rate of Withholding

Refer to important notes on the back of this form before completing this part. Please indicate the rate of withholding below.

1 Does the payee have a Commissioner's Instalment Rate (CIR)?

Yes The CIR is . % - Go to 2

No Flat rate of withholding is 20%

2 Is the CIR greater than 20%?

Yes The rate of withholding will be the CIR

No We agree the rate of withholding will be 20% OR CIR

Please select one box only

Part D - The Agreement

We, the undersigned, agree that payments, as described below, made by the payer to the payee are subject to withholding under section 12-55 of Schedule 1 Part 2-5 of the *Taxation Administration Act 1953*. The rate of withholding is notified at Part C above.

This agreement relates to all payments made for (indicate the nature of payments)

on or after (indicate date) / /

DECLARATION: I declare that the information I have given on this form is complete and correct.

Payee's Signature

Print name

Date / /

Payer's Signature

Print name

Position held

Date / /

PLEASE NOTE: There are penalties for deliberately making a false or misleading statement.

NAT 2772-5.2000

In Confidence when completed

See reverse for additional information

Form 3.3 [1005] Weekly tax

Schedule 2 **Pay as you go (PAYG) withholding** NAT 1005

Weekly tax table

Incorporating Medicare levy with and without leave loading.

FOR PAYMENTS MADE ON OR AFTER 1 JULY 2008.

This document is a withholding schedule made by the Commissioner of Taxation in accordance with sections 15-25 and 15-30 of Schedule 1 to the *Taxation Administration Act 1953*. It applies to withholding payments covered by Subdivisions 12-B (except sections 12-50 and 12-55), and 12-D of Schedule 1.

For more information visit **www.ato.gov.au**

NAT 1005-05.2008

Australian Government
Australian Taxation Office

Form 3.3 [1005] *continued*

WHO SHOULD USE THIS TABLE?

Use this table if you make any of the following payments on a weekly basis:

- salary, wages, allowances and leave loading to employees
- director's fees
- salary and allowances to office holders (including Members of Parliament, statutory office holders, defence force members and police officers)
- payments to labour hire workers
- payments to religious practitioners
- Commonwealth education or training payments
- compensation, sickness or accident payments that are calculated at a periodical rate and made because a person is unable to work (unless the payment is made under an insurance policy to the policy owner).

Also use this table for payments to foreign residents. See page 3 for more information.

Some payees (shearers, fruit and vegetable harvesters, performing artists and those engaged on a daily or casual basis) may be subject to different withholding arrangements.

There are also special arrangements for withholding from payments made under voluntary agreements.

For more information on other tax tables, see *PAYG withholding essentials* at **www.ato.gov.au**

USING FORMULAS

Withholding amounts shown in this table can be expressed in a mathematical form.

If you have developed your own payroll software package, you will need to use the *PAYG withholding – Statement of formulas for calculating amounts to be withheld* (NAT 1004). A copy of this schedule is available from **www.ato.gov.au**

WHEN THERE ARE 53 PAY PERIODS IN A FINANCIAL YEAR

In some years you may pay your payees 53 times instead of the usual 52. As this table is based on 52 pays, the extra pay may result in insufficient amounts being withheld. Tell your payees when this occurs so those who are concerned about a shortfall can ask you to withhold the additional amounts shown in the table below:

Weekly earnings $	Additional withholding $
600 to 1,499	2
1,500 to 3,449	5
3,450 & over	8

TAX FILE NUMBER (TFN) DECLARATIONS

The answers payees provide on a *Tax file number declaration* (NAT 3092) primarily determine the amount to be withheld from payments. A *Tax file number declaration* applies to payments made after the declaration is provided to you. A later declaration provided by a payee overrides an earlier declaration.

If a payee does not give you a valid *Tax file number declaration* within **14 days** of starting a payer/payee relationship, you must fill in a *Tax file number declaration* with all available details of the payee and send it to the Tax Office.

If you have *Employment declarations* that were valid at 30 June 2000, they will continue to be valid under PAYG.

NO TFN PROVIDED

You must withhold 46.5% of the payment (ignoring any cents) if you make a payment to a payee and the payee has not:

- quoted their TFN
- claimed an exemption from quoting, or
- advised that they have applied for a TFN or have made an enquiry with the Tax Office.

If a payee states at question 1 of the *Tax file number declaration* that they have lodged a *Tax file number application or enquiry* with the Tax Office, the payee has **28 days** to give you their TFN.

If the payee has not given you their TFN within **28 days**, you must withhold 46.5% from the total amount of all payments made to the payee (ignoring any cents) unless the Tax Office tells you not to.

Do not allow for any tax offsets or Medicare levy adjustment. Do not add amounts for Higher Education Loan Programme (HELP) or Student Financial Supplement Scheme (SFSS).

WITHHOLDING DECLARATIONS

A payee may use a *Withholding declaration* to advise their entitlement to a tax offset, which they choose to claim through reduced withholding. See page 3 for more information.

Payees can also use *Withholding declarations* to advise you of changes to their situation since providing a valid *Tax file number declaration*, which may affect the amount to be withheld from their payments.

Changes which may affect the amount to be withheld include:

- becoming or ceasing to be an Australian resident for tax purposes
- claiming or discontinuing a claim for the tax-free threshold
- advising a HELP or SFSS debt, or changes to them
- entitlement to a senior Australians tax offset, and
- upward variation to increase the rate or amount to be withheld.

A *Withholding declaration* takes effect from the first payment you make after the payee has provided the declaration. A later declaration provided by a payee overrides an earlier declaration.

A valid *Tax file number declaration* (or *Employment declaration*) must be in place before a payee can authorise you to vary their withholding by providing a *Withholding declaration*.

MEDICARE LEVY ADJUSTMENT

To claim the Medicare levy adjustment available to some low income earners with dependants, a payee must lodge a *Medicare levy variation declaration* (NAT 0929) along with their *Tax file number declaration*.

Some payees may be liable for an increased rate of Medicare levy or the Medicare levy surcharge on reportable fringe benefits. These payees can lodge a *Medicare levy variation declaration*, requiring you to increase the amount to be withheld from payments you make to them.

For instructions on how to work out the Medicare levy adjustment, use the *PAYG withholding – Medicare levy adjustment weekly tax table* (NAT 1010).

ALLOWANCES

Generally, allowances are added to normal earnings and the amount to be withheld is calculated on the total amount of earnings and allowances.

Refer to *PAYG bulletin no. 1 – Taxing of allowances for the 2000/01 and future income years*.

Form 3.3 [1005] *continued*

FOREIGN RESIDENTS

Foreign resident tax rates apply where a payee has answered 'NO' to the question 'Are you an Australian resident for tax purposes?' on their *Tax file number declaration*.

There are two ways to withhold from the earnings of a foreign resident:

- if the payee has not given you a valid TFN, you need to withhold 45 cents for each $1 of earnings (ignoring any cents) or
- if the payee has given you a valid TFN, withhold the amount calculated from 'Foreign resident tax rates' below, rounding any cents to the nearest dollar.

Foreign resident payees cannot claim any tax offsets. If a foreign resident payee has claimed any tax offsets on the *Tax file number declaration*, **do not** make any adjustment to the weekly amount to be withheld.

Foreign resident tax rates

Weekly earnings $	Weekly rate
0 to 653	29 cents for each dollar of earnings
654 to 1,538	$190 plus 30 cents for each $1 of earnings over $653
1,539 to 3,461	$455 plus 40 cents for each $1 of earnings over $1,538
3,462 & over	$1,224 plus 45 cents for each $1 of earnings over $3,461

HELP AND SFSS DEBTS

On 1 June 2006, all accumulated Higher Education Contribution Scheme (HECS) debts became accumulated Higher Education Loan Programme (HELP) debts.

Individuals with an accumulated HELP or Student Financial Supplement Scheme (SFSS) debt may be required to have additional amounts withheld from payments you make to them. A payee with a HELP or SFSS debt will notify you of this on their *Tax file number declaration* or *Withholding declaration*.

Use *PAYG withholding – HELP weekly tax table* (NAT 2173) to calculate additional withholding amounts for HELP debts.

Use *PAYG withholding – SFSS weekly tax table* (NAT 3306) to calculate additional withholding amounts for SFSS debts.

Do not add amounts for HELP or SFSS when no TFN has been provided.

HOLIDAY PAY, LONG SERVICE LEAVE AND EMPLOYMENT TERMINATION PAYMENTS

Payees who continue working for you

For withholding purposes you must include holiday pay (including any leave loading) and long service leave payments as part of normal earnings, except when they are paid on termination of employment. Payment for leave loading is subject to withholding if it exceeds the current threshold of **$320**. Only that part of the payment which exceeds this threshold should be subject to withholding, unless your payee asks you to withhold from the full amount.

Refer to *PAYG withholding – calculation sheet – holiday and long service leave payments for continuing employment* (Index No. 6209).

Payees who cease working for you

Lump sum payments made when a payee ceases working for you are not covered by this table.

If a payee has unused annual leave, leave loading or long service leave, see *PAYG withholding – Tax table for unused leave payments on termination of employment* (NAT 3351).

Any other payments made may be employment termination payments and you should refer to *PAYG withholding – Tax table for employment termination payments* (NAT 70980).

Do not withhold any amount for HELP or SFSS debts from lump sum termination payments.

CHANGE TO FAMILY TAX BENEFIT (FTB) 2008–09

If a payee has claimed Family Tax Benefit (FTB) on their *Withholding declaration* **do not** reduce their withholding amount. FTB cannot be claimed through the Tax System from 1 July 2008. Claims for FTB should be made through the Family Assistance Office.

TAX OFFSETS

Payees who choose to claim their entitlement to a tax offset through reduced withholding, must provide you with a *Withholding declaration*. Tax offsets include:

- dependent spouse
- zone
- parent, spouse's parent or invalid relative
- housekeeper, and
- child-housekeeper.

Use the 'Ready reckoner for tax offsets' on page 4 to convert the payee's annual tax offset entitlement into a weekly value. Deduct this amount from the amount shown in column 2 or 3 of the table beginning on page 5.

Do not allow for any tax offsets if using column 4 or foreign resident rates, or when no TFN has been provided.

EXAMPLE

A payee has weekly earnings of $563 and, if using column 2, the amount to be withheld is $66.

The payee claims a tax offset entitlement of $1,000 on their *Withholding declaration*.

Use the 'Ready reckoner for tax offsets' on page 4 to find the weekly value of $19.

The total amount to be withheld is worked out as follows:

Amount to be withheld on $563	$66.00
Deduct weekly value	$19.00
Total amount to be withheld	**$47.00**

Form 3.3 [1005] *continued*

HOW TO WORK OUT WITHHOLDING AMOUNTS

1 Add any allowances and irregular payments that are to be included in this week's pay to the normal weekly earnings, ignoring any cents.

2 Find the payee's total weekly earnings in **column 1**.

3 Use the appropriate column to find the correct amount to be withheld. If the payee is:
- claiming the tax-free threshold and is entitled to a leave loading, use **column 2**
- claiming the tax-free threshold and is not entitled to a leave loading, use **column 3**, or
- not claiming the tax-free threshold, whether or not entitled to a leave loading, use **column 4**.

4 If the payee has an end-of-year entitlement to a tax offset, use the 'Ready reckoner for tax offsets' shown below to convert the payee's estimate of their full-year entitlement into a weekly value. Then subtract this value from the withholding amount found in step 3.

5 If the payee is entitled to make an adjustment for the Medicare levy, subtract the value of the adjustment, determined from the *PAYG withholding – Medicare levy adjustment weekly tax table* (NAT 1010), from the amount found in step 4.

6 If the payee has advised you of a HELP or SFSS debt, add the amount determined from the *PAYG withholding – HELP weekly tax table* (NAT 2173) or *PAYG withholding – SFSS weekly tax table* (NAT 3306) to the amount you calculated in step 5.

! If you use column 4 or foreign resident tax rates, or no TFN has been provided, do not allow for any tax offsets or Medicare levy adjustment.

EXAMPLE

A payee has weekly earnings of $563.60.

To work out the correct amount to withhold, ignore cents, use column 1 and find $563.

If the payee is:
- claiming the tax-free threshold and is entitled to a leave loading, use column 2 to find the correct amount to withhold = $66.
- claiming the tax-free threshold and is not entitled to a leave loading, use column 3 to find the correct amount to withhold = $65.
- not claiming the tax-free threshold, whether or not entitled to a leave loading, use column 4 to find the correct amount to withhold = $138.

Resident income tax rates from 1 July 2008 (not including Medicare levy)

Taxable income range $	Tax rate %
0 to 6,000	0
6,001 to 34,000	15
34,001 to 80,000	30
80,001 to 180,000	40
Greater than 180,000	45

PAYG WITHHOLDING PUBLICATIONS

All PAYG withholding tax tables and other PAYG publications can be accessed quickly and easily from **www.ato.gov.au**

Copies of weekly and fortnightly tax tables are available from most newsagents. Newsagents also hold copies of the *Tax file number declaration* (NAT 3092) and the *Withholding declaration* (NAT 3093).

READY RECKONER FOR TAX OFFSETS

Amount claimed $	Weekly value $	Amount claimed $	Weekly value $	Amount claimed $	Weekly value $	Amount claimed $	Weekly value $	Amount claimed $	Weekly value $
1	—	20	—	200	4.00	1000	19.00	1759	33.00
2	—	30	1.00	300	6.00	1100	21.00	1800	34.00
3	—	40	1.00	338	6.00	1173	22.00	1900	36.00
4	—	50	1.00	400	8.00	1200	23.00	2000	38.00
5	—	57	1.00	500	10.00	1300	25.00	2500	48.00
6	—	60	1.00	600	11.00	1400	27.00	3000	57.00
7	—	70	1.00	700	13.00	1500	29.00		
8	—	80	2.00	792	15.00	1583	30.00		
9	—	90	2.00	800	15.00	1600	30.00		
10	—	100	2.00	900	17.00	1700	32.00		

If the exact tax offset amount claimed is not shown in the ready reckoner, add the values for an appropriate combination

Example: Tax offsets of $425 claimed. Add values of $400, $20 and $5 = $8.00 + $0.00 + $0.00 = $8.00.
Therefore, reduce the amount to be withheld by $8.00.

Form 3.3 [1005] *continued*

WEEKLY TAX TABLE

Weekly earnings 1 $	Amount to be withheld: With tax-free threshold with leave loading 2 $	Amount to be withheld: With tax-free threshold no leave loading 3 $	Amount to be withheld: No tax-free threshold 4 $
1	—	—	—
2	—	—	—
3	—	—	—
4	—	—	1.00
5	—	—	1.00
6	—	—	1.00
7	—	—	1.00
8	—	—	1.00
9	—	—	1.00
10	—	—	2.00
11	—	—	2.00
12	—	—	2.00
13	—	—	2.00
14	—	—	2.00
15	—	—	2.00
16	—	—	3.00
17	—	—	3.00
18	—	—	3.00
19	—	—	3.00
20	—	—	3.00
21	—	—	3.00
22	—	—	4.00
23	—	—	4.00
24	—	—	4.00
25	—	—	4.00
26	—	—	4.00
27	—	—	4.00
28	—	—	5.00
29	—	—	5.00
30	—	—	5.00
31	—	—	5.00
32	—	—	5.00
33	—	—	5.00
34	—	—	6.00
35	—	—	6.00
36	—	—	6.00
37	—	—	6.00
38	—	—	6.00
39	—	—	6.00
40	—	—	7.00
41	—	—	7.00
42	—	—	7.00
43	—	—	7.00
44	—	—	7.00
45	—	—	7.00
46	—	—	8.00
47	—	—	8.00
48	—	—	8.00
49	—	—	8.00
50	—	—	8.00
51	—	—	8.00
52	—	—	9.00
53	—	—	9.00
54	—	—	9.00
55	—	—	9.00
56	—	—	9.00
57	—	—	9.00
58	—	—	10.00
59	—	—	10.00
60	—	—	10.00
61	—	—	10.00
62	—	—	10.00
63	—	—	10.00
64	—	—	11.00
65	—	—	11.00
66	—	—	11.00
67	—	—	11.00
68	—	—	11.00
69	—	—	11.00
70	—	—	12.00
71	—	—	12.00
72	—	—	12.00
73	—	—	12.00
74	—	—	12.00
75	—	—	12.00
76	—	—	13.00
77	—	—	13.00
78	—	—	13.00
79	—	—	13.00
80	—	—	13.00

Weekly earnings 1 $	Amount to be withheld: With tax-free threshold with leave loading 2 $	Amount to be withheld: With tax-free threshold no leave loading 3 $	Amount to be withheld: No tax-free threshold 4 $
81	—	—	13.00
82	—	—	14.00
83	—	—	14.00
84	—	—	14.00
85	—	—	14.00
86	—	—	14.00
87	—	—	14.00
88	—	—	15.00
89	—	—	15.00
90	—	—	15.00
91	—	—	15.00
92	—	—	15.00
93	—	—	15.00
94	—	—	16.00
95	—	—	16.00
96	—	—	16.00
97	—	—	16.00
98	—	—	16.00
99	—	—	16.00
100	—	—	16.00
101	—	—	17.00
102	—	—	17.00
103	—	—	17.00
104	—	—	17.00
105	—	—	17.00
106	—	—	17.00
107	—	—	18.00
108	—	—	18.00
109	—	—	18.00
110	—	—	18.00
111	—	—	18.00
112	—	—	18.00
113	—	—	19.00
114	—	—	19.00
115	—	—	19.00
116	—	—	19.00
117	—	—	19.00
118	—	—	19.00
119	—	—	20.00
120	—	—	20.00
121	—	—	20.00
122	—	—	20.00
123	—	—	20.00
124	—	—	20.00
125	—	—	21.00
126	—	—	21.00
127	—	—	21.00
128	—	—	21.00
129	—	—	21.00
130	—	—	21.00
131	—	—	22.00
132	—	—	22.00
133	—	—	22.00
134	—	—	22.00
135	—	—	22.00
136	—	—	22.00
137	—	—	23.00
138	—	—	23.00
139	—	—	23.00
140	—	—	23.00
141	—	—	23.00
142	—	—	23.00
143	—	—	24.00
144	—	—	24.00
145	—	—	24.00
146	—	—	24.00
147	—	—	24.00
148	—	—	24.00
149	—	—	25.00
150	—	—	25.00
151	—	—	25.00
152	—	—	25.00
153	—	—	25.00
154	—	—	25.00
155	—	—	26.00
156	—	—	26.00
157	—	—	26.00
158	—	—	26.00
159	—	—	26.00
160	—	—	26.00

Weekly earnings 1 $	Amount to be withheld: With tax-free threshold with leave loading 2 $	Amount to be withheld: With tax-free threshold no leave loading 3 $	Amount to be withheld: No tax-free threshold 4 $
161	—	—	27.00
162	—	—	27.00
163	—	—	27.00
164	—	—	27.00
165	—	—	27.00
166	—	—	27.00
167	—	—	28.00
168	—	—	28.00
169	—	—	28.00
170	—	—	28.00
171	—	—	28.00
172	—	—	28.00
173	—	—	29.00
174	—	—	29.00
175	—	—	29.00
176	—	—	29.00
177	—	—	29.00
178	—	—	29.00
179	—	—	30.00
180	—	—	30.00
181	—	—	30.00
182	—	—	30.00
183	—	—	30.00
184	—	—	30.00
185	—	—	31.00
186	—	—	31.00
187	—	—	31.00
188	—	—	31.00
189	—	—	31.00
190	1.00	—	31.00
191	1.00	1.00	32.00
192	1.00	1.00	32.00
193	1.00	1.00	32.00
194	1.00	1.00	32.00
195	1.00	1.00	32.00
196	2.00	1.00	32.00
197	2.00	1.00	33.00
198	2.00	2.00	33.00
199	2.00	2.00	33.00
200	2.00	2.00	33.00
201	2.00	2.00	33.00
202	2.00	2.00	33.00
203	3.00	2.00	33.00
204	3.00	2.00	34.00
205	3.00	3.00	34.00
206	3.00	3.00	34.00
207	3.00	3.00	34.00
208	3.00	3.00	34.00
209	4.00	3.00	34.00
210	4.00	3.00	35.00
211	4.00	4.00	35.00
212	4.00	4.00	35.00
213	4.00	4.00	35.00
214	4.00	4.00	35.00
215	4.00	4.00	35.00
216	5.00	4.00	36.00
217	5.00	4.00	36.00
218	5.00	5.00	36.00
219	5.00	5.00	36.00
220	5.00	5.00	36.00
221	5.00	5.00	36.00
222	5.00	5.00	37.00
223	6.00	5.00	37.00
224	6.00	5.00	37.00
225	6.00	6.00	37.00
226	6.00	6.00	37.00
227	6.00	6.00	37.00
228	6.00	6.00	38.00
229	7.00	6.00	38.00
230	7.00	6.00	38.00
231	7.00	7.00	38.00
232	7.00	7.00	38.00
233	7.00	7.00	38.00
234	7.00	7.00	39.00
235	7.00	7.00	39.00
236	8.00	7.00	39.00
237	8.00	7.00	39.00
238	8.00	8.00	39.00
239	8.00	8.00	39.00
240	8.00	8.00	40.00

Weekly earnings 1 $	Amount to be withheld: With tax-free threshold with leave loading 2 $	Amount to be withheld: With tax-free threshold no leave loading 3 $	Amount to be withheld: No tax-free threshold 4 $
241	8.00	8.00	40.00
242	9.00	8.00	40.00
243	9.00	8.00	40.00
244	9.00	8.00	40.00
245	9.00	9.00	40.00
246	9.00	9.00	41.00
247	9.00	9.00	41.00
248	9.00	9.00	41.00
249	10.00	9.00	41.00
250	10.00	9.00	41.00
251	10.00	10.00	41.00
252	10.00	10.00	42.00
253	10.00	10.00	42.00
254	10.00	10.00	42.00
255	10.00	10.00	42.00
256	11.00	10.00	42.00
257	11.00	10.00	42.00
258	11.00	11.00	43.00
259	11.00	11.00	48.00
260	11.00	11.00	48.00
261	11.00	11.00	48.00
262	12.00	11.00	48.00
263	12.00	11.00	48.00
264	12.00	11.00	49.00
265	12.00	12.00	49.00
266	12.00	12.00	49.00
267	12.00	12.00	49.00
268	12.00	12.00	49.00
269	13.00	12.00	50.00
270	13.00	12.00	50.00
271	13.00	13.00	50.00
272	13.00	13.00	50.00
273	13.00	13.00	50.00
274	13.00	13.00	50.00
275	14.00	13.00	51.00
276	14.00	13.00	51.00
277	14.00	13.00	51.00
278	14.00	14.00	51.00
279	14.00	14.00	51.00
280	14.00	14.00	52.00
281	14.00	14.00	52.00
282	15.00	14.00	52.00
283	15.00	14.00	52.00
284	15.00	14.00	52.00
285	15.00	15.00	52.00
286	15.00	15.00	53.00
287	15.00	15.00	53.00
288	15.00	15.00	53.00
289	16.00	15.00	53.00
290	16.00	15.00	53.00
291	16.00	16.00	54.00
292	16.00	16.00	54.00
293	16.00	16.00	54.00
294	16.00	16.00	54.00
295	17.00	16.00	54.00
296	17.00	16.00	55.00
297	17.00	16.00	55.00
298	17.00	17.00	55.00
299	17.00	17.00	55.00
300	17.00	17.00	55.00
301	17.00	17.00	55.00
302	18.00	17.00	56.00
303	18.00	17.00	56.00
304	18.00	17.00	56.00
305	18.00	18.00	56.00
306	18.00	18.00	56.00
307	18.00	18.00	57.00
308	19.00	18.00	57.00
309	19.00	18.00	57.00
310	19.00	18.00	57.00
311	19.00	19.00	57.00
312	19.00	19.00	57.00
313	19.00	19.00	58.00
314	19.00	19.00	58.00
315	20.00	19.00	58.00
316	20.00	19.00	58.00
317	20.00	19.00	58.00
318	20.00	20.00	59.00
319	20.00	20.00	59.00
320	20.00	20.00	59.00

Form 3.3 [1005] *continued*

WEEKLY TAX TABLE

Weekly earnings	Amount to be withheld		
	With tax-free threshold with leave loading	With tax-free threshold no leave loading	No tax-free threshold
1	2	3	4
$	$	$	$
321	20.00	20.00	59.00
322	21.00	20.00	59.00
323	21.00	20.00	60.00
324	21.00	20.00	60.00
325	21.00	21.00	60.00
326	21.00	21.00	60.00
327	21.00	21.00	60.00
328	22.00	21.00	60.00
329	22.00	21.00	61.00
330	22.00	21.00	61.00
331	22.00	22.00	61.00
332	22.00	22.00	61.00
333	23.00	22.00	61.00
334	23.00	22.00	62.00
335	23.00	22.00	62.00
336	24.00	23.00	62.00
337	24.00	23.00	62.00
338	24.00	23.00	63.00
339	24.00	23.00	63.00
340	25.00	24.00	63.00
341	25.00	24.00	64.00
342	25.00	24.00	64.00
343	25.00	24.00	64.00
344	26.00	25.00	65.00
345	26.00	25.00	65.00
346	26.00	25.00	65.00
347	26.00	25.00	66.00
348	27.00	26.00	66.00
349	27.00	26.00	66.00
350	27.00	26.00	67.00
351	27.00	26.00	67.00
352	28.00	27.00	67.00
353	28.00	27.00	68.00
354	28.00	27.00	68.00
355	28.00	27.00	68.00
356	29.00	28.00	69.00
357	29.00	28.00	69.00
358	29.00	28.00	69.00
359	29.00	28.00	70.00
360	30.00	29.00	70.00
361	30.00	29.00	70.00
362	30.00	29.00	71.00
363	30.00	29.00	71.00
364	31.00	30.00	71.00
365	31.00	30.00	72.00
366	31.00	30.00	72.00
367	31.00	30.00	72.00
368	32.00	31.00	73.00
369	32.00	31.00	73.00
370	32.00	31.00	73.00
371	32.00	31.00	74.00
372	33.00	32.00	74.00
373	33.00	32.00	74.00
374	33.00	32.00	75.00
375	33.00	32.00	75.00
376	34.00	33.00	75.00
377	34.00	33.00	76.00
378	34.00	33.00	76.00
379	34.00	33.00	76.00
380	35.00	34.00	77.00
381	35.00	34.00	77.00
382	35.00	34.00	77.00
383	35.00	34.00	78.00
384	36.00	35.00	78.00
385	36.00	35.00	78.00
386	36.00	35.00	79.00
387	36.00	35.00	79.00
388	37.00	36.00	79.00
389	37.00	36.00	80.00
390	37.00	36.00	80.00
391	37.00	36.00	80.00
392	37.00	37.00	81.00
393	37.00	37.00	81.00
394	38.00	37.00	81.00
395	38.00	37.00	82.00
396	38.00	37.00	82.00
397	38.00	37.00	82.00
398	38.00	38.00	83.00
399	38.00	38.00	83.00
400	39.00	38.00	83.00

Weekly earnings	Amount to be withheld		
	With tax-free threshold with leave loading	With tax-free threshold no leave loading	No tax-free threshold
1	2	3	4
$	$	$	$
401	39.00	38.00	84.00
402	39.00	38.00	84.00
403	39.00	38.00	84.00
404	39.00	39.00	85.00
405	39.00	39.00	85.00
406	40.00	39.00	85.00
407	40.00	39.00	86.00
408	40.00	39.00	86.00
409	40.00	39.00	86.00
410	40.00	40.00	87.00
411	40.00	40.00	87.00
412	41.00	40.00	87.00
413	41.00	40.00	88.00
414	41.00	40.00	88.00
415	41.00	40.00	88.00
416	41.00	41.00	89.00
417	41.00	41.00	89.00
418	42.00	41.00	89.00
419	42.00	41.00	90.00
420	42.00	41.00	90.00
421	42.00	41.00	90.00
422	42.00	42.00	91.00
423	42.00	42.00	91.00
424	43.00	42.00	91.00
425	43.00	42.00	92.00
426	43.00	42.00	92.00
427	43.00	42.00	92.00
428	43.00	43.00	93.00
429	43.00	43.00	93.00
430	44.00	43.00	93.00
431	44.00	43.00	94.00
432	44.00	43.00	94.00
433	44.00	43.00	94.00
434	44.00	44.00	95.00
435	44.00	44.00	95.00
436	45.00	44.00	95.00
437	45.00	44.00	96.00
438	45.00	44.00	96.00
439	45.00	44.00	96.00
440	45.00	44.00	97.00
441	45.00	45.00	97.00
442	46.00	45.00	97.00
443	46.00	45.00	98.00
444	46.00	45.00	98.00
445	46.00	45.00	98.00
446	46.00	45.00	99.00
447	46.00	46.00	99.00
448	47.00	46.00	99.00
449	47.00	46.00	100.00
450	47.00	46.00	100.00
451	47.00	46.00	101.00
452	47.00	46.00	101.00
453	47.00	47.00	101.00
454	48.00	47.00	102.00
455	48.00	47.00	102.00
456	48.00	47.00	102.00
457	48.00	47.00	103.00
458	48.00	47.00	103.00
459	48.00	48.00	103.00
460	49.00	48.00	104.00
461	49.00	48.00	104.00
462	49.00	48.00	104.00
463	49.00	48.00	105.00
464	49.00	48.00	105.00
465	49.00	49.00	105.00
466	50.00	49.00	106.00
467	50.00	49.00	106.00
468	50.00	49.00	106.00
469	50.00	49.00	107.00
470	50.00	49.00	107.00
471	50.00	50.00	107.00
472	51.00	50.00	108.00
473	51.00	50.00	108.00
474	51.00	50.00	108.00
475	51.00	50.00	109.00
476	51.00	50.00	109.00
477	51.00	51.00	109.00
478	52.00	51.00	110.00
479	52.00	51.00	110.00
480	52.00	51.00	110.00

Weekly earnings	Amount to be withheld		
	With tax-free threshold with leave loading	With tax-free threshold no leave loading	No tax-free threshold
1	2	3	4
$	$	$	$
481	52.00	51.00	111.00
482	52.00	51.00	111.00
483	52.00	52.00	111.00
484	53.00	52.00	112.00
485	53.00	52.00	112.00
486	53.00	52.00	112.00
487	53.00	52.00	113.00
488	53.00	52.00	113.00
489	53.00	53.00	113.00
490	54.00	53.00	114.00
491	54.00	53.00	114.00
492	54.00	53.00	114.00
493	54.00	53.00	115.00
494	54.00	53.00	115.00
495	54.00	54.00	115.00
496	55.00	54.00	116.00
497	55.00	54.00	116.00
498	55.00	54.00	116.00
499	55.00	54.00	117.00
500	55.00	54.00	117.00
501	55.00	55.00	117.00
502	56.00	55.00	118.00
503	56.00	55.00	118.00
504	56.00	55.00	118.00
505	56.00	55.00	119.00
506	56.00	55.00	119.00
507	56.00	56.00	119.00
508	57.00	56.00	120.00
509	57.00	56.00	120.00
510	57.00	56.00	120.00
511	57.00	56.00	121.00
512	57.00	56.00	121.00
513	57.00	57.00	121.00
514	58.00	57.00	122.00
515	58.00	57.00	122.00
516	58.00	57.00	122.00
517	58.00	57.00	123.00
518	58.00	57.00	123.00
519	58.00	58.00	123.00
520	59.00	58.00	124.00
521	59.00	58.00	124.00
522	59.00	58.00	124.00
523	59.00	58.00	125.00
524	59.00	58.00	125.00
525	59.00	59.00	125.00
526	60.00	59.00	126.00
527	60.00	59.00	126.00
528	60.00	59.00	126.00
529	60.00	59.00	127.00
530	60.00	59.00	127.00
531	60.00	60.00	127.00
532	61.00	60.00	128.00
533	61.00	60.00	128.00
534	61.00	60.00	128.00
535	61.00	60.00	129.00
536	61.00	60.00	129.00
537	61.00	60.00	129.00
538	62.00	61.00	130.00
539	62.00	61.00	130.00
540	62.00	61.00	130.00
541	62.00	61.00	131.00
542	62.00	61.00	131.00
543	62.00	61.00	131.00
544	63.00	62.00	132.00
545	63.00	62.00	132.00
546	63.00	62.00	132.00
547	63.00	62.00	133.00
548	63.00	62.00	133.00
549	63.00	62.00	133.00
550	64.00	63.00	134.00
551	64.00	63.00	134.00
552	64.00	63.00	134.00
553	64.00	63.00	135.00
554	64.00	63.00	135.00
555	64.00	63.00	135.00
556	65.00	64.00	136.00
557	65.00	64.00	136.00
558	65.00	64.00	136.00
559	65.00	64.00	137.00
560	65.00	64.00	137.00

Weekly earnings	Amount to be withheld		
	With tax-free threshold with leave loading	With tax-free threshold no leave loading	No tax-free threshold
1	2	3	4
$	$	$	$
561	65.00	64.00	137.00
562	66.00	65.00	138.00
563	66.00	65.00	138.00
564	66.00	65.00	138.00
565	66.00	65.00	139.00
566	66.00	65.00	139.00
567	66.00	65.00	139.00
568	67.00	66.00	140.00
569	67.00	66.00	140.00
570	67.00	66.00	140.00
571	67.00	66.00	141.00
572	67.00	66.00	141.00
573	67.00	66.00	141.00
574	68.00	67.00	142.00
575	68.00	67.00	142.00
576	68.00	67.00	142.00
577	68.00	67.00	143.00
578	68.00	67.00	143.00
579	69.00	67.00	143.00
580	69.00	68.00	144.00
581	69.00	68.00	144.00
582	69.00	68.00	144.00
583	69.00	68.00	145.00
584	69.00	68.00	145.00
585	70.00	69.00	145.00
586	70.00	69.00	146.00
587	70.00	69.00	146.00
588	70.00	69.00	146.00
589	70.00	69.00	147.00
590	71.00	70.00	147.00
591	71.00	70.00	147.00
592	71.00	70.00	148.00
593	71.00	70.00	148.00
594	71.00	70.00	148.00
595	72.00	70.00	149.00
596	72.00	71.00	149.00
597	72.00	71.00	149.00
598	72.00	71.00	150.00
599	72.00	71.00	150.00
600	72.00	71.00	150.00
601	73.00	72.00	151.00
602	73.00	72.00	151.00
603	73.00	72.00	151.00
604	73.00	72.00	152.00
605	73.00	72.00	152.00
606	74.00	72.00	152.00
607	74.00	73.00	153.00
608	74.00	73.00	153.00
609	74.00	73.00	153.00
610	74.00	73.00	154.00
611	75.00	73.00	154.00
612	75.00	74.00	154.00
613	75.00	74.00	155.00
614	75.00	74.00	155.00
615	75.00	74.00	155.00
616	75.00	74.00	156.00
617	76.00	75.00	156.00
618	76.00	75.00	156.00
619	76.00	75.00	157.00
620	76.00	75.00	157.00
621	76.00	75.00	157.00
622	77.00	75.00	158.00
623	77.00	76.00	158.00
624	77.00	76.00	158.00
625	77.00	76.00	159.00
626	77.00	76.00	159.00
627	78.00	76.00	159.00
628	78.00	77.00	160.00
629	78.00	77.00	160.00
630	78.00	77.00	160.00
631	78.00	77.00	161.00
632	78.00	77.00	161.00
633	79.00	77.00	161.00
634	79.00	78.00	162.00
635	79.00	78.00	162.00
636	79.00	78.00	162.00
637	79.00	78.00	163.00
638	80.00	78.00	163.00
639	80.00	79.00	163.00
640	80.00	79.00	164.00

6 **SCHEDULE 2** WEEKLY TAX TABLE

Form 3.3 [1005] *continued*

WEEKLY TAX TABLE

Weekly earnings	Amount to be withheld			Weekly earnings	Amount to be withheld			Weekly earnings	Amount to be withheld			Weekly earnings	Amount to be withheld		
	With tax-free threshold with leave loading	With tax-free threshold no leave loading	No tax-free threshold		With tax-free threshold with leave loading	With tax-free threshold no leave loading	No tax-free threshold		With tax-free threshold with leave loading	With tax-free threshold no leave loading	No tax-free threshold		With tax-free threshold with leave loading	With tax-free threshold no leave loading	No tax-free threshold
1	2	3	4	1	2	3	4	1	2	3	4	1	2	3	4
$	$	$	$	$	$	$	$	$	$	$	$	$	$	$	$
641	80.00	79.00	164.00	721	106.00	104.00	191.00	801	133.00	131.00	218.00	881	160.00	158.00	244.00
642	80.00	79.00	164.00	722	106.00	104.00	191.00	802	133.00	131.00	218.00	882	160.00	158.00	244.00
643	80.00	79.00	165.00	723	107.00	105.00	192.00	803	134.00	131.00	218.00	883	160.00	158.00	244.00
644	81.00	80.00	165.00	724	107.00	105.00	192.00	804	134.00	132.00	219.00	884	161.00	159.00	245.00
645	81.00	80.00	165.00	725	107.00	105.00	192.00	805	134.00	132.00	219.00	885	161.00	159.00	245.00
646	81.00	80.00	166.00	726	108.00	106.00	193.00	806	135.00	132.00	219.00	886	161.00	159.00	245.00
647	81.00	80.00	166.00	727	108.00	106.00	193.00	807	135.00	133.00	220.00	887	162.00	160.00	246.00
648	82.00	80.00	166.00	728	108.00	106.00	193.00	808	135.00	133.00	220.00	888	162.00	160.00	246.00
649	82.00	80.00	167.00	729	109.00	107.00	194.00	809	136.00	133.00	220.00	889	162.00	160.00	246.00
650	82.00	81.00	167.00	730	109.00	107.00	194.00	810	136.00	134.00	221.00	890	163.00	161.00	246.00
651	83.00	81.00	168.00	731	109.00	107.00	194.00	811	136.00	134.00	221.00	891	163.00	161.00	247.00
652	83.00	81.00	168.00	732	110.00	108.00	195.00	812	137.00	134.00	221.00	892	163.00	161.00	247.00
653	83.00	81.00	168.00	733	110.00	108.00	195.00	813	137.00	135.00	222.00	893	164.00	162.00	247.00
654	84.00	82.00	169.00	734	110.00	108.00	195.00	814	137.00	135.00	222.00	894	164.00	162.00	248.00
655	84.00	82.00	169.00	735	111.00	109.00	196.00	815	138.00	135.00	222.00	895	164.00	162.00	248.00
656	84.00	82.00	169.00	736	111.00	109.00	196.00	816	138.00	136.00	223.00	896	165.00	163.00	248.00
657	85.00	83.00	170.00	737	111.00	109.00	196.00	817	138.00	136.00	223.00	897	165.00	163.00	249.00
658	85.00	83.00	170.00	738	112.00	110.00	197.00	818	139.00	136.00	223.00	898	165.00	163.00	249.00
659	85.00	83.00	170.00	739	112.00	110.00	197.00	819	139.00	137.00	224.00	899	166.00	164.00	249.00
660	86.00	84.00	171.00	740	112.00	110.00	197.00	820	139.00	137.00	224.00	900	166.00	164.00	250.00
661	86.00	84.00	171.00	741	113.00	111.00	198.00	821	140.00	137.00	224.00	901	166.00	164.00	250.00
662	86.00	84.00	171.00	742	113.00	111.00	198.00	822	140.00	138.00	225.00	902	167.00	165.00	250.00
663	87.00	85.00	172.00	743	113.00	111.00	198.00	823	140.00	138.00	225.00	903	167.00	165.00	251.00
664	87.00	85.00	172.00	744	114.00	112.00	199.00	824	141.00	138.00	225.00	904	167.00	165.00	251.00
665	87.00	85.00	172.00	745	114.00	112.00	199.00	825	141.00	139.00	226.00	905	168.00	166.00	251.00
666	88.00	86.00	173.00	746	114.00	112.00	199.00	826	141.00	139.00	226.00	906	168.00	166.00	252.00
667	88.00	86.00	173.00	747	115.00	113.00	200.00	827	142.00	139.00	226.00	907	168.00	166.00	252.00
668	88.00	86.00	173.00	748	115.00	113.00	200.00	828	142.00	140.00	227.00	908	169.00	167.00	252.00
669	89.00	87.00	174.00	749	115.00	113.00	200.00	829	142.00	140.00	227.00	909	169.00	167.00	252.00
670	89.00	87.00	174.00	750	116.00	114.00	201.00	830	143.00	140.00	227.00	910	169.00	167.00	253.00
671	89.00	87.00	174.00	751	116.00	114.00	201.00	831	143.00	141.00	228.00	911	170.00	168.00	253.00
672	90.00	88.00	175.00	752	116.00	114.00	201.00	832	143.00	141.00	228.00	912	170.00	168.00	253.00
673	90.00	88.00	175.00	753	117.00	115.00	202.00	833	144.00	142.00	228.00	913	170.00	168.00	254.00
674	90.00	88.00	175.00	754	117.00	115.00	202.00	834	144.00	142.00	229.00	914	171.00	169.00	254.00
675	91.00	89.00	176.00	755	117.00	115.00	202.00	835	144.00	142.00	229.00	915	171.00	169.00	254.00
676	91.00	89.00	176.00	756	118.00	116.00	203.00	836	145.00	143.00	229.00	916	171.00	169.00	255.00
677	91.00	89.00	176.00	757	118.00	116.00	203.00	837	145.00	143.00	230.00	917	172.00	170.00	255.00
678	92.00	90.00	177.00	758	118.00	116.00	203.00	838	145.00	143.00	230.00	918	172.00	170.00	255.00
679	92.00	90.00	177.00	759	119.00	117.00	204.00	839	146.00	144.00	230.00	919	172.00	170.00	256.00
680	92.00	90.00	177.00	760	119.00	117.00	204.00	840	146.00	144.00	231.00	920	173.00	171.00	256.00
681	93.00	91.00	178.00	761	119.00	117.00	204.00	841	146.00	144.00	231.00	921	173.00	171.00	256.00
682	93.00	91.00	178.00	762	120.00	118.00	205.00	842	147.00	145.00	231.00	922	173.00	171.00	257.00
683	93.00	91.00	178.00	763	120.00	118.00	205.00	843	147.00	145.00	232.00	923	174.00	172.00	257.00
684	94.00	92.00	179.00	764	120.00	118.00	205.00	844	147.00	145.00	232.00	924	174.00	172.00	257.00
685	94.00	92.00	179.00	765	121.00	119.00	206.00	845	148.00	146.00	232.00	925	174.00	172.00	258.00
686	94.00	92.00	179.00	766	121.00	119.00	206.00	846	148.00	146.00	233.00	926	175.00	173.00	258.00
687	95.00	93.00	180.00	767	121.00	119.00	206.00	847	148.00	146.00	233.00	927	175.00	173.00	258.00
688	95.00	93.00	180.00	768	122.00	120.00	207.00	848	149.00	147.00	233.00	928	175.00	173.00	258.00
689	95.00	93.00	180.00	769	122.00	120.00	207.00	849	149.00	147.00	234.00	929	176.00	174.00	259.00
690	96.00	94.00	181.00	770	122.00	120.00	207.00	850	149.00	147.00	234.00	930	176.00	174.00	259.00
691	96.00	94.00	181.00	771	123.00	121.00	208.00	851	150.00	148.00	234.00	931	176.00	174.00	259.00
692	96.00	94.00	181.00	772	123.00	121.00	208.00	852	150.00	148.00	235.00	932	177.00	175.00	260.00
693	97.00	95.00	182.00	773	123.00	121.00	208.00	853	150.00	148.00	235.00	933	177.00	175.00	260.00
694	97.00	95.00	182.00	774	124.00	122.00	209.00	854	151.00	149.00	235.00	934	177.00	175.00	260.00
695	97.00	95.00	182.00	775	124.00	122.00	209.00	855	151.00	149.00	235.00	935	178.00	176.00	261.00
696	98.00	96.00	183.00	776	124.00	122.00	209.00	856	151.00	149.00	236.00	936	178.00	176.00	261.00
697	98.00	96.00	183.00	777	125.00	123.00	210.00	857	152.00	150.00	236.00	937	178.00	176.00	261.00
698	98.00	96.00	183.00	778	125.00	123.00	210.00	858	152.00	150.00	236.00	938	179.00	177.00	262.00
699	99.00	97.00	184.00	779	125.00	123.00	210.00	859	152.00	150.00	237.00	939	179.00	177.00	262.00
700	99.00	97.00	184.00	780	126.00	124.00	211.00	860	153.00	151.00	237.00	940	179.00	177.00	262.00
701	99.00	97.00	184.00	781	126.00	124.00	211.00	861	153.00	151.00	237.00	941	180.00	178.00	263.00
702	100.00	98.00	185.00	782	126.00	124.00	211.00	862	153.00	151.00	238.00	942	180.00	178.00	263.00
703	100.00	98.00	185.00	783	127.00	125.00	212.00	863	154.00	152.00	238.00	943	180.00	178.00	263.00
704	100.00	98.00	185.00	784	127.00	125.00	212.00	864	154.00	152.00	238.00	944	181.00	179.00	263.00
705	101.00	99.00	186.00	785	127.00	125.00	212.00	865	154.00	152.00	239.00	945	181.00	179.00	264.00
706	101.00	99.00	186.00	786	128.00	126.00	213.00	866	155.00	153.00	239.00	946	181.00	179.00	264.00
707	101.00	99.00	186.00	787	128.00	126.00	213.00	867	155.00	153.00	239.00	947	182.00	180.00	264.00
708	102.00	100.00	187.00	788	128.00	126.00	213.00	868	155.00	153.00	240.00	948	182.00	180.00	265.00
709	102.00	100.00	187.00	789	129.00	127.00	214.00	869	156.00	154.00	240.00	949	182.00	180.00	265.00
710	102.00	100.00	187.00	790	129.00	127.00	214.00	870	156.00	154.00	240.00	950	183.00	181.00	265.00
711	103.00	101.00	188.00	791	129.00	127.00	214.00	871	156.00	154.00	240.00	951	183.00	181.00	266.00
712	103.00	101.00	188.00	792	130.00	128.00	215.00	872	157.00	155.00	241.00	952	183.00	181.00	266.00
713	103.00	101.00	188.00	793	130.00	128.00	215.00	873	157.00	155.00	241.00	953	184.00	182.00	266.00
714	104.00	102.00	189.00	794	130.00	128.00	215.00	874	157.00	155.00	241.00	954	184.00	182.00	267.00
715	104.00	102.00	189.00	795	131.00	129.00	216.00	875	158.00	156.00	242.00	955	184.00	182.00	267.00
716	104.00	102.00	189.00	796	131.00	129.00	216.00	876	158.00	156.00	242.00	956	185.00	183.00	267.00
717	105.00	103.00	190.00	797	132.00	129.00	216.00	877	158.00	156.00	242.00	957	185.00	183.00	268.00
718	105.00	103.00	190.00	798	132.00	130.00	217.00	878	159.00	157.00	243.00	958	185.00	183.00	268.00
719	105.00	103.00	190.00	799	132.00	130.00	217.00	879	159.00	157.00	243.00	959	186.00	184.00	268.00
720	106.00	104.00	191.00	800	133.00	130.00	217.00	880	159.00	157.00	243.00	960	186.00	184.00	269.00

Form 3.3 [1005] *continued*

WEEKLY TAX TABLE

Weekly earnings	Amount to be withheld		
	With tax-free threshold with leave loading	With tax-free threshold no leave loading	No tax-free threshold
1	2	3	4
$	$	$	$
961	186.00	184.00	269.00
962	187.00	185.00	269.00
963	187.00	185.00	269.00
964	187.00	185.00	270.00
965	188.00	186.00	270.00
966	188.00	186.00	270.00
967	188.00	186.00	271.00
968	189.00	187.00	271.00
969	189.00	187.00	271.00
970	189.00	187.00	272.00
971	190.00	188.00	272.00
972	190.00	188.00	272.00
973	190.00	188.00	273.00
974	191.00	189.00	273.00
975	191.00	189.00	273.00
976	191.00	189.00	274.00
977	192.00	190.00	274.00
978	192.00	190.00	274.00
979	192.00	190.00	275.00
980	193.00	191.00	275.00
981	193.00	191.00	275.00
982	193.00	191.00	275.00
983	194.00	192.00	276.00
984	194.00	192.00	276.00
985	194.00	192.00	276.00
986	195.00	193.00	277.00
987	195.00	193.00	277.00
988	195.00	193.00	277.00
989	196.00	194.00	278.00
990	196.00	194.00	278.00
991	196.00	194.00	278.00
992	197.00	195.00	279.00
993	197.00	195.00	279.00
994	197.00	195.00	279.00
995	198.00	196.00	280.00
996	198.00	196.00	280.00
997	199.00	196.00	280.00
998	199.00	197.00	280.00
999	199.00	197.00	281.00
1000	200.00	197.00	281.00
1001	200.00	198.00	281.00
1002	200.00	198.00	282.00
1003	201.00	198.00	282.00
1004	201.00	199.00	282.00
1005	201.00	199.00	283.00
1006	202.00	199.00	283.00
1007	202.00	200.00	283.00
1008	202.00	200.00	284.00
1009	203.00	200.00	284.00
1010	203.00	201.00	284.00
1011	203.00	201.00	285.00
1012	204.00	201.00	285.00
1013	204.00	202.00	285.00
1014	204.00	202.00	286.00
1015	205.00	202.00	286.00
1016	205.00	203.00	286.00
1017	205.00	203.00	286.00
1018	206.00	203.00	287.00
1019	206.00	204.00	287.00
1020	206.00	204.00	287.00
1021	207.00	204.00	288.00
1022	207.00	205.00	288.00
1023	207.00	205.00	288.00
1024	208.00	205.00	289.00
1025	208.00	206.00	289.00
1026	208.00	206.00	289.00
1027	209.00	206.00	290.00
1028	209.00	207.00	290.00
1029	209.00	207.00	290.00
1030	210.00	207.00	291.00
1031	210.00	208.00	291.00
1032	210.00	208.00	291.00
1033	211.00	209.00	292.00
1034	211.00	209.00	292.00
1035	211.00	209.00	292.00
1036	212.00	210.00	292.00
1037	212.00	210.00	293.00
1038	212.00	210.00	293.00
1039	213.00	211.00	293.00
1040	213.00	211.00	294.00
1041	213.00	211.00	294.00
1042	214.00	212.00	294.00
1043	214.00	212.00	295.00
1044	214.00	212.00	295.00
1045	215.00	213.00	295.00
1046	215.00	213.00	296.00
1047	215.00	213.00	296.00
1048	216.00	214.00	296.00
1049	216.00	214.00	297.00
1050	216.00	214.00	297.00
1051	217.00	215.00	297.00
1052	217.00	215.00	298.00
1053	217.00	215.00	298.00
1054	218.00	216.00	298.00
1055	218.00	216.00	298.00
1056	218.00	216.00	299.00
1057	219.00	217.00	299.00
1058	219.00	217.00	299.00
1059	219.00	217.00	300.00
1060	220.00	218.00	300.00
1061	220.00	218.00	300.00
1062	220.00	218.00	301.00
1063	221.00	219.00	301.00
1064	221.00	219.00	301.00
1065	221.00	219.00	302.00
1066	222.00	220.00	302.00
1067	222.00	220.00	302.00
1068	222.00	220.00	303.00
1069	223.00	221.00	303.00
1070	223.00	221.00	303.00
1071	223.00	221.00	303.00
1072	224.00	222.00	304.00
1073	224.00	222.00	304.00
1074	224.00	222.00	304.00
1075	225.00	223.00	305.00
1076	225.00	223.00	305.00
1077	225.00	223.00	305.00
1078	226.00	224.00	306.00
1079	226.00	224.00	306.00
1080	226.00	224.00	306.00
1081	227.00	225.00	307.00
1082	227.00	225.00	307.00
1083	227.00	225.00	307.00
1084	228.00	226.00	308.00
1085	228.00	226.00	308.00
1086	228.00	226.00	308.00
1087	229.00	227.00	309.00
1088	229.00	227.00	309.00
1089	229.00	227.00	309.00
1090	230.00	228.00	309.00
1091	230.00	228.00	310.00
1092	230.00	228.00	310.00
1093	231.00	229.00	310.00
1094	231.00	229.00	311.00
1095	231.00	229.00	311.00
1096	232.00	230.00	311.00
1097	232.00	230.00	312.00
1098	232.00	230.00	312.00
1099	233.00	231.00	312.00
1100	233.00	231.00	313.00
1101	233.00	231.00	313.00
1102	234.00	232.00	313.00
1103	234.00	232.00	314.00
1104	234.00	232.00	314.00
1105	235.00	233.00	314.00
1106	235.00	233.00	315.00
1107	235.00	233.00	315.00
1108	236.00	234.00	315.00
1109	236.00	234.00	315.00
1110	236.00	234.00	316.00
1111	237.00	235.00	316.00
1112	237.00	235.00	316.00
1113	237.00	235.00	317.00
1114	238.00	236.00	317.00
1115	238.00	236.00	317.00
1116	238.00	236.00	318.00
1117	239.00	237.00	318.00
1118	239.00	237.00	318.00
1119	239.00	237.00	319.00
1120	240.00	238.00	319.00
1121	240.00	238.00	319.00
1122	240.00	238.00	320.00
1123	241.00	239.00	320.00
1124	241.00	239.00	320.00
1125	241.00	239.00	321.00
1126	242.00	240.00	321.00
1127	242.00	240.00	321.00
1128	242.00	240.00	321.00
1129	243.00	241.00	322.00
1130	243.00	241.00	322.00
1131	243.00	241.00	322.00
1132	244.00	242.00	323.00
1133	244.00	242.00	323.00
1134	244.00	242.00	323.00
1135	245.00	243.00	324.00
1136	245.00	243.00	324.00
1137	245.00	243.00	324.00
1138	246.00	244.00	325.00
1139	246.00	244.00	325.00
1140	246.00	244.00	325.00
1141	247.00	245.00	326.00
1142	247.00	245.00	326.00
1143	247.00	245.00	326.00
1144	248.00	246.00	326.00
1145	248.00	246.00	327.00
1146	248.00	246.00	327.00
1147	249.00	247.00	327.00
1148	249.00	247.00	328.00
1149	249.00	247.00	328.00
1150	250.00	248.00	328.00
1151	250.00	248.00	329.00
1152	250.00	248.00	329.00
1153	251.00	249.00	329.00
1154	251.00	249.00	330.00
1155	251.00	249.00	330.00
1156	252.00	250.00	330.00
1157	252.00	250.00	331.00
1158	252.00	250.00	331.00
1159	253.00	251.00	331.00
1160	253.00	251.00	332.00
1161	253.00	251.00	332.00
1162	253.00	252.00	332.00
1163	254.00	252.00	332.00
1164	254.00	252.00	333.00
1165	254.00	252.00	333.00
1166	255.00	253.00	333.00
1167	255.00	253.00	334.00
1168	255.00	253.00	334.00
1169	256.00	254.00	334.00
1170	256.00	254.00	335.00
1171	256.00	254.00	335.00
1172	257.00	255.00	335.00
1173	257.00	255.00	336.00
1174	257.00	255.00	336.00
1175	258.00	256.00	336.00
1176	258.00	256.00	337.00
1177	258.00	256.00	337.00
1178	259.00	257.00	337.00
1179	259.00	257.00	338.00
1180	259.00	257.00	338.00
1181	259.00	258.00	338.00
1182	260.00	258.00	338.00
1183	260.00	258.00	339.00
1184	260.00	258.00	339.00
1185	261.00	259.00	339.00
1186	261.00	259.00	340.00
1187	261.00	259.00	340.00
1188	262.00	260.00	340.00
1189	262.00	260.00	341.00
1190	262.00	260.00	341.00
1191	263.00	261.00	341.00
1192	263.00	261.00	342.00
1193	263.00	261.00	342.00
1194	264.00	262.00	342.00
1195	264.00	262.00	343.00
1196	264.00	262.00	343.00
1197	264.00	263.00	343.00
1198	265.00	263.00	343.00
1199	265.00	263.00	344.00
1200	265.00	264.00	344.00
1201	266.00	264.00	344.00
1202	266.00	264.00	345.00
1203	266.00	264.00	345.00
1204	267.00	265.00	345.00
1205	267.00	265.00	346.00
1206	267.00	265.00	346.00
1207	268.00	266.00	346.00
1208	268.00	266.00	347.00
1209	268.00	266.00	347.00
1210	269.00	267.00	347.00
1211	269.00	267.00	348.00
1212	269.00	267.00	348.00
1213	270.00	268.00	348.00
1214	270.00	268.00	349.00
1215	270.00	268.00	349.00
1216	270.00	269.00	349.00
1217	271.00	269.00	349.00
1218	271.00	269.00	350.00
1219	271.00	269.00	350.00
1220	272.00	270.00	350.00
1221	272.00	270.00	351.00
1222	272.00	270.00	351.00
1223	273.00	271.00	352.00
1224	273.00	271.00	352.00
1225	273.00	271.00	352.00
1226	274.00	272.00	353.00
1227	274.00	272.00	353.00
1228	274.00	272.00	354.00
1229	275.00	273.00	354.00
1230	275.00	273.00	355.00
1231	275.00	273.00	355.00
1232	276.00	274.00	355.00
1233	276.00	274.00	356.00
1234	276.00	274.00	356.00
1235	276.00	275.00	357.00
1236	277.00	275.00	357.00
1237	277.00	275.00	357.00
1238	277.00	275.00	358.00
1239	278.00	276.00	358.00
1240	278.00	276.00	359.00
1241	278.00	276.00	359.00
1242	279.00	277.00	360.00
1243	279.00	277.00	360.00
1244	279.00	277.00	360.00
1245	280.00	278.00	361.00
1246	280.00	278.00	361.00
1247	280.00	278.00	362.00
1248	281.00	279.00	362.00
1249	281.00	279.00	362.00
1250	281.00	279.00	363.00
1251	282.00	280.00	363.00
1252	282.00	280.00	364.00
1253	282.00	280.00	364.00
1254	282.00	281.00	365.00
1255	283.00	281.00	365.00
1256	283.00	281.00	365.00
1257	283.00	281.00	366.00
1258	284.00	282.00	366.00
1259	284.00	282.00	367.00
1260	284.00	282.00	367.00
1261	285.00	283.00	367.00
1262	285.00	283.00	368.00
1263	285.00	283.00	368.00
1264	286.00	284.00	369.00
1265	286.00	284.00	369.00
1266	286.00	284.00	370.00
1267	287.00	285.00	370.00
1268	287.00	285.00	370.00
1269	287.00	285.00	371.00
1270	287.00	286.00	371.00
1271	288.00	286.00	372.00
1272	288.00	286.00	372.00
1273	288.00	286.00	372.00
1274	289.00	287.00	373.00
1275	289.00	287.00	373.00
1276	289.00	287.00	374.00
1277	290.00	288.00	374.00
1278	290.00	288.00	374.00
1279	290.00	288.00	375.00
1280	291.00	289.00	375.00

Form 3.3 [1005] *continued*

WEEKLY TAX TABLE

Weekly earnings	Amount to be withheld			Weekly earnings	Amount to be withheld			Weekly earnings	Amount to be withheld			Weekly earnings	Amount to be withheld		
	With tax-free threshold with leave loading	With tax-free threshold no leave loading	No tax-free threshold		With tax-free threshold with leave loading	With tax-free threshold no leave loading	No tax-free threshold		With tax-free threshold with leave loading	With tax-free threshold no leave loading	No tax-free threshold		With tax-free threshold with leave loading	With tax-free threshold no leave loading	No tax-free threshold
1	2	3	4	1	2	3	4	1	2	3	4	1	2	3	4
$	$	$	$	$	$	$	$	$	$	$	$	$	$	$	$
1281	291.00	289.00	376.00	1361	316.00	314.00	409.00	1441	341.00	339.00	442.00	1521	367.00	365.00	475.00
1282	291.00	289.00	376.00	1362	316.00	315.00	409.00	1442	342.00	340.00	443.00	1522	367.00	365.00	476.00
1283	292.00	290.00	377.00	1363	317.00	315.00	410.00	1443	342.00	340.00	443.00	1523	367.00	365.00	476.00
1284	292.00	290.00	377.00	1364	317.00	315.00	410.00	1444	342.00	340.00	443.00	1524	368.00	366.00	477.00
1285	292.00	290.00	377.00	1365	317.00	315.00	411.00	1445	343.00	341.00	444.00	1525	368.00	366.00	477.00
1286	293.00	291.00	378.00	1366	318.00	316.00	411.00	1446	343.00	341.00	444.00	1526	368.00	366.00	477.00
1287	293.00	291.00	378.00	1367	318.00	316.00	411.00	1447	343.00	341.00	445.00	1527	368.00	367.00	478.00
1288	293.00	291.00	379.00	1368	318.00	316.00	412.00	1448	344.00	342.00	445.00	1528	369.00	367.00	478.00
1289	293.00	292.00	379.00	1369	319.00	317.00	412.00	1449	344.00	342.00	445.00	1529	369.00	367.00	479.00
1290	294.00	292.00	379.00	1370	319.00	317.00	413.00	1450	344.00	342.00	446.00	1530	369.00	367.00	479.00
1291	294.00	292.00	380.00	1371	319.00	317.00	413.00	1451	345.00	343.00	446.00	1531	370.00	368.00	479.00
1292	294.00	292.00	380.00	1372	320.00	318.00	413.00	1452	345.00	343.00	447.00	1532	370.00	368.00	480.00
1293	295.00	293.00	381.00	1373	320.00	318.00	414.00	1453	345.00	343.00	447.00	1533	371.00	368.00	480.00
1294	295.00	293.00	381.00	1374	320.00	318.00	414.00	1454	345.00	344.00	448.00	1534	371.00	369.00	481.00
1295	295.00	293.00	382.00	1375	321.00	319.00	415.00	1455	346.00	344.00	448.00	1535	371.00	369.00	481.00
1296	296.00	294.00	382.00	1376	321.00	319.00	415.00	1456	346.00	344.00	448.00	1536	372.00	369.00	482.00
1297	296.00	294.00	382.00	1377	321.00	319.00	416.00	1457	346.00	344.00	449.00	1537	372.00	370.00	482.00
1298	296.00	294.00	383.00	1378	322.00	320.00	416.00	1458	347.00	345.00	449.00	1538	373.00	370.00	482.00
1299	297.00	295.00	383.00	1379	322.00	320.00	416.00	1459	347.00	345.00	450.00	1539	373.00	370.00	483.00
1300	297.00	295.00	384.00	1380	322.00	320.00	417.00	1460	347.00	345.00	450.00	1540	373.00	371.00	483.00
1301	297.00	295.00	384.00	1381	322.00	321.00	417.00	1461	348.00	346.00	450.00	1541	374.00	371.00	484.00
1302	298.00	296.00	384.00	1382	323.00	321.00	418.00	1462	348.00	346.00	451.00	1542	374.00	372.00	484.00
1303	298.00	296.00	385.00	1383	323.00	321.00	418.00	1463	348.00	346.00	451.00	1543	375.00	372.00	484.00
1304	298.00	296.00	385.00	1384	323.00	321.00	418.00	1464	349.00	347.00	452.00	1544	375.00	373.00	485.00
1305	299.00	297.00	386.00	1385	324.00	322.00	419.00	1465	349.00	347.00	452.00	1545	375.00	373.00	485.00
1306	299.00	297.00	386.00	1386	324.00	322.00	419.00	1466	349.00	347.00	453.00	1546	376.00	373.00	486.00
1307	299.00	297.00	387.00	1387	324.00	322.00	420.00	1467	350.00	348.00	453.00	1547	376.00	374.00	486.00
1308	299.00	298.00	387.00	1388	325.00	323.00	420.00	1468	350.00	348.00	453.00	1548	377.00	374.00	487.00
1309	300.00	298.00	387.00	1389	325.00	323.00	421.00	1469	350.00	348.00	454.00	1549	377.00	375.00	487.00
1310	300.00	298.00	388.00	1390	325.00	323.00	421.00	1470	350.00	349.00	454.00	1550	378.00	375.00	487.00
1311	300.00	298.00	388.00	1391	326.00	324.00	421.00	1471	351.00	349.00	455.00	1551	378.00	375.00	488.00
1312	301.00	299.00	389.00	1392	326.00	324.00	422.00	1472	351.00	349.00	455.00	1552	378.00	376.00	488.00
1313	301.00	299.00	389.00	1393	326.00	324.00	422.00	1473	351.00	349.00	455.00	1553	379.00	376.00	489.00
1314	301.00	299.00	389.00	1394	327.00	325.00	423.00	1474	352.00	350.00	456.00	1554	379.00	377.00	489.00
1315	302.00	300.00	390.00	1395	327.00	325.00	423.00	1475	352.00	350.00	456.00	1555	380.00	377.00	489.00
1316	302.00	300.00	390.00	1396	327.00	325.00	423.00	1476	352.00	350.00	457.00	1556	380.00	377.00	490.00
1317	302.00	300.00	391.00	1397	327.00	326.00	424.00	1477	353.00	351.00	457.00	1557	380.00	378.00	490.00
1318	303.00	301.00	391.00	1398	328.00	326.00	424.00	1478	353.00	351.00	457.00	1558	381.00	378.00	491.00
1319	303.00	301.00	391.00	1399	328.00	326.00	425.00	1479	353.00	351.00	458.00	1559	381.00	379.00	491.00
1320	303.00	301.00	392.00	1400	328.00	327.00	425.00	1480	354.00	352.00	458.00	1560	382.00	379.00	492.00
1321	304.00	302.00	392.00	1401	329.00	327.00	426.00	1481	354.00	352.00	459.00	1561	382.00	380.00	492.00
1322	304.00	302.00	393.00	1402	329.00	327.00	426.00	1482	354.00	352.00	459.00	1562	383.00	380.00	492.00
1323	304.00	302.00	393.00	1403	329.00	327.00	426.00	1483	355.00	353.00	460.00	1563	383.00	380.00	493.00
1324	305.00	303.00	394.00	1404	330.00	328.00	427.00	1484	355.00	353.00	460.00	1564	383.00	381.00	493.00
1325	305.00	303.00	394.00	1405	330.00	328.00	427.00	1485	355.00	353.00	460.00	1565	384.00	381.00	494.00
1326	305.00	303.00	394.00	1406	330.00	328.00	428.00	1486	356.00	354.00	461.00	1566	384.00	382.00	494.00
1327	305.00	304.00	395.00	1407	331.00	329.00	428.00	1487	356.00	354.00	461.00	1567	385.00	382.00	494.00
1328	306.00	304.00	395.00	1408	331.00	329.00	428.00	1488	356.00	354.00	462.00	1568	385.00	382.00	495.00
1329	306.00	304.00	396.00	1409	331.00	329.00	429.00	1489	356.00	355.00	462.00	1569	385.00	383.00	495.00
1330	306.00	304.00	396.00	1410	332.00	330.00	429.00	1490	357.00	355.00	462.00	1570	386.00	383.00	496.00
1331	307.00	305.00	396.00	1411	332.00	330.00	430.00	1491	357.00	355.00	463.00	1571	386.00	384.00	496.00
1332	307.00	305.00	397.00	1412	332.00	330.00	430.00	1492	357.00	355.00	463.00	1572	387.00	384.00	496.00
1333	307.00	305.00	397.00	1413	333.00	331.00	431.00	1493	358.00	356.00	464.00	1573	387.00	385.00	497.00
1334	308.00	306.00	398.00	1414	333.00	331.00	431.00	1494	358.00	356.00	464.00	1574	388.00	385.00	497.00
1335	308.00	306.00	398.00	1415	333.00	331.00	431.00	1495	358.00	356.00	465.00	1575	388.00	385.00	498.00
1336	308.00	306.00	399.00	1416	333.00	332.00	432.00	1496	359.00	357.00	465.00	1576	388.00	386.00	498.00
1337	309.00	307.00	399.00	1417	334.00	332.00	432.00	1497	359.00	357.00	465.00	1577	389.00	386.00	499.00
1338	309.00	307.00	399.00	1418	334.00	332.00	433.00	1498	359.00	357.00	466.00	1578	389.00	387.00	499.00
1339	309.00	307.00	400.00	1419	334.00	332.00	433.00	1499	360.00	358.00	466.00	1579	390.00	387.00	499.00
1340	310.00	308.00	400.00	1420	335.00	333.00	433.00	1500	360.00	358.00	467.00	1580	390.00	387.00	500.00
1341	310.00	308.00	401.00	1421	335.00	333.00	434.00	1501	360.00	358.00	467.00	1581	390.00	388.00	500.00
1342	310.00	308.00	401.00	1422	335.00	333.00	434.00	1502	361.00	359.00	467.00	1582	391.00	388.00	501.00
1343	310.00	309.00	401.00	1423	336.00	334.00	435.00	1503	361.00	359.00	468.00	1583	391.00	389.00	501.00
1344	311.00	309.00	402.00	1424	336.00	334.00	435.00	1504	361.00	359.00	468.00	1584	392.00	389.00	501.00
1345	311.00	309.00	402.00	1425	336.00	334.00	435.00	1505	362.00	360.00	469.00	1585	392.00	390.00	502.00
1346	311.00	309.00	403.00	1426	337.00	335.00	436.00	1506	362.00	360.00	469.00	1586	393.00	390.00	502.00
1347	312.00	310.00	403.00	1427	337.00	335.00	436.00	1507	362.00	360.00	470.00	1587	393.00	390.00	503.00
1348	312.00	310.00	404.00	1428	337.00	335.00	437.00	1508	362.00	361.00	470.00	1588	393.00	391.00	503.00
1349	312.00	310.00	404.00	1429	338.00	336.00	437.00	1509	363.00	361.00	470.00	1589	394.00	391.00	504.00
1350	313.00	311.00	404.00	1430	338.00	336.00	438.00	1510	363.00	361.00	471.00	1590	394.00	392.00	504.00
1351	313.00	311.00	405.00	1431	338.00	336.00	438.00	1511	363.00	361.00	471.00	1591	395.00	392.00	504.00
1352	313.00	311.00	405.00	1432	339.00	337.00	438.00	1512	364.00	362.00	472.00	1592	395.00	392.00	505.00
1353	314.00	312.00	406.00	1433	339.00	337.00	439.00	1513	364.00	362.00	472.00	1593	395.00	393.00	505.00
1354	314.00	312.00	406.00	1434	339.00	337.00	439.00	1514	364.00	362.00	472.00	1594	396.00	393.00	506.00
1355	314.00	312.00	406.00	1435	339.00	338.00	440.00	1515	365.00	363.00	473.00	1595	396.00	394.00	506.00
1356	315.00	313.00	407.00	1436	340.00	338.00	440.00	1516	365.00	363.00	473.00	1596	397.00	394.00	506.00
1357	315.00	313.00	407.00	1437	340.00	338.00	440.00	1517	365.00	363.00	474.00	1597	397.00	395.00	507.00
1358	315.00	313.00	408.00	1438	340.00	338.00	441.00	1518	366.00	364.00	474.00	1598	397.00	395.00	507.00
1359	316.00	314.00	408.00	1439	341.00	339.00	441.00	1519	366.00	364.00	474.00	1599	398.00	395.00	508.00
1360	316.00	314.00	409.00	1440	341.00	339.00	442.00	1520	366.00	364.00	475.00	1600	398.00	396.00	508.00

Form 3.3 [1005] *continued*

WEEKLY TAX TABLE

Weekly earnings	Amount to be withheld		
	With tax-free threshold with leave loading	With tax-free threshold no leave loading	No tax-free threshold
1	2	3	4
$	$	$	$
1601	399.00	396.00	509.00
1602	399.00	397.00	509.00
1603	400.00	397.00	509.00
1604	400.00	397.00	510.00
1605	400.00	398.00	510.00
1606	401.00	398.00	511.00
1607	401.00	399.00	511.00
1608	402.00	399.00	511.00
1609	402.00	399.00	512.00
1610	402.00	400.00	512.00
1611	403.00	400.00	513.00
1612	403.00	401.00	513.00
1613	404.00	401.00	514.00
1614	404.00	402.00	514.00
1615	405.00	402.00	514.00
1616	405.00	402.00	515.00
1617	405.00	403.00	515.00
1618	406.00	403.00	516.00
1619	406.00	404.00	516.00
1620	407.00	404.00	516.00
1621	407.00	404.00	517.00
1622	407.00	405.00	517.00
1623	408.00	405.00	518.00
1624	408.00	406.00	518.00
1625	409.00	406.00	518.00
1626	409.00	407.00	519.00
1627	410.00	407.00	519.00
1628	410.00	407.00	520.00
1629	410.00	408.00	520.00
1630	411.00	408.00	521.00
1631	411.00	409.00	521.00
1632	412.00	409.00	521.00
1633	412.00	409.00	522.00
1634	412.00	410.00	522.00
1635	413.00	410.00	523.00
1636	413.00	411.00	523.00
1637	414.00	411.00	523.00
1638	414.00	412.00	524.00
1639	414.00	412.00	524.00
1640	415.00	412.00	525.00
1641	415.00	413.00	525.00
1642	416.00	413.00	526.00
1643	416.00	414.00	526.00
1644	417.00	414.00	526.00
1645	417.00	414.00	527.00
1646	417.00	415.00	527.00
1647	418.00	415.00	528.00
1648	418.00	416.00	528.00
1649	419.00	416.00	528.00
1650	419.00	417.00	529.00
1651	419.00	417.00	529.00
1652	420.00	417.00	530.00
1653	420.00	418.00	530.00
1654	421.00	418.00	531.00
1655	421.00	419.00	531.00
1656	422.00	419.00	531.00
1657	422.00	419.00	532.00
1658	422.00	420.00	532.00
1659	423.00	420.00	533.00
1660	423.00	421.00	533.00
1661	424.00	421.00	533.00
1662	424.00	421.00	534.00
1663	424.00	422.00	534.00
1664	425.00	422.00	535.00
1665	425.00	423.00	535.00
1666	426.00	423.00	536.00
1667	426.00	424.00	536.00
1668	427.00	424.00	536.00
1669	427.00	424.00	537.00
1670	427.00	425.00	537.00
1671	428.00	425.00	538.00
1672	428.00	426.00	538.00
1673	429.00	426.00	538.00
1674	429.00	426.00	539.00
1675	429.00	427.00	539.00
1676	430.00	427.00	540.00
1677	430.00	428.00	540.00
1678	431.00	428.00	540.00
1679	431.00	429.00	541.00
1680	432.00	429.00	541.00
1681	432.00	429.00	542.00
1682	432.00	430.00	542.00
1683	433.00	430.00	543.00
1684	433.00	431.00	543.00
1685	434.00	431.00	543.00
1686	434.00	431.00	544.00
1687	434.00	432.00	544.00
1688	435.00	432.00	545.00
1689	435.00	433.00	545.00
1690	436.00	433.00	545.00
1691	436.00	434.00	546.00
1692	436.00	434.00	546.00
1693	437.00	434.00	547.00
1694	437.00	435.00	547.00
1695	438.00	435.00	548.00
1696	438.00	436.00	548.00
1697	439.00	436.00	548.00
1698	439.00	436.00	549.00
1699	439.00	437.00	549.00
1700	440.00	437.00	550.00
1701	440.00	438.00	550.00
1702	441.00	438.00	550.00
1703	441.00	439.00	551.00
1704	441.00	439.00	551.00
1705	442.00	439.00	552.00
1706	442.00	440.00	552.00
1707	443.00	440.00	553.00
1708	443.00	441.00	553.00
1709	444.00	441.00	553.00
1710	444.00	441.00	554.00
1711	444.00	442.00	554.00
1712	445.00	442.00	555.00
1713	445.00	443.00	555.00
1714	446.00	443.00	555.00
1715	446.00	443.00	556.00
1716	446.00	444.00	556.00
1717	447.00	444.00	557.00
1718	447.00	445.00	557.00
1719	448.00	445.00	557.00
1720	448.00	446.00	558.00
1721	449.00	446.00	558.00
1722	449.00	446.00	559.00
1723	449.00	447.00	559.00
1724	450.00	447.00	560.00
1725	450.00	448.00	560.00
1726	451.00	448.00	560.00
1727	451.00	448.00	561.00
1728	451.00	449.00	561.00
1729	452.00	449.00	562.00
1730	452.00	450.00	562.00
1731	453.00	450.00	562.00
1732	453.00	451.00	563.00
1733	454.00	451.00	563.00
1734	454.00	451.00	564.00
1735	454.00	452.00	564.00
1736	455.00	452.00	565.00
1737	455.00	453.00	565.00
1738	456.00	453.00	565.00
1739	456.00	453.00	566.00
1740	456.00	454.00	566.00
1741	457.00	454.00	567.00
1742	457.00	455.00	567.00
1743	458.00	455.00	567.00
1744	458.00	456.00	568.00
1745	458.00	456.00	568.00
1746	459.00	456.00	569.00
1747	459.00	457.00	569.00
1748	460.00	457.00	570.00
1749	460.00	458.00	570.00
1750	461.00	458.00	570.00
1751	461.00	458.00	571.00
1752	461.00	459.00	571.00
1753	462.00	459.00	572.00
1754	462.00	460.00	572.00
1755	463.00	460.00	572.00
1756	463.00	460.00	573.00
1757	463.00	461.00	573.00
1758	464.00	461.00	574.00
1759	464.00	462.00	574.00
1760	465.00	462.00	575.00
1761	465.00	463.00	575.00
1762	466.00	463.00	575.00
1763	466.00	463.00	576.00
1764	466.00	464.00	576.00
1765	467.00	464.00	577.00
1766	467.00	465.00	577.00
1767	468.00	465.00	577.00
1768	468.00	465.00	578.00
1769	468.00	466.00	578.00
1770	469.00	466.00	579.00
1771	469.00	467.00	579.00
1772	470.00	467.00	579.00
1773	470.00	468.00	580.00
1774	471.00	468.00	580.00
1775	471.00	468.00	581.00
1776	471.00	469.00	581.00
1777	472.00	469.00	582.00
1778	472.00	470.00	582.00
1779	473.00	470.00	582.00
1780	473.00	470.00	583.00
1781	473.00	471.00	583.00
1782	474.00	471.00	584.00
1783	474.00	472.00	584.00
1784	475.00	472.00	584.00
1785	475.00	473.00	585.00
1786	476.00	473.00	585.00
1787	476.00	473.00	586.00
1788	476.00	474.00	586.00
1789	477.00	474.00	587.00
1790	477.00	475.00	587.00
1791	478.00	475.00	587.00
1792	478.00	475.00	588.00
1793	478.00	476.00	588.00
1794	479.00	476.00	589.00
1795	479.00	477.00	589.00
1796	480.00	477.00	589.00
1797	480.00	478.00	590.00
1798	480.00	478.00	590.00
1799	481.00	478.00	591.00
1800	481.00	479.00	591.00
1801	482.00	479.00	592.00
1802	482.00	480.00	592.00
1803	483.00	480.00	592.00
1804	483.00	480.00	593.00
1805	483.00	481.00	593.00
1806	484.00	481.00	594.00
1807	484.00	482.00	594.00
1808	485.00	482.00	594.00
1809	485.00	482.00	595.00
1810	485.00	483.00	595.00
1811	486.00	483.00	596.00
1812	486.00	484.00	596.00
1813	487.00	484.00	597.00
1814	487.00	485.00	597.00
1815	488.00	485.00	597.00
1816	488.00	485.00	598.00
1817	488.00	486.00	598.00
1818	489.00	486.00	599.00
1819	489.00	487.00	599.00
1820	490.00	487.00	599.00
1821	490.00	487.00	600.00
1822	490.00	488.00	600.00
1823	491.00	488.00	601.00
1824	491.00	489.00	601.00
1825	492.00	489.00	601.00
1826	492.00	490.00	602.00
1827	493.00	490.00	602.00
1828	493.00	490.00	603.00
1829	493.00	491.00	603.00
1830	494.00	491.00	604.00
1831	494.00	492.00	604.00
1832	495.00	492.00	604.00
1833	495.00	492.00	605.00
1834	495.00	493.00	605.00
1835	496.00	493.00	606.00
1836	496.00	494.00	606.00
1837	497.00	494.00	606.00
1838	497.00	495.00	607.00
1839	497.00	495.00	607.00
1840	498.00	495.00	608.00
1841	498.00	496.00	608.00
1842	499.00	496.00	609.00
1843	499.00	497.00	609.00
1844	500.00	497.00	609.00
1845	500.00	497.00	610.00
1846	500.00	498.00	610.00
1847	501.00	498.00	611.00
1848	501.00	499.00	611.00
1849	502.00	499.00	611.00
1850	502.00	500.00	612.00
1851	502.00	500.00	612.00
1852	503.00	500.00	613.00
1853	503.00	501.00	613.00
1854	504.00	501.00	614.00
1855	504.00	502.00	614.00
1856	505.00	502.00	614.00
1857	505.00	502.00	615.00
1858	505.00	503.00	615.00
1859	506.00	503.00	616.00
1860	506.00	504.00	616.00
1861	507.00	504.00	616.00
1862	507.00	504.00	617.00
1863	507.00	505.00	617.00
1864	508.00	505.00	618.00
1865	508.00	506.00	618.00
1866	509.00	506.00	619.00
1867	509.00	507.00	619.00
1868	510.00	507.00	619.00
1869	510.00	507.00	620.00
1870	510.00	508.00	620.00
1871	511.00	508.00	621.00
1872	511.00	509.00	621.00
1873	512.00	509.00	621.00
1874	512.00	509.00	622.00
1875	512.00	510.00	622.00
1876	513.00	510.00	623.00
1877	513.00	511.00	623.00
1878	514.00	511.00	623.00
1879	514.00	512.00	624.00
1880	515.00	512.00	624.00
1881	515.00	512.00	625.00
1882	515.00	513.00	625.00
1883	516.00	513.00	626.00
1884	516.00	514.00	626.00
1885	517.00	514.00	626.00
1886	517.00	514.00	627.00
1887	517.00	515.00	627.00
1888	518.00	515.00	628.00
1889	518.00	516.00	628.00
1890	519.00	516.00	628.00
1891	519.00	517.00	629.00
1892	519.00	517.00	629.00
1893	520.00	517.00	630.00
1894	520.00	518.00	630.00
1895	521.00	518.00	631.00
1896	521.00	519.00	631.00
1897	522.00	519.00	631.00
1898	522.00	519.00	632.00
1899	522.00	520.00	632.00
1900	523.00	520.00	633.00
1901	523.00	521.00	633.00
1902	524.00	521.00	633.00
1903	524.00	522.00	634.00
1904	524.00	522.00	634.00
1905	525.00	522.00	635.00
1906	525.00	523.00	635.00
1907	526.00	523.00	636.00
1908	526.00	524.00	636.00
1909	527.00	524.00	636.00
1910	527.00	524.00	637.00
1911	527.00	525.00	637.00
1912	528.00	525.00	638.00
1913	528.00	526.00	638.00
1914	529.00	526.00	638.00
1915	529.00	526.00	639.00
1916	529.00	527.00	639.00
1917	530.00	527.00	640.00
1918	530.00	528.00	640.00
1919	531.00	528.00	640.00
1920	531.00	529.00	641.00

Form 3.3 [1005] *continued*

WEEKLY TAX TABLE

Weekly earnings	Amount to be withheld: With tax-free threshold with leave loading	With tax-free threshold no leave loading	No tax-free threshold	Weekly earnings	Amount to be withheld: With tax-free threshold with leave loading	With tax-free threshold no leave loading	No tax-free threshold	Weekly earnings	Amount to be withheld: With tax-free threshold with leave loading	With tax-free threshold no leave loading	No tax-free threshold	Weekly earnings	Amount to be withheld: With tax-free threshold with leave loading	With tax-free threshold no leave loading	No tax-free threshold
1	2	3	4	1	2	3	4	1	2	3	4	1	2	3	4
$	$	$	$	$	$	$	$	$	$	$	$	$	$	$	$
1921	532.00	529.00	641.00	2001	565.00	562.00	675.00	2081	598.00	595.00	708.00	2161	631.00	629.00	741.00
1922	532.00	529.00	642.00	2002	565.00	563.00	675.00	2082	598.00	596.00	708.00	2162	632.00	629.00	741.00
1923	532.00	530.00	642.00	2003	566.00	563.00	675.00	2083	599.00	596.00	709.00	2163	632.00	629.00	742.00
1924	533.00	530.00	643.00	2004	566.00	563.00	676.00	2084	599.00	597.00	709.00	2164	632.00	630.00	742.00
1925	533.00	531.00	643.00	2005	566.00	564.00	676.00	2085	600.00	597.00	709.00	2165	633.00	630.00	743.00
1926	534.00	531.00	643.00	2006	567.00	564.00	677.00	2086	600.00	597.00	710.00	2166	633.00	631.00	743.00
1927	534.00	531.00	644.00	2007	567.00	565.00	677.00	2087	600.00	598.00	710.00	2167	634.00	631.00	743.00
1928	534.00	532.00	644.00	2008	568.00	565.00	677.00	2088	601.00	598.00	711.00	2168	634.00	631.00	744.00
1929	535.00	532.00	645.00	2009	568.00	565.00	678.00	2089	601.00	599.00	711.00	2169	634.00	632.00	744.00
1930	535.00	533.00	645.00	2010	568.00	566.00	678.00	2090	602.00	599.00	711.00	2170	635.00	632.00	745.00
1931	536.00	533.00	645.00	2011	569.00	566.00	679.00	2091	602.00	600.00	712.00	2171	635.00	633.00	745.00
1932	536.00	534.00	646.00	2012	569.00	567.00	679.00	2092	602.00	600.00	712.00	2172	636.00	633.00	745.00
1933	537.00	534.00	646.00	2013	570.00	567.00	680.00	2093	603.00	600.00	713.00	2173	636.00	634.00	746.00
1934	537.00	534.00	647.00	2014	570.00	568.00	680.00	2094	603.00	601.00	713.00	2174	637.00	634.00	746.00
1935	537.00	535.00	647.00	2015	571.00	568.00	680.00	2095	604.00	601.00	714.00	2175	637.00	634.00	747.00
1936	538.00	535.00	648.00	2016	571.00	568.00	681.00	2096	604.00	602.00	714.00	2176	637.00	635.00	747.00
1937	538.00	536.00	648.00	2017	571.00	569.00	681.00	2097	605.00	602.00	714.00	2177	638.00	635.00	748.00
1938	539.00	536.00	648.00	2018	572.00	569.00	682.00	2098	605.00	602.00	715.00	2178	638.00	636.00	748.00
1939	539.00	536.00	649.00	2019	572.00	570.00	682.00	2099	605.00	603.00	715.00	2179	639.00	636.00	748.00
1940	539.00	537.00	649.00	2020	573.00	570.00	682.00	2100	606.00	603.00	716.00	2180	639.00	636.00	749.00
1941	540.00	537.00	650.00	2021	573.00	570.00	683.00	2101	606.00	604.00	716.00	2181	639.00	637.00	749.00
1942	540.00	538.00	650.00	2022	573.00	571.00	683.00	2102	607.00	604.00	716.00	2182	640.00	637.00	750.00
1943	541.00	538.00	650.00	2023	574.00	571.00	684.00	2103	607.00	605.00	717.00	2183	640.00	638.00	750.00
1944	541.00	539.00	651.00	2024	574.00	572.00	684.00	2104	607.00	605.00	717.00	2184	641.00	638.00	750.00
1945	541.00	539.00	651.00	2025	575.00	572.00	684.00	2105	608.00	605.00	718.00	2185	641.00	639.00	751.00
1946	542.00	539.00	652.00	2026	575.00	573.00	685.00	2106	608.00	606.00	718.00	2186	642.00	639.00	751.00
1947	542.00	540.00	652.00	2027	576.00	573.00	685.00	2107	609.00	606.00	719.00	2187	642.00	639.00	752.00
1948	543.00	540.00	653.00	2028	576.00	573.00	686.00	2108	609.00	607.00	719.00	2188	642.00	640.00	752.00
1949	543.00	541.00	653.00	2029	576.00	574.00	686.00	2109	610.00	607.00	719.00	2189	643.00	640.00	753.00
1950	544.00	541.00	653.00	2030	577.00	574.00	687.00	2110	610.00	607.00	720.00	2190	643.00	641.00	753.00
1951	544.00	541.00	654.00	2031	577.00	575.00	687.00	2111	610.00	608.00	720.00	2191	644.00	641.00	753.00
1952	544.00	542.00	654.00	2032	578.00	575.00	687.00	2112	611.00	608.00	721.00	2192	644.00	641.00	754.00
1953	545.00	542.00	655.00	2033	578.00	575.00	688.00	2113	611.00	609.00	721.00	2193	644.00	642.00	754.00
1954	545.00	543.00	655.00	2034	578.00	576.00	688.00	2114	612.00	609.00	721.00	2194	645.00	642.00	755.00
1955	546.00	543.00	655.00	2035	579.00	576.00	689.00	2115	612.00	609.00	722.00	2195	645.00	643.00	755.00
1956	546.00	543.00	656.00	2036	579.00	577.00	689.00	2116	612.00	610.00	722.00	2196	646.00	643.00	755.00
1957	546.00	544.00	656.00	2037	580.00	577.00	689.00	2117	613.00	610.00	723.00	2197	646.00	644.00	756.00
1958	547.00	544.00	657.00	2038	580.00	578.00	690.00	2118	613.00	611.00	723.00	2198	646.00	644.00	756.00
1959	547.00	545.00	657.00	2039	580.00	578.00	690.00	2119	614.00	611.00	723.00	2199	647.00	644.00	757.00
1960	548.00	545.00	658.00	2040	581.00	578.00	691.00	2120	614.00	612.00	724.00	2200	647.00	645.00	757.00
1961	548.00	546.00	658.00	2041	581.00	579.00	691.00	2121	615.00	612.00	724.00	2201	648.00	645.00	758.00
1962	549.00	546.00	658.00	2042	582.00	579.00	692.00	2122	615.00	612.00	725.00	2202	648.00	646.00	758.00
1963	549.00	546.00	659.00	2043	582.00	580.00	692.00	2123	615.00	613.00	725.00	2203	649.00	646.00	758.00
1964	549.00	547.00	659.00	2044	583.00	580.00	692.00	2124	616.00	613.00	726.00	2204	649.00	646.00	759.00
1965	550.00	547.00	660.00	2045	583.00	580.00	693.00	2125	616.00	614.00	726.00	2205	649.00	647.00	759.00
1966	550.00	548.00	660.00	2046	583.00	581.00	693.00	2126	617.00	614.00	726.00	2206	650.00	647.00	760.00
1967	551.00	548.00	660.00	2047	584.00	581.00	694.00	2127	617.00	614.00	727.00	2207	650.00	648.00	760.00
1968	551.00	548.00	661.00	2048	584.00	582.00	694.00	2128	617.00	615.00	727.00	2208	651.00	648.00	760.00
1969	551.00	549.00	661.00	2049	585.00	582.00	694.00	2129	618.00	615.00	728.00	2209	651.00	648.00	761.00
1970	552.00	549.00	662.00	2050	585.00	583.00	695.00	2130	618.00	616.00	728.00	2210	651.00	649.00	761.00
1971	552.00	550.00	662.00	2051	585.00	583.00	695.00	2131	619.00	616.00	728.00	2211	652.00	649.00	762.00
1972	553.00	550.00	662.00	2052	586.00	583.00	696.00	2132	619.00	617.00	729.00	2212	652.00	650.00	762.00
1973	553.00	551.00	663.00	2053	586.00	584.00	696.00	2133	620.00	617.00	729.00	2213	653.00	650.00	763.00
1974	554.00	551.00	663.00	2054	587.00	584.00	697.00	2134	620.00	617.00	730.00	2214	653.00	651.00	763.00
1975	554.00	551.00	664.00	2055	587.00	585.00	697.00	2135	620.00	618.00	730.00	2215	654.00	651.00	763.00
1976	554.00	552.00	664.00	2056	588.00	585.00	697.00	2136	621.00	618.00	731.00	2216	654.00	651.00	764.00
1977	555.00	552.00	665.00	2057	588.00	585.00	698.00	2137	621.00	619.00	731.00	2217	654.00	652.00	764.00
1978	555.00	553.00	665.00	2058	588.00	586.00	698.00	2138	622.00	619.00	731.00	2218	655.00	652.00	765.00
1979	556.00	553.00	665.00	2059	589.00	586.00	699.00	2139	622.00	619.00	732.00	2219	655.00	653.00	765.00
1980	556.00	553.00	666.00	2060	589.00	587.00	699.00	2140	622.00	620.00	732.00	2220	656.00	653.00	765.00
1981	556.00	554.00	666.00	2061	590.00	587.00	699.00	2141	623.00	620.00	733.00	2221	656.00	653.00	766.00
1982	557.00	554.00	667.00	2062	590.00	587.00	700.00	2142	623.00	621.00	733.00	2222	656.00	654.00	766.00
1983	557.00	555.00	667.00	2063	590.00	588.00	700.00	2143	624.00	621.00	733.00	2223	657.00	654.00	767.00
1984	558.00	555.00	667.00	2064	591.00	588.00	701.00	2144	624.00	622.00	734.00	2224	657.00	655.00	767.00
1985	558.00	556.00	668.00	2065	591.00	589.00	701.00	2145	624.00	622.00	734.00	2225	658.00	655.00	767.00
1986	559.00	556.00	668.00	2066	592.00	589.00	702.00	2146	625.00	622.00	735.00	2226	658.00	656.00	768.00
1987	559.00	556.00	669.00	2067	592.00	590.00	702.00	2147	625.00	623.00	735.00	2227	659.00	656.00	768.00
1988	559.00	557.00	669.00	2068	593.00	590.00	702.00	2148	626.00	623.00	736.00	2228	659.00	656.00	769.00
1989	560.00	557.00	670.00	2069	593.00	590.00	703.00	2149	626.00	624.00	736.00	2229	659.00	657.00	769.00
1990	560.00	558.00	670.00	2070	593.00	591.00	703.00	2150	627.00	624.00	736.00	2230	660.00	657.00	770.00
1991	561.00	558.00	670.00	2071	594.00	591.00	704.00	2151	627.00	624.00	737.00	2231	660.00	658.00	770.00
1992	561.00	558.00	671.00	2072	594.00	592.00	704.00	2152	627.00	625.00	737.00	2232	661.00	658.00	770.00
1993	561.00	559.00	671.00	2073	595.00	592.00	704.00	2153	628.00	625.00	738.00	2233	661.00	658.00	771.00
1994	562.00	559.00	672.00	2074	595.00	592.00	705.00	2154	628.00	626.00	738.00	2234	661.00	659.00	771.00
1995	562.00	560.00	672.00	2075	595.00	593.00	705.00	2155	629.00	626.00	738.00	2235	662.00	659.00	772.00
1996	563.00	560.00	672.00	2076	596.00	593.00	706.00	2156	629.00	626.00	739.00	2236	662.00	660.00	772.00
1997	563.00	561.00	673.00	2077	596.00	594.00	706.00	2157	629.00	627.00	739.00	2237	663.00	660.00	772.00
1998	563.00	561.00	673.00	2078	597.00	594.00	706.00	2158	630.00	627.00	740.00	2238	663.00	661.00	773.00
1999	564.00	561.00	674.00	2079	597.00	595.00	707.00	2159	630.00	628.00	740.00	2239	663.00	661.00	773.00
2000	564.00	562.00	674.00	2080	598.00	595.00	707.00	2160	631.00	628.00	741.00	2240	664.00	661.00	774.00

SCHEDULE 2 WEEKLY TAX TABLE 11

Form 3.3 [1005] *continued*

WEEKLY TAX TABLE

Weekly earnings	Amount to be withheld		
	With tax-free threshold with leave loading	With tax-free threshold no leave loading	No tax-free threshold
1 $	2 $	3 $	4 $
2241	664.00	662.00	774.00
2242	665.00	662.00	775.00
2243	665.00	663.00	775.00
2244	666.00	663.00	775.00
2245	666.00	663.00	776.00
2246	666.00	664.00	776.00
2247	667.00	664.00	777.00
2248	667.00	665.00	777.00
2249	668.00	665.00	777.00
2250	668.00	666.00	778.00
2251	668.00	666.00	778.00
2252	669.00	666.00	779.00
2253	669.00	667.00	779.00
2254	670.00	667.00	780.00
2255	670.00	668.00	780.00
2256	671.00	668.00	780.00
2257	671.00	668.00	781.00
2258	671.00	669.00	781.00
2259	672.00	669.00	782.00
2260	672.00	670.00	782.00
2261	673.00	670.00	782.00
2262	673.00	670.00	783.00
2263	673.00	671.00	783.00
2264	674.00	671.00	784.00
2265	674.00	672.00	784.00
2266	675.00	672.00	785.00
2267	675.00	673.00	785.00
2268	676.00	673.00	785.00
2269	676.00	673.00	786.00
2270	676.00	674.00	786.00
2271	677.00	674.00	787.00
2272	677.00	675.00	787.00
2273	678.00	675.00	787.00
2274	678.00	675.00	788.00
2275	678.00	676.00	788.00
2276	679.00	676.00	789.00
2277	679.00	677.00	789.00
2278	680.00	677.00	789.00
2279	680.00	678.00	790.00
2280	681.00	678.00	790.00
2281	681.00	678.00	791.00
2282	681.00	679.00	791.00
2283	682.00	679.00	792.00
2284	682.00	680.00	792.00
2285	683.00	680.00	792.00
2286	683.00	680.00	793.00
2287	683.00	681.00	793.00
2288	684.00	681.00	794.00
2289	684.00	682.00	794.00
2290	685.00	682.00	794.00
2291	685.00	683.00	795.00
2292	685.00	683.00	795.00
2293	686.00	683.00	796.00
2294	686.00	684.00	796.00
2295	687.00	684.00	797.00
2296	687.00	685.00	797.00
2297	688.00	685.00	797.00
2298	688.00	685.00	798.00
2299	688.00	686.00	798.00
2300	689.00	686.00	799.00
2301	689.00	687.00	799.00
2302	690.00	687.00	799.00
2303	690.00	688.00	800.00
2304	690.00	688.00	800.00
2305	691.00	688.00	801.00
2306	691.00	689.00	801.00
2307	692.00	689.00	802.00
2308	692.00	690.00	802.00
2309	693.00	690.00	802.00
2310	693.00	690.00	803.00
2311	693.00	691.00	803.00
2312	694.00	691.00	804.00
2313	694.00	692.00	804.00
2314	695.00	692.00	804.00
2315	695.00	692.00	805.00
2316	695.00	693.00	805.00
2317	696.00	693.00	806.00
2318	696.00	694.00	806.00
2319	697.00	694.00	806.00
2320	697.00	695.00	807.00
2321	698.00	695.00	807.00
2322	698.00	695.00	808.00
2323	698.00	696.00	808.00
2324	699.00	696.00	809.00
2325	699.00	697.00	809.00
2326	700.00	697.00	809.00
2327	700.00	697.00	810.00
2328	700.00	698.00	810.00
2329	701.00	698.00	811.00
2330	701.00	699.00	811.00
2331	702.00	699.00	811.00
2332	702.00	700.00	812.00
2333	703.00	700.00	812.00
2334	703.00	700.00	813.00
2335	703.00	701.00	813.00
2336	704.00	701.00	814.00
2337	704.00	702.00	814.00
2338	705.00	702.00	814.00
2339	705.00	702.00	815.00
2340	705.00	703.00	815.00
2341	706.00	703.00	816.00
2342	706.00	704.00	816.00
2343	707.00	704.00	816.00
2344	707.00	705.00	817.00
2345	707.00	705.00	817.00
2346	708.00	705.00	818.00
2347	708.00	706.00	818.00
2348	709.00	706.00	819.00
2349	709.00	707.00	819.00
2350	710.00	707.00	819.00
2351	710.00	707.00	820.00
2352	710.00	708.00	820.00
2353	711.00	708.00	821.00
2354	711.00	709.00	821.00
2355	712.00	709.00	821.00
2356	712.00	709.00	822.00
2357	712.00	710.00	822.00
2358	713.00	710.00	823.00
2359	713.00	711.00	823.00
2360	714.00	711.00	824.00
2361	714.00	712.00	824.00
2362	715.00	712.00	824.00
2363	715.00	712.00	825.00
2364	715.00	713.00	825.00
2365	716.00	713.00	826.00
2366	716.00	714.00	826.00
2367	717.00	714.00	826.00
2368	717.00	714.00	827.00
2369	717.00	715.00	827.00
2370	718.00	715.00	828.00
2371	718.00	716.00	828.00
2372	719.00	716.00	828.00
2373	719.00	717.00	829.00
2374	720.00	717.00	829.00
2375	720.00	717.00	830.00
2376	720.00	718.00	830.00
2377	721.00	718.00	831.00
2378	721.00	719.00	831.00
2379	722.00	719.00	831.00
2380	722.00	719.00	832.00
2381	722.00	720.00	832.00
2382	723.00	720.00	833.00
2383	723.00	721.00	833.00
2384	724.00	721.00	833.00
2385	724.00	722.00	834.00
2386	725.00	722.00	834.00
2387	725.00	722.00	835.00
2388	725.00	723.00	835.00
2389	726.00	723.00	836.00
2390	726.00	724.00	836.00
2391	727.00	724.00	836.00
2392	727.00	724.00	837.00
2393	727.00	725.00	837.00
2394	728.00	725.00	838.00
2395	728.00	726.00	838.00
2396	729.00	726.00	838.00
2397	729.00	727.00	839.00
2398	729.00	727.00	839.00
2399	730.00	727.00	840.00
2400	730.00	728.00	840.00
2401	731.00	728.00	841.00
2402	731.00	729.00	841.00
2403	732.00	729.00	841.00
2404	732.00	729.00	842.00
2405	732.00	730.00	842.00
2406	733.00	730.00	843.00
2407	733.00	731.00	843.00
2408	734.00	731.00	843.00
2409	734.00	731.00	844.00
2410	734.00	732.00	844.00
2411	735.00	732.00	845.00
2412	735.00	733.00	845.00
2413	736.00	733.00	846.00
2414	736.00	734.00	846.00
2415	737.00	734.00	846.00
2416	737.00	734.00	847.00
2417	737.00	735.00	847.00
2418	738.00	735.00	848.00
2419	738.00	736.00	848.00
2420	739.00	736.00	848.00
2421	739.00	736.00	849.00
2422	739.00	737.00	849.00
2423	740.00	737.00	850.00
2424	740.00	738.00	850.00
2425	741.00	738.00	850.00
2426	741.00	739.00	851.00
2427	742.00	739.00	851.00
2428	742.00	739.00	852.00
2429	742.00	740.00	852.00
2430	743.00	740.00	853.00
2431	743.00	741.00	853.00
2432	744.00	741.00	853.00
2433	744.00	741.00	854.00
2434	744.00	742.00	854.00
2435	745.00	742.00	855.00
2436	745.00	743.00	855.00
2437	746.00	743.00	855.00
2438	746.00	744.00	856.00
2439	746.00	744.00	856.00
2440	747.00	744.00	857.00
2441	747.00	745.00	857.00
2442	748.00	745.00	858.00
2443	748.00	746.00	858.00
2444	749.00	746.00	858.00
2445	749.00	746.00	859.00
2446	749.00	747.00	859.00
2447	750.00	747.00	860.00
2448	750.00	748.00	860.00
2449	751.00	748.00	860.00
2450	751.00	749.00	861.00
2451	751.00	749.00	861.00
2452	752.00	749.00	862.00
2453	752.00	750.00	862.00
2454	753.00	750.00	863.00
2455	753.00	751.00	863.00
2456	754.00	751.00	863.00
2457	754.00	751.00	864.00
2458	754.00	752.00	864.00
2459	755.00	752.00	865.00
2460	755.00	753.00	865.00
2461	756.00	753.00	865.00
2462	756.00	753.00	866.00
2463	756.00	754.00	866.00
2464	757.00	754.00	867.00
2465	757.00	755.00	867.00
2466	758.00	755.00	868.00
2467	758.00	756.00	868.00
2468	759.00	756.00	868.00
2469	759.00	756.00	869.00
2470	759.00	757.00	869.00
2471	760.00	757.00	870.00
2472	760.00	758.00	870.00
2473	761.00	758.00	870.00
2474	761.00	758.00	871.00
2475	761.00	759.00	871.00
2476	762.00	759.00	872.00
2477	762.00	760.00	872.00
2478	763.00	760.00	872.00
2479	763.00	761.00	873.00
2480	764.00	761.00	873.00
2481	764.00	761.00	874.00
2482	764.00	762.00	874.00
2483	765.00	762.00	875.00
2484	765.00	763.00	875.00
2485	766.00	763.00	875.00
2486	766.00	763.00	876.00
2487	766.00	764.00	876.00
2488	767.00	764.00	877.00
2489	767.00	765.00	877.00
2490	768.00	765.00	877.00
2491	768.00	766.00	878.00
2492	768.00	766.00	878.00
2493	769.00	766.00	879.00
2494	769.00	767.00	879.00
2495	770.00	767.00	880.00
2496	770.00	768.00	880.00
2497	771.00	768.00	880.00
2498	771.00	768.00	881.00
2499	771.00	769.00	881.00
2500	772.00	769.00	882.00

Where the tax-free threshold is claimed with leave loading and the payee earns:
- more than $2,500 but less than $3,455, withhold $772 plus 41.50 cents for each $1 of earnings in excess of $2,500
- more than $3,454, withhold $1,168 plus 46.50 cents for each $1 of earnings in excess of $3,454.

Where the tax-free threshold is claimed with no leave loading and the payee earns:
- more than $2,500 but less than $3,461, withhold $769 plus 41.50 cents for each $1 of earnings in excess of $2,500
- more than $3,460, withhold $1,168 plus 46.50 cents for each $1 of earnings in excess of $3,460.

Where the tax-free threshold is **not** claimed and the payee earns:
- more than $2,500 but less than $3,144, withhold $882, plus 41.50 cents for each $1 of earnings in excess of $2,500
- more than $3,143, withhold $1,149 plus 46.50 cents for each $1 of earnings in excess of $3,143.

For all withholding amounts calculated, round the result to the nearest dollar.

PUBLISHED BY

Australian Taxation Office, Canberra, May 2008

OUR COMMITMENT TO YOU

We are committed to providing you with advice and information you can rely on.

If you feel this publication does not fully cover your circumstances, seek help from the Tax Office or a professional adviser.

The information in this publication was current in May 2008. We regularly revise our publications to take account of any changes to the law, so make sure that you have the latest information. If you are unsure, you can check for a more recent version on our website at **www.ato.gov.au** or contact us.

JS 10914

Form 3.4 [1006] Fortnightly tax

FORTNIGHTLY TAX TABLE

Fortnightly earnings	Amount to be withheld		
	With tax-free threshold with leave loading	With tax-free threshold no leave loading	No tax-free threshold
1	2	3	4
$	$	$	$
2	—	—	—
4	—	—	—
6	—	—	—
8	—	—	2.00
10	—	—	2.00
12	—	—	2.00
14	—	—	2.00
16	—	—	2.00
18	—	—	2.00
20	—	—	4.00
22	—	—	4.00
24	—	—	4.00
26	—	—	4.00
28	—	—	4.00
30	—	—	4.00
32	—	—	6.00
34	—	—	6.00
36	—	—	6.00
38	—	—	6.00
40	—	—	6.00
42	—	—	6.00
44	—	—	8.00
46	—	—	8.00
48	—	—	8.00
50	—	—	8.00
52	—	—	8.00
54	—	—	8.00
56	—	—	10.00
58	—	—	10.00
60	—	—	10.00
62	—	—	10.00
64	—	—	10.00
66	—	—	10.00
68	—	—	12.00
70	—	—	12.00
72	—	—	12.00
74	—	—	12.00
76	—	—	12.00
78	—	—	12.00
80	—	—	14.00
82	—	—	14.00
84	—	—	14.00
86	—	—	14.00
88	—	—	14.00
90	—	—	14.00
92	—	—	16.00
94	—	—	16.00
96	—	—	16.00
98	—	—	16.00
100	—	—	16.00
102	—	—	16.00
104	—	—	18.00
106	—	—	18.00
108	—	—	18.00
110	—	—	18.00
112	—	—	18.00
114	—	—	18.00
116	—	—	20.00
118	—	—	20.00
120	—	—	20.00
122	—	—	20.00
124	—	—	20.00
126	—	—	20.00
128	—	—	22.00
130	—	—	22.00
132	—	—	22.00
134	—	—	22.00
136	—	—	22.00
138	—	—	22.00
140	—	—	24.00
142	—	—	24.00
144	—	—	24.00
146	—	—	24.00
148	—	—	24.00
150	—	—	24.00
152	—	—	26.00
154	—	—	26.00
156	—	—	26.00
158	—	—	26.00
160	—	—	26.00
162	—	—	26.00
164	—	—	28.00
166	—	—	28.00
168	—	—	28.00
170	—	—	28.00
172	—	—	28.00
174	—	—	28.00
176	—	—	30.00
178	—	—	30.00
180	—	—	30.00
182	—	—	30.00
184	—	—	30.00
186	—	—	30.00
188	—	—	32.00
190	—	—	32.00
192	—	—	32.00
194	—	—	32.00
196	—	—	32.00
198	—	—	32.00
200	—	—	32.00
202	—	—	34.00
204	—	—	34.00
206	—	—	34.00
208	—	—	34.00
210	—	—	34.00
212	—	—	34.00
214	—	—	36.00
216	—	—	36.00
218	—	—	36.00
220	—	—	36.00
222	—	—	36.00
224	—	—	36.00
226	—	—	38.00
228	—	—	38.00
230	—	—	38.00
232	—	—	38.00
234	—	—	38.00
236	—	—	38.00
238	—	—	40.00
240	—	—	40.00
242	—	—	40.00
244	—	—	40.00
246	—	—	40.00
248	—	—	40.00
250	—	—	42.00
252	—	—	42.00
254	—	—	42.00
256	—	—	42.00
258	—	—	42.00
260	—	—	42.00
262	—	—	44.00
264	—	—	44.00
266	—	—	44.00
268	—	—	44.00
270	—	—	44.00
272	—	—	44.00
274	—	—	46.00
276	—	—	46.00
278	—	—	46.00
280	—	—	46.00
282	—	—	46.00
284	—	—	46.00
286	—	—	48.00
288	—	—	48.00
290	—	—	48.00
292	—	—	48.00
294	—	—	48.00
296	—	—	48.00
298	—	—	50.00
300	—	—	50.00
302	—	—	50.00
304	—	—	50.00
306	—	—	50.00
308	—	—	50.00
310	—	—	52.00
312	—	—	52.00
314	—	—	52.00
316	—	—	52.00
318	—	—	52.00
320	—	—	52.00
322	—	—	54.00
324	—	—	54.00
326	—	—	54.00
328	—	—	54.00
330	—	—	54.00
332	—	—	54.00
334	—	—	56.00
336	—	—	56.00
338	—	—	56.00
340	—	—	56.00
342	—	—	56.00
344	—	—	56.00
346	—	—	58.00
348	—	—	58.00
350	—	—	58.00
352	—	—	58.00
354	—	—	58.00
356	—	—	58.00
358	—	—	60.00
360	—	—	60.00
362	—	—	60.00
364	—	—	60.00
366	—	—	60.00
368	—	—	60.00
370	—	—	62.00
372	—	—	62.00
374	—	—	62.00
376	—	—	62.00
378	—	—	62.00
380	2.00	—	62.00
382	2.00	2.00	64.00
384	2.00	2.00	64.00
386	2.00	2.00	64.00
388	2.00	2.00	64.00
390	2.00	2.00	64.00
392	4.00	2.00	64.00
394	4.00	2.00	66.00
396	4.00	4.00	66.00
398	4.00	4.00	66.00
400	4.00	4.00	66.00
402	4.00	4.00	66.00
404	4.00	4.00	66.00
406	6.00	4.00	66.00
408	6.00	4.00	68.00
410	6.00	6.00	68.00
412	6.00	6.00	68.00
414	6.00	6.00	68.00
416	6.00	6.00	68.00
418	8.00	6.00	68.00
420	8.00	6.00	70.00
422	8.00	8.00	70.00
424	8.00	8.00	70.00
426	8.00	8.00	70.00
428	8.00	8.00	70.00
430	8.00	8.00	70.00
432	10.00	8.00	72.00
434	10.00	8.00	72.00
436	10.00	10.00	72.00
438	10.00	10.00	72.00
440	10.00	10.00	72.00
442	10.00	10.00	72.00
444	10.00	10.00	74.00
446	12.00	10.00	74.00
448	12.00	10.00	74.00
450	12.00	12.00	74.00
452	12.00	12.00	74.00
454	12.00	12.00	74.00
456	12.00	12.00	76.00
458	14.00	12.00	76.00
460	14.00	12.00	76.00
462	14.00	14.00	76.00
464	14.00	14.00	76.00
466	14.00	14.00	76.00
468	14.00	14.00	78.00
470	14.00	14.00	78.00
472	16.00	14.00	78.00
474	16.00	14.00	78.00
476	16.00	16.00	78.00
478	16.00	16.00	78.00
480	16.00	16.00	80.00
482	16.00	16.00	80.00
484	18.00	16.00	80.00
486	18.00	16.00	80.00
488	18.00	16.00	80.00
490	18.00	18.00	80.00
492	18.00	18.00	82.00
494	18.00	18.00	82.00
496	18.00	18.00	82.00
498	20.00	18.00	82.00
500	20.00	18.00	82.00
502	20.00	20.00	82.00
504	20.00	20.00	84.00
506	20.00	20.00	84.00
508	20.00	20.00	84.00
510	20.00	20.00	84.00
512	22.00	20.00	84.00
514	22.00	20.00	84.00
516	22.00	22.00	86.00
518	22.00	22.00	96.00
520	22.00	22.00	96.00
522	22.00	22.00	96.00
524	24.00	22.00	96.00
526	24.00	22.00	96.00
528	24.00	22.00	98.00
530	24.00	24.00	98.00
532	24.00	24.00	98.00
534	24.00	24.00	98.00
536	24.00	24.00	98.00
538	26.00	24.00	100.00
540	26.00	24.00	100.00
542	26.00	26.00	100.00
544	26.00	26.00	100.00
546	26.00	26.00	100.00
548	26.00	26.00	100.00
550	28.00	26.00	102.00
552	28.00	26.00	102.00
554	28.00	26.00	102.00
556	28.00	28.00	102.00
558	28.00	28.00	102.00
560	28.00	28.00	104.00
562	28.00	28.00	104.00
564	30.00	28.00	104.00
566	30.00	28.00	104.00
568	30.00	28.00	104.00
570	30.00	30.00	104.00
572	30.00	30.00	106.00
574	30.00	30.00	106.00
576	30.00	30.00	106.00
578	32.00	30.00	106.00
580	32.00	30.00	106.00
582	32.00	32.00	108.00
584	32.00	32.00	108.00
586	32.00	32.00	108.00
588	32.00	32.00	108.00
590	34.00	32.00	108.00
592	34.00	32.00	110.00
594	34.00	32.00	110.00
596	34.00	34.00	110.00
598	34.00	34.00	110.00
600	34.00	34.00	110.00
602	34.00	34.00	110.00
604	36.00	34.00	112.00
606	36.00	34.00	112.00
608	36.00	34.00	112.00
610	36.00	36.00	112.00
612	36.00	36.00	112.00
614	36.00	36.00	114.00
616	38.00	36.00	114.00
618	38.00	36.00	114.00
620	38.00	36.00	114.00
622	38.00	38.00	114.00
624	38.00	38.00	114.00
626	38.00	38.00	116.00
628	38.00	38.00	116.00
630	40.00	38.00	116.00
632	40.00	38.00	116.00
634	40.00	38.00	116.00
636	40.00	40.00	118.00
638	40.00	40.00	118.00
640	40.00	40.00	118.00

Form 3.4 [1006] *continued*

FORTNIGHTLY TAX TABLE

	Amount to be withheld		
Fortnightly earnings 1 $	With tax-free threshold with leave loading 2 $	With tax-free threshold no leave loading 3 $	No tax-free threshold 4 $
642	40.00	40.00	118.00
644	42.00	40.00	118.00
646	42.00	40.00	120.00
648	42.00	40.00	120.00
650	42.00	42.00	120.00
652	42.00	42.00	120.00
654	42.00	42.00	120.00
656	44.00	42.00	120.00
658	44.00	42.00	122.00
660	44.00	42.00	122.00
662	44.00	44.00	122.00
664	44.00	44.00	122.00
666	46.00	44.00	122.00
668	46.00	44.00	124.00
670	46.00	44.00	124.00
672	48.00	46.00	124.00
674	48.00	46.00	124.00
676	48.00	46.00	126.00
678	48.00	46.00	126.00
680	50.00	48.00	126.00
682	50.00	48.00	128.00
684	50.00	48.00	128.00
686	50.00	48.00	128.00
688	52.00	50.00	130.00
690	52.00	50.00	130.00
692	52.00	50.00	130.00
694	52.00	50.00	132.00
696	54.00	52.00	132.00
698	54.00	52.00	132.00
700	54.00	52.00	134.00
702	54.00	52.00	134.00
704	56.00	54.00	134.00
706	56.00	54.00	136.00
708	56.00	54.00	136.00
710	56.00	54.00	136.00
712	58.00	56.00	138.00
714	58.00	56.00	138.00
716	58.00	56.00	138.00
718	58.00	56.00	140.00
720	60.00	58.00	140.00
722	60.00	58.00	140.00
724	60.00	58.00	142.00
726	60.00	58.00	142.00
728	62.00	60.00	142.00
730	62.00	60.00	144.00
732	62.00	60.00	144.00
734	62.00	60.00	144.00
736	64.00	62.00	146.00
738	64.00	62.00	146.00
740	64.00	62.00	146.00
742	64.00	62.00	148.00
744	66.00	64.00	148.00
746	66.00	64.00	148.00
748	66.00	64.00	150.00
750	66.00	64.00	150.00
752	68.00	66.00	150.00
754	68.00	66.00	152.00
756	68.00	66.00	152.00
758	68.00	66.00	152.00
760	70.00	68.00	154.00
762	70.00	68.00	154.00
764	70.00	68.00	154.00
766	70.00	68.00	156.00
768	72.00	70.00	156.00
770	72.00	70.00	156.00
772	72.00	70.00	158.00
774	72.00	70.00	158.00
776	74.00	72.00	158.00
778	74.00	72.00	160.00
780	74.00	72.00	160.00
782	74.00	72.00	160.00
784	74.00	74.00	162.00
786	74.00	74.00	162.00
788	76.00	74.00	162.00
790	76.00	74.00	164.00
792	76.00	74.00	164.00
794	76.00	74.00	164.00
796	76.00	76.00	166.00
798	76.00	76.00	166.00
800	78.00	76.00	166.00

	Amount to be withheld		
Fortnightly earnings 1 $	With tax-free threshold with leave loading 2 $	With tax-free threshold no leave loading 3 $	No tax-free threshold 4 $
802	78.00	76.00	168.00
804	78.00	76.00	168.00
806	78.00	76.00	168.00
808	78.00	78.00	170.00
810	78.00	78.00	170.00
812	80.00	78.00	170.00
814	80.00	78.00	172.00
816	80.00	78.00	172.00
818	80.00	78.00	172.00
820	80.00	80.00	174.00
822	80.00	80.00	174.00
824	82.00	80.00	174.00
826	82.00	80.00	176.00
828	82.00	80.00	176.00
830	82.00	80.00	176.00
832	82.00	82.00	178.00
834	82.00	82.00	178.00
836	84.00	82.00	178.00
838	84.00	82.00	180.00
840	84.00	82.00	180.00
842	84.00	82.00	180.00
844	84.00	84.00	182.00
846	84.00	84.00	182.00
848	86.00	84.00	182.00
850	86.00	84.00	184.00
852	86.00	84.00	184.00
854	86.00	84.00	184.00
856	86.00	86.00	186.00
858	86.00	86.00	186.00
860	88.00	86.00	186.00
862	88.00	86.00	188.00
864	88.00	86.00	188.00
866	88.00	86.00	188.00
868	88.00	88.00	190.00
870	88.00	88.00	190.00
872	90.00	88.00	190.00
874	90.00	88.00	192.00
876	90.00	88.00	192.00
878	90.00	88.00	192.00
880	90.00	88.00	194.00
882	90.00	90.00	194.00
884	92.00	90.00	194.00
886	92.00	90.00	196.00
888	92.00	90.00	196.00
890	92.00	90.00	196.00
892	92.00	90.00	198.00
894	92.00	92.00	198.00
896	94.00	92.00	198.00
898	94.00	92.00	200.00
900	94.00	92.00	200.00
902	94.00	92.00	202.00
904	94.00	92.00	202.00
906	94.00	94.00	202.00
908	96.00	94.00	204.00
910	96.00	94.00	204.00
912	96.00	94.00	204.00
914	96.00	94.00	206.00
916	96.00	94.00	206.00
918	96.00	96.00	206.00
920	98.00	96.00	208.00
922	98.00	96.00	208.00
924	98.00	96.00	208.00
926	98.00	96.00	210.00
928	98.00	96.00	210.00
930	98.00	98.00	210.00
932	100.00	98.00	212.00
934	100.00	98.00	212.00
936	100.00	98.00	212.00
938	100.00	98.00	214.00
940	100.00	98.00	214.00
942	100.00	100.00	214.00
944	102.00	100.00	216.00
946	102.00	100.00	216.00
948	102.00	100.00	216.00
950	102.00	100.00	218.00
952	102.00	100.00	218.00
954	102.00	102.00	218.00
956	104.00	102.00	220.00
958	104.00	102.00	220.00
960	104.00	102.00	220.00

	Amount to be withheld		
Fortnightly earnings 1 $	With tax-free threshold with leave loading 2 $	With tax-free threshold no leave loading 3 $	No tax-free threshold 4 $
962	104.00	102.00	222.00
964	104.00	102.00	222.00
966	104.00	104.00	222.00
968	106.00	104.00	224.00
970	106.00	104.00	224.00
972	106.00	104.00	224.00
974	106.00	104.00	226.00
976	106.00	104.00	226.00
978	106.00	106.00	226.00
980	108.00	106.00	228.00
982	108.00	106.00	228.00
984	108.00	106.00	228.00
986	108.00	106.00	230.00
988	108.00	106.00	230.00
990	108.00	108.00	230.00
992	110.00	108.00	232.00
994	110.00	108.00	232.00
996	110.00	108.00	232.00
998	110.00	108.00	234.00
1000	110.00	108.00	234.00
1002	110.00	110.00	234.00
1004	112.00	110.00	236.00
1006	112.00	110.00	236.00
1008	112.00	110.00	236.00
1010	112.00	110.00	238.00
1012	112.00	110.00	238.00
1014	112.00	112.00	238.00
1016	114.00	112.00	240.00
1018	114.00	112.00	240.00
1020	114.00	112.00	240.00
1022	114.00	112.00	242.00
1024	114.00	112.00	242.00
1026	114.00	114.00	242.00
1028	116.00	114.00	244.00
1030	116.00	114.00	244.00
1032	116.00	114.00	244.00
1034	116.00	114.00	246.00
1036	116.00	114.00	246.00
1038	116.00	116.00	246.00
1040	118.00	116.00	248.00
1042	118.00	116.00	248.00
1044	118.00	116.00	248.00
1046	118.00	116.00	250.00
1048	118.00	116.00	250.00
1050	118.00	118.00	250.00
1052	120.00	118.00	252.00
1054	120.00	118.00	252.00
1056	120.00	118.00	252.00
1058	120.00	118.00	254.00
1060	120.00	118.00	254.00
1062	120.00	120.00	254.00
1064	122.00	120.00	256.00
1066	122.00	120.00	256.00
1068	122.00	120.00	256.00
1070	122.00	120.00	258.00
1072	122.00	120.00	258.00
1074	122.00	120.00	258.00
1076	124.00	122.00	260.00
1078	124.00	122.00	260.00
1080	124.00	122.00	260.00
1082	124.00	122.00	262.00
1084	124.00	122.00	262.00
1086	124.00	122.00	262.00
1088	126.00	124.00	264.00
1090	126.00	124.00	264.00
1092	126.00	124.00	264.00
1094	126.00	124.00	266.00
1096	126.00	124.00	266.00
1098	126.00	124.00	266.00
1100	128.00	126.00	268.00
1102	128.00	126.00	268.00
1104	128.00	126.00	268.00
1106	128.00	126.00	270.00
1108	128.00	126.00	270.00
1110	128.00	126.00	270.00
1112	130.00	128.00	272.00
1114	130.00	128.00	272.00
1116	130.00	128.00	272.00
1118	130.00	128.00	274.00
1120	130.00	128.00	274.00

	Amount to be withheld		
Fortnightly earnings 1 $	With tax-free threshold with leave loading 2 $	With tax-free threshold no leave loading 3 $	No tax-free threshold 4 $
1122	130.00	128.00	274.00
1124	132.00	130.00	276.00
1126	132.00	130.00	276.00
1128	132.00	130.00	276.00
1130	132.00	130.00	278.00
1132	132.00	130.00	278.00
1134	132.00	130.00	278.00
1136	134.00	132.00	280.00
1138	134.00	132.00	280.00
1140	134.00	132.00	280.00
1142	134.00	132.00	282.00
1144	134.00	132.00	282.00
1146	134.00	132.00	282.00
1148	136.00	134.00	284.00
1150	136.00	134.00	284.00
1152	136.00	134.00	284.00
1154	136.00	134.00	286.00
1156	136.00	134.00	286.00
1158	138.00	134.00	286.00
1160	138.00	136.00	288.00
1162	138.00	136.00	288.00
1164	138.00	136.00	288.00
1166	138.00	136.00	290.00
1168	138.00	136.00	290.00
1170	140.00	138.00	290.00
1172	140.00	138.00	292.00
1174	140.00	138.00	292.00
1176	140.00	138.00	292.00
1178	140.00	138.00	294.00
1180	142.00	140.00	294.00
1182	142.00	140.00	294.00
1184	142.00	140.00	296.00
1186	142.00	140.00	296.00
1188	142.00	140.00	296.00
1190	144.00	140.00	298.00
1192	144.00	142.00	298.00
1194	144.00	142.00	298.00
1196	144.00	142.00	300.00
1198	144.00	142.00	300.00
1200	144.00	142.00	300.00
1202	146.00	144.00	302.00
1204	146.00	144.00	302.00
1206	146.00	144.00	302.00
1208	146.00	144.00	304.00
1210	146.00	144.00	304.00
1212	148.00	144.00	304.00
1214	148.00	146.00	306.00
1216	148.00	146.00	306.00
1218	148.00	146.00	306.00
1220	148.00	146.00	308.00
1222	150.00	146.00	308.00
1224	150.00	148.00	308.00
1226	150.00	148.00	310.00
1228	150.00	148.00	310.00
1230	150.00	148.00	310.00
1232	150.00	148.00	312.00
1234	152.00	150.00	312.00
1236	152.00	150.00	312.00
1238	152.00	150.00	314.00
1240	152.00	150.00	314.00
1242	152.00	150.00	314.00
1244	154.00	150.00	316.00
1246	154.00	152.00	316.00
1248	154.00	152.00	316.00
1250	154.00	152.00	318.00
1252	154.00	152.00	318.00
1254	156.00	152.00	318.00
1256	156.00	154.00	320.00
1258	156.00	154.00	320.00
1260	156.00	154.00	320.00
1262	156.00	154.00	322.00
1264	156.00	154.00	322.00
1266	158.00	154.00	322.00
1268	158.00	156.00	324.00
1270	158.00	156.00	324.00
1272	158.00	156.00	324.00
1274	158.00	156.00	326.00
1276	160.00	156.00	326.00
1278	160.00	158.00	326.00
1280	160.00	158.00	328.00

6 SCHEDULE 3 FORTNIGHTLY TAX TABLE

Form 3.4 [1006] *continued*

FORTNIGHTLY TAX TABLE

Fortnightly earnings 1 $	Amount to be withheld: With tax-free threshold with leave loading 2 $	With tax-free threshold no leave loading 3 $	No tax-free threshold 4 $
1282	160.00	158.00	328.00
1284	160.00	158.00	328.00
1286	160.00	158.00	330.00
1288	162.00	160.00	330.00
1290	162.00	160.00	330.00
1292	162.00	160.00	332.00
1294	162.00	160.00	332.00
1296	164.00	160.00	332.00
1298	164.00	160.00	334.00
1300	164.00	162.00	334.00
1302	166.00	162.00	336.00
1304	166.00	162.00	336.00
1306	166.00	162.00	336.00
1308	168.00	164.00	338.00
1310	168.00	164.00	338.00
1312	168.00	164.00	338.00
1314	170.00	166.00	340.00
1316	170.00	166.00	340.00
1318	170.00	166.00	340.00
1320	172.00	168.00	342.00
1322	172.00	168.00	342.00
1324	172.00	168.00	342.00
1326	174.00	170.00	344.00
1328	174.00	170.00	344.00
1330	174.00	170.00	344.00
1332	176.00	172.00	346.00
1334	176.00	172.00	346.00
1336	176.00	172.00	346.00
1338	178.00	174.00	348.00
1340	178.00	174.00	348.00
1342	178.00	174.00	348.00
1344	180.00	176.00	350.00
1346	180.00	176.00	350.00
1348	180.00	176.00	350.00
1350	182.00	178.00	352.00
1352	182.00	178.00	352.00
1354	182.00	178.00	352.00
1356	184.00	180.00	354.00
1358	184.00	180.00	354.00
1360	184.00	180.00	354.00
1362	186.00	182.00	356.00
1364	186.00	182.00	356.00
1366	186.00	182.00	356.00
1368	188.00	184.00	358.00
1370	188.00	184.00	358.00
1372	188.00	184.00	358.00
1374	190.00	186.00	360.00
1376	190.00	186.00	360.00
1378	190.00	186.00	360.00
1380	192.00	188.00	362.00
1382	192.00	188.00	362.00
1384	192.00	188.00	362.00
1386	194.00	190.00	364.00
1388	194.00	190.00	364.00
1390	194.00	190.00	364.00
1392	196.00	192.00	366.00
1394	196.00	192.00	366.00
1396	196.00	192.00	366.00
1398	198.00	194.00	368.00
1400	198.00	194.00	368.00
1402	198.00	194.00	368.00
1404	200.00	196.00	370.00
1406	200.00	196.00	370.00
1408	200.00	196.00	370.00
1410	202.00	198.00	372.00
1412	202.00	198.00	372.00
1414	202.00	198.00	372.00
1416	204.00	200.00	374.00
1418	204.00	200.00	374.00
1420	204.00	200.00	374.00
1422	206.00	202.00	376.00
1424	206.00	202.00	376.00
1426	206.00	202.00	376.00
1428	208.00	204.00	378.00
1430	208.00	204.00	378.00
1432	208.00	204.00	378.00
1434	210.00	206.00	380.00
1436	210.00	206.00	380.00
1438	210.00	206.00	380.00
1440	212.00	208.00	382.00

Fortnightly earnings 1 $	Amount to be withheld: With tax-free threshold with leave loading 2 $	With tax-free threshold no leave loading 3 $	No tax-free threshold 4 $
1442	212.00	208.00	382.00
1444	212.00	208.00	382.00
1446	214.00	210.00	384.00
1448	214.00	210.00	384.00
1450	214.00	210.00	384.00
1452	216.00	212.00	386.00
1454	216.00	212.00	386.00
1456	216.00	212.00	386.00
1458	218.00	214.00	388.00
1460	218.00	214.00	388.00
1462	218.00	214.00	388.00
1464	220.00	216.00	390.00
1466	220.00	216.00	390.00
1468	220.00	216.00	390.00
1470	222.00	218.00	392.00
1472	222.00	218.00	392.00
1474	222.00	218.00	392.00
1476	224.00	220.00	394.00
1478	224.00	220.00	394.00
1480	224.00	220.00	394.00
1482	226.00	222.00	396.00
1484	226.00	222.00	396.00
1486	226.00	222.00	396.00
1488	228.00	224.00	398.00
1490	228.00	224.00	398.00
1492	228.00	224.00	398.00
1494	230.00	226.00	400.00
1496	230.00	226.00	400.00
1498	230.00	226.00	400.00
1500	232.00	228.00	402.00
1502	232.00	228.00	402.00
1504	232.00	228.00	402.00
1506	234.00	230.00	404.00
1508	234.00	230.00	404.00
1510	234.00	230.00	404.00
1512	236.00	232.00	406.00
1514	236.00	232.00	406.00
1516	236.00	232.00	406.00
1518	238.00	234.00	408.00
1520	238.00	234.00	408.00
1522	238.00	234.00	408.00
1524	240.00	236.00	410.00
1526	240.00	236.00	410.00
1528	240.00	236.00	410.00
1530	242.00	238.00	412.00
1532	242.00	238.00	412.00
1534	242.00	238.00	412.00
1536	244.00	240.00	414.00
1538	244.00	240.00	414.00
1540	244.00	240.00	414.00
1542	246.00	242.00	416.00
1544	246.00	242.00	416.00
1546	246.00	242.00	416.00
1548	248.00	244.00	418.00
1550	248.00	244.00	418.00
1552	248.00	244.00	418.00
1554	250.00	246.00	420.00
1556	250.00	246.00	420.00
1558	250.00	246.00	420.00
1560	252.00	248.00	422.00
1562	252.00	248.00	422.00
1564	252.00	248.00	422.00
1566	254.00	250.00	424.00
1568	254.00	250.00	424.00
1570	254.00	250.00	424.00
1572	256.00	252.00	426.00
1574	256.00	252.00	426.00
1576	256.00	252.00	426.00
1578	258.00	254.00	428.00
1580	258.00	254.00	428.00
1582	258.00	254.00	428.00
1584	260.00	256.00	430.00
1586	260.00	256.00	430.00
1588	260.00	256.00	430.00
1590	262.00	258.00	432.00
1592	262.00	258.00	432.00
1594	264.00	258.00	432.00
1596	264.00	260.00	434.00
1598	264.00	260.00	434.00
1600	266.00	260.00	434.00

Fortnightly earnings 1 $	Amount to be withheld: With tax-free threshold with leave loading 2 $	With tax-free threshold no leave loading 3 $	No tax-free threshold 4 $
1602	266.00	262.00	436.00
1604	266.00	262.00	436.00
1606	268.00	262.00	436.00
1608	268.00	264.00	438.00
1610	268.00	264.00	438.00
1612	270.00	264.00	438.00
1614	270.00	266.00	440.00
1616	270.00	266.00	440.00
1618	272.00	266.00	440.00
1620	272.00	268.00	442.00
1622	272.00	268.00	442.00
1624	274.00	268.00	442.00
1626	274.00	270.00	444.00
1628	274.00	270.00	444.00
1630	276.00	270.00	444.00
1632	276.00	272.00	446.00
1634	276.00	272.00	446.00
1636	278.00	272.00	446.00
1638	278.00	274.00	448.00
1640	278.00	274.00	448.00
1642	280.00	274.00	448.00
1644	280.00	276.00	450.00
1646	280.00	276.00	450.00
1648	282.00	276.00	450.00
1650	282.00	278.00	452.00
1652	282.00	278.00	452.00
1654	284.00	278.00	452.00
1656	284.00	280.00	454.00
1658	284.00	280.00	454.00
1660	286.00	280.00	454.00
1662	286.00	282.00	456.00
1664	286.00	282.00	456.00
1666	288.00	284.00	456.00
1668	288.00	284.00	458.00
1670	288.00	284.00	458.00
1672	290.00	286.00	458.00
1674	290.00	286.00	460.00
1676	290.00	286.00	460.00
1678	292.00	288.00	460.00
1680	292.00	288.00	462.00
1682	292.00	288.00	462.00
1684	294.00	290.00	462.00
1686	294.00	290.00	464.00
1688	294.00	290.00	464.00
1690	296.00	292.00	464.00
1692	296.00	292.00	466.00
1694	296.00	292.00	466.00
1696	298.00	294.00	466.00
1698	298.00	294.00	468.00
1700	298.00	294.00	468.00
1702	300.00	296.00	468.00
1704	300.00	296.00	470.00
1706	300.00	296.00	470.00
1708	302.00	298.00	470.00
1710	302.00	298.00	470.00
1712	302.00	298.00	472.00
1714	304.00	300.00	472.00
1716	304.00	300.00	472.00
1718	304.00	300.00	474.00
1720	306.00	302.00	474.00
1722	306.00	302.00	474.00
1724	306.00	302.00	476.00
1726	308.00	304.00	476.00
1728	308.00	304.00	476.00
1730	308.00	304.00	478.00
1732	310.00	306.00	478.00
1734	310.00	306.00	478.00
1736	310.00	306.00	480.00
1738	312.00	308.00	480.00
1740	312.00	308.00	480.00
1742	312.00	308.00	480.00
1744	314.00	310.00	482.00
1746	314.00	310.00	482.00
1748	314.00	310.00	482.00
1750	316.00	312.00	484.00
1752	316.00	312.00	484.00
1754	316.00	312.00	484.00
1756	318.00	314.00	486.00
1758	318.00	314.00	486.00
1760	318.00	314.00	486.00

Fortnightly earnings 1 $	Amount to be withheld: With tax-free threshold with leave loading 2 $	With tax-free threshold no leave loading 3 $	No tax-free threshold 4 $
1762	320.00	316.00	488.00
1764	320.00	316.00	488.00
1766	320.00	316.00	488.00
1768	322.00	318.00	490.00
1770	322.00	318.00	490.00
1772	322.00	318.00	490.00
1774	324.00	320.00	492.00
1776	324.00	320.00	492.00
1778	324.00	320.00	492.00
1780	326.00	322.00	492.00
1782	326.00	322.00	494.00
1784	326.00	322.00	494.00
1786	328.00	324.00	494.00
1788	328.00	324.00	496.00
1790	328.00	324.00	496.00
1792	330.00	326.00	496.00
1794	330.00	326.00	498.00
1796	330.00	326.00	498.00
1798	332.00	328.00	498.00
1800	332.00	328.00	500.00
1802	332.00	328.00	500.00
1804	334.00	330.00	500.00
1806	334.00	330.00	502.00
1808	334.00	330.00	502.00
1810	336.00	332.00	502.00
1812	336.00	332.00	504.00
1814	336.00	332.00	504.00
1816	338.00	334.00	504.00
1818	338.00	334.00	504.00
1820	338.00	334.00	506.00
1822	340.00	336.00	506.00
1824	340.00	336.00	506.00
1826	340.00	336.00	508.00
1828	342.00	338.00	508.00
1830	342.00	338.00	508.00
1832	342.00	338.00	510.00
1834	344.00	340.00	510.00
1836	344.00	340.00	510.00
1838	344.00	340.00	512.00
1840	346.00	342.00	512.00
1842	346.00	342.00	512.00
1844	346.00	342.00	514.00
1846	348.00	344.00	514.00
1848	348.00	344.00	514.00
1850	348.00	344.00	516.00
1852	350.00	346.00	516.00
1854	350.00	346.00	516.00
1856	350.00	346.00	516.00
1858	352.00	348.00	518.00
1860	352.00	348.00	518.00
1862	352.00	348.00	518.00
1864	354.00	350.00	520.00
1866	354.00	350.00	520.00
1868	354.00	350.00	520.00
1870	356.00	352.00	522.00
1872	356.00	352.00	522.00
1874	356.00	352.00	522.00
1876	358.00	354.00	524.00
1878	358.00	354.00	524.00
1880	358.00	354.00	524.00
1882	360.00	356.00	526.00
1884	360.00	356.00	526.00
1886	360.00	356.00	526.00
1888	362.00	358.00	526.00
1890	362.00	358.00	528.00
1892	362.00	358.00	528.00
1894	364.00	360.00	528.00
1896	364.00	360.00	530.00
1898	364.00	360.00	530.00
1900	366.00	362.00	530.00
1902	366.00	362.00	532.00
1904	366.00	362.00	532.00
1906	368.00	364.00	532.00
1908	368.00	364.00	534.00
1910	368.00	364.00	534.00
1912	370.00	366.00	534.00
1914	370.00	366.00	536.00
1916	370.00	366.00	536.00
1918	372.00	368.00	536.00
1920	372.00	368.00	538.00

SCHEDULE 3 FORTNIGHTLY TAX TABLE 7

Form 3.5 [1007] Monthly tax

MONTHLY TAX TABLE

Monthly earnings	Amount to be withheld		
	With tax-free threshold with leave loading	With tax-free threshold no leave loading	No tax-free threshold
1	2	3	4
$	$	$	$
4.33	—	—	—
8.67	—	—	—
13.00	—	—	—
17.33	—	—	4.00
21.67	—	—	4.00
26.00	—	—	4.00
30.33	—	—	4.00
34.67	—	—	4.00
39.00	—	—	4.00
43.33	—	—	9.00
47.67	—	—	9.00
52.00	—	—	9.00
56.33	—	—	9.00
60.67	—	—	9.00
65.00	—	—	9.00
69.33	—	—	13.00
73.67	—	—	13.00
78.00	—	—	13.00
82.33	—	—	13.00
86.67	—	—	13.00
91.00	—	—	13.00
95.33	—	—	17.00
99.67	—	—	17.00
104.00	—	—	17.00
108.33	—	—	17.00
112.67	—	—	17.00
117.00	—	—	17.00
121.33	—	—	22.00
125.67	—	—	22.00
130.00	—	—	22.00
134.33	—	—	22.00
138.67	—	—	22.00
143.00	—	—	22.00
147.33	—	—	26.00
151.67	—	—	26.00
156.00	—	—	26.00
160.33	—	—	26.00
164.67	—	—	26.00
169.00	—	—	26.00
173.33	—	—	30.00
177.67	—	—	30.00
182.00	—	—	30.00
186.33	—	—	30.00
190.67	—	—	30.00
195.00	—	—	30.00
199.33	—	—	35.00
203.67	—	—	35.00
208.00	—	—	35.00
212.33	—	—	35.00
216.67	—	—	35.00
221.00	—	—	35.00
225.33	—	—	39.00
229.67	—	—	39.00
234.00	—	—	39.00
238.33	—	—	39.00
242.67	—	—	39.00
247.00	—	—	39.00
251.33	—	—	43.00
255.67	—	—	43.00
260.00	—	—	43.00
264.33	—	—	43.00
268.67	—	—	43.00
273.00	—	—	43.00
277.33	—	—	48.00
281.67	—	—	48.00
286.00	—	—	48.00
290.33	—	—	48.00
294.67	—	—	48.00
299.00	—	—	48.00
303.33	—	—	52.00
307.67	—	—	52.00
312.00	—	—	52.00
316.33	—	—	52.00
320.67	—	—	52.00
325.00	—	—	52.00
329.33	—	—	56.00
333.67	—	—	56.00
338.00	—	—	56.00
342.33	—	—	56.00
346.67	—	—	56.00

Monthly earnings	Amount to be withheld		
	With tax-free threshold with leave loading	With tax-free threshold no leave loading	No tax-free threshold
1	2	3	4
$	$	$	$
351.00	—	—	56.00
355.33	—	—	61.00
359.67	—	—	61.00
364.00	—	—	61.00
368.33	—	—	61.00
372.67	—	—	61.00
377.00	—	—	61.00
381.33	—	—	65.00
385.67	—	—	65.00
390.00	—	—	65.00
394.33	—	—	65.00
398.67	—	—	65.00
403.00	—	—	65.00
407.33	—	—	69.00
411.67	—	—	69.00
416.00	—	—	69.00
420.33	—	—	69.00
424.67	—	—	69.00
429.00	—	—	69.00
433.33	—	—	69.00
437.67	—	—	74.00
442.00	—	—	74.00
446.33	—	—	74.00
450.67	—	—	74.00
455.00	—	—	74.00
459.33	—	—	74.00
463.67	—	—	78.00
468.00	—	—	78.00
472.33	—	—	78.00
476.67	—	—	78.00
481.00	—	—	78.00
485.33	—	—	78.00
489.67	—	—	82.00
494.00	—	—	82.00
498.33	—	—	82.00
502.67	—	—	82.00
507.00	—	—	82.00
511.33	—	—	82.00
515.67	—	—	87.00
520.00	—	—	87.00
524.33	—	—	87.00
528.67	—	—	87.00
533.00	—	—	87.00
537.33	—	—	87.00
541.67	—	—	91.00
546.00	—	—	91.00
550.33	—	—	91.00
554.67	—	—	91.00
559.00	—	—	91.00
563.33	—	—	91.00
567.67	—	—	95.00
572.00	—	—	95.00
576.33	—	—	95.00
580.67	—	—	95.00
585.00	—	—	95.00
589.33	—	—	95.00
593.67	—	—	100.00
598.00	—	—	100.00
602.33	—	—	100.00
606.67	—	—	100.00
611.00	—	—	100.00
615.33	—	—	100.00
619.67	—	—	104.00
624.00	—	—	104.00
628.33	—	—	104.00
632.67	—	—	104.00
637.00	—	—	104.00
641.33	—	—	104.00
645.67	—	—	108.00
650.00	—	—	108.00
654.33	—	—	108.00
658.67	—	—	108.00
663.00	—	—	108.00
667.33	—	—	108.00
671.67	—	—	113.00
676.00	—	—	113.00
680.33	—	—	113.00
684.67	—	—	113.00
689.00	—	—	113.00
693.33	—	—	113.00

Monthly earnings	Amount to be withheld		
	With tax-free threshold with leave loading	With tax-free threshold no leave loading	No tax-free threshold
1	2	3	4
$	$	$	$
697.67	—	—	117.00
702.00	—	—	117.00
706.33	—	—	117.00
710.67	—	—	117.00
715.00	—	—	117.00
719.33	—	—	117.00
723.67	—	—	121.00
728.00	—	—	121.00
732.33	—	—	121.00
736.67	—	—	121.00
741.00	—	—	121.00
745.33	—	—	121.00
749.67	—	—	126.00
754.00	—	—	126.00
758.33	—	—	126.00
762.67	—	—	126.00
767.00	—	—	126.00
771.33	—	—	126.00
775.67	—	—	130.00
780.00	—	—	130.00
784.33	—	—	130.00
788.67	—	—	130.00
793.00	—	—	130.00
797.33	—	—	130.00
801.67	—	—	134.00
806.00	—	—	134.00
810.33	—	—	134.00
814.67	—	—	134.00
819.00	—	—	134.00
823.33	4.00	—	134.00
827.67	4.00	4.00	139.00
832.00	4.00	4.00	139.00
836.33	4.00	4.00	139.00
840.67	4.00	4.00	139.00
845.00	4.00	4.00	139.00
849.33	9.00	4.00	139.00
853.67	9.00	4.00	143.00
858.00	9.00	9.00	143.00
862.33	9.00	9.00	143.00
866.67	9.00	9.00	143.00
871.00	9.00	9.00	143.00
875.33	9.00	9.00	143.00
879.67	13.00	9.00	143.00
884.00	13.00	9.00	147.00
888.33	13.00	13.00	147.00
892.67	13.00	13.00	147.00
897.00	13.00	13.00	147.00
901.33	13.00	13.00	147.00
905.67	17.00	13.00	147.00
910.00	17.00	13.00	152.00
914.33	17.00	17.00	152.00
918.67	17.00	17.00	152.00
923.00	17.00	17.00	152.00
927.33	17.00	17.00	152.00
931.67	17.00	17.00	152.00
936.00	22.00	17.00	156.00
940.33	22.00	17.00	156.00
944.67	22.00	22.00	156.00
949.00	22.00	22.00	156.00
953.33	22.00	22.00	156.00
957.67	22.00	22.00	156.00
962.00	22.00	22.00	160.00
966.33	26.00	22.00	160.00
970.67	26.00	22.00	160.00
975.00	26.00	26.00	160.00
979.33	26.00	26.00	160.00
983.67	26.00	26.00	160.00
988.00	26.00	26.00	165.00
992.33	30.00	26.00	165.00
996.67	30.00	26.00	165.00
1001.00	30.00	30.00	165.00
1005.33	30.00	30.00	165.00
1009.67	30.00	30.00	165.00
1014.00	30.00	30.00	169.00
1018.33	30.00	30.00	169.00
1022.67	35.00	30.00	169.00
1027.00	35.00	30.00	169.00
1031.33	35.00	35.00	169.00
1035.67	35.00	35.00	169.00
1040.00	35.00	35.00	173.00

Monthly earnings	Amount to be withheld		
	With tax-free threshold with leave loading	With tax-free threshold no leave loading	No tax-free threshold
1	2	3	4
$	$	$	$
1044.33	35.00	35.00	173.00
1048.67	39.00	35.00	173.00
1053.00	39.00	35.00	173.00
1057.33	39.00	35.00	173.00
1061.67	39.00	39.00	173.00
1066.00	39.00	39.00	178.00
1070.33	39.00	39.00	178.00
1074.67	39.00	39.00	178.00
1079.00	43.00	39.00	178.00
1083.33	43.00	39.00	178.00
1087.67	43.00	43.00	178.00
1092.00	43.00	43.00	182.00
1096.33	43.00	43.00	182.00
1100.67	43.00	43.00	182.00
1105.00	43.00	43.00	182.00
1109.33	48.00	43.00	182.00
1113.67	48.00	43.00	182.00
1118.00	48.00	48.00	186.00
1122.33	48.00	48.00	208.00
1126.67	48.00	48.00	208.00
1131.00	48.00	48.00	208.00
1135.33	52.00	48.00	208.00
1139.67	52.00	48.00	208.00
1144.00	52.00	48.00	212.00
1148.33	52.00	52.00	212.00
1152.67	52.00	52.00	212.00
1157.00	52.00	52.00	212.00
1161.33	52.00	52.00	212.00
1165.67	56.00	52.00	217.00
1170.00	56.00	52.00	217.00
1174.33	56.00	56.00	217.00
1178.67	56.00	56.00	217.00
1183.00	56.00	56.00	217.00
1187.33	56.00	56.00	217.00
1191.67	61.00	56.00	221.00
1196.00	61.00	56.00	221.00
1200.33	61.00	56.00	221.00
1204.67	61.00	61.00	221.00
1209.00	61.00	61.00	221.00
1213.33	61.00	61.00	225.00
1217.67	61.00	61.00	225.00
1222.00	65.00	61.00	225.00
1226.33	65.00	61.00	225.00
1230.67	65.00	61.00	225.00
1235.00	65.00	65.00	225.00
1239.33	65.00	65.00	230.00
1243.67	65.00	65.00	230.00
1248.00	65.00	65.00	230.00
1252.33	69.00	65.00	230.00
1256.67	69.00	65.00	230.00
1261.00	69.00	69.00	234.00
1265.33	69.00	69.00	234.00
1269.67	69.00	69.00	234.00
1274.00	69.00	69.00	234.00
1278.33	74.00	69.00	234.00
1282.67	74.00	69.00	238.00
1287.00	74.00	69.00	238.00
1291.33	74.00	74.00	238.00
1295.67	74.00	74.00	238.00
1300.00	74.00	74.00	238.00
1304.33	74.00	74.00	238.00
1308.67	78.00	74.00	243.00
1313.00	78.00	74.00	243.00
1317.33	78.00	74.00	243.00
1321.67	78.00	78.00	243.00
1326.00	78.00	78.00	243.00
1330.33	78.00	78.00	247.00
1334.67	82.00	78.00	247.00
1339.00	82.00	78.00	247.00
1343.33	82.00	78.00	247.00
1347.67	82.00	82.00	247.00
1352.00	82.00	82.00	247.00
1356.33	82.00	82.00	251.00
1360.67	82.00	82.00	251.00
1365.00	87.00	82.00	251.00
1369.33	87.00	82.00	251.00
1373.67	87.00	82.00	251.00
1378.00	87.00	87.00	256.00
1382.33	87.00	87.00	256.00
1386.67	87.00	87.00	256.00

Form 3.5 [1007] *continued*

MONTHLY TAX TABLE

Monthly earnings 1 $	Amount to be withheld: With tax-free threshold with leave loading 2 $	With tax-free threshold no leave loading 3 $	No tax-free threshold 4 $
1391.00	87.00	87.00	256.00
1395.33	91.00	87.00	256.00
1399.67	91.00	87.00	260.00
1404.00	91.00	87.00	260.00
1408.33	91.00	91.00	260.00
1412.67	91.00	91.00	260.00
1417.00	91.00	91.00	260.00
1421.33	95.00	91.00	260.00
1425.67	95.00	91.00	264.00
1430.00	95.00	91.00	264.00
1434.33	95.00	95.00	264.00
1438.67	95.00	95.00	264.00
1443.00	100.00	95.00	264.00
1447.33	100.00	95.00	269.00
1451.67	100.00	95.00	269.00
1456.00	104.00	100.00	269.00
1460.33	104.00	100.00	269.00
1464.67	104.00	100.00	273.00
1469.00	104.00	100.00	273.00
1473.33	108.00	104.00	273.00
1477.67	108.00	104.00	277.00
1482.00	108.00	104.00	277.00
1486.33	108.00	104.00	277.00
1490.67	113.00	108.00	282.00
1495.00	113.00	108.00	282.00
1499.33	113.00	108.00	282.00
1503.67	113.00	108.00	286.00
1508.00	117.00	113.00	286.00
1512.33	117.00	113.00	286.00
1516.67	117.00	113.00	290.00
1521.00	117.00	113.00	290.00
1525.33	121.00	117.00	290.00
1529.67	121.00	117.00	295.00
1534.00	121.00	117.00	295.00
1538.33	121.00	117.00	295.00
1542.67	126.00	121.00	299.00
1547.00	126.00	121.00	299.00
1551.33	126.00	121.00	299.00
1555.67	126.00	121.00	303.00
1560.00	130.00	126.00	303.00
1564.33	130.00	126.00	303.00
1568.67	130.00	126.00	308.00
1573.00	130.00	126.00	308.00
1577.33	134.00	130.00	308.00
1581.67	134.00	130.00	312.00
1586.00	134.00	130.00	312.00
1590.33	134.00	130.00	312.00
1594.67	139.00	134.00	316.00
1599.00	139.00	134.00	316.00
1603.33	139.00	134.00	316.00
1607.67	139.00	134.00	321.00
1612.00	143.00	139.00	321.00
1616.33	143.00	139.00	321.00
1620.67	143.00	139.00	325.00
1625.00	143.00	139.00	325.00
1629.33	147.00	143.00	325.00
1633.67	147.00	143.00	329.00
1638.00	147.00	143.00	329.00
1642.33	147.00	143.00	329.00
1646.67	152.00	147.00	334.00
1651.00	152.00	147.00	334.00
1655.33	152.00	147.00	334.00
1659.67	152.00	147.00	338.00
1664.00	156.00	152.00	338.00
1668.33	156.00	152.00	338.00
1672.67	156.00	152.00	342.00
1677.00	156.00	152.00	342.00
1681.33	160.00	156.00	342.00
1685.67	160.00	156.00	347.00
1690.00	160.00	156.00	347.00
1694.33	160.00	156.00	347.00
1698.67	160.00	160.00	351.00
1703.00	160.00	160.00	351.00
1707.33	165.00	160.00	351.00
1711.67	165.00	160.00	355.00
1716.00	165.00	160.00	355.00
1720.33	165.00	160.00	355.00
1724.67	165.00	165.00	360.00
1729.00	165.00	165.00	360.00
1733.33	169.00	165.00	360.00

Monthly earnings 1 $	Amount to be withheld: With tax-free threshold with leave loading 2 $	With tax-free threshold no leave loading 3 $	No tax-free threshold 4 $
1737.67	169.00	165.00	364.00
1742.00	169.00	165.00	364.00
1746.33	169.00	165.00	364.00
1750.67	169.00	169.00	368.00
1755.00	169.00	169.00	368.00
1759.33	173.00	169.00	368.00
1763.67	173.00	169.00	373.00
1768.00	173.00	169.00	373.00
1772.33	173.00	169.00	373.00
1776.67	173.00	173.00	377.00
1781.00	173.00	173.00	377.00
1785.33	178.00	173.00	377.00
1789.67	178.00	173.00	381.00
1794.00	178.00	173.00	381.00
1798.33	178.00	173.00	381.00
1802.67	178.00	178.00	386.00
1807.00	178.00	178.00	386.00
1811.33	182.00	178.00	386.00
1815.67	182.00	178.00	390.00
1820.00	182.00	178.00	390.00
1824.33	182.00	178.00	390.00
1828.67	182.00	182.00	394.00
1833.00	182.00	182.00	394.00
1837.33	186.00	182.00	394.00
1841.67	186.00	182.00	399.00
1846.00	186.00	182.00	399.00
1850.33	186.00	182.00	399.00
1854.67	186.00	186.00	403.00
1859.00	186.00	186.00	403.00
1863.33	191.00	186.00	403.00
1867.67	191.00	186.00	407.00
1872.00	191.00	186.00	407.00
1876.33	191.00	186.00	407.00
1880.67	191.00	191.00	412.00
1885.00	191.00	191.00	412.00
1889.33	195.00	191.00	412.00
1893.67	195.00	191.00	416.00
1898.00	195.00	191.00	416.00
1902.33	195.00	191.00	416.00
1906.67	195.00	191.00	420.00
1911.00	195.00	195.00	420.00
1915.33	199.00	195.00	420.00
1919.67	199.00	195.00	425.00
1924.00	199.00	195.00	425.00
1928.33	199.00	195.00	425.00
1932.67	199.00	195.00	429.00
1937.00	199.00	199.00	429.00
1941.33	204.00	199.00	429.00
1945.67	204.00	199.00	433.00
1950.00	204.00	199.00	433.00
1954.33	204.00	199.00	438.00
1958.67	204.00	199.00	438.00
1963.00	204.00	204.00	438.00
1967.33	208.00	204.00	442.00
1971.67	208.00	204.00	442.00
1976.00	208.00	204.00	442.00
1980.33	208.00	204.00	446.00
1984.67	208.00	204.00	446.00
1989.00	208.00	208.00	446.00
1993.33	212.00	208.00	451.00
1997.67	212.00	208.00	451.00
2002.00	212.00	208.00	451.00
2006.33	212.00	208.00	455.00
2010.67	212.00	208.00	455.00
2015.00	212.00	212.00	455.00
2019.33	217.00	212.00	459.00
2023.67	217.00	212.00	459.00
2028.00	217.00	212.00	459.00
2032.33	217.00	212.00	464.00
2036.67	217.00	212.00	464.00
2041.00	217.00	217.00	464.00
2045.33	221.00	217.00	468.00
2049.67	221.00	217.00	468.00
2054.00	221.00	217.00	468.00
2058.33	221.00	217.00	472.00
2062.67	221.00	217.00	472.00
2067.00	221.00	221.00	472.00
2071.33	225.00	221.00	477.00
2075.67	225.00	221.00	477.00
2080.00	225.00	221.00	477.00

Monthly earnings 1 $	Amount to be withheld: With tax-free threshold with leave loading 2 $	With tax-free threshold no leave loading 3 $	No tax-free threshold 4 $
2084.33	225.00	221.00	481.00
2088.67	225.00	221.00	481.00
2093.00	225.00	225.00	481.00
2097.33	230.00	225.00	485.00
2101.67	230.00	225.00	485.00
2106.00	230.00	225.00	485.00
2110.33	230.00	225.00	490.00
2114.67	230.00	225.00	490.00
2119.00	230.00	230.00	490.00
2123.33	234.00	230.00	494.00
2127.67	234.00	230.00	494.00
2132.00	234.00	230.00	494.00
2136.33	234.00	230.00	498.00
2140.67	234.00	230.00	498.00
2145.00	234.00	234.00	498.00
2149.33	238.00	234.00	503.00
2153.67	238.00	234.00	503.00
2158.00	238.00	234.00	503.00
2162.33	238.00	234.00	507.00
2166.67	238.00	234.00	507.00
2171.00	238.00	238.00	507.00
2175.33	243.00	238.00	511.00
2179.67	243.00	238.00	511.00
2184.00	243.00	238.00	511.00
2188.33	243.00	238.00	516.00
2192.67	243.00	238.00	516.00
2197.00	243.00	243.00	516.00
2201.33	247.00	243.00	520.00
2205.67	247.00	243.00	520.00
2210.00	247.00	243.00	520.00
2214.33	247.00	243.00	524.00
2218.67	247.00	243.00	524.00
2223.00	247.00	247.00	524.00
2227.33	251.00	247.00	529.00
2231.67	251.00	247.00	529.00
2236.00	251.00	247.00	529.00
2240.33	251.00	247.00	533.00
2244.67	251.00	247.00	533.00
2249.00	251.00	251.00	533.00
2253.33	256.00	251.00	537.00
2257.67	256.00	251.00	537.00
2262.00	256.00	251.00	537.00
2266.33	256.00	251.00	542.00
2270.67	256.00	251.00	542.00
2275.00	256.00	256.00	542.00
2279.33	260.00	256.00	546.00
2283.67	260.00	256.00	546.00
2288.00	260.00	256.00	546.00
2292.33	260.00	256.00	550.00
2296.67	260.00	256.00	550.00
2301.00	260.00	260.00	550.00
2305.33	264.00	260.00	555.00
2309.67	264.00	260.00	555.00
2314.00	264.00	260.00	555.00
2318.33	264.00	260.00	559.00
2322.67	264.00	260.00	559.00
2327.00	264.00	260.00	559.00
2331.33	269.00	264.00	563.00
2335.67	269.00	264.00	563.00
2340.00	269.00	264.00	563.00
2344.33	269.00	264.00	568.00
2348.67	269.00	264.00	568.00
2353.00	269.00	269.00	568.00
2357.33	273.00	269.00	572.00
2361.67	273.00	269.00	572.00
2366.00	273.00	269.00	572.00
2370.33	273.00	269.00	576.00
2374.67	273.00	269.00	576.00
2379.00	273.00	269.00	576.00
2383.33	277.00	273.00	581.00
2387.67	277.00	273.00	581.00
2392.00	277.00	273.00	581.00
2396.33	277.00	273.00	585.00
2400.67	277.00	273.00	585.00
2405.00	277.00	273.00	585.00
2409.33	282.00	277.00	589.00
2413.67	282.00	277.00	589.00
2418.00	282.00	277.00	589.00
2422.33	282.00	277.00	594.00
2426.67	282.00	277.00	594.00

Monthly earnings 1 $	Amount to be withheld: With tax-free threshold with leave loading 2 $	With tax-free threshold no leave loading 3 $	No tax-free threshold 4 $
2431.00	282.00	277.00	594.00
2435.33	286.00	282.00	598.00
2439.67	286.00	282.00	598.00
2444.00	286.00	282.00	598.00
2448.33	286.00	282.00	602.00
2452.67	286.00	282.00	602.00
2457.00	286.00	282.00	602.00
2461.33	290.00	286.00	607.00
2465.67	290.00	286.00	607.00
2470.00	290.00	286.00	607.00
2474.33	290.00	286.00	611.00
2478.67	290.00	286.00	611.00
2483.00	290.00	286.00	611.00
2487.33	295.00	290.00	615.00
2491.67	295.00	290.00	615.00
2496.00	295.00	290.00	615.00
2500.33	295.00	290.00	620.00
2504.67	295.00	290.00	620.00
2509.00	299.00	290.00	620.00
2513.33	299.00	295.00	624.00
2517.67	299.00	295.00	624.00
2522.00	299.00	295.00	624.00
2526.33	299.00	295.00	628.00
2530.67	299.00	295.00	628.00
2535.00	303.00	299.00	628.00
2539.33	303.00	299.00	633.00
2543.67	303.00	299.00	633.00
2548.00	303.00	299.00	633.00
2552.33	303.00	299.00	637.00
2556.67	308.00	303.00	637.00
2561.00	308.00	303.00	637.00
2565.33	308.00	303.00	641.00
2569.67	308.00	303.00	641.00
2574.00	308.00	303.00	641.00
2578.33	312.00	303.00	646.00
2582.67	312.00	308.00	646.00
2587.00	312.00	308.00	646.00
2591.33	312.00	308.00	650.00
2595.67	312.00	308.00	650.00
2600.00	312.00	308.00	650.00
2604.33	316.00	312.00	654.00
2608.67	316.00	312.00	654.00
2613.00	316.00	312.00	654.00
2617.33	316.00	312.00	659.00
2621.67	316.00	312.00	659.00
2626.00	321.00	312.00	659.00
2630.33	321.00	316.00	663.00
2634.67	321.00	316.00	663.00
2639.00	321.00	316.00	663.00
2643.33	321.00	316.00	667.00
2647.67	325.00	316.00	667.00
2652.00	325.00	321.00	667.00
2656.33	325.00	321.00	672.00
2660.67	325.00	321.00	672.00
2665.00	325.00	321.00	672.00
2669.33	325.00	321.00	676.00
2673.67	329.00	325.00	676.00
2678.00	329.00	325.00	676.00
2682.33	329.00	325.00	680.00
2686.67	329.00	325.00	680.00
2691.00	329.00	325.00	680.00
2695.33	334.00	325.00	685.00
2699.67	334.00	329.00	685.00
2704.00	334.00	329.00	685.00
2708.33	334.00	329.00	689.00
2712.67	334.00	329.00	689.00
2717.00	338.00	329.00	689.00
2721.33	338.00	334.00	693.00
2725.67	338.00	334.00	693.00
2730.00	338.00	334.00	693.00
2734.33	338.00	334.00	698.00
2738.67	338.00	334.00	698.00
2743.00	342.00	334.00	698.00
2747.33	342.00	338.00	702.00
2751.67	342.00	338.00	702.00
2756.00	342.00	338.00	702.00
2760.33	342.00	338.00	706.00
2764.67	347.00	338.00	706.00
2769.00	347.00	342.00	706.00
2773.33	347.00	342.00	711.00

Form 3.5 [1007] *continued*

MONTHLY TAX TABLE

Monthly earnings	Amount to be withheld: With tax-free threshold with leave loading	With tax-free threshold no leave loading	No tax-free threshold
1	2	3	4
$	$	$	$
2777.67	347.00	342.00	711.00
2782.00	347.00	342.00	711.00
2786.33	347.00	342.00	715.00
2790.67	351.00	347.00	715.00
2795.00	351.00	347.00	715.00
2799.33	351.00	347.00	719.00
2803.67	351.00	347.00	719.00
2808.00	355.00	347.00	719.00
2812.33	355.00	347.00	724.00
2816.67	355.00	351.00	724.00
2821.00	360.00	351.00	728.00
2825.33	360.00	351.00	728.00
2829.67	360.00	351.00	728.00
2834.00	364.00	355.00	732.00
2838.33	364.00	355.00	732.00
2842.67	364.00	355.00	732.00
2847.00	368.00	360.00	737.00
2851.33	368.00	360.00	737.00
2855.67	368.00	360.00	737.00
2860.00	373.00	364.00	741.00
2864.33	373.00	364.00	741.00
2868.67	373.00	364.00	741.00
2873.00	377.00	368.00	745.00
2877.33	377.00	368.00	745.00
2881.67	377.00	368.00	745.00
2886.00	381.00	373.00	750.00
2890.33	381.00	373.00	750.00
2894.67	381.00	373.00	750.00
2899.00	386.00	377.00	754.00
2903.33	386.00	377.00	754.00
2907.67	386.00	377.00	754.00
2912.00	390.00	381.00	758.00
2916.33	390.00	381.00	758.00
2920.67	390.00	381.00	758.00
2925.00	394.00	386.00	763.00
2929.33	394.00	386.00	763.00
2933.67	394.00	386.00	763.00
2938.00	399.00	390.00	767.00
2942.33	399.00	390.00	767.00
2946.67	399.00	390.00	767.00
2951.00	403.00	394.00	771.00
2955.33	403.00	394.00	771.00
2959.67	403.00	394.00	771.00
2964.00	407.00	399.00	776.00
2968.33	407.00	399.00	776.00
2972.67	407.00	399.00	776.00
2977.00	412.00	403.00	780.00
2981.33	412.00	403.00	780.00
2985.67	412.00	403.00	780.00
2990.00	416.00	407.00	784.00
2994.33	416.00	407.00	784.00
2998.67	416.00	407.00	784.00
3003.00	420.00	412.00	789.00
3007.33	420.00	412.00	789.00
3011.67	420.00	412.00	789.00
3016.00	425.00	416.00	793.00
3020.33	425.00	416.00	793.00
3024.67	425.00	416.00	793.00
3029.00	429.00	420.00	797.00
3033.33	429.00	420.00	797.00
3037.67	429.00	420.00	797.00
3042.00	433.00	425.00	802.00
3046.33	433.00	425.00	802.00
3050.67	433.00	425.00	802.00
3055.00	438.00	429.00	806.00
3059.33	438.00	429.00	806.00
3063.67	438.00	429.00	806.00
3068.00	442.00	433.00	810.00
3072.33	442.00	433.00	810.00
3076.67	442.00	433.00	810.00
3081.00	446.00	438.00	815.00
3085.33	446.00	438.00	815.00
3089.67	446.00	438.00	815.00
3094.00	451.00	442.00	819.00
3098.33	451.00	442.00	819.00
3102.67	451.00	442.00	819.00
3107.00	455.00	446.00	823.00
3111.33	455.00	446.00	823.00
3115.67	455.00	446.00	823.00
3120.00	459.00	451.00	828.00

Monthly earnings	Amount to be withheld: With tax-free threshold with leave loading	With tax-free threshold no leave loading	No tax-free threshold
1	2	3	4
$	$	$	$
3124.33	459.00	451.00	828.00
3128.67	459.00	451.00	828.00
3133.00	464.00	455.00	832.00
3137.33	464.00	455.00	832.00
3141.67	464.00	455.00	832.00
3146.00	468.00	459.00	836.00
3150.33	468.00	459.00	836.00
3154.67	468.00	459.00	836.00
3159.00	472.00	464.00	841.00
3163.33	472.00	464.00	841.00
3167.67	472.00	464.00	841.00
3172.00	477.00	468.00	845.00
3176.33	477.00	468.00	845.00
3180.67	477.00	468.00	845.00
3185.00	481.00	472.00	849.00
3189.33	481.00	472.00	849.00
3193.67	481.00	472.00	849.00
3198.00	485.00	477.00	854.00
3202.33	485.00	477.00	854.00
3206.67	485.00	477.00	854.00
3211.00	490.00	481.00	858.00
3215.33	490.00	481.00	858.00
3219.67	490.00	481.00	858.00
3224.00	494.00	485.00	862.00
3228.33	494.00	485.00	862.00
3232.67	494.00	485.00	862.00
3237.00	498.00	490.00	867.00
3241.33	498.00	490.00	867.00
3245.67	498.00	490.00	867.00
3250.00	503.00	494.00	871.00
3254.33	503.00	494.00	871.00
3258.67	503.00	494.00	871.00
3263.00	507.00	498.00	875.00
3267.33	507.00	498.00	875.00
3271.67	507.00	498.00	875.00
3276.00	511.00	503.00	880.00
3280.33	511.00	503.00	880.00
3284.67	511.00	503.00	880.00
3289.00	516.00	507.00	884.00
3293.33	516.00	507.00	884.00
3297.67	516.00	507.00	884.00
3302.00	520.00	511.00	888.00
3306.33	520.00	511.00	888.00
3310.67	520.00	511.00	888.00
3315.00	524.00	516.00	893.00
3319.33	524.00	516.00	893.00
3323.67	524.00	516.00	893.00
3328.00	529.00	520.00	897.00
3332.33	529.00	520.00	897.00
3336.67	529.00	520.00	897.00
3341.00	533.00	524.00	901.00
3345.33	533.00	524.00	901.00
3349.67	533.00	524.00	901.00
3354.00	537.00	529.00	906.00
3358.33	537.00	529.00	906.00
3362.67	537.00	529.00	906.00
3367.00	542.00	533.00	910.00
3371.33	542.00	533.00	910.00
3375.67	542.00	533.00	910.00
3380.00	546.00	537.00	914.00
3384.33	546.00	537.00	914.00
3388.67	546.00	537.00	914.00
3393.00	550.00	542.00	919.00
3397.33	550.00	542.00	919.00
3401.67	550.00	542.00	919.00
3406.00	555.00	546.00	923.00
3410.33	555.00	546.00	923.00
3414.67	555.00	546.00	923.00
3419.00	559.00	550.00	927.00
3423.33	559.00	550.00	927.00
3427.67	559.00	550.00	927.00
3432.00	563.00	555.00	932.00
3436.33	563.00	555.00	932.00
3440.67	563.00	555.00	932.00
3445.00	568.00	559.00	936.00
3449.33	568.00	559.00	936.00
3453.67	572.00	559.00	936.00
3458.00	572.00	563.00	940.00
3462.33	572.00	563.00	940.00
3466.67	576.00	563.00	940.00

Monthly earnings	Amount to be withheld: With tax-free threshold with leave loading	With tax-free threshold no leave loading	No tax-free threshold
1	2	3	4
$	$	$	$
3471.00	576.00	568.00	945.00
3475.33	576.00	568.00	945.00
3479.67	581.00	568.00	945.00
3484.00	581.00	572.00	949.00
3488.33	581.00	572.00	949.00
3492.67	585.00	572.00	949.00
3497.00	585.00	576.00	953.00
3501.33	585.00	576.00	953.00
3505.67	589.00	576.00	953.00
3510.00	589.00	581.00	958.00
3514.33	589.00	581.00	958.00
3518.67	594.00	581.00	958.00
3523.00	594.00	585.00	962.00
3527.33	594.00	585.00	962.00
3531.67	598.00	585.00	962.00
3536.00	598.00	589.00	966.00
3540.33	598.00	589.00	966.00
3544.67	602.00	589.00	966.00
3549.00	602.00	594.00	971.00
3553.33	602.00	594.00	971.00
3557.67	607.00	594.00	971.00
3562.00	607.00	598.00	975.00
3566.33	607.00	598.00	975.00
3570.67	611.00	598.00	975.00
3575.00	611.00	602.00	979.00
3579.33	611.00	602.00	979.00
3583.67	615.00	602.00	979.00
3588.00	615.00	607.00	984.00
3592.33	615.00	607.00	984.00
3596.67	620.00	607.00	984.00
3601.00	620.00	611.00	988.00
3605.33	620.00	611.00	988.00
3609.67	624.00	615.00	988.00
3614.00	624.00	615.00	992.00
3618.33	624.00	615.00	992.00
3622.67	628.00	620.00	992.00
3627.00	628.00	620.00	997.00
3631.33	628.00	620.00	997.00
3635.67	633.00	624.00	997.00
3640.00	633.00	624.00	1001.00
3644.33	633.00	624.00	1001.00
3648.67	637.00	628.00	1001.00
3653.00	637.00	628.00	1005.00
3657.33	637.00	628.00	1005.00
3661.67	641.00	633.00	1005.00
3666.00	641.00	633.00	1010.00
3670.33	641.00	633.00	1010.00
3674.67	646.00	637.00	1010.00
3679.00	646.00	637.00	1014.00
3683.33	646.00	637.00	1014.00
3687.67	650.00	641.00	1014.00
3692.00	650.00	641.00	1018.00
3696.33	650.00	641.00	1018.00
3700.67	654.00	646.00	1018.00
3705.00	654.00	646.00	1018.00
3709.33	654.00	646.00	1023.00
3713.67	659.00	650.00	1023.00
3718.00	659.00	650.00	1023.00
3722.33	659.00	650.00	1027.00
3726.67	663.00	654.00	1027.00
3731.00	663.00	654.00	1027.00
3735.33	663.00	654.00	1031.00
3739.67	667.00	659.00	1031.00
3744.00	667.00	659.00	1031.00
3748.33	667.00	659.00	1036.00
3752.67	672.00	663.00	1036.00
3757.00	672.00	663.00	1036.00
3761.33	672.00	663.00	1040.00
3765.67	676.00	667.00	1040.00
3770.00	676.00	667.00	1040.00
3774.33	676.00	667.00	1040.00
3778.67	680.00	672.00	1044.00
3783.00	680.00	672.00	1044.00
3787.33	680.00	672.00	1044.00
3791.67	685.00	676.00	1049.00
3796.00	685.00	676.00	1049.00
3800.33	685.00	676.00	1049.00
3804.67	689.00	680.00	1053.00
3809.00	689.00	680.00	1053.00
3813.33	689.00	680.00	1053.00

Monthly earnings	Amount to be withheld: With tax-free threshold with leave loading	With tax-free threshold no leave loading	No tax-free threshold
1	2	3	4
$	$	$	$
3817.67	693.00	685.00	1057.00
3822.00	693.00	685.00	1057.00
3826.33	693.00	685.00	1057.00
3830.67	698.00	689.00	1062.00
3835.00	698.00	689.00	1062.00
3839.33	698.00	689.00	1062.00
3843.67	702.00	693.00	1066.00
3848.00	702.00	693.00	1066.00
3852.33	702.00	693.00	1066.00
3856.67	706.00	698.00	1066.00
3861.00	706.00	698.00	1070.00
3865.33	706.00	698.00	1070.00
3869.67	711.00	702.00	1070.00
3874.00	711.00	702.00	1075.00
3878.33	711.00	702.00	1075.00
3882.67	715.00	706.00	1075.00
3887.00	715.00	706.00	1079.00
3891.33	715.00	706.00	1079.00
3895.67	719.00	711.00	1079.00
3900.00	719.00	711.00	1083.00
3904.33	719.00	711.00	1083.00
3908.67	724.00	715.00	1083.00
3913.00	724.00	715.00	1088.00
3917.33	724.00	715.00	1088.00
3921.67	728.00	719.00	1088.00
3926.00	728.00	719.00	1092.00
3930.33	728.00	719.00	1092.00
3934.67	732.00	724.00	1092.00
3939.00	732.00	724.00	1092.00
3943.33	732.00	724.00	1096.00
3947.67	737.00	728.00	1096.00
3952.00	737.00	728.00	1096.00
3956.33	737.00	728.00	1101.00
3960.67	741.00	732.00	1101.00
3965.00	741.00	732.00	1101.00
3969.33	741.00	732.00	1105.00
3973.67	745.00	737.00	1105.00
3978.00	745.00	737.00	1105.00
3982.33	745.00	737.00	1109.00
3986.67	750.00	741.00	1109.00
3991.00	750.00	741.00	1109.00
3995.33	750.00	741.00	1114.00
3999.67	754.00	745.00	1114.00
4004.00	754.00	745.00	1114.00
4008.33	754.00	745.00	1118.00
4012.67	758.00	750.00	1118.00
4017.00	758.00	750.00	1118.00
4021.33	758.00	750.00	1118.00
4025.67	763.00	754.00	1122.00
4030.00	763.00	754.00	1122.00
4034.33	763.00	754.00	1122.00
4038.67	767.00	758.00	1127.00
4043.00	767.00	758.00	1127.00
4047.33	767.00	758.00	1127.00
4051.67	771.00	763.00	1131.00
4056.00	771.00	763.00	1131.00
4060.33	771.00	763.00	1131.00
4064.67	776.00	767.00	1135.00
4069.00	776.00	767.00	1135.00
4073.33	776.00	767.00	1135.00
4077.67	780.00	771.00	1140.00
4082.00	780.00	771.00	1140.00
4086.33	780.00	771.00	1140.00
4090.67	784.00	776.00	1140.00
4095.00	784.00	776.00	1144.00
4099.33	784.00	776.00	1144.00
4103.67	789.00	780.00	1144.00
4108.00	789.00	780.00	1148.00
4112.33	789.00	780.00	1148.00
4116.67	793.00	784.00	1148.00
4121.00	793.00	784.00	1153.00
4125.33	793.00	784.00	1153.00
4129.67	797.00	789.00	1153.00
4134.00	797.00	789.00	1157.00
4138.33	797.00	789.00	1157.00
4142.67	802.00	793.00	1157.00
4147.00	802.00	793.00	1161.00
4151.33	802.00	793.00	1161.00
4155.67	806.00	797.00	1161.00
4160.00	806.00	797.00	1166.00

Form 3.6 [2036] Tax withholding variation

Australian Government
Australian Taxation Office

2009 PAYG income tax withholding variation (ITWV) application

1 July 2008 to 30 June 2009

Office use only

Complete the application if you want to vary the rate or amount of PAYG tax withheld from payments made to you for the year ending 30 June 2009. You must also complete the *2009 PAYG ITWV supplement* (NAT 5423) if you have business income or non-commercial business or partnership losses.

Read the instructions for this application before you fill it in.

Please print in BLOCK LETTERS in ink.

If you wish to have additional amounts withheld, complete *Withholding declaration – upwards variation* (NAT 5367).

2009 applications may be lodged during the income year. The last date for lodgment is **15 May 2009.**

Section A: Your details

The Tax Office is authorised by the *Taxation Administration Act 1953* to collect your tax file number (TFN). It is not an offence not to quote your TFN but not quoting it could increase the chance of a delay or error in processing your application.

A1 Your tax file number (TFN) ☐☐☐ ☐☐☐ ☐☐☐

A2 Have you lodged an *Employment declaration* or *TFN declaration* with your payer that quotes your TFN? Yes ☐ No ☐ Exempt ☐ Tick one of the reason boxes ☐ Under 18 years old and earn below the tax-free threshold ☐ Pension recipient

A3 Will you be receiving payments under a labour hire arrangement under subsection 12-60(1) in Schedule 1 to the *Taxation Administration Act 1953*? Yes ☐ No ☐
If you are an employee, tick **No**.

A4 Your date of birth Day ☐☐ / Month ☐☐ / Year ☐☐☐☐

A5 Your name Title: Mr ☐ Mrs ☐ Miss ☐ Ms ☐ Other ☐

Family name

Given names

A6 Your postal address

Suburb/town

State/territory

Postcode

Country if other than Australia

A7 Your phone number/s (if we need to contact you about your application, it is quicker by phone).

Work

Home

Mobile

A8 Tax agent's or other contact phone number and name

Only if this application is not completed by you. By completing this item you are authorising us to deal with this person as the first point of contact.

Phone number

Contact name

A9 Tax agent's registration number ☐☐☐☐☐-☐☐☐

Only if this application is completed by your tax agent.

A10 Your occupation

A11 Are you an Australian resident for tax purposes? Yes ☐ No ☐

A12 Reason for your application

A13 Reason codes See the instructions for a list of the codes.

NAT 2036-04.2008

IN-CONFIDENCE — when completed

Page 1

Form 3.6 [2036] *continued*

Section B: **Your payer's details**

If you have more than two payers, attach a separate sheet with the required details.

Payer 1

B1 (b) Will you be receiving payments from this payer for the full year?

Yes ☐ Go to B2.

No ☐ Provide one or both of the following dates.

Starting date Day / Month / Year

Finishing date Day / Month / Year

B2 Have you made a voluntary agreement with this payer to withhold amounts under section 12-55 in Schedule 1 to the *Taxation Administration Act 1953*?

Yes ☐ You must complete all relevant details in section G on the *2009 PAYG ITWV supplement* (NAT 5423) and attach a copy of your voluntary agreement.

No ☐

B3 Payer's Australian business number (ABN)

B4 Payer's business name

B5 Pay office postal address (for privacy reasons, this should preferably be a PO box, locked bag or similar address).

Suburb/town State/territory Postcode

B6 Your pay officer's direct phone number

B7 Your payroll ID, employee or policy number

The details for items B8 to B13 are on your most recent payslip. If you do not complete these items, your application will be returned to you.

B8 Gross payment per payment period $ .00 Do not include reportable fringe benefits or non-assessable amounts. For example, salary sacrifice amounts.

B9 Tax withheld per payment $ .00

B10 Payment frequency

Weekly ☐ Fortnightly ☐ Monthly ☐ Half-monthly ☐ 4-weekly ☐ 6-weekly ☐

2-monthly ☐ 3-monthly ☐ 4-monthly ☐ 6-monthly ☐ Yearly ☐

B11 Dates of last payment and next payment

Last payment Day / Month / Year Next payment Day / Month / Year

If your last payment date shown above at item B11 is on or before 30 June 2008, you do not need to complete items B12 and B13 below.

B12 Gross payments received since 1 July 2008 (as per date of last payment shown at item B11 above)

Include any bonus payments received at this item. $ .00

B13 Tax withheld since 1 July 2008 (as per date of last payment shown at item B11 above)

Include tax withheld from any bonus payments at this item. $ .00

Also include at items B12 and B13 the total of your gross assessable payments received and tax withheld since 1 July 2008 for any previous payers.

Page 2 IN-CONFIDENCE — when completed

Form 3.6 [2036] *continued*

Section B: **Your payer's details** – *continued*

Attach your payslip here

Payer 2

B1 (a) Is this variation to apply to this payer?

Yes ☐ Go to B1(b).

No ☐ Provide an estimate of the annual gross income and annual tax for this payer, then go to the next page.

Annual gross income $ ______ ·00 Annual tax $ ______ ·00

(b) Will you be receiving payments from this payer for the full year?

Yes ☐ Go to B2.

No ☐ Provide one or both of the following dates.

Starting date Day / Month / Year ☐☐ / ☐☐ / ☐☐☐☐ Finishing date Day / Month / Year ☐☐ / ☐☐ / ☐☐☐☐

B2 Have you made a voluntary agreement with this payer to withhold amounts under section 12-55 in Schedule 1 to the *Taxation Administration Act 1953*?

Yes ☐ You must complete all relevant details in section G on the *2009 PAYG ITWV supplement* (NAT 5423) and attach a copy of your voluntary agreement.

No ☐

B3 Payer's Australian business number (ABN) ☐☐ ☐☐☐ ☐☐☐ ☐☐☐ / ☐☐☐

B4 Payer's business name

B5 Pay office postal address (for privacy reasons, this should preferably be a PO box, locked bag or similar address).

Suburb/town State/territory Postcode

B6 Your pay officer's direct phone number ☐☐ ☐☐☐☐☐☐☐☐

B7 Your payroll ID, employee or policy number

The details for items B8 to B13 are on your most recent payslip. If you do not complete these items, your application will be returned to you.

B8 Gross payment per payment period $ ______ ·00 Do not include reportable fringe benefits or non-assessable amounts. For example, salary sacrifice amounts.

B9 Tax withheld per payment $ ______ ·00

B10 Payment frequency

Weekly ☐ Fortnightly ☐ Monthly ☐ Half-monthly ☐ 4-weekly ☐ 6-weekly ☐

2-monthly ☐ 3-monthly ☐ 4-monthly ☐ 6-monthly ☐ Yearly ☐

B11 Dates of last payment and next payment

Last payment Day / Month / Year ☐☐ / ☐☐ / ☐☐☐☐ Next payment Day / Month / Year ☐☐ / ☐☐ / ☐☐☐☐

If your last payment date shown above at item B11 is on or before 30 June 2008, you do not need to complete items B12 and B13 below.

B12 Gross payments received since 1 July 2008 (as per date of last payment shown at item B11 above)

Include any bonus payments received at this item. $ ______ ·00

B13 Tax withheld since 1 July 2008 (as per date of last payment shown at item B11 above)

Include tax withheld from any bonus payments at this item. $ ______ ·00

Form 3.6 [2036] *continued*

Section C: **Rental details**

Have your rental details (other than the dates available for rent) changed since you lodged your last application? You must tick one of the boxes below.

NO ☐ You do not need to complete this section. Go to section D.

YES ☐
N/A New applicant ☐ You must complete this section for all rental properties or the application will be returned to you.

If you have more than three properties, attach a separate sheet with the required details.

Property 1

Full name/s appearing on title deed (write the full name/s exactly as it appears on the title deed).

Address of rental property

Suburb/town | State/territory | Postcode

Date you purchased the property Day / Month / Year | **Is the property under construction?** Yes ☐ No ☐ | **Percentage owned** %

Dates available for rent in 2008–09 Day / Month / Year to Day / Month / Year | **Year building constructed**

Property 2

Full name/s appearing on title deed (write the full name/s exactly as it appears on the title deed).

Address of rental property

Suburb/town | State/territory | Postcode

Date you purchased the property Day / Month / Year | **Is the property under construction?** Yes ☐ No ☐ | **Percentage owned** %

Dates available for rent in 2008–09 Day / Month / Year to Day / Month / Year | **Year building constructed**

Property 3

Full name/s appearing on title deed (write the full name/s exactly as it appears on the title deed).

Address of rental property

Suburb/town | State/territory | Postcode

Date you purchased the property Day / Month / Year | **Is the property under construction?** Yes ☐ No ☐ | **Percentage owned** %

Dates available for rent in 2008–09 Day / Month / Year to Day / Month / Year | **Year building constructed**

Page 4 IN-CONFIDENCE — when completed

Form 3.6 [2036] *continued*

Section D: **Investment details**

DO NOT complete this section if the income or loss is derived from a business activity you conduct as a sole trader or in partnership. Income or loss from this source is to be shown at items E6 or E7.

If your investment is related to shares in publicly listed companies, do not list each company. Just write 'Own share portfolio' at item D1 and the total amount of deductions at item D6. For all other investments, provide full details for each investment.

If you have more than two investments, attach a separate sheet with the required details.

Product rulings were introduced to enable the Commissioner to rule publicly on the availability of claimed tax benefits from products. A 'product' refers to an arrangement in which a number of taxpayers individually enter into substantially the same transactions with a common entity or a group of entities. A product ruling provides participants with a binding ruling on the tax consequences of the particular product, but can provide no guarantee as to the commercial viability of the product.

Investment 1

D1 Name of investment or film venture (provide the full name, including any project numbers or specific year details).

D2 Product ruling number and/or private binding ruling number (if applicable) ☐☐☐☐ / ☐☐☐

D3 Date you initially entered into this investment or film venture Day ☐☐ / Month ☐☐ / Year ☐☐☐☐

D4 Has the Commissioner's discretion been ruled on in your favour, either in a product or private ruling, for this deduction? Yes ☐ What income years have been ruled on? Year ☐☐☐☐ to Year ☐☐☐☐ No ☐

D5 Has a prospectus, an information memorandum or a product disclosure statement been issued for this investment? Yes ☐ Indicate which one. ☐ Prospectus ☐ Information memorandum ☐ Product disclosure statement No ☐

D6 Amount of deduction relating to this investment you have included in F2 $ .00

D7 Number of investment units purchased

Investment 2

D1 Name of investment or film venture (provide the full name, including any project numbers or specific year details).

D2 Product ruling number and/or private binding ruling number (if applicable) ☐☐☐☐ / ☐☐☐

D3 Date you initially entered into this investment or film venture Day ☐☐ / Month ☐☐ / Year ☐☐☐☐

D4 Has the Commissioner's discretion been ruled on in your favour, either in a product or private ruling, for this deduction? Yes ☐ What income years have been ruled on? Year ☐☐☐☐ to Year ☐☐☐☐ No ☐

D5 Has a prospectus, an information memorandum or a product disclosure statement been issued for this investment? Yes ☐ Indicate which one. ☐ Prospectus ☐ Information memorandum ☐ Product disclosure statement No ☐

D6 Amount of deduction relating to this investment you have included in F2 $ .00

D7 Number of investment units purchased

Form 3.6 [2036] *continued*

Section E: **Annual income and tax offsets**

The estimates you provide on this application should be the amounts you expect to provide on your 2009 income tax return. If your reason code begins in the range 05–17, you must complete this section or the application will be returned to you.

E1 Payments for work and services

(a) Payments to you as an employee:

(i) total gross annual salary or wages $ .00

(ii) allowances $ .00

(iii) overtime $ .00

(iv) bonuses $ .00

Do not include reportable fringe benefits amounts. For example, salary sacrifice amounts.

How do you want your bonuses taxed?
☐ Normal tax to be taken out of bonuses
☐ Varied rate to apply to bonuses.

See the notes for this item in the instructions.

(v) commission $ .00

(b) Payment to a company director (director's fees) $ .00

(c) Payment to an office holder $ .00

(d) Return to work payment $ .00

(e) Payment under a labour hire arrangement $ .00

(f) Personal services attributed income $ .00

(g) Specified payment to performing artist $ .00

(h) Payments to religious practitioners $ .00

E2 Australian government pensions and allowances

(a) Pensions $ .00 ☐ Office use only

(b) Education or training payment or other allowance (for example, Newstart, Austudy payments) $ .00

E3 Compensation, sickness or accident payments $ .00

E4 Australian superannuation income and annuities

(a) Australian superannuation income streams (taxed element) $ .00

(b) Australian superannuation income streams (untaxed element) $ .00

(c) Superannuation lump sums (taxed element) $ .00

(d) Superannuation lump sums (untaxed element) $ .00

(e) Australian annuities $ .00

E5 Employment related payments

(a) Employment termination payments (ETP). Attach your *ETP payment summary*, or an estimated summary from your payer, and also include any ETP tax offset at item E13. $ .00

(b) Payment for unused annual leave or unused long service leave. (If this is a termination payment, attach a copy of your final payment summary.) $ .00

For items E6 and E7: Do not include any losses from investments. Include investment income at item E8, E10 or E11, and investment deductions at items F2(a) to F2(c).

E6 Partnership/trust income or partnership loss

If the amount is a loss, write **L** in the **LOSS** box. Attach a separate sheet including the full name of the partnership or trust, the tax file number, the nature of the principal partnership or trust activity (for example, rental property ownership or primary production) and an estimated profit and loss statement for the period 1 July 2008 to 30 June 2009. $ .00 ☐ LOSS

If either of these amounts is a loss, complete section H on the *2009 PAYG ITWV supplement* (NAT 5423) or your application may be returned to you.

E7 Net income or loss from business

To arrive at this amount, you must complete all relevant income and expense items in section G on the *2009 PAYG ITWV supplement* (NAT 5423). If the amount is a loss, write **L** in the **LOSS** box. $ .00 ☐ LOSS

Form 3.6 [2036] *continued*

Section E: **Annual income and tax offsets** – *continued*

E8 Interest $ .00

E9 Gross rent $ .00
If amounts for rent are included, make sure you complete section C.

E10 Dividends
(a) Unfranked amount $ .00
(b) Franked amount $ .00
(c) Franking credit $ .00

E11 Other income
Specify the nature of amounts for other income (including net capital gains). Do not include any amounts for business income or payments covered by a voluntary agreement to withhold. These must be included at item E7 (herein) and item G6, on the *2009 PAYG ITWV supplement* (NAT 5423), respectively.
Specify and attach details.
$ .00

You must complete item E12 if your reason code begins in the range 05–17. If you do not complete this item, your application will be returned to you.

E12 Total income
Calculate by adding all the amounts for items E1 to E11. If the amount is a loss, write **L** in the **LOSS** box. $ .00 LOSS

E13 Tax offsets
For example, employment termination payment tax offset, superannuation income stream offset, dependent spouse without children and zone tax offsets. Do not include the 30% child care tax rebate, franking credits or the 30% private health insurance rebate.
Specify
$ .00

E14 Family tax benefit (FTB)

Do not complete this item if you or your spouse are receiving fortnightly payments from the Family Assistance Office (FAO). If you need help to estimate your FTB entitlement, contact your nearest FAO, visit **www.familyassist.gov.au** or phone **13 61 50**.

(a) Your FTB entitlement $ .00
(b) Number of dependent children

E15 Spouse's taxable income $ .00

E16 Medicare
You can claim an exemption from the Medicare levy only in the following circumstances:

Medicare levy exemption categories	CODE
You are a blind pensioner or you receive the sickness allowance from Centrelink.	A
You are entitled to full free medical treatment for all conditions under Defence Force arrangements or Veterans' Affairs Repatriation Health Card (Gold Card) or repatriation arrangements.	B
You are not an Australian resident for tax purposes.	C
You are a resident of Norfolk Island.	D
You are a member of a diplomatic mission or consular post in Australia – or a member of such a person's family and you are living with them – and you are not an Australian citizen and you do not ordinarily live in Australia.	E

See *TaxPack* for more information on full or half exemption. EXEMPTION CODE
(a) Full exemption: estimated number of days
(b) Half exemption: estimated number of days

Form 3.6 [2036] *continued*

Section F: **Annual deductions**

You can claim deductions for expenses incurred in earning your assessable income, including the following.

F1 Work-related expenses

(a) Motor vehicle $ .00 See *TaxPack* for more information.

(b) Travel expenses $ .00 Travel expenses, for example, costs of overnight accommodation, meals not reimbursed by payer.

(c) Home office $ .00 If the **home office** is used in connection with your income producing activities, but does not constitute a 'place of business', only a proportion of the running expenses can be claimed.

(d) Self-education $ .00

(e) Other $ .00 Specify and attach details.

F2 Investment deductions (excluding expenses related to rental property)

If you are claiming amounts for investment deductions, you must complete the investment details in section D. If the Commissioner's discretion has not been ruled on favourably for you, either in a product or private ruling, you may not be entitled to this deduction.

(a) Investment interest $ .00

(b) Management fees $ .00

(c) Other $ .00 Specify and attach details.

F3 Expenses related to rental property

(a) Interest $ .00 See our publication *Rental properties* (NAT 1729) for more information.

(b) Rates and insurance $ .00 Expenses of a capital or private nature are not deductible.

(c) Agents commission and management fees $ .00

(d) Repairs and maintenance $ .00

(e) Decline in value of depreciating assets $ .00

(f) Capital works $ .00

(g) Other $ .00 Specify and attach details.

F4 Tax losses of earlier income years claimed this income year $ .00

You cannot claim a tax loss from an earlier income year if your taxable income for the year ended 30 June 2008 is more than zero.

Do not include at this item:
- this year's rental loss
- amounts for allowable deferred non-commercial losses (see instructions for completing section H on the *2009 PAYG ITWV supplement*).

F5 Other deductions
Include any donations, tax agent fees, deductible amount of a non-superannuation annuity or foreign pension or annuity. $ .00 Specify and attach details.

You must complete items F6 and F7 if your reason code begins in the range 05–17. If you do not complete these items, your application will be returned to you.

F6 TOTAL DEDUCTIONS $ .00 Calculate by adding deductions at items F1 to F5.

F7 TAXABLE INCOME $ .00 LOSS Calculate by taking your **Total deductions** (item F6) away from your **Total income** (item E12). If the amount is a loss, write **L** in the **LOSS** box.

Taxpayer's declaration

Read and sign the declaration after completing your application. Even though someone else may have helped you complete your application, you are responsible for the information provided and you must sign the declaration.

I declare that:
- All the information I have given on this application, including any attachments, is true and correct.
- I have shown all my income (including net capital gains) for tax purposes for 2008–09.

SIGNATURE (Applicant's original signature only)

Date Day / Month / Year

The tax law imposes heavy penalties for giving false or misleading information.

Privacy
The Tax Office is authorised by taxation laws to collect the information requested on this form. For further information see **Privacy** in the attached instructions.

Attach your completed *2009 PAYG ITWV supplement* (NAT 5423) if required

Send your completed application to:
ITWV
Australian Taxation Office
Locked Bag 1515
UPPER MT GRAVATT QLD 4122

Page 8 **IN-CONFIDENCE — when completed**

Form 3.7 [2954] Add a new business

Australian Government
Australian Business Register
Australian Taxation Office

SHEET 1 OF 2 Initial sheet here

Add a new business account

Use this form if the entity has an ABN and needs to register for, or be eligible to claim:
- goods and services tax (GST)
- fuel tax credits
- pay as you go (PAYG) withholding
- luxury car tax (LCT), or
- wine equalisation tax (WET).

29540408

We will only process this form if you are recorded with us as being authorised to make changes or update details on behalf of the entity.

OTHER WAYS OF ADDING A NEW BUSINESS ACCOUNT

Besides using this form, you can add some new accounts by:
- using an online option
- phoning us
- using your tax agent.

Online options

You can add some business accounts online through the:
- Australian Business Register (if you already have an ABN) at **www.abr.gov.au** or
- business and tax agent portals.

To add a new business account online you need to register for a free digital certificate. For more information go to **www.ato.gov.au/onlineservices**

By phone

Phone **13 28 66** between 8.00am and 6.00pm, Monday to Friday.

To add a new account over the phone, you must be recorded with us as being authorised to make changes or update details on behalf of the entity.

INSTRUCTIONS FOR COMPLETING THIS FORM

- Initial the form where directed.
- Print clearly using a black pen.
- Use BLOCK LETTERS and print one character per box.

S M I T H S T

- Place X in all applicable boxes.

AFTER COMPLETING THE FORM

- Check you have signed and dated the declaration.
- Make a copy for your records.
- Mail your completed form to the address shown on the last page of this form.

MORE INFORMATION

The following products may help you complete this form or be useful to your business:
- *GST for small business* (NAT 3014)
- *Fuel tax credits expanded from 1 July 2008* (NAT 15231).

To obtain a copy of these products:
- order through **www.ato.gov.au**, or
- phone **1300 720 092**.

If you need help completing this form phone **13 28 66** between 8.00am and 6.00pm, Monday to Friday.

Section A: **Entity information** – this section is compulsory

When the term 'entity' is used on this form, it refers to the sole trader, partnership, company, trust, superannuation fund or other type of organisation that is adding a new business account.

1 What is the entity's Australian business number (ABN)?

2 If the entity has a GST or PAYG branch and wants to add a new account to this branch, provide the branch number.

3 What is the entity's legal name as it appears on the Australian Business Register?

Form 3.7 [2954] *continued*

Section B: **Do you want to register for goods and services tax (GST)?**

No ☐ Go to section C **Yes** ☐ Complete this section

Entities cannot register for GST if they are not carrying on an enterprise.

Some entities are required by law to register, while others may choose to voluntarily register for GST.

It is recommended that you read *GST for small business* (NAT 3014) if you are unfamiliar with GST.

4 Is the entity required by law to register for GST?

An entity is required to register if it:
- is carrying on an enterprise and its GST turnover is $75,000 or more ($150,000 or more if the entity is a non-profit organisation)
- supplies taxi or limousine travel for fares
- is a representative of an incapacitated entity (where the incapacitated entity is registered or required to be registered), or
- is a resident agent acting for a non-resident (where the non-resident is registered or required to be registered).

No ☐ **Yes** ☐ Go to question 6

5 If the entity is not required by law to register for GST, is the entity volunteering to register for GST?

An entity that is not required by law to register for GST can choose to register voluntarily if it is carrying on an enterprise or intends to carry on an enterprise in the near future.

No ☐ Go to section D **Yes** ☐

6 What is the entity's date of registration for GST?

If an entity is required by law to register for GST its date of registration is the date that:
- its GST turnover met or exceeded the registration turnover threshold of $75,000 (or $150,000 for non-profit organisations). The turnover threshold is GST exclusive.
- it commenced supplying taxi or limousine travel for fares
- it commenced representation of an incapacitated entity, or
- it commenced in its capacity as a resident agent for a non-resident.

An entity that is voluntarily registering for GST, can choose its date of registration.

Day ☐☐ / Month ☐☐ / Year ☐☐☐☐

If the entity's GST registration is backdated more than 21 days it may be liable for 'failure to register on time' penalties, 'failure to lodge on time' penalties, and general interest charge (GIC) on GST owed.

7 What is the entity's GST turnover?

The entity's GST turnover is the greater of its current and projected GST turnovers.
- Current GST turnover – the value of all supplies made or likely to be made in the current month plus the previous 11 months.
- Projected GST turnover – the value of all supplies made or likely to be made in the current month plus the next 11 months.

(Place X in one box only)

$0 to $74,999 ☐ $75,000 to $149,999 ☐ $150,000 to $1,999,999 ☐ $2 million $19,999,999 ☐

$20 million and over ☐ If your GST turnover is greater than $20 million, you must select 'Monthly' at question 8, register for online services at question 11, and provide an email address at question 12.

8 How often will the entity lodge its activity statements?

If the entity's GST turnover is:
- $20 million or more, it must lodge monthly
- less than $20 million, it can choose to lodge monthly or quarterly, or
- expected to be less than $75,000 (or less than $150,000 for non-profit entities), it can choose to lodge monthly, quarterly or annually (once a year).

An entity that is registering voluntarily can choose to lodge monthly, quarterly or annually.

Taxi and limousine drivers and agents for non-residents must lodge monthly or quarterly.

An entity that elects to report GST annually and has other obligations such as PAYG withholding for employees will still need to report those obligations either monthly or quarterly.

Monthly ☐ Quarterly ☐ Annually ☐

Form 3.7 [2954] *continued*

SHEET 2 OF 2 Initial sheet here

9 Does the entity intend to account for GST on a cash or a non-cash (accruals) basis?

Cash accounting

Accounting for GST on a cash basis means the entity accounts for the GST for its sales when it receives payment for them.

Entities can choose to use a cash basis of accounting for GST purposes if they are properly accounting on a cash basis for income tax purposes or are:

- an endorsed charitable institution
- a trustee of an endorsed charitable fund
- a gift deductible entity, or
- a government school.

Entities can also use a cash basis of accounting for GST if:

- they are a small business entity (refer to **www.ato.gov.au** to determine if you are a small business entity) with an annual turnover (including the turnover of their related entities) of $2 million or less, or
- they are not operating a business, but are carrying on an enterprise with a GST turnover of $2 million or less.

> If you do not meet any of the criteria mentioned above and want to account for GST on a cash basis, phone **13 28 66** between 8.00am and 6.00pm, Monday to Friday.

Non-cash (accruals) accounting

Accounting for GST on a non-cash (accruals) basis means that the entity will account for GST on its sales when it has issued an invoice or received any part of the payment, whichever occurs first.

Cash ☐ Non-cash (accruals) ☐

10 Does the entity import goods or services into Australia?

No ☐ Yes ☐ ▶ For information about deferring GST on imports, phone **1300 130 915** between 8.00am and 6.00pm, Monday to Friday.

11 Does the entity wish to register for access to the Tax Office's online services for business?

Going online is a fast, convenient and secure way to do business with us. We offer a range of online services to make it easier for business.

You can go online to lodge and revise activity statements, perform some superannuation transactions, request payment summary report information, update your ABN details on the Australian Business Register and access the Business Portal.

No ☐ Yes ☐ ▶ You must provide an email address at question 12. We will send you a CD-ROM and more information about your online services registration.

> An entity must register for the Tax Office's online services if:
> - its GST turnover is $20 million or more, as indicated at question 7
> - it is an importer, intending to defer the payment of GST on imported goods, or
> - it wants to maintain its details on the Australian Business Register over the internet.

12 What is the entity's email address?

Use BLOCK LETTERS and print one character per box. Provide only one email address.

IN-CONFIDENCE – when completed

Form 3.7 [2954] *continued*

Section C: **Do you need to register for a fuel tax credits?**

No ☐ Go to section D **Yes** ☐ Complete this section

From 1 July 2008, most fuel used in your business is eligible for fuel tax credits, including fuel used in equipment, tools, machinery and heavy vehicles.

The only exceptions are:

- fuel used in vehicles of 4.5 tonne gross vehicle mass (GVM) or less travelling on a public road (for example, passenger cars, small delivery vans, or utes), and
- alternative fuels.

For information about fuel tax credits:
- visit **www.ato.gov.au**, or
- phone **13 28 66** between 8.00am and 6.00pm, Monday to Friday.

To register for fuel tax credits, the entity must also be registered for GST.

13 From what date is the entity eligible for fuel tax credits?

This date cannot be before the entity's GST registration date or 1 July 2006 (when fuel tax credits commenced).

Day Month Year

☐☐ / ☐☐ / ☐☐☐☐

14 Which fuel does the entity use in its business activities?

(Place X in all applicable boxes)

Diesel ☐ Petrol ☐ Other ☐

15 Does the entity use fuel in a vehicle with a GVM greater than 4.5 tonnes travelling on a public road?

No ☐

Yes ☐

Form 3.7 [2954] *continued*

Section D: **Do you need to register for pay as you go (PAYG) withholding?**

No ☐ ▸ Go to section E **Yes** ☐ ▸ Complete this section

Register for PAYG withholding if the entity is required to withhold amounts from payments it makes to payees, such as:

- employees (salary and wages)
- contractors or sub-contractors under a voluntary agreement, or
- labour hire workers.

The entity will also need to register if it is required to withhold an amount from payments:

- to suppliers who have not provided an ABN
- of investment income to Australian residents, or
- of royalties, dividends, interest or fund payments to non-residents.

16 Is the entity required by law to register for PAYG withholding?

No ☐ ▸ Go to section E **Yes** ☐ ▸ When will withholding commence? Day ☐☐ / Month ☐☐ / Year ☐☐☐☐

If the entity's PAYG withholding registration is backdated it may be liable for general interest charge (GIC) on amounts withheld.

17 How many employees does the entity estimate it will pay? ☐☐☐☐,☐☐☐

Do not include people under a voluntary agreement or labour hire arrangement in your estimate.

18 What amount does the entity expect to withhold from payments to its payees each year?

This is the estimated annual withholding amount and it is used to determine how often the entity will pay withholding amounts to us.

Where the withholding amount is expected to be:

- less than or equal to $25,000, the entity will be required to pay quarterly
- between $25,001 and $1,000,000, the entity will be required to pay monthly, or
- greater than $1,000,000, the entity will be required to pay more frequently. (If the entity falls in this group we will send more information.)

$ ☐☐☐,☐☐☐,☐☐☐.✕✕

19 How will the entity provide its PAYG withholding payment summary annual report to the Tax Office?

Entities that have made withholding payments have to lodge an annual report with us at the end of each year. There are different annual reports for different payments. Entities that have employees and other workers will need to lodge a PAYG withholding payment summary annual report.

This annual report can be lodged electronically, or by paper using forms we supply.

Indicate the method you plan to use to lodge the entity's PAYG payment summary annual report.

Paper form supplied by the Tax Office ☐ ▸ Go to question 21 Electronically ☐

20 How will the entity provide payment summaries to its payees?

Print its own payment summaries ☐ Use payment summaries supplied by the Tax Office ☐

21 Will the entity pay royalties, dividends, interest or fund payments to non-residents, or are you an investment body that will pay investment income to Australian residents? No ☐ Yes ☐

Investment income includes interest and dividends.

A 'fund payment' is a defined term in tax law and is a payment generally made by managed investment trusts.

IN-CONFIDENCE – when completed

Form 3.7 [2954] *continued*

22 What is the main industry that the entity operates in? (Place X in one box only)

Agriculture	Construction	Financial and insurance services	Health care and social assistance
Forestry	Wholesale trade	Rental, hiring and real estate services	Arts and recreation services
Fishing (including aquaculture)	Retail trade	Professional, scientific and technical services	Other services
Mining	Accommodation and food services	Administrative and support services	
Manufacturing	Transport, postal and warehousing	Public administration and safety	
Electricity, gas, water and waste	Information media and telecommunications	Education and training	

23 Describe the main activity from which the entity derives the majority of its business income.
Also describe the main goods produced or the main services provided by the entity.

Section E: **Do you need to register for luxury car tax (LCT)?**

No ▶ Go to section F   Yes ▶ Complete this section

The entity must register for luxury car tax if it intends to sell luxury cars. A luxury car is a car with a retail price, including GST, that exceeds the luxury car tax threshold.

This threshold is the car depreciation limit for income tax purposes. To find out about the current car depreciation limit contact us or visit **www.ato.gov.au**

If your LCT registration is backdated you may be liable for general interest charge (GIC) on LCT owed.

The entity must also be registered for GST to register for a luxury car tax account.

24 From what date did, or will, the entity become involved in manufacturing, wholesaling, importing or retailing luxury cars? Day / Month / Year

25 Which of the following best describes the entity's activity in the luxury car industry?

Manufacturer   Wholesaler   Importer   Retailer

26 What percentage of the entity's total activity do the following activities represent?

Manufacturing %   Wholesaling %   Importing %   Retailing %

27 What is the entity's estimated annual luxury car tax liability? (Place X in one box only)

$0 to $49,999 $50,000 to $99,999 $100,000 to $499,999 $500,000 to $5 million   More than $5 million

28 Does the entity expect to have a luxury car tax liability on every activity statement? No   Yes

IN-CONFIDENCE – when completed

Form 3.7 [2954] *continued*

Section F: **Do you need to register for wine equalisation tax (WET)?**

No ☐ Go to section G **Yes** ☐ Complete this section

The entity will need to register for wine equalisation tax (WET) if it manufactures, wholesales, imports or exports wine.
This tax applies to the following alcoholic beverages:

- grape wine
- grape wine products such as marsala, vermouth, wine cocktails and creams
- other fruit wines and vegetable wines
- cider and perry, and
- mead and sake.

If your WET registration is backdated you may be liable for general interest charge (GIC) on WET owed.

The entity must also be registered for GST to register for a wine equalisation tax account.

29 On what date did, or will, the entity become involved in manufacturing, wholesaling, importing or exporting alcoholic beverages?

Day / Month / Year

30 Which of the following best describes the entity's activity in the alcoholic beverages industry?

Manufacturer ☐ Wholesaler ☐ Importer ☐ Exporter ☐ Indirect marketer retailer ☐

31 What percentage of the entity's total turnover do the following products represent?

Wine % Beer % Spirits % Other alcoholic beverages %

Section G: **Financial account details**

Only complete this section if the entity has not provided these details previously. If you do not provide these details we cannot refund money owed. If you do not need to complete this section, go to section H.

32 What are the entity's financial institution account details for Tax Office refunds?

Refunds will only be paid directly into a recognised financial institution account located in Australia.
The account details provided must be held by:

- the entity (solely or jointly)
- the entity's registered tax agent, or
- a legal practitioner acting as trustee or executor for the entity.

BSB number (must be 6 digits) Account number

Full account name – for example, JQ Citizen. Do not show the account type, such as cheque, savings, mortgage offset.

Is the account held by:

the entity ☐

the entity jointly with others ☐

a tax agent for the entity ☐

a legal practitioner as trustee or executor for the entity ☐

If the account you wish to nominate for refunds is not one of the four complying account options presented above, you can request the Commissioner of Taxation to exercise his discretion to pay electronic funds into the account of a third party. For more information phone **13 28 66** between 8.00am and 6.00pm, Monday to Friday.

IN-CONFIDENCE – when completed

Form 3.7 [2954] *continued*

Section H: **Declaration** – this section is compulsory and must be completed by an individual authorised by the entity

Before you sign this form
Check that you have provided accurate and complete information.

Penalties
Penalties may be imposed for giving false or misleading information.

Privacy
The collection of information on this form is authorised by taxation laws, including the *A New Tax System (Australian Business Number) Act 1999*, for the administration of those laws. Some of the information collected will be used to update the entity's details on the Australian Business Register (ABR). Selected information may be made publicly available and some may be passed to other government agencies, including Commonwealth, state, territory and local agencies, authorised by law to receive it.

You can find details of the government agencies regularly receiving information from the Australian Business Register at **www.abr.gov.au**. You can also phone us on **13 28 66** between 8.00am and 6.00pm, Monday to Friday and have a list of agencies sent to you.

Name of signatory

Position held (for example, director, tax agent, trustee or partner)

Business hours phone number

I declare that:

- *I am authorised to make this application on behalf of the entity whose ABN appears on this form, and*
- *that the information given on this form is accurate and complete.*

Only a person on our records as having authority to make changes or update registration details on behalf of the entity can sign this declaration.

Signature

Day / Month / Year

How to lodge this form

Send your completed application to:
Australian Taxation Office
PO Box 3373
PENRITH NSW 2740

Make a copy of this application for your own records before you mail it.

Form 3.8 [46] PAYG payment summary—individual non-business

Australian Government
Australian Taxation Office

PAYG payment summary – individual non-business

00460208

Both sections of this form must be completed. For help, refer to *How to complete the PAYG payment summary – individual non-business form* (NAT 3388).

Are you **amending a payment summary** you have already sent? If so, place X in this box. ☐

Payment summary for year ending 30 June ☐☐☐☐

Section A: **Payee details and payments**

Payee's surname or family name

Payee's given name/s

Payee's residential address

Suburb/town/locality | State/territory | Postcode

Date of birth (if known) Day / Month / Year

Period during which payments were made Day / Month / Year to Day / Month / Year

Payee's tax file number

TOTAL TAX WITHHELD $, , .XX

GROSS PAYMENTS (do not include amounts shown under 'Allowances', 'Lump sum payments', 'CDEP payments' and 'Other income')	$, , .XX	Lump sum A	$, , .XX
Community Development Employment Projects (CDEP) payments	$, , .XX	Lump sum B	$, , .XX
Other income (eg exempt income or foreign source salary and wages)	$, , .XX	Lump sum D	$, , .XX
Reportable fringe benefits amount FBT year 1 April to 31 March	$, , .XX	Lump sum E	$, , .XX

Allowances (provide details) — Amount

$, , .XX
$, , .XX
$, , .XX
$, , .XX

Total allowances $, , .XX

Union/Professional association fees – Name of organisation — Amount

$, .XX
$, .XX

Workplace giving etc – Name of organisation

$, .XX

Tax Office original

Section B: **Payer details**

! You **must** also complete this section

Payer's Australian business number (ABN) or withholding payer number (WPN) — Branch number

Payer's name (use the same name that appears on your activity statement)

DECLARATION – *I declare that the information given on this form is complete and correct.*

Signature of authorised person

Date Day / Month / Year

NAT 0046-02.2008

Sample only

Form 3.9 [3223] PAYG payment summary—voluntary agreement

Australian Government
Australian Taxation Office

PAYG payment summary – voluntary agreement

32230606

Tax Office copy
Send this copy to the Tax Office

About this form

This form is used to provide details of amounts withheld from payments made under a voluntary agreement.

Print clearly in BLOCK LETTERS using a black pen.

Do not use rubber stamps to show payer details.

You can report the information on this form electronically.

Payment summary for year ending 30 June ☐☐☐☐

Payer details

Your Australian business number (ABN) or withholding payer number ☐☐ ☐☐☐ ☐☐☐ ☐☐☐ **Branch number** ☐☐☐

Payer's name

Payee details

Payee's Australian business number

Payee's date of birth (optional) Day / Month / Year

Full name of payee

Surname or family name

Given name

Other given name/s

Payee's address

Street number and name

Suburb/town

State/territory

Postal code

Country, if other than Australia

Payment details

Period during which payments were made Day / Month / Year to Day / Month / Year

Total tax withheld (whole dollars)
$ ☐☐☐,☐☐☐,☐☐☐ .00

Total tax withheld (whole dollars only in words)
Millions Thousands Hundreds Tens Units

Gross payments (whole dollars)
(including the market value of non-cash benefits)
$ ☐☐☐,☐☐☐,☐☐☐ .00

Withholding rate
☐☐☐.☐☐ %

Declaration

I declare that the information given on this form is complete and correct.

Signature

Date Day / Month / Year

NAT 3223-06.2006

IN-CONFIDENCE — when completed

Form 3.10 [3447] PAYG payment summary statement

Australian Government
Australian Taxation Office

PAYG payment summary statement

34470707

WHAT THIS FORM IS FOR

This form is part of the annual report that must be lodged by pay as you go withholding payers, when they choose to report on paper.

This form should only be completed for the 2008 financial year or later.

Please see over for how to complete this form.

Print clearly in BLOCK LETTERS with a black pen only. Do not use rubber stamps to show payer details.

Complete and send this form to us by **14 August** with the **Tax Office originals** of the payment summaries issued. Do not use this form if you report using electronic media.

If your business is located in NSW, ACT, QLD or NT:	If your business is located in VIC, SA, WA or TAS:
Australian Taxation Office Locked Bag 50 PENRITH NSW 2740	Australian Taxation Office Locked Bag 6007 ALBURY NSW 2640

If this is an **AMENDED *PAYG payment summary statement*** please place X in this box ☐

Statement for year ending 30 June

Payer details — **Payer's ABN or withholding payer number** — **Branch number**

Payer's name

Payer's address

Street number and street name

Suburb, town or locality — State — Postcode

Contact name — **Contact phone number**

Payment summaries issued

Payment summary type	Total number of payment summaries issued	Total of gross payments or taxable components (whole dollars)	Total of amounts of tax withheld (whole dollars)
Individual non-business (includes salaries or wages paid to employees)		$	$
Employment termination payment		$	$
Superannuation lump sum		$	$
Superannuation income stream		$	$
Business and personal services income		$	$

Payment summaries you have issued for **voluntary agreements, labour hire and other specified payments**, and **personal services attributed income** should be included at 'Business and personal services income'.

Declaration I declare that the information given on this form is complete and correct.

Signature

Date Day / Month / Year

Photocopy this form. You will need to keep a copy of this completed form, together with the **PAYG payer's copy** of the payment summaries issued, for your records.

NAT 3447-07.2007

Form 5.1 [1067] FBT return

Australian Government
Australian Taxation Office

Fringe benefits tax (FBT) return 2008

1 April 2007 to 31 March 2008

10670208

WHEN COMPLETING THIS RETURN

For help with completing this return refer to *How to complete your 2008 fringe benefits tax return* (NAT 2376).

- Print clearly using a black pen only.
- Use BLOCK LETTERS and print one character in each box. S M I T H S T
- Place X in ALL relevant boxes.

Business details

1 Tax file number (TFN)

It is not an offence not to quote your TFN but not quoting it may increase the risk of administrative error and/or delay this return. If you do not have a TFN, refer to *How to complete your 2008 fringe benefits tax return* (NAT 2376) for more information.

2 Australian business number (ABN) (if applicable)

3 Name of trustee or senior partner

INDIVIDUAL

Title: Mr Mrs Miss Ms Other

Surname or family name

Given name/s

OR

NON-INDIVIDUAL (company, partnership, trust etc)

Name of corporate trustee/senior partner

4 Name of employer

INDIVIDUAL

Title: Mr Mrs Miss Ms Other

Surname or family name

Given name/s

OR

NON-INDIVIDUAL (company, partnership, trust etc)

5 Postal address

Suburb/town/locality

State/territory (Australia only)

Postcode (Australia only)

Country if outside Australia

NAT 1067-02.2008

IN-CONFIDENCE – when completed

Page 1

Form 5.1 [1067] ***continued***

9 **Name of the person to contact**

Provide the name, daytime contact phone number and email address (if applicable) of the person we can contact, if needed, regarding the information in this return.

Title: Mr Mrs Miss Ms Other

Surname or family name

Given name/s

Daytime contact phone number

Email address (please use BLOCK LETTERS)

10 **Number of employees receiving fringe benefits during the period 1 April 2007 to 31 March 2008**

11 **Hours taken to prepare and complete this form**

Refer to *How to complete your 2008 fringe benefits tax return* (NAT 2376) for more information. Do not include tax agent's time. hours

12 **Do you expect to lodge an FBT return for 2008–09 or future years?** No Yes

Return calculation details

Refer to *How to complete your 2008 fringe benefits tax return* (NAT 2376) for more information.

13 **Calculated fringe benefits taxable amounts** (whole dollars only)

A Type 1 aggregate amount $ x 2.0647 = $ A

B Type 2 aggregate amount $ x 1.8692 = $ B

C Aggregate non-exempt amount (hospitals, ambulances, public benevolent institutions and health promotion charities only) or $ C

14 **Fringe benefits taxable amount** *(A + B)* or *C* $

15 **Amount of tax payable** (46.5% of item 14 amount) $

If you are not a rebatable employer, **go to question 18 Sub-total.**

16 **Aggregate non-rebatable amount** $

Refer to *How to complete your 2008 fringe benefits tax return* (NAT 2376) for more information.

17 **Amount of rebate: 48% of** (item 15 amount less item 16 amount) $

18 **Sub-total** (item 15 amount less item 17 amount) $

19 **Less instalment amounts reported on activity statements** $

Refer to *How to complete your 2008 fringe benefits tax return* (NAT 2376) for more information.

20 **Payment due** Send this amount with your payment advice $

or

21 **Credit due to you** $

IN-CONFIDENCE – when completed

Form 5.1 [1067] *continued*

22 Details of fringe benefits provided

Type of benefits provided (1 April 2007 to 31 March 2008)		Number	WHOLE DOLLARS ONLY Gross taxable value (a)	Employee contribution (b)	Value of reductions (c)	Taxable value of benefits (a) – (b) – (c)
Cars using the statutory formula	A					
Cars using the operating cost method	B					
Loans granted	C					
Debt waiver	D					
Expense payments	E					
Housing – units of accommodation provided	F					
Employees receiving living-away-from-home allowance (show total paid including exempt components)	G					
Airline transport (airlines and travel agents only)	H					
Board	J					
Property	K					
Income tax exempt body – entertainment	L					
Other benefits (residual)	M					
Car parking	N					
Meal entertainment	P					

Declarations

Before you sign this form
Please check that you have provided accurate and complete information.

Penalties
Please be aware that penalties may be imposed for giving false or misleading information.

Privacy
The Australian Taxation Office is authorised by the *Fringe Benefits Tax (Assessment) Act 1986* and the *Taxation Administration Act 1953* to ask for information on this return. We need this information to help us to administer the taxation laws. We may give this information to other government agencies authorised in taxation law – for example, the Australian Bureau of Statistics and the Reserve Bank of Australia.

23 Tax agent's declaration

I declare that this return has been prepared in accordance with information supplied by my client, that my client has given me a declaration stating that the information provided to me is true and correct and that my client has authorised me to lodge the return.

Name of tax agent

Tax agent registration number

Signature of tax agent*

Date Day / Month / Year

* Where the tax agent is a partnership or a company, this declaration must be signed in the name of the partnership or company by a person who is registered as a nominee of that partnership or company.

24 Employer's declaration – where the employer lodges the return

I declare that the information in this return is true and correct.

Name of employer

Signature of employer*

Date Day / Month / Year

* Proprietor, partner, public officer, trustee or, for government departments and authorities, the delegated officer.

This return will not be regarded as having been lodged unless the appropriate declaration has been signed by the tax agent or the employer.

Page 4 **IN-CONFIDENCE – when completed**

Statement of account for FBT

The Statement of account for FBT generated from Integrated Core Processing (ICP), has a new format.
This will only be for FBT accounts and commenced on April 1, 2008.
Transactions processed on the account prior to this date are rolled into the Statement opening balance.

The Statement of account is divided into sections (pages).
The coloured boxes below show the contents of each page and how the information appears.
Select a box to view a page in more detail.

Instructions

Select the red boxes to reveal more details about the Statement of account

Format of Statement of account for FBT

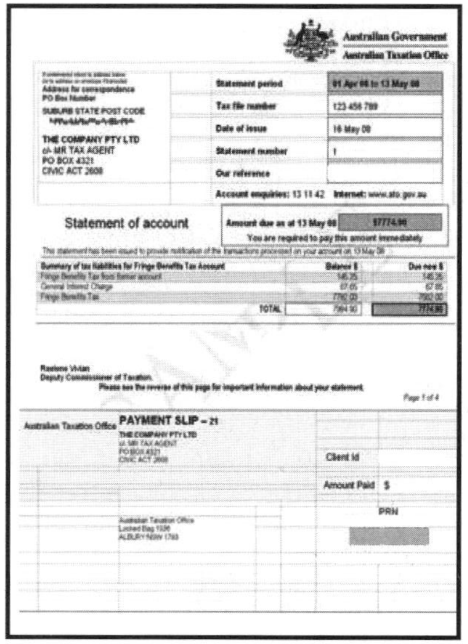

Page 1of 4

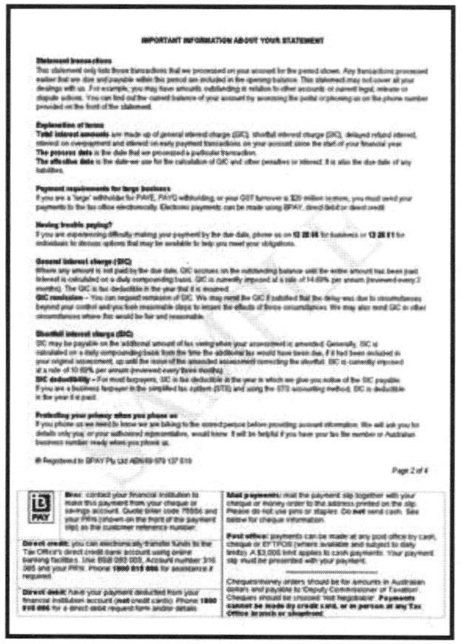

Page 2 of 4

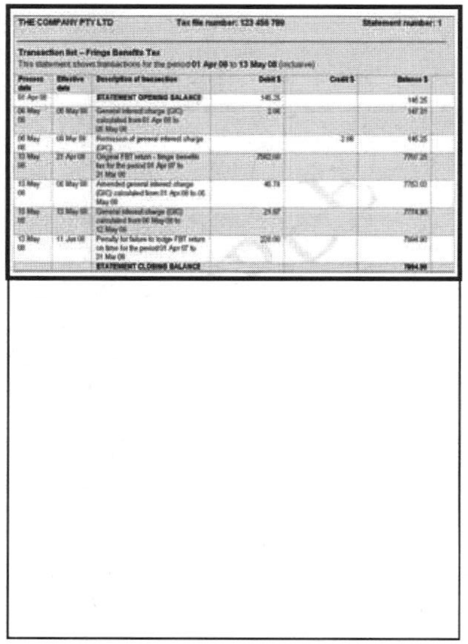

Page 3 of 4

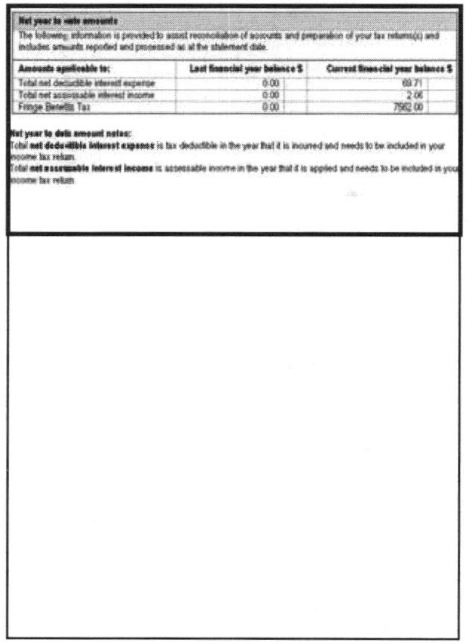

Page 4 of 4

NEXT

Form 6.1 [4203] BAS general worksheet

GST calculation worksheet for BAS

(If you want to use the calculation sheet method to work out GST amounts)

Tax period

Name

Do not lodge the calculation sheet with your BAS

We recommend you file it with a copy of the BAS to which it relates

Show amounts at these labels on your BAS

GST amounts you owe the Tax Office from sales

				Show on BAS
G1	Total sales (including any GST)		G1 $	G1 on the BAS
G2	Export sales	G2 $		G2 on the BAS
G3	Other GST-free sales	G3 $		G3 on the BAS
G4	Input taxed sales	G4 $		
G5	G2 + G3 + G4		G5 $	
G6	Total sales subject to GST (G1 minus G5)		G6 $	
G7	Adjustments (if applicable)		G7 $	
G8	Total sales subject to GST after adjustments (G6 + G7)		G8 $	
G9	GST on sales (G8 divided by eleven)		G9 $	1A in the Summary section of the BAS

GST amounts the Tax Office owes you from purchases

				Show on BAS
G10	Capital purchases (including any GST)	G10 $		G10 on the BAS
G11	Non-capital purchases (including any GST)	G11 $		G11 on the BAS
G12	G10 + G11		G12 $	
G13	Purchases for making input taxed sales	G13 $		
G14	Purchases without GST in the price	G14 $		
G15	Estimated purchases for private use or not income tax deductible	G15 $		
G16	G13 + G14 + G15		G16 $	
G17	Total purchases subject to GST (G12 minus G16)		G17 $	
G18	Adjustments (if applicable)		G18 $	
G19	Total purchases subject to GST after adjustments (G17 + G18)		G19 $	
G20	GST on purchases (G19 divided by eleven)		G20 $	1B in the Summary section of the BAS

Now go to the GST section on the front of the BAS and follow the instructions on the form. You will need to transfer amounts from this calculation sheet to the BAS.

NAT 4203-4.2004

Form 6.2 [4195] BAS summary report

C

Office use only

41950404

Business activity statement

Document ID

ABN

Form due on

Payment due on

GST accounting method

Contact phone number

Contact person who completed the form

When completing this form, please
- use a BLACK pen only (to help with processing)
- leave boxes blank if not applicable (do not use N/A, NIL)
- show whole dollars only (do not show cents)
- do not use symbols such as +, –, /, $

Goods and services tax (GST)

Complete Option 1 OR 2 OR 3 (indicate one choice with an X)

Option 1: Calculate GST and report quarterly

Total sales	G1	$ .00
Does the amount shown at G1 include GST? (indicate with **X**)		Yes / No
Export sales	G2	$ .00
Other GST-free sales	G3	$ .00
Capital purchases	G10	$ .00
Non-capital purchases	G11	$ .00

Report GST on sales at 1A and GST on purchases at 1B in the Summary section over the page and then complete the other sections

OR

Option 2: Calculate GST quarterly and report annually

Total sales	G1	$ .00
Does the amount shown at G1 include GST? (indicate with **X**)		Yes / No

Report GST on sales at 1A and GST on purchases at 1B in the Summary section over the page and then complete the other sections

OR

Option 3: Pay GST instalment amount quarterly

	G21	$

Write this amount at 1A in the Summary section over the page (leave 1B blank)

OR if varying this amount, complete G22, G23, G24

Estimated net GST for the year	G22	$ .00
Varied amount for the quarter	G23	$ .00

Write the G23 amount at 1A in the Summary section over the page and then complete the other sections (leave 1B blank)

Reason code for variation	G24

PAYG tax withheld

Total salary, wages and other payments	W1	$ .00
Amount withheld from payments shown at W1	W2	$ .00
Amount withheld where no ABN is quoted	W4	$ .00
Other amounts withheld (excluding any amount shown at W2 or W4)	W3	$ .00
Total amounts withheld (W2 + W4 + W3)	W5	$ .00

Write the W5 amount at 4 in the Summary section over the page and then complete the other sections

NAT 4195-4.2004

How to pay

BPAY: contact your bank, credit union or building society to make this payment from your cheque or savings account. Quote biller code **75556** and your EFT code (shown on the other side of this payment slip) as the customer reference number.

Direct credit: transfer funds directly to the Tax Office using computer based banking software.

Direct debit: have your payment deducted from your nominated bank account (excluding credit cards).

Mail payments: mail this payment slip together with your cheque / money order using the envelope provided. Please do not use pins or staples. Do NOT send cash.

Post Office: payments can be made at any Post Office by cash, cheque or EFTPOS (subject to daily limits). A $3,000 cash limit applies. Your payment slip must be presented with your payment.

- Cheques/money orders should be made payable to the 'Deputy Commissioner of Taxation' and crossed 'Not Negotiable'.
- All cheques must be tendered in Australian currency.

Payments cannot be made by credit card or in person at any Tax Office branch or shopfront.

Form 6.2 [4195] *continued*

PAYG income tax instalment

Only complete Option 1 OR 2 (indicate one choice with **X**)

☐ **Option 1: Pay a PAYG instalment amount quarterly**

T7 $ ______

Write the T7 amount at 5A in the Summary section
OR if varying this amount, complete T8, T9, T4

Estimated tax for the year **T8** $ ☐☐☐☐☐☐☐☐☐ .00

Varied amount for the quarter **T9** $ ☐☐☐☐☐☐☐☐☐ .00

Write the T9 amount at 5A in the Summary section

Reason code for variation **T4** ☐☐

OR

☐ **Option 2: Calculate PAYG instalment using income times rate**

PAYG instalment income **T1** $ ☐☐☐☐☐☐☐☐☐ .00

T2 ______ %

OR
New varied rate **T3** ☐☐☐.☐☐ %

T1 x T2 (or x T3) **T11** $ ☐☐☐☐☐☐☐☐☐ .00

Write the T11 amount at 5A in the Summary section

Reason code for variation **T4** ☐☐

Fringe benefits tax (FBT) instalment

F1 $ ______

Write the F1 amount at 6A in the Summary section
OR if varying this amount, complete F2, F3, F4

Estimated FBT for the year **F2** $ ☐☐☐☐☐☐☐☐☐ .00

Varied amount for the quarter **F3** $ ☐☐☐☐☐☐☐☐☐ .00

Write the F3 amount at 6A in the Summary section

Reason code for variation **F4** ☐☐

Summary

If you are using GST Option 3 leave 1B, 1C, 1D, 1E, 1F blank

Amounts you owe the Tax Office

GST on sales or GST instalment	**1A**	$ ☐☐☐☐☐☐☐☐☐ .00
Wine equalisation tax	**1C**	$ ☐☐☐☐☐☐☐☐☐ .00
Luxury car tax	**1E**	$ ☐☐☐☐☐☐☐☐☐ .00
PAYG tax withheld	**4**	$ ☐☐☐☐☐☐☐☐☐ .00
PAYG income tax instalment	**5A**	$ ☐☐☐☐☐☐☐☐☐ .00
FBT instalment	**6A**	$ ☐☐☐☐☐☐☐☐☐ .00
Deferred company/fund instalment	**7**	$ ☐☐☐☐☐☐☐☐☐ .00
1A + 1C + 1E + 4 + 5A + 6A + 7	**8A**	$ ☐☐☐☐☐☐☐☐☐ .00

Amounts the Tax Office owes you

GST on purchases	**1B**	$ ☐☐☐☐☐☐☐☐☐ .00
Wine equalisation tax refundable	**1D**	$ ☐☐☐☐☐☐☐☐☐ .00
Luxury car tax refundable	**1F**	$ ☐☐☐☐☐☐☐☐☐ .00
Credit from PAYG income tax instalment variation	**5B**	$ ☐☐☐☐☐☐☐☐☐ .00
Credit from FBT instalment variation	**6B**	$ ☐☐☐☐☐☐☐☐☐ .00
1B + 1D + 1F + 5B + 6B	**8B**	$ ☐☐☐☐☐☐☐☐☐ .00

Payment or refund?

Is 8A more than 8B? (indicate with **X**)

☐ Yes, then write the result of **8A minus 8B** at 9. **This amount is payable to the Tax Office.**

☐ No, then write the result of **8B minus 8A** at 9. **This amount is refundable to you** (or offset against any other tax debt you have).

Your payment or refund amount

9 $ ☐☐☐☐☐☐☐☐☐ .00

Do not use symbols such as +, –, /, $

Declaration I declare that the information given on this form is true and correct, and that I am authorised to make this declaration. The tax invoice requirements have been met.

Signature   Date   /   /

Please return this completed form to

HRS ☐☐ MINS ☐☐
Please estimate the time taken to complete this form. Include the time taken to collect any information.

Activity statement instructions are available from **www.ato.gov.au** or can be ordered by phoning **13 28 66**. The Tax Office is authorised by the tax laws to collect this information to administer those laws and may pass information to other government agencies. More information about privacy and access to your tax information is available from **www.ato.gov.au**

Australian Government
Australian Taxation Office

Form 7.1 [9599] Superannuation guarantee

Australian Government
Australian Taxation Office

Superannuation guarantee charge statement – quarterly

HOR 27

OFFICE USE ONLY

Amount received $

Date received Day / Month / Year

Before filling in this statement, please read *How to complete the Superannuation guarantee charge statement – quarterly* (NAT 9600).

- The instructions include examples and calculation worksheets to help you to complete this statement. Instructions and statements are available at **www.ato.gov.au/super** or by phoning our information line on **13 10 20**.
- Cheques should be made payable to the 'Deputy Commissioner of Taxation' and crossed 'Not Negotiable'.

Section A: **Employer details**

For use for any quarter starting on or after 1 July 2003. A separate statement must be used for each quarter.

1 This statement is for the quarter ended Day / Month / Year

Quarter	*Period covered*	*Quarter*	*Period covered*
1	1 July to **30 September**	3	1 January to **31 March**
2	1 October to **31 December**	4	1 April to **30 June**

2 Employer's tax file number (TFN)

The Tax Office is authorised by the *Taxation Administration Act 1953* to request your TFN. You do not have to quote your TFN, however not providing it may lead to delays in processing your statement.

3 Employer's Australian business number (ABN)

4 Employer's full legal business name (See page 10 of the instructions)

5 Employer's trading name (If applicable)

6 Employer's postal address for service of superannuation guarantee (SG) notices

Suburb/town State/territory Postcode

7 Employer's main business address (This must be a street address, **not** a post office box)

Suburb/town State/territory Postcode

8 Authorised contact name and phone numbers

Authorised contact name

Telephone number Mobile number Facsimile number

Do not send this statement and payment to a superannuation fund. This statement and payment **MUST** be sent to the address below:

Australian Taxation Office
PO Box 277
WORLD TRADE CENTRE VIC 8005

The tax law imposes heavy penalties for giving false or misleading information.

Privacy

The Tax Office is authorised by the *Superannuation Guarantee (Administration) Act 1992* to collect the information in this form. The information is needed to determine your superannuation guarantee obligations. These obligations include your choice of superannuation fund obligations. The employer name and the amount of an individual employee's individual shortfall provided on the form may be disclosed to that employee. We are very careful to protect your privacy. More details about privacy are in the free brochure *Safeguarding your privacy*, available at any Tax Office.

NAT9599-01.2006 **IN-CONFIDENCE – when completed**

Form 7.1 [9599] *continued*

Section B: **Employee details**

EMPLOYEE ONE

9 Employee's TFN

10 Employee's full name

Title: Mr Mrs Miss Ms Other

Family name

First given name

Other given name

11 Employee's date of birth Day / Month / Year

12 Employee's postal address

Suburb/town State/territory Postcode

For information about questions 13 to 15, see page 11 of the instructions. For help to complete these questions, go to pages 14 to 20 for examples and a blank calculation worksheet.

13 Employee's SG shortfall (excluding choice) **H** $, .

14 Your choice liability for this employee (If this does not apply for this employee, write '0'.)

Do not show more than $500 in this box as the choice liability for each employee is capped at $500 per notice period. See page 3 of the instructions for more information. The Tax Office may reduce this liability in some circumstances.

I $.

15 Employee's subtotal (H + I) **J** $, .

16 Employee's nominated fund details (See page 11 of the instructions)

Fund name

Fund's ABN

Fund's SPIN

Employee's member number

Fund's SFN

Obtain this information from your employee or the superannuation fund.

Section C: **Offset for late payment**

To determine if you are eligible, see Part 4, page 21, of the instructions. For more information on how to complete this section see page 11 and the calculation sheet on page 24.

17 Do you want to claim an offset amount for this employee?

No ▸ Go to next employee

Yes ▸ Complete questions 18 and 19

18 Your late payment election amount
(See page 11 of the instructions) **N** $, .

This amount cannot be greater than the sum of the late contributions paid for the employee.

19 Your offset amount
(See page 12 of the instructions) **S** $, .

This amount cannot be greater than the late payment amount (label N) claimed for the employee nor greater than the total of the employee's subtotal (label J) plus nominal interest (label Q from the calculation worksheet on page 24 of the instructions).

Page 2 **IN-CONFIDENCE – when completed**

Form 7.1 [9599] ***continued***

Section D: **Employee details totals** (for all employees included in this statement)

See page 12 of the instructions.

20 Number of employees included in this statement ☐☐☐☐

21 Total SG shortfalls (excluding choice) for the quarter H $☐☐☐,☐☐☐.☐☐

22 Total choice liabilities for the quarter + I $☐☐☐,☐☐☐.☐☐

23 Subtotal for the quarter (H + I) = J $☐☐☐,☐☐☐.☐☐
This will be referred to as 'Total individual shortfalls' on any notice of assessment you may receive.

24 Nominal interest component + K $☐☐☐,☐☐☐.☐☐
(See page 12 of the instructions)

25 Administration component ($20 for each employee recorded in this statement) + L $☐☐☐,☐☐☐.☐☐
(See page 12 of the instructions)

26 Superannuation guarantee charge for the quarter (J + K + L) = M $☐☐☐,☐☐☐.☐☐
This is the superannuation guarantee charge you send to us with this statement, when you have not elected any late payment offsets. Go to section F.
If you have filled in questions 18 and 19 in section C, complete section E below.

Section E: **Late payment offset totals**

To determine if you are eligible, see Part 4, page 21, of the instructions. For more information on how to complete this section see page 12 of the instructions.

I understand that by making this election for a late payment offset:

- I will not be able to withdraw the election nor change the late contribution election amount
- late contributions used to offset part of the superannuation guarantee charge remain non-tax deductible for income tax purposes, and
- any offset amount cannot be used as a prepayment for current or future contributions.

27 Number of employees included in the late payment offset questions in section C ☐☐☐☐

28 Total late payment amount N $☐☐☐,☐☐☐.☐☐
Total of all amounts recorded at question 18 for each employee
(See page 13 of the instructions)

29 Total offset amount S $☐☐☐,☐☐☐.☐☐
Total of all amounts recorded at question 19 for each employee
(See page 13 of the instructions)

30 Total superannuation guarantee charge payable (M – S) T $☐☐☐,☐☐☐.☐☐
This is the superannuation guarantee charge you send to us with this statement when you have elected a late payment offset.

Form 7.1 [9599] *continued*

Section F: **Employer's declaration**

I declare that the particulars shown in Sections A, B, C, D & E of this statement and the relevant records used to determine the superannuation guarantee charge, as shown, are correct.

The tax law imposes heavy penalties for giving false or misleading information.

See page 13 of the instructions for details on who may sign this declaration.

Details of person making this declaration

Print name

Telephone number

Facsimile number

Signature

Date Day Month Year

If you have less than 20 employees, please provide an estimate of the time taken to complete this statement. HRS MINS

Section G: **Agent's declaration**

Having charged a fee directly or indirectly for preparing or assisting in the preparation of this statement, I hereby certify that this statement has been prepared in accordance with the information supplied by the employer.

Print name

Tax agent registration number

Signature

Date Day Month Year

Agent's authorised contact person

Print name

Telephone number

Facsimile number

IN-CONFIDENCE – when completed

Australian Taxation Office

Payment slip – 27

You must complete this payment slip if you are attaching a cheque. Enclose your cheque with this statement, please do not staple or pin the cheque to the statement.

Superannuation guarantee quarterly statement

For the quarter ended Day / Month / Year

Australian business number (ABN)

Full legal name of employer

Amount $

Tax file number

Office use only

27

HOR

Form 7.2 [2476] Lost super enquiry

Instructions and form for **super account holders** Individuals

Searching for lost super

WHO SHOULD COMPLETE THIS FORM?

You should complete this form if you want to search our lost members register for any super you may have lost. Your super fund will report you as a lost member if:

- they have not been able to contact you
- they have not received any contributions or rollover amounts for you in the last five years, or
- your account was transferred from another fund as a lost member account and no new address has been found.

WHEN COMPLETING THIS FORM

When completing this form:

- Print clearly in BLOCK LETTERS using a black or blue pen.
- Use BLOCK LETTERS and print one character in each box.

S M I T H   S T

- Place X in ALL applicable boxes.

AFTER COMPLETING THIS FORM

After you complete this form, send it to us at:

PO Box 3578
ALBURY NSW 2640

We will use the information you provide to check for any possible matches on the lost members register. We will write to you to let you know whether or not we have found a possible match or if we need more information.

ACCOUNT BALANCES LESS THAN $200

If we successfully match your details with an entry on our lost members register, and the balance of your lost super account is less than $200, you may withdraw this amount from your super fund tax-free regardless of your age.

HOW ELSE CAN I SEARCH FOR LOST SUPER?

You can also search for your lost super by:

- phoning **13 28 65** and following the prompts (you will need your TFN to use this service)
- phoning us on **13 10 20**
- using SuperSeeker on our website at **www.ato.gov.au**, or
- asking your current super fund to conduct a search on your behalf using SuperMatch.

NAT 2476-05.2008

Australian Government
Australian Taxation Office

Form 7.2 [2476] *continued*

Australian Government
Australian Taxation Office

Searching for lost super

OFFICE USE ONLY
Enquiry number
LMR reference numbers
Form keyed by: Name (please print)
Date Day / Month / Year

Section A: **Your personal details**

1 Tax file number (TFN)

You do not have to provide us with your TFN but doing so will help us process your enquiry.

2 Name

Title: Mr ☐ Mrs ☐ Miss ☐ Ms ☐ Other

Family name

First given name

Other given names

3 Gender Male ☐ Female ☐

4 Date of birth Day / Month / Year

5 Residency

Were you an eligible temporary resident visa holder who has now permanently departed Australia? No ☐ Yes ☐

Section B: **Your contact details**

6 Current postal address

Street number and name

Suburb/town

State/territory

Postal code

Country, if other than Australia

7 Daytime phone number

8 Email address (if applicable)

NAT2476-05.2008

IN CONFIDENCE – when completed

Form 7.2 [2476] *continued*

Section C: **Your super fund details**

9 Super fund details Provide details of any super fund where contributions may have been made on your behalf.

Superannuation fund name	Account number	Beneficiaries	Period of contributions

Section D: **Your previous details**

➔ If you have additional information for the following questions, attach it to this form. If you can't provide responses to any of these questions we will still search for your lost super.

10 Previous name details Provide details of all previous names and any names you are commonly known by.

Family name	Given name	Other given names	Date of change
			/ /
			/ /
			/ /

11 Previous address details Provide details of all previous addresses you lived at in Australia.

Address	State	Postcode	Period of residence

12 Previous employment details Provide details of all your previous employers.

Employer name	Employer address	Occupation	Period of employment

Section E: **Declaration**

13 Declaration Either you or a person authorised to act on your behalf must complete this declaration.

I declare that the information given on this form is complete and correct.

Name of signatory

Signature

Date Day / Month / Year

IN CONFIDENCE – when completed

Form 8.1 [2173] HELP—weekly

Schedule 11 **Pay as you go (PAYG) withholding** NAT 2173

Higher Education Loan Programme (HELP) weekly tax table

Including statement of formulas.

FOR PAYMENTS MADE ON OR AFTER 1 JULY 2008.

This document is a withholding schedule made by the Commissioner of Taxation in accordance with sections 15-25 and 15-30 of Schedule 1 to the *Taxation Administration Act 1953*. It applies to withholding payments covered by Subdivisions 12-B (except sections 12-50 and 12-55), 12-C (except sections 12-85 and 12-90) and 12-D of Schedule 1.

For more information visit **www.ato.gov.au**

NAT 2173-05.2008

Australian Government
Australian Taxation Office

Form 8.1 [2173] *continued*

HECS IS NOW HELP
On 1 June 2006, all accumulated Higher Education Contribution Scheme (HECS) debts became accumulated Higher Education Loan Programme (HELP) debts.

WHO SHOULD USE THIS TABLE?
Use this table if you make weekly payments and the payee has provided you with a *Tax file number declaration* or *Withholding declaration* and has:

- answered 'YES' to the question 'Do you have an accumulated Higher Education Loan Programme (HELP) debt?'
- not applied for an exemption or reduction of the Medicare levy on a *Medicare levy variation declaration* due to low family income
- claimed the tax-free threshold and has weekly earnings of $799 or more, or
- not claimed the tax-free threshold and has weekly earnings of $482 or more.

The HELP component is to be withheld from all earnings, including taxable allowances, bonuses and commissions.

Do not withhold any amount for HELP from lump sum termination payments.

HOW TO WORK OUT WITHHOLDING AMOUNTS

1 Use the appropriate weekly tax table to calculate the weekly withholding amount for the payee's earnings, allowing for any tax offsets claimed.
2 Use this HELP weekly tax table to calculate the HELP component to be withheld.
3 Add the HELP component to the withholding amount. Withhold the result from the payee's earnings.
4 If the payee also has a Financial Supplement debt, add the Student Financial Supplement Scheme (SFSS) component (calculated using the SFSS tax tables) as well as the HELP component to the amounts to be withheld. Withhold the result from the payee's earnings.

HOW TO FIND THE HELP COMPONENT IN THE FOLLOWING TABLE
Find the payee's weekly earnings in **column 1** (ignoring any cents) and use the appropriate column to find the HELP component.

If the payee is claiming the tax-free threshold, use **column 2**.

If the payee is not claiming the tax-free threshold, use **column 3**.

EXAMPLE

The payee has claimed the tax-free threshold and has weekly earnings of $876.54. Ignoring cents, find $876 in column 1. The HELP component in column 2 is $35.00.

USING FORMULAS
Withholding amounts shown in this table can be expressed in a mathematical form. If you have developed your own payroll software package, you can use the formulas and coefficients outlined below.

The formulas comprise linear equations of the form **y = ax**, where:

- **y** is the weekly HELP component
- **x** is the weekly earnings expressed in whole dollars plus 99 cents, and
- the value of the coefficient **a** is as shown in the tables on this page.

Tax-free threshold claimed

Weekly earnings — x $	Component rate — a %
0 to 798.99	0.0
799.00 to 890.99	4.0
891.00 to 981.99	4.5
982.00 to 1,032.99	5.0
1,033.00 to 1,110.99	5.5
1,111.00 to 1,202.99	6.0
1,203.00 to 1,265.99	6.5
1,266.00 to 1,393.99	7.0
1,394.00 to 1,484.99	7.5
1,485.00 & over	8.0

No tax-free threshold claimed

Weekly earnings — x $	Component rate — a %
0 to 481.99	0.0
482.00 to 572.99	4.0
573.00 to 663.99	4.5
664.00 to 715.99	5.0
716.00 to 792.99	5.5
793.00 to 885.99	6.0
886.00 to 948.99	6.5
949.00 to 1,075.99	7.0
1,076.00 to 1,167.99	7.5
1,168.00 & over	8.0

ROUNDING OF COMPONENT AMOUNTS
Component amounts calculated as a result of applying the above formulas should be rounded to the nearest dollar. Values ending in 50 cents are rounded to the next higher dollar. Do this rounding directly – that is, do not make a preliminary rounding to the nearest cent.

EXAMPLE

The payee has claimed the tax-free threshold and has weekly earnings of $808.62.

HELP component = $808.99 × 4.0% = $32.00 rounded to the nearest dollar.

ACCOUNTING SOFTWARE
Software written in accordance with the formulas in this schedule should be tested for accuracy against the table in the following pages. You should only use such software if it produces the exact amounts shown in the table.

Form 8.1 [2173] *continued*

HELP WEEKLY TAX TABLE

Weekly earnings 1 $	Tax-free threshold weekly component 2 $	No tax-free threshold weekly component 3 $	Weekly earnings 1 $	Tax-free threshold weekly component 2 $	No tax-free threshold weekly component 3 $	Weekly earnings 1 $	Tax-free threshold weekly component 2 $	No tax-free threshold weekly component 3 $	Weekly earnings 1 $	Tax-free threshold weekly component 2 $	No tax-free threshold weekly component 3 $
482	—	19.00	552	—	22.00	622	—	28.00	692	—	35.00
483	—	19.00	553	—	22.00	623	—	28.00	693	—	35.00
484	—	19.00	554	—	22.00	624	—	28.00	694	—	35.00
485	—	19.00	555	—	22.00	625	—	28.00	695	—	35.00
486	—	19.00	556	—	22.00	626	—	28.00	696	—	35.00
487	—	20.00	557	—	22.00	627	—	28.00	697	—	35.00
488	—	20.00	558	—	22.00	628	—	28.00	698	—	35.00
489	—	20.00	559	—	22.00	629	—	28.00	699	—	35.00
490	—	20.00	560	—	22.00	630	—	28.00	700	—	35.00
491	—	20.00	561	—	22.00	631	—	28.00	701	—	35.00
492	—	20.00	562	—	23.00	632	—	28.00	702	—	35.00
493	—	20.00	563	—	23.00	633	—	29.00	703	—	35.00
494	—	20.00	564	—	23.00	634	—	29.00	704	—	35.00
495	—	20.00	565	—	23.00	635	—	29.00	705	—	35.00
496	—	20.00	566	—	23.00	636	—	29.00	706	—	35.00
497	—	20.00	567	—	23.00	637	—	29.00	707	—	35.00
498	—	20.00	568	—	23.00	638	—	29.00	708	—	35.00
499	—	20.00	569	—	23.00	639	—	29.00	709	—	35.00
500	—	20.00	570	—	23.00	640	—	29.00	710	—	36.00
501	—	20.00	571	—	23.00	641	—	29.00	711	—	36.00
502	—	20.00	572	—	23.00	642	—	29.00	712	—	36.00
503	—	20.00	573	—	26.00	643	—	29.00	713	—	36.00
504	—	20.00	574	—	26.00	644	—	29.00	714	—	36.00
505	—	20.00	575	—	26.00	645	—	29.00	715	—	36.00
506	—	20.00	576	—	26.00	646	—	29.00	716	—	39.00
507	—	20.00	577	—	26.00	647	—	29.00	717	—	39.00
508	—	20.00	578	—	26.00	648	—	29.00	718	—	40.00
509	—	20.00	579	—	26.00	649	—	29.00	719	—	40.00
510	—	20.00	580	—	26.00	650	—	29.00	720	—	40.00
511	—	20.00	581	—	26.00	651	—	29.00	721	—	40.00
512	—	21.00	582	—	26.00	652	—	29.00	722	—	40.00
513	—	21.00	583	—	26.00	653	—	29.00	723	—	40.00
514	—	21.00	584	—	26.00	654	—	29.00	724	—	40.00
515	—	21.00	585	—	26.00	655	—	30.00	725	—	40.00
516	—	21.00	586	—	26.00	656	—	30.00	726	—	40.00
517	—	21.00	587	—	26.00	657	—	30.00	727	—	40.00
518	—	21.00	588	—	27.00	658	—	30.00	728	—	40.00
519	—	21.00	589	—	27.00	659	—	30.00	729	—	40.00
520	—	21.00	590	—	27.00	660	—	30.00	730	—	40.00
521	—	21.00	591	—	27.00	661	—	30.00	731	—	40.00
522	—	21.00	592	—	27.00	662	—	30.00	732	—	40.00
523	—	21.00	593	—	27.00	663	—	30.00	733	—	40.00
524	—	21.00	594	—	27.00	664	—	33.00	734	—	40.00
525	—	21.00	595	—	27.00	665	—	33.00	735	—	40.00
526	—	21.00	596	—	27.00	666	—	33.00	736	—	41.00
527	—	21.00	597	—	27.00	667	—	33.00	737	—	41.00
528	—	21.00	598	—	27.00	668	—	33.00	738	—	41.00
529	—	21.00	599	—	27.00	669	—	33.00	739	—	41.00
530	—	21.00	600	—	27.00	670	—	34.00	740	—	41.00
531	—	21.00	601	—	27.00	671	—	34.00	741	—	41.00
532	—	21.00	602	—	27.00	672	—	34.00	742	—	41.00
533	—	21.00	603	—	27.00	673	—	34.00	743	—	41.00
534	—	21.00	604	—	27.00	674	—	34.00	744	—	41.00
535	—	21.00	605	—	27.00	675	—	34.00	745	—	41.00
536	—	21.00	606	—	27.00	676	—	34.00	746	—	41.00
537	—	22.00	607	—	27.00	677	—	34.00	747	—	41.00
538	—	22.00	608	—	27.00	678	—	34.00	748	—	41.00
539	—	22.00	609	—	27.00	679	—	34.00	749	—	41.00
540	—	22.00	610	—	27.00	680	—	34.00	750	—	41.00
541	—	22.00	611	—	28.00	681	—	34.00	751	—	41.00
542	—	22.00	612	—	28.00	682	—	34.00	752	—	41.00
543	—	22.00	613	—	28.00	683	—	34.00	753	—	41.00
544	—	22.00	614	—	28.00	684	—	34.00	754	—	42.00
545	—	22.00	615	—	28.00	685	—	34.00	755	—	42.00
546	—	22.00	616	—	28.00	686	—	34.00	756	—	42.00
547	—	22.00	617	—	28.00	687	—	34.00	757	—	42.00
548	—	22.00	618	—	28.00	688	—	34.00	758	—	42.00
549	—	22.00	619	—	28.00	689	—	34.00	759	—	42.00
550	—	22.00	620	—	28.00	690	—	35.00	760	—	42.00
551	—	22.00	621	—	28.00	691	—	35.00	761	—	42.00

SCHEDULE 11 HIGHER EDUCATION LOAN PROGRAMME (HELP) WEEKLY TAX TABLE 3

Form 8.1 [2173] *continued*

HELP WEEKLY TAX TABLE

Weekly earnings 1 $	Tax-free threshold weekly component 2 $	No tax-free threshold weekly component 3 $	Weekly earnings 1 $	Tax-free threshold weekly component 2 $	No tax-free threshold weekly component 3 $	Weekly earnings 1 $	Tax-free threshold weekly component 2 $	No tax-free threshold weekly component 3 $	Weekly earnings 1 $	Tax-free threshold weekly component 2 $	No tax-free threshold weekly component 3 $
762	—	42.00	832	33.00	50.00	902	41.00	59.00	972	44.00	68.00
763	—	42.00	833	33.00	50.00	903	41.00	59.00	973	44.00	68.00
764	—	42.00	834	33.00	50.00	904	41.00	59.00	974	44.00	68.00
765	—	42.00	835	33.00	50.00	905	41.00	59.00	975	44.00	68.00
766	—	42.00	836	33.00	50.00	906	41.00	59.00	976	44.00	68.00
767	—	42.00	837	34.00	50.00	907	41.00	59.00	977	44.00	68.00
768	—	42.00	838	34.00	50.00	908	41.00	59.00	978	44.00	69.00
769	—	42.00	839	34.00	50.00	909	41.00	59.00	979	44.00	69.00
770	—	42.00	840	34.00	50.00	910	41.00	59.00	980	44.00	69.00
771	—	42.00	841	34.00	51.00	911	41.00	59.00	981	44.00	69.00
772	—	43.00	842	34.00	51.00	912	41.00	59.00	982	49.00	69.00
773	—	43.00	843	34.00	51.00	913	41.00	59.00	983	49.00	69.00
774	—	43.00	844	34.00	51.00	914	41.00	59.00	984	49.00	69.00
775	—	43.00	845	34.00	51.00	915	41.00	60.00	985	49.00	69.00
776	—	43.00	846	34.00	51.00	916	41.00	60.00	986	49.00	69.00
777	—	43.00	847	34.00	51.00	917	41.00	60.00	987	49.00	69.00
778	—	43.00	848	34.00	51.00	918	41.00	60.00	988	49.00	69.00
779	—	43.00	849	34.00	51.00	919	41.00	60.00	989	49.00	69.00
780	—	43.00	850	34.00	51.00	920	41.00	60.00	990	50.00	69.00
781	—	43.00	851	34.00	51.00	921	41.00	60.00	991	50.00	69.00
782	—	43.00	852	34.00	51.00	922	42.00	60.00	992	50.00	70.00
783	—	43.00	853	34.00	51.00	923	42.00	60.00	993	50.00	70.00
784	—	43.00	854	34.00	51.00	924	42.00	60.00	994	50.00	70.00
785	—	43.00	855	34.00	51.00	925	42.00	60.00	995	50.00	70.00
786	—	43.00	856	34.00	51.00	926	42.00	60.00	996	50.00	70.00
787	—	43.00	857	34.00	51.00	927	42.00	60.00	997	50.00	70.00
788	—	43.00	858	34.00	52.00	928	42.00	60.00	998	50.00	70.00
789	—	43.00	859	34.00	52.00	929	42.00	60.00	999	50.00	70.00
790	—	44.00	860	34.00	52.00	930	42.00	61.00	1000	50.00	70.00
791	—	44.00	861	34.00	52.00	931	42.00	61.00	1001	50.00	70.00
792	—	44.00	862	35.00	52.00	932	42.00	61.00	1002	50.00	70.00
793	—	48.00	863	35.00	52.00	933	42.00	61.00	1003	50.00	70.00
794	—	48.00	864	35.00	52.00	934	42.00	61.00	1004	50.00	70.00
795	—	48.00	865	35.00	52.00	935	42.00	61.00	1005	50.00	70.00
796	—	48.00	866	35.00	52.00	936	42.00	61.00	1006	50.00	70.00
797	—	48.00	867	35.00	52.00	937	42.00	61.00	1007	50.00	71.00
798	—	48.00	868	35.00	52.00	938	42.00	61.00	1008	50.00	71.00
799	32.00	48.00	869	35.00	52.00	939	42.00	61.00	1009	50.00	71.00
800	32.00	48.00	870	35.00	52.00	940	42.00	61.00	1010	51.00	71.00
801	32.00	48.00	871	35.00	52.00	941	42.00	61.00	1011	51.00	71.00
802	32.00	48.00	872	35.00	52.00	942	42.00	61.00	1012	51.00	71.00
803	32.00	48.00	873	35.00	52.00	943	42.00	61.00	1013	51.00	71.00
804	32.00	48.00	874	35.00	52.00	944	43.00	61.00	1014	51.00	71.00
805	32.00	48.00	875	35.00	53.00	945	43.00	61.00	1015	51.00	71.00
806	32.00	48.00	876	35.00	53.00	946	43.00	62.00	1016	51.00	71.00
807	32.00	48.00	877	35.00	53.00	947	43.00	62.00	1017	51.00	71.00
808	32.00	49.00	878	35.00	53.00	948	43.00	62.00	1018	51.00	71.00
809	32.00	49.00	879	35.00	53.00	949	43.00	66.00	1019	51.00	71.00
810	32.00	49.00	880	35.00	53.00	950	43.00	67.00	1020	51.00	71.00
811	32.00	49.00	881	35.00	53.00	951	43.00	67.00	1021	51.00	72.00
812	33.00	49.00	882	35.00	53.00	952	43.00	67.00	1022	51.00	72.00
813	33.00	49.00	883	35.00	53.00	953	43.00	67.00	1023	51.00	72.00
814	33.00	49.00	884	35.00	53.00	954	43.00	67.00	1024	51.00	72.00
815	33.00	49.00	885	35.00	53.00	955	43.00	67.00	1025	51.00	72.00
816	33.00	49.00	886	35.00	58.00	956	43.00	67.00	1026	51.00	72.00
817	33.00	49.00	887	36.00	58.00	957	43.00	67.00	1027	51.00	72.00
818	33.00	49.00	888	36.00	58.00	958	43.00	67.00	1028	51.00	72.00
819	33.00	49.00	889	36.00	58.00	959	43.00	67.00	1029	51.00	72.00
820	33.00	49.00	890	36.00	58.00	960	43.00	67.00	1030	52.00	72.00
821	33.00	49.00	891	40.00	58.00	961	43.00	67.00	1031	52.00	72.00
822	33.00	49.00	892	40.00	58.00	962	43.00	67.00	1032	52.00	72.00
823	33.00	49.00	893	40.00	58.00	963	43.00	67.00	1033	57.00	72.00
824	33.00	49.00	894	40.00	58.00	964	43.00	68.00	1034	57.00	72.00
825	33.00	50.00	895	40.00	58.00	965	43.00	68.00	1035	57.00	73.00
826	33.00	50.00	896	40.00	58.00	966	44.00	68.00	1036	57.00	73.00
827	33.00	50.00	897	40.00	58.00	967	44.00	68.00	1037	57.00	73.00
828	33.00	50.00	898	40.00	58.00	968	44.00	68.00	1038	57.00	73.00
829	33.00	50.00	899	40.00	58.00	969	44.00	68.00	1039	57.00	73.00
830	33.00	50.00	900	41.00	59.00	970	44.00	68.00	1040	57.00	73.00
831	33.00	50.00	901	41.00	59.00	971	44.00	68.00	1041	57.00	73.00

4 **SCHEDULE 11** HIGHER EDUCATION LOAN PROGRAMME (HELP) WEEKLY TAX TABLE

Form 9.1 [CSA 4057] Child support worksheet

The new
Child Support Scheme
A better balance for separated families

Child support worksheet

Use this worksheet to estimate the child support payable for each child from 1 July 2008. If you have different care levels for the children, you'll need to estimate the child support for each child separately.

For help and information, click on the hyperlinks throughout this worksheet.

Step 1: Work out your child support income	**Parent 1**	**Parent 2**
Work out each parent's adjusted taxable income	$	$
Deduct the self-support amount from each parent's adjusted taxable income	– $	– $
Deduct a relevant dependent child amount	– $	– $
Deduct a multi-case allowance amount	– $	– $
Each parent's child support income	= $	= $
Step 2: Work out the combined child support income	**Parent 1**	**Parent 2**
Add each parent's child support income together	$	$
Combined child support income	= $	
Step 3: Work out each parent's income percentage	**Parent 1**	**Parent 2**
Each parent's child support income	$	$
Divide each parent's child support income by the combined child support income	$	$
Multiply the resulting amount by 100	x 100	x 100
Each parent's income percentage	=	=
Step 4: Work out each parent's care percentage	**Parent 1**	**Parent 2**
Each parent's care percentage	= %	= %
Step 5: Work out each parent's cost percentage	**Parent 1**	**Parent 2**
Each parent's cost percentage	= %	= %
Step 6: Work out each parent's child support percentage	**Parent 1**	**Parent 2**
Each parent's income percentage	%	%
Deduct each parent's cost percentage	%	%
Each parent's child support percentage	= %	= %

If it's a positive child support percentage, that parent needs to pay child support.
We go on to stages 7 and 8 using only the positive child support percentage.

Step 7: Work out the cost of the children	**Child**	
Cost of all the child support children	= $	
Step 8: Work out the child support payable	**Parent 1**	**Parent 2**
Each parent's child support percentage	%	%
Multiply this amount by the total cost of the children	$	$
Amount of child support for each child	= $	= $

If you have two or more child support cases, follow these steps

Work out the effect of the multi-case cap	**Parent 1**	**Parent 2**
Insert the multi-case cap for the child	%	%
Insert the child support amount for the child	$	$
The lesser amount of the two is the child support payable for the child	$	$

CSA4057.02.08

ABN The abbreviation for *Australian Business Number*.
accounts method The cash book method of accounting for GST.
accrual accounting method The method that must be adopted for activity reporting when gross sales are over $2 million.
accrued annual leave Leave due to the employee for annual leave owing.
accrued sick leave Leave from sick days not taken and sometimes made available to the employee on termination of employment.
activity statement The ATO form for reporting business taxes such as GST, FBT, PAYG withholdings and instalment tax. Can be either a 'business' or an 'instalment' statement.
additional family payment An extra payment to families in need, over and above the basic family payment. It is subject to means testing.
additional tax Generally a penalty for the late payment or avoidance of tax, charged at some rate on the amount originally assessed. It could be the extra amount of tax to cover a HELP debt.
adjusted income The income amount arrived at after applying the CSA formula. This amount includes any reportable fringe benefits and rental losses.
adjustment factor A multiplication factor periodically determined by the Valuer-General of Tasmania under the *Land Valuation Act 1971*. This is used to adjust land values in Tasmania in an attempt to bring all properties into a common valuation band.
adjustment note The documentary evidence required for GST purposes to support a change of business activity details.
administration component A flat fee of $20 per shortfall employee, charged by the ATO when a superannuation guarantee charge is made.
ad valorem rate A tax rate expressed as a percentage of the total value of output of the commodity in question.
allowable deductions Deductions, either specific or general, that the Commissioner of Taxation allows to be subtracted from assessable income.
annual leave loading The additional amount of 17.5% leave loading payable by some employers for annual leave due every year to an employee.
annual withholding The amount of tax withheld from all sources in a year.
annualised Calculated as if for a year.
annuities Fixed sums of money paid to a person every year for life; generally the result of insurance or superannuation.
anti-avoidance provisions Sections in the ITAA 1936 that make deliberate schemes to avoid tax liable for penalties.
arms-length transaction (payee) A transaction (or payee) that is made by one person to another where neither one of the parties to the event has any power over the other.
assessable dealings Any transactions for the sale or application to own use of wine or alcoholic beverages to which WET applies.
assessable income All amounts under the provisions of both the ITAA 1936 and 1997 that are deemed assessable income.
assessed land value Used for land tax purposes, this is the value of land as set out by the Commissioner of Land Tax or the adjusted land value using equalisation factors.
assessment The ascertainment of taxable income or, in the case of land tax, the taxable value. For Higher Education Support it is the amount of contribution according to student workload for the half-year.
ATO The abbreviation commonly used for the Australian Taxation Office.
Australian Business Number (ABN) The unique number issued by the ATO to entities that register. Also used when registered for GST.
Australian Business Register A public listing of all registered enterprises, with ABN and GST status disclosed. Also listed are details of place of business, type of entity, trading name, legal name and postal and business address.
average unimproved value The value for land tax liability in the Australian Capital Territory.
BAS The abbreviation for *Business Activity Statement*.

prime tax assessed The amount of tax calculated by applying the tax rates to the taxable income of a taxpayer, before adding any levies or deducting any rebates or credits of tax.

Principal Place of Residence (PPR) For the purposes of duties, the main residence or home where purchasers intend living.

private ruling Ruling requested by the taxpayer and given on a specific topic and which relates only to that taxpayer.

pro rata Dividing tax between buyer and seller or making a division over periods.

progressive tax Tax that takes an increasing proportion of the tax base as the base rises; for example, the system currently in use in Australia.

proof of identity Appropriate documents required to establish beyond doubt a person's identity.

property tax For land tax purposes, both Victoria and Western Australia levy property taxes over and above the land tax rates payable.

proportional tax Constant or flat rate regardless of the change in the tax base.

protected earnings amount The minimum amount of wages below which the employer cannot make deductions for child support.

public key technology (PKT) For e-commerce with the ATO, special keys to ensure that the e-commerce system provides integrity and confidentiality.

public ruling Ruling usually initiated by the ATO and that generally has application for all applicable taxpayers.

quarterly instalments Remittances four times per year.

quotations Declarations of a TFN or an ABN made by persons for GST purposes, investment purposes, employment purposes or other requirements.

rateable land The aggregate of all land owned by a person or an entity on which land tax may be levied.

rates of tax The rates set by the government under the Rating Acts and applied to taxable income. In the case of GST, this is the rate applied to the taxable value of goods; and for land tax and payroll tax, this is the rate applied in those circumstances.

rebate of tax A credit of tax that is deducted from the tax payable.

rebateable dealings Dealings that include wholesale sales of wine, cellar door and mail order retail sales, wine used for tastings and promotions, and other applications to own use eligible for a rebate of WET.

receipts The taxation term used to indicate all consideration received by a firm or individual, whether capital or revenue in nature.

registered Term given by the ATO to an entity that by law has to be registered. The practical implication of this is a requirement to fully participate in the PAYG withholding system, withholding tax from employees or others, regularly remitting such to the ATO and supplying all employees with a payment summary by the prescribed time.

registered for GST An entity that has applied for an ABN and has been granted registration for GST purposes.

regressive tax A tax rate that falls as the value of the tax base rises.

relevant records Any records that should evidence transactions or events in a business.

reportable fringe benefit A benefit with a taxable value greater than $2000 that must be grossed-up and reported on the annual payment summary of an employee.

representative member The nominated member of a GST group that is liable for all GST matters affecting the group.

resident For tax purposes, a resident is a person who resides or is domiciled in Australia for at least six months of the year of tax, or a company that is incorporated or carries on business in Australia.

residential premises For tax purposes, residential premises are those in which persons reside permanently.

returns For tax purposes, these refer to statements giving details of income, profits, sales, payrolls, land held, fringe benefits given or capital gains accrued, and that are required to be lodged with the relevant authority on certain required dates.

revenue The amounts collected by either the federal or state governments that are used to meet the welfare objectives for Australian society.

safety net letter A letter issued by the ATO to a business that does not yet have an ABN but has recently applied for one to enable the business to deal with other businesses without the need to have tax withheld at the 46.5% rate.

secondary assessment The issue of a second assessment for land tax purposes, where a taxpayer both jointly and separately owns rateable land.

second-hand goods Goods that are not new, but have been used before.

self-support amount The indexed amount set by the CSA that is deducted from a parent's relevant income for child support purposes.

self-assess The act of assessing by the taxpayer the amount of a required levy or tax.

shifted backwards The shifting of the tax burden back to some other person or entity, either partially or fully; generally caused by changes in the behaviour of a person induced by the levying of the tax.

small withholder Employer with annual PAYG withholdings of less than $25 000.

specific rate The tax rate expressed as a fixed money sum per unit or volume of output.

standard annual program The standard program that a particular education institution expects a student to complete in one full calendar year in the course of gaining a higher education qualification.

statutes The written laws of Parliament, either federal or state.

statutory formula One method of calculating car fringe benefit.

statutory fraction The fraction used in the calculation of a car fringe benefit as set out in section 9(2) of the *Fringe Benefits Tax Assessment Act 1986*.

Student Learning Entitlement (SLE) The program set by the government that identifies the student's entitlement to a Commonwealth-supported place.

substantiation Being able to produce a document or entry which gives evidence that the transaction took place, its value and date.

superannuation contributions Contributions from an employee's wage in accordance with instructions given to the employer, or contributions by the employer in accordance with the superannuation levy.

superannuation guarantee charge A non-deductible payment that must be made to the ATO whenever an employer has not satisfactorily met the minimum level of superannuation support for employees.

superannuation guarantee levy The amount that must be set aside for each employee every year based on the ordinary time earnings multiplied by the charge percentage. This is a deductible payment that must be made to a complying fund.

superannuation guarantee shortfall The difference between the legislated amount that must be set aside for each employee every year and the actual amount set aside.

superannuation guarantee statement An ATO form that, if required, is the formal basis of self-assessing the amount of liability for the superannuation guarantee charge.

SuperMatch An ATO initiative designed to provide superannuation funds with electronic access to data about persons who may have superannuation entitlements but have lost contact with the relevant superannuation fund.

support assessment Under the *Child Support Act*, this is an assessment of the paying parent's ability to maintain the child.

support income percentage The ratio of a parent's support income to combined support income.

support payments The payments made by the paying parent in response either to a support assessment or to an agreement.

Tax Agent Portal A web-based support system that enables tax agents to interact directly with their client files at the ATO.

tax A compulsory levy mainly designed to raise revenue.

tax avoidance The legal minimisation of tax liability, but against the spirit of the law.

tax base The measure to which the tax rate can be applied or levied.

tax burden Generally refers to the individual or entity who bears the final burden of the tax, regardless of where it was levied.

tax evasion The illegal minimisation of taxation and against the letter of the law.

tax file number (TFN) The unique number issued by the ATO to each taxpayer.

tax incidence The study of who really pays the tax or bears the burden of tax.

tax instalment A portion of a tax liability paid to the ATO.

tax invoice Required by the ATO in specific detail, to evidence all creditable transactions made by a GST-registered business that wishes to claim GST input tax credits.

tax period The specific reporting period for businesses registered for GST.

tax threshold The amount often given as tax-free, as in income, payroll tax, first home purchase stamp duty or land tax.

taxable Any income, rateable land, payroll, goods or services to which a tax may be applied.

taxable income The result of deducting any allowable deductions from assessable income.

taxable supply The supply of goods and services that have a 10% rating for GST.

taxable value The amount of a benefit determined for fringe benefits purposes, which is then grossed up for FBT to be assessed.

taxable wages Any wages paid in a state for payroll tax purposes.

tax-free threshold The first step of income granted tax-free to taxpayers.

termination payments Payments made to employees on resignation, redundancy or dismissal.

TFN The abbreviation for *tax file number*.

TFN declaration Form to advise an employer of the taxpayer's tax file number.

TFN notification forms Various ATO forms that advise financial institutions of the taxpayer's tax file number.

TFN reporting system A system wherein information about assessable income is reported to the ATO and an applicable TFN is also reported, thus enabling cross-checking by the ATO.

unit The particular person or group that forms a unit. For Australian tax purposes it is a single legal entity, whereas in Britain it is a couple or partnership.

untaxed portion That part of the aggregate value of the benefit added to the net benefit to produce the grossed-up value.

valuations For land tax purposes, these are used in each state to record the rateable value of land.

variations only return This form is used for land tax purposes and is completed and lodged only if there has been a change in the beneficial ownership of rateable land from the previous assessment.

vertical equity Persons in different situations are treated differently by the tax system.

vested In full legal possession.

VET FEE-HELP The loan available to eligible students for certain higher award courses at TAFE institutes.

vocational education and training (VET) The combination of academic studies with more practical training and workplace experience. Courses are delivered at VET-accredited institutions.

voluntary agreement An agreement entered into between an individual registered for GST and a business registered for GST. Voluntary amounts can be withheld from payments made to the individual to relieve the individual from having to pay PAYG instalments on that income.

wages The meaning for payroll purposes is wider than the general meaning and includes any fringe benefits given to an employee, as well as wages or salary.

weighted average The calculation including both GST and WET used for reporting the wine equalisation tax.

weighted units Units in any course for higher education are given a weighting to attest to the degree of difficulty of the particular subject. This weighting will be a percentage of the standard annual full-time program or EFTSU (which is 1).

WET The abbreviation for *wine equalisation tax*.

wholesale sale The amount on which WET is calculated, being the last wholesale sale of wine.

wine equalisation tax (WET) The specific amount of tax that is payable to the ATO on wine sales.

workers compensation Money paid to a worker who is injured or falls sick as a result of a workplace accident, generally from the employer's insurance company as a result of compulsory insurance paid.

Page numbers in *italics* indicate figures and tables.